ALL ABOUT LAW

ALL ABOUT

EXPLORING THE CANADIAN LEGAL SYSTEM

ALL ABOUT LAW

EXPLORING THE CANADIAN LEGAL SYSTEM

Terry G. Murphy, BCom, MEd
Limestone District School Board (retired)

Kathleen Ryan Elliott, BBA, LLB, BEd
Kawartha Pine Ridge District School Board

Agi Mete, BA, MSEd
Niagara Catholic District School Board

Jamie Glass, BA, BEd, LLB *Juris Doctor*
York Region District School Board

NELSON EDUCATION

NELSON / EDUCATION

All About Law: Exploring the Canadian Legal System
Sixth Edition

Authors
Terry G. Murphy, Kathleen Ryan Elliott, Agi Mete, Jamie Glass

General Manager, Social Studies and Business Studies
Carol Stokes

Publisher, Social Studies and Business Studies
Doug Panasis

Managing Editor, Development
Karin Fediw

Product Manager, Social Studies and Business Studies
Doug Morrow

Assistant Editor
Kimberly Murphy

Editorial Assistant
Jordana Camerman

Production Manager
Helen Jager-Locsin

Senior Production Coordinators
Kathrine Pummell,
Sharon Latta Paterson

Design Director
Ken Phipps

Interior Design
Studio Montage

Cover Design
Rocket Design

Cover Image
Karin Fediw

Printer
RR Donnelley

Focus Strategic Communications Inc.

Project Manager
Adrianna Edwards

Developmental Editors
Ron Edwards, Adrianna Edwards

Copy Editors
Leanne Rancourt, Ann Firth

Proofreaders
Linda Szostak, Susan McNish,
Layla Moola

Index
Carol Roberts

Art Director
Adrianna Edwards

Compositor
Valentino Sanna

Photo Research and Permissions
Elizabeth Kelly

About the Cover

The image on the cover is the *Pillars of Justice*, a 10-ton sculpture representing a stylized, 11-person jury standing in two rows under a roof representing a courthouse. A vacant space has been left for the twelfth juror to enable the viewer to imagine filling that role as a partner in the justice system. This sculpture was created by Edwina Sandys, a noted international sculptor and granddaughter of Sir Winston Churchill. In the past 20 years, she has produced four monumental sculptures that were commissioned by the United Nations for their centres in Geneva, Vienna, Rio de Janeiro, Dublin, and New York.

The sculpture is the first of several that will be displayed in the McMurtry Gardens of Justice in an outdoor gallery between Osgoode Hall and the courthouse at 361 University Avenue in Toronto. Upon completion, the sculpture garden will depict various values underlying our system of justice, particularly those reflected in the *Charter of Rights and Freedoms,* in celebration of the rule of law and the administration of justice in Ontario. The Gardens is a permanent tribute to the Honourable Roy McMurtry, Ontario's chief justice from 1996 until his retirement in 2007. Roy McMurtry has dedicated his life and career to public service and has been a long-standing advocate for the province's most vulnerable.

An outdoor classroom space will be incorporated into the Gardens to provide a meeting place for the many thousands of students who visit these courthouses each year and to assist them in their understanding of and respect for our system of justice and of the power of artistic expression.

Reviewers/Consultants

The authors and the publisher wish to thank the consultants and reviewers for their input—advice, ideas, directions, and suggestions—that helped to make this learning resource more student-friendly and teacher-useful. Their contribution in time, effort, and expertise was invaluable.

James Biss
Teacher
Erindale Secondary School
Peel District School Board

Fred Bortolussi
Teacher
St. Michael Catholic High School
Catholic District School Board of Eastern Ontario

Nancy Christoffer
Bias Reviewer

Brenda Davis
Education Consultant
Six Nations of the Grand River

Cynthia Fromstein, BA, LLB
Barrister & Solicitor
Toronto, Ontario

Allen C. Gerstl, BSc, LLB
Barrister & Solicitor
Toronto, Ontario

Lynne Polon Howard, BA, LLB, BEd, MEd
Law Teacher, Social Science Department Head
Tanenbaum Community Hebrew Academy of Toronto
Richmond Hill, Ontario

Marlyn Keaschuck
Teacher (retired)
Chinook School Division, Saskatchewan

Angelo Kontos
Teacher
Rick Hansen Secondary School
Peel District School Board

Peter Legge
Teacher
St. Thomas Aquinas Secondary School
London District Catholic School Board

Tracey McBride
Teacher
Port Colborne High School
District School Board of Niagara

Sarah McCoubrey, BFA, MEd, LLB
Executive Director
Ontario Justice Education Network

Joshua S. Phillips, BA, LLB
Green & Chercover
Toronto, Ontario

Celeste Poltak, LLM
Koskie Minsky LLP Barristers and Solicitors

Jessica Price
Teacher
St. Joseph Secondary School
Dufferin–Peel Catholic District School Board

G. Paul Renwick, BA, LLB
Assistant Crown Attorney
Toronto, Ontario

Jorge Resende
Teacher
Archbishop Romero Catholic Secondary School
Toronto Catholic District School Board

Andrea B. Scharf, BA, LLB
Barrister & Solicitor
Toronto, Ontario

Robert Schrofel
Teacher
John Taylor Collegiate
St. James Assiniboia School Division #2, Manitoba

Catherine Sharp
Teacher
Markville Secondary School
York Region District School Board

Seth Weinstein BA, LLB
Greenspan Humphrey Lavine
Toronto, Ontario

Mark Younger-Lewis
Teacher
John McCrae Secondary School
Ottawa Carleton District School Board

Acknowledgments

All About Law, 6th edition, is the work of a committed team: four dedicated authors and an amazing support team whose contributions must be recognized. First and foremost, we authors want to thank Adrianna Edwards and Ron Edwards of Focus Strategic Communications Inc. for their involvement in this project above and beyond what was expected as project manager and developmental editor respectively. Thanks for guiding us through the writing process and for keeping us on track with your valuable input. Much of the final vision in this text is the result of their commitment to making this the best edition ever of *All About Law* and a book that we know students and teachers will enjoy. Others on the Focus team, Leanne Rancourt, Elizabeth Kelly, Ann Firth, Linda Szostak, and Val Sanna, must be thanked for the look and style of this text.

We are extremely grateful to the many educators who participated in focus groups arranged by Doug Morrow at Nelson Education and who offered suggestions that are reflected in some of this text's new features. As well, several educators, lawyers, and consultants reviewed all of the manuscript, and their names are listed on a separate page. We thank you most sincerely for your suggestions and contributions.

We also want to thank Carol Stokes and the Nelson Education team for their commitment and support for this project. Their names and titles appear on the copyright page. It has been wonderful to have Nelson Education's continuous support for so many editions of *All About Law*.

Finally, we acknowledge and thank Madame Justice Gloria Epstein, Paul Emond, Fred Jarman, and Amber Lynch. We appreciate their involvement in *All About Law*, 6th edition.

Terry G. Murphy, Kathleen Ryan Elliott,
Agi Mete, and Jamie Glass
March 2009

Dedications

To my wife Katherine (Kit); Jamie, Laura, and their new beautiful daughter Jordan Sophia; and to Karen, Russ, and our wonderful granddaughters Macy and Ella; thanks for all your love and support.—*TGM*

To Grant, Ryan, and Alexander, with love and appreciation.—*KRE*

To my wife Nadia and my three lovely daughters, Emma, Olivia, and Alissa, for their patience, understanding, love, and support during the writing process. I am truly blessed. A special thank you to all of the law students I have had the privilege of teaching over the years and who have inspired me to do what I love and love what I do. Finally, to my co-authors, an amazing group of talented and dedicated educators who were so incredibly committed to writing this wonderful text.—*AM*

For my wee boy, Adrian; I hope you enjoy your university studies. Thank you to Sophie, my lovely wife, for your invaluable input in the writing process. You are my rock. Switching careers from lawyer to law teacher has brought me much happiness and inner peace, and I thank my police officer Dad and my teacher Mum for all their love and support over the years. *Dieu et mon droit.*—*JMSG*

Table of Contents

How to Use This Book   x

Unit 1: An Introduction to Law   3

Chapter 1
Law: Its Purpose and History   4

1.1 Introduction   5
1.2 What Is Law, and Why Do We Have It?   6
1.3 Divisions of Law   9
1.4 The Development of Canadian Law   12
1.5 How Rights Have Developed in Canada   21
1.6 The Development of Canada's Constitution   27
1.7 How Laws Are Made   29
ISSUE: *Mediation: An Effective Form of Dispute Resolution?*   32
Chapter Review   34

Chapter 2
The *Canadian Charter of Rights and Freedoms*   36

2.1 Introduction   37
2.2 Reasonable Limits and Notwithstanding Clauses   38
2.3 Fundamental Freedoms   41
2.4 Democratic and Mobility Rights   46
2.5 Legal Rights   48
2.6 Equality Rights   60
2.7 Language and General Rights   61
2.8 Remedies   64
2.9 The Courts and the Legislature   65
ISSUE: *Do the Courts Have Too Much Power Compared to Legislatures?*   66
Chapter Review   68

Chapter 3
Human Rights in Canada   70

3.1 Introduction   71
3.2 Women's Rights   72
3.3 Aboriginal Rights   79
3.4 Rights of Other Groups   84
3.5 Human Rights   92
3.6 Human Rights Legislation   94
3.7 Enforcing Human Rights Laws   102
Careers in Human Rights   105
ISSUE: *Should Aboriginal Peoples Have Their Own System of Justice?*   106
Chapter Review   108

Unit 2: Criminal Law   111

Chapter 4
Introduction to Criminal Law   112

4.1 Introduction   113
4.2 The Nature of Criminal Law   114
4.3 The Power to Make Criminal Law   118
4.4 Summary Conviction and Indictable Offences   121
4.5 The Elements of a Criminal Offence   124
4.6 Parties to an Offence   131
4.7 Our Criminal Court System   134
Careers in Criminal Law   139
ISSUE: *Should Marijuana Be Legalized?*   140
Chapter Review   142

Chapter 5
The Police—Investigation, Arrest, and Bringing the Accused to Trial   144

5.1 Introduction   145
5.2 Arrest   146
5.3 Duties of Police Officers   149
5.4 Legal Rights and Search Laws   154
5.5 Release and Bail Procedures   164
5.6 Awaiting Trial   168
ISSUE: *Should the Police Be Allowed to Use Tasers?*   176
Chapter Review   178

Chapter 6
Trial Procedures 180

6.1	Introduction	181
6.2	Courtroom Participants	181
6.3	Juries and Jury Selection	187
6.4	Presentation of Evidence	194
6.5	Reaching a Verdict	208
ISSUE:	*Should We Have Trials by Jury?*	212
Chapter Review		214

Chapter 7
***Criminal Code* Offences** 216

7.1	Introduction	217
7.2	Violent Crimes	218
7.3	Property Crimes	231
7.4	Other Crimes	237
7.5	The *Controlled Drugs and Substances Act*	244
7.6	Driving Offences	250
ISSUE:	*Do Mandatory Minimum Sentences Work?*	258
Chapter Review		260

Chapter 8
Criminal Defences 262

8.1	Introduction	263
8.2	The Alibi Defence	263
8.3	Automatism	265
8.4	Intoxication	270
8.5	Defences That Provide a Reason for the Offence	274
8.6	Other Defences	281
ISSUE:	*Should Buy-and-Bust Police Operations Be Unconstitutional?*	284
Chapter Review		286

Chapter 9
From Sentencing to Release 288

9.1	Introduction	289
9.2	The Process and Objectives of Sentencing	290
9.3	Sentencing an Offender	298
9.4	Restorative Justice and Victims of Crime	310
9.5	Appeals	314
9.6	Canada's Prison System	316
9.7	Conditional Release	318
ISSUE:	*Are Restorative Justice Programs Good for Victims?*	322
Chapter Review		324

Chapter 10
The Youth Criminal Justice System 326

10.1	Introduction	327
10.2	The *Youth Criminal Justice Act*	331
10.3	Legal Rights of Youths	334
10.4	Trial Procedures	341
10.5	Youth Sentencing Options	345
ISSUE:	*Bullying, Drugs, and School Safety: Do Schools Need Heightened Security?*	352
Chapter Review		354

Unit 3: Civil Law 357

Chapter 11
Resolving Civil Disputes 358

11.1	Introduction	359
11.2	Crimes and Torts	360
11.3	Civil Courts and Trial Procedures	361
11.4	Judgment and Civil Remedies	372
11.5	Alternative Dispute Resolution	380
ISSUE:	*Should the Criminal or Civil Justice System Regulate Violence in Sports?*	384
Chapter Review		386

Chapter 12
Negligence and Other Torts   388

12.1   Introduction   389
12.2   The Elements of Negligence   391
12.3   Defences for Negligence   398
12.4   Special Types of Negligence   402
12.5   Trespass to Persons and Land   413
12.6   Defences for Trespass   419
12.7   Defamation of Character and Its Defences   422
12.8   The Need for Insurance   426
ISSUE: *Safety or Religion: Which Is More Important When Wearing Helmets?*   428
Chapter Review   430

Unit 4: Family Law   433

Chapter 13
Marriage, Divorce, and the Family   434

13.1   Introduction   435
13.2   The Changing Family Structure   435
13.3   Legal Requirements of Marriage   439
13.4   Annulment, Separation, and Divorce   448
13.5   Children and Divorce   453
13.6   Children in Need of Protection   464
ISSUE: *Should Polygamy Be Legalized?*   470
Chapter Review   472

Chapter 14
Division of Property and Support   474

14.1   Introduction   475
14.2   Dividing Family Property   475
14.3   Common Law Relationships   484
14.4   Spousal Support   490
14.5   Child Support   497
14.6   Domestic Contracts   506
Careers in Family Law   509
ISSUE: *Should Canadians Have Universal Daycare?*   510
Chapter Review   512

Unit 5: Contract Law   515

Chapter 15
Elements of a Contract   516

15.1   Introduction   517
15.2   Agreement or Contract?   517
15.3   Elements of a Contract   520
15.4   Discharging a Contract   536
15.5   Breach of Contract   538
15.6   Sale-of-Goods Legislation   542
ISSUE: *E-Commerce: The Changing Nature of Business Transactions*   548
Chapter Review   550

Chapter 16
Dispute Resolution   552

16.1   Introduction   553
16.2   Consumer Protection   553
16.3   Landlord and Tenant Law   563
16.4   Employment Law   574
Careers in Contract Law   593
ISSUE: *Should Alcohol and Drug Tests of Employees Be Allowed?*   594
Chapter Review   596

Appendix A: *Canadian Charter of Rights and Freedoms*   598
Appendix B: Citation References   602
Appendix C: Table of Cases   604
Glossary   606
Index   618
Credits   626

How to Use This Book

Law is an essential part of Canada's culture. Without law, we cannot function effectively in our daily lives. A broad knowledge and understanding of law is not only a vital part of your education, but is also an important factor in the operation of a democratic and orderly society.

The authors are pleased to present the sixth edition of *All About Law*, which has been thoroughly revised. Unit 1 explores the purpose, history, and types of Canadian law. Chapter 1 outlines the development of Canada's constitution and how laws are made. Laws that protect civil and human rights are covered in Chapter 2.

Chapter 3 examines groups that have experienced discrimination and looks at the legal initiatives proposed to remedy the injustices.

In Unit 2, you will be introduced to criminal law and the major legislative amendments made recently to the *Criminal Code*, particularly the *Youth Criminal Justice Act* and the *Controlled Drugs and Substances Act*.

Various aspects of tort law, family law, and contract law will likely affect you throughout your life. Units 3, 4, and 5 provide in-depth coverage of these types of law.

Features of the Sixth Edition

What You Should Know
Each chapter starts with an outline of key questions.

Chapter at a Glance
The main topics of the chapter are previewed.

Selected Key Terms
A list of selected key terms is found on the first page of each chapter. These are the most important legal terms used in the chapter.

Case

Case Name, 2009 SCC 000 (CanLII)

For more information, Go to Nelson Social Studies

Case features provide an extensive collection of relevant case studies from across Canada. We have used as many recent cases as possible. Precedent-setting and historically valuable cases are also included.

Each case has been identified with a complete citation so that you are aware of the date of the case and the court in which it was heard. Abbreviations used in case citations are explained in **Citation References** in **Appendix B** on pages 602 to 603.

For a complete list of cases in this book, see the **Table of Cases** in **Appendix C** on pages 604 to 605.

For Discussion

1. Each case ends with four questions covering points of law and giving you the opportunity to clarify and analyze reasons for judgments. In answering these questions, you will consider the information you have learned in the chapter, along with the details presented in the case itself. You will soon recognize that concepts covered in other chapters are interrelated.

You Be the Judge

Case Name, 2009 ONCA 000 (CanLII)

For more information, Go to Nelson Social Studies

This feature presents a brief legal scenario (real or fictional). Actual cases have been identified with complete citations.

- Each You Be the Judge feature ends with a question, which invites you to interpret the case or scenario and consider a course of action, as if you were the judge.

margin definitions Brief margin definitions appear near bolded key terms throughout the chapters.

 Did You Know?

This feature offers relevant and interesting facts that correspond to the main text.

 ## Looking Back

Feature Title

This feature provides a historical perspective on specific aspects of Canadian law.

For Discussion

1. Each Looking Back feature ends with four questions. In answering these questions, you will consider the information presented in this feature.

 You and the Law

This new feature appears in each chapter and highlights ways in which various aspects of Canadian law affect you as a student and as a vital member of society.

 ## Agents of Change

Feature Title

This feature profiles a person, organization, institution, or event that has helped to bring about change in Canadian law.

For Discussion

1. Each Agents of Change feature ends with four questions. In answering these questions, you will consider the information presented in this feature.

Review Your Understanding

1. This feature, which contains five questions, follows each major section within a chapter. These questions will help you to check your knowledge and understanding of the material you have just covered.

CAREERS

Feature Title

This feature explores the career opportunities within a particular area of law, such as human rights commissioner, correctional services officer, or small claims court clerk.

Career Exploration Activity

Each Careers feature includes a career exploration activity.

1. Several questions follow the career exploration activity.

 All About Law DVD

DVD icons appear throughout the chapters and link to a new DVD program series from CBC news programs and archives. These DVDs can be used to introduce, illustrate, and/or summarize concepts presented in the text. Each DVD program comes with a print support package to assist teachers when using this feature.

ISSUE

Feature Title

This feature, near the end of each chapter, explores a "hot topic" related to the chapter content. Both sides of challenging issues are presented.

What Do You Think?

1. Each Issue feature ends with several thought-provoking questions.

Chapter Review

Each chapter concludes with a Chapter Review, consisting of the following:

Chapter Highlights, summarizing the main points of the chapter—a useful study aid

Check Your Knowledge, containing knowledge and understanding questions and emphasizing the skills of summarizing, identifying, and comparing

Apply Your Learning, providing additional case studies and questions for analysis

Communicate Your Understanding, offering further opportunities for presenting arguments in oral or written form, justifying opinions, and debating ideas

Develop Your Thinking, presenting opportunities for more in-depth research projects, role plays, and simulations

Appendices

Appendix A, on pages 598 to 601, contains the *Canadian Charter of Rights and Freedoms*. Appendix B, on pages 602 to 603, provides a list of Citation References. Appendix C, on pages 604 to 605, contains the Table of Cases. You will be asked to refer to these appendices throughout your study of law.

Index

A comprehensive index, on pages 618 to 625, lists subjects covered in this book and the pages on which they can be found. Use the index as a quick reference guide to the book's contents.

Glossary

The Glossary, on pages 606 to 617, gives meanings for difficult legal terms and concepts that are printed in **bold** throughout the book. It is like a mini-dictionary.

Learning Outcomes

Learning to reason logically and to make informed decisions are important goals of education. The study of law is a major step to achieving these goals. The questions and activities throughout the book will give you opportunities to develop legal knowledge and understanding, as well as skills in thinking and inquiry. You will also improve your communication skills and apply what you have learned to your academic, personal, and professional life.

Chapter 1
Law: Its Purpose and History 4

Chapter 2
The *Canadian Charter of Rights and Freedoms* 36

Chapter 3
Human Rights in Canada 70

Whatever our goals—peace, an end to discrimination, a better environment, a greater prosperity for the citizens of the world—the law is an essential tool for achieving them.

—Beverley McLachlin
Chief Justice, Supreme Court of Canada

1 Law: Its Purpose and History

The Lady Justice is a familiar image, especially around courthouses and courtrooms. This statue is located outside of the Supreme Court of Canada building in Ottawa. It is an interpretation of the more traditional version of a blindfolded Lady Justice carrying a sword and scales.

What You Should Know

- What is law?
- Why do societies have laws?
- What are the historical roots of Canadian law?
- Who is responsible for making law in Canada?
- How have our rights developed in Canada?

Chapter at a Glance

1.1 Introduction

1.2 What Is Law, and Why Do We Have It?

1.3 Divisions of Law

1.4 The Development of Canadian Law

1.5 How Rights Have Developed in Canada

1.6 The Development of Canada's Constitution

1.7 How Laws Are Made

Selected Key Terms

bill	plaintiff
case law	precedent
citation	private law
civil law	procedural law
Code of Hammurabi	public law
common law	rule of law
defendant	statute
lobby	substantive law

1.1 Introduction

Laws affect your lives each day. In fact, we all seem to be fascinated with laws. Every day we hear about local, national, and international events that involve law. On television or in newspapers, we follow cases where suspected criminals are charged with outrageous crimes. We might even read or watch video footage about the most recent crimes on Internet news websites. We are fascinated by stories of criminal activity but are shocked when it happens in our own neighbourhoods. People talk about legal issues and trials and want to know what happens in the courts. Many books, television shows, movies, and documentaries all have legal themes—just think of the number of *CSI* and *Law and Order* shows on television. But, do we really understand the justice system? How are laws developed in Canada? How does the legal system work?

 Did You Know?

Often, the fictionalized versions of the law on TV tend to distort and sensationalize real law. The media contribute to this hype by giving extensive coverage to crime in newspapers, on the radio, and on television.

The number of television crime dramas, such as Canadian-produced CSI: NY, show how fascinated our society is with the legal system.

Because laws affect every aspect of your lives, it is important for you to understand the law. Knowing your rights and responsibilities makes you a more informed citizen. In our Canadian democracy, citizens elect politicians. They make the laws. By voting, you help select the people who will represent your needs and values during the lawmaking process.

In this chapter, you will learn what law is and the various divisions of law. You will also examine the early history of law and the developments that have occurred to shape Canadian law as it is today.

1.2 What Is Law, and Why Do We Have It?

Laws change in response to changes in society. Cyberbullying is the use of electronic communications technologies, such as your e-mail or cellphone, to intentionally and repeatedly harass or threaten others. Such acts could result in your suspension or expulsion from school, and the use of threats might even end up with you being charged with the serious crime of "uttering threats."

Laws reflect the values and beliefs of a society. As society's values change, so do its laws. For example, you no longer have to wear a bathing suit that covers you from your neck to your ankles when you sunbathe on a public beach, as was the case a century or so ago. We have traffic laws about how fast you can drive, drug laws on possession and trafficking of illegal substances, criminal laws related to stealing, and environmental laws that punish us for polluting, to name just a few. Even the development of new technology has resulted in the creation of laws. For example, we now have criminal laws that punish people if they try to steal your credit card information or your whole identity. But what exactly is a law?

Laws versus Rules

When people get together in groups, whether at school, at work, at home, or in a social situation, some rules are needed to keep order. Imagine playing sports without rules! You may be familiar with the consequences of not following these rules. However, when you break these rules, even if you suffer consequences for doing so, they are not as serious as the consequences you will experience if you break the law. For example, shoplifting from your favourite store could result in you being charged with theft and having a criminal record. So, when does a rule become a law?

True, we do talk about the "laws" of physics or economics. But, when we talk about a law, it refers to a rule that is enforced by the government. A law is intended to be obeyed by everyone living within that society. As a society, we have banned some activities because of their consequences for other citizens. Laws strike a balance between individual freedom and the needs of society. If a member of society breaks the law by stealing from another person, he or she is punished. As an individual, you are free to do whatever you want, with one exception: You must not do those things the law forbids or prohibits. The characteristics of laws are summarized in the illustration on the next page.

What Is Law?

1. Laws are a set of rules established and enforced by the government.

2. Laws are mandatory.

3. Laws involve a detailed system of consequences.

These three characteristics are what make laws different from rules.

Although most people willingly accept laws about highway speed limits or restrictions on certain drugs, some people do not. If Canadians do not agree with one of the country's laws, they can join pressure groups and **lobby** the government to change the law. Lobby groups try to raise public awareness about changing laws to reflect their opinions and needs. For example, victims' rights groups have pushed for stronger gun control laws. Lobby groups may also challenge laws by going to court or by organizing peaceful demonstrations. Canada is a free country, so people can oppose the laws in a number of ways, but only up to a certain point. If protesters break the law, they can be arrested.

lobby attempt to influence government to benefit a particular group or organization

Why Do We Have Laws?

Society needs laws to limit the behaviour of its citizens. To enforce those laws, society has created punishments for breaking criminal law. Society tries to develop fitting penalties depending on the severity of the offence. Sometimes penalties change. For example, a society concerned with street racing may increase penalties to include long-term suspensions of drivers' licences. It may permanently take licences away from those caught racing.

Laws not only try to protect us from harm, but they also provide a system for settling disputes. For example, suppose you paid money to a bicycle repair shop to fix your mountain bike, but then found out that the store did not fix your bike. What could you do? You could go to a small claims court to try to get your money back (those under 18 would need the help of a responsible adult to do so). As a guide to help you better understand why we have laws in Canada, see the illustration on the next page describing the functions of law.

 You and the Law

Every day, laws and rules impact your lives. Can you think of any laws or rules that affected you on your way to school today? Explain.

Five Functions of Law

2. Provide a System of Enforcement

3. Protect Rights and Freedoms

1. Establish Rules of Conduct

4. Protect Society

5. Resolve Disputes

Why we have laws in Canada

 Did You Know?

Another function of law is to bring order to social relations. Contract, family, and other aspects of civil law establish practices and make it easier to predict how others will act. For example, if you loan someone money, under the law, he or she must pay you back.

1. **Establish Rules of Conduct:** Laws try to outline guidelines for individuals living with others in society to reduce conflicts between them. For example, in order for you to get your driver's licence, you must pass a written test and a road test to demonstrate that you know traffic safety rules. Imagine what would happen if there were no rules for our roads. The resulting chaos would be a danger to everyone.

2. **Provide a System of Enforcement:** For laws to have any meaning, they must be enforced. Police and the courts oversee the operation of laws. For example, if you break a law such as speeding in your car, police may charge you, and then you will have to answer for your actions in a court.

3. **Protect Rights and Freedoms:** In our free and democratic society, laws protect our rights and freedoms. Laws help encourage the values of tolerance and respect. In Canada, we have basic freedoms such as freedom of expression or of peaceful assembly. These rights cannot be limited unless there is a solid legal reason for doing so. For example, your freedom of expression does not allow you to harass or verbally disrespect someone in your school. You will learn more about your rights and freedoms in Chapter 2.

4. **Protect Society:** Criminal laws are designed to protect people from harm. Our society defines what we consider wrong and sets out punishments for those who break the law. For example, we have criminal laws that prevent you from carrying an unlicensed handgun or beating up your neighbour. Civil laws also protect individuals from being harmed or taken advantage of. For example, we have labour and occupational safety laws that protect you from harm when you are working.

5. **Resolve Disputes:** An important function of law is to settle conflicts. Disputes can be settled through negotiation or through the court system. Laws help to create order and ensure that disagreements are solved fairly. For example, if you went on someone's property without the owner's permission, you could be sued for trespass.

Review Your Understanding

1. What is law?
2. Distinguish between laws and rules.
3. Summarize the five functions of law.
4. What factors might cause laws to change?
5. Justify the importance of law enforcement in society.

substantive law the laws that outline your rights and obligations in society

procedural law the legal processes involved in protecting our rights

1.3 Divisions of Law

Law can be divided into two basic types:

- substantive law
- procedural law

Substantive and Procedural Law

Substantive law consists of rules that outline your rights and obligations in society. Substantive laws in the *Criminal Code* outline the activities or actions that are considered crimes in our society. For example, it is a crime to beat up another person. The *Criminal Code* describes the various types of assault. The offence of aggravated assault is defined as an action that "wounds, maims, disfigures or endangers the life" of another person.

Procedural law outlines the steps involved in protecting our rights. For example, there are formal legal processes that the police must follow to obtain a legal search warrant. There are formal procedures they must perform to conduct a proper alcohol or drug spot check on a suspected impaired driver.

Public Law and Private Law

Substantive law is divided into the areas of public law and private law, also known as civil law. Public law controls the relationships between governments and the people who live in society. It represents laws that apply to all individuals. The main types of public law are criminal, constitutional, and administrative law.

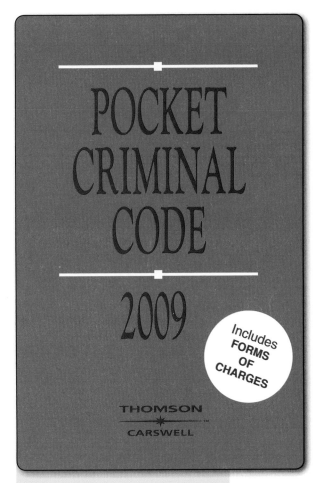

POCKET CRIMINAL CODE 2009

Includes FORMS OF CHARGES

THOMSON CARSWELL

The *Criminal Code* lists the activities that are considered crimes in Canada.

Private law outlines the legal relationship between private citizens, and between citizens and organizations. Its main purpose is to manage the behaviour of persons and organizations in conflict with each other. It also manages payment of damages to those who have been wronged. Private (civil) law can be further subdivided into tort, family, contract, property, and labour and employment law. Refer to the illustration below to discover the divisions of Canadian law.

criminal law the body of public law that defines crimes and punishments

constitutional law outlines the structure and powers of the federal and provincial governments and addresses all issues concerning the Charter

administrative law outlines the relationship between citizens and government bodies

public law controls the relationships between individuals and the state

Public law controls the relationships between governments and society.

Divisions of Public Law and Private Law

PUBLIC LAW: Controls the relationship between the government and the people. It represents laws that apply to all individuals.

Criminal Law: Outlines offences against society and prescribes punishments. Crimes include murder, kidnapping, sexual assault, break and enter, and theft. Criminal acts and their punishments are detailed in the *Criminal Code of Canada*. For example, murder carries a maximum penalty of life imprisonment. Criminal laws about drugs are found in the *Controlled Drugs and Substances Act*. Criminal laws for youths are found in the *Youth Criminal Justice Act*. Criminal law is discussed in greater detail in Unit 2.

Constitutional Law: Outlines the structure and powers of the federal and provincial governments. The Constitution is the supreme law in Canada. Rights in the *Charter of Rights and Freedoms* are part of constitutional law. For example, if a law violates equality rights that are guaranteed in our Constitution, the law could be declared invalid. In legal terms, this is known as "struck down as unconstitutional." The *Charter of Rights and Freedoms* is discussed in greater detail near the end of this chapter in the section Constitutional Protection of Civil Rights and in Chapter 2.

Administrative Law: Outlines the relationship between citizens and government boards and agencies. It is a set of rules for procedural fairness when taking a complaint to a government board or agency. In other words, it is a way to make sure that legal hearings and reviews are fair for all parties. For example, if people feel that they are discriminated against, they can file a complaint with a human rights commission. Other boards and agencies involve licensing activities. Liquor control boards manage the consumption and sale of alcoholic beverages. They also grant liquor licences. Administrative agencies help people resolve disputes without the cost and delay of going to court. For example, disputes between landlords and tenants can be resolved at tribunals.

PRIVATE LAW: (also known as **civil law**): Outlines the rights and responsibilities of private individuals and organizations. In a private (civil) law case, the person who starts the lawsuit is called the **plaintiff**, and the person who is being sued is called the **defendant**. The plaintiff sues because he or she believes that the defendant has caused him or her harm, loss, or injury.

Tort Law: Holds a person or organization responsible for the damage they cause to another person. Torts are wrongs that one person commits against another. For example, a dental surgeon does not live up to the profession's standard of care during an operation. The patient can sue for malpractice or negligence (carelessness). Tort law is discussed in greater detail in Unit 3.

Family Law: Regulates aspects of family life. It deals with the relationship between persons living together as spouses or partners, and among parents, grandparents, and children. Family law may deal with separation and divorce, division of property, and child custody. It may also deal with unpaid support payments to spouses and children. Family law is discussed in greater detail in Unit 4.

Contract Law: Outlines the requirements for legally binding agreements. For example, a contract may be for something as simple as buying a DVD— you offer to pay for it and the store accepts your money. But contracts may also involve complex agreements between companies and governments. If someone does not fulfill the terms of the contract, this is known in legal terms as a breach of contract. That means that the legal agreement is broken. The injured party can take legal action in the courts and sue for damages. Contract law is discussed in greater detail in Chapter 15.

Property Law: Outlines the relationship between individuals and property. For example, property laws may cover the use, enjoyment, sale, and lease of property. So, when you finish school and decide to rent your first apartment some day, you will be asked to sign a lease agreement. Property law is discussed in greater detail in Chapter 16.

Labour and Employment Law: Governs the relationship between employers and employees. For example, labour laws may control the actions of unions and management during a strike. Employment laws deal with issues such as minimum wage, pay equity, working conditions, and workers' compensation. They also deal with disputes between workers and employers when there is no union. For example, if an employer pays below the legal minimum wage, you can challenge this using employment standards laws. Labour and employment laws are discussed in greater detail in Chapter 16.

private law outlines the relationship between private individuals and organizations

civil law the private law governing the relationships between individuals

plaintiff the person suing in a civil action

defendant in civil law, the person who is being sued; in criminal law, the person charged with an offence

tort law the area of law dealing with damages caused by a person or organization

family law the area of law that regulates aspects of family life

contract law outlines the requirements for legally binding agreements and remedies if the agreement is breached

property law outlines the rights and responsibilities of owning, acquiring, and maintaining property

labour and employment law labour law governs the relationships between employers and unions; employment law governs the relationship between employers and employees

1.4 The Development of Canadian Law

Canadian law is based upon the laws of France and England, the countries that colonized Canada. However, there are important differences between the legal systems of the two countries. Early on, French law was codified and written down. English law, on the other hand, was known as customary law, as it was based on custom or what had been done in the past. It was not codified or written down until quite late in England's history. Over hundreds of years, the English Parliament has passed laws codifying many customs and court decisions. However, much of English law has still not been written down.

The Evolution of Law

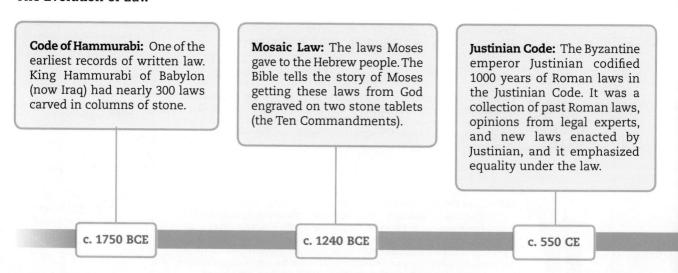

Code of Hammurabi: One of the earliest records of written law. King Hammurabi of Babylon (now Iraq) had nearly 300 laws carved in columns of stone.

Mosaic Law: The laws Moses gave to the Hebrew people. The Bible tells the story of Moses getting these laws from God engraved on two stone tablets (the Ten Commandments).

Justinian Code: The Byzantine emperor Justinian codified 1000 years of Roman laws in the Justinian Code. It was a collection of past Roman laws, opinions from legal experts, and new laws enacted by Justinian, and it emphasized equality under the law.

c. 1750 BCE   c. 1240 BCE   c. 550 CE

Modern Canadian law is influenced by the Aboriginal peoples. When the British and French came to Canada, the Aboriginal peoples had their own systems of government and legal systems. These included the ideas of elected leaders, government by consensus, and concepts of equality and equality before the law. They can all be found in the Constitution of the Iroquois Nations (also known as the Great Binding Law).

The Early History of Law

The laws of ancient civilizations greatly influenced modern Canadian law. In early societies, local customs and beliefs were the law. It was not necessary to write the customs down because everyone was aware of them. They were passed on by word of mouth to future generations. As societies grew, the laws became more complex. It became too difficult for many citizens to know and understand these laws. So, it became necessary for existing laws to be written down in a permanent form. The timeline below across pages 12 and 13 shows some of the most important early records of law. Many of the laws referred to in the timeline are called "codes." A code is a written collection of a country's laws, arranged so that they can be used and understood. This process of preparing a code is called **codification**. The **Code of Hammurabi**, for example, was organized under headings such as family, criminal, labour, property, and so on. Babylonian judges could match a person's offence and punishment by looking at the written law rather than deciding for themselves what punishment to pass.

codification the process of assembling a system of laws into a body of statutes

Code of Hammurabi one of the earliest known sets of written laws, recorded by King Hammurabi of Babylon in 1750 BCE

 Did You Know?

Under the Code of Hammurabi, if a man destroyed the eye of another man, the victim was entitled to destroy his assailant's eye. This is the origin of the expression, "An eye for an eye, a tooth for a tooth."

Magna Carta: A famous document that the English nobility forced King John to sign in 1215. The Magna Carta recognized the principle of the rule of law, which is the idea that all people—rulers and commoners alike—have to follow the same laws.

Napoleonic Code: Also called the French Civil Code, the Napoleonic Code was a revised set of civil laws for all French people. Because Napoleon conquered much of Europe around this time, this new set of laws became the legal model for many European countries.

It is important to remember that law is constantly evolving. Each of these records of law had an impact on laws written hundreds or even thousands of years later. For example, the Napoleonic Code was based heavily on the Justinian Code, and civil law in Québec is based on the Napoleonic Code.

| 1215 | 1804 |

Activity

To learn more about the Code of Hammurabi,

Go to Nelson Social Studies

retribution a deserved punishment for a wrong

restitution the act of making good, restoring, or compensating a person for a wrong that was done to him or her

feudal system a political, social, and economic system prevalent in Europe between the ninth and fifteenth centuries

Both the Code of Hammurabi and Mosaic law illustrate systems that followed the concept of **retribution**. For every crime there should be a deserved punishment. In early law, most crimes had harsh punishments. For example, under the Code of Hammurabi, the penalty for receiving stolen goods was death. Under Mosaic law, hitting your mother or father was punishable by death.

Mosaic law also introduced the concept of **restitution.** This is paying back the victim for the harm done by an offender. If you were found guilty of theft, you were required to repay the victim for the goods stolen. In recent years, restitution has become a more common punishment in Canadian law and is discussed further in Chapter 9.

The Feudal System and Common Law

In 1066, William, Duke of Normandy (in what is now France), invaded and conquered England. As the king of England, William introduced a system of government from Europe called the **feudal system.** The king owned all the land and divided much of it among his lords and nobles. In return, the lords became the king's vassals (servants) and promised him loyalty and military service. These lords had vassals of their own who farmed the lands and gave part of their produce to the lords and the Church. Some of them also served in the armies of the lords.

In this historic illustration, vassals receive their lord's orders before going to the fields to farm.

A lord's land was called his manor, or estate, and he ran it as he saw fit. For example, a lord acted as the judge in any trial of a vassal accused of breaking the law. Injustice often resulted. One lord might find a vassal guilty of theft and order repayment plus compensation for trouble to the victim. Another might sentence the vassal to death for the same crime. To eliminate these inconsistencies, the king appointed a number of judges who travelled throughout England and held hearings on controversial or disputed cases. These judges met regularly in London to discuss cases and share experiences. By the thirteenth century, the laws and punishments were more similar for both criminal and civil cases. When similar legal issues arose, judges began to decide similar cases in the same way, which were recorded and became known as **case law**.

As judges developed standard punishments for specific crimes, these legal decisions became the basis of English **common law**, so called because it was common to the whole of England. Common law relied on case law or **precedent** cases. As the legal system became more just, it earned new respect. This common law system was introduced to North America by the colonists who first travelled here.

When a legal case was hard to decide, the judge would sometimes order a new trial to be "determined" by God. Trial by combat was one way to choose the winner. The victor was assumed innocent, and the loser, guilty.

Common Law

The common law system developed in England. It relied on case law and was common for all people.

case law recorded written decisions of judges; also known as common law

common law a system of law based on past legal decisions; also known as case law

precedent a legal decision that serves as an example and authority in subsequent similar cases

appeal referring a case to a higher court to reconsider the lower court's decision

Common law is based upon the important principle of the rule of precedent. A precedent is something that has been done before. For example, a ruling in one case can later determine how future cases are handled. The rule of precedent is part of the English law that has been passed down to Canada. A case and its decision became common knowledge in the English legal community. Then, all judges who heard cases with similar facts would give similar decisions. By treating similar cases alike, English judges established the same standard of judging offences throughout the country. At first, these case decisions existed only in the judges' memories. They were known as "unwritten law." This system was considered an improvement over the feudal system. In it, a lord had the right to judge cases however he chose. People who were dissatisfied with court decisions could **appeal** to the monarch, who had the authority to overrule judges' decisions. Today, the legal system still has an appeal process of applying to a higher court to review a decision of a lower court. Each province has a court of appeal. The highest court is the Supreme Court of Canada.

Precedent

Our Canadian legal system relies heavily on precedent, ensuring that similar facts result in similar decisions.

Did You Know?

Sometimes the rule of precedent is known as *stare decisis*, a Latin phrase that means "to stand by earlier decisions."

Today, lawyers and judges still refer to earlier decisions on cases that are identical or similar to the one they are dealing with as precedents. These earlier cases are considered examples that should be followed. They influence and guide judges when they reach a verdict and pass sentence.

The rule of precedent introduces some certainty into the law. It means that everyone, including the accused, can examine similar cases and arguments and expect a similar result. Today, trial lawyers spend much time submitting precedents, hoping to persuade the judge to reach a similar decision. Many older cases in this text are landmark judgments that set precedents that are still followed by the courts today. Of course, following earlier cases too closely can cause a problem if the precedent is not recent. Henry VIII of England issued a law that cats should be allowed to roam at will. He did so because of the huge numbers of rodents in England at the time. This law is not a suitable precedent for modern apartment building rules.

Activity

To learn how to access written Canadian court decisions on the Internet,

Go to Nelson Social Studies

Case Law Citation

As the number of judges and court cases increased in Canada, it became necessary to record the decisions. Many court case decisions are recorded and published. You can find them in paper and electronic form. Thus, common law is often called case law. You can retrieve these cases from sources such as *Canadian Criminal Cases* (C.C.C.), *Reports of Family Law* (R.F.L.), or *Supreme Court Reports* (S.C.R.). You can also use case reporting websites, such as CanLII, the Canadian Legal Information Institute.

citation the reference for a legal case

Each recorded case is given a title, or **citation**. The citation lists basic information: who is involved in the case, whether the case is public or private (civil) law, and the year the court decision was reached. It also identifies which court heard the case and the name of the published book (the law reporting series of books) in which the court decision appears. This information makes it easy to locate the case in a law library.

Most high school students cannot access a law library. Therefore, this textbook uses neutral citations. These specify the case name, the year of the decision, the court hearing the case, and a court-assigned number for an Internet case-reporting website. You can find the citations online at an Internet case-reporting website, or by visiting the Nelson Social Studies website.

Did You Know?

Today, the term "common law" relates to law based on judges' decisions, precedent, and reported case law. It is distinct from the law passed by governments, and it serves as a major part of Canadian law today.

Elements of a Citation

NEUTRAL (Online) CITATION

R.	v.	Ferguson,	2008	SCC	6	CanLII
Regina or *Rex* (Latin for "queen" or "king") represents society	*versus* (Latin for "against")	defendant (accused)	year of decision	Supreme Court of Canada; the court hearing the case	number assigned by the court	Canadian Legal Information Institute, which provides access to full case decisions on the Internet

Cowles	v.	Balac,	2006	CanLII	34916	(ON C.A.)
plaintiff (person suing)	*versus* (Latin for "against")	defendant (person being sued)	year of decision	Canadian Legal Information Institute, which provides access to full case decisions on the Internet	number assigned by the legal information service	Ontario Court of Appeal

CASE-REPORTING SERIES CITATION

R.	v.	Bates	(2000),	35	C.R.	(5th)	327	(Ont. C.A.)
Regina or *Rex* (Latin for "queen" or "king") represents society	*versus* (Latin for "against")	defendant (accused)	year of decision	volume number	name of reporter where case is reported (e.g., *Criminal Reports*)	series	page number	jurisdiction (federal, province, or territory) and court (e.g., Ontario Court of Appeal)

Langille et al.	v.	McGrath	(2000),	233	N.B.R.	(2d)	29	(N.B.Q.B.)
plaintiff and others (Latin *et alia* for "and others")	*versus* (Latin for "against")	defendant	year of decision	volume number	name of reporter where case is reported (e.g., *New Brunswick Reports*)	series	page number	jurisdiction (federal, province, or territory) and court (e.g., New Brunswick Court of Queen's Bench)

These charts show the elements of a citation for a neutral online citation and for a citation in a case-reporting series of books. In this text, most cases use a neutral citation followed by a reference to the Nelson Social Studies website.

Case

Grant v. Dempsey, 2001 NSSC 20 (CanLII)

For more information, Go to Nelson Social Studies

On October 14, 1995, the 18-year-old plaintiff, Adrian Grant, was lying in the middle of a street in Middleton, Nova Scotia, severely intoxicated, wearing dark clothing. At 1:30 a.m., he was run over and seriously injured by a van operated by Garth Dempsey. Dempsey had been working late and was driving home at the legal speed. It was a dark, dry night with no streetlights in the area. Dempsey had just put his lights low before meeting an oncoming vehicle. He did not have time to put his high-beam lights on before he saw an object right in front of him. Dempsey thought it was a duffle bag or a garbage bag on the road. When he realized he had run over a person he called 911.

Evidence at trial indicated that Adrian Grant had a blood-alcohol level about two and one-half times the legal limit for driving and he had no recollection of how he came to be lying on the road. Adrian Grant sued for personal injuries.

For Discussion

1. Explain the components of the case citation.
2. What type of law is involved in this case?
3. Was Grant responsible for his own injuries? Explain.
4. Was Dempsey's driving at fault? Explain.

 Case

R. v. Kerr, 2004 SCC 44 (CanLII)

For more information, Go to Nelson Social Studies

The accused, Jason Kerr, was serving time for armed robbery in a maximum security prison in Edmonton, Alberta, where Joseph Garon, a fellow inmate, made death threats against him. Garon had been a member of a criminal gang that controlled inmates inside the prison through intimidation and assaults. After Garon threatened to "smash his head in," Kerr was worried that Garon might carry out the threat, and so he concealed two weapons in his pants. When Kerr went to the dining area, Garon approached him holding out a homemade knife. A fight resulted where both Kerr and Garon stabbed each other multiple times. Garon was killed by a stab wound to the head. Kerr was charged with second degree murder and possession of a dangerous weapon.

Kerr was acquitted at trial on the basis that the murder was self-defence and he had the weapons for defence. The Crown appealed to the Alberta Court

of Appeal on January 30, 2003. The Court of Appeal upheld the trial decision of self-defence but convicted Kerr on the weapons charge. Kerr appealed to the Supreme Court of Canada. In a 6–1 judgment released June 23, 2004, the Supreme Court allowed the appeal and acquitted Kerr on the weapons charge.

For Discussion

1. Explain the components of the case citation.
2. What type of law is involved in this case?
3. Do you think the accused planned the attack? Explain.
4. What factors do you think the trial judge and court of appeal judges took into consideration in acquitting the accused on the charge of second-degree murder?

The Rule of Law and the Magna Carta

When King John ruled England (1199–1216), there was an important development in English law. The king thought he was above the law and abused the power of his position. Eventually, the English nobility forced King John to sign the Magna Carta, the "Great Charter," in 1215. This famous document recognized the principle of the **rule of law**. This principle required that all rulers obey the law. In addition, no ruler could restrict the freedoms of the people without reason. The people's legal rights could not be changed without their consent. The Magna Carta also guaranteed the right of **habeas corpus**. This meant that any person who was imprisoned was entitled to appear before the courts within a reasonable time. The accused could be released if held unlawfully, or tried by peers (equals) if charged with an offence. The right of habeas corpus is guaranteed in today's Charter, section 10(c).

rule of law the fundamental principle that the law applies equally to all persons

habeas corpus a document that requires a person to be brought to court to determine if he or she is being legally detained

King John receives the Magna Carta. The Magna Carta recognized the principle of the rule of law.

The Magna Carta was first issued in 1215 and reissued throughout the thirteenth century by England's rulers. This photo shows the 1297 version.

Canadians are governed by the rule of law. Government officials cannot make up or change the rules without consulting anyone else. The rule of law exists because our society believes that there should be equality under the law and that decisions should not be made arbitrarily (without reason or justification).

Parliament and Statute Law

Although King John and his successors had to obey the law, they still struggled for power with the English nobles. Around 1265, a group of nobles revolted against King Henry III to make him reform the English legal process. These nobles wanted to reduce the king's power and acquire more power for themselves. As a result, representatives were called together from all parts of England, forming the first Parliament. The job of Parliament was to help make laws for the country. Over the next four centuries, Parliament struggled for power with the monarchs of Great Britain.

statute a law passed by a legislative body

One of the most important functions of Parliament is to pass laws, known as **statutes**. As British society changed, common law and case law could not address every legal situation. Parliament filled the gaps and made new laws to deal with new situations. In addition, many common law decisions made by the courts were codified by Parliament and became statute law. One important outcome of recording laws and court decisions was that it allowed the public to read the laws and know what they said.

In making a decision in any case, courts must consider both the common law and the statute law. Canadian law is made up of both common law decisions and statute laws passed by government.

Review Your Understanding

1. Explain the significance of the Code of Hammurabi and Mosaic law.
2. How did the English common law system develop?
3. How is the rule of precedent used in today's system of law?
4. Why is a case citation useful in law?
5. Explain the significance of statute law as a source of law.

1.5 How Rights Have Developed in Canada

civil rights the rights of citizens that limit the power of governments

Canada is often thought of as one of the best countries in the world in which to live. It ranks near the top of the UN Human Development Index report. The report measures things like standard of living, life expectancy, and literacy. One reason for its rank is that Canada highly values **civil rights** and freedoms, which limit the power that a government has over its citizens. Canada also respects human rights. These protect people from unfair discrimination by other individuals. Compared to people in many other countries, Canadians can feel secure in almost all areas of their lives. Canadians are free because laws are passed and enforced to protect their rights and freedoms. In fact, many other countries look to Canada as an example of what a free society can be.

Wealth, gender, race, age, beliefs, family status, and so on are not supposed to determine how you are treated in Canada. Today, everyone is considered equal under the law. This belief is a foundation of Canadian society and Canadian law. As a result, Canadians expect their laws to be fair and just for everyone. This situation is quite new. In Chapter 2 you will learn more about the *Charter of Rights and Freedoms*, and in Chapter 3 you will learn that Canada has not always treated different groups of people equally.

Being equal under the law is a very recent legal concept in human history. If you were born a slave in ancient Babylon in 1700 BCE, you had few legal rights—unless you married someone of a higher class. If you were born a peasant in sixteenth-century France, you would probably die a peasant. For thousands of years, the vast majority of people had few, if any, rights. People had little opportunity to improve their lives. It took many hundreds of years for the concept of human rights and freedoms to take root and spread. Many wars and revolutions had to be fought in order to win these rights. In the next section, a few major events in that struggle will be examined.

The United Nations Human Development Index, 2007–2008

Country	HDI Ranking
Iceland	1
Norway	2
Australia	3
Canada	4
Ireland	5
Sweden	6
Switzerland	7
Japan	8
Netherlands	9
France	10
Finland	11
United States	12

Canada ranked fourth on the Human Development Index for 2007 to 2008.

The Development of Human Rights and Freedoms

As you previously learned in this chapter, the earliest legal codes imposed laws and punishments that most Canadians today would consider cruel. These laws were meant to ensure that these societies would survive. Human rights simply were not an issue. The Magna Carta and later the *Bill of Rights* helped lay the groundwork for our modern legal system.

These and other events showed that beliefs about rights could lead to changes in governing. By the end of the seventeenth century, many Western legal and moral thinkers believed that human beings had rights to life, liberty, and security. Such rights were thought to exist independently of any rights or duties created by a ruler, government, church, or society. Those in power felt threatened by these ideas, which spread quickly in Europe and North America.

Rights and Revolutions

In this historic painting, John Hancock signs the U.S. Declaration of Independence in 1776, during the American Revolution.

The American Revolution broke out in 1775. People in 13 colonies were angry over new taxes and lack of representation in Parliament. They fought for independence from Great Britain. The U.S. Declaration of Independence was issued on July 4, 1776. The revolution did not end until 1783. In 1788, the U.S. Constitution was written and became law. Criticized for not containing a bill of rights, 10 changes were made to the Constitution in 1791. These changes became the U.S. *Bill of Rights*. They are still the basis of freedom and civil rights for Americans.

New ideas spread throughout Europe and North America in the centuries leading up to the American Revolution. Perhaps the most radical idea was that the rules governing people must change if they do not protect citizens' rights.

In the eighteenth century, a group of French thinkers known as the *philosophes* wrote books and pamphlets attacking the power of the French king, the nobles, and the Church. They wanted an end to the feudal system and more freedom for the French people. These ideas helped start the American Revolution.

France also sent ships and troops to help the Americans. Returning soldiers brought back stories of the successful American Revolution and the ideas of liberty and equality. This fed the growing demands for change in France.

Ultimately, in 1789, just one year after the U.S. Constitution became law, the common people in France rose up against their king. The people were rebelling against the power of the nobles and the Church. The feudal system and the privileges of rulers and Church were abolished during the French Revolution. A National Assembly (similar to the House of Commons) was set up, and its members were elected by the people. The Western idea of a "nation-state," as we understand it today, came out of these revolutions.

On August 26, 1789, the National Assembly passed the Declaration of the Rights of Man and of the Citizen. It guaranteed all French citizens their basic freedoms and became the basis of future modern democracies.

 Did You Know?

Article 1 of the Declaration of the Rights of Man and of the Citizen states: Men are born and remain free and equal in rights.

The Declaration of the Rights of Man and of the Citizen was a document that influenced the development of rights and freedoms in other democracies.

The Universal Declaration of Human Rights

World War II was the most destructive war in history and one that truly spanned the globe. Many groups of people were rounded up and sent to camps, where millions of prisoners were killed, including more than 6 million Jews. There were also at least 5 million non-Jewish victims, including Gypsies, political enemies, gays, and disabled people. People around the world were horrified when the camps were discovered near the end of the war.

In 1945, world leaders formed the United Nations. One of the United Nations' first steps was to try to guarantee all people certain rights and freedoms. The UN Commission on Human Rights was set up to produce a list of human rights and freedoms for people all over the world. The Universal Declaration of Human Rights was adopted by the United Nations on December 10, 1948.

The Universal Declaration of Human Rights was the first time nations from around the world had signed a formal agreement on specific rights and freedoms for all human beings. For billions of people—perhaps the majority of people—the guarantees contained in the Declaration are unfulfilled. More than 60 years after it was passed, however, the Declaration remains a standard that many countries have tried to live up to and put into effect.

The Universal Declaration of Human Rights

Some of the rights guaranteed under the Universal Declaration of Human Rights:

- All human beings are born free and equal in dignity and rights.

- Everyone is entitled to all the rights set forth in this Declaration, without distinction of any kind, such as race, colour, sex, language, religion, political or other opinion, national or social origin, property, birth, or other status.

- Everyone has the right to life, liberty, and security of person.

- No one shall be held in slavery or servitude.

- No one shall be subjected to torture or to cruel, inhuman, or degrading treatment or punishment.

- All are equal before the law and are entitled without any discrimination to equal protection of the law.

- No one shall be subjected to arbitrary arrest, detention, or exile.

- Everyone charged with a penal offence has the right to be presumed innocent until proved guilty according to law in a public trial.

- Everyone has the right to freedom of movement.

- Everyone has the right to freedom of thought, conscience, and religion.

- Everyone has the right to freedom of opinion and expression.

- Everyone has the right to freedom of peaceful assembly and association.

- Everyone, without any discrimination, has the right to equal pay for equal work.

John Diefenbaker and the *Canadian Bill of Rights*

As you have learned, much of Canadian law is based on English common law. Common law is unwritten and based on customs and earlier court decisions. As a result, for many years, Canadians had legal rights that were not written down but simply understood to exist. One example of this was the right to be charged and tried in a court of law if accused of a crime. After the rights abuses of World War II, many Canadians came to believe that legal rights had to be written down.

John Diefenbaker holds the *Canadian Bill of Rights*.

In 1945, John Diefenbaker, a young Member of Parliament (MP), led a movement to have these rights made into law. He was defeated by MPs who thought that Canada's tradition of common law was good enough. Diefenbaker later became leader of the Progressive Conservative Party. In federal election campaigns in 1957 and 1958, he promised a bill of rights for all Canadians.

As prime minister, Diefenbaker kept his promise. Parliament passed the *Canadian Bill of Rights* on August 10, 1960. This federal legislation was not revolutionary. It merely set down in legislation the civil rights and freedoms that Canadians had already enjoyed under common law. It also reminded Canadians of the importance of individual rights.

The *Canadian Bill of Rights*

Rights guaranteed under the *Canadian Bill of Rights* include the following:

- the right to life, liberty, and security of the person and enjoyment of property, and the right not to be deprived thereof except by due process of law
- the right to equality before the law and its protection
- freedom of religion, speech, assembly and association, and the press
- the right not to be arbitrarily detained, imprisoned, or exiled
- the right not to receive cruel and unusual treatment or punishment
- the right to be informed promptly of the reason for arrest
- the right to retain and instruct counsel without delay
- the right to obtain a writ of habeas corpus to determine the validity of detention
- the right not to give evidence if denied counsel, and protection against self-incrimination
- the right to a fair hearing
- the right to be presumed innocent until proven guilty
- the right to reasonable bail
- the right to an interpreter in any legal proceedings

For Discussion

1. Why was the *Canadian Bill of Rights* an important step in the development of civil liberties in Canada?

2. A fundamental principle identified in the *Canadian Bill of Rights* is "the right to be presumed innocent until proven guilty." Why is this principle important to our justice system?

3. Compare the rights identified in the *Canadian Bill of Rights* with the rights provided in the Universal Declaration of Human Rights in the figure on page 24. What similarities are there?

4. Which right do you think was most important under the *Canadian Bill of Rights*? Why?

The *Canadian Bill of Rights* gave Canadians human rights and fundamental freedoms without discrimination by reason of race, national origin, colour, religion, or sex.

Constitutional Protection of Civil Rights

The *Canadian Bill of Rights* did not stop demands for stronger protection of rights and was criticized for several reasons. As a federal statute (law), it applied only to federal matters, and Parliament could change it at any time. Not only that, it did little to protect equality rights.

In the mid-1960s, the new leader of the Liberal Party, Pierre Elliott Trudeau, captured Canadians' imaginations. He spoke of a "just society." He promised greater social justice and stronger guarantees of individual rights. Trudeau was prime minister for most of the time between 1968 and 1984. He was largely responsible for the *Constitution Act, 1982*.

Many Canadians consider the *Canadian Charter of Rights and Freedoms* to be the most important part of the *Constitution Act, 1982*. It lists the civil rights and freedoms of all Canadians. It guarantees them at every level of government. The Charter is not ordinary statute law, it is constitutional law. Parliament cannot vote to change or abolish it. In order to change constitutional law, the federal government and at least two-thirds of the provinces with 50 percent of the population must agree. This is called the **amending formula**. The rights and freedoms listed in the Charter are part of the Constitution. The entire Charter can be found in Appendix A, pages 598–601.

Section 24 of the Charter details the enforcement of guaranteed rights and freedoms. It states that anyone whose Charter rights or freedoms are violated may go to court to seek a remedy. For example, police must carry out fair and reasonable investigations when searching for evidence. If they improperly search for drugs and violate your Charter rights, you can apply to the court to have the drug evidence thrown out. The court may decide to exclude the evidence, especially if allowing it makes the trial unfair.

Pierre Elliott Trudeau was victorious at the 1968 Liberal leadership convention. On April 20, 1968, he was sworn in as the next prime minister of Canada.

amending formula the procedure to change (amend) Canada's Constitution

All About Law DVD

"Police Diversity: To Serve and Protect the Changing Face of Canada" from *All About Law DVD*

Review Your Understanding

1. Explain the difference between civil rights and human rights.

2. What impact did the U.S. *Bill of Rights* have on the development of rights laws?

3. Explain the significance of the Declaration of the Rights of Man and of the Citizen.

4. What factors contributed to the passing of the Universal Declaration of Human Rights? Why is this document significant today?

5. Explain the amending formula necessary to change Canada's Constitution.

1.6 The Development of Canada's Constitution

The powers and levels of government that make law are described in the Canadian Constitution. The British Parliament passed our first constitution, the *British North America Act (BNA Act)*. It came into effect on July 1, 1867 and the Dominion of Canada was born. Four provinces made up the country: Ontario, Québec, New Brunswick, and Nova Scotia. Canada was not fully independent—Britain still controlled Canada's foreign affairs. For example, Canada could not make its own treaties with other countries. When Britain declared war, Canada was automatically at war. Canada's highest court was in Britain, the Judicial Committee of the Privy Council (JCPC). It could overrule decisions made by the Canadian courts.

Gradually, Canada assumed more control over its own affairs. In 1931, British Parliament passed the Statute of Westminster, giving Canada control over its foreign affairs. When World War II broke out in 1939, Canada declared war on Germany independent of Britain. Then, in 1949, the Supreme Court of Canada became Canada's highest court of appeal. However, one link to Britain prevented Canada from being truly independent. The *BNA Act* was a British statute and only the British Parliament could change (amend) it. Canada had to ask Britain about any changes it wanted to make. For example, in 1940, the Canadian federal government wanted to include unemployment insurance in the *BNA Act* as one of its powers. The British Parliament had to pass the amendment.

In the twentieth century, Britain was willing to give Canada its own constitution and allow it to be independent. However, the federal and provincial governments were suspicious of each other and unwilling to risk losing any powers. They could not agree on a formula to amend the Constitution, if change became necessary.

patriation the process of bringing legislation back under the legal authority of the country to which it applies

The Constitution was transferred to Canada from Britain on April 17, 1982, and Canada finally became an independent country. This process was called **patriation**. The Queen, shown here with Prime Minister Pierre Elliott Trudeau, signed the *Constitution Act, 1982,* in Ottawa.

Division of Powers

jurisdiction authority to do
something, such as make laws

The Constitution Act, 1867, lists federal, provincial, and territorial government powers. It outlines which government has **jurisdiction**, or authority, to make laws in specific areas. The federal government's powers are outlined in section 91. Provincial government powers are outlined in section 92. Section 93 gives the provinces control over education. The chart below gives specific examples of some of the federal and provincial government powers.

Federal and Provincial Government Powers	
Federal Government Powers (Section 91)	Provincial Government Powers (Section 92)
• peace, order, and good government • criminal law • unemployment insurance • banking, currency, and coinage • federal penitentiaries • marriage and divorce • postal services • Aboriginal peoples and their lands	• property and civil rights • marriage ceremonies • police forces and provincial courts • highways and roads • provincial jails • hospitals

Federal and provincial government powers as set forth in the *Constitution Act, 1867*

All About Law DVD

"What Happened" from *All About Law DVD*

The Constitution clearly spells out the division of powers. However, there are still many disputes between levels of government. For example, providing health care is a provincial responsibility. But the federal government tries to set national standards that guarantee all Canadians equal access to health care. Some provinces argue that if the federal government wants to set standards for provincial systems, it should provide more money. Sometimes, these disputes end up in court.

Cities and Townships: A Third Level of Government

The *Constitution Act, 1867*, established only two levels of government. The provinces gave some of their powers to a third level, local municipalities. Municipalities include cities, towns, townships, villages, and counties. The laws that govern the activities of a local community are called bylaws. They are passed by municipal governments and relate to local issues such as emergency services, building permits, the use of pesticides on your lawn, and so on.

Review Your Understanding

1. Explain the significance of the *British North America Act*.
2. Why is the Statute of Westminster important in Canadian law?
3. Why did it take so long for Canada to get control of its own Constitution?
4. Distinguish between sections 91 and 92 of the *Constitution Act, 1867*, and identify three important powers contained in each section.
5. What is the third level of government in Canada? What type of laws does it pass?

1.7 How Laws Are Made

When Canadian governments want to make or change laws, they must consider what effect that might have. An unpopular law might cause a Member of Parliament (MP) to be defeated in the next election. Before a law is changed or a new law is created, governments spend time and money researching the effects the law is likely to have. A law that the government has proposed is called a **bill**. Once a bill is passed, it becomes a statute or an act.

bill a proposed law; a draft form of an act or statute

How Federal Laws Are Passed

Parliament, which makes our federal laws, consists of three parts: the House of Commons, the Senate, and the governor general, who represents Canada's head of state, Queen Elizabeth II. The House of Commons is the part of Parliament that has the most important role in making laws. Its representatives are elected by the citizens of Canada.

Each Member of Parliament (MP) is an elected representative of a riding or electoral district. Canada is divided into 308 ridings. There is an MP for every geographical area. The political party with the most members elected to the House of Commons forms the government. The other parties in the House are called opposition parties. The leader of the governing party is the prime minister. He or she appoints MPs from his or her party to the Cabinet, which is the executive committee that controls government policy. Cabinet ministers are the heads of government departments that employ thousands of civil servants. They see that federal laws are carried out (refer to the chart on page 28 for the list of federal powers).

Examples of Statute Law

Federal Statutes

- *Criminal Code of Canada*
- *Controlled Drugs and Substances Act*
- *Youth Criminal Justice Act*
- *Hazardous Products Act*
- *Anti-terrorism Act*
- *Income Tax Act*

Provincial Statutes

- *Alberta Highway Traffic Act*
- *Ontario Child and Family Services Act*
- *British Columbia Marriage Act*
- *Saskatchewan Sale of Goods Act*
- *Nova Scotia Hospitals Act*
- *New Brunswick Jury Act*

The federal Parliament and provincial legislatures pass their own statute laws, generally referred to as acts.

The Three Branches of Government in Canada		
Branches	**Federal**	**Provincial**
Executive	Governor General (Monarch)	Lieutenant-Governor (Monarch)
	Prime Minister	Premier
	Federal Cabinet	Cabinet
	Civil Service	Civil Service
Legislative	Parliament	Provincial Legislature
	Governor General (Monarch)	Lieutenant-Governor (Monarch)
	House of Commons	Elected House
	Senate	
Judiciary	Federal Judiciary	Provincial Judiciary

The three branches of government—executive, legislative, and judiciary—each plays a role in changing or interpreting the law.

 Did You Know?

The judiciary is an independent part of the government made up of judges who are appointed to hear legal cases in our court system, interpret the laws, and make unbiased legal decisions.

When a government wants to introduce a new law in Canada, a Cabinet minister introduces a bill into the House of Commons. If the prime minister's party has a majority government (more than half the elected MPs), there is usually no difficulty getting the bill passed. But, if it does not have a majority, it will have to make deals with the opposition to get the bill passed. Once approved, the bill is sent to the Senate. If approved there, it is sent to the governor general, who signs it into law. When a bill becomes law, all Canadians have to obey it or face the consequences.

Passage of a Bill into Law at the Federal Level

Who	Stage
House of Commons	**First Reading** • Bill introduced by a Cabinet minister or private member • First vote taken **Second Reading** • Bill introduced again and debated in general • Second vote taken **Committee Stage** • Bill usually sent to a select committee, standing committee, or committee of the whole House • Bill studied in detail, and changes (amendments) often made; each section may be voted on separately **Third Reading** • Bill briefly debated • Third vote taken
Senate	• Bill goes through three readings and committees, as in the House of Commons
Governor General	• Signs bill to become a law (royal assent)

The legislative branch of government makes the laws. It consists of the House of Commons and the Senate. Why do you think it is important to have three readings of a bill in the House of Commons?

The House of Commons

Governor General Michaëlle Jean represents the Queen in Canada as head of state.

How Provincial Laws Are Passed

Provincial and territorial legislatures pass bills similarly to Parliament. However, they do not have Senates. Once bills pass through three readings, they go to the lieutenant-governor, the Queen's representative, for signature.

How Municipal Bylaws Are Passed

Elected councils, led by a mayor or reeve, vote on municipal bylaws. Procedures vary from one municipality to the next. Municipal bylaws may regulate activities such as garbage collection and water services, local police services, and municipal road maintenance.

Review Your Understanding

1. Why is the House of Commons the most powerful part of Parliament?
2. What are the responsibilities of Cabinet ministers?
3. Briefly summarize how a bill becomes a law at the federal level.
4. What is the responsibility of the governor general with respect to the law-making process?
5. What is the responsibility of a provincial lieutenant-governor?

Mediation: An Effective Form of Dispute Resolution?

Traditionally, courts handle legal disputes over issues such as property matters, inheritance, or child custody. However, in recent years, overcrowding of the courts has created a backlog of cases. Delays can result in injustice for many. The cost of court cases can deny justice to people with moderate incomes. Some interests may be ignored when more than two parties are involved in a dispute. Alternatives to using the courts to solve disputes have become more popular.

Several methods of alternative dispute resolution (ADR) have been developed to settle legal conflicts outside the courts:

- **Negotiation:** The parties communicate with each other until a decision is reached.

- **Mediation:** A third party (a mediator) listens to the parties in the dispute and helps them make a decision that all will accept.

- **Arbitration:** A third party (an arbitrator) listens to the parties and makes a decision. Often, the arbitrator is a respected expert, and the parties must agree in advance to accept the arbitrator's decision.

The most commonly used ADR method is mediation. Mediators are neutral parties who are trained to help the people involved in the dispute come up with solutions to their problems. The mediator hopes that if the parties find a solution that seems fair to both of them, they will abide by it.

Mediation is not new. Labour and management use it to resolve disputes. ADR is now used in family law for separations or divorce. It is also used in administrative law issues, such as landlord and tenant disputes. The Canadian Bar Association, the professional association of lawyers, encourages its members to gain expertise in ADR methods. Its journal has referred to ADR as a "growth industry."

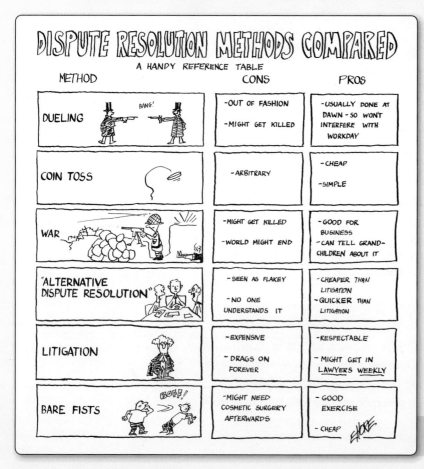

From war to ADR, this cartoon summarizes the options.

On One Side

Mediation program supporters argue that the court system takes too long, is too expensive, and does not guarantee satisfaction. People learning how to use ADR, including anger and stress management, will be better listeners and communicators. They will come to accept and expect to settle differences through conflict resolution programs. Mediation creates positive situations. Parties in dispute can participate in achieving acceptable solutions. Court cases often result in a winner and a loser.

On the Other Side

ADR critics believe that mediation is fine for small disagreements. It is not suitable for battles such as medical negligence. They argue that each party wants to win the case. Parties prefer to gamble on winning the case in court. Some disputes involve parties who are extremely hostile toward each other. Sometimes, hostility and anger prevent a mediator from effectively helping parties reach a settlement.

Critics also point out that ADR methods are not always cheaper because the same lawyers representing the disputants (the people involved in the dispute) in court now offer mediation services. They believe that ADR creates another layer of bureaucracy and expense for disputants.

Instead of ADR, critics support speeding up the legal system and making it more efficient. They suggest creating more courts and appointing more judges to handle the case backlog.

The Bottom Line

Long delays in Canada's justice system must be fixed. Unethical landlords and employers, for example, sometimes depend on the fact that their victims cannot afford the long wait for justice from the civil courts. People suffering discrimination want their complaints settled quickly.

What Do You Think?

1. Assume that you have been consulted as a legal expert to recommend whether a mediation or court process should be used in a particular case. For each situation below, explain why you have selected either mediation or the court system to resolve the case:

   • Divorced parents both want sole custody of their child.
   • A teenage girl accuses a man of stalking her, but he denies it.
   • A university student wants a landlord to fix the leaking ceiling in her apartment.
   • A teen is caught shoplifting a pair of jeans.
   • A youth believes he has been wrongly dismissed from his job.

2. Assume that your parents are involved in legal separation or divorce proceedings and are having difficulty splitting up their household property. Explain the advantages and disadvantages of using mediation as a form of dispute resolution.

Chapter Review

Chapter Highlights

- The citizens of Canada elect lawmakers who make laws that suit the majority of Canadians.
- Laws are rules established and enforced by the government.
- Rules and laws are necessary to keep peace and order in society and to settle disputes.
- Public law controls the relationship between the government and the people and includes criminal, administrative, and constitutional law.
- Private (civil) law outlines the rights and responsibilities of private citizens and organizations, and includes family law, contract law, tort law, property law, and labour law.
- Old laws are often the basis of modern laws. Some important sources of modern law are the Code of Hammurabi, Mosaic law, Roman law, and the Napoleonic Code.
- Lawyers and judges refer to earlier court decisions called precedents.
- A law passed by Parliament is called a statute or an act.
- There are two types of rights: civil rights and human rights. Civil rights outline the power that a government has over its citizens. Human rights protect us from being discriminated against by private individuals, businesses, and institutions.
- The Universal Declaration of Human Rights influenced rights development in Canada.
- Canada's first constitution was called the *British North America Act, 1867*. It was renamed the *Constitution Act, 1867*, in 1982.
- The Statute of Westminster gave Canada control over its foreign affairs.
- The *Constitution Act, 1867*, set out the division of powers for the government. Section 91 details federal matters while section 92 details provincial concerns.
- The name of Canada's constitution today is the *Constitution Act, 1982*.
- The *Canadian Charter of Rights and Freedoms* helps to protect the rights of Canadians. It is part of the *Constitution Act, 1982*.
- The House of Commons is the most powerful branch of Parliament because it passes most laws.

Check Your Knowledge

1. Explain precedent. Why is it important in Canadian law?
2. Explain rule of law. Why is it important in Canadian law?
3. Explain the difference between criminal law and civil law.
4. What is one of the most important functions of Parliament?

Apply Your Learning

5. State whether each of the following is an example of substantive or procedural law:
   a) a law that makes it illegal to assault another person
   b) a law that outlines the steps to follow in making an arrest
   c) a law that makes it illegal to possess a controlled drug
   d) a law that outlines the steps in obtaining a search warrant
6. Indicate whether each of the following is an example of public law or private law:
   a) A youth is arrested for committing a break and enter.

b) A store owner agrees to sell you a chocolate bar at a specified price.

c) Your job as a cashier pays you at the provincial minimum-wage rate.

d) You are arrested for underage drinking in a public park.

e) You sue a doctor for causing you extensive throat injury while operating to remove your tonsils.

f) Your parents have divorced and agree on issues related to custody and support payments.

g) Your parents are considering buying a new home or leasing a new apartment.

h) You attend a demonstration and are arrested for unlawful assembly.

7. For each example in question 6 above, indicate the specific type of law involved.

Communicate Your Understanding

8. Using newspapers, magazines, or Internet news sources, research three examples of criminal law and three examples of civil law. Summarize the legal events that occurred in each article, and explain why it relates to criminal or civil law. Identify the title of each article, and document the source of your information.

9. In pairs, select one of the topics below. One student will prepare an argument in favour of the statement, and the other student will prepare an argument against the statement. Support your position with examples.

a) Social networking sites on the Internet should be regulated by the government.

b) Punishments for youth offenders in Canada are too weak.

c) There should be harsh punishments for identity theft in Canada.

d) People are basically bad. They need laws and punishments to control them.

e) Canadian lawmakers should bring in punishments similar to those in the Code of Hammurabi and Mosaic law.

10. Prepare a timeline summarizing significant events in the development of Canadian rights history.

Develop Your Thinking

11. You have been asked to create a brief legal history lesson for students in an introductory history course at your high school. Create an organizer chart that identifies the various historic legal systems that have contributed to contemporary Canadian law. In your chart, identify the system, briefly summarize its main beliefs and values, and identify the influence on our current laws.

12. Article 4 of the Declaration of the Rights of Man and of the Citizen states "Liberty consists of the power to do whatever is not injurious to others." Explain, in your own words, the significance of this right.

13. How have laws and rules affected your daily activities today? Develop your answer by indicating examples where rules have influenced your actions, and areas where laws have influenced your conduct.

14. Review a copy of your school's code of conduct. Which school rules are related to criminal laws that we have in society?

2

The Canadian Charter of Rights and Freedoms

What You Should Know

- What are your rights and freedoms under the *Charter of Rights and Freedoms*?
- Are there limits to your rights and freedoms under the Charter?
- What happens if your rights are violated under the Charter?
- Has the Charter given the courts too much power?

Chapter at a Glance

2.1 Introduction

2.2 Reasonable Limits and Notwithstanding Clauses

2.3 Fundamental Freedoms

2.4 Democratic and Mobility Rights

2.5 Legal Rights

2.6 Equality Rights

2.7 Language and General Rights

2.8 Remedies

2.9 The Courts and the Legislature

Selected Key Terms

burden of proof
democratic rights
entrenched
equality rights
fundamental freedoms
infringed

legal rights
mobility rights
notwithstanding clause
reasonable limits clause
remedy
rights and freedoms

Police and activists clash at the Québec City Summit of the Americas in April 2001. Should police be allowed to use force during demonstrations? How do you respect both the rights of delegates and the rights of protesters during talks?

2.1 Introduction

Imagine if you were arrested and not given an opportunity to contact a lawyer. What if you were thrown in jail and never told the reason. Fortunately, Canadians live in a society where rights and freedoms are guaranteed under the *Charter of Rights and Freedoms*. Your rights can be described as what you are entitled to expect from the government. For example, you have legal rights that must be respected if you are arrested or charged with an offence. Your freedoms (s.7 right to liberty) involve your ability to conduct your affairs without government interference. You have various fundamental freedoms, including freedom of expression and freedom of religion. Since April 17, 1982, your rights and freedoms have been entrenched (safeguarded) in the Canadian Constitution. In other words, your rights and freedoms are protected in the Constitution, and they can only be changed by an amendment to it, which is very difficult to do. In this chapter, you will explore the meaning of these rights and freedoms and discover cases where Charter rights and freedoms have been infringed (violated).

While your rights and freedoms are guaranteed in the Constitution, definitions are not provided; the courts have interpreted the meaning of the words used in the Charter. For example, you are protected against unreasonable search and seizure. Does this mean that police cannot use sniffer dogs to conduct random searches in schools and other public places, such as malls and sports arenas? Is it constitutional for the police to use helicopter fly-overs to determine whether someone is running an illegal marijuana-growing operation? What does "unreasonable" really mean in law?

A cornerstone of the *Charter of Rights and Freedoms* is the reasonable limits clause (s.1). Your rights and freedoms are not absolute; they can be limited if it can be justified in our free and democratic society. Further, in some situations, the federal, provincial, or territorial governments can use the notwithstanding clause (s.33) to pass laws that override certain rights and freedoms in the Charter. (See Appendix A.)

What can you do if you think that your rights or freedoms have been infringed? First, you go to court to see if a judge agrees with you. Then, you can figure out a way to have your rights enforced. In law, this is known as a remedy.

As a helpful four-step guide to exploring Charter cases in this chapter, refer to the figure and guide on the next page. To better understand Charter cases, follow the guide and ask the four questions in sequence.

Should helicopter fly-overs be permitted to search for criminal activities?

 You and the Law

In Canada, we have rights and freedoms that are recognized and admired worldwide. Which rights and freedoms do you feel are the most important? Explain.

Four-Step Guide: How to Analyze a Charter Case

☑ **1. Does the Charter Apply?** The Charter covers only matters involving the government. For example, a Charter case may challenge a law passed by the government. It may question a government action, such as the way police officers made a search or seizure. If the matter concerns only private individuals with no aspect of the government involved, the Charter does not apply. The question may have to be settled through other means. For example, if a dispute involved a landlord refusing to rent an apartment to a tenant because of his or her race, the dispute would have to be settled under the human rights legislation of the province or territory on the grounds of racial discrimination.

☑ **2. Has a Charter Right or Freedom Been Infringed?** In each Charter case, the court must examine the facts. A government action or law can be challenged in court. Does it violate a particular right or freedom guaranteed under the Charter? In this chapter, you will examine your fundamental freedoms, democratic rights, mobility rights, legal rights, equality rights, language rights, Aboriginal rights, and multicultural rights. You will also discover how the courts have interpreted the meaning of these rights in cases brought before them.

☑ **3. Does the Reasonable Limits Clause Justify the Infringement?** Your Charter rights are not absolute; they can be limited if it can be justified in our free and democratic society. Section 1 of the Charter is a critical section because it provides the authority for the government to limit your Charter rights and freedoms.

☑ **4. If Not, Is There a Remedy under the Charter?** What happens if your rights have been infringed, and the courts will not allow section 1 of the Charter to be used to limit your rights? You may be able to apply to the court for a remedy, such as having the evidence excluded under section 24(2) of the Charter (see page 26). The court may even declare a law unconstitutional and strike it down.

4. If not, is there a remedy provided under the Charter?

3. Does the reasonable limits clause justify the infringement?

2. Has a Charter right or freedom been infringed?

1. Does the Charter apply?

When considering a legal case that involves the *Charter of Rights and Freedoms*, ask these four questions in sequence.

2.2 Reasonable Limits and Notwithstanding Clauses

reasonable limits clause the provision (clause) in the Charter stating that the Charter rights and freedoms are not absolute, so they can be limited if there is justification

rights and freedoms legal entitlements that people can expect from the government

burden of proof the onus of bringing forth proof (evidence) to prove someone's legal argument to the court

Can you say anything you want? No, because your ability to say whatever you want might harm others. For example, writing racist or sexist comments that promote hatred on an Internet blog is not only against the law, but it also results in harm to the specific group targeted by the comment.

Section 1 of the Charter contains a **reasonable limits clause**, which guarantees your **rights and freedoms** subject only to "reasonable limits." Simply put, this means that your rights and freedoms are limited in certain situations. Unfortunately, the Charter does not define the term "reasonable." Therefore, the courts have had to interpret the meaning. Read the landmark case of *R. v. Oakes*, 1986, on the next page, and learn about the test involving the **burden of proof** used by the courts to limit rights and freedoms under the Charter.

R. v. Oakes, 1986 CanLII 46 (S.C.C.)

For more information, Go to Nelson Social Studies

In 1982, David Oakes was charged with unlawful possession of a narcotic for the purpose of trafficking under section 8 of the *Narcotic Control Act* (now referred to as the *Controlled Drugs and Substances Act*.) It was the job of the Crown attorney to prove that Mr. Oakes had the drugs in his possession. Once that was done, it was up to Mr. Oakes to prove that he did not have them for the purpose of trafficking. Mr. Oakes argued that it should not be his responsibility to prove himself innocent of trafficking. In legal tradition, the accused is presumed innocent until proven guilty. The Crown attorney generally has the responsibility of proving the case against the accused. This is known as the burden of proof. Oakes argued that when the burden of proof switched to him, his legal right under section 11(d) of the Charter, the right to be presumed innocent until proven guilty, was violated. At trial and later at appeal, the courts accepted Mr. Oakes's argument that "reverse burden of proof" was unconstitutional. The Crown appealed to the Supreme Court of Canada.

In 1986, the Supreme Court of Canada accepted the argument that Mr. Oakes's legal right to be presumed innocent until proven guilty was violated. In its reasoning, the Supreme Court set out a test to determine how section 1 of the Charter, the reasonable limits clause, should be interpreted. First, the court asked whether the law enforced an important government objective. Society is concerned about drug trafficking, so the federal government has enacted laws against it. The court must then perform a balancing test. In this proportionality test, the courts must balance individual rights against the rights of society. The proportionality test consists of three questions:

1. Is there a rational connection between limiting an individual's rights and the objective of the law in question? (The objective of the law is to reduce drug trafficking.)
2. Does the law or government action interfere with rights and freedoms as little as possible?

3. Are the effects of the limitation proportional to the objective? (Is there a balance between meeting the objective of the law and limiting individual rights?)

The court ruled that just because the accused had a small quantity of narcotics, that was no reason to assume that he intended to traffic it. The appeal was dismissed, and section 8 of the *Narcotic Control Act* was declared unconstitutional.

For Discussion

1. What was the charge against David Oakes?
2. Why did he argue that his Charter rights were violated?
3. Explain the four parts used in the Oakes test to limit Charter rights.
4. Why do you think the presumption of innocence is so highly valued in Canadian society?

Burden of Proof

In a criminal trial, the Crown must prove the case against the accused.

Chapter 2 **The Canadian Charter of Rights and Freedoms** **39**

notwithstanding clause the provision (clause) in the Charter that allows governments to create certain laws that contradict some Charter rights

Negotiations for the *Constitution Act, 1982,* were very intense. Several provinces feared that the Constitution would give the federal government too much power over provincial matters. They also worried that the Charter would allow courts to change provincial laws. At the last minute, the federal government and the provinces agreed to the **notwithstanding clause**. It became section 33 of the Charter. The clause applies only to the fundamental freedoms (section 2), legal rights (sections 7–14), and equality rights (section 15) aspects of the Charter. It allows governments to enact legislation in spite of the fact (notwithstanding) that it may violate those rights and freedoms. As a safety feature, the law must be reviewed every five years.

The notwithstanding clause is sometimes referred to as the override clause or the opt-out clause. It has rarely been used. In one significant case, *Ford v. Québec (Attorney General)*, 1988, the Québec government passed Bill 101, requiring all public signs to be only in French. That same year, the Supreme Court of Canada ruled that Québec's Bill 101 violated the Charter's guarantees of freedom of expression. The government of Québec argued that the law was necessary to protect the survival of the French language. Using the notwithstanding clause, the Québec government passed Bill C-178, which allowed Québec's French-only law on public signs to stay in effect.

Today, signs in Québec can include English, but at only half the size of the French. Do you agree with this law? Justify your answer.

Review Your Understanding

1. What is the purpose of the reasonable limits clause?
2. When can freedom of expression be limited? Provide an example.
3. Our rights and freedoms can be limited if it is "demonstrably justified." What do you think these words mean?
4. Explain the purpose of the notwithstanding clause.
5. What rights and freedoms apply under section 33?

2.3 Fundamental Freedoms

Section 2 of the Charter lists the basic freedoms of all people in Canada. These are called the **fundamental freedoms**: freedom of conscience and religion; freedom of thought, belief, opinion, and expression; freedom of peaceful assembly; and freedom of association. As previously mentioned, these freedoms are not absolute and can be subject to reasonable limits.

Freedom of Conscience and Religion

Freedom of conscience and religion means that, in Canada, you are free to practise your religion. You cannot be forced to act in a way that goes against your beliefs or conscience. The courts have ruled on many significant cases involving freedom of religion. For example, Canada used to have a law called the *Lord's Day Act*, dating from 1906. It prohibited businesses from opening on Sundays. In the case of *R. v. Big M Drug Mart*, 1985, the Supreme Court of Canada declared the act to be in conflict with section 2(a) of the Charter. Compelling everyone to observe Sunday as a day of rest violated freedom of religion, since Canada is a nation of many faiths.

In Canada, freedom of religion allows retailers to have their stores open 24 hours, seven days a week.

Sometimes legal conflicts arise because basic beliefs of a religion may conflict with other rights and freedoms. In one case, the Supreme Court upheld the right of a practising Sikh to wear a kirpan on school property. The case was *Multani v. Commission scolaire Marguerite-Bourgeoys*, 2006.

Wearing a kirpan (a ceremonial dagger) is part of the Sikh religion. Why do you think allowing practising Sikhs to wear a kirpan is such a controversial issue?

⚖ Case

Multani v. Commission scolaire Marguerite-Bourgeoys, 2006 SCC 6 (CanLII)

For more information, **Go to Nelson Social Studies** 🌐

Gurbaj Singh Multani immigrated to Canada from Pakistan in 2000. He attended a francophone school in LaSalle, Québec. In November 2001, the school administration became aware that Multani had been carrying a metal ceremonial dagger that is part of his religious faith. It is known as a kirpan. He had dropped it in the schoolyard. At first, school authorities decided to prohibit Multani from attending school if he carried his kirpan. In December 2001, the school board proposed a compromise: he would be allowed to wear his kirpan as long as it was wrapped and sealed under his clothing, in order to protect school security.

In February 2002, Multani and his family agreed to the conditions. Then, the school board backed out. It refused to allow the agreement, stating that the school code of conduct prohibited carrying weapons and dangerous objects. The board informed Multani and his family that a symbolic kirpan in the form of a harmless pendant, for example, would be acceptable in place of the metal kirpan. Multani and his father argued that the ban went against the freedom of religion and freedom of equality guarantees under Québec's human rights laws. It also went against the freedom of conscience and religion guaranteed in section 2(a) of the Charter.

continues...

Multani v. Commission scolaire Marguerite-Bourgeoys, 2006 SCC 6 (CanLII)

In May 2002, the Québec Superior Court ruled that Multani be allowed to wear the kirpan to school. However, it had to be wrapped in cloth and a wooden sheath and concealed under his clothes. School officials could conduct reasonable inspections to ensure conditions were being followed. Failure to follow these conditions would result in the loss of the right to wear the kirpan.

The case was appealed to the Québec Court of Appeal. The court unanimously ruled that while freedom of religion had been infringed, it was not possible to accommodate Mr. Multani reasonably without compromising the school board's security rules. The Québec Court of Appeal upheld the ban on kirpans in schools.

The Multani family appealed the case to the Supreme Court of Canada. In March 2006, the Supreme Court of Canada set out a two-part test for determining whether freedom of religion had been violated. The appellant (the person seeking a remedy in court) must establish the following:

1. that he or she sincerely believes in the practice or belief that has a connection with religion;
2. that his or her ability with the practice or religious belief is being interfered with.

The court held that Multani sincerely believed that his faith required him to wear the kirpan at all times. For Orthodox Sikhs, the kirpan is a religious symbol; Multani genuinely believed that he would not be complying with the requirements of his religion if he wore a plastic or wooden kirpan. The judgment was unanimous. The court stated that the school board's policy on banning the kirpan clearly violated Multani's freedom of religion under section 2(a) of the Charter.

For Discussion

1. What is the two-part test used by the Supreme Court of Canada to determine whether freedom of religion is violated?
2. Why did the Québec Superior Court allow Multani to wear the kirpan?
3. What was the decision of the Québec Court of Appeal? Why did they arrive at that decision?
4. The Supreme Court commented in its decision that allowing Multani to wear his kirpan under certain conditions demonstrates the importance that our society attaches to protecting freedom of religion and to showing respect for its minorities. Do you agree with this statement? Why or why not?

Gurbaj Singh Multani shows his kirpan after winning his appeal at the Supreme Court of Canada.

Freedom of Thought, Belief, Opinion, and Expression

Activist Judy Rebick addresses a crowd of students outside Concordia University on November 15, 2002. A judge granted an injunction to Concordia, allowing the school to bar NDP MPs from using its downtown campus to discuss the Middle East conflict. Under what circumstances might a person's freedom of expression be limited?

 Did You Know?

Canada's obscenity laws restrict freedom of expression. The Supreme Court of Canada has held material to be obscene if it contains any of the following:

- explicit sex with violence
- explicit sex without violence but that is degrading or dehumanizing
- explicit sex that does not contain violence, is not degrading or dehumanizing, but employs children in producing it (*R. v. Butler*, 1992)

The Charter covers all forms of communication and expression, including the mass media, writing, painting, sculpture, and film. However, there are limits on your freedom of expression. For example, it is illegal to target groups because of their colour, race, religion, or ethnic origin and to spread hate. Governments also ban material they consider to be obscene to protect people.

In *R. v. Keegstra*, 1990, James Keegstra was convicted of wilfully promoting hatred. He taught his Alberta high school students that the Holocaust, in which 6 million Jews were killed during World War II, had never happened. His case went to the Supreme Court of Canada. The court agreed that Canada's hate laws did infringe on the Charter guarantee of freedom of expression. However, the majority of the court believed that the infringement could be justified. It would protect people from hate propaganda.

In the case of *R. v. Butler*, 1992, the Supreme Court agreed to limit freedom of expression. Butler was charged with over 200 crimes, involving possessing, selling, and exposing obscene material. The court agreed that Canada's obscenity laws did infringe the freedom of expression under the Charter. It also felt that it was reasonable for the government to impose those laws out of concern for possible victims (see Chapter 7 for more information).

The courts have often agreed to limit freedom of expression in the area of advertising. See the case on the next page of *Canada (Attorney General) v. JTI-Macdonald Corp.*, 2007. The Supreme Court of Canada placed limits on tobacco advertising and promotion by tobacco manufacturers.

 Activity

To learn more about your freedom of expression,

Go to Nelson
Social Studies

Canada (Attorney General) v. JTI-Macdonald Corp., 2007 SCC 30 (CanLII)

For more information, Go to Nelson Social Studies

Why do you think the government increased the size of the health warning on cigarette packages?

In 1997, the federal government changed the laws governing tobacco. The law forbade certain types of advertising, such as lifestyle ads appealing to young persons. It also banned sponsorship promotion. The tobacco manufacturers argued against the limits imposed on tobacco advertising. They claimed they violated their freedom of expression under the Charter. The initial trial found the new laws to be constitutional. Then, the Québec Court of Appeal ruled some parts to be unconstitutional. Both the attorney general and the tobacco manufacturers appealed.

In 2007, the Supreme Court of Canada ruled that the ban on promotion clearly infringed freedom of expression. However, the ban on misleading advertising was justified. The government was concerned with promoting health, protecting consumers, and preventing young people from smoking. The court agreed that the ban on lifestyle advertising was justified. It linked a product with a lifestyle to create an image that might lead more people to smoke. The court spoke about sponsorship promotion being lifestyle advertising in disguise. It upheld the ban on using corporate names in sponsorship promotion. Finally, the requirement that the government health warning occupy at least half of the package display surface did infringe freedom of expression. However, it met the government's objective of reminding people about the health hazards.

For Discussion

1. What restrictions were placed on tobacco advertising under the legislation?

2. Why did the tobacco manufacturers challenge the ruling?

3. In a unanimous 9–0 judgment, the Supreme Court upheld the bans on advertising. Why did they rule that the limits on tobacco advertising and promotion were justified under section 1 of the Charter?

4. Do you think that warning labels will discourage people from consuming tobacco or prevent young smokers from taking up the habit? Explain your reasoning.

Freedom of Peaceful Assembly

The freedom of peaceful assembly is usually associated with the right to participate in a public demonstration. Examples might include the following:

- environmental protesters condemning logging of old-growth forests or the use of pesticides in lawn fertilizers

- workers protesting their working conditions
- social justice activists protesting international trade issues
- community residents protesting the site of a new dump in their community

The key word is "peaceful." If a public display threatens to turn violent, the police may charge the participants with unlawful assembly. If things get disorderly or chaotic, police may charge participants with rioting.

Freedom of Association

Freedom of association refers to the right of individuals to join together in groups. These can include sports clubs, cultural organizations, or trade unions. The Supreme Court of Canada has expanded the interpretation of freedom of association. It recognizes workers' rights to collective bargaining. They have the right to be represented by a union. The union negotiates with employers on behalf of its members. Any law or government action that interferes with collective bargaining violates freedom of association under the Charter. The case was *Health Services and Support-Facilities Subsector Bargaining Assn. v. British Columbia*, 2007. (This case will be discussed further in Chapter 16.)

Your freedom of association can also be limited. For example, if a youth criminal is arrested and charged with assaulting people, the court may issue an order preventing the youth from associating with the victims of the assaults or with any co-accused or other gang members.

Protesters hurl part of a fence at riot police during the Summit of the Americas in Québec City on April 20, 2001. This is an example of a demonstration that turned violent. Under what circumstances can a person be charged with unlawful assembly?

Chapter 2 **The Canadian Charter of Rights and Freedoms**

Review Your Understanding

1. Explain the four fundamental freedoms in the Charter.
2. Explain the meaning of freedom of religion, and provide examples.
3. Why were limits placed on freedom of expression in the Keegstra and Butler cases?
4. Distinguish between freedom of association and freedom of peaceful assembly.
5. What limits are placed on freedom of peaceful assembly?

2.4 Democratic and Mobility Rights

democratic rights the right of Canadian citizens to vote

Sections 3, 4, and 5 of the Charter guarantee the **democratic rights** of Canadians. For example, every Canadian citizen over the age of 18 has the right to vote. In addition to voting rights, the Charter guarantees that an election will be held every five years. It further provides that the federal Parliament and provincial legislatures must sit at least once every 12 months.

entrenched fixed firmly or securely in law

Before 1982, the right to vote was included in various election acts. Since these were ordinary statutes, they could be changed at any time by Parliament or provincial legislatures. Today, the democratic right to vote is **entrenched** in the Charter. That means that it cannot be removed without an amendment to the Constitution. Many people—women, Aboriginal peoples, Chinese Canadians, and Japanese Canadians—have fought long, hard battles over the years to get the right to vote in Canada. For example, inmates in federal prisons have won the right to vote in federal elections.

 Did You Know?

The federal government, British Columbia, Ontario, and Newfoundland and Labrador have all adopted fixed election dates.

Even so, many people do not take advantage of their right to vote. Voter turnout for Canada's federal elections has dropped steadily. In 1979, 75.7 percent of those qualified voted. In the January 2006 election, just 64.7 percent did so.

Voter Turnout at Canada's Federal Elections, 1979–2006

Percent turnout (y-axis, 0 to 80)

Years (x-axis): 1979, 1980, 1984, 1988, 1993, 1997, 2000, 2004, 2006

Why do you suppose voter turnout has been dwindling over the past 20 years?

Sauvé v. Canada (Chief Electoral Officer), 2002 SCC 68 (CanLII)

For more information, Go to Nelson Social Studies

Richard Sauvé, an inmate of a federal prison, challenged a section of the *Canada Elections Act* that denied federal inmates serving a sentence of more than two years the right to vote in federal elections. The Supreme Court of Canada ruled that the law violated Sauvé's democratic rights (s.3 right to vote) and could not be justified by section 1 of the Charter.

- Do you agree with the court's decision? Why or why not?

This inmate casts his ballot for the federal election at the Montréal Detention Centre. All inmates in federal and provincial institutions now have the right to vote in federal elections. Should they be allowed to vote? Explain your reasoning.

Section 6 of the Charter guarantees your right to move freely inside and outside of Canada. This is known as **mobility rights**. The Charter guarantees the right of every citizen to enter, leave, or remain in Canada. It also allows Canadian citizens and permanent residents to live and work in any province. (Permanent residents have the right to enter or remain in Canada as long as Canada's immigration laws are followed. They are not Canadian citizens.) The Charter does allow provincial governments to impose restrictions on mobility rights. Provinces with lower than average employment rates can prevent citizens from other provinces coming to look for work. This would protect the province's citizens from losing their jobs to outsiders.

mobility rights the right to enter and leave Canada, and the right to move between the provinces

Review Your Understanding

1. Explain your democratic rights under the Charter.
2. When are you eligible to vote in Canada?
3. What are mobility rights?
4. Summarize the exception to being able to seek employment in any province.
5. How do mobility rights apply to permanent residents of Canada?

2.5 Legal Rights

legal rights Charter sections that protect personal and privacy rights and safeguard procedural rights in the criminal justice system

The **legal rights** section of the Charter provides legal safeguards to ensure that proper procedures are followed in the criminal justice system in areas such as searches, arrests, detention, and interrogation. For example, police cannot randomly stop you in a mall and proceed with a physical body search. The police must be able to justify a search by providing a legally valid reason for conducting it. Further, if you are being arrested, police must tell you immediately the reason for the arrest and not wait until they have brought you to the police station. You must also be notified of your right to a lawyer. Such safeguards are designed to protect you from being unfairly treated by our criminal justice system. If police do not follow proper procedure and provide an accused with his or her Charter rights, they run the risk of having their actions challenged in a court. If the rights of the accused are violated, the accused may seek a **remedy**, such as applying to the court to have the evidence thrown out. Without the evidence, there may not be a case against the accused. You will learn more about your legal rights in Chapter 5.

remedy the way in which a wrongdoing is fixed by the court or other judicial body

Life, Liberty, and Security of the Person

The Crown is required by law to tell an accused and his or her lawyer what evidence and other information they have against that person. For example, say you decide to go for a ride with your friend. Your friend is driving his car when he is stopped by a police officer during a roadside

Do you think this person's rights are being violated? Under what circumstances would it be justified to conduct a search?

check for alcohol. The police officer notices drugs on the car dashboard, and your friend confesses that the drugs are his. You are sitting immediately beside your friend in the passenger seat. Despite your friend's confession, you are both charged with possession of narcotics. During the trial, the Crown attorney neglects to tell your lawyer about the driver's confession. If a Crown attorney withholds key information from an accused and his or her lawyer, it may prevent the accused from making a full defence to the charges. In the case of *R. v. Stinchcombe*, 1991, a witness questioned by the Crown made statements that were favourable to the defence, but during the trial, the Crown did not call that witness, nor did it disclose the statements to the defence. Stinchcombe argued that, because of this failure, he was denied his rights to life, liberty, and security of the person under section 7 of the Charter. The court ruled that it is a duty of the Crown to disclose all relevant information it has in its possession before the case goes to trial to allow the defence to answer charges in full.

In *R. v. Morgentaler*, 1988, the Supreme Court declared Canada's abortion laws unconstitutional. It ruled that they violated section 7 of the Charter. This guaranteed the security of the person. As a result, Canada's abortion laws are no longer in effect.

 Did You Know?

In *Chaoulli v. Québec (Attorney General)*, 2005, in a 4–3 decision, the Supreme Court ruled that failing to provide public health care of a reasonable standard within a reasonable time violated section 7 of the Charter.

 Did You Know?

On July 1, 2008, Henry Morgentaler was awarded the Order of Canada. It was a controversial appointment.

 You Be the Judge

Rodriguez v. British Columbia (Attorney General), 1993 CanLII 75 (S.C.C.)

For more information, **Go to Nelson Social Studies**

Sue Rodriguez was a victim of a terminal disease that would soon leave her helpless. She was told that she had no more than three years to live. Once she was unable to enjoy life, she hoped that someone would be able to help her end her life. In Canada, it is not illegal to commit suicide. However, it is illegal for anyone to assist in a suicide.

Rodriguez argued that the law denying assisted suicide violated her right to life, liberty, and security of the person. The Supreme Court disagreed with Rodriguez. It kept the law on assisted suicide in the *Criminal Code*. The court commented that the objective of the law was to preserve life and protect the vulnerable in society.

On February 12, 1994, Rodriguez committed suicide with the help of an anonymous doctor.

- Do you agree with the Supreme Court's decision in this case? Do you think the assisted suicide law should still be in the *Criminal Code*? Justify your answer.

All About Law DVD

"Sue Rodriguez: Choosing Death" from *All About Law DVD*

Sue Rodriguez is pushed in her wheelchair by Right to Die activist John Hofsess as they prepare to enter a downtown Victoria hotel for a news conference in 1993.

Activity

To learn more about search and seizure laws,

Go to Nelson Social Studies

Search and Seizure Laws

Many criminal cases involve section 8 of the Charter: "Everyone has the right to be secure against an unreasonable search and seizure." Police must have a good reason for searching your person, your home, or your possessions, and they must also be able to justify the taking of any evidence from these locations. What if police pulled your vehicle over during a RIDE (Reduce Impaired Driving Everywhere) spot check and began searching for drugs? Would that search be considered unreasonable if it were challenged in court? By law, the police must have reasonable grounds to search the vehicle, such as seeing the drugs in plain view or receiving a tip that this vehicle may have been involved in drug trafficking. They also must act fairly while conducting searches. Evidence obtained during an illegal search may be thrown out under section 24(2) of the Charter, as you read on page 26.

 You Be the Judge

R. v. A.M., 2008 SCC 19 (CanLII)

For more information, **Go to Nelson Social Studies**

In 2006, the Ontario Court of Appeal ruled that police officers had conducted an unreasonable search and seizure when they entered a high school with a sniffer dog and conducted a warrantless and random search for drugs. The case was appealed to the Supreme Court of Canada, and the court ruled that completely random drug searches violate privacy rights.

• Do you agree with the court's decision? Why or why not?

Police often use dogs to assist in drug searches.

We are not surprised when police officers search someone they have arrested. They must make sure that she or he has no weapons. See the case on the next page of *R. v. Mann*, 2004. Searches can be reasonable even prior to an arrest. However, the individual must be detained on reasonable grounds. Also, the searches must be part of a justified investigation to ensure police safety.

R. v. Mann, 2004 SCC 52 (CanLII)

For more information, **Go to Nelson Social Studies**

In December 2000, as Philip Mann was walking near the site of a reported break and enter, two police officers asked him to identify himself because he matched the description of the suspect. He complied, gave his name and date of birth, and consented to a pat-down search in which police officers searched for weapons. During the search, one police officer felt a soft object in Mann's sweater pocket. The officer reached in Mann's pocket and discovered a small bag containing marijuana. The officer continued the search and found further marijuana and two valium pills.

Mann was arrested and charged with possession of marijuana for the purpose of trafficking. The trial judge concluded that there was no evidence to suggest that it was reasonable for the officer to search Mann's pocket for security reasons. Therefore, the evidence was excluded under section 24(2) of the Charter. Mann was acquitted.

The Crown appealed to the Manitoba Court of Appeal, which ordered a new trial. The Court of Appeal was concerned with creating a safe environment for police officers and did not want to restrict police officers from carrying out pat-down searches in the course of exercising their police duties. Mann appealed to the Supreme Court of Canada.

In its 2004 decision, the Supreme Court held that the search was a violation of section 8 of the Charter. The evidence was excluded. The court ruled that Mann was detained as the police officers began their investigation into the reported break and enter. Common law allows police to detain someone and then to search him or her for the purposes of protection. However, the Supreme Court held that the police officers did not have the right to search for anything other than weapons. When the officer reached into the pocket of Mann's sweater, he actually shifted the purpose of the pat-down search from ensuring safety to detecting and collecting evidence.

Two of the seven judges dissented. They agreed that the search was a violation of section 8 of the Charter. Still, they argued that the evidence need not be excluded. They did not accept the argument that allowing the drug evidence would bring the administration of justice into disrepute and make the trial unfair.

For Discussion

1. Pat-down searches are often used by police officers to ensure that the suspect is not carrying a weapon. Do you think a pat-down search was reasonable in this case? Explain why or why not.

2. Why did the Supreme Court rule in Mann's favour?

3. How was section 24(2) used in the *Mann* case?

4. Do you think the evidence should be excluded in this case? Explain.

In Chapter 5, you will learn more about the authority of police officers to conduct searches. That chapter also discusses the need for search warrants. If police showed up at your door and wanted to search your home without a warrant, you might see this as a violation of your privacy rights.

Television shows such as CSI and *Law and Order* have also taught us to expect police to look for physical evidence such as weapons or hair, blood, or fibre samples.

Forensic investigators search for evidence at a crime scene.

For example, suppose police use a heat-sensing device to uncover a suspected illegal marijuana-growing operation. Could the recorded heat pattern images be enough evidence for a judge to grant a search warrant? Would the use of the helicopter fly-over be an invasion of privacy? The case below of *R. v. Tessling*, 2004, will tell you more about your privacy rights.

Case

R. v. Tessling, 2004 SCC 67 (CanLII)

For more information, Go to Nelson Social Studies

In February 1999, police got a tip about a possible marijuana-growing operation. It was on the property of Walter Tessling in Windsor, Ontario. The lights used in growing marijuana use great amounts of electricity. The police asked Ontario Hydro to check Tessling's electrical meter. It showed no unusual electricity usage. However, it is common for criminals to bypass the hydro meters. They do this to hide high electricity readings.

Marijuana-growing usually requires large amounts of heat. So, the police decided to use heat sensors to see the heat patterns at Tessling's home. This technology is known as forward-looking infrared (FLIR). The police were hoping to find evidence of a marijuana-growing operation. In April 1999, the RCMP did a helicopter fly-over above Tessling's home.

The heat image data and the information from the informants were used to obtain a search warrant, which the police used to enter Tessling's home. They found marijuana worth between $15 000 and $22 500. They also found scales, freezer bags, and some guns. Tessling was charged with trafficking marijuana and possession of weapons.

continues...

R. v. Tessling, 2004 SCC 67 (CanLII)

Tessling was convicted in December 2000. He appealed. In January 2003, the Ontario Court of Appeal held that the helicopter fly-over had violated Tessling's privacy rights. These are defined in section 8 of the Charter. The court also concluded that the search was illegal. The marijuana evidence was excluded under section 24(2) of the Charter. Tessling was acquitted.

The Crown appealed the case. In a unanimous verdict, the Supreme Court of Canada held that the evidence from the RCMP fly-over was admissible. It was not unreasonable under section 8 of the Charter, nor did it infringe on Tessling's privacy rights. Tessling's conviction was restored. He was sentenced to 18 months for trafficking in marijuana and possessing weapons.

For Discussion

1. What was the decision at trial?
2. What was the decision of the Ontario Court of Appeal?
3. Why did the Supreme Court of Canada restore Tessling's conviction?
4. Mr. Justice Ian Binnie commented: "The respondent had no reasonable expectation of privacy in the heat distribution information." What do you think Mr. Justice Binnie meant by "reasonable expectation of privacy"?

In Canada, illegal marijuana-growing operations have become a significant problem. Here, an RCMP officer investigates a marijuana-growing operation in the basement of a Moncton, New Brunswick, house on July 27, 2004. The RCMP executed search warrants at 14 homes in the greater Moncton area as part of an organized crime investigation into commercial marijuana-growing operations.

Review Your Understanding

1. How has section 7 of the Charter, the right to life, liberty, and security of the person, been used to support proper disclosure during a criminal trial?
2. What type of information could give the police reasonable and probable grounds for a search?
3. When is a search reasonable?
4. If evidence is obtained and the search is declared unreasonable under section 8 of the Charter, what Charter remedy is available to challenge whether the drug evidence can be admitted in court?
5. Should police be allowed to conduct pat-down searches? Explain.

 Did You Know?

It is technically legal, within the meaning of the law, for police to stop drivers to check for sobriety as part of a RIDE program. The courts have held this detention to be a reasonable limit on a person's rights to protect society from harm caused by drunk drivers. The precedent case on this issue is *R. v. Hufsky*, 1988.

Detention and Arrest

Section 9 of the Charter guarantees that "everyone has the right not to be arbitrarily detained or imprisoned." In this case, "arbitrarily" means not having a sufficient legal reason for stopping or restricting someone's movement or putting him or her in jail. To detain someone does not necessarily mean to imprison or put him or her in jail. When your liberty is restricted, you are detained. For example, if you were stopped by police for questioning and believed you had no choice but to comply, then you could be detained within the meaning of the law. A detention could become an arrest once police establish reasonable and probable grounds for the arrest.

Section 10 of the Charter guarantees that everyone has the right to be informed "promptly" of the reasons for the arrest or the detention. In Canada, this is known as a police caution. Furthermore, the accused must be told of the right in a manner that he or she can understand. For example, if you do not speak English, an officer can arrange for an interpreter. Another legal right is the right to consult a lawyer—known in legal terms as the right to retain and instruct counsel—in a reasonable amount of time. Also, the accused has the right to be informed of that right. This right to counsel includes the right to be informed about legal aid. Legal aid is available to help people who do not have enough money to pay for a lawyer. A person seeking legal aid may apply for a certificate through a local legal aid office in his or her community. This certificate is awarded based on financial need and allows the holder of the certificate to hire a legal aid lawyer of her or his choice. Often, legal aid cases deal with criminal law or family law matters, such

Do you think it is reasonable for police officers to stop drivers randomly to check for driving under the influence of alcohol or drugs? Justify your response.

as child custody and access and support payment issues. The third component of section 10 allows a court to determine if a person was held in custody legally. In legal terms, this is called lawful detention.

The Charter sections on detention and arrest have also been used to challenge aspects of Canada's anti-terrorism legislation. See the case of *Charkaoui v. Canada*, 2007. There, the Supreme Court struck down portions of the *Immigration and Refugee Protection Act*. These dealt with security certificates. It gave the government one year to write a new law. This case provides an excellent example of how the courts try to balance individual rights against national security.

 Case

Charkaoui v. Canada (Citizenship and Immigration), 2007 SCC 9 (CanLII)

For more information, Go to Nelson Social Studies

In May 2003, Adil Charkaoui, a Moroccan citizen, was arrested. He was detained for two and a half years on a security certificate under the *Immigration and Refugee Protection Act*. Security certificates are used to detain individuals who are considered to be threats to national security. Charkaoui, along with Algerian Mohamed Harkat and Syrian Hassan Almrei, were detained under security certificates. The three men were never charged with criminal offences. They did not have any connection to each other. They were all accused, however, of having ties to al Qaeda and other terrorist groups. They were believed to be a threat to Canada's security.

A security certificate must be signed by two cabinet ministers. A judge of the Federal Court must decide if the certificate is "reasonable." The hearings to determine this are held in secret. Only the judge, government lawyers, and witnesses are present. The detainees and their lawyers are given only a summary of the allegations. They are not given any specific details of the government's case against them. They are also not allowed to be present at the hearing. Once the security certificate is declared reasonable by the Federal Court judge, the detainee can be deported from Canada on the grounds of being a danger to the security of Canada. The decision of the Federal Court judge is final and cannot be appealed.

Charkaoui, Harkat, and Almrei argued that they should be charged with a crime if they are to be detained. Once charged, they should be brought to trial. They challenged the validity of the secret hearings. They also questioned the fact that they were not allowed to have someone present to represent their interests. In December 2003, the Federal Court of Canada declared security certificates lawful. The men appealed to the Federal Court of Appeal. The court was concerned that information released might harm national security. That is why it also upheld the secret process of reviewing the security certificates.

The men appealed to the Supreme Court of Canada. In the interim, Charkaoui was freed on bail in February 2005 but placed under strict house arrest. Harkat, who had been detained for three and a half years, was freed on bail under strict conditions in June 2006. Almrei, who had been detained since October 2001, was held at an immigration holding centre and not granted bail.

In 2007, the Supreme Court of Canada struck down parts of the *Immigration and Refugee Protection Act*. The process for reviewing the validity of a security certificate violated section 7 of the Charter. So did the procedures for reviewing the detention. The act permitted the use of evidence that was not disclosed to the detainees during secret hearings. That meant that the detainees were not given the opportunity for a fair hearing. The detainees were also denied the right to know the full case against them. Thus, they were not able to make a full defence to the charges. Under the law, foreign nationals could be detained without a review

continues...

Charkaoui v. Canada (Citizenship and Immigration), 2007 SCC 9 (CanLII)

until 120 days after the security certificate was deemed reasonable. Permanent resident detainees had a review within 48 hours. The court determined that the time limits in the provisions for continuing detention of a foreign national violated sections 9 and 10(c) of the Charter because they were arbitrary. While the detentions were not arbitrary when they were first applied, the court considered it arbitrary to continue the detention without a process of review. The security certificate and detention system was held to be unconstitutional. The court gave the federal government one year to write a new law.

Adil Charkaoui holds the security certificate that was found to be unconstitutional.

For Discussion

1. What is the purpose of a security certificate?
2. What section of the Charter did the detainees allege was violated by the security certificate system?
3. Why did the detention review procedure violate the Charter?
4. Do you think a government-appointed lawyer would fairly represent a suspected terrorist's interests? Explain.

Review Your Understanding

1. Explain your rights under section 9 of the Charter.
2. In your own words, what does "arbitrarily" mean?
3. Why are your section 9 rights limited during a random police stop that checks for the sobriety of drivers?
4. Identify three rights everyone has on arrest.
5. Distinguish between a detention and an arrest.

Rights on Being Charged with an Offence

Section 11 of the Charter — Rights at Trial — provides specific rights for any person charged with an offence. These rights include the right to be told what the specific offence is without an unreasonable delay and the right to be tried within a reasonable time. In the *R. v. Askov*, 1990, case, the accused was charged with conspiracy to commit extortion. But two years later, his trial date had still not been set. The accused argued that his right to be tried within a reasonable time was violated. The court agreed to a **stay of proceedings**. In other words, the proceedings in court were stopped, and no further action was taken against the accused. It effectively halted the case. After the *R. v. Askov* ruling, the Ontario court system stayed over 50 000 cases on the basis of unreasonable delay. (See Chapter 6, page 186, for more about this case.)

Under section 11 of the Charter, an accused cannot be forced to testify. He or she may discuss the pros and cons of testifying with his or her lawyer. However, no one can be forced to take the witness stand. Furthermore, under section 11, anyone charged cannot be denied reasonable bail without good reason. Also, everybody has the right to a trial by jury if the case involves serious criminal charges.

Cruel and Unusual Treatment or Punishment

Section 12 of the Charter outlaws "cruel and unusual" punishment. Generally, our criminal laws set limits on penalties. For example, the maximum sentence for arson (intentionally causing fires) is 14 years in jail. Assault causing bodily harm carries a maximum of 10 years. However, the *Criminal Code* also includes mandatory minimum punishments. For example, there is a minimum term of 4 years for weapons-related offences and a 10-year minimum sentence for second-degree murder. First-degree murder has a minimum term of 25 years. Chapter 9 discusses the topic of sentencing in greater detail.

Did You Know?

Any person charged with an offence has the right to be presumed innocent until proven guilty. You do not have to be a Canadian citizen to be guaranteed this right under section 11(d) of the *Charter of Rights and Freedoms*.

stay of proceedings a court order to stop the trial proceedings until a certain condition is met

Criminal Code Offences and Maximum Penalties

Sample *Criminal Code of Canada* Offences	Maximum Penalties
Murder	Life imprisonment
Kidnapping	Life imprisonment
Sexual assault using a weapon, causing bodily harm	14 years
Assault causing bodily harm	10 years
Uttering threats	5 years

This table shows various *Criminal Code* offences and their maximum penalties. These offences and others will be discussed in Chapter 7.

The Charter Since 1982

When the *Charter of Rights and Freedoms* was proclaimed in 1982, the winds of change were rustling through the Canadian justice system. It was a bold new statement of rights and freedoms that became entrenched in our Constitution. Chief Justice Beverley McLachlin has referred to the passing of our Charter as Canada's legal coming of age. The Charter was created through a hands-on, made-in-Canada process. The Charter acted as an expression of who we are as a people.

With the proclamation of the Charter in 1982, Canadians could now challenge laws and government actions that violated Charter rights and freedoms.

Section 24 of the Charter details the enforcement of guaranteed rights and freedoms. It states that anyone whose Charter rights have been infringed (violated) may seek a "remedy" in court. For example, evidence must be gathered in a way that respects Charter rights and freedoms. Under section 24(2), anyone can apply to the court to have evidence excluded if that person's rights have been violated. In making such decisions, judges must consider the circumstances of the case. They have to decide whether allowing the evidence in would make the trial unfair.

Some significant challenges lay on the road ahead as the courts struggled with interpreting the Charter. What is a "reasonable limit"? What is freedom of religion and expression? What constitutes an "unreasonable search and seizure"? These and other questions had to be answered.

Since 1982, the Supreme Court of Canada has issued many landmark decisions based on the Charter. Some of the rulings have been controversial. This is particularly true in cases where rulings changed existing laws. Several cases that have changed the legal landscape in Canada are summarized below.

***R. v. Oakes*, 1986:** David Oakes was charged with possession of a narcotic for the purpose of trafficking. He challenged a law requiring him to prove he was not trafficking drugs. He argued that this reverse burden of proof, requiring him to prove himself innocent of trafficking, violated his right under the Charter to be presumed innocent until proven guilty. The court agreed and declared the law to be unconstitutional. The Oakes case is regularly used in courts as a precedent because it sets out the test—often referred to as the "Oakes test"—in deciding when your rights and freedoms can be limited under the Charter.

***R. v. Morgentaler*, 1988:** The Supreme Court entered a legal, moral, and ethical debate when Dr. Henry Morgentaler challenged Canada's abortion law. The court struck down Canada's abortion law because it violated section 7 of the Charter. That section confirms everyone's right to life, liberty, and security of the person. Since the abortion law restricted a woman's ability and right to obtain an abortion legally, it was struck down. The case created controversy. People debated whether the Supreme Court had too much power in interpreting laws.

***R. v. Collins*, 1987:** Undercover police officers used a choke hold to search Ruby Collins for drugs. It turned out that she did not have any drugs in her mouth, although she did have some in her hand. Collins argued that the search and seizure violated section 8 of the Charter. The Supreme Court ruling established a test for a reasonable search. The police must have reasonable grounds for carrying out a search and must act fairly while conducting it. The court also declared that evidence obtained in an unreasonable manner cannot be used in court if it would interfere with the fairness of the trial.

***Irwin Toy Ltd. v. Québec (Attorney General)*, 1989:** Irwin Toy challenged a Québec law that banned television advertising to children under the age

continues...

The Charter Since 1982

of 13. The court ruled that the law protected children from manipulation by advertising. As such, it was a reasonable limit on freedom of expression. Freedom of expression was recognized as a guaranteed right. Still, it was subject to reasonable limits under section 1 of the Charter.

***R. v. Keegstra*, 1990:** James Keegstra was an Alberta high school teacher. He was charged with promoting hatred toward an identifiable group—in this case, Jewish people. He argued that his freedom of expression was violated. However, the court allowed section 1 of the Charter to limit freedom of expression. Canada's hate-crime laws are a reasonable limit on our freedom of expression. They protect groups from hate speech.

***Vriend v. Alberta*, 1998:** Delwin Vriend was an Alberta Christian college teacher. He was fired because he was gay. Vriend wanted to challenge his dismissal as discrimination under provincial human rights legislation. However, Alberta's *Human Rights, Citizenship, and Multiculturalism Act* only recognized discrimination on the basis of sex, not sexual orientation. Vriend argued at the Supreme Court that the act violated his equality rights. It did not protect him from discrimination on the basis of his sexual orientation. The court agreed. However, it did not rule that the human rights law was unconstitutional. Instead, the court ordered the Alberta government to include sexual orientation as a prohibited ground of discrimination under the law. The Alberta government complied.

Perhaps the same comments made by Chief Justice Beverley McLachlin on the twentieth anniversary of the Charter hold true today: "While the Charter is no longer in its infancy, these are still early years in its life. The Charter is still a work in progress, an unfinished project. Perhaps, it will always be. Future generations will have a great role to play in shaping it." It remains to be seen what new cases will come before the courts and what effect they will have on our rights and freedoms.

For Discussion

1. In which of the cases were fundamental freedoms denied?
2. In which of the cases was the law held to be a reasonable limit on individual rights?
3. What is the test for a reasonable search under the *R. v. Collins* case?
4. What step did the court take in the *Vriend v. Alberta* case to uphold the human rights law?

Chief Justice Beverley McLachlin

Self-Incrimination and Interpreter Rights

Section 13 of the Charter protects witnesses who testify in court from having the evidence used against them in later court proceedings. In other words, they cannot incriminate themselves by such testimony. This is known legally as self-incrimination. This right is suspended if witnesses lie while giving evidence. Lying under oath is known as perjury. If they are charged with perjury, the testimony they gave could be used against them.

Anyone involved in a proceeding who does not understand or speak the language of the court has the right to an interpreter. This is guaranteed in section 14 of the Charter. This section also applies to persons who are hearing impaired. In the case of *R. v. Tran*, 1994, an interpreter gave the accused a summary of the testimony and did not translate all of it. Therefore, the accused was not given a full opportunity to respond to the case against him. The Supreme Court held that the interpretation does not have to be perfect, but it must be continuous, precise, impartial, competent, and occur at the same time as the proceeding.

Did You Know?

In April 2007, in *Wynberg v. Ontario*, 2006, the Supreme Court of Canada refused to hear an appeal in a case that involved 28 families wanting the Ontario government to pay for expensive treatment for their autistic children. The original court had ruled that the government was violating Charter equality rights by not providing the treatment. The Ontario Court of Appeal reversed the decision and denied the funding.

Review Your Understanding

1. Summarize five of your rights when charged with an offence.
2. For what types of offences does Canada have a mandatory minimum sentence?
3. What protection do witnesses have in court?
4. When can the evidence given by a witness be used against him or her in court?
5. Summarize your rights under section 14 of the Charter.

2.6 Equality Rights

equality rights protection from discrimination

All About Law DVD

"Same-Sex Marriage" from *All About Law DVD*

Section 15 of the Charter provides **equality rights** to every individual. The specific grounds for discrimination include race, national or ethnic origin, colour, religion, sex, age, or mental or physical disability. The courts have added citizenship, marital status, and sexual orientation. For example, the courts held that a provincial law that allowed only Canadian citizens to practise law in British Columbia violated equality rights. The case was *Andrews v. Law Society of BC*, 1989. Ontario family law did not give same-sex couples the right to claim spousal support from each other when they split up. The court ruled this to be discrimination under section 15 of the Charter. The case was *M. v. H.*, 1999. As we saw above, in the case of *Vriend v. Alberta*, 1998, the Supreme Court required the Alberta government to include "sexual orientation" as grounds for discrimination. However, not all cases arguing for equality rights have been successful.

Equality Rights

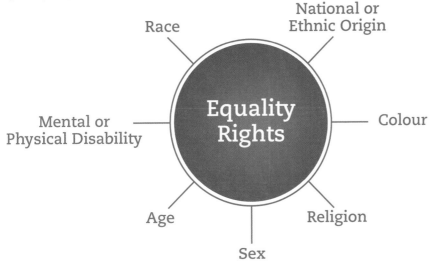

Race

National or
Ethnic Origin

Equality Rights

Mental or
Physical Disability

Colour

Age

Religion

Sex

Section 15 of the Charter
provides equality rights to
every individual without
discrimination.

Review Your Understanding

1. In what four ways is equality guaranteed under section 15 of the Charter?
2. List the grounds of discrimination that are covered by section 15 of the Charter.
3. What additional grounds of discrimination have been considered by the courts because they are related to those grounds of discrimination listed under section 15?
4. The courts often speak of the concept of "human dignity" when they are ruling on discrimination cases. What qualities would you associate with the concept of human dignity?
5. Is it a good idea to help groups that have historically been discriminated against by using a quota system for government jobs? Why or why not?

language rights protection
of the provinces' and Canada's
official languages in all
government institutions

2.7 Language and General Rights

Language Rights

The Charter guarantees **language rights**. It proclaims that English and French are Canada's two official languages. The Charter's official language sections, 16 to 22, provide that both languages have equal importance in Parliament and in all of Canada's institutions. The laws of Canada must be printed in English and French. Either language can be used in federal courts. Canadians also have the right to use either language when dealing with federal government offices where there is sufficient demand for bilingual services.

These stop signs
appear throughout
New Brunswick, the
only officially bilingual
province in Canada.

Official documents, such as these documents on Canadian passports, must be printed in both English and French.

Section 23 of the Charter guarantees rights for minority language education. These rights apply only to Canada's official languages (English and French). Also, they only apply to Canadian citizens. Education is a provincial matter. That means that each province decides whether to provide education in a language other than English or French.

 ## You Be the Judge

Arsenault-Cameron v. Prince Edward Island, 2000 SCC 1 (CanLII)

For more information, Go to Nelson Social Studies

A group of parents in Summerside, Prince Edward Island, argued that they were entitled to have their children educated in French. As there were enough students in the area to justify setting up a French school using public funds, they applied to the French Language School Board to establish a French school for Grades 1 to 6. The minister of education refused to set up the school but agreed to bus students to an existing school an hour's drive away. The parents took legal action against the provincial government, arguing that they had the right under the Charter to have their children educated in French.

• How do you think the Supreme Court of Canada decided the case?

Aboriginal and Multicultural Rights

Section 25 of the Charter guarantees the existing rights of Aboriginal peoples. In other words, the rights and freedoms in the Charter cannot interfere with any Aboriginal rights, treaty rights, or other rights of the Aboriginal peoples of Canada. Section 35 of the *Constitution Act, 1982* recognizes existing Aboriginal and treaty rights. However, it does not define these rights. The courts have the task of interpreting the meaning of the law. These constitutional protections set the stage for a variety of cases to be heard on the nature and scope of **Aboriginal rights**. These include such issues as the Aboriginal right to hunt and fish. Other important areas are Aboriginal land claims and self-government. Chapter 3 deals with the legal issues of Aboriginal peoples in greater detail.

Aboriginal rights the guarantee of the rights and freedoms of the Aboriginal peoples of Canada, entrenched in the Charter

In 2000, after a struggle of more than 100 years, a land claims treaty with the Pacific coast Nisga'a people was signed. Indian Affairs Minister Jane Stewart, Tribal Council President Joe Gosnell, and British Columbia Premier Glen Clark celebrate the signing of the Nisga'a Treaty.

Section 27 of the Charter recognizes the multicultural nature of Canada. Canadians come from many ethnic backgrounds and have a variety of needs. Courts and governments must consider these varying cultural backgrounds at all times.

1. Explain the purpose of section 25 of the Charter.
2. What groups are included as Aboriginal peoples in Canada under the Charter?
3. How does the *Constitution Act, 1982*, recognize Aboriginal rights?
4. Why do existing Aboriginal and treaty rights have to be interpreted by the courts?
5. How does the Charter respect multicultural rights?

2.8 Remedies

There are two methods of enforcing rights and freedoms guaranteed by the Charter:

1. using the authority under section 52 of the *Constitution Act, 1982*
2. seeking a remedy under section 24 of the *Charter of Rights and Freedoms*

strike down to rule in court that a law is invalid and no longer in effect

read down to rule in court that a law is generally acceptable, but a specific part of the law is invalid and thus removed

read in to add a term to a law that changes the law, but still allows the law to be upheld as constitutional

Under section 52 of the *Constitution Act, 1982*, the Constitution is set out as the most powerful law in Canada. If a law is passed in Canada, and all or part of the law goes against the Constitution, the entire law or part of it can be declared unconstitutional. The courts have the option to **strike down** a law, which means that the law is no longer in effect. They can also **read down** a law, which allows for a narrow interpretation of the law and generally considers what is written in the statute. The courts can also **read in** a term that changes the law, but allows the law to be upheld as constitutional and does not need to be struck down. (See the case of *Vriend v. Alberta*, 1998, on page 59.)

Strike down, read in, and read down are three types of remedies when legislation is found to be unconstitutional.

STRIKE DOWN

READ IN

READ DOWN

The second method of enforcing rights allows anyone who thinks his or her rights and freedoms have been **infringed** to apply to a court for a remedy under section 24 of the Charter. For example, a court may decide that your right to a trial within a reasonable time was violated. The court may then order a stop to the criminal proceedings. This order would prevent a Crown attorney from taking any additional steps against you. In another case, police may have searched your home and gathered evidence without a proper search warrant. The courts may find the search unreasonable. Then, you could apply to have the evidence thrown out under section 24(2) of the Charter. The courts must decide whether allowing the evidence would make the trial unfair, or whether it would make the justice system look bad. In legal terms, would allowing the evidence bring the administration of justice into disrepute?

infringed broken or violated, as in an agreement or right that is infringed

Review Your Understanding

1. What is a remedy?
2. What remedy is provided under section 52 of the *Constitution Act, 1982*?
3. Distinguish between "striking down" and "reading down" a law.
4. Explain the remedy provided under section 24 of the Charter.
5. What is the meaning of "to bring the administration of justice into disrepute?"

2.9 The Courts and the Legislature

You have already learned in Chapter 1 that the legislatures of the federal, provincial, and territorial governments have the power to make laws. Those bodies also have the power to change laws. Under the *Constitution Act, 1867*, the courts decided who had the power to enforce the laws. This depended on the division of powers by level of government. Since the Charter, the courts also decide whether or not these laws or government actions are unconstitutional.

We elect politicians to represent our interests at the various levels of government. We expect politicians to make the laws. However, our Charter allows our courts to interpret these same laws. Sometimes the courts have been accused of taking too much power away from the legislatures. The courts have sometimes been accused of taking over the lawmaking power and putting their own personal viewpoints and values into their court judgments. This is known as **judicial activism**. Others argue that the elected governments are avoiding controversial issues, forcing the courts to protect basic rights. Read the Issue on pages 66–67 to gain a better understanding of the role of courts and legislatures in making Canadian law.

judicial activism when judges put their own personal views and values into their court judgments

Do the Courts Have Too Much Power Compared to Legislatures?

The *Charter of Rights and Freedoms* gave courts broad new powers. It means that if a court finds that any provincial, territorial, or federal law trespasses on rights protected in the Charter, it can declare the law unconstitutional and no longer in effect. This has made the Supreme Court very powerful. The Supreme Court of Canada decisions below have been very controversial because of the social and moral issues relating to the cases.

> **R. v. Morgentaler, 1988:** The Supreme Court struck down Canada's abortion law on the grounds that it violated a woman's right to control her own body. The government chose not to create a new abortion law.
>
> **R. v. Butler, 1992:** The Supreme Court upheld Canada's obscenity laws but allowed the defence of artistic merit to be used in some cases where freedom of expression is being challenged (for example, a justification that material in question may have some artistic purpose).
>
> **R. v. Daviault, 1994:** The court ruled that extreme drunkenness may be a defence in rape (now sexual assault). According to that decision, convicting someone who did not know what he or she was doing is a violation of his or her Charter rights.

In *Doucet-Boudreau v. Nova Scotia (Minister of Education)*, 2003, a group of francophone parents wanted to educate their children in French. They claimed that the Nova Scotia government was violating their minority language rights. The trial judge agreed. The judge also ordered the government to report back to the court on its progress in providing French-language facilities and programs at the secondary level. The provincial government appealed. However,

the Supreme Court of Canada agreed that this was a suitable procedure.

In other cases, the courts have been criticized for their power when dealing with subjects like anti-terrorism legislation. Should the court be telling lawmakers what to do? Should they be giving governments time limits for rewriting a law? Or should the governments be given the exclusive authority to make the laws for the safety and security of Canada?

In *Charkaoui v. Canada (Citizenship and Immigration)*, 2007, the Supreme Court struck down part of the *Immigration and Refugee Protection Act* dealing with security certificates and detentions. The accused were suspected of having terrorist ties. The court held that they were denied their right to a fair hearing. They were not informed of the case against them. They were not allowed to be represented by a lawyer in a secret hearing. The Supreme Court gave the government one year to create a new law that would not be in violation of the Charter.

Similarly, in *M. v. H.*, 1999, the court ruled that equality rights were being denied to same-sex couples. The Ontario government was given six months to rewrite its family law legislation so as not to discriminate against same-sex partners. It did so.

As you can see, the court's decision varies depending on the case. Sometimes the court protects individual rights guaranteed in the Charter. Sometimes laws are struck down. Sometimes governments are given the opportunity to create new laws.

On One Side

Some Canadians believe that the Supreme Court of Canada has become too powerful. It may be time to re-examine the role that the justices play. These people are opposed to the idea that nine appointed judges can overrule laws made by elected representatives. They say that if laws need to be updated and changed, elected lawmakers should do this. That is the very heart of democracy.

Other people believe that the Supreme Court is protecting individual rights at the expense of the needs of society. According to these critics, the Charter guarantees too many individual rights. They see it as threatening the welfare and safety of Canadians. They argue that it does too much to protect criminals. It does not do enough to guarantee the rights and freedoms of law-abiding Canadians.

On the Other Side

Many Canadians who support the Charter point out that it protects their rights and freedoms from government interference. They believe that the courts can respond to changing social attitudes and beliefs much more quickly than elected governments. Politicians want to be re-elected. That is why they often avoid passing controversial legislation. The appointed justices of the Supreme Court do not have this pressure. They do have professional legal backgrounds and they can be trusted to know the law and fairly interpret its provisions. Their ability to use the Charter to overrule certain laws ensures greater fairness and justice.

Supreme Court of Canada

Federal Parliament Buildings

The Bottom Line

The Charter has changed life and law in Canada. It has often placed judges and their decisions in the media spotlight. Supreme Court decisions are especially important because they affect all Canadians. As the *Charkaoui* decision indicates, the courts are now being asked to consider security versus individual rights in light of anti-terrorism laws. When does security outweigh civil liberties, or should it ever? When the courts strike down a law, are they practising judicial activism? When the courts give the legislatures one year to create a new law, are they participating in a creative dialogue to allow laws to be upheld?

Freedoms and rights may be expanded or limited. This will depend on new cases brought before the courts. The courts will continue to interpret rights and freedoms. They will also balance individual and societal interests when they make decisions about which rights to expand and which to limit. The bottom-line question is, although the legislatures have the prime lawmaking power, should the courts have the power to overrule them?

Who do you think should have more power: the courts or the legislatures?

What Do You Think?

1. Examine the cases mentioned and identify whether the court decisions are in favour of individual rights or the needs of society.

2. In groups, discuss whether Supreme Court decisions are having a negative or positive effect on Canadian society. Share your conclusions.

3. What types of issues might require the court to limit individual rights in favour of the needs of society?

4. Should the needs of society be more important than individual rights, or should individual rights be protected at all costs? Explain.

Chapter 2 **The Canadian Charter of Rights and Freedoms**

Chapter Review

Chapter Highlights

- The *Canadian Charter of Rights and Freedoms* guarantees the rights and freedoms of all Canadians.
- The Charter is a part of the *Constitution Act, 1982*.
- Since April 17, 1982, your rights and freedoms have been entrenched in the Canadian Constitution.
- The *Constitution Act, 1982*, is the most important law in Canada.
- The rights and freedoms guaranteed in the Charter are not absolute but are subject to reasonable limits that can be justified in our free and democratic society.
- The Supreme Court of Canada interprets the rights and freedoms listed in the Charter.
- Section 2 of the Charter lists the fundamental freedoms of all Canadians.
- Democratic rights include the right to vote.
- Mobility rights include the right to enter, remain in, and leave Canada.
- Legal rights provide protection if you are involved with the criminal justice system.
- A cornerstone of the Canadian justice system is the right to be presumed innocent until proven guilty.
- Equality rights provide you with freedom from discrimination.
- Language rights define French and English as the two official languages in Canada.
- Minority language education rights apply to the two official languages, French and English.
- The Charter provides for Aboriginal and multicultural rights.
- A constitutional remedy used by the courts includes striking down a law that violates the Charter.
- To save laws from being struck down as unconstitutional, courts can "read in" a term or "read down" the law.
- Federal, provincial, or territorial governments can use the notwithstanding clause to pass laws that override certain rights and freedoms in the Charter.

Check Your Knowledge

1. Prepare a chart outlining your rights and freedoms under the Charter.
2. Explain the purpose of the reasonable limits clause.
3. Explain how the notwithstanding clause makes it possible to override rights and freedoms under the Charter.
4. Explain the purpose of section 24 of the Charter.

Apply Your Learning

5. Refer to the *R. v. Oakes*, 1986, case on page 39 and apply the four-step guide to analyzing a Charter case.
   a) Does the Charter apply?
   b) Has a Charter right or freedom been infringed?
   c) Does the reasonable limits clause justify the infringement?
   d) If not, is there a remedy provided under the Charter?
6. Use the Internet to research a Supreme Court of Canada Charter decision. Identify the name of the case and the Charter issue that the court was asked to consider.

Communicate Your Understanding

7. You have been asked to draft proposed changes to the Charter. Prepare an argument that poverty should be included as a ground for discrimination in equality rights.

8. Civil liberties are freedoms that protect individuals from unwanted government interference. Why are civil liberties, such as freedom of expression and freedom of religion, protected in our society? Should your civil liberties be reasonably limited in a democratic society?

9. Assume that your local town council is proposing to install video surveillance cameras on all major street corners in your community. Prepare a debate arguing that video camera surveillance technology is justifiable for security reasons. Be sure to consider a counterargument that the use of video camera surveillance technology violates your privacy rights.

10. In pairs, select one of the topics below. One student will prepare an argument in favour of the statement, and the other student will prepare a counterargument against the statement. Support your position with examples. Share your opinions with your partner.

    a) Canadian society is going to break down and the court system will become ineffective because Canadians have too many civil rights, and far too many minority groups are protected under the law.

    b) Because people who talk on cellphones while driving are dangerous to themselves and others, the use of cellphones while driving should be banned.

    c) Because they have so much power, the justices of the Supreme Court of Canada should be elected.

    d) Police officers should not be allowed to conduct random searches of schools, malls, and other public places using sniffer dogs.

Develop Your Thinking

11. On the twenty-fifth anniversary of the Charter, Chief Justice Beverley McLachlin of the Supreme Court of Canada commented: "The most important thing I think is to educate the children and young people. The basics of the Canadian Constitution —including the Charter—should be mandatory learning in our schools and high schools." Why is it important to have an understanding of our rights and freedoms under the Charter?

12. In the case of *Charkaoui v. Canada (Citizenship and Immigration)*, 2007, the court tried to balance liberty and security. The Supreme Court ruled that the indefinite jailing of a foreign national (non-citizen) suspected of being a terrorist is legitimate, as long as the detention is subject to a meaningful and regular review. What do you think would constitute a "meaningful and regular review"?

13. Mr. Justice Marc Rosenberg of the Ontario Court of Appeal has stated that "it is because of the Charter that the criminal justice system is out from under the shadow of capital punishment." Which sections of the Charter do you think support his comments?

14. In the case of *R. v. M. (M.R.)*, 1998, a vice-principal was justified in searching a junior high school student who was suspected of drug dealing. In its majority decision, the court stated: "Students know that their teachers and other school authorities are responsible for providing a safe environment and maintaining order and discipline in the school. They must know that this may sometimes require personal searches of students and their personal effects and the seizure of prohibited items." Research more about your reasonable expectation of privacy. When should privacy rights be limited?

3 Human Rights in Canada

What You Should Know

- Which groups of Canadians have experienced discrimination?
- Who are some of the people who have worked to make Canada a more just society?
- What forms of discrimination still exist in Canada? What is being done to eliminate them?
- What rights do the *Canadian Human Rights Act* and provincial human rights codes protect, and how are they enforced?

Selected Key Terms

accommodation

assimilation

barrier to equality

bona fide occupational requirement

complainant

discrimination

employment equity

grounds of discrimination

human rights

intentional discrimination

pay equity

prejudice

stereotyping

unintentional discrimination

Chapter at a Glance

3.1 Introduction

3.2 Women's Rights

3.3 Aboriginal Rights

3.4 Rights of Other Groups

3.5 Human Rights

3.6 Human Rights Legislation

3.7 Enforcing Human Rights Laws

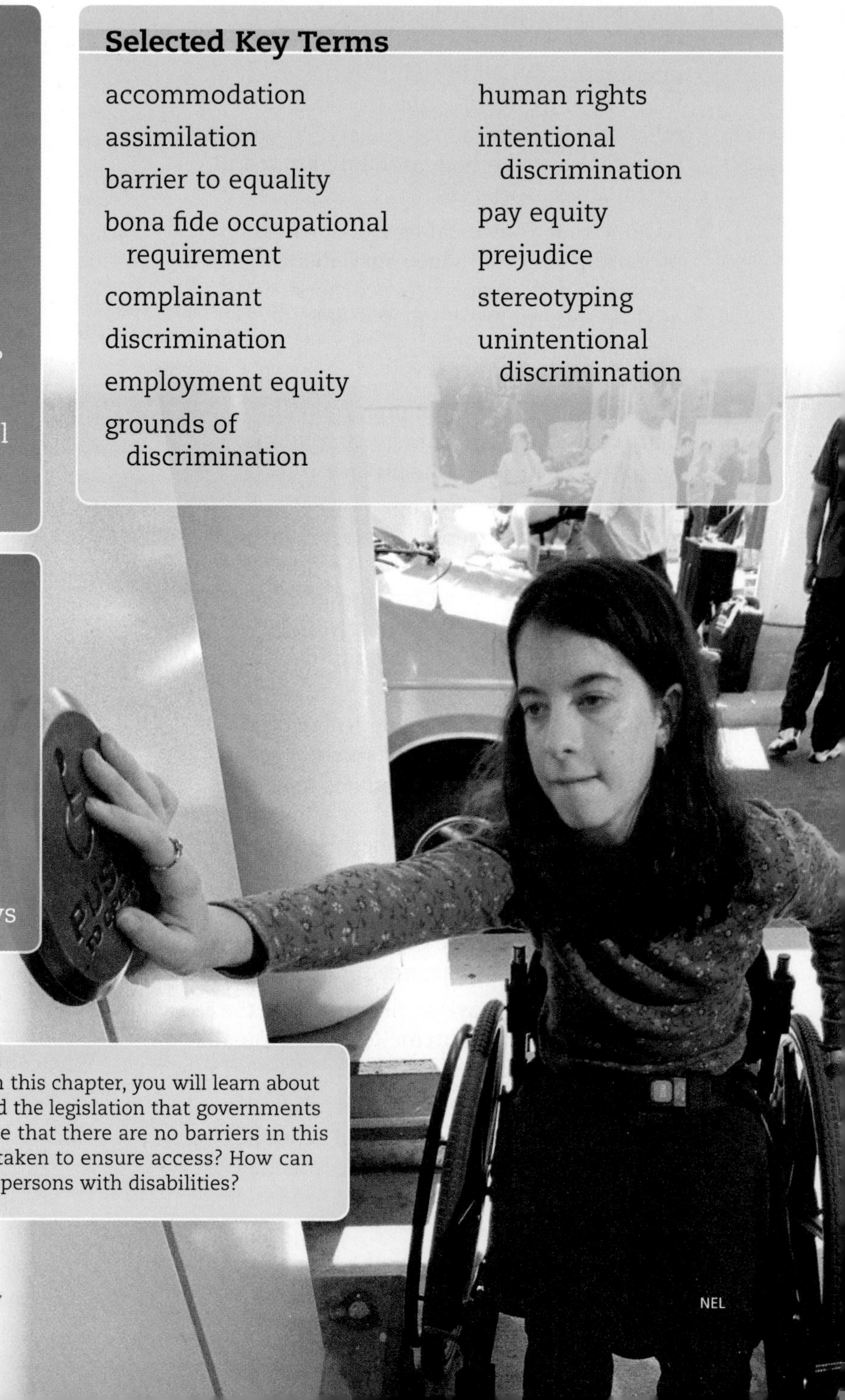

Barriers come in all shapes and sizes. In this chapter, you will learn about different types of barriers to equality and the legislation that governments have passed to try to remove them. Note that there are no barriers in this photo. Can you imagine the measures taken to ensure access? How can we ensure better access to facilities for persons with disabilities?

3.1 Introduction

Individuals should be treated equally and fairly as human beings regardless of the group to which they belong. All Canadians are supposed to be equal under the law. However, equality has not been won without a fight, especially for some groups.

In this chapter, you will read about several groups that have historically faced barriers to equality. Those barriers are anything that prevents someone from participating fully in society. For example, today most people take the right to vote for granted. However, for years, women and Aboriginal peoples were denied this basic right. That meant they could not participate fully in the democracy of Canada.

Many groups have faced barriers in their struggle to achieve equality. Women fought for many years to achieve the right to vote and the right to hold public office. Immigrants faced **discrimination** on the basis of race. Canada had an immigration policy that was not open to everyone. The Canadian government limited immigration from certain countries. It even barred some races from entering certain professions. In this chapter, you will explore the barriers experienced by women, Aboriginal people, immigrants, gay men and lesbians, and people with disabilities.

You will also explore **human rights** laws. These protect people from being treated unfairly by others. Human rights laws have been passed in Canada by the federal, provincial, and territorial governments. They make it illegal for people to treat others unfairly. Discrimination occurs when individuals or groups are treated unfairly or differently because of such characteristics as race, sex, religion, age, or disability. You will learn about the prohibited grounds of discrimination (types of discrimination). You will also discover how to make a human rights complaint.

Human rights laws protect people from discrimination.

discrimination treating individuals or groups unfairly or differently because of such characteristics as race, sex, religion, age, or disability

human rights rights that protect a person from unfair treatment by other individuals and governments, but are not always upheld by a country's justice system

Chapter 3 **Human Rights in Canada**

3.2 Women's Rights

One hundred and fifty years ago, women had few rights. They were excluded from universities and professional schools, and they could not vote or run for political office. Working-class women often worked beside their husbands on the farm or in factories, but most middle-class women stayed at home to take care of their husbands and children. Outside of nursing and teaching, there were few career opportunities for middle-class women.

Toward the end of the nineteenth century (the 1800s), attitudes toward women slowly began to change. Small groups of women in Canada, the United States, and Europe joined together to fight for **suffrage**—the right to vote. They were known as suffragettes. At first, they were regarded as radicals, or extremists. Almost everyone, including other women, disapproved of them because they challenged old laws and customs.

suffrage the right to vote in political elections; franchise

In 1876, Dr. Emily Stowe established the first suffrage organization in Canada—the Toronto Women's Literary Club. She was a **feminist** who believed that women should have the same rights as men. She and others worked hard to convince Canadians that women should have the right to vote. However, it would take time to persuade most people that adult women should be able to vote and hold positions held by men.

feminist one who believes in the social, economic, and political equality of the sexes

In 1912, Nellie McClung, a teacher and author, helped to establish the Winnipeg Political Equality League. It became one of the most effective suffrage organizations in Canada. When the league appealed to the Manitoba premier to give women the vote, he replied that "nice women" did not want to vote. It was not until 1916 that Manitoba became the first province to give women the right to vote. Other Canadian provinces quickly followed Manitoba's example. In 1920, the *Dominion Elections Act* gave most women in Canada the right to vote and the right to be elected to Parliament.

Women and the Right to Vote

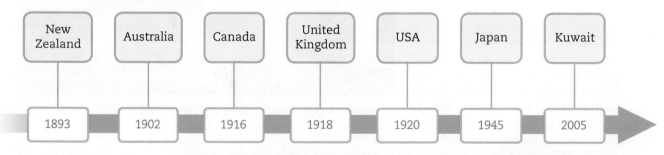

New Zealand	Australia	Canada	United Kingdom	USA	Japan	Kuwait
1893	1902	1916	1918	1920	1945	2005

Women from around the world have had to fight for the right to vote—and many are still fighting for that right today. The dates in this timeline represent the first time when women in various countries obtained that right. Keep in mind, though, that most countries placed restrictions and conditions on women's suffrage, and sometimes these restrictions were not lifted for several years or even decades.

Development of Women's Rights

World War I (1914–1918) was a turning point for women's rights. While the men were fighting in Europe, thousands of Canadian women took up jobs on farms and in factories. These efforts helped to win the war and earned women new respect. By the end of the war, Canadian women, except for Aboriginal women, had won the right to vote.

When World War I ended, Canadian men came home and reclaimed their jobs, and most Canadian women returned to their traditional role as homemakers. In 1921, the federal government passed a regulation preventing married women from holding jobs in the government unless they had no support from their husband's income. Female civil servants had to quit their jobs when they married. The only exception to this rule occurred if no man was available to fill the job. It seemed to many women that they had rights and freedoms only when their country needed them.

That same year, Agnes Macphail became the first woman to be elected to the House of Commons. She believed in women's rights and worked hard to improve them. But women did not rush into politics to try to get elected. They were educated to believe that politics was a "man's occupation" and that their responsibilities lay elsewhere.

WOMEN
ARE PERSONS
LES FEMMES SONT
DES PERSONNES

EMILY MURPHY

Women have not always had the right to vote in Canada. This 1985 commemorative stamp is of Emily Murphy, a feminist from Alberta who fought for women's rights. In 1916, she became Canada's first woman magistrate.

Political Equality for Women

Province/Territory	Suffrage as of	Right to Hold Office as of
Manitoba	January 28, 1916	January 28, 1916
Saskatchewan	March 14, 1916	March 14, 1916
Alberta	April 19, 1916	April 19, 1916
British Columbia	April 5, 1917	April 5, 1917
Ontario	April 12, 1917	April 24, 1919
Nova Scotia	April 26, 1918	April 26, 1919
New Brunswick	April 17, 1919	March 9, 1934
Yukon Territory	May 20, 1919	May 20, 1919
Prince Edward Island	May 3, 1922	May 3, 1922
Newfoundland and Labrador (not yet part of Canada)	April 13, 1925	April 13, 1925
Québec	April 25, 1940	April 25, 1940
Northwest Territories	June 12, 1951	June 12, 1951
Nunavut	April 1, 1999*	April 1, 1999

This chart shows when women in different Canadian provinces and territories won the right to vote and the right to hold office.

* Date Nunavut was created

 Did You Know?

By 1973, only 22 women had ever been elected to the House of Commons, including Agnes Macphail. In February 2008, there were 69 female members out of 308 seats in the House of Commons.

Chapter 3 **Human Rights in Canada**

Did You Know?

In 1930, Cairine Wilson became the first woman appointed to the Senate. By 2008, 31 of the 93 Canadian senators were female.

Not only did women fight for the right to vote and hold political office. They also fought for the right to sit in the Canadian Senate. In fact, women were not considered "persons" in Canada prior to 1929. That meant that they were not allowed to become senators. See the Looking Back feature below on the Persons Case. Explore the legal battle fought in the Canadian and British courts by five strong-minded women. They wanted women declared qualified persons for the purposes of being appointed to the Canadian Senate.

 Looking Back

The Persons Case

These statues of the "Famous Five" are located on Parliament Hill in Ottawa. Nellie McClung, Emily Murphy, Irene Parlby, Henrietta Muir Edwards, and Louise McKinney were all part of the "Famous Five" who took the Persons Case to the Supreme Court of Canada and eventually to the Judicial Committee of the Privy Council, the highest court of the time in Britain.

In 1927, five Alberta feminists asked Parliament to define the term "person." It was used in section 24 of the *British North America Act, 1867.* That was Canada's first constitution. They wanted to know if "persons" who qualified for appointment to the Senate included women. No woman had ever been appointed to the Senate up until this time. In 1928, the Supreme Court of Canada decided that the word "person"

meant male persons only. Women were not legal persons and could therefore not hold any appointed office. Canadian law, as interpreted at the time, actually prevented women from achieving equality.

The Supreme Court said that section 24 of the *British North America Act, 1867,* had to be read in light of the times when it was written. Women could not vote or hold office in 1867. Further, only male nouns and pronouns were used in the act.

This famous case came to be known as the "Persons Case." Five determined women appealed this decision to the highest court of the time. That was the Judicial Committee of the Privy Council in Britain. Canada was still not completely independent of Britain in 1928. This British court could overrule any decision made by the Supreme Court of Canada. In 1929, it overruled the Supreme Court of Canada's decision. It said that women were indeed legal "persons" who qualified for appointment to the Senate.

The five women, listed on the next page, came to be known as the Famous Five because of the importance of the Persons Case. They not only advanced women's rights, but other important social issues as well.

The Famous Five worked tirelessly to make Canada a more just society with respect to women's rights. They recognized that both women and men make valuable contributions to society.

However, despite being progressive about women's rights, the Famous Five did not lobby for everyone's rights. Today, some people object to their opinions about the equality of people of different races. This is a good example of the slow evolution of human rights protection in Canada.

continues...

The Persons Case

The Famous Five	
Nellie McClung	An influential politician who fought for "equal pay for equal work." She was also the author of 16 books and the first woman to sit on the board of governors of the Canadian Broadcasting Corporation (CBC).
Emily Murphy	The first female judge to be appointed in Canada in 1916 and the first woman appointed to the Edmonton Hospital Board. She was a writer and politician and a strong promoter of women's rights.
Irene Parlby	Elected to the Legislative Assembly of Alberta in 1921 and appointed to the Cabinet. She was also Canada's representative to the League of Nations in 1930 and was the first woman to receive an Honorary Doctor of Law degree from the University of Alberta in 1935.
Henrietta Muir Edwards	An expert on the legal status of women and children in Canada, she fought for mother's allowance (government money to help families raise children).
Louise McKinney	The first woman elected to a provincial legislature in Alberta in 1917. She was a suffragette and strong supporter of the temperance movement (a movement dedicated to outlawing the consumption of alcohol).

For Discussion

1. What was the legal issue in the Persons Case?
2. What did the Supreme Court of Canada decide? Why?
3. How did the Judicial Committee of the Privy Council in Great Britain decide the case? Why do you think they came to that decision?
4. Identify a significant contribution of each of the Famous Five to achieving women's equality in Canada.

During World War II (1939–1945), 45 000 Canadian women joined the military. Their jobs included nurses, drivers, firefighters, and radio technicians. They wore uniforms and had military training, but they were not allowed to fight in combat. In addition, they were paid 20 percent less than men who held the same rank.

Back home, more than 1 million women entered the workforce to help with the war effort. However, when the war ended, they encountered the same old attitudes. A 1944 Gallup opinion poll showed that most people believed that returning soldiers should be hired over women. Seventy-five percent of men felt this way. Sixty-eight percent of women agreed. It was not until 1955 that legislation favouring the hiring of men was abolished.

Women were instrumental to the war effort during World War II. Many joined the military and served overseas in a variety of jobs.

You learned in Chapter 1 that in 1960, Prime Minister John Diefenbaker's government passed the *Canadian Bill of Rights*, the first human rights legislation in Canada. The Bill of Rights stated that it was illegal to discriminate against people because of their sex, race, religion, or colour. The Bill of Rights also helped to pave the way for the *Canadian Charter of Rights and Freedoms*. In 1982, protection of women's rights was enshrined (set forth) in section 28 of the Charter, which guarantees rights and freedoms "equally to male and female persons."

Review Your Understanding

1. Identify some of the historic barriers to achieving women's equality.
2. Identify the social attitudes that created barriers to women achieving equality.
3. What is suffrage?
4. What effect did World War I have on women in the Canadian workforce?
5. Why is the Persons Case important in Canadian history?

Women's Issues Today

Today, the women's movement in Canada is still working to resolve a number of equality issues. One organization at the forefront of legal reform is the Women's Legal Education and Action Fund (LEAF). It describes itself as "a national, non-profit organization working to promote equality for women and girls in Canada." LEAF safeguards women's rights. It uses the equality provisions from the *Charter of Rights and Freedoms* to do so. It also intervenes in legal cases where women's rights are an issue. These include employment and **pay equity, sexual harassment**, and discrimination against pregnant women. Many people are surprised to hear that some of these basic issues are not yet resolved.

pay equity equal payment for work evaluated as equal in worth

sexual harassment unwelcome actions or conduct of a sexual nature toward another person

Audrey Johnson, Executive Director for LEAF National, speaks at the 2007 Persons Day Event. This is LEAF's signature event, attracting almost 1000 individuals every year.

Pay Equity

Pay equity is the principle of equal payment for work of equal value. It is guaranteed under section 11 of the *Canadian Human Rights Act*. Federal employers must establish the value of particular jobs. This is done by comparing the skill, effort, responsibility, and working conditions for various jobs. Then, female- and male-dominated jobs are examined. Once a value of a job is determined, the employer must then see if there is a wage gap between the women and men performing work of equal value.

Traditional attitudes are one reason for inequalities. In 1983, a civil servants' union complained that women were not being paid the same as men. In 1998, the Canadian Human Rights Tribunal ruled that these female employees had been treated unfairly for years. It ordered the federal government to pay billions of dollars in back wages. The following year, the federal government agreed to pay $3.5 billion to 230 000 current and retired workers. Such highly publicized cases indicate that progress is being made in reducing the wage gap between men and women. Still, pay equity cases often involve a long legal struggle. Equity is still not guaranteed.

Employment Equity

Employment equity means the equal treatment of all employees based on their abilities. In 1995, the federal government passed the *Employment Equity Act*. It is meant to correct unfairness to certain groups. These include women, Aboriginal peoples, people with disabilities, and visible minorities. This law applies to the federal government itself. It also applies to Crown companies run by it.

Employment equity law requires employers to identify **barriers to equality** in the workplace. They must remedy situations in which barriers exist. They must also actively hire and promote minority groups. The federal government is committed to removing all forms of unfairness in the workplace. (See Chapter 16 for more about these issues.)

employment equity the principle that treatment of all employees should be based on their abilities and be fair, just, and impartial; generally aimed at women, Aboriginal peoples, visible minorities, and people with disabilities

barrier to equality anything that prevents someone from participating fully and equally in society

Canadian soldiers distributed food to Kandahar families in Afghanistan. Women have not always had the same employment opportunities in the Canadian Forces as men have. Women were first allowed to work in combat jobs in infantry, artillery, and armoured divisions in 1987. Two years later, a Canadian Human Rights Tribunal ordered the military to permit women to serve in most combat jobs. By 2000, the military announced it was lifting its ban on women serving in submarines. Do you agree that women should be allowed to serve in all combat roles? Justify your position.

Did You Know?

In 2006, women made up approximately 15 percent of Canada's armed forces and about 2 percent of Canada's regular force combat troops.

Review Your Understanding

1. What are some of the current barriers to equality facing women?
2. What is pay equity?
3. How are different jobs compared under pay equity?
4. What is employment equity?
5. What groups are protected under employment equity laws?

3.3 Aboriginal Rights

When Aboriginal peoples talk about achieving equality, they are usually not referring to individual rights and freedoms. They are referring to their **collective rights**. Those rights have come from having occupied Canada for thousands of years as distinct nations. These rights focus on land and the right to self-government.

Development of Aboriginal Rights

Europeans began arriving in North America in the 1600s. They formed military alliances and partnerships with a number of **First Nations**. Those were the first peoples of Canada. This helped to maintain the lucrative fur trade and to support military conflicts such as the Seven Years' War (1756–1763). That war ended French rule in what is now Canada. It also led to the founding of Canada's present system of Aboriginal treaties. (Treaties are agreements made between two or more groups.) This system had its roots in the Royal Proclamation of 1763. That Royal Proclamation remains an important legal document. It has been described as a kind of "Magna Carta" that recognizes Aboriginal peoples as nations. In fact, section 25(a) of Canada's Constitution does guarantee "any rights or freedoms that have been recognized by the Royal Proclamation of October 7, 1763."

By Confederation in 1867, European immigrants flooded the country. Between 1871 and 1921, the Canadian government concluded a series of land agreements with Aboriginal peoples. They were designed to force the peaceful removal of Aboriginal peoples from their traditional lands to reserve lands. This would allow for European settlement. Canada's official policy toward Aboriginal peoples was that they were to be "protected" on reserves, "civilized" by being taught European ways and beliefs, and eventually assimilated (being absorbed fully) into European Canadian society.

In 1868, the federal government passed the *Indian Act*. It defined who was "**Indian**" and who was not. It banned some traditional cultural practices. It replaced traditional Aboriginal self-government with elected band councils, and rejected Aboriginal ways of justice.

collective rights the rights of the group, rather than the individual

First Nations a term originated by Aboriginal peoples to describe themselves and to recognize that they belong to distinct cultural groups with sovereign rights based on being Canada's first inhabitants

The Royal Proclamation of 1763

Indian the term used in the *Constitution Act, 1982*, to describe First Nations peoples who are not Inuit or Métis

Development of Aboriginal Rights

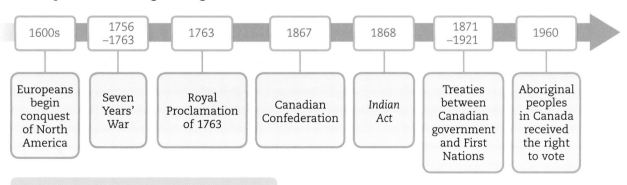

1600s	1756–1763	1763	1867	1868	1871–1921	1960
Europeans begin conquest of North America	Seven Years' War	Royal Proclamation of 1763	Canadian Confederation	*Indian Act*	Treaties between Canadian government and First Nations	Aboriginal peoples in Canada received the right to vote

Aboriginal rights have evolved since the 1600s.

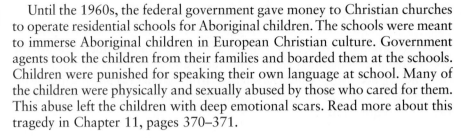
All About Law DVD

"Aboriginal Abuse" from
All About Law DVD

Until the 1960s, the federal government gave money to Christian churches to operate residential schools for Aboriginal children. The schools were meant to immerse Aboriginal children in European Christian culture. Government agents took the children from their families and boarded them at the schools. Children were punished for speaking their own language at school. Many of the children were physically and sexually abused by those who cared for them. This abuse left the children with deep emotional scars. Read more about this tragedy in Chapter 11, pages 370–371.

Aboriginal Leaders and Lobby Groups

Since the 1950s, Aboriginal peoples have fought to reverse the policy of **assimilation** and be recognized as distinct nations within Canada. In 1951, Aboriginal leaders formed the Native Indian Brotherhood to lobby the federal government on Aboriginal rights and to press for the settlement of **land claims** (a claim to land long-used by Aboriginal peoples).

The Aboriginal justice movement was set back in 1969. At that time, the Trudeau government released its policy document, or White Paper. The document showed Trudeau's emphasis on individual rights over collective rights. It said that Aboriginal peoples had no special status and called for the repeal (withdrawal) of the *Indian Act* and existing treaties. It proposed to "enable the Indian people to be free—free to develop Indian culture in an environment of legal, social, and economic equality with other Canadians." The White Paper only made Aboriginal peoples more determined to fight for their rights.

In 1982, Aboriginal leaders replaced the Native Indian Brotherhood with the Assembly of First Nations (AFN). This better reflected the Aboriginal people's diversity. The AFN is a national lobby organization and represents over 630 First Nations communities across Canada. The AFN presents Aboriginal views on such matters as Aboriginal and treaty rights, economic development, health, housing, justice, and social development. There are other provincial lobby groups that deal with particular First Nations, Métis or Inuit concerns within the provinces.

Did You Know?

In June 2008, Prime Minister Harper officially apologized to former students of native residential schools, calling it "a sad chapter in our history."

assimilation the process of absorbing a minority into the prevailing culture

land claim assertion of the right to certain lands, as in claim to land long used by Aboriginal peoples

Did You Know?

The AFN defines Aboriginal peoples as First Nations, Inuit, and Métis, each having their own distinct history, culture, and political organization.

Activity

To learn more about the Assembly of First Nations,

Go to Nelson Social Studies

On July 10, 2007, National Chief Phil Fontaine spoke in Halifax at AFN's 28th annual general assembly. The symbols in the AFN logo represent and embody the strength, culture, and beliefs of the First Nations peoples.

Landmark Aboriginal Rights Decisions

In 1973, the Supreme Court of Canada handed down an influential decision. In *Calder v. Attorney-General of British Columbia*, 1973, the Nisga'a people of northwestern British Columbia claimed that they had always held legal title to their ancestral lands. In other words, they claimed that ownership of their land had never been given or taken away. The British Columbia Supreme Court and Court of Appeal ruled against them. The Nisga'a appealed their case to the Supreme Court of Canada. Seven judges heard the appeal.

The Supreme Court dismissed the Nisga'a appeal on a technicality. Yet this case was significant for Aboriginal rights. Six judges agreed that the concept of "Aboriginal title" was a valid one, but were split evenly on whether Nisga'a Aboriginal title still existed. The three judges who sided with the Nisga'a claim said that, where title had not been extinguished (cancelled), it might exist wherever land had been occupied and used by Aboriginal peoples.

The Trudeau government recognized the significance of the *Calder* decision. It reversed the stand it took in the White Paper (see page 80). It introduced a process for negotiating land claims settlements. Since 1973, several comprehensive land claims settlements have been achieved.

In 1997, the Supreme Court of Canada handed down another important decision on Aboriginal rights and treaty rights. The case of *Delgamuukw v. British Columbia*, 1997, represented a great victory for First Nations. The case was launched in 1984. Fifty-one Wet'suwet'en and Gitxsan hereditary chiefs took Canada and British Columbia to court. They tried to gain ownership of their ancestral lands. After a lengthy court battle, the case finally went to the Supreme Court. The court did not determine whether the Wet'suwet'en and Gitxsan established title in any of the territories they claimed. The court sent that issue back to trial.

 Did You Know?

The Nunavut Land Claims Agreement called for the division of the Northwest Territories to create Nunavut. On April 1, 1999, Nunavut became Canada's third territory, with the first Inuit-led government in Canadian history.

 Did You Know?

There are two types of Aboriginal land claims: comprehensive land claims deal with areas that have not been covered by treaty or other legal means. Specific land claims are those dealing with breaches of obligations under treaties and the like.

Members of The Gitxsan Dancers performed in front of the Supreme Court of Canada building in Ottawa on June 16, 1997, while their land claim case was being presented to the Supreme Court.

However, the court did something important. It described a test to prove Aboriginal title. It showed how Canada's Constitution protects that title. According to the test, an Aboriginal group has title if it can show it exclusively occupied the land before Britain declared sovereignty over that land. The court held that Aboriginal oral histories were acceptable as evidence in a court of law.

The court noted that Aboriginal title and rights are not absolute. Governments may interfere with these rights. But they must justify it and show that their action meets a strict test. The Delgamuukw decision was important to Aboriginal peoples. It outlined what they can demand in treaty negotiations once they establish Aboriginal title.

Case

Guerin v. The Queen, 1984 CanLII 25 (S.C.C.)

For more information, **Go to Nelson Social Studies**

In 1957, the Indian affairs branch officer for the Musqueam band in Vancouver negotiated a long-term lease of band land to a local golf club. The *Indian Act* required that leases or sales of Aboriginal land to non-Aboriginals must have the approval of the Indian Affairs department.

In 1975, the Musqueam band sued the federal government. They claimed that the branch officer had violated his position of trust. They argued that the lease omitted the terms that had been orally conveyed to him at a special meeting. Specifically, the band wanted $2900 annual rent for 15 years. This was to be followed by 10-year renewal periods with rents to be determined at the time of renewal. The lease that the branch officer signed was for renewal periods of 15 years. Increases were limited to 15 percent of the previous rental.

The Supreme Court of Canada ruled unanimously in favour of the Musqueam band. It noted that Aboriginal peoples had no choice in their land dealings but to work through Indian Affairs department officials. They relied on these officials to represent their interests. By altering the terms of the Musqueam offer without the band's knowledge or approval, the branch officer had failed in his basic duties to the Musqueam band. Moreover, there was a breach of trust by the federal government.

This map of southwest Vancouver shows the Musqueam reserve land in question.

For Discussion

1. Does the *Indian Act* give Aboriginal groups an unrestricted right to sell or lease reserve land? Explain.

2. Why was the Musqueam band dissatisfied with the agreement the branch officer had negotiated?

3. Why did the Supreme Court of Canada rule in favour of the Musqueam band?

4. How might the decision in this case be used by other Aboriginal groups to prove that they have received unjust treatment?

Aboriginal Rights and Canada's Constitution

Canada's Constitution addresses Aboriginal rights in section 25 of the *Charter of Rights and Freedoms* and section 35 of the *Constitution Act, 1982*. In 1987, Prime Minister Brian Mulroney and the 10 provincial premiers agreed on a plan to reform Canada's Constitution. Known as the Meech Lake Accord, the agreement had to be ratified (signed into agreement) by Parliament and the provincial legislatures before becoming law.

In 1990, ratification came to an abrupt end when Elijah Harper, a Cree member of the Manitoba legislature, refused to make the vote on the Accord unanimous. A unanimous vote was required by law. This meant that there was no vote on ratification in the legislature. Harper strongly opposed the Accord. It did not recognize the First Nations as equal founding partners of Canada. His concerns were addressed in the subsequent Charlottetown Accord, but this Accord also failed as a result of a national referendum.

Aboriginal Issues Today

Despite winning recognition of Aboriginal and treaty rights, Aboriginal peoples still face major barriers to equality. Poverty is widespread and educational achievement is generally low. Serious health and social problems afflict many. In recent years, many Aboriginal leaders have declared their communities to be in a state of crisis. Their major concerns are drug and alcohol abuse, high rates of youth suicide, low employment, and appalling housing conditions. In addition, racism directed at Aboriginal peoples continues to be a problem.

Most Canadians do not deny the serious nature of the problems. But, the solutions are the subject of heated debate. Most Aboriginal peoples feel they will gain their rightful place in society once their rights as distinct peoples are recognized in law and interpreted in treaties. They also feel that prosperity will result from self-government and the settlement of land claims.

Settling outstanding land claims will be costly for the provincial and federal governments. It may require expropriating (taking away) land that other Canadians have lived and worked on for many years. Opponents argue that the rights of local residents and non-Aboriginal peoples are often not considered in these processes. Most Canadians want to see these issues resolved, but disagree on how to do so.

Elijah Harper, a Cree member of the Manitoba legislature, voted down the Meech Lake Accord.

 Did You Know?

Section 25 of the Charter and section 35 of the *Constitution Act, 1982*, protect Aboriginal rights and treaty rights in the Canadian Constitution, but these rights are not defined; Canadian courts must interpret the meaning of Aboriginal rights.

Review Your Understanding

1. Distinguish between collective rights and individual rights.
2. What are some historic barriers to equality for Aboriginal peoples?
3. What was the significance of the 1969 White Paper released by the Trudeau government?
4. What was the Meech Lake Accord? Why did Elijah Harper oppose the Meech Lake Accord?
5. Summarize the significance of the *Calder* decision.

Did You Know?

Canadian 2006 census data revealed that the number of visible minorities in Canada has passed 5 million people, representing 16.2 percent of the entire Canadian population. The largest visible minority group are South Asians, representing 1.3 million people. The growth in the visible minority population in Canada increased 26.2 percent between 2001 and 2006.

3.4 Rights of Other Groups

Rights of Immigrants

Canada is a nation of newcomers. In the twentieth century, more than 10 million immigrants came to Canada from all over the world. Today we receive over 250 000 immigrants a year. They have a profound effect in shaping Canadian society and culture. In 1971, Prime Minister Trudeau proclaimed "a policy of multiculturalism within a bilingual framework." This policy was supposed to help Canada's ethnic groups preserve their cultural heritage. Today, Canadians are proud of the cultural diversity of their country.

Canada has not always embraced the idea of a multicultural society. Until the 1960s, Canadian immigration laws were not truly open. Canada used its legal powers to keep certain groups of people out, and to keep them from gaining equality.

Immigrant Population in Canada

Place of Birth	Total Immigrant Population	Period of Immigration				
		Before 1961	1961–1970	1971–1980	1981–1990	1991–2001
United States	237 920	34 805	46 880	62 835	41 965	51 435
Central and South America	304 650	5910	17 155	62 925	102 655	116 005
Caribbean and Bermuda	294 050	6990	42 740	91 475	68 840	84 005
United Kingdom	606 000	217 175	160 005	126 030	60 145	42 645
Other Northern and Western Europe	494 825	248 830	86 820	56 345	45 595	57 235
Eastern Europe	471 365	135 425	36 595	30 055	104 825	164 465
Southern Europe	715 370	207 900	232 255	126 095	55 620	93 500
Africa	282 600	4635	23 830	54 655	59 710	139 770
West-Central Asia and Middle East	285 585	4445	13 360	29 675	75 885	162 220
Eastern Asia	730 600	18 325	36 360	97 610	155 070	423 235
South-East Asia	469 105	2240	14 095	107 445	159 660	185 665
Southern Asia	503 895	3845	26 600	77 230	101 110	295 110
Oceania and other countries	52 525	3950	8870	13 910	10 415	15 380

What does this table reveal about changes in Canada's immigrant population over time? Based on the trends you see here, predict what the 2011 census results will reveal about the immigrant population.

Today, Canada is one of the most multicultural countries in the world, and new citizens are sworn in daily all across the country.

Selective Immigration

In the early 1880s, the Canadian Pacific Railway (CPR) started building Canada's first national railroad. More than 10 000 workers came from China to help, and earned $1 a day. Non-Chinese workers earned almost twice as much money for doing the same job. By 1885, the railroad was complete. The Chinese workers were no longer welcome in Canada. That year, Parliament imposed a $50 head tax on every Chinese person entering Canada. The tax was designed to discourage them from entering the country. In 1903, the tax was increased to $500.

In 1923, the Canadian government passed the *Chinese Exclusion Act*, abolishing the head tax. However, it was almost impossible for Chinese citizens to move to Canada. Between 1931 and 1941, the Chinese population in Canada dropped from 46 519 to 34 627 people.

Ralph Lung Kee Lee was 106 at the time he boarded the "Redress Express" train in 2006 to be compensated for the injustice of paying the discriminatory Chinese head tax. He presented the government with a "Last Spike" from the CPR railway.

Chapter 3 **Human Rights in Canada**

Anti-Asian sentiment in Canada was not limited to the Chinese. In the early 1900s, the British Columbia government discouraged most Asian immigration. They barred Asians from certain professions and denied them the right to vote. In 1908, Wilfrid Laurier's government introduced a regulation requiring all immigrants to travel to Canada by "direct continuous passage" from their country of origin. This regulation was passed to stop immigration from India. There was no direct travel between the two countries at the time.

In 1910, the federal government passed a new *Immigration Act* that gave it sweeping powers to reject "immigrants belonging to any race deemed unsuitable to the climate or requirements of Canada." In 1917, the newly created Department for Immigration and Colonization created a list of "preferred" and "non-preferred" countries. Legal discrimination continued against Asian immigrants.

Wartime Discrimination

During World War I, Ukrainian Canadians were branded as "enemy aliens." Many came to Canada from Austria–Hungary, Britain's enemy during the war. Thousands of Ukrainian Canadians were interned (confined) under the *War Measures Act* of 1914. Robert Borden's government passed the act shortly after the war broke out. It gave the government extraordinary powers. For example, they could arrest people without charging them with an offence and detain them indefinitely. About 5000 Ukrainians were imprisoned under the act. Another 80 000 were classified as enemy aliens. They had to wear special identification badges and report to the police regularly.

Japanese Canadians were similarly targeted during World War II. Before the war, they endured anti-Asian discrimination. When the Japanese attacked Pearl Harbor, this resentment gave way to hysteria in the United States and Canada.

? Did You Know?

Between 1885 and 1923, 81 000 Chinese immigrants paid $23 million in head tax, worth more than $1 billion in today's currency. On June 22, 2006, Prime Minister Stephen Harper offered an apology and compensation of $20 000 for surviving Chinese immigrants or their spouses who had once paid the head tax.

Canadian-born children of Japanese descent were forced to leave their homes and live in one of eight internment camps in British Columbia, such as the Lemon Creek Internment Camp. David Suzuki, world-famous broadcaster and environmentalist, lived in this camp for a time.

OCT-28-1945-LEMON CREEK B.C.

Despite RCMP reports that Japanese Canadians did not threaten Canadian security, the Canadian government began rounding them up in March of 1942. Men were sent to work camps where they were forced to work for 25 cents per day. Women and children were sent to internment camps in the interior of British Columbia, where they stayed until the end of the war. The Canadian government seized their property and sold it at government auctions. After the war, many Japanese families had no homes or possessions. They were forcibly resettled in the Prairies and Ontario. Approximately 4300 individuals were deported to Japan, despite the fact that they were English speaking, natural-born Canadians who had no ties to Japan.

Canada also refused entry to thousands of Jewish refugees escaping persecution in Nazi Germany on the eve of World War II. It did so on the grounds that their presence would upset Canada's ethnic balance. Anti-Semitism and anti-immigrant feelings were strong in Canada at the time. The refugees were forced to return to Europe, where many died during the Holocaust.

Immigration Following World War II

In 1947, Prime Minister Mackenzie King announced a new immigration policy. It was designed to attract new immigrants. Its purpose was to increase the population and expand Canada's economy. However, King used a careful selection process. He said that it was not a "fundamental right" for everyone to immigrate to Canada. Only persons whom the government regarded as "desirable future citizens" would be admitted. King considered immigration of non-Europeans undesirable. He said it would "make a fundamental alteration in the character of our population."

King's new policy brought about a wave of immigrants from Europe. Between 1947 and 1962, Canada admitted nearly 250 000 persons. They were escaping the dreadful conditions that resulted from World War II. In 1956 and 1957, Canada accepted 37 500 Hungarian refugees fleeing a failed uprising against communist rule in their country.

Starting in the 1960s, Canada's immigration policy underwent a major change. By 1967, the federal government eliminated race, religion, and national origin as a basis for choosing immigrants. The end of this discrimination meant that a major barrier to equality in Canada was gone.

Prime Minster Mackenzie King's 1947 immigration policy was responsible for a new wave of immigration from Europe.

Did You Know?

In 1988, the federal government issued a public apology to Japanese Canadians for their ill treatment during World War II and announced a $400 million compensation package. On May 9, 2008, the federal government announced a $10 million grant as an apology for the part it played in interning Ukrainian and other Eastern European immigrants in Canadian camps during World War I.

Did You Know?

Asian Canadians did not get the right to vote in Canada until 1949.

Did You Know?

The 2006 census identified 6 186 950 foreign-born people in Canada. Approximately one in five (19.8 percent) of the Canadian population were foreign born, the highest proportion since 1931.

The Immigration Act

In 1976, a new *Immigration Act* introduced a **points system**. It looked at an applicant's education, skills, personal qualities such as resourcefulness and motivation, and occupational demand. Canada was still careful about who was chosen, but now immigrants were selected based on their ability to contribute to the economy. Large numbers of immigrants from non-European countries arrived in Canada for the first time as a result of the new regulations. The long-term effect has been a dramatic change in Canada's cultural and social fabric. A multicultural society has emerged.

The *Immigration Act* also sets out who may not enter Canada:

- immigrant applicants who are suffering from illnesses that pose a public danger or may place an undue financial burden on health services
- persons who lack the funds to support themselves
- convicted criminals or those who pose a risk of committing serious crimes
- potential or known terrorists
- persons who have been convicted of war crime

Sometimes officials have to decide whether to keep someone from entering Canada. To do so, they perform security checks with police in the person's home country. Before entering Canada, the person must have a medical exam that meets Canadian standards.

points system a method of evaluating applicants for independent immigration, using categories and points

 Did You Know?

On November 1, 2001, the *Immigration and Refugee Protection Act* replaced the *Immigration Act* from 1976. The act includes measures to curb abuse of the immigration and refugee system, to strengthen obligations for immigrants to have sponsors, and to allow the refugee system to process refugees more easily. The act also has new selection criteria to attract more highly skilled and adaptable independent immigrants. It also has more "front-end" screening measures to better identify and deal with suspected criminals, terrorists, and any others who present security risks.

Review Your Understanding

1. How were Ukrainian Canadians and Japanese Canadians the victims of wartime discrimination in Canada?
2. How did Prime Minister Mackenzie King's immigration policy affect immigration in Canada?
3. When did Canada officially end its discriminatory immigration practices?
4. How does the points system work?
5. When might an immigration applicant not be admitted to Canada?

Rights of Gay Men and Lesbians

At the end of the twentieth century, attitudes changed toward homosexuality and legal rights of gay men and lesbians. In the past, homosexuality was a crime. Punishments included fines, going to prison, and even death. In Britain, any man convicted of having sex with another man could receive the death penalty. In 1861 the law changed, and convicted men received prison sentences of 10 years to life. Today, some nations still have harsh punishments. Until 1967, homosexuality was a crime in Canada and was dealt with in the *Criminal Code*.

Changing Attitudes and Legal Rights

Several things happened to change views and start the gay rights movement. The movement is about legal rights and being socially accepted. One of the factors was timing. In the 1960s, young people rebelled against previous generations' values and traditions. Interest in women's rights and civil rights for black people grew. Pierre Trudeau became the justice minister in 1967. He liberalized Canada's divorce laws. He rewrote abortion and prostitution laws. He decriminalized homosexuality. That meant that gay and lesbian relationships were no longer a crime. He noted, "There's no place for the state in the bedrooms of the nation. I think what's done in private between adults doesn't concern the *Criminal Code*."

South of the border, another important event occurred. In 1969, police raided the Stonewall Inn, a gay bar in New York City. (Gay bars in Canada and the United States were often raided in the 1950s and 1960s.) A riot followed, involving about 400 people. Four police officers were injured and 13 rioters were arrested. This was the first time that a group of gay people had resisted arrest and fought back. This event is widely acknowledged as the start of the gay rights movement in North America. It was only a matter of time before people organized to press for rights in the legal arena. Eventually, laws were changed in Canada to protect gay men and lesbians from discrimination.

The Pride Parade is an annual event in Toronto that attracts hundreds of thousands of parade watchers and is an international tourist attraction.

In 1996, the federal government added "sexual orientation" to the *Canadian Human Rights Act*. Gay men and lesbians are now protected from discrimination in federal government matters. In *Moore v. Canada (Treasury Board)*, 1996, the Canadian Human Rights Tribunal ordered the federal government to extend employment benefits, such as medical and dental benefits, to partners in same-sex couples. In 1997, the federal government offered same-sex benefits to its gay and lesbian employees. In 1999, the Supreme Court of Canada ruled in the case of *M. v. H.*, 1999, that same-sex couples have the same legal rights and responsibilities as heterosexual couples. In a unanimous 9–0 decision, the Supreme Court concluded that Ontario's *Family Law Act* was unconstitutional. Its definition of "spouse" excluded same-sex relationships (see Chapter 14, page 488 for more detail). The Ontario government changed dozens of laws, giving same-sex couples equal standing with heterosexual couples. Several other provinces followed suit.

In 2002, many cases appeared before Canadian courts. They argued that the definition of "spouse" under marriage laws was prejudiced against same-sex couples. The definition at the time was the union of one man and one woman, excluding all others. Marriage acts were challenged in the courts. They denied equality rights based on sexual orientation. In 2003, both the Ontario and British Columbia courts struck down marriage laws as unconstitutional. Eventually, the *Civil Marriage Act* legalized same-sex marriage in Canada on July 20, 2005. You will learn more about Canada's marriage laws in Chapter 13.

 Did You Know?

In March 2007, in *Canada (Attorney General) v. Hislop*, 2007, the Supreme Court ruled that the federal government had violated the equality rights of same-sex partners by granting survivor benefits only to same-sex persons whose partners had died after January 1, 1998.

Douglas Elliott (left), one of the leading lawyers in Canada's same-sex marriage dispute, married his long-time partner, Greg Lawrence, in Toronto in 2008. Many dignitaries, including judges and cabinet ministers, attended the ceremony.

As with feminism, the gay rights movement depends on people and effective organizing to demand legal equality. One of the most effective organizations is Egale Canada (Equality for Gays and Lesbians Everywhere). It has fought for equality since 1986, mostly at the federal level. Egale pressed the federal government to act on its commitment to add "sexual orientation" to the *Canadian Human Rights Act*. It has also intervened in cases before the Supreme Court of Canada in support of legal recognition for same-sex relationships.

Review Your Understanding

1. What attitudes and social conditions have created barriers to achieving equality for gay men and lesbians?
2. Why is "Stonewall" an important event in the gay rights movement?
3. What significant change was made in Canadian law with respect to homosexuality in 1967?
4. What change was made to the *Canadian Human Rights Act* in 1996?
5. What is the significance of the *Civil Marriage Act* of 2005?

Rights of People with Disabilities

There are 600 million people around the world who have mental and physical disabilities. Most face barriers to gaining social and legal equality. Such barriers include unequal access to schools, services, and employment. Lack of suitable transportation and poor building access prevent them from easily getting around. Only recently has attention been focused on their rights and the barriers they face.

In many countries today, children born with disabilities are abandoned and left to die. People with disabilities have been rejected throughout history. Even in the twentieth century, children with disabilities were put in government-run institutions. By the end of World War II, parents were more interested in having their children fit into society. Also, adults with disabilities wanted a say in their futures.

The United Nations proclaimed 1981 the International Year of Disabled Persons. The spotlight shone on the legal rights of people with disabilities. Across Canada in the 1980s, there was a move to close institutions that housed people with disabilities and mental illnesses. The goal was to allow everyone in Canada to live with dignity in the community, with proper support. Increasingly, Canadians started asking their governments to help meet these needs.

 Did You Know?

Under the Participation and Activity Limitation Survey (PALS), an estimated 4.4 million Canadians, or one out of every seven Canadians, reported having a disability in 2006.

 Did You Know?

In 2006, 41 percent of the signed complaints to the Canadian Human Rights Commission cited disability as the ground of discrimination.

Legal Disabilities in Ontario

- Brain injury
- Deafness
- Epilepsy
- Mental illness
- Developmental disability
- Behaviour problems
- Physical disability
- Substance abuse
- Learning problems
- Blindness
- Obesity

Disabilities are not just physical but can include mental, social, and emotional conditions

People with Disabilities Today

People with disabilities still face barriers today. Although they are guaranteed equal rights under the *Canadian Charter of Rights and Freedoms*, many schools cannot meet their needs.

Today in Canada, businesses and government institutions do not have to provide complete building access to people with disabilities. For example, buildings are not legally required to have wheelchair ramps. It is left up to the company or organization to provide this service. People with disabilities can complain to their provincial human rights commission regarding accessibility issues.

David Onley, Ontario's twenty-eighth lieutenant-governor, is an advocate for persons with disabilities. Onley uses a motorized scooter and crutches because he had polio as a child and became paralyzed from the waist down.

These cases are heard individually. Sometimes, human rights cases are settled, and the barrier disappears. For example, wheelchair access is created. However, more access is needed so that people with disabilities can participate equally in society.

In Ontario, that is the goal of the *Accessibility for Ontarians with Disabilities Act (AODA), 2005*. The aim is to provide accessibility for goods, services, accommodation, employment, and premises by 2025.

David Lepofsky, a lawyer who is blind, fought the Toronto Transit Commission (TTC) for more than a decade to have subways, buses, and streetcars announce stops. It cost Toronto taxpayers $450 000 in legal fees. The TTC subsequently installed an automated announcement system on their subways.

Review Your Understanding

1. What is "access"?
2. Why is access a key issue when arguing for the rights of people with disabilities?
3. What types of conditions are included as legal disabilities?
4. What is being done in your school to accommodate persons with disabilities?
5. What is the aim of the *Accessibility for Ontarians with Disabilities Act, 2005*?

3.5 Human Rights

The *Charter of Rights and Freedoms* is discussed in Chapter 2. The Charter lists and protects your civil rights. Civil rights involve matters between persons and government. As you read in the introduction to this chapter, human rights are different. They involve matters between people. Different levels of government have passed laws making discrimination illegal. In order to understand the concept of discrimination, it is important to know the difference between **prejudice** and **stereotyping**.

Prejudice and Stereotyping

prejudice a preconceived opinion of a person based on the person's belonging to a certain group

stereotyping judging, or forming an opinion of one person of a group and applying that judgment to all members of the group

Prejudice involves making a judgment about a person who belongs to a certain group. A prejudiced person pre-judges another person based on the fact that he or she belongs to a group. It is not based on actual character, skill, or personality. Prejudiced opinions are based on ignorance, not fact. They are often negative. Prejudiced beliefs about a group often influence the way a person deals with members of the group. For instance, Fred refuses to play baseball with some friends because they chose Chantal to be the pitcher. Fred believes that women cannot play baseball. He is demonstrating prejudice. He is applying a belief about a group (women) to a person in that group (Chantal).

Stereotyping involves judging one member of a group and applying that judgment to the entire group. Stereotypes are the labels that prejudiced people apply to members of certain groups. It does not matter what the person is like. Examples include saying that all women are dangerous drivers, that all

Asian people are good at mathematics, and that all teenagers have negative attitudes. Many people deny they are prejudiced. However, they tell jokes about minority groups. They use stereotypes to ridicule others. These jokes are not harmless. They feed on prejudice and help it spread.

Discrimination

Prejudice and stereotyping are not illegal. They are part of a belief system that leads to discrimination. Human rights laws prohibit discrimination. Discrimination happens when people act on a prejudice or stereotype and treat others unfairly. In a discrimination case, the **complainant** is the person who must prove that he or she is the victim of discrimination. The respondent is the person who is alleged to have acted in a manner that discriminates.

There are two types of discrimination in law: intentional and unintentional. **Intentional discrimination** happens when a person or organization knowingly commits a discriminatory act. Sometimes it is called "differential treatment." In other words, the discrimination is on purpose. For example, a man refuses to hire the most fully qualified candidate for an engineering job. The person is a woman and he believes that women do not make good engineers. Human rights laws say the employer discriminated against the woman. Human rights laws make it illegal for persons and organizations to discriminate against others. **Unintentional discrimination** is sometimes called "adverse effect discrimination." It occurs when people or organizations treat others unfairly but are not aware that they are discriminating. For example, a woman applies to become a firefighter. She may have to pass a fitness test that is impossible for her or any woman to pass. Therefore, she is denied access to the job as a firefighter.

Sometimes employers have standards that are necessary to perform a job safely and efficiently. An employer will be asked to justify that the standard is a **bona fide occupational requirement**. That is, they must justify that the standard is necessary to perform the job effectively. For example, stating that intake counsellors be female in a crisis centre for abused women could be argued to be a bona fide occupational requirement.

One of the leading cases on discrimination is *British Columbia (Public Service Employee Relation Commission) v. BCGSEU*, 1999 (see case on next page). In this case, the Province of British Columbia did not intentionally discriminate when they used a minimum fitness aerobic running standard for forest firefighters. However, the standard effectively eliminated women who were otherwise qualified for the job. Further, the employer could not justify that the standard was a bona fide occupational requirement.

complainant a person who makes an allegation of discrimination

intentional discrimination treatment of others that is unfair (on the basis of prejudice or stereotype) and on purpose

unintentional discrimination actions that appear to be neutral but that have the effect of discriminating against most members of a group

bona fide occupational requirement a legitimate, reasonable necessity (requirement) of a job; a possible defence against unfair discrimination in hiring and other employment situations

a • un sentiment d'appartenance • a sense of belonging

A Sense of Belonging is a project of the United Nations Association in Canada. Its aim is to fight discrimination in communities across Canada through outreach and public education.

British Columbia (Public Service Employee Relation Commission) v. BCGSEU, 1999 CanLII 652 (S.C.C.)

For more information, Go to Nelson Social Studies

Tawney Meiorin appealed to the Supreme Court of Canada.

Tawney Meiorin was hired to work as a forest firefighter in British Columbia. After working for two years, her employer, the Province of British Columbia, set up fitness requirements that all forest firefighters had to meet. Meiorin tried four times to pass the aerobic running test. She could not run 2.5 kilometres in 11 minutes. She missed meeting the running standard by 49.4 seconds. She was dismissed from her job.

Meiorin filed a complaint with her union. There was an arbitration hearing between the union and her employer. An arbitrator ruled that the use of this aerobic standard discriminated against Meiorin. The requirement had an unequal negative effect on women as a group. Studies were presented that indicated women have lower aerobic capacities than men. Most women, even through increased training, could not meet the standard required. The government was not able to justify that the aerobic running standard was absolutely necessary for the performance of the job. That is, it could not justify that the standard was a bona fide occupational requirement. The arbitrator ordered the government to reinstate Meiorin in her job and to give back lost wages and benefits.

The government appealed the case to the British Columbia Court of Appeal. The court overturned the initial ruling saying that there was no discrimination, the standard was necessary for firefighters to safely and efficiently perform their jobs, and the same standard applied to all individuals tested.

- Meiorin appealed the case to the Supreme Court of Canada. What do you think was the Supreme Court's decision?

You and the Law

Treating people respectfully is shown by your words and actions. How can discrimination be prevented by careful consideration of what you do and what you say?

Review Your Understanding

1. Explain the difference between civil rights and human rights.
2. How do prejudice and stereotyping lead to discrimination?
3. Explain the difference between a complainant and a respondent.
4. What is the difference between intentional and unintentional discrimination?
5. What is a bona fide occupational requirement?

3.6 Human Rights Legislation

Federal, provincial, and territorial governments have passed legislation to protect human rights in matters involving private individuals. In 1977, the federal *Canadian Human Rights Act* came into effect. It guarantees that all Canadians receive fair and equal treatment from all institutions under federal control. This includes airlines, banks, and television and radio stations.

(You will recall federal responsibilities were listed in Chapter 1 on page 28). All federally licensed companies and their employees are also covered by the *Canadian Human Rights Act*.

The provinces and territories have human rights legislation that covers situations that are under their authority. Ontario's *Human Rights Code*, Nova Scotia's *Human Rights Act*, Québec's *Charter of Human Rights and Freedoms*, and Alberta's *Human Rights, Citizenship, and Multiculturalism Act* are a few examples. Human rights laws generally apply to certain areas. For example, the law prohibits discrimination in employment or renting an apartment. Employers cannot advertise for jobs and indicate that members of one sex need not apply. Further, landlords cannot refuse to rent apartments based on race.

Human rights laws also protect people from discrimination at work. See the illustration below for discrimination issues in the workplace.

Discrimination Issues in the Workplace

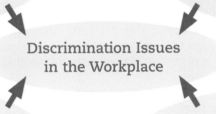

Sexual Harassment:
Unwelcome actions or conduct toward another person of a sexual nature, such as repeated rude jokes

Poisoned Environment:
Workplace where the employer allows inappropriate conduct, such as racially or sexually offensive insults, remarks, or jokes

Discrimination Issues in the Workplace

Accommodation:
When the employer removes a barrier or changes a policy so discrimination does not occur, such as by installing a large-print monitor for a visually impaired employee

Undue Hardship:
When accommodation puts the employer at such great risk—either financial (threatening the company's ability to survive) or health and safety—that it makes addressing the employee's needs impossible; the employer must not suffer undue hardship

Four issues that pertain to discrimination in the workplace include sexual harassment, poisoned environment, accommodation, and undue hardship.

As a helpful five-step guide to exploring human rights cases in this chapter, refer to the figure below. In order to better understand human rights cases, follow the guide and ask the five questions in sequence.

Five-Step Guide: How to Analyze a Human Rights Case

5. If not, is there a remedy under human rights law?

4. Is there a reasonable accommodation up to the point of undue hardship?

3. Is there discrimination?

2. Does federal or provincial human rights law apply?

1. Is the matter a human rights issue?

When considering a legal case that involves alleged discrimination, ask these five questions in sequence.

accommodation removing a barrier or changing a policy to avoid discrimination

undue hardship a financial or health and safety risk that makes it impossible to accommodate a complainant in a discrimination case

☑ **1. Is the Matter a Human Rights Issue?** Both human rights law and the *Charter of Rights and Freedoms* equality rights section deal with discrimination. If the matter concerns only persons or groups with no aspect of the government involved, human rights laws apply. For example, a landlord refuses to rent an apartment because of a person's race. The dispute will be settled under the provincial or territorial human rights law on the grounds of racial discrimination. If the government passes a law that discriminates against an individual or group, the Charter applies.

☑ **2. Does Federal or Provincial Human Rights Law Apply?** Human rights law in Canada falls under the federal *Canadian Human Rights Act* or a provincial human rights code. Matters dealing with federal institutions, such as banks, airlines, or television and radio stations, use the *Canadian Human Rights Act*. In matters concerning provincial institutions, such as hospitals or schools, a provincial human rights code applies. For example, if an airline discriminates against an employee, the *Canadian Human Rights Act* applies. If a teacher or student is a victim of discrimination in a school, a provincial or territorial human rights code applies. Provinces and territories deal with education.

☑ **3. Is There Discrimination?** In human rights cases, the court must review the facts to see if discrimination or harassment occurred. Federal, provincial, and territorial human rights laws list the grounds (categories) of discrimination. For example, the *Canadian Human Rights Act* includes such grounds as race, religion, age, sex, and disability. You will learn more about grounds of discrimination later in this chapter.

☑ **4. Is There a Reasonable Accommodation up to the Point of Undue Hardship?** In some circumstances, an **accommodation** may exist. Accommodation involves removing a barrier or changing a policy so discrimination does not happen. For example, an employer may make a workplace wheelchair accessible. Employers are required to accommodate up to the point of **undue hardship**. For example, an employer could argue undue hardship by showing that the business would suffer financial losses or a safety risk by trying to make an accommodation.

☑ **5. If Not, Is There a Remedy under Human Rights Law?** Under human rights law, remedies such as money can be made to compensate for damaging a complainant's self-respect. Money can also be awarded for lost wages or benefits. It may include medical or other expenses resulting from the damage. You will learn more about human rights remedies later in this chapter.

Canadian Human Rights Act

The *Canadian Human Rights Act* was passed in 1977. It protects people from discrimination and harassment. The act applies to federal government departments. It also applies to businesses falling under federal control, such as postal services, banks, airlines, and rail services. (See the chart on page 28 of Chapter 1 for a list of divisions under federal and provincial control.) The act bans discrimination on various grounds. They are race, national or ethnic origin, colour, religion, age, sex, marital status, family status, sexual orientation, disability, and a conviction for which a pardon has been granted.

Did You Know?

In a 6-2 judgment in August 2008 in *Montréal (City) v. Québec (Commission des droits de la personne et des droits de la jeunesse)*, 2008 SCC 48, the Supreme Court ruled that Montréal police violated a woman's rights by rejecting her job application as a police officer because of a prior shoplifting conviction for which she had been pardoned. Her application was rejected on the grounds she did not satisfy the criterion of "good moral behaviour" imposed by the *Police Act*. The court held that the rejection of her application was improper because it simply dismissed it due to her criminal history.

Grounds of Discrimination Cited in Signed Complaints to the Canadian Human Rights Commission

Type of Discrimination	2002		2003		2004		2005		2006	
	#	%	#	%	#	%	#	%	#	%
Disability	438	44	495	37	389	39	429	50	344	41
Sex	188	19	204	16	165	17	102	12	138	16
National or ethnic origin	94	9	141	11	109	11	73	8	84	10
Race	71	7	146	11	105	11	74	8	80	10
Age	65	7	159	12	60	6	51	6	55	7
Family status	30	3	38	3	61	6	45	5	40	5
Colour	30	3	59	4	26	3	14	2	33	4
Religion	30	3	35	3	34	3	40	5	28	3
Sexual orientation	31	3	27	2	21	2	23	3	25	3
Marital status	14	2	15	1	14	1	13	1	12	1
Pardon	3	—	1	—	5	1	2	—	—	—
Total	994	100	1320	100	989	100	866	100	839	100

grounds of discrimination
categories or types of discrimination protected by law

What were the top three **grounds of discrimination** cited in complaints to the Canadian Human Rights Commission in 2006?

In which area were most of the complaints made to the Canadian Human Rights Commission in 2006? In which area were the fewest complaints made?

Did You Know?

If you were denied a job working at a radio station because of your race, the *Canadian Human Rights Act* would apply.

Type of Allegations Cited in Complaints Made to the Canadian Human Rights Commission

Type of Allegation	2002		2003		2004		2005		2006	
	#	%	#	%	#	%	#	%	#	%
Employment-related	666	65	1048	66	834	67	821	75	782	73
Services-related	128	13	195	12	179	14	132	12	102	10
Harassment—employment	164	16	249	16	175	14	95	9	126	12
Harassment—services	26	3	31	2	18	1	7	1	16	2
Hate messages	4	—	10	1	10	1	13	1	20	2
Retaliation	15	2	33	2	22	2	12	1	13	1
Union membership	7	0.5	2	—	7	1	7	1	3	—
Pay equity	7	0.5	7	—	—	—	2	—	2	—
Notices, signs, symbols	2	—	9	1	—	—	2	—	—	—
Total	1019	100	1584	100	1245	100	1091	100	1064	100

You saw in the *British Columbia (Public Service Employee Relation Commission) v. BCGSEU*, 1999, case (see the You Be the Judge feature on page 94) how a British Columbia firefighter was discriminated against by a fitness test policy. Read the case below of *Council of Canadians with Disabilities v. VIA Rail Canada Inc.*, 2007, to see how people with disabilities were discriminated against.

⚖️ **Case**

Council of Canadians with Disabilities v. VIA Rail Canada Inc., 2007 SCC 15 (CanLII)

For more information, Go to Nelson Social Studies

In 2000, VIA Rail purchased 139 rail cars known as Renaissance cars for $29.8 million. The Council of Canadians with Disabilities complained to the Canadian Transportation Agency (the "Agency"). They said that the cars were inaccessible to people with disabilities. They argued that the Renaissance cars must meet modern accessibility standards. VIA Rail argued that the cars were sufficiently wheelchair accessible. Its employees would transfer passengers into onboard wheelchairs and assist them with services such as getting to the washrooms.

The Agency agreed with the Council of Canadians with Disabilities. In a 2003 decision, they gave VIA Rail a chance to show why the identified obstacles were not barriers to people with disabilities. They also asked that VIA Rail provide information to show the cost to modify the cars. Two months later, VIA Rail replied that the cost to modify the cars was

continues...

Council of Canadians with Disabilities v. VIA Rail Canada Inc., 2007 SCC 15 (CanLII)

not reasonable. It gave the Agency a vague estimate ("over $35 million") in a three-page letter. It did not provide any supporting evidence. In June 2003, the Agency advised VIA Rail that its response lacked detail. They gave VIA Rail more time to prepare a response. VIA Rail indicated its cost estimates and asked for the Agency to make a decision.

The Agency ruled for VIA Rail to renovate 30 of the 139 cars for better wheelchair accessibility. As the Renaissance trains were narrow, the doorways were not big enough for standard wheelchairs. The wheelchair tie-downs only accommodated a child's wheelchair, and there were no accessible washrooms in the coach cars. This barrier to people with disabilities had to be removed unless VIA could prove that it tried to accommodate to the point of undue hardship. Undue hardship can be shown by such factors as cost, economic viability, safety, and the quality of service to the passengers. The Agency decided that the changes needed did not justify a finding of undue hardship based on financial cost.

VIA appealed the case to the Federal Court of Appeal, which allowed the appeal. The federal court ruled that the Agency violated fairness rules. They failed to give VIA Rail enough time to respond to requests for cost and feasibility details. The Council of Canadians with Disabilities appealed the decision to the Supreme Court of Canada.

In a 5–4 judgment in March 2007, the Supreme Court ruled that VIA Rail must make changes. It must ensure that the trains can accommodate people with disabilities. The Renaissance car design was an undue barrier for them. The Supreme Court found the decision of the Canadian Transportation Agency to be reasonable and allowed the appeal.

For Discussion

1. Why did the Council of Canadians with Disabilities complain to the Canadian Transportation Agency?
2. What specific barriers to equality did the Renaissance cars present?
3. How could undue hardship be shown?
4. How did the Supreme Court of Canada decide the case?

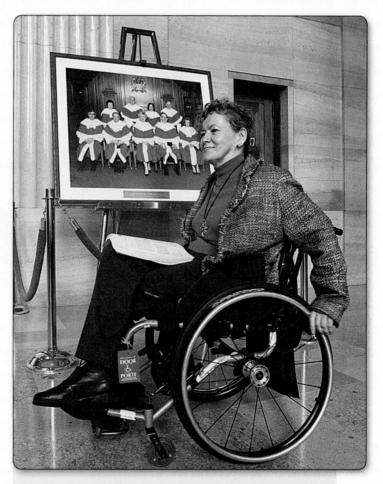

Pat Danforth of the Council of Canadians with Disabilities celebrates at the Supreme Court of Canada after the ruling came out in March 2007.

Did You Know?

In late November 2008, the Supreme Court of Canada rejected an application from Air Canada and WestJet for permission to appeal a January 2008 ruling from the Canadian Transportation Agency. The court's decision meant that airlines must offer a free extra seat to people with disabilities who require room for an attendant during the flight, or who require extra room for a wheelchair, or who are clinically obese and require two seats. This "one person, one fare" policy had a deadline of January 10, 2009, for implementation.

Activity

To learn more about discrimination and harassment,

Go to Nelson Social Studies

Provincial Human Rights Laws

All provincial and territorial human rights laws are based on the United Nations *Universal Declaration of Human Rights*, which you were introduced to in Chapter 1. Within each province and territory, the human rights laws can overrule any other provincial or territorial law. This means that if a law goes against the human rights law of a province or territory, it can be challenged as discriminatory.

The Ontario Human Rights Code

In Ontario, the *Human Rights Code* protects every resident's right to be free from discrimination. This includes race, sex, ethnic origin, ancestry, creed, marital or family status, sexual orientation, age, disability, or citizenship. Human rights laws are constantly updated and expanded. In Ontario, there are persons with physical, mental, and learning disabilities. Disabilities also include alcoholism, drug dependency, or environmental sensitivities.

Human rights laws can reflect changing social attitudes and awareness. In Ontario, mandatory retirement ended as of December 12, 2006. Before that, the *Human Rights Code* did not stop workplace discrimination against persons aged 65 and older. Now, those aged 65 or older can challenge mandatory retirement policies. They can file complaints based on age discrimination. Employers cannot make decisions about employees on the basis of age.

People with disabilities have the right to easy access of services and facilities.

Discrimination complaints on the basis of disability are common in Ontario. In 2006, disability complaints made up 29 percent of decisions by the Ontario Human Rights Commission. Accessibility is a key area of concern, as we discussed earlier in this chapter. When people with disabilities visit public places, such as restaurants and shops, they have the right to equality in accessibility. Human rights complaints can result from not providing accessibility. When barriers exist, such as those preventing someone in a wheelchair from entering a building, owners may have to accommodate complainants. For example, a building owner may have to replace steps with a wheelchair ramp. As discussed earlier, the respondent must accommodate to the point of undue hardship: Would the financial cost outweigh the need to accommodate the complainant? Maintaining a person's dignity and respect are also key factors when human rights tribunals assess whether an accommodation is reasonable. If an employer offers to lift persons out of wheelchairs so they can enter a building, does that preserve dignity and respect for people with disabilities?

In the case of the British Columbia firefighters, the required fitness test discriminated against female firefighters. It was considered a form of indirect discrimination. The case of *Siadat v. Ontario College of Teachers*, 2007 is another example of indirect discrimination.

 You Be the Judge

Siadat v. Ontario College of Teachers, 2007 CanLII 253 (ON S.C.D.C.)

For more information, **Go to Nelson Social Studies**

Fatima Siadat was born and educated in Iran and practised as a teacher for 16 years. While teaching literature in Iran, she commented on the right to freedom of expression. She lost her job because of her political views and threats were made to her life. She fled to Canada as a refugee. A refugee is a person who has a well-founded fear of persecution because of their beliefs in their country and flees to another country for protection. In Iran, Siadat was considered an enemy because of her political views.

In 2001, Siadat applied to the Ontario College of Teachers for her teaching licence. The college required original official documents to prove her teaching qualifications. Unfortunately, her university degree and university records showing the equivalent of a teacher's certificate were held by the Ministry of Education in Iran. Siadat was concerned that her family in Iran would be harmed if she pressed to have

continues...

Fatima Siadat

Siadat v. Ontario College of Teachers, 2007 CanLII 253 (ON S.C.D.C.)

these original documents sent to her. As she could not provide official documentation of her qualifications to teach, the college refused to certify her as a teacher. That was in 2001. The following year, the Registration Appeals Committee of the Ontario College of Teachers also refused her application. In 2004, she appealed again to the Registration Appeals Committee, asking the college to find another way of assessing her qualifications (that is, to accommodate her) without requiring original documents. Her request was denied.

Siadat argued that the Ontario *Human Rights Code* applied to the case before the college, quoting section 6. It allows for every person to be treated equally with respect to membership in a self-governing profession, without discrimination because of place of origin. She argued that the Ontario College of Teachers failed to accommodate her. This resulted in

discrimination based on place of origin. Siadat wanted to be accommodated from the usual original document requirement. She asked that other documents be considered. She produced an Iran Ministry of Education identification card that had her name and picture. She also provided photocopies of her bachelor's degree in teaching and her employment order, translated into English. Her resumé outlined 16 years of teaching experience in Iran. The Ontario College of Teachers argued that these documents were not sufficient.

The Ontario Superior Court of Justice, Divisional Court, reviewed the college's Registration Appeals Committee decision. It decided that discrimination based on place of origin did occur. The Ontario College of Teachers had to prove that it was impossible to accommodate Siadat. They had to prove undue hardship if they used other documentation.

- How do you think the court decided?

Review Your Understanding

1. When does the *Canadian Human Rights Act* apply?
2. What are the grounds of discrimination listed under the Ontario *Human Rights Code*?
3. What conditions constitute a disability under human rights law?
4. Is mandatory retirement discriminatory? Explain.
5. What is a barrier to accessibility? Provide an example.

Did You Know?

As of June 2008, the Human Rights Tribunal of Ontario (HRTO) has the power to deal with discrimination complaints in Ontario.

3.7 Enforcing Human Rights Laws

In Ontario, the process for filing human rights complaints was criticized for creating a huge case backlog and lengthy wait times. The Ontario government passed the *Human Rights Code Amendment Act, 2006*, to address these concerns. It came into effect on June 30, 2008. Until then, when you filed a complaint with the Ontario Human Rights Commission, a human rights officer interviewed you to get the facts. If the complaint had merit and fell within the Commission's jurisdiction, you filled out a formal statement about the alleged incident. Since 1997, the Commission has used a mediation process to try to settle the majority of complaints. However, if mediation is unsuccessful, the Commission investigates the complaint to decide whether it should go on to a formal board of inquiry or tribunal. The complaint has to be brought before the Commission within six months of the last incident of discrimination.

The Commission still exists to promote human rights in Ontario. Now, it focuses on public education, developing policies, and research. Discrimination claims are now filed directly with the tribunal. The aim is to resolve issues fairly and quickly. The tribunal can also refer matters to the Commission to conduct an inquiry. Under the new system, complaints must be filed within one year of the alleged discrimination. For example, assume you walk into your favourite restaurant. A waiter makes a racist comment about you and refuses to serve you. You must file your discrimination complaint, based on race, with the tribunal within one year.

Remedies

The purpose of human rights laws is not to punish the respondent. It is to compensate victims of discrimination and prevent similar incidents from happening again. A legal remedy is a mechanism for enforcing someone's rights. There are several remedies available under human rights laws. They include issuing letters of apology, paying lost wages or benefits, and paying for mental anguish. They can also include compelling employers to rehire employees, or setting up anti-discrimination or anti-harassment programs. If respondents refuse to obey tribunal or board of inquiry orders, they face criminal charges and a heavy fine. Either party can appeal a tribunal decision to the courts as a civil case.

The Process of Filing a Human Rights Complaint in Ontario

| Filing a Human Rights Complaint in Ontario | ➡ | Human Rights Tribunal of Ontario | ➡ | Remedy |

It is now simpler to file a human rights complaint in Ontario.

Chapter 3 **Human Rights in Canada**

Did You Know?

After June 30, 2008, the human rights system in Ontario was expanded to include the Human Rights Legal Support Centre, an independent, publicly funded corporation that offers legal and support services for individuals filing human rights complaints throughout Ontario.

Under which social area did most of the complaints to the Ontario Human Rights Commission fall in 2006–2007?

Cases Completed or Referred, by Disposition and Social Area

	Accommodation	Contract	Employment	Services	Vocational Associations	Sum of Categories	Percentage of All Complaints (%)
Withdrawn by the complainant	12	1	320	54	4	391	18.46
Settled by the Commission	34	1	769	92	2	898	42.40
Resolved between parties	15		279	48	7	349	16.48
Dismissed based on preliminary objections (s.34)	7	2	111	27	4	151	7.13
Referred to Human Rights Tribunal (s. 36)	8		95	37		140	6.61
Dismissed on the merits (s. 36)	6	1	137	40	5	189	8.92
Total	82	5	1711	298	22	2118	100
Percentage (%)	3.87	0.24	80.78	14.07	1.04	100	

Cases Completed or Referred by the Commission

In 2006–2007, what percentage of cases were settled by the Ontario Human Rights Commission compared to cases that were actually decided by a human rights tribunal?

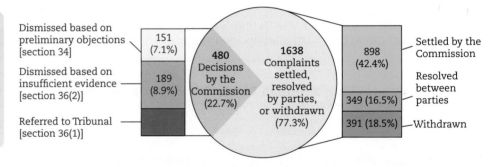

Dismissed based on preliminary objections [section 34]
151 (7.1%)

Dismissed based on insufficient evidence [section 36(2)]
189 (8.9%)

Referred to Tribunal [section 36(1)]

480 Decisions by the Commission (22.7%)

1638 Complaints settled, resolved by parties, or withdrawn (77.3%)

898 (42.4%) — Settled by the Commission

349 (16.5%) — Resolved between parties

391 (18.5%) — Withdrawn

Review Your Understanding

1. What is the current role of the Ontario Human Rights Commission?
2. What is the role of the Human Rights Tribunal of Ontario?
3. In Ontario, within what time period must a human rights complaint be filed?
4. In general, what is the purpose of human rights laws?
5. What types of remedies are available under human rights law?

In Human Rights

There are a surprising number of careers in the human rights field. These include working in the public service, with agencies charged with protecting public interests, or in human resource management. You can also work for private organizations advocating for human rights.

For more information about careers in human rights,

 Go to Nelson Social Studies

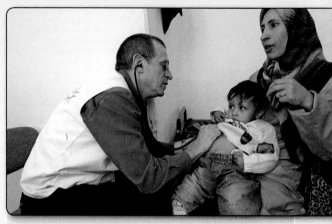

Physicians for Human Rights is an international advocacy group that mobilizes health professionals to promote the right to health for all.

In Focus

Human Rights Commissioner

Human rights commissioners serve on the federal Canadian Human Rights Commission or on provincial human rights commissions. Most are appointed and work on a part-time basis while working at other jobs. Their duty is to ensure everyone has equal opportunity and freedom from discrimination. They hear individual complaints from the public. Sometimes they conduct general inquiries. For example, in November 2007, the Ontario Human Rights Chief Commissioner Barbara Hall launched a public inquiry. She reviewed media reports and public concerns about alleged incidents in Ontario affecting Asian-Canadian anglers. They were alleged victims of racism and racial discrimination.

Employment Equity Officer

Employment equity specialists work in private and public human resources divisions. They help develop and advise on policies and programs. They ensure that their employers comply with human rights laws and standards. They also assist in investigating discrimination and harassment complaints from women, Aboriginal peoples, people with disabilities, and visible minorities, among others.

Advocacy Group Staff Member/ Volunteer

Human rights advocacy groups operate at the local, national, and international levels. They include the Canadian Civil Liberties Association, the Human Rights Institute of Canada, Amnesty International, Human Rights Watch, and Physicians for Human Rights. These groups fight for human rights. They mount campaigns against human rights abuses. These organizations often operate with small staffs and rely heavily on volunteers. Volunteering with an advocacy group could lead to a career in the human rights field.

Career Exploration Activity

As a class, explore career opportunities in the human rights field. Compile a human rights career bulletin board or run a law-related career fair.

1. Research careers related to human rights. Use the Internet or your nearest employment information centre.
2. Select a human rights career and explain the type of work that would be performed in that career.

Should Aboriginal Peoples Have Their Own System of Justice?

Recently, many countries, including Canada, have considered officially recognizing Aboriginal justice systems. Canada has been experimenting with Aboriginal justice. In some communities, Aboriginal police officers have replaced the local police. These officers understand Aboriginal offenders and their lives better. They can deal with situations more effectively.

Experiments have also extended to prisons to help Aboriginal inmates. The Stony Mountain Penitentiary in Manitoba has four sweat lodges in the exercise yard. The Aboriginal prisoners gather once a week to participate in the spiritual program of sweat-lodge ceremonies. According to the prison's warden, the healing process works. He has seen prisoners who have participated in the program completely changed.

This is a sentencing circle for a 20-year-old shoplifter in Winnipeg in September 1998. It was the first sentence handed down by a sentencing circle after Manitoba introduced a provincial program for Aboriginal offenders.

Fines and imprisonment are usually not an effective deterrent to most Aboriginal offenders. Aboriginal peoples in some Canadian communities use their own traditions to deal with lawbreakers. Aboriginal justice emphasizes treatment and healing through sentencing and healing circles instead of imprisonment. This form of justice is often called restorative justice. (See Chapter 9, pages 310 and 322–323 for more information about restorative justice.) Instead of punishing the offender, it is an approach to law and crime that emphasizes healing, forgiveness, and community involvement. Both types of circles are examples of restorative justice approaches to law.

In a sentencing circle, the offender is brought before victims and their families, friends, band Elders, witnesses, lawyers, and the judge to discuss sentencing. Everyone has an equal say in the sentencing. Although the setting is more relaxed than a courtroom, the encounter between victim and offender can be intense. The sentence can range from community work to banishment to the woods for a set period of time. In the woods, offenders must live off the land as their ancestors did. They must be spiritually cleansed and rehabilitated.

Healing circles are alternatives to traditional punishment. If an offender pleads guilty and agrees to participate in a healing circle, the conventional sentence is usually suspended. The offender must meet with the victim(s), their families, and other offenders. The offender works with them to share their experiences. He or she seeks forgiveness for the wrongdoings. The offender might agree to take courses in anger management, parenting, or other topics related to the offence. Other community members, such as Elders and the offender's family, might be asked to participate.

On One Side

Some Canadians oppose the concept of a separate Aboriginal justice system. They believe that all Canadians should be treated equally under the criminal justice system. The *Charter of Rights and Freedoms* guarantees equal treatment to all Canadians. Members of Aboriginal communities should not be treated differently from other Canadians.

This side would argue that a separate justice system will lead to lobbying by other ethnic groups for their own justice systems. Denying these factions could lead to resentment, but agreeing to them could lead to chaos in the Canadian justice system.

There is an additional complication: there are legal distinctions among Aboriginal peoples themselves. There are **Status Indians**, First Nations people who are registered legally under the *Indian Act*. **Treaty Indians** are individuals not registered under the *Indian Act* but who can show legal descent from a band that signed a treaty with the federal government in Canada. They have more rights than non-status and non-treaty Indians. The Métis and Inuit have also won recognition of certain rights, such as special hunting and fishing rights.

These legal distinctions raise a difficult question: Should the distinctions be preserved, or do they stand in the way of achieving true equality? For some, the answer lies in recognizing the rights of self-government of Aboriginal peoples.

On the Other Side

Canada's criminal justice system has not solved the problems found in Aboriginal communities. Rates of suicide, alcoholism, crime, and imprisonment are key concerns among Aboriginal peoples.

Those who support an Aboriginal justice system claim that many Aboriginal people have turned to alcohol and drugs to block out painful memories of degradation and sexual abuse. Criminal activity followed, taking them in and out of jail. Instead of imprisonment, these offenders need to reconnect with themselves and their people through a healing process.

There was a concern about so many Aboriginal peoples in Canadian prisons. This was addressed when one of the *Criminal Code* sentencing provisions was changed in 1996. As a result, when sentencing Aboriginal offenders, judges may consider "the unique systemic background factors that may have played a part in bringing the particular Aboriginal offender before the courts." They can also look at "the types of sentencing procedures and sanctions that may be appropriate in the circumstances for the offender because of his or her particular Aboriginal heritage or connection."

The Supreme Court of Canada confirmed in *R. v. Gladue*, 1999, that restorative justice measures can be considered in the sentencing process. Restorative justice and how it pertains to the *Youth Criminal Justice Act* is discussed in detail in Chapter 9.

The Bottom Line

Aboriginal self-government and a separate justice system seem to be compatible objectives. Aboriginal peoples have unique needs and concerns. They are striving to meet these needs in a way that reflects their history and culture as well as the demands of the twenty-first century.

What Do You Think?

1. Explain how sweat-lodge ceremonies and healing and sentencing circles work to achieve Aboriginal justice.

2. Explain the concept of restorative justice.

3. Outline the pros and cons of an Aboriginal justice system in Canada.

4. Should healing circles and sentencing circles be considered for non-Aboriginal offenders? Explain.

Status Indian First Nations person who is registered legally under the *Indian Act*

Treaty Indian a person not registered under the *Indian Act* but who can show legal descent from a band that signed a treaty with the federal government in Canada

Chapter Review

Chapter Highlights

- A barrier to equality is anything that prevents someone from participating fully in society.
- The Persons Case of 1929 established that women were legal persons in Canada and could be appointed to political office.
- Women continue to fight for pay equity and employment equity.
- Aboriginal peoples are fighting for their collective rights as distinct nations within Canada.
- The courts have played a major role in defining Aboriginal rights.
- Self-government is the goal of many Aboriginal leaders.
- Immigration laws restrict who may enter the country.
- Canada's early immigration laws were often discriminatory against certain groups.
- Refugee claimants must establish that they have a "well-founded" fear of being persecuted in their country of origin.
- Immigration has transformed Canada into a multicultural society.
- The Supreme Court ruled in the *M. v. H.*, 1999, case that under Canada's Constitution, same-sex couples must be treated the same as married couples.
- Access issues continue to be a problem for persons with disabilities.
- Prejudice involves making a predetermined judgment about a person who belongs to a certain group.
- Stereotyping involves judging one member of a group and applying that judgment to the entire group.
- Discrimination includes direct (intentional) and indirect (adverse effect) discrimination.
- A bona fide occupational requirement is a standard or requirement that is considered necessary to perform a job effectively.
- Accommodation involves removing a barrier or changing a policy so discrimination does not occur.
- Undue hardship can be used as a defence to a discrimination claim.
- The *Canadian Human Rights Act* (1977) protects human rights at the federal level of government.
- Provincial or territorial human rights laws protect individuals from discrimination or harassment.

Check Your Knowledge

1. Prepare a chart outlining historical barriers faced by the following groups in Canada: women, Aboriginal peoples, immigrants, gay men and lesbians, and people with disabilities.
2. Explain discrimination. How do prejudice and stereotyping contribute to discrimination?
3. Explain accommodation. Provide an example.
4. Explain undue hardship. Provide an example.

Apply Your Learning

5. In *Smith v. Ontario (Human Rights Commission)*, 2005, Mark Smith had started a part-time job with a Mr. Lube outlet in Brampton, Ontario, in September 1992. He became a supervisor in 1993 but was terminated in 1995. As an employee who was black, Smith alleged he was a victim of name-calling and racial taunts in the workplace, which started almost immediately after he began his job and lasted until he was terminated. The Board of Inquiry of the Ontario Human Rights Commission found that Smith had been subject to racial harassment in a poisoned work environment and ordered the respondent to pay Smith $8000 for general damages for the time period of his employment. The board also directed the respondent to post notices that racial harassment and/or name-calling are against the Ontario *Human Rights Code* and will result in a justified termination. The board further ordered the respondent to write a letter to each of its employees stating that they had been found guilty of racial

discrimination and harassment under the Code. The board decided that race was not a factor in Smith's termination, so he was not compensated for lost wages. Further, the board did not award any money to Smith for mental anguish because they said that the respondent did not act willfully or recklessly.

Smith appealed the part of the decision that said that the termination was not racially motivated. On appeal, the Ontario Superior Court decided that claim of racial discrimination does not require proof of racial motivation, simply that race need only be a factor in the termination of an employee; in other words, Smith did not have to prove that he was terminated *solely* because of his race. He was awarded over $25 000 plus interest as compensation for his lost income. The court also concluded that the respondents were reckless in violating Smith's right to be free from a poisoned work environment and awarded Smith a further $10 000 for mental anguish.

a) What remedies were ordered against the respondent by the Ontario Human Rights Commission?

b) Why did the Ontario Superior Court alter that decision?

6. In the fall of 2005, Balpreet Singh, a law student at the University of Ottawa, was removed from an Ottawa–Toronto train. A passenger on the train complained about him wearing a kirpan (a ceremonial dagger that is part of the Sikh faith). Singh was told by VIA Rail employees that he was not allowed to wear the kirpan on the train. Singh lodged a complaint with the Canadian Human Rights Commission and eventually settled the complaint in April 2007 for a full refund of $316, the value of a six-pack book of tickets. VIA subsequently made changes to their policy on kirpans. The current policy requires that the kirpan can only be worn by Sikhs and that it must be kept in a protective covering at all times.

a) Why did Singh file a complaint with the Canadian Human Rights Commission?

b) Prepare an argument that Singh was the victim of discrimination.

Communicate Your Understanding

7. Assume you are the owner of the Mr. Lube outlet in question 5 above. Write a letter to your employees explaining the concepts of discrimination and harassment. Include in your letter what constitutes a poisoned work environment and indicate the consequences of engaging in discriminatory comments or conduct.

8. Design an appropriate remedy in a complaint case where it is apparent that an employer condoned a poisoned environment by allowing sexual comments and jokes to be made in the workplace.

Develop Your Thinking

9. As part of a forum for International Women's Day, you have been asked to develop and present a timeline highlighting significant achievements in the rights of women over the past 100 years. Where possible, include the names of the individuals and organizations involved in each achievement and evaluate their contributions in developing increased awareness of the rights of women in Canadian society.

10. Poverty can be considered a barrier to equality. Canada's House of Commons voted unanimously in 1989 "to seek to achieve the goal of eliminating poverty among Canadian children by the year 2000." The 2007 Child and Family Poverty Report Card indicated that the child poverty rate had stayed exactly the same as the rate in 1989. The study also indicated that poverty hits children in visible minority, First Nations, and immigrant communities more often. Homelessness is an extreme form of poverty. Without a home, people may find that they have even fewer rights. Research what is being done in your local community to improve the lives of those living in poverty.

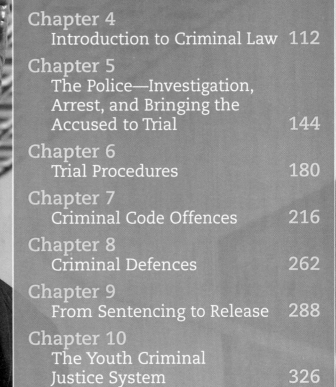

Criminal Law

Chapter 4
Introduction to Criminal Law 112

Chapter 5
The Police—Investigation,
Arrest, and Bringing the
Accused to Trial 144

Chapter 6
Trial Procedures 180

Chapter 7
Criminal Code Offences 216

Chapter 8
Criminal Defences 262

Chapter 9
From Sentencing to Release 288

Chapter 10
The Youth Criminal
Justice System 326

❝Canadians look to governments to ensure that the justice system is working effectively and that Canadians are safe. Our government will take tough action against crime and work with partners to improve the administration of justice. Serious offences will be met with serious penalties. More broadly, Canada's criminal justice system will be made more efficient.❞

—Speech from the Throne
November 19, 2008

4 Introduction to Criminal Law

What You Should Know

- What is a crime?
- What is the difference between summary conviction and indictable offences?
- What elements or conditions must exist for an action to be considered a crime?
- What is the purpose of the criminal justice system?
- How do the changing values of Canadians influence criminal law?

Chapter at a Glance

4.1 Introduction

4.2 The Nature of Criminal Law

4.3 The Power to Make Criminal Law

4.4 Summary Conviction and Indictable Offences

4.5 The Elements of a Criminal Offence

4.6 Parties to an Offence

4.7 Our Criminal Court System

Selected Key Terms

actus reus	impartiality
Criminal Code	indictable offence
criminal offence	legalize
criminalize	*mens rea*
decriminalize	prosecute
hybrid offence	summary conviction offence

When does a conflict between two persons become a criminal offence? Criminal law is in place to deal with wrongs committed against individuals and society. This helps Canadians live safely and not be subject to physical harm.

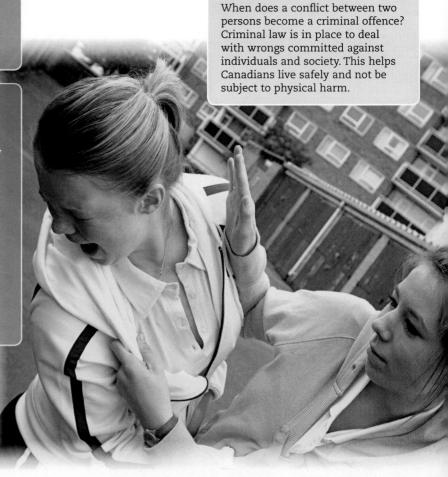

4.1 Introduction

What if you lived in a society where a person's actions had no consequences? What if a fellow student could beat you up or break into your locker and steal from you, and there were no way to punish this person? What would your school be like?

The law exists to protect individuals and society as a whole by keeping order. Criminal law deals with wrongs committed against society. Individuals and society are linked because any wrong committed against an individual is a wrong against everyone. It disturbs the safety of society. Thus, even though an individual is a crime victim, society (in the form of the criminal justice system) prosecutes and punishes the offender. Even if the victim does not want to testify and wants the charges dropped, the police and the Crown attorney can still go ahead with the prosecution.

Civil law deals with wrongs committed against an individual. That may sound abstract and a bit confusing, given our definition of criminal law above. The distinction between criminal and civil law should be clearer with this example. Suppose Sam

attacks Ameer, throwing the first punch and hitting Ameer several times. The *Criminal Code* describes Sam's offence as assault and sets a penalty for it. For this assault, Sam is charged under criminal law. He has done something that society considers unacceptable. Canadian citizens want to live safely and not be subject to physical harm, and criminal law is in place to safeguard these needs.

If Sam is found guilty at trial, he may have to pay a fine, perform community work, or be imprisoned. None of these penalties compensate Ameer for any personal distress or economic loss (for example, physical or emotional pain, missed work, and medical expenses not covered by provincial health care). Criminal law does not help the individual victim. Under civil law, Ameer could sue Sam for damages. This case would be heard at a different time and in civil court. (For more information on civil law, see Chapter 11.)

Would it make a difference if Sam had been under severe emotional distress? For example, what if he had just failed an important test, been fired from his job, or broken up with his girlfriend recently? Or what if Ameer had been provoking him by calling him names? Should any of these circumstances make a difference in the criminal case?

Did You Know?

The Law Reform Commission of Canada was established in 1971 as an independent reviewer of Canadian law. It was disbanded in 1993, but reinstated in 1996 as the Law Commission of Canada. It provides strategic advice on legal policy and law reform issues. It was dissolved by the Conservative government in December 2006.

Criminal Code the body of public law that defines crimes and prescribes punishments

criminal offence an action, omission, or state of being that is considered a crime, as defined in the *Criminal Code* or other criminal statute

4.2 The Nature of Criminal Law

What Is a Crime?

The *Criminal Code* is the main source of criminal law in Canada. It describes which acts are considered **criminal offences** and what the punishments are for crimes. The legal definition of a crime is any act that is prohibited (considered illegal) by the federal *Criminal Code*. But what exactly is a prohibited, or illegal, act in Canada? The Law Reform Commission of Canada states that four conditions must exist for an act to be considered a crime:

1. The actions or behaviour of the person must be considered immoral (wrong) by most Canadians.
2. The person's actions must cause harm to society and any individual victims.
3. The harm caused by the person's actions must be serious.
4. The person must be punished by the criminal justice system for his or her actions.

Any reforms (changes) to the *Criminal Code* must take these four conditions into consideration. The federal government creates the laws that are in the *Criminal Code* and is supposed to represent what Canadians want. If enough people want a new criminal law, or if they want to get rid of a current law, it is the government's job to do so.

A case in point would be the 2006 reforms to the *Criminal Code* regarding street racing. As a society, we expect drivers to act responsibly behind the wheel and not put others at risk. We view any behaviour that endangers people and makes us question the safety of our roads as immoral or wrong. When street racing increasingly resulted in injury and death, the government decided to put a stop to it. As the justice minister at the time said, "There is

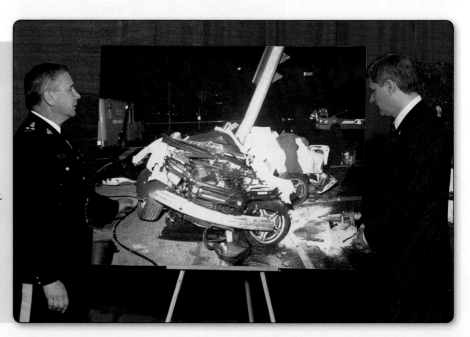

Assistant RCMP Commissioner Al McIntyre (left) explains the circumstances of a street racing accident to Prime Minister Stephen Harper on May 25, 2006. Two days later, a 19-year-old was charged for suspected street racing in the deaths of Rob and Lisa Manchester. The Manchesters, who had been out celebrating their seventeenth wedding anniversary, were killed instantly when their car was struck by the suspect's car. They left behind a seven-year-old daughter.

no task more important to any government than the protection of its citizens. That is why the government is sending a strong message that street racing on Canada's roads and highways will not be tolerated."

On June 15, 2006, the federal government introduced a bill (proposed law) in the House of Commons to make street racing a crime. Members of Parliament voted in favour of this bill, and it was passed into law. To reflect this new law, two new sections specific to street racing were added to the *Criminal Code*: section 249.2, criminal negligence causing death, and section 249.3, criminal negligence causing bodily harm. Street racing is now a crime under the *Criminal Code*. There is a maximum penalty of 14 years in prison if someone is injured. The penalty if someone is killed is up to life imprisonment. See Chapter 7 for more on street racing.

What Is Immoral Behaviour?

The *Criminal Code* reflects what actions the government, and often the majority of Canadians, consider to be immoral behaviour. The government amends or makes new laws according to what most Canadians want. The federal government attempts to forbid and punish immoral behaviour by making it illegal. For example, theft, murder, and assault are considered immoral behaviour and are therefore included in the *Criminal Code*. Possession of marijuana and euthanasia (assisted suicide) are still in the *Criminal Code*. However, some people may not agree that these activities are immoral. Grey areas such as these are debated all the time.

Canadian citizens have different beliefs on what constitutes immoral behaviour. The government can respond by **criminalizing, decriminalizing,** or **legalizing** specific types of behaviour. Legal behaviour is anything that is not against the law and does not harm others (for example, wearing blue jeans). Smoking on school property, for which you could be fined or suspended from school, is illegal behaviour, but it is not criminalized. Driving faster than the speed limit is another example of behaviour that is unlawful, but not criminal. Illegal behaviour that is criminalized involves acts such as theft or assault for which you could be imprisoned.

You and the Law

Are there street racers at your school? Do you think it was necessary to criminalize this activity? Why or why not?

criminalize to make a behaviour a criminal offence in the *Criminal Code* or other criminal statute

decriminalize to make a behaviour that was illegal punishable only by fines

legalize to make an act completely legal by removing it from the *Criminal Code* or other criminal statute

Legal, Illegal, and Criminal Behaviour

Legal	Illegal	Criminal
• Dying your hair blue	• Purchasing cigarettes if you are 18 or younger	• Theft
• Wearing religious clothing	• Speeding	• Assault
• Drinking alcohol when you turn 19	• Drinking in public places	• Possessing marijuana
• Using a cellphone in the movie theatre	• Cutting down certain trees	• Kidnapping
• Protesting with pickets	• Burning leaves	• Trespassing

Behaviour that some people consider immoral, such as smoking, is not necessarily illegal (although it is illegal to purchase tobacco if you are 18 years of age or less).

Did You Know?

Any action found in the *Criminal Code* has been criminalized. As morals and values change, so must our criminal laws.

The Purpose of the Criminal Justice System

- to protect people from harm

- to protect property from harm

- to provide retribution (punish the prohibited act by "paying back society" and balancing the scales of justice)

- to enforce moral standards based on the norms and beliefs of Canadians

- to provide rehabilitation (help an individual who has committed a crime to see that his or her actions were wrong and reintegrate him or her into the community as a productive member of Canadian society)

- to maintain order in society

- to deter people from committing crimes through precautionary measures such as community policing, social programs, and education, but also by having criminal trials open to the public; showing people who have committed crimes being tried and punished for their wrongs helps prevent future crime

The criminal justice system in Canada attempts to protect Canadians in many different ways.

Is There Justice in the Canadian Criminal Justice System?

procedural justice fairness in the processes that resolve disputes

The Greek philosopher Plato (427 BCE to 347 BCE) wrote that justice is fairness. But what exactly is fairness? The Law Reform Commission of Canada defines fairness in the criminal justice system as **procedural justice**. The entire procedure must be just for the accused—from police investigation, to the judge's trial decisions; from sentencing, to the treatment a convicted offender receives by corrections officials while in jail or prison. To achieve justice, this procedure must reflect the following principles:

- Fairness: The process must be impartial toward the accused. Also, similar cases should be treated alike and different cases differently. The courts must consider the facts and circumstances of each case.

- Efficiency: The process must be timely.

- Clarity: The accused must understand the charges and the process.

- Restraint: Government officials (the police, the prosecutor, judges, and corrections officers) must show self-discipline in their treatment of the accused.

- Accountability: Government officials must be held responsible for their actions.

- Participation: The accused must be allowed to play an active part in the process, and this process must be open to public scrutiny.

- Protection: To guard the accused from harm, all procedures of government officials must be regulated.

These are the core values of our criminal justice system, which are held up to the rest of the world as an example of the rule of law. The rule of law guarantees freedom and security in that it allows no one to be above the law; every individual is subject to the law regardless of his or her power or importance. For example, if the prime minister were caught shoplifting, he or she would be charged with theft. The Canadian criminal justice system is also a good example of **impartiality**. In general, impartiality means that the judges should be open-minded and not biased for or against the person on trial.

impartiality a principle that judicial decisions should be based on objective criteria and be free from bias or conflicts of interest

Lady Justice is the symbol of fairness in the criminal justice system, and can be seen in many courthouses. The sword in her right hand represents decisiveness in the sense that she has the authority to make a final decision in the case she is hearing. In her left hand, Lady Justice holds a pair of scales. If a crime goes unpunished, the scales are out of balance. But, once the person who committed the crime is held accountable, balance is restored. Lady Justice also wears a blindfold as she presides over trials. This covering of the eyes represents impartiality as she is blind to all factors that may bias her —such as economic status, race, ethnicity, religion, sex, or sexual orientation. To ensure the procedure is fair, all Lady Justice will hear or see is the evidence presented at trial.

Activity

To learn more about the purpose of the criminal justice system,

Go to Nelson Social Studies

We can be proud of Canada's legal system compared to justice systems in other countries. However, that does not mean it is flawless. We must be watchful citizens in our democracy and make sure that our legal system remains fair. The United Nations (UN) and Amnesty International note that Canada still has justice system issues to address when it comes to fairness and equality. These include racial profiling in police activities, the treatment of Aboriginal peoples, gender inequality, and the unequal distribution of our nation's wealth.

Review Your Understanding

1. Explain the purpose of criminal law. Provide brief examples to support your understanding.
2. According to the Law Reform Commission of Canada, what conditions must exist for an action to be considered a crime? Provide examples.
3. What influences the federal government when it decides what behaviours to criminalize, decriminalize, or legalize?
4. When the government decides that crimes are to be added, deleted, or changed in the *Criminal Code*, why is it important to have a free and open debate about the proposed changes?
5. What are activities that you think should be criminalized and decriminalized?

4.3 The Power to Make Criminal Law

The *Criminal Code*

enact to pass a proposed law into legislation

Criminal law is **enacted** (made into law) by a democratically elected federal Parliament. For that reason, criminal offences are treated the same across Canada. Canada's criminal law is found in the *Criminal Code*. It governs society by prohibiting certain acts. If these acts are carried out, the person who committed them is punished.

amend to change existing legislation (laws)

The *Criminal Code* is written and **amended** (changed) by the federal Parliament, but the Supreme Court of Canada still has a major influence on criminal law. When the Supreme Court makes a decision in an important case (after first ruling that the case is of national importance), this decision becomes a precedent. This means that it acts as an example or guide for future decisions in similar cases. In this sense, even though the courts do not make the law, the Supreme Court still has a significant impact on criminal law in Canada.

Cabinet minister Beverley Oda responds to questions in the House of Commons. The power to make criminal law lies with the federal government. Members of Parliament, who are elected by Canadians, try to make laws based on what Canadians think should be illegal.

 Did You Know?

Canada's first *Criminal Code* was enacted in 1892. Read the following excerpts from the first *Criminal Code*, and reflect on how attitudes have changed:

"Whenever whipping may be awarded for any offence ... the number of strokes shall be specified in the sentence and the instrument to be used for whipping shall be a cat-o'-nine-tails."

"In all cases where an offender is sentenced to death, the sentence shall be that he be hanged by the neck until he is dead."

Public Law

Canada has a democratic system of government, and its citizens elect Members of Parliament to represent them. Those politicians are supposed to reflect the wishes of Canadians in the laws they write and amend. This means that Canadian criminal law is public law. The power to make criminal law is given to the federal government in the first half of the Canadian Constitution. This part of the Constitution was originally called the *British North America Act*. It is now referred to as the *Constitution Act, 1982*. The power to make law is outlined in section 91 of the *Constitution Act*.

The second half of the Canadian Constitution is the *Charter of Rights and Freedoms*. The *Criminal Code* restrictions must not infringe upon a citizen's legal rights as defined in the Charter. For example, section 7 guarantees the right to security of the person, which means that police cannot harm suspects during their investigation.

Criminal law is also public law because it concerns the actions of the government against an individual. In Canada, when someone is **prosecuted** in a criminal law trial, he or she is brought to trial by the Crown attorney. The Crown attorney represents the government, which in turn represents us, the public. Canadians refer to a criminal court case as *R. v. (name of accused, e.g., Smith)*. See Chapter 1, page 17, for an explanation of the elements of a citation.

prosecute to initiate and carry out a legal action

Legal Rights in the *Charter of Rights and Freedoms*

The Charter was created in 1982. Canadian citizens were still protected before that time by decisions of our courts. Court decisions are known as the common law. Many of the rights found in the Charter are long-established precedents set by Canadian courts. Since the Charter's creation, these rights have been constitutionally entrenched (set and protected). It would be difficult now to infringe upon these rights. Former Prime Minister Pierre Trudeau entrenched the Charter in our Constitution. He believed, as do many Canadians, that a written constitution, or "bill of rights," is stronger and safer than rights based solely on precedent or the common law.

The rights contained in the *Charter of Rights and Freedoms* are not absolute. According to section 1 of the Charter, our rights are only subject to "such reasonable limits prescribed by law as can be demonstrably justified in a free and democratic society." Sometimes an individual's Charter rights conflict with the duties and limits (restrictions) of the *Criminal Code*. If the courts feel that the *Criminal Code* limit on a person's behaviour has gone too far, they will rule that the law is unconstitutional. In these cases, the criminal court needs to weigh what is best for society against an individual's rights.

Did You Know?

The English philosopher John Stuart Mill (1806–1873) wrote, "The freedom to swing your arm ends where your neighbour's nose begins." In other words, every Canadian citizen is entitled to the right of bodily expression, but this right cannot outweigh the *Criminal Code* restriction on assault. Can you think of any other laws in the *Criminal Code* that may conflict with an individual's Charter rights?

Did You Know?

There is no *Good Samaritan Act* in Canada. The *Criminal Code* does not specify that it is an individual's duty to help someone in trouble (a person drowning, for example). Do you think we should have such an act in Canada? Explain.

Limits, Duties, and Rights of Individuals

The *Criminal Code* restricts what an individual can do (steal, assault someone, smoke marijuana, and so on).

The *Criminal Code* identifies specific duties that an individual must do. If an individual fails to carry out these specific duties (for example, by failing to care for a newborn baby), he or she is criminally responsible.

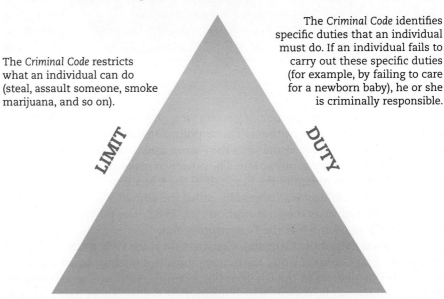

LIMIT

DUTY

RIGHT

The Charter states what an individual is free to do (the right to liberty, the right not to be arbitrarily detained, and so on).

Sometimes, the limits and duties set out by the *Criminal Code* can conflict with an individual's Charter rights.

Review Your Understanding

1. Why is criminal law considered "public law"?
2. What is the purpose of the *Criminal Code* of Canada?
3. When might a criminal law be ruled unconstitutional by the courts?
4. How does the Charter limit or restrict people's rights?
5. What happens when an individual's Charter rights conflict with the *Criminal Code*?

4.4 Summary Conviction and Indictable Offences

If you visit a courthouse, you may be able to observe a criminal trial. There, people are charged with **summary conviction offences** or **indictable offences**, depending on the severity of the crime. These are the terms we use in Canada to differentiate between severe and less serious crimes. You may be familiar with the terms "felonies" and "misdemeanours" from American TV shows and films. We do not use these terms in the Canadian legal system. In Canada, less serious crimes (misdemeanours) may be summary conviction offences. More serious crimes (felonies) are indictable offences. The term **hybrid offences** refers to offences that may be treated as either summary conviction or indictable offences, depending on the decision of the prosecutor.

summary conviction offence a minor criminal offence with less severe punishments, which is usually tried soon after the charge is laid (summarily) without a preliminary hearing or jury

indictable offence a serious criminal offence with a severe penalty, proceeding by way of a formal court document called an indictment

hybrid offence a criminal offence proceeding by way of a summary conviction or an indictable offence; the Crown decides which way to proceed

Summary Conviction Offences

Summary conviction offences are minor criminal offences. If Robin plays a telephone prank or yells loudly at a passerby in a mall, she can be charged with a summary conviction offence. Both telephone harassment and causing a public disturbance are summary conviction offences. A person accused of this type of offence can be arrested and charged. Under the *Criminal Code*, the maximum penalty for most summary conviction offences is a fine of $2000 and/or six months in jail.

Unlike indictable offences, there is a six-month limitation period for laying a charge for a summary conviction offence. This means that a person must be charged within six months of the offence or she or he is free and clear. A provincial court judge hears the evidence and gives the verdict for summary conviction offences.

Heckling or bullying can be summary conviction offences. However, if these offences escalate into serious acts of violence, offenders could be charged with indictable offences.

A variety of offences are always categorized as summary conviction offences. They include causing a disturbance, taking a motor vehicle without the owner's consent, and possession of a certain amount of marijuana. (For more on the issue of marijuana and the law, see the Issue feature on page 140.)

Indictable Offences

Indictable offences are serious crimes that carry more severe penalties than summary conviction offences. The *Criminal Code* sets a maximum penalty for each offence. For example, with manslaughter, the maximum penalty is life imprisonment. However, the trial judge ultimately decides on the actual time spent behind bars. Other examples of indictable offences are robbery, breaking and entering, and murder. The *Criminal Code* sets a minimum penalty for some specific offences. For example, a person convicted of an offence using a firearm as a first offender must serve a term of at least one year of imprisonment. Unlike summary conviction offences, there is no **statute of limitations** (time limit) for laying a charge of an indictable offence. For serious indictable offences, the accused can choose whether to be tried by a provincial court judge alone, by a judge of the superior court of the province or territory alone, or by a judge of the higher court with a jury.

Did You Know?

The courts must impose the maximum penalty—life imprisonment without becoming eligible for parole for 25 years—for only two indictable offences: high treason and first-degree murder. Treason is disloyalty to one's nation, such as giving Canadian government secrets to another country.

statute of limitations a time limit imposed by law within which a specific action must be taken

You and the Law

Journalists' coverage of real crimes is very different from the fictional portrayal of crime on TV. What law-related TV shows do you watch and why? What are the main differences between real criminal law and TV law?

Stealing a bicycle may be prosecuted as an indictable offence.

Hybrid Offences

Most offences defined in the *Criminal Code* are hybrid offences. This means that they can end up as either indictable or summary conviction charges. The Crown attorney decides whether to seek a less severe punishment (known as proceeding summarily) or to proceed by indictment. This is done to give local prosecutors some leeway in their decisions. Until the Crown makes its decision, hybrid offences remain indictable. The Crown often bases its decision on the previous record of the accused, the date of the offence (if the offence occurred less than six months in the past), and whether lesser penalties are appropriate if a conviction is obtained. Hybrid offences include impaired driving, assault, public mischief, and theft under $5000. Maximum penalties will vary for hybrid offences from two years imprisonment to 10 years.

Sometimes, the prosecutor decides to reduce an indictable offence to a summary conviction charge.

? Did You Know?

In Canada, unlike in the United States, cameras are rarely allowed in the courtroom.

Review Your Understanding

1. What is the difference between a summary conviction and an indictable offence?
2. What are the equivalent terms for summary conviction and indictable offences in the United States?
3. Compare the maximum penalties for summary conviction and indictable offences.
4. What choices does a Crown attorney have in dealing with a hybrid offence?
5. Why would the Crown decide to proceed summarily rather than proceed by indictment?

4.5 The Elements of a Criminal Offence

Actus non facit reum nisi mens sit rea

This phrase is Latin for "the act will not make a person guilty unless the mind is also guilty." In other words, you must consciously intend to commit a crime; you cannot commit a crime unknowingly or by accident. Thus, to find someone guilty of an offence, the Crown must prove that a criminal act occurred—the *actus reus* (external, voluntary act meaning "wrongful deed")—and that the accused had a criminal intention—the *mens rea* (internal act meaning "guilty mind"). If the Crown cannot prove both of these elements beyond a reasonable doubt, the accused will be acquitted and set free. For example, in any criminal case, the Crown must prove the identity of the accused. If the Crown cannot prove, beyond a reasonable doubt, that the accused was the one who actually committed the crime, then the Crown did not prove the *actus reus*. See the case below of *R. v. Parks*, 1992, for an interesting example of the need for proof of the *mens rea* in a crime.

actus reus a Latin phrase meaning "a wrongful deed"; the physical or guilty act, omission, or state of being that constitutes a crime

mens rea a Latin phrase meaning "a guilty mind"; the mental element of one's criminal actions

 Case

R. v. Parks, 1992 CanLII 78 (S.C.C.)

For more information, **Go to Nelson Social Studies**

In 1987, Kenneth Parks got up from his bed, drove over 20 kilometres to his in-laws' house, and stabbed both his mother-in-law and father-in-law, killing her and seriously injuring him. Immediately afterwards, Parks drove to a nearby police station and reported what he had done. Parks was charged with first-degree murder and attempted murder even though he claimed to have been sleepwalking throughout the incident. Parks testified that he had always been a deep sleeper and had a great deal of trouble waking up. (Several members of his family also suffer from sleep problems.) The year prior to the incident was particularly stressful for him, and his personal life suffered. Parks's in-laws were aware of his problems, supported him, and had excellent relations with him.

At the trial, Parks presented a defence of automatism. It is unconscious movement or functioning without conscious control. (Automatism and other defences will be discussed further in Chapter 8.) The defence called five psychiatrists and psychologists. They testified that these acts of violence were done in

continues...

Kenneth Parks (shown here with his wife) leaves the court on bail.

R. v. Parks, 1992 CanLII 78 (S.C.C.)

a genuinely hypnotic state. At issue here was whether sleepwalking should be classified as non-insane automatism, resulting in an acquittal, or as a "disease of the mind" (insane automatism), giving rise to the special verdict of not guilty by reason of insanity.

The judge and jury acquitted Parks of the charges of murder and attempted murder in the original trial. The Crown appealed, but the Court of Appeal upheld the acquittal. Upon further appeal by the Crown, the Supreme Court agreed with the acquittal because Parks had no intent or knowledge of what he was doing. It was found that the accused was genuinely sleepwalking at the time he committed murder. His somnambulism was ruled a sleep disorder, not a form of insanity.

For Discussion

1. Were *actus reus* and *mens rea* present at the time this crime was committed? Explain.

2. Why do you think the Supreme Court dismissed the Crown's appeal?

3. Should a person be able to use a severe sleep disorder as a reason to nullify criminal responsibility? Explain your opinion.

4. Why should epileptics not be allowed to use the defence of automatism in the case of a car accident? Explain.

At trial, the Crown will first try to prove that the accused was the one who actually committed the crime. Then they move on to proving intent or knowledge. Intent is the true purpose of the accused. No one can know for sure what was in another person's mind, but the court will make its decision based on the facts of the case at hand and on what a reasonable person would believe under the circumstances. For example, Rosanna is arrested at the airport with several balloons filled with cocaine that she had swallowed. If she tells the judge that she thought the substance was baking soda, and this is how she likes to transport it, the judge would simply not believe her as no reasonable person would do such a thing. The court will conclude that the true purpose of this act was to import narcotics.

A woman is arrested for possession of illegal drugs. No reasonable person would swallow balloons in order to carry their baking soda, making it unlikely that a judge would believe someone was *not* intentionally importing narcotics as a mule.

Intention

If Shivonne goes into the store and deliberately puts a lipstick in her purse, she intends to commit the act of theft. On the other hand, if she absentmindedly puts the lipstick in her purse without intending to steal it, then forgets about it, she would be found not guilty. She did not intend to commit a crime. If one student deliberately punches another in the stomach, he or she is guilty of assault. But if a group of students are playing soccer and during the game Brian kicks the ball toward the goal and strikes the goalkeeper in the stomach, criminal law would not consider this an assault. Brian had no **intent** to cause harm.

intent the state of the mind of a person who commits an action deliberately and on purpose

Criminal State of Mind

Accused persons may not intend the outcome of their actions, but they may have a certain "state of mind." This criminal state of mind means that the accused persons knew they were doing something illegal. For example, Sharon has just shoplifted and runs from the store. She bumps into Maheen, knocking her to the ground and causing serious injuries. Sharon is not only guilty of theft, but of assault as well. Even though Sharon did not intend to assault Maheen and she did not intend this outcome, she had a "criminal state of mind" while committing the offence of theft.

willful blindness the act of deliberately choosing to ignore certain facts or information

Willful Blindness

Willful blindness is pretending not to know something. If you "turn a blind eye" and say "I don't see anything," but you really know what is going on, you are guilty of willful blindness. For example, if Courtney is offered $100 to deliver a package a couple of blocks away for Zack, a known drug dealer, but does not ask what is in the package, then she could be charged and convicted of drug trafficking. The average person would be suspicious of Zack and would ask appropriate questions, such as, "What is in the package?" They would not turn a blind eye.

Packages used to smuggle drugs can take many forms, including plush toys and dolls.

Recklessness

Recklessness is the careless disregard for the possible results of an action. For example, a person who knows he or she has AIDS has unprotected sex with others without informing them of his or her medical condition. The person with AIDS could be charged with assault, attempted murder, or even murder if the victim eventually dies. The careless disregard for the possible results of an action, even though the person may not intend to hurt anyone, would result in the required *mens rea* being proven at trial. The offence was committed with knowledge and recklessness.

recklessness a state of acting carelessly without regard for the consequences of one's actions

criminal negligence wanton and reckless disregard for the lives and safety of other people

Criminal Negligence

Criminal negligence is the wanton and reckless disregard for the lives and safety of other people. For example, head chef Samad works on his science experiments in his restaurant's kitchen. A waiter picks up what appears to be the soup of the day and serves it to a customer who dies from poisoning. Samad may be guilty of manslaughter and would be charged. A reasonable person would have realized the possible consequences of her or his actions and the fact that the restaurant soup bowls are normally filled with harmless liquid.

The Supreme Court of Canada has defined the required state of mind in the case of criminal negligence. The court decided that if a reasonable, objective analysis were made, and the act would carry the risk of harm, then the person was negligent. In this case, the Crown must show that Samad's actions were unreasonable, as the average person would have known that this action could cause harm. See the case on the next page of *R. v. Williams,* 2003, for a real-life example of criminal negligence.

A reasonable person would expect the contents of a restaurant soup bowl to be harmless.

You Be the Judge

R. v. Collins and French, 2006 BCSC 1531 (CanLII)

For more information, Go to Nelson Social Studies

Sometime in the afternoon of December 2, 2004, victim Thelma Pete was brutally beaten, receiving approximately 25 blows to the head. Later, she was with the accused, Richard Collins and James French, in a darkened entrance to an abandoned school building where the pair were drinking alcohol. At approximately 10:00 p.m., Collins and French took Pete by taxi to French's apartment. They laid her on the apartment floor and continued to drink. She died from her injuries sometime during the night.

Collins and French were charged with manslaughter. The Crown did not allege that they had anything to do with her beating. The Crown argued that they were guilty of manslaughter because their actions amounted to criminal negligence. Interestingly, they would have been in less trouble if they had left Pete to freeze to death instead of taking her with them. This is because the *Criminal Code* states that everyone is under a legal duty to provide the necessities of life to a person under his or her charge if that person is unable to care for themselves.

- How do you think the court ruled? Explain.

R. v. Williams, 2003 SCC 41 (CanLII)

For more information, Go to Nelson Social Studies

Harold Williams and the victim were in a relationship for a year that ended in November 1992. Williams had tested positive for HIV but did not tell the victim. Williams received counselling by health care professionals about HIV, its transmission, safer practices, and his duty to disclose his HIV status to sexual partners. However, he continued to practise unprotected sex with the victim. After the relationship ended, Williams's partner tested positive for HIV. Williams was arrested, charged, and convicted of aggravated assault but was acquitted on appeal. The Court of Appeal substituted a conviction for attempted aggravated assault. It ruled that the crime of attempted aggravated assault must establish intent. Intent was established but only for attempt, not the actual assault. The Crown did not like this decision and appealed to the Supreme Court of Canada. In 2001, the Supreme Court of Canada unanimously (7–0) upheld this decision. There was no way to prove the victim did not have AIDS before having sexual relations with Williams.

For Discussion

1. Was there intent, recklessness, or criminal negligence in this case? Explain.

2. When you hear the word "assault," what do you think of? How does this case make you think of assault in a different way?

3. If Williams had a common sexually transmitted disease, would the charge still be aggravated assault? Why or why not?

4. Critics have denounced the Supreme Court decision as sexist and a setback for female victims of sexual abuse. Do you agree or disagree? Justify your opinion by using the facts from the case to support your view.

Knowledge

The knowledge of certain facts can also provide the necessary *mens rea* for a criminal conviction. For example, the *Criminal Code* states that anyone knowingly using a revoked or cancelled credit card is guilty of the indictable offence of fraud. The Crown only needs to prove that the person used the credit card and that he or she knew the card was not good. It is not necessary to prove that there was intent to defraud.

Motive

motive the reason for committing a certain act

If an accused had a reason to commit the offence, it is called his or her **motive.** Having a reason or motive, however, does not establish the guilt of the accused. Motive is not knowledge. The fact that Rosanna was in financial difficulty is not relevant to her guilt in the earlier example of cocaine smuggling. Many of us have motives, but never follow through on them with a criminal act. Suppose that a married woman, who is having an affair, is killed in a suspicious fire. Her husband may have had a motive to kill her, but unless it can be shown that he caused the fire, he has not committed an offence.

During a trial, the Crown may refer to the motive of the accused for committing the crime. This is called indirect or circumstantial evidence. The Crown must try to make the judge or jury conclude that the accused is guilty with no direct evidence such as an eyewitness. If a guilty verdict is returned, the judge may also consider the motive during sentencing.

 Did You Know?

If a husband sets a fire as part of an insurance fraud scheme, and does not know that his wife was in the building, he would still be guilty of first-degree murder because he was committing an indictable offence at the time.

Might this be a good way for security guards to look for shoplifters?

Attempt

A person who intends to commit a crime but fails to complete the act may still be guilty of a criminal offence. In Rosanna's case (the woman smuggling cocaine into the country by swallowing balloons containing the drugs), if she vomited up the cocaine balloons on the plane, she would still be charged with attempted importation (and possession for the purpose of trafficking). Even though she failed to actually import the drug, it was the **attempt** that was important.

As with any crime, proving attempt means showing that there was intent to commit the offence. The *actus reus* for an attempt begins when the person takes the first step toward committing the crime. It is the judge who decides—even in trial by jury—when the preparation stage ends and the attempt stage begins. For example, Rosanna prepared for her crime by buying plane tickets, balloons, milk to coat her stomach, and a laxative to help her retrieve the drugs. She further prepared by swallowing the drug-filled balloons. However, it was only when she stepped onto the plane that she attempted the crime of importation. If she was arrested just after she swallowed the drugs, she would not be charged with importing, but with possession. If she threw up on the plane and did not actually step onto Canadian soil, she would be charged with attempted importation.

During a trial, if the Crown is unable to prove that the offence was committed but only that an attempt was made, the accused may be convicted of the attempt. If the accused was originally charged with the attempt, but the evidence indicates that the offence was actually committed, the judge may order the accused to be tried for the offence itself.

attempt an act done with the intent to commit a criminal offence but without success

 Did You Know?

The law considers some people to be incapable of forming the intent necessary to commit a crime. Examples include people suffering from some forms of mental illness and children under the age of 12.

Conspiracy

conspiracy an agreement between two or more people to commit an unlawful act

A **conspiracy** is an agreement between two or more people to commit a crime or to achieve something legal by doing something illegal. For example, if Roberto and Hank discuss their plans to break into Katiya's house to steal her credit cards, they have conspired to commit a crime. Even if they do not carry out the plan, they have agreed to a conspiracy to commit the crime. In a conspiracy, all the people involved must be serious in their intention to commit the crime. Jokes or threats are not considered conspiracy.

Conspiracy is the agreement to commit an illegal act, whether the individuals carry out the crime or not.

Did You Know?

The *Anti-Terrorism Act* states that someone who knowingly takes in a terrorist, takes part in terrorism, or is an accomplice to terrorism commits an indictable offence and could receive up to 10 years of imprisonment. Facilitating a terrorist act could get someone up to 14 years. Convicted leaders of terrorist acts can receive up to life imprisonment.

Review Your Understanding

1. Identify the two elements that must exist for a crime to be committed.
2. *Actus reus* does not always require an action to be committed. Give an example of such a circumstance.
3. Distinguish among the different categories of *mens rea*, and provide an example for each.
4. How is motive used in a criminal trial?
5. When does an attempt begin? Provide an example of a situation where a criminal charge of attempt could be made.

4.6 Parties to an Offence

Aiding or Abetting

If you help someone to commit a crime, you are guilty of **aiding** that person to commit the crime. If you encourage a person to commit a crime, you are guilty of **abetting** that person. In other words, to advise or give suggestions about a crime is aiding. To incite, instigate, or urge someone to commit a crime is abetting. To be convicted of aiding or abetting, you must believe that the other person truly intended to commit the offence. Onlookers who merely witness a criminal act are not guilty of aiding or abetting. However, if onlookers do anything that could be seen as urging or inciting a criminal act, they could be guilty of abetting.

Under section 21(2) of the *Criminal Code*, a person who aids or abets a criminal is just as guilty of the crime as the person who actually carries it out. For example, Patrick urges Paolo to take a wallet from the gym change room. Patrick is inciting Paolo to commit an offence (abetting). If Paolo is caught trying to steal the wallet, Patrick would receive the same charge (attempted theft) and the same penalty as Paolo because he encouraged Paolo to commit the crime.

aiding assisting someone to commit a criminal offence

abetting encouraging or urging another person to commit a crime

A person who urges someone to steal is just as guilty as the person who actually steals.

 ## You Be the Judge

R. v. Goodine, 1993 CanLII 5379 (NB C.A.)

For more information, **Go to Nelson Social Studies** 🌐

One summer afternoon in 1992, Todd Johnston went for a ride with his girlfriend and two friends, Jason Boyd and Cory Goodine. After driving on country roads near Arthurette, New Brunswick, Johnston stopped the truck. Without warning, he shot Boyd in the head with a revolver. He then removed Boyd's body from the truck and dragged it a short distance.

Still holding the revolver, Johnston ordered Goodine to "get off the truck and help me because you are in on this, too." Goodine obeyed Johnston's orders to drag the body into the woods. When the victim moaned, Johnston shot Boyd again in the back of the head. Medical evidence at trial indicated that either shot would have caused Boyd's death.

A few days later, Goodine told two of his friends about the murder and led them to Boyd's body. The next day, the friends reported the incident to the police. They arrested Goodine and charged him with being an accessory after the fact to murder. The jury acquitted the accused following a trial. The Crown appealed to the Court of Appeal, but the appeal was dismissed.

• Goodine was not charged with aiding and abetting. Why do you think that was? Explain your reasoning.

Accessory after the Fact

If you knowingly help a person to escape or hide from the police after a crime, you are an **accessory after the fact**. Even providing food, clothing, or shelter to the offender is an offence.

accessory after the fact someone who knows that a crime has been committed and who helps the person who committed the crime to hide or escape from the police

Organized Crime

A group is three or more individuals who share a common identity. This could be comprised of Scouts, members of a gymnastics team, political protesters, *Canadian Idol* groupies, or Facebook friends. As soon as a group defines itself by opposing authority and engaging in ongoing criminal activity, the group becomes a criminal organization that defies our mainstream values. For example, see the case below of *R. v. Lindsay*, 2005.

 Case

R. v. Lindsay, 2005 CanLII 24240 (ON S.C.)

For more information, Go to Nelson Social Studies

In 2002, Stephen (Tiger) Lindsay and Raymond (Razor) Bonner wore their Hells Angels' jackets when they visited a Barrie, Ontario, businessman in his home. They demanded $75 000 to settle a dispute over a satellite TV system. The businessman testified to their threats. He tape-recorded Lindsay saying, "If you toy with me, your days are numbered."

Lindsay and Bonner were charged with extortion. The Crown sought to have the Hells Angels formally declared a "criminal organization" under the federal anti-gang legislation. At the conclusion of the trial in June 2005, the Ontario Superior Court of Justice ruled that Lindsay and Bonner had

continues...

In an effort to combat organized crime, the Ontario Superior Court of Justice declared the Hells Angels a criminal organization.

R. v. Lindsay, 2005 CanLII 24240 (ON S.C.)

committed extortion in association with a criminal organization and had used the Hells Angels' reputation as a weapon. This was the first time a Canadian court declared a group, as opposed to individuals, to be "criminal" in a move to combat organized crime. The government also added new penalties for being part of a criminal gang. They include an extra 14 years in prison on top of the sentence you received for the crime you were convicted of in the first place.

For Discussion

1. Should organized criminals and gang members face stiffer penalties than individuals?

2. Do you think that organized crime is a problem in our society?

3. How do people act differently in a group than when they are alone? Explain your answer.

4. Do you believe the Hells Angels is a criminal organization? Why or why not?

Canadians are becoming more concerned with gangs that commit crime. There are media reports about organized crime almost every day. It is becoming a more complex phenomenon. Criminal organizations have evolved into intricate international networks where they combine illegal activities with legal businesses. They take advantage of open markets and the differing levels of commitment and ability that various governments have to combat them. In 2008, the Ontario government continued to focus on putting an end to gang violence. It included building a $26-million operation centre for the Anti-Guns and Gangs Task Force. Two years earlier, Criminal Intelligence Service Canada (CISC) issued its annual report, focusing on organized crime and street gangs. The report provided a provincial breakdown of crime. Gang activity continues to thrive in the Greater Toronto Area, home to roughly 80 of the country's 300-plus gangs.

To help put a stop to gangs and organized crime, section 467.11 of the *Criminal Code* states that a person who facilitates a gang-related offence is just as guilty as the person who actually commits it. This is known as a criminal organization offence.

> **? Did You Know?**
>
> Criminal Intelligence Service Canada (CISC) said the Hells Angels motorcycle gang remains the largest and most powerful outlaw gang in Canada.

 All About Law DVD

"Gang Wars: Bloodbath in Vancouver" from *All About Law DVD*

Review Your Understanding

1. According to the *Criminal Code*, who may be a party to an offence?
2. Distinguish between "aiding" and "abetting."
3. Identify who may be considered an accessory after the fact.
4. What is the significance of anti-gang legislation?
5. What is a criminal organization offence?

4.7 Our Criminal Court System

Thousands of cases go to trial each year. The cost of operating the criminal justice system, which is paid for by taxpayers, is very high. As a result, the structure and procedures of Canadian courts are constantly being revised to provide greater efficiency.

The *British North America Act, 1867*, gave the federal government the power to make criminal law and establish the procedures to be followed in criminal matters. The federal and provincial governments divide jurisdiction over the court system. The provincial governments control the administration of justice. This means that they organize and maintain their provincial courts. For example, they provide courthouses and court staff. The criminal court system in Canada consists of several levels, listed below. See also the diagram on page 136. Trial procedures will be discussed in greater detail in Chapter 6.

Ontario Court of Justice

Alberta Court of
Queen's Bench

The Criminal Court System in Canada

Provincial Courts—Criminal Division

(example: the Ontario Court of Justice)

This is the trial court that most students will be familiar with as it involves the finding of facts, witness testimony, and the introduction of evidence. If a mistake is made at this stage, then an appeal can be made to a higher court. This court

- arraigns the accused (reads the charge and enters the plea) in all criminal cases
- holds preliminary hearings for most severe indictable offences, where the accused elects to have the case tried in a higher court
- hears and tries criminal summary conviction cases and the least serious indictable offences such as theft under $5000

The judges in this court are appointed by the provincial governments.

Provincial Superior Court—Appeals and Trials (names vary)

(example: the Superior Court of Justice for the province of Ontario or the Court of Queen's Bench for the province of Alberta)

This court is the court of first appeal with respect to criminal cases arising in the provincial court. This court

- tries the more severe crimes such as manslaughter and sexual assault, and the most severe indictable offences such as murder and armed robbery
- hears criminal appeals in summary conviction cases
- sets provincial precedent; decisions must be followed by provincial court judges in that province
- can be composed of a judge alone or a judge and jury

The judges in this court are appointed by the federal government.

The Criminal Court System in Canada (continued)

Provincial Court of Appeal (names vary)

(example: the British Columbia Court of Appeal)

This is the highest court and the final court of appeal in the province. Many appeals stop here as the Supreme Court of Canada accepts only appeals that are deemed to be of great importance. Appeals are heard by three or more judges, depending on the case. Their decisions may be either unanimous or majority judgments. Split two-to-one judgments are not uncommon. When the court releases its decision, it also provides explanations for the majority vote, and dissenting judges provide their reasons for disagreeing.

This court

- hears appeals from the trial division of provincial superior courts
- sets provincial precedent; decisions must be followed by all judges in that province
- has three to five judges to hear all appeals

The judges in this court are appointed by the federal government.

British Columbia
Court of Appeal

Federal Courts

This is Canada's national court system that hears legal disputes with the federal government. In 2003, the former Federal Court of Canada was separated into two distinct courts: the Federal Court, and the Federal Court of Appeal.

The Federal Court has jurisdiction over cases involving federal government boards, tribunals and commissions, and issues within federal jurisdiction. These include immigration and citizenship matters, and intellectual property (such as copyright and trademark issues), as well as cases involving the federal government. The Federal Court of Appeal hears appeals of decisions by the Federal Court. Decisions of this court may be appealed to the Supreme Court of Canada.

Both the Federal Court and the Federal Court of Appeal have regional offices in all major cities in Canada, although the judges and the main court facilities are located in Ottawa.

The Federal Court of Appeal

Supreme Court of Canada

The Supreme Court of Canada (SCC) is the final court of appeal in our country. Even though the SCC is the highest court in the land, not all parties—individuals, organizations, or even governments—have the right to appeal to it. Before it agrees to hear an appeal, the court determines if the issue is of great importance or if a question of law must be decided or interpreted. However, there is an automatic right of appeal when there is a split decision from a provincial court of appeal. Like the provincial courts of appeal, the SCC may be either unanimous or split.

The Supreme Court of Canada

- has unlimited jurisdiction in criminal matters
- hears appeals from provincial appeal courts and the Federal Court of Appeal

continues…

Supreme Court of Canada

Chapter 4   **Introduction to Criminal Law**   **135**

The Criminal Court System in Canada (continued)

Supreme Court of Canada (continued)

- hears cases of national importance (for example, interprets the *Charter of Rights and Freedoms* or clarifies a criminal law matter)
- generally grants leave (permission) before the appeal will be heard
- sets a national precedent in its judgments; these decisions must be followed by all judges in all courts of Canada

The nine judges of the Supreme Court are appointed by the federal government and can serve until age 75.

There are several levels in the Canadian criminal court system. Distinguish between the "highest" and "lowest" courts in Canada. Identify the jurisdiction for each level of court.

e Activity

To learn more about the Supreme Court of Canada,

Go to Nelson Social Studies

This diagram shows the general structure of the criminal court system in Canada. However, the court names vary from province to province.

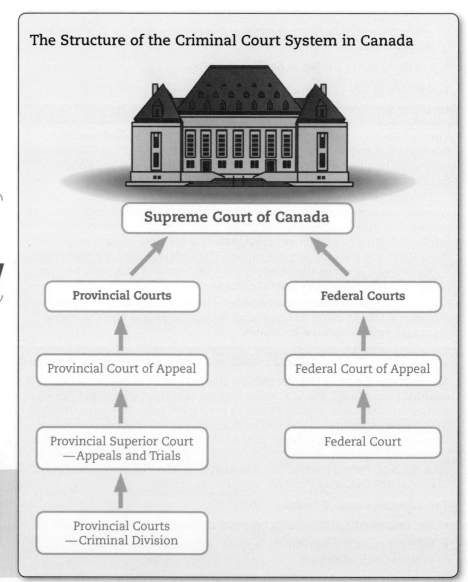

The Structure of the Criminal Court System in Canada

Supreme Court of Canada

Provincial Courts

Federal Courts

Provincial Court of Appeal

Federal Court of Appeal

Provincial Superior Court
—Appeals and Trials

Federal Court

Provincial Courts
—Criminal Division

The Association in Defence of the Wrongly Convicted (AIDWYC)

The AIDWYC is a Canadian-based organization. It fights against wrongful convictions that are miscarriages of justice when an innocent person goes to jail. The group began in support of Guy Paul Morin immediately following his wrongful conviction in the summer of 1992. For some 10 years ending in 2004, AIDWYC's executive director was Rubin "Hurricane" Carter. He is the American boxer who spent 20 years in prison for crimes he did not commit. (His ordeal was told in Canadian director Norman Jewison's film *The Hurricane*, which starred Denzel Washington.) The AIDWYC directors include lawyers, academics, and other interested members of the public.

The AIDWYC has investigated such leading cases as the Milgaard and Truscott cases. David Milgaard was released in 1992 after serving 22 years in jail for the rape and murder of Gail Miller, a crime that he did not commit. Five years later, he was fully exonerated (freed from guilt) through DNA testing. This was a new tool in forensic science at that time. Milgaard was awarded $10 million in damages and an apology for the injustice that had been done to him. At that time, this was the largest settlement in Canadian history. The AIDWYC played a major role in the Milgaard public inquiry in 2005–2006. The inquiry looked into all aspects of the police investigation and the subsequent criminal proceedings that resulted in Milgaard's wrongful conviction.

Then in 2007, the AIDWYC helped Steven Truscott clear his name. In 1959, 14-year-old Truscott was wrongfully convicted of murdering 12-year-old Lynne Harper. Truscott was sentenced to death by hanging. This was later changed to life imprisonment. Truscott was released on parole after 10 years in prison. In 2000, after more than 20 years of maintaining a low profile, he publicly proclaimed his innocence. With AIDWYC assistance, he renewed the fight to clear his name. The federal justice minister referred the case to the Ontario Court of Appeal. In August 2007, that court acquitted Truscott and pronounced the case a miscarriage of justice in a 5–0 decision. Truscott was awarded $6.5 million.

Denzel Washington (left) and Rubin "Hurricane" Carter

For Discussion

1. How did the evolution of forensic science influence these two cases?

2. What is a "miscarriage of justice"? Why did the courts call these wrongful convictions "miscarriages of justice" rather than declaring the accused not guilty or innocent? What is the difference between "miscarriage of justice," "innocent," and "not guilty," and why is this final resolution important?

3. When asked about his wrongful conviction, Milgaard replied, "The question shouldn't be how I feel about this. The question should be how did this happen?" Why do you think wrongful convictions occur?

4. How much money should wrongfully convicted people receive in compensation for the time they spent in jail and the fact that they lived with the stigma of a criminal conviction for many years?

Criminal Offences and Procedures

As noted earlier, summary conviction offences and more serious indictable offences have different trial procedures. These will be examined in more detail in later chapters.

Examples of Categories of Indictable Offences

Least Serious Trial procedure similar to summary conviction offences	More Serious Accused selects one of three trial procedures	Most Serious Trial is usually held before judge and jury
• theft (under $5000)	• manslaughter	• murder
• mischief (under $5000)	• assault	• treason
• fraud (under $5000)	• sexual assault	• piracy
• possession of property obtained by crime (under $5000)	• weapons offences	• bribing a judicial official
• keeping a common bawdy house	• driving while impaired (over 80 mg)	• driving while impaired (over 80 mg) causing death
• cheating at play	• resisting arrest	• robbery with firearm
• failing to comply with probation	• threatening to cause death or harm	• fleeing police (causing injury)

Why do you think there are different trial procedures for different types of offences?

Review Your Understanding

1. What types of cases does the Supreme Court of Canada handle?
2. What is the legal effect when a decision is made by the Supreme Court of Canada?
3. What types of cases are handled by the provincial courts?
4. What functions do the provincial superior courts perform?
5. Why do different criminal offences end up with different procedures?

In Criminal Law

Careers in police work or correctional services are well suited to people who are self-confident and assertive and who can remain calm in hazardous situations. Being a keen observer of people and having an ability to work both independently and as part of a team are other desirable qualities for this line of work.

For more information about different programs in criminology offered by Canadian colleges and universities,

Correctional services officer

Police officer at work

In Focus

Police Officer

Police officers are responsible for maintaining public safety and order. They enforce laws and regulations. Police assigned to criminal investigations gather evidence from crime scenes, interview witnesses, make arrests, and testify in court. Police assigned to traffic patrol enforce traffic laws, provide emergency assistance, and investigate traffic accidents. Police also visit classrooms or community centres to talk about crime prevention and safety.

Court Officer

Court officers maintain security and control of persons in custody while they are on trial. They escort the accused from jail to the court. While in court, they maintain security and order in courtrooms. They watch prisoners and all persons entering, exiting, and being held in cell areas.

A key qualification to become a court officer is the ability to work in a stressful and diverse environment. Court officers must also possess good oral communication skills to deal with members of police services and the public in a professional and tactful manner.

Correctional Services Officer

Correctional services officers watch over prisoners. They also maintain order in correctional facilities. They supervise prisoners during work periods, mealtimes, and recreational breaks. They also guard prisoners moving between correctional facilities. They monitor any potential prison disturbances and escape attempts. These officers work outdoors in all kinds of weather conditions. Indoor conditions can be noisy and overcrowded.

Career Exploration Activity

As a class, explore the career opportunities in police work and correctional services. The information you compile can be used to profile various law-related careers for a guidance bulletin-board display, or you may choose to run a law-related career fair.

1. Use the Internet or your local employment information centre, or contact the local authorities to conduct research into these careers.
2. Briefly summarize the training requirements, wage rates, working conditions, and future job prospects for police, court, and correctional officers. Record the information on index cards.

Should Marijuana Be Legalized?

Drug crimes are costly to Canadian society. More tax dollars are spent on police enforcement and trial costs than on any other type of crime. These costs include courtroom overhead; judges', prosecutors', and court officers' salaries; and legal aid. The Canadian government spends millions of dollars investigating and arresting people involved in the marijuana drug trade. Do you think this money is well spent? Recent polls showed that over 75 percent of adult Canadians think that marijuana should be decriminalized—that is, punishable by a fine instead of imprisonment. Close to 60 percent of Canadians think that marijuana should be legalized completely.

Furthermore, criminalizing marijuana raises its price. It encourages bad people to get involved. This leads to an increase in other crimes such as property damage, assaults, theft, robbery, and murder. Revenue from growing and selling marijuana in Canada is estimated at over $30 billion a year. Annual production in British Columbia alone is valued at $6 billion, making it the largest industry in the province! Some people feel that we should legalize possessing and using marijuana, and let the government regulate and tax its use as it does with alcohol.

Substances that alter a person's cognitive functions are classified as illegal drugs. Otherwise, tea, beer, cola, and aspirin would be lumped in with heroin and cocaine. Marijuana users often experience relaxation and are more aware of things. They may feel that time is slowing down, and have a rapid heartbeat. But, marijuana is not a narcotic. This fact has been ruled by the courts to be irrelevant in its legal definition, because marijuana is still on the list of substances classified as a controlled drug by the federal government. Controlled drugs are classified as criminal because the Canadian government has decided that they are harmful.

According to the *Controlled Drugs and Substances Act*, it is an offence to possess one single marijuana cigarette (joint). For a first-time summary conviction offence, the punishment is a fine up to $1000 and/or six months in jail. Often, police simply confiscate the marijuana and send the person on his or her way. If possessing a small amount is mostly ignored by the police, then is this law legitimate (that is, is it really a law)?

The debate over whether marijuana should be decriminalized is a hot topic in Canada today.

On One Side

Many people think drug use is a serious criminal offence. They believe that higher fines and longer jail sentences for drug users and traffickers would reduce drug use. They point to the *Controlled Drugs and Substances Act*. They argue that marijuana use is a crime. Since the federal government has criminalized this activity, these Canadians want the police to have greater powers to search for illegal drugs so that the laws can be better enforced. They feel that the $100 million a year it costs Canadian taxpayers to enforce Canada's drug laws is money well spent. They believe that drug use is immoral. If *Criminal Code* drug laws are not enforced, society will be weakened and eventually will begin to crumble. People on this side of the debate believe that individuals have choices. If they choose to take illegal drugs, they must suffer the consequences of the criminal justice system.

On the Other Side

Other Canadians feel that stiffer penalties will not rehabilitate drug users. Those who fall victim to drug abuse should be treated rather than punished. They applaud a 2000 Ontario Court of Appeal ruling. It stated that the sections on marijuana in the *Controlled Drugs and Substances Act* are unconstitutional. These sections fail to recognize the medicinal uses of the drug (such as treating glaucoma). In fact, many important organizations think the government should decriminalize the use and possession of marijuana. The Canadian Medical Association, the Canadian Bar Association, and the Canadian Council of Churches are some of the groups that favour decriminalization.

The Bottom Line

Questions about decriminalizing marijuana are not black and white with easy answers. Should adults who smoke small amounts of marijuana once in a while be free to choose for themselves, as long as they do not harm anyone else? Should drug addicts be considered victims who require treatment? What about driving and doing drugs? Canada's lawmakers have been reluctant to deal with the issue. There is great pressure from our neighbour to the south, the United States, to maintain marijuana as an illegal substance. The courts have consistently refused to overturn possession convictions. They also send a clear message to the federal government when they write, "It is up to Parliament to change the law, not the courts." The federal government was considering decriminalizing possession of small amounts of marijuana in 2005. The "anti-drug" pressure from the various sources quickly ended these reforms.

More details on drug laws in Canada will be discussed in Chapter 7.

For Discussion

1. Section 7 of the *Charter of Rights and Freedoms* guarantees liberty. What does this mean in relation to marijuana use?

2. Why do you think support for the legalization of marijuana has grown steadily over the past few years?

3. Why are alcohol and tobacco legal, but marijuana is illegal?

4. What does the *Controlled Drugs and Substances Act* say about marijuana use and possession?

5. What are the costs to Canadian society of criminalizing marijuana use?

6. What do you think is the difference between the terms "legalized" and "decriminalized"? Explain.

Chapter Review

Chapter Highlights

- Criminal law deals with offences against society and may punish those found guilty of a crime with imprisonment.
- Through punishment, the criminal law aims to deter people from committing offences.
- Criminal law is the responsibility of the federal government and is found in the *Criminal Code*.
- Some activities are prohibited by provincial laws, but they are not criminalized. Examples include traffic violations, loitering, and drinking alcohol in public, for which fines are levied.
- Summary conviction offences are minor criminal offences (called misdemeanours in the United States).
- Indictable offences are more serious criminal offences (called felonies in the United States).
- The Crown attorney must prove its case beyond a reasonable doubt.
- *Actus reus* (the external act) and *mens rea* (the internal intention) must exist to prove someone is guilty of a crime.
- Aiding and abetting a criminal is a crime.
- All criminal cases start in the criminal division of a provincial court.
- Provincial court judges try summary conviction and minor indictable offences.
- The superior court of each province has a trial division and an appeal division for important criminal cases.
- An accused has a choice of trial procedures for more serious indictable offences.
- The most serious indictable offences are tried by judge and jury.
- Supreme Court of Canada decisions must be followed by all lower courts across the country.

Check Your Knowledge

1. What is a crime, and how is it dealt with in Canadian society?
2. Explain the types of criminal offences and provide an example of each.
3. Distinguish between the *actus reus* and *mens rea* in a criminal offence and provide an example for each.
4. Summarize the structure of the criminal court system and identify the types of cases heard in each court.

Apply Your Learning

5. In groups, examine the Law Reform Commission of Canada's four conditions that must exist for something to be considered a crime. Apply them to cyberbullying. What are your conclusions regarding each of the four conditions as they relate to this offence?
6. In the famous case of *R. v. Wilkins*, 1964, a police officer parked his motorcycle but left it running while he went to write a ticket. Wilkins hopped on and drove the motorcycle a short distance away to play a joke on the officer. His motive was to play a prank, but he was charged with the theft of the motorcycle. Theft requires "the intent to convert an object to one's own use." Should the accused be found guilty of theft or not? Explain why.

Communicate Your Understanding

7. Online "cyber abetting" was at issue in the 2008 murder of Toronto teen Stefanie Rengel, who was stabbed six times in the stomach and left to die on the sidewalk near her family's home. The accused is a teenage girl who cannot be named under the *Youth Criminal Justice Act*. Based on the Internet

postings of the accused in this case, the Crown attorney alleges that she incited the heinous murder out of jealousy. Police searched through her Facebook account, cellphone records, and online communications and found evidence that she encouraged (abetted) her boyfriend to commit the murder.

Should your e-mail, MSN conversations, Facebook profile, and other Internet communications be your private affair, or should the authorities be able to monitor what is happening online? At issue is your constitutional right to freedom of expression versus the *Criminal Code* restrictions on aiding, abetting, counselling, and conspiring. Develop arguments to either support or criticize the use of online postings in criminal cases.

8. "The law exists to protect society and individuals and keep order." Based on the following 2004 statistics from Statistics Canada, develop arguments that would support the above statement:

- 94 percent of Canadians stated they were satisfied with their personal safety; this is up from 86 percent in 1993 and 91 percent in 1999.

- 42 percent of women were confident using public transportation after work (compared to 71 percent of men).

- People in the Atlantic provinces felt the most secure in their personal safety—ranging from 99 percent in Newfoundland and Labrador to 95 percent in Nova Scotia.

9. From the Internet or sources such as newspapers and magazines, collect five criminal law articles on cases that have not yet gone to trial. Write a brief summary of the facts of each case. Consult the *Criminal Code* and do the following:

a) For each case, indicate the offence committed, the *actus reus*, the *mens rea*, and the maximum penalty for the offence.

b) Summarize the evidence that you think the Crown prosecutor and defence counsel might present.

c) Indicate whether you think the accused will be found guilty or not guilty at trial. Give reasons for your decision.

Develop Your Thinking

10. Topics such as gangs, organized crime, group assault, or "teen swarmings" have received increased attention from the media. The Toronto Police Service statistics suggest that, on average, six swarmings a day occur in Toronto.

a) Has there been an increase in the frequency, brutality, and random nature of group assaults in your area?

b) Should there be an 11:00 p.m. curfew placed on teens aged 16 and under?

c) Does goth, heavy metal, or hip-hop music incite teens to commit crimes in groups?

d) Are all gangs "organized criminals"?

e) Should there be a restriction placed on who and how many other youths teens can associate with?

11. In groups, brainstorm and list some of the causes of crime. Develop a second list of suggestions about how these causes could be eliminated. How realistic are these suggestions? What limitations exist? Share your conclusions.

5

The Police—Investigation, Arrest, and Bringing the Accused to Trial

What You Should Know

- What is a proper and lawful arrest in criminal law?
- What are the legal rights of a person accused of committing a crime?
- What procedure do police follow in the investigation of a suspect?
- What are the various pre-trial legal procedures?

Chapter at a Glance

5.1 Introduction

5.2 Arrest

5.3 Duties of Police Officers

5.4 Legal Rights and Search Laws

5.5 Release and Bail Procedures

5.6 Awaiting Trial

Selected Key Terms

accused

appearance notice

arrest

bail hearing

citizen's arrest

custody

detain

disclosure

evidence

plea negotiation

preliminary hearing

reasonable and probable grounds

search

search warrant

warrant

This man was one of six people arrested after police found 2500 kilograms of hashish in a sailboat docked at Tangier, Nova Scotia. What do you already know about the steps involved in making an arrest?

5.1 Introduction

An arrest can happen either at the same time a crime is committed or after a long police investigation. In other words, the police may catch the suspect in the heat of the moment. In such cases, the suspect is "caught in the act." Or, they may gather evidence over time and then get a warrant to arrest the suspect.

In either case, the person charged has certain legal rights to protect him or her during the arrest and trial procedures. The person charged is now referred to as the accused, and no longer as the suspect. These rights are listed in sections 7 to 14 of the *Charter of Rights and Freedoms*. They ensure that the accused is protected as he or she moves through our criminal justice system. These rights protect the accused against possible unfair treatment from police officers, judges, and correctional officers, and even from the lawmakers in the federal government. (For more about the Charter, see Chapter 2, pages 48–60.)

Section 7 of the Charter guarantees the life, liberty, and personal security of all Canadians. It also demands that governments respect the basic principles of justice whenever they intrude on (interfere with) those rights. Section 7 has an impact in criminal matters. An accused person risks losing his or her liberty if convicted. The accused must have done something serious that is prohibited by the *Criminal Code* for it to be justifiable to take away her or his freedom. Imprisoning a person who has acted reasonably and has not done anything illegal offends the principles of fundamental justice.

Also in section 7, there is the right to security of the person. This means that Canadians have the right to be safe from physical and psychological harm. In criminal matters, this could apply to police officers using excessive force or other means such as threats or verbal abuse in their investigation to gain information or a confession from a suspect. This would be an example of harming the well-being of an accused person.

When police place someone under arrest, they have to follow certain rules to ensure that the person's Charter rights are being upheld.

Limits on Police Behaviour

During a police investigation, limits are placed on police officers and the actions they can take to arrest someone. One of the most important limits is that officers usually must obtain a search warrant properly before conducting a search. To do so, the officers must apply to a judge or justice of the peace and show concrete reasons—known in legal terms as **reasonable and probable grounds**—that there is evidence of a crime. To establish whether or not the

reasonable and probable grounds facts that would cause an average person to believe beyond a mere suspicion

police acted on reasonable and probable grounds, the officers must show that they were objective. They also must show that a clear connection between the search and a criminal offence was evident. The court will consider whether the officers were being reasonable; that is, what the average person would believe to be sensible and logical. It also considers whether the connection to the **accused** was probable. It cannot be random, impulsive, or even based on a hunch.

At trial, if the judge decides the evidence was obtained unlawfully by the police, in most cases it is not allowed (known as inadmissible) in the court of law. This may be the case if the accused was searched improperly, either without a warrant or in violation of the Charter.

accused the person charged with an offence; the defendant in a criminal trial

  Activity

To learn more about arrest procedures,

 Go to Nelson Social Studies

5.2 Arrest

Even if the police think that a suspect has committed a crime, they cannot simply **arrest** that suspect; they must have reasonable and probable grounds that the person was involved in a crime. When police have established that they have grounds, they are then ready to apprehend and charge the suspect. At this point, the police can do one of three things:

1. Issue an appearance notice.
2. Arrest the suspect.
3. Obtain a warrant for arrest.

arrest to detain a person legally and to charge him or her with a criminal offence

Mother Goose and Grimm

If arrested by police, you are required to give only your name and address.

Appearance Notice

If the police believe that the accused is not a threat to others and will show up at a bail hearing, they issue an **appearance notice** for summary conviction offences and less serious indictable offences. This notice includes the offence(s) the accused has been charged with and the time and place of the required court appearance. This notice will be issued by the police officer only if he or she believes that the accused will appear in court on the given date. The officer will then swear a complaint under oath that a crime has been committed. This is known as swearing an **information** before a judge or justice of the peace. The information is the basis of all charges.

appearance notice a legal document stating the criminal charge and the court date

information the starting document for a less serious offence

Arresting the Suspect

For more serious indictable offences, the police arrest the suspect and take him or her into custody. The purpose of the arrest is to lay charges, preserve evidence, and prevent the accused from fleeing or committing further offences. Any officer can arrest a suspect without a warrant if there are reasonable grounds to believe that someone has committed or is about to commit an offence. The familiar Miranda warning heard on American television shows and movies—"You have the right to remain silent. Anything you say can and will be used against you in a court of law…"—is similar to what in Canada is called reading the caution to the accused.

Steps in a Lawful Arrest

1. Notice on arrest (identifying herself or himself): "I am Police Constable Lemieux."

2. Advising the accused that he or she is under arrest and the offence charged with: "I am arresting you, (suspect's name), for (brief description of the criminal act(s) the officer believes the suspect has committed)."

3. Caution 1, right to counsel (lawyer): "It is my duty to inform you that you have the right to retain and instruct counsel without delay. Do you understand?" This includes the right to free advice from a legal aid lawyer and a phone number to reach such a person.

4. Caution 2, right to remain silent: "You are charged with (state the criminal offence). Do you wish to say anything in answer to the charge? You are not obligated to say anything unless you wish to do so, but whatever you say may be given in as evidence…."

5. Physically touching the accused to signify custody (this often involves handcuffs).

When arresting a suspect, the police must do all these things.

If the accused resists arrest, the police have the legal authority to use "as much force as is necessary" to prevent an escape. The trial judge decides if the police used necessary force, or if they unfairly harmed the accused (infringing on his or her "security of the person"). The use of more force than necessary can result in criminal or civil assault charges against the officer.

In certain circumstances, police are allowed to use serious or deadly force. They can do so in the following situations:

- The behaviour of a suspect might cause serious harm or death to others.

- The suspect flees to escape arrest.

- There are no alternative means to prevent escape.

If a suspect tries to escape, the police may be allowed to use serious and even deadly force in certain situations.

summons an order to appear in criminal court

warrant an order by a judge to arrest the accused for listed alleged offences

citizen's arrest detainment by a civilian of a person believed to have committed a crime

Warrant for Arrest

If they have difficulty finding the accused, police can go before a judge or justice of the peace and receive a document called a **summons**. It orders the accused to appear in court at a certain time and place. It is delivered to the accused by a sheriff or a deputy.

If the police can demonstrate to the judge that the accused will not appear in court voluntarily, the judge will issue an arrest **warrant**. It names the accused (or describes the accused if the name is unknown), lists the offence(s), and orders the arrest of the accused. If the judge does not think the police have provided reasonable grounds to believe that the accused has committed the offence, he or she will not issue a summons or a warrant.

Citizen's Arrest

A regular citizen can make an arrest if he or she witnesses a criminal act or believes that a suspect has just committed one. This belief must be reasonable. The arresting citizen cannot use excessive force and must surrender the suspect to the police as soon as possible. The arresting citizen should state clearly that she or he is placing the suspect under arrest. If the arresting citizen acts in an unreasonable way, he or she can be sued. **Citizen's arrest** is covered in section 494 of the *Criminal Code*.

A security officer or a store detective is allowed to make a citizen's arrest.

R. v. Asante-Mensah, 2003 SCC 38 (CanLII)

For more information, Go to Nelson Social Studies

In 1991, a taxi driver repeatedly "scooped" fares at Pearson International Airport in Toronto, contrary to regulations. He jumped the line in front of other taxis and picked up passengers ahead of his turn. An airport inspector approached the accused, touched his shoulder, and told him that he was under arrest for trespassing, and that he would be **detained** for police. The accused attempted to get into his taxi, but the inspector blocked his way. During the confrontation, the accused shoved his car door into the inspector. The inspector backed off, and the accused fled. The driver was charged with resisting arrest. At trial, the judge acquitted the accused because the inspector was not authorized to make an arrest. The Ontario Court of Appeal disagreed, setting aside the acquittal and substituting a conviction.

In a 9–0 judgment in July 2003, the Supreme Court of Canada upheld the conviction. The court wrote that the word "arrest" is well understood in common law. It is initiated by words accompanied by physical touching or submission, and ends with delivery to the police. As with all arrests, force may be employed if it is reasonable under the circumstances.

- Do you think regular citizens should be allowed to make an arrest? Explain.

Review Your Understanding

1. Why is there sometimes conflict between the police and the public when arrests are made?

2. Why is it important to know your legal rights?

3. Describe in detail the three choices available to police when they believe an offence has been committed.

4. Why must police swear an information before a judge or justice of the peace?

5. a) How much force may police use when making an arrest?

   b) What can happen if police use too much force?

   c) Should police be forbidden to use any kind of force when making an arrest? Explain.

 Did You Know?

Section 494 of the *Criminal Code* gives store detectives, security guards, private detectives, and ordinary citizens the authority to make arrests.

5.3 Duties of Police Officers

Adequate and effective police services must include a minimum of all of the following core police services:

- crime prevention
- law enforcement
- assistance to victims of crime
- maintenance of public order
- emergency response
- investigation of crime

In Canada, policing is carried out at three levels: federal, provincial, and municipal. The Royal Canadian Mounted Police (RCMP) is the federal (national) police force. Its counterpart in the United States is the Federal Bureau of Investigation (FBI). The provincial police forces in Ontario and Québec are the Ontario Provincial Police (OPP) and the Sûreté du Québec (SQ). Their counterparts in the United States are the state troopers, such as the New York State Police. In all other provinces and territories, the RCMP also serves as the provincial police force because of smaller populations. Municipal police, such as the Vancouver Police Department, enforce criminal and municipal laws. They mainly work within the city's boundaries. The RCMP across Canada, the OPP in Ontario, and the SQ in Québec act as municipal police in towns that do not have their own police force.

Policing in Canada is carried out at three levels. In Toronto, for example, policing is done by the Toronto Police Service, the OPP, and the RCMP.

Police Conduct and the Police Services Act

Police conduct is controlled in four main ways:

1. legislatively (through statutes such as the *Police Services Act*)
2. judicially (years of common law precedents)
3. administratively (the Ontario Civilian Commission on Police Services oversees police conduct in Ontario)
4. constitutionally (legal rights in sections 7 to 10 of the Charter)

Police officers often have to make quick decisions to save lives—their own as well as others. They have to act reasonably because they are held responsible for their conduct and behaviour when carrying out their duties. If they break the rules of police conduct, their evidence may be refused, which can result in an acquittal. In rare situations, the officers involved can be charged under criminal law or sued under civil law.

Each province has a public board that oversees police operations and reviews citizen complaints about police conduct. Each province also has a provincial police services act that provides the legal framework governing police officers and services. The legislation sets out the duties of police officers. It governs what happens if officers do not discharge their duties and are charged with misconduct. These acts also include the procedures for dealing with public complaints about the conduct of police officers. Police Services also discipline their officers when appropriate.

? Did You Know?

In 2006, Bill 103 created the Police Complaints Commissioner.

Principles of Canadian Police Services

1. the need to ensure the safety and security of all persons and property
2. the importance of safeguarding the fundamental rights guaranteed by the *Canadian Charter of Rights and Freedoms* and the various provincial human rights laws
3. the need for co-operation between the providers of police services and the communities they serve
4. the importance of respecting victims of crime and understanding their needs
5. the need to be sensitive about the pluralistic (diverse) and multicultural character of our society
6. the need to ensure that police forces are representative of the communities they serve

Canadian police services are provided according to these six principles.

It is important for police officers to respect victims of crime and understand their needs.

 Case

R. v. Harrison, 2008 ONCA 85 (CanLII)

For more information, **Go to Nelson Social Studies**

On October 22, 2004, Bradley Harrison was driving his car, which was registered in Alberta, through Ontario on a trip from Vancouver to Toronto. A police officer decided to stop the accused's car for no legal reason; Harrison was driving at the speed limit but was missing a front licence plate. The officer testified that he realized that in Alberta it was not an offence to drive a vehicle without a front plate. After stopping the car, the officer did a search of the vehicle. He found 35 kilograms (77 pounds) of cocaine, and Harrison was charged with trafficking. The street value was determined to be between $2.5 and $5 million.

continues...

R. v. Harrison, 2008 ONCA 85 (CanLII)

Justice Eleanore Cronk, who was appointed to the Ontario Court of Appeal on July 31, 2001, was one of the judges who presided over the appeal.

A key issue for the trial judge was the admissibility into evidence of the seized cocaine. He allowed the cocaine as evidence despite his finding of serious and flagrant breaches of the accused's sections 8 and 9 Charter rights. The trial judge felt that the officer had no legal grounds to stop the vehicle and seriously infringed the accused's Charter rights by searching the car.

On appeal to the Ontario Court of Appeal, the majority of the court held that, even though it considered the officer's conduct to be "extremely serious," it would not keep the evidence out of court. The court recognized that the officer knew he did not have reasonable or probable grounds to stop the car or search it, but proceeded anyway. Thus, the court approved using evidence obtained through police misconduct. The court's reasoning was that, even though this diminishing of Charter protections makes our justice system look bad, it is outweighed by the need to keep a large amount of cocaine off the streets.

The court noted that, under the *Charter of Rights and Freedoms*, improperly obtained evidence is not automatically excluded. In Canada, such evidence is to be excluded if its admission "would bring the administration of justice into disrepute." According to the judges in this case, the officer's actions, as bad as they were, "pale in comparison to the criminality involved in the possession for the purpose of distribution of 77 pounds of cocaine."

In her dissent, Justice Cronk was critical of the majority. She said they were minimizing the seriousness of the Charter violations. She felt that, if courts continue to weaken Charter protections, the public may become accustomed to police misconduct. This may cause Canadians to question our justice system. This will eventually "bring the administration of justice into disrepute." The court's decision was appealed to the Supreme Court of Canada.

For Discussion

1. Does this case mean that the courts are condoning police misconduct?

2. What is worse, a breach of Charter rights by admitting tainted evidence, or allowing a serious crime to go unpunished?

3. In 2007, Supreme Court of Canada Justice Binnie said, "A society that valued police efficiency and effectiveness above other values would be a police state." What do you think Justice Binnie would say about this case?

4. Conduct an Internet search to see what decision the Supreme Court reached. Do you agree with the court's decision? Why or why not?

Police Duties

Police officers have many duties to perform, all of which help ensure public safety. Police officers are usually the first persons at a crime scene, and a large part of their duty is to establish and maintain order. To protect evidence from being tampered with, they must secure the scene of the crime from any public interference. In addition, officers must keep an accurate log (written record) of what they see and hear at the scene of the crime. These logs may provide important evidence in court.

 Activity

To learn about the Special Investigations Unit (SIU),

Go to Nelson Social Studies

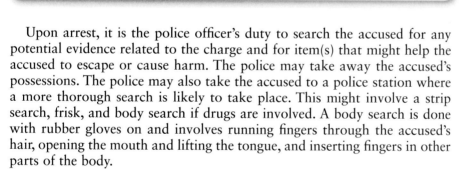

The Duties of Police Officers

- preserving the peace
- preventing crimes
- assisting victims
- apprehending criminals
- laying charges
- participating in prosecutions
- executing warrants
- performing duties that the police chief assigns
- enforcing laws
- completing training

The duties of Ontario Provincial Police (OPP) officers

Upon arrest, it is the police officer's duty to search the accused for any potential evidence related to the charge and for item(s) that might help the accused to escape or cause harm. The police may take away the accused's possessions. The police may also take the accused to a police station where a more thorough search is likely to take place. This might involve a strip search, frisk, and body search if drugs are involved. A body search is done with rubber gloves on and involves running fingers through the accused's hair, opening the mouth and lifting the tongue, and inserting fingers in other parts of the body.

These extensive body searches must be conducted by officers of the same sex as the accused. They cannot be done without reasonable and probable grounds that the accused has drugs on his or her person. Again, whether the officer had sufficient reason to conduct an invasive body search is determined by the trial judge. The police are also authorized to fingerprint and photograph the accused at this time.

The accused may also be asked to take part in a **lineup**. This is where several individuals, including the accused, line up to be identified by victims or eyewitnesses. The accused may also be asked to take a **polygraph test** (a lie detector test), or give blood, urine, DNA, or breath samples. The accused can refuse all of these requests, except in cases of impaired driving offences where blood/breath samples are required. However, the *Criminal Code* does allow police to obtain DNA samples from a suspect if a court-issued warrant is granted, even if the suspect is unwilling to provide the samples.

 Did You Know?

The *Anti-Terrorism Act* permits police to hold those suspected of planning acts of terrorism in custody. These suspects can be imprisoned without a warrant, but they must be brought before a judge within 24 hours. They can then be released after 72 hours, but only if they accept a judge's conditions for a supervised life (a type of parole without a conviction) in the community for the next 12 months. If they refuse to accept these conditions, they can be imprisoned for a year.

lineup a line of people formed by the police for identification

polygraph test a test using a device to determine if a person is telling the truth

This photograph shows how a polygraph test would be conducted. Polygraph tests are also used by the RCMP. They require that all potential recruits take a pre-employment polygraph test to verify an individual's honesty and integrity. Polygraph tests are not admissible in court as they are not considered reliable.

You and the Law

Since 2008, several Toronto-area schools have had full-time, armed, uniformed police officers assigned to develop programs to fight bullying and crime and to build relationships with students. What do you think of this idea? Should police be assigned to all city schools across Canada? Why or why not?

Review Your Understanding

1. Refer to sections 7 through 11 of the *Canadian Charter of Rights and Freedoms* (see Appendix A, pages 598–601), and summarize the legal rights of Canadians.

2. Why is it important to co-operate with the police? Under what circumstances might this not be advisable?

3. For each of the duties of a police officer, state the corresponding right of a citizen:

   a) questioning prior to arrest

   b) searching a person before arrest

   c) questioning the accused after arrest

   d) searching a person after arrest

4. What powers do the police have concerning the following: fingerprinting, requesting a lineup, administering a polygraph test, or collecting a blood sample?

5. Why would the police want to detain people and search them prior to arrest?

5.4 Legal Rights and Search Laws

The *Charter of Rights and Freedoms* outlines many rights and freedoms that all people in Canada are entitled to. The legal rights of citizens who are **detained** or arrested are outlined in sections 7 to 11 of the Charter.

detain to stop a person from leaving, or to confine someone

One of the most important rights in Canada is the right to privacy. Section 8 of the Charter states that everyone has the right to be secure against unreasonable search or seizure. Thus, the police cannot search you or your property, record you speaking, or seize your property (take by force) unless they have reasonable and probable grounds to do so.

But what does "reasonable and probable" mean? For example, the police receive a 911 call that an electronics store has just been held up at gunpoint and you are found running from the store with a laptop in one hand and a gun in the other. It is reasonable to assume that you just committed a theft and that the laptop is stolen merchandise. However, if you are standing outside the store at the time of the robbery, with nothing clearly on you to incriminate you, it is unreasonable to search you. There is no reason to believe that you have stolen any merchandise. Even if the police have a hunch that you are part of this robbery, it is not a sufficient reason for them to search you. The police must be fair because the privacy of Canadians is very important.

The police can **search** a person without a warrant if they have arrested that person or if they believe he or she is carrying a concealed weapon. This is known as "police search incident to arrest." Other than that, police cannot demand that you tell them your name or even make you stand still for a moment. The only exception is if you are driving a car. In this case, they can ask for your licence, ownership, and insurance papers. Police can also stop your car to check for the mechanics of the vehicle, but they cannot conduct a search for this reason alone. In addition, if the police can see something in your car "in plain view" (for example, alcohol, drugs, weapons, and the like), they may ask about it. However, the object of their interest must be clearly visible. For example, if you are driving a vehicle, police are not allowed to look inside a gym bag that is visible in the vehicle. They may ask you what is in the bag, but you do not have to tell them.

The police can arrest without first obtaining a **search warrant** only if they catch the person in the act or if they have reasonable and probable grounds to believe that the person has committed a crime, or is about to do so.

Did You Know?

The main purposes of a "police search incident to arrest" are as follows:

- to ensure the safety of the police and the public
- to prevent the destruction of evidence
- to discover evidence of the offence for which the accused was arrested

search the police procedure in which officers look for evidence that may be used in court

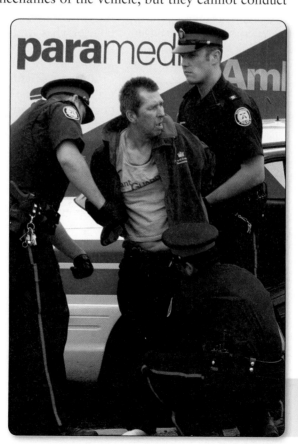

search warrant a court order authorizing police to search a specific place at a specified time

Police can search someone after placing that person under arrest.

R. v. Clayton, 2007 SCC 32 (CanLII)

For more information, **Go to Nelson Social Studies**

Early one morning in September 1999, police received a 911 call from a man who reported that he had seen four men with handguns standing near four cars in the parking lot of a night club in Brampton, Ontario. The men were described as being among a group of 10 "black guys" in the parking area. In response to the call, officers arrived immediately at the scene and set up roadblocks at both of the club's two exits. A car that did not match any of the descriptions provided by the 911 caller drove toward the exit. After stopping the car, the officers observed that the two occupants, Wendell Clayton and Troy Farmer, were black males. One officer approached the driver (Farmer), informed him about the gun complaint, and asked him to step out of the car. He protested before getting out of the car, and the officer became concerned for his own safety. The passenger, Clayton, fled but was tackled a short distance away. Once the two officers regained control of the scene, they searched the driver and passenger and found they were each carrying loaded, prohibited handguns. The men were arrested and charged with gun-related offences under the *Criminal Code*.

At trial in 2001, the judge found that the initial roadblock and stop of the accused's car was lawful. However, detaining both men and searching for handguns violated their sections 8 and 9 Charter rights. Although the judge believed there were Charter violations, he admitted the guns into evidence under section 24(2) of the Charter. Both men were convicted.

The two men appealed their convictions to the Ontario Court of Appeal. The appeal was heard in September 2004 and a unanimous judgment was given. The appellate court excluded the guns as evidence and acquitted the men on all charges.

The Crown appealed this decision to the Supreme Court of Canada, where the appeal was heard in June 2006. In a 9–0 judgment in July 2007, the top court allowed the Crown's appeal and restored the convictions. The Supreme Court dealt with the issue of what kind of reputation our criminal justice system would have if the guns were or were not allowed as evidence. Which looks worse: infringing on a person's rights, or allowing people with guns to get off? In this case, the court felt that excluding the guns would be worse. Civil liberties activists such as Alan Borovoy (you will read about him later in this chapter) felt that it was worse for the reputation of our justice system to allow unreasonable searches.

For Discussion

1. Should police be allowed to detain and question suspects if reasonable and probable grounds do not exist? Why or why not?

2. Why did the trial judge rule that the roadblock was lawful and admit the guns as evidence?

3. How do we balance an individual's Charter rights in a way that allows the police to do their job in high-pressure, dangerous situations?

4. Do you agree with the Supreme Court decision? Explain.

Police officers question a suspect at a police roadblock.

Rights on Being Searched

When someone is arrested for a crime, the police may wish to search the accused's residence to look for evidence related to the charge. Police can enter your home only with a search warrant. It is a legal court-issued document giving them authority to search. On the other hand, government officials, such as inspectors, also need warrants to enter business grounds, but it is a very different process.

Obtaining a Search Warrant

Before a warrant can be issued, police officers must swear before a justice of the peace or a judge that an offence has been committed. They must have reasonable grounds to believe that evidence of the crime exists on the property. If the information about the evidence was received from an informant, the officer must outline to the court why the informant is reliable before a warrant is issued. If the officer's testimony is accepted, a search warrant is issued.

Before searching a private residence, police must obtain a search warrant from a judge or justice of the peace.

Using a Search Warrant

A warrant can be used to search a residence only on the date indicated. The search can involve only those areas and items outlined in the warrant. A warrant is an order, issued by a justice, authorizing the officer(s) to enter a specified place to search for and seize specified property. Only the items mentioned in the warrant can be seized, unless other illegal items are found during the search. For example, the police may get a warrant to search for stolen cash from a bank robbery. If they stumble across that individual's stash of marijuana, they can legally seize that and charge the person with possession. The officers must have reasonable and probable grounds that any items seized were used when committing a crime or were obtained illegally. The officers cannot go beyond the terms of the warrant in hope of finding something illegal that would justify laying a charge. The items seized can be kept for up to three months, or for a longer period if they are needed as evidence at trial.

To obtain a search warrant, a police officer must swear an information (a document containing the evidence police have of a crime). This document must

- identify the premises specifically
- identify the criminal offence
- describe the goods they are looking for
- be signed by a judge or justice of the peace

Search Laws and Rules

Police can demand to enter a property when they are carrying a search warrant. If permission is refused, or if no one is home, the police have the right to break into the premises. However, the police are liable for any excessive force used. For example, most courts would rule it excessive if the officers took out their guns and shot the door handle off, only to find out that the door was unlocked in the first place. Anyone who answers the door can ask the police for a copy of the search warrant. If the document is not correct in every detail (for example, the wrong date or address), entry can be refused. Once inside, the police can search individuals on the premises only after arrest, unless they believe that the person possesses illegal drugs or weapons. In this case, the search can be conducted immediately. Again, the police must have reasonable and probable grounds for the search.

Police need a warrant when using electronic surveillance equipment—such as videotapes, tracking devices, or all types of recorders—that intercept private conversations. Most warrants issued to police for this purpose involve the illegal drug trade.

telewarrant a court order issued by phone, fax, or e-mail to search a place or arrest a person

This tiny microphone is concealed in a tie and can be used to collect vital evidence about drug trafficking or other crimes.

A new type of warrant is a **telewarrant**. It can be obtained by telephone, fax, or e-mail. To obtain a search warrant, a police officer usually must appear in person before a justice. Telewarrants were created for remote areas of Canada where personal appearance is too difficult. However, urban police officers are starting to use these as well. Telewarrants have enhanced police powers as they allow warrants to be obtained quickly.

Exceptions to Search Laws

There are some important exceptions to the search laws you have just learned about. Under the *Controlled Drugs and Substances Act*, the police may search any place that is not a private residence (someone's home) without a warrant if there are reasonable and probable grounds to believe that it contains illegal drugs. Anyone found inside these premises can also be searched without a warrant. These types of searches usually take place when there is no time to obtain a warrant or because of the need for a surprise entry. The police may also search for illegal weapons without a warrant in any place that is not a private residence, such as a car. Again, the police must prove to a judge that they had reasonable and probable grounds, which is not always an easy task.

R. v. Shankar, 2007 ONCA 280 (CanLII)

For more information, Go to Nelson Social Studies

Corey Shankar was driving his car without its tail lights illuminated when police pulled him over at 2:30 a.m. in late October 2004. The police asked for his licence, registration, and insurance. Shankar gave them a driver's licence in the name of Jason Singh, a yellow sticky note with insurance information handwritten on it, and a photocopy of the vehicle registration. When questioned about his name on the licence, Shankar spelled the name "Sing" rather than "Singh" and gave the wrong unit number of the address.

Based on this, the police arrested Shankar for attempting to mislead them about his identity and physically removed him from the car. Shankar told them that they were not allowed to search the car. When the police patted him down for weapons, they discovered that Shankar was wearing two bulletproof vests. He explained that he needed them because people "want to kill me." A search of the car revealed a semi-automatic hand pistol, a fully loaded ammunition clip in the trunk, and a hunting knife and fully loaded revolver in the locked glove box. At trial, Shankar did not testify or call any evidence. He was convicted on two counts of possession of loaded, prohibited firearms and public mischief.

Shankar appealed his conviction to the Ontario Court of Appeal, where the appeal was heard in March 2007. In a unanimous judgment on April 17, 2007, the court dismissed his appeal.

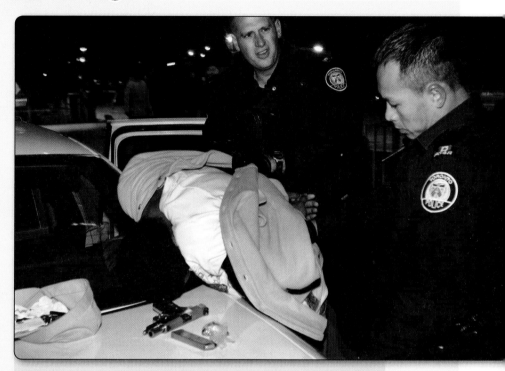

Police require reasonable and probable grounds to search a suspect.

For Discussion

1. Although the trial judge stated that the extended search was not reasonably necessary and was a section 8 Charter breach, he still admitted the guns into evidence. Why do you think he did this?

2. What arguments do you think Shankar could make to support his view that the evidence should not have been admitted pursuant to section 24(2) of the Charter?

3. What does "police search incident to arrest" mean?

4. How does "police search incident to arrest" apply in this case? Explain.

Rights on Being Detained

Section 9 of the Charter states that everyone has the right not to be arbitrarily detained or imprisoned. In other words, a person cannot be stopped, held for questioning, arrested, or put in jail unless the police have a good reason to do so. If you agree to stop and talk, however, the police have not unfairly detained you. Again, automobiles are an exception, as police are allowed to stop drivers.

Before arresting a person, police officers often ask questions to explore and gather information. Thus, when an officer stops someone for questioning, that person has been detained. For example, if the officer says, "Wait there a moment, I would like to speak with you," you have been detained. In actuality, people who are detained, but not arrested, do not have to answer any questions, including giving their names. In fact, a person can keep walking and just say, "Sorry officer, I do not wish to answer any of your questions."

Unless there are reasonable and probable grounds, a police officer is not allowed to detain and question a pedestrian.

Detention should either lead quickly (within seconds or minutes) to arrest, or the person should be free to go. Police officers are allowed to ask you, "Would you mind answering some questions?" If you refuse, they cannot stop you for longer than it takes to ask this initial question. Sometimes a police officer insists on questioning or searching an unco-operative individual. That person should immediately demand to see a lawyer and write down the officer's badge number and the names of any witnesses. There are certain situations, such as a police spot check of your car, in which you do have to give some information, such as your licence and car registration.

Citizens detained against their will have been detained illegally. They may make a complaint about police conduct, or, if arrested, challenge the validity of any evidence collected.

 Did You Know?

Although you have the right to remain silent and not answer any questions, it is generally advisable to co-operate with the police rather than antagonize them.

R. v. Dillon, 2006 CanLII 10745 (ON S.C.)

For more information, Go to Nelson Social Studies

In March 2005, two Toronto police officers became suspicious of a car they saw in the parking lot of a bar known to police as a frequent trouble spot. The officers stopped to investigate and found the accused, Duane Dillon, sitting in the driver's seat with the engine running and the car lights on. The officers pulled in behind his car, blocking it from leaving until they could determine the driver's sobriety. After talking to Dillon and seeing his red, bloodshot eyes, the officers believed that he was intoxicated. They arrested him for impaired care and control of a motor vehicle. As an incident to the arrest, the officers searched the vehicle. They found a large quantity of cocaine, marijuana, crack cocaine, and a small digital scale.

Later, at the police station, Dillon provided breath samples. The resulting Breathalyzer readings were 108 and 105 milligrams. He was then charged with possession of cocaine for the purpose of trafficking, and care and control of a motor vehicle with a blood/alcohol concentration of more than 80 milligrams of alcohol per 100 millilitres of blood (the legal limit).

At trial in the Superior Court of Justice in late November 2005, the accused argued that his section 9 Charter rights were violated. The evidence seized and the Breathalyzer readings should be excluded from trial.

- What do you think the court decided? Explain.

Rights on Being Arrested

An accused's request to contact a lawyer must be honoured immediately. A duty counsel is a criminal defence lawyer employed by the government or legal aid, to assist accused persons at their first appearance. Police stations also provide a list of defence lawyers' phone numbers and a private phone for consultation at the station. The accused can refuse to answer any further questions, apart from the basic information necessary to complete the charge, such as name, address, occupation, and date of birth.

A request by an accused to speak with a lawyer must be granted in a reasonable amount of time.

One study found that almost 60 percent of accused persons gave verbal statements and 70 percent gave written statements to police before contacting a lawyer. Why do people make these statements? One reason is that police are good at encouraging people to talk. Another reason is that people often believe they can talk themselves out of the situation. A third reason is that people think that not talking creates a bad impression. However, any statements volunteered to the police will be used as evidence against the person.

Section 10 of the Charter states that on arrest or detention, everyone has the right to the following:

- to be informed of the reasons

- to retain and instruct counsel (and to be informed of that right)

- to have the validity of the detention determined by way of habeas corpus (Latin for "produce the body") and to be released if the detention is not lawful (illegal)

If you are arrested or detained, you must be told the reason right away. You must be aware of the seriousness of the situation so the police cannot just put you in handcuffs and say, "Oh, we want to chat with you for a moment" without telling you what the charges are. Also, the police must tell you of your right to a lawyer. If you say you want a lawyer, police must stop questioning you until you have had a chance to speak privately with a lawyer. The police must tell you about **legal aid** and **duty counsel** and give you a phone book and a phone. Police must also provide you with the toll-free number for legal aid.

legal aid legal services paid for by taxpayers, available to persons unable to afford a lawyer

duty counsel a government lawyer who provides legal advice to those just arrested or brought before the court

Why does this cartoon not apply in Canada? Explain.

R. v. Singh, 2007 SCC 48 (CanLII)

For more information, Go to Nelson Social Studies

Jagrup Singh was charged with second-degree murder in April 2002 after an innocent bystander was killed by a stray bullet while standing just inside the door of a pub in Surrey, British Columbia. Police never found a murder weapon or any forensic evidence linking Singh to the shooting. However, he was identified from a police photo lineup by a doorman and a witness who were shown videotape footage of three Indo-Canadian men who had been in the pub earlier that night.

Singh was advised of his section 10(b) Charter right to counsel and privately consulted with a lawyer. The police officer questioning Singh knew this. Although Singh invoked his constitutional right to remain silent 18 times, the officer continued to interrogate Singh, urging him to ignore his lawyer's advice. Singh never confessed to the murder, but made incriminating statements by admitting to being in the pub and by identifying himself in the videotape.

At trial, Singh's defence lawyer challenged the admissibility of his statements as they infringed on Singh's Charter rights. The judge admitted the statements, believing that the admissions came freely and were not the result of the police breaking down the accused. The jury convicted Singh. He appealed his conviction to the British Columbia Court of Appeal, where his appeal was heard in May 2006. In a unanimous judgment in June 2006, the appellate court upheld the trial judgment and affirmed Singh's conviction.

Singh appealed this decision to the Supreme Court of Canada, where the appeal was heard on May 23, 2007. In a sharply divided 5–4 judgment on November 1, 2007, the court upheld his conviction. The four dissenting judges were very critical of expanding police interrogation powers and lessening an accused person's right to silence.

For Discussion

1. What specific Charter right did Singh argue was violated?

2. The Supreme Court majority stated that, while the individual has the right to remain silent, it does not mean that the authorities cannot question him. Do you agree? Why or why not?

3. The Supreme Court minority stated that the individual has the right to remain silent and that the police were wrong to continue to question Singh after he had invoked his constitutional right. Do you agree? Why or why not?

4. This decision increases police powers as it suggests that an accused's right to silence is not always protected. Is this a good thing or a bad thing? Explain.

Legal Aid

According to the Charter, all Canadians have the "right to retain and instruct counsel without delay" for criminal cases. If the accused cannot afford a lawyer, he or she can apply for legal aid. Legal services are provided free of charge to those accused of crimes who cannot afford to hire a lawyer. Court-appointed lawyers are paid for by tax dollars. Legal aid is generally granted to individuals who receive social assistance or to those whose family incomes are low. People receiving legal aid can choose which lawyer will represent them. Critics argue that the justice system is flawed. Only the very poor or very rich in our society have easy access to lawyers. It is for this reason that people have pushed for a public legal insurance program, similar to provincial health care, since legal costs can quickly skyrocket.

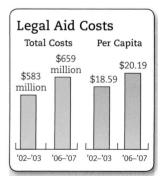

Legal aid spending in Canada, 2002–2007

custody in criminal law, actual imprisonment or physical detention

bail hearing a hearing to decide whether an accused can be released from jail before trial and with what conditions

Finally, section 10(c) states that all accused persons have the right to tell their story to a judge or justice of the peace, who will decide within 24 hours if they should remain in **custody**. This is called a **bail hearing**. If the judge decides that your detention is not legal, you must be released. This is called habeas corpus. It was originally used in medieval Britain and was a writ requiring that a prisoner be brought to court to determine the legality of the confinement. Today, it guarantees that the accused be brought before a judge. Habeas corpus has been incorporated into many international covenants on civil and political rights.

Review Your Understanding

1. Describe how a search warrant is obtained and used.
2. What is a telewarrant and how does it increase police powers?
3. Outline the important exceptions to search laws for illegal drug and gun offences.
4. List and explain the steps a police officer must go through when making a lawful arrest.
5. List three rights a Canadian has on being detained or arrested.

5.5 Release and Bail Procedures

After being arrested, a person may be released on the spot. This may be when police officers believe that the accused presents no further danger and will appear on the trial date. Others are taken to the police station, where the police record the criminal charges and take fingerprints and photographs. Some of these people will also be released, usually if they are charged with less serious offences. If the police believe that an accused may commit further offences, is a threat to the victim or witness, will interfere with the investigation, or will not appear in court, she or he may be detained until a bail hearing takes place.

When a person is arrested and taken to the police station, police take fingerprints of the accused.

Accused persons must be brought before a judge or justice of the peace for a bail hearing within 24 hours. Bail is money or property guaranteed to the court to ensure that the accused will return to court at a later date. If the accused fails to appear on the court date, the person who posted bail (called the surety) will lose his or her money or property. If an accused person is considered to be dangerous or a flight risk (likely not to appear on the court date, known as skipping bail), the bail is denied and the accused must remain in custody until trial.

There is now less emphasis on the payment of money as a condition of being released. This discriminates against the poor. Generally, if a person pleads not guilty and promises to appear at the court date, the judge will release the accused on bail conditions. Conditions can include a curfew, restrictions on where the accused can be (school, work), and that he or she cannot be in the company of any co-accused or the victim.

For more serious offences such as murder, or if the accused were charged while out on bail on another charge, that person must convince the court that he or she should not stay in custody and should be released until the court date appearance. This is known as **reverse onus**. It is now up to the accused to prove this to the court. Normally, he or she would be considered innocent until proven guilty by the Crown. On a murder charge, for example, the accused is responsible for proving that he or she poses no threat to society and will appear in court when so ordered before being released. For lesser criminal offences, it is up to the assistant Crown attorney to "show cause" (prove) that the accused should not be released.

reverse onus when the burden of proof is placed on the defence rather than the Crown

undertaking a document in which the accused agrees to appear in court as required

recognizance a signed guarantee by the accused to appear in court as required and to abide by the terms

Judicial Release Procedures

If released, the accused is required to sign an **undertaking** and to live up to the conditions set by the court. These conditions might include a curfew, orders not to associate with certain friends or go to certain places, and having to report to a police station once a week. These regulations are designed to help the accused avoid further trouble with the law before the court hearing. The accused might also be required to sign a **recognizance**. This document states that the accused recognizes that he or she is charged with an offence and that he or she promises to appear in court on a certain date.

An accused may need to sign a recognizance. A signed recognizance document is a promise that an accused will appear in court on a specific day and time.

Release Denied

If the accused is not released by the judge or justice of the peace, he or she is entitled to appeal the decision to a higher court. If, for any reason, the accused is kept in prison without being arrested, or is denied a bail hearing, an application for a writ of habeas corpus can be made. As you have already learned, this writ requires the accused to appear in court, to swear that he or she has been denied these rights, and to ask for release. A judge rules on the application, and, if the writ is granted, the accused is released.

You Be the Judge

R. v. Hall, 2002 SCC 64 (CanLII)

For more information, Go to Nelson Social Studies

In 1999, a woman's body was found with 37 wounds, and her assailant had tried to cut off her head. The brutal murder caused much public concern and general fear. Based on compelling evidence linking the accused to the crime, David Scott Hall was charged with first-degree murder. He applied for bail and was denied. This was not because of fears for public safety or concerns that he would not appear in court. The judge denied bail "to maintain confidence in the administration of justice."

Hall appealed this decision. The Superior Court judge dismissed his writ of habeas corpus application. The Ontario Court of Appeal affirmed the decision. The Supreme Court of Canada upheld this decision by a 5–4 decision. Five judges agreed that denying bail in order to maintain confidence in the administration of justice infringes on the presumption of innocence and section 11(e) of the *Charter of Rights and Freedoms*. Section 11(e) guarantees a right "not

to be denied reasonable bail without just cause." But they felt that because public confidence is essential to the proper functioning of the bail system and the justice system as a whole, Hall should not be granted bail. A reasonable member of the community would be satisfied that denying Hall bail is necessary to maintain confidence in the administration of justice. The provision is not too broad. It strikes an appropriate balance between the rights of the accused and the need to maintain justice in the community.

Four judges disagreed, saying that liberty was at the heart of a free and democratic society. This includes the right to be presumed innocent until proven guilty and specifically the right to bail. The dissenting justices held that the presumption of innocence was the principle behind the bail system. It was harmed by not granting Hall bail.

- What judgment would you render on Hall's request to be released on bail? Explain your answer.

Fingerprints, Photographs, and Biometrics

People who are charged with indictable offences and are released may be fingerprinted and photographed before being released. Biometrics can also be used. This is a science that establishes individuals' identity by measuring their physical features, for example, their nose, eyes, lips, ears, and hairline. It is based on the idea that the distances between someone's features can be represented by a mathematical pattern.

If people are acquitted of a crime, they do not automatically have the right to have those records removed from police files. The federal government has not addressed this issue. It is even difficult to have files destroyed in cases where someone is mistakenly arrested and fingerprinted.

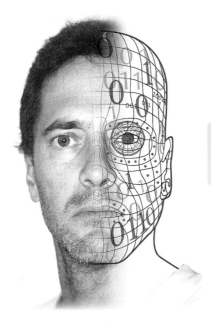

Why do you think gambling casinos and some police forces are using biometric technology?

Security or Freedom in Our Society?

Maintaining the balance between individual rights and society's safety and security is a concern raised in many criminal cases. Too much emphasis on individual rights and freedoms can make police work too difficult. It can leave society at risk because dangerous criminals may not be captured. However, too much emphasis on protecting society can result in a "police state," where individuals have limited rights and are powerless against the state and police intrusion. It is up to us, the voting public, to maintain the proper balance between freedom and security. The public can contribute by taking part in public affairs and holding police and politicians to the high standards set by our laws. In addition, police must remain aware of their duty to society and to individuals and improve their practices to comply with the powers granted to them.

 You and the Law

The police see several students hanging around in a park. With no reasonable or probable grounds, the police search all of the students' backpacks. A gun is found in one of the backpacks. Which is more important in this case: the student's legal rights, or society's security and safety? Explain.

Review Your Understanding

1. Following arrest, under what circumstances is the accused more likely to be released until his or her court appearance? When is someone not likely to be released?

2. How could it be argued that reverse onus breaks the rule that someone is presumed innocent until proven guilty? How could its use be justified in our society?

3. Why is habeas corpus an important legal right in a civil democracy?

4. What happens to the fingerprints and photographs of people who are acquitted of a crime? Do you agree with this procedure?

5. Why is it important to maintain the balance of individual rights and the protection of society as a whole? In your opinion, is this balance being achieved?

5.6 Awaiting Trial

When awaiting trial, the accused should consult a criminal defence lawyer. He or she should reveal everything that is connected to the case, allowing the lawyer to prepare the best possible defence. However, if the accused admits to the lawyer, "I did it," the lawyer cannot say that his or her client did not commit the crime. All the lawyer can do is attack the Crown's case. To prepare for trial, lawyers will study legal texts and laws related to the offence. They interview witnesses, and examine previous court decisions and precedents to gather the necessary background for the case. The accused has the right to make suggestions to the lawyer. If there is a serious disagreement, the accused can change lawyers, or the lawyer can withdraw from the case.

An accused should consult with a lawyer so that his or her lawyer can prepare the best possible defence.

Disclosure

disclosure all evidence against the accused that the Crown must reveal to the defence early in the proceedings

Disclosure is one of the most important features of our criminal justice system. It ensures a fair trial for the accused. Prior to trial, Crown attorneys must disclose all evidence to the defence, whether they intend to use it or not. However, the only thing the defence attorney has to disclose to the Crown is if he or she plans to put forward an alibi defence (that the accused was somewhere else when the offence occurred). This is so the Crown has time to investigate the alibi. The Crown must show its evidence to ensure justice for the accused. The accused needs to fully understand the Crown's case and properly prepare a defence.

After disclosure has been received, there will be a preliminary hearing at which the expected evidence is shown to a judge. If the judge or Crown concludes that there is not enough evidence to proceed, the charges might be dropped.

Collecting Evidence

Before a criminal trial, both the Crown and the defence may examine all the items and information collected by the police in their investigation. The items and information are collectively known as **evidence**. Evidence might include weapons, clothing, traces of blood or other fluids, or fingerprints. Some of these items will be tendered (submitted) to the court as evidence in the trial. Evidence may also include DNA and other **forensic science** tests. Often shortened to forensics, this is the application of science to legal problems. The term is used most often in connection with an autopsy. An autopsy is an examination by a coroner to determine the cause of death. Forensic scientists can find clues in samples of blood and other bodily fluids. They can also find clues in teeth, bones, hair, fingerprints, handwriting, clothing fibres, and other items. These clues can help to determine the guilt or innocence of the accused.

evidence anything that is used to determine the truth in a court of law

forensic science the application of scientific techniques to criminal investigations

Forensic scientists gather clues to a case by examining evidence left at the scene of a crime such as bodily fluids, hair, fingerprints, clothing, and so on. These clues can help establish the guilt or innocence of an accused.

All About Law DVD

"Cold Case" from
All About Law DVD

DNA matching is a technique based on the fact that every individual's cell contains a unique form of the complex chemical deoxyribonucleic acid (DNA). The unique profile of each person's DNA makes DNA matching possible. This is a powerful tool that allows the Crown to enter a DNA match as evidence. For example, a hair sample matching that of the accused found on the victim's body at the scene of the crime is strong evidence in a murder trial. DNA matching can also be used by the defence to show that there is no match between the accused and the crime scene evidence. Police obtain DNA samples from suspects with consent, or on rare occasions, when a warrant is issued. Collecting DNA is considered one of the most invasive searches as it collects the most private information.

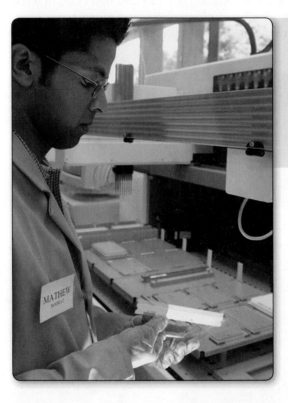

The RCMP has a National DNA Data Bank in Ottawa that stores the genetic profiles of people convicted of serious crimes. The data bank has been used to solve many past crimes and to uncover wrongful convictions.

DNA is now so important in solving crime that there is an RCMP National DNA Data Bank in Ottawa. It stores the genetic profiles of people convicted of serious crimes. The data bank was created in response to the *DNA Identification Act* of 2000. It contributes to the administration of justice. It helps law enforcement agencies from across the country do the following:

- link crimes together where there are no suspects

- help identify suspects

- eliminate suspects where there is no match between crime scene DNA and a DNA profile in the data bank

- determine whether a serial offender is involved in a crime

Did You Know?

Forensic investigators can tell a person's gender and race from a hair root or follicle and determine the probable make, model, and year of a vehicle from a speck of paint. The RCMP's forensic scientists handle thousands of cases a year in their crime laboratories.

Case

R. v. Feeney, 1997 CanLII 342 (S.C.C.)

For more information, **Go to Nelson Social Studies** 🌐

In 1991 in British Columbia, Michael Feeney was accused of murdering an 85-year-old man by striking him repeatedly on the head with a crowbar. The deceased's truck was found later in a ditch, with a bloody crowbar beside it. A cigarette butt and fingerprints not belonging to the victim were also found at the victim's mobile home.

The police forcibly entered Feeney's home while he slept, and seized a bloody shirt, but they did not have a search warrant. The trial judge found that both the arrest and the resulting search were legal, and Feeney was convicted of second-degree murder. His appeal was dismissed unanimously. Then, the Supreme Court of Canada set aside the conviction and ordered a new trial. Since the police had not obtained a search warrant before entering Feeney's home, the search was illegal. The bloody shirt could not be used as evidence, even though the blood stains matched the victim's blood type and proved Feeney's guilt.

Although the bloody shirt was inadmissible in court, the RCMP obtained other evidence to prove Feeney's guilt for the second trial. A warrant was issued under section 487.05 of the *Criminal Code* to obtain a blood sample from Feeney. The RCMP had legally obtained a set of fingerprints from the Calgary Police Service. They had fingerprinted Feeney the previous year for a break and enter. Feeney's fingerprints were the same as those found at the scene of the crime.

The second trial jury heard all of this evidence and found Feeney guilty of second-degree murder. On appeal, the British Columbia Court of Appeal upheld his conviction.

But the most important part of this case was the Supreme Court's protection of a person's home and section 8 Charter rights. To search someone's home, police now have to get a "Feeney Warrant." This is also one of the reasons that telewarrants came to be.

For Discussion

1. Why do you think the RCMP did not obtain a search warrant before searching Feeney's home?

2. Why did the Supreme Court order a new trial?

3. Why did the RCMP have to obtain new evidence for Feeney's second trial? What evidence did they obtain?

4. How does section 8 of the Charter protect the privacy of your home?

British Columbia Court of Appeal

ALAN BOROVOY

Alan Borovoy is an advocate for the civil rights of individuals.

Alan Borovoy has been general counsel of the Canadian Civil Liberties Association (CCLA) since May 1968. Prior to the CCLA, Borovoy worked with other human rights and civil liberties organizations such as the Canadian Labour Congress's human rights department, the Ontario Federation of Labour Human Rights Committee, and the Toronto and District Labour Committee for Human Rights.

Borovoy has made presentations to public inquiries. He has given testimony on issues such as mandatory drug testing in the workplace, wiretapping, and police race relations. He has also participated in delegations to the federal and provincial governments on issues of capital punishment, religious education in public schools, the *War Measures Act*, campus free speech, and national security and intelligence.

Borovoy's work in the areas of police power and political oversight includes the following:

- police powers and practices relating to such matters as detaining, arresting, searching, secretly surveilling, questioning, and using force
- the relationship between police officers and those investigating possible police wrongdoing
- the need for improved mechanisms to increase the accountability of police to civilian authorities

For Discussion

1. Alan Borovoy considers it important to have an independent civilian oversight board to monitor police conduct. Why do you think he believes this?

2. What do you think Borovoy might say about the way in which police powers and practices relating to such matters as detaining, arresting, searching, questioning, and using force have been regulated?

3. Should the police be allowed to "police" themselves?

4. Launching a complaint against the police is a long, complicated, and expensive process that has been heavily criticized by civil rights advocates such as Borovoy. In 2005, this led the Ontario government to appoint a senior judge, retired Chief Justice Patrick LeSage, to review the police complaints system and suggest how it can be changed. LeSage concluded the following:

   - The police should ultimately be accountable to civilian authority.

   - The public complaints system must be fair, effective, and transparent, and seen to be so.

   - Any model of resolving public complaints about police should have the confidence of the public and the respect of the police.

   In your own words, explain what LeSage's three recommendations mean.

Court Appearances

When the accused appears in court, the provincial court judge sets a trial date. If the accused has no lawyer, he or she may speak to duty counsel or ask for an **adjournment** in order to apply for legal aid. The judge also indicates in which court the case will be tried. As you learned in the criminal court structure in Chapter 4, the possibilities are determined by the type of offence, as shown in the diagram below.

adjournment a postponement of court business

Courts and Offences

Provincial Court	Provincial Superior Court
• summary conviction and minor indictable offences (theft, fraud, and mischief —all under $5000) • more serious indictable offences (assault, sexual assault, and weapons offences); judge alone without jury	• the most serious indictable offences (listed in section 469 of the *Criminal Code*, including treason, murder, and piracy); judge and jury • more serious indictable offences (assault, sexual assault, and weapons offences); judge alone without jury, or judge and jury

Depending on the type of offence, the accused may be able to elect whether he or she wants the trial to be heard by a judge alone or a judge and jury.

The Plea

Someone charged with committing a criminal offence enters a plea in provincial court. The charge is read in court, and the person pleads guilty or not guilty. At this stage of the process, about 90 percent of accused Canadians enter a plea of guilty. If the accused pleads guilty to a summary conviction or minor indictable offence, he or she is usually sentenced immediately. If the accused pleads not guilty, the provincial court judge sets a trial date.

Preliminary Hearing

A **preliminary hearing** occurs for very serious offences. It lets the provincial court judge decide whether there is sufficient evidence to proceed with a trial in a higher court. During the preliminary hearing, the judge hears Crown evidence and Crown witness testimony to determine if a reasonable case can be made against the accused. The defence does not need to present evidence at the preliminary hearing, but can cross-examine the Crown witnesses. If the Crown cannot produce enough evidence, the charges are dropped, and the accused is free to go. If there is sufficient evidence, the judge sets the trial date.

preliminary hearing a court hearing to determine if there is enough evidence to proceed to trial

How the System Works: Ontario Provincial Court

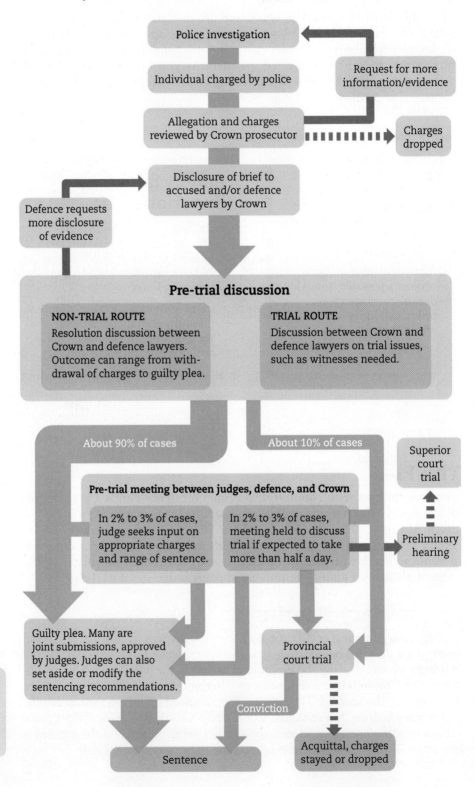

This diagram shows the process a case goes through, from the initial police investigation to sentencing.

Resolution Discussions

resolution discussion a pretrial meeting between the defence and Crown to try to resolve the case without a trial

plea negotiation a deal between the Crown and the defence for a guilty plea to a lesser charge and/or penalty

Before trial, defence lawyers and Crown attorneys participate in **resolution discussions**. The result can be a **plea negotiation**, known in the United States as plea bargaining. Plea and sentencing decisions are discussed in these pre-trial discussions. If there is strong evidence against the accused, the defence may encourage its client to plead guilty to a lesser charge in hope of receiving a lighter sentence. A guilty plea to a lesser charge benefits the court by saving time and the Canadian taxpayers' money.

Plea negotiations are often regarded as compromising justice. Less than 10 percent of cases make it to trial. The other 90 percent are plea negotiated. The most infamous in Canadian history was Karla Homolka's plea negotiation. The "deal with the devil" resulted in a 12-year sentence for Homolka and led many people to question its value and legitimacy. Homolka was sentenced before the public became aware of many of the gruesome facts that were revealed during her ex-husband Paul Bernardo's trial. (The pair had tortured and killed several teenage girls.) By court order, testimony in her case could not be reported until his trial was complete. Those who support the Homolka plea negotiation point out that her evidence, made available through plea negotiations, was needed to establish the strongest possible case against Bernardo.

Plea negotiations greatly reduce the number of cases going to trial. Plea negotiations often seem sordid, but in the end, justice is usually served. The Crown gets a conviction, and the accused receives a penalty, although not the maximum one. This process can save victims or their families a great deal of suffering. They do not have to take the witness stand and relive their ordeals. On the other hand, innocent defendants may feel pressured to "cop a plea" out of fear that, if convicted at trial, they will receive a more severe penalty. A lawyer cannot encourage a client to plead guilty if they are not in fact guilty. A judge cannot accept a guilty plea if the accused indicates that he or she did not do it, but wants the matter cleaned up quickly.

Karla Homolka is pictured here outside the courtroom during her 1993 trial. After serving a 12-year sentence, Karla Homolka was released on July 4, 2005. Since then, Homolka married, gave birth to a son, and moved to the Antilles with her husband and child, where she is trying to make a new life for herself under the assumed name of Leanne Teale.

Review Your Understanding

1. What does a defence lawyer do to prepare for a case?
2. Why is disclosure an essential part of the criminal justice system?
3. How is forensic science used in the criminal justice process?
4. On what basis does the *Criminal Code* establish the court in which a case is tried?
5. Explain plea negotiation, and outline the advantages and disadvantages of the process. In your opinion, is justice served by plea negotiations?

Should the Police Be Allowed to Use Tasers?

Tasers are weapons that use nitrogen gas capsules to shoot two electrified probes attached to an insulated wire that has a range of over 10 metres. The projectiles attach to the suspect, penetrating the skin and anchoring themselves at a depth of about 10 millimetres. Once the probes have attached, the police officer pulls the trigger. Electrical charges are sent through the suspect's body, disrupting the central nervous system and rendering the person immobile. Tasers use a timing feature that delivers an initial shock for about seven seconds. This is followed by shock waves every one-and-a-half seconds afterwards. These periodic jolts keep the suspect from regaining his or her wits.

On One Side

Tasers are a non-deadly option that allow police to disable suspects without having to be close enough to touch them, as required with a stun gun or baton. Police commonly use Tasers as an effective means of self-defence, especially when someone threatens the officer with a knife or other weapon. There are also cases where a suspect's violent behaviour cannot be controlled by pepper spray or blows by a baton. In these cases, a Taser is an option short of deadly force. Suspects in this case, who might otherwise have been shot with a gun, are probably very happy to be alive.

On the Other Side

Some people do not like the idea of using Tasers because they deliberately cause the attacker pain. For many people, the idea of shocking a person to incapacity is not right. Furthermore, more that 20 people have died in Canada from complications after being "tasered." In a growing number of cases, coroners have ruled that the Taser may have contributed to a victim's death. These cases generally occurred when the attacker had a history of health problems, such as heart trouble. For example, in September 2007, Robert Dziekanski, a Polish immigrant, was killed by RCMP using Tasers at the Vancouver International Airport.

Some people feel that Tasers are used too quickly and unnecessarily by overeager police officers. They see this as a serious abuse of power. Increased use leads to increased police powers and, potentially, a police state where citizens' section 7 right to security of their bodies is reduced.

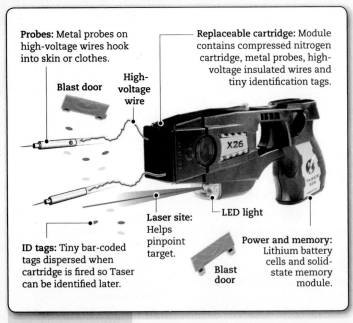

Probes: Metal probes on high-voltage wires hook into skin or clothes.

Blast door

High-voltage wire

Replaceable cartridge: Module contains compressed nitrogen cartridge, metal probes, high-voltage insulated wires and tiny identification tags.

Laser site: Helps pinpoint target.

LED light

ID tags: Tiny bar-coded tags dispersed when cartridge is fired so Taser can be identified later.

Blast door

Power and memory: Lithium battery cells and solid-state memory module.

How a Taser works

The Bottom Line

There is a social contract between the police and the general public. We agree to allow the police to enforce the laws of this country. In exchange, the police agree to do so fairly and without the use of excessive force. If you want to know whether the police stepped over the line, ask yourself this question: "Would I agree to the use of the same level of force against me as was used against Robert Dziekanski?" This is precisely the question being asked at the 2008 British Columbia public inquiry on Taser use. The first phase of this inquiry will look at the rules of police use of the weapon, the training they receive, and any medical evidence about the effects of the weapon. The second phase will look specifically at the circumstances surrounding Dziekanski's death.

"Taser" is an acronym made up from the first letters in "Thomas A. Swift Electric Rifle." John H. Cover, former NASA scientist and original inventor of the Taser, named the weapon after his favourite book character, Tom Swift. It was one of the books in the series, *Tom Swift and His Electric Rifle*, that inspired Cover to coin the acronym "Taser." The term has become so common today that it even spawned the verb form, "to tase." In fact, "Don't tase me!" has become part of our pop-culture vocabulary.

All About Law DVD

"Taser Doc." from
All About Law DVD

What Do You Think?

1. Does the "social contract" between the public and police include the use of Tasers?

2. Should the voltage of Tasers be reduced? Should Tasers be classified as "impact weapons" such as guns?

3. What is more important for the police: the obligation to protect or the duty to punish?

4. Conduct an Internet search and find out the outcome of the 2008 public inquiry on Tasers. Do you agree with the inquiry's decisions? Why or why not?

> **Did You Know?**
>
> In December 2008, the Ontario government ordered police departments to test their X26 model Tasers (those made before December 31, 2005) to ensure that they were not producing greater electrical currents than expected.

Chapter Review

Chapter Highlights

- Being aware of your constitutional legal rights in the Charter will protect you.
- Being aware of police powers will protect you.
- The police are there to serve and protect the people by enforcing the law, particularly the *Criminal Code*.
- When making an arrest, the police must have reasonable and probable grounds that the suspect committed the offence.
- When apprehending a suspect, the police can issue an appearance notice, arrest the suspect, or obtain a warrant.
- Police can use as much force as necessary to prevent an escape.
- Citizens can make an arrest under certain circumstances.
- Police are responsible for their behaviour and conduct when carrying out their duties.
- The *Police Service Act* governs police conduct.
- Police must inform those under arrest of their rights.
- The police do not have to warn an arrested person that he or she has the right to silence.
- Police must obtain a search warrant to search a private residence.
- Before trial, the accused can apply to be released on bail.
- Some accused persons may qualify for legal aid.
- Prior to a trial, the assistant Crown attorney and the defence meet to review the Crown's evidence.
- DNA testing has become an important part of collecting evidence.
- A preliminary hearing enables the provincial court to decide whether there is enough evidence to be tried by a higher court.

Check Your Knowledge

1. Outline the requirements for a legal arrest.
2. Identify the legal rights of an accused on arrest or detention.
3. Identify the powers of the police with regard to a proper legal search.
4. Identify the different types of pre-trial release, and provide an example of each.

Apply Your Learning

5. Puneeta was sitting with some friends at the park when two police officers walked over to the group. When the police noticed several open beer cans near Puneeta, they demanded identification, assuming that she was guilty of drinking in public. Puneeta told the officers that the beer cans were not hers and that she had not been drinking. She demanded to be let go, but the police grabbed her by the arm. Puneeta became frightened and noisy, and struggled to get free. The police then fined her for drinking in public and arrested her for causing a disturbance. When the officers began to handcuff her, a shoving and pushing match broke out. Puneeta was charged with two counts of assault.

   a) Why was Puneeta charged with assault?
   b) Should Puneeta be found guilty of assault? Explain.

Communicate Your Understanding

6. In groups, role-play an arrest by outlining the dialogue that should take place between a police officer and a suspect. Select a *Criminal Code* offence in which you are interested and identify the section number from the Code. Ensure that the requirements of the *Charter of Rights and Freedoms* are met with your arrest procedure.

7. It is an amazing thing for a person to confess to a serious crime, to accept the stigma of a criminal conviction and give up their freedom willingly, without a fight, passing up the Charter guarantee to a fair trial. And yet, every day in Canada, thousands of accused do just that. Close to 90 percent of criminal cases end in a guilty plea. Most of those have been negotiated with Crown prosecutors in return for a lesser charge, a lighter sentence, a more comfortable prison, or an agreement to testify against someone else. The plea negotiation has become the primary means of dispensing justice in Canada. It is effective, both for accused criminals looking to minimize their punishment and for prosecutors coping with the torrent of cases sloshing through the courts.

   Is it morally correct to trade the legal rights guaranteed by the Charter for convenience and cost savings? Write a one-paragraph explanation about how the process of plea negotiating is used in the criminal process.

8. In pairs, select one of the topics listed below. One student should prepare an argument in favour of the statement, and the other student should prepare a counterargument against the statement. Support your arguments with examples. Share your opinions.

   a) Police should have the right to go on strike.

   b) Everyone in Canada should be photographed and fingerprinted to make law enforcement easier.

   c) Police should not carry guns except under special circumstances.

   d) Anyone with a criminal record should not be released on bail.

   e) Police should be forbidden from engaging in high-speed chases.

Develop Your Thinking

9. Assume that you are a member of a civil liberties association that wants to ensure that individual rights are protected at all costs. Outline the legal rights that you feel must be given to an accused person. Now, assume that you are the head of a police services board and you want to make sure that society is protected at all costs. Outline the types of actions that you feel police are justified in using to protect society. Use examples from the text or other sources to support each position.

6 Trial Procedures

What You Should Know

- What is the adversarial system, and how does it work?
- What procedures are followed in selecting a jury?
- What different types of evidence can be used by the Crown and the defence?
- What sections of the Charter apply to evidence and the rights of the accused?
- What is the significance of the judge's charge to the jury?

Selected Key Terms

adversarial system

challenge for cause

circumstantial evidence

credibility

Crown attorney

defence counsel

direct evidence

hung jury

jury panel

oath

peremptory challenge

perjury

sequester

voir dire

Chapter at a Glance

6.1 Introduction

6.2 Courtroom Participants

6.3 Juries and Jury Selection

6.4 Presentation of Evidence

6.5 Reaching a Verdict

The judges of the Supreme Court of Canada are formally called "justices." They are chosen from the highest courts in the provinces and territories.

6.1 Introduction

Have you ever watched criminal trials on television or in movies and seen the prosecutors and defence lawyers argue their cases in court? What other people were involved in the courtroom process? Were there many witnesses, or only the accused? Did the trial involve a jury or a judge sitting alone?

In this chapter, you will learn about trial procedures in criminal courts in Canada. This exploration will include learning about the people involved in the criminal trial process and understanding what is expected of each of them. You will also learn about the jury selection process and examine the role that juries play in determining the guilt or innocence of an accused. Finally, you will discover that the criminal trial process is a complex system with strict rules about what can be used as evidence in a trial.

6.2 Courtroom Participants

Trial procedures in Canada are based on the **adversarial system,** which involves two opposing sides: the Crown (representing society) and the defence (representing the accused). In a criminal trial, the burden is on the Crown to prove beyond a reasonable doubt that the accused committed the offence. For a conviction, both the *actus reus* ("wrongful deed") and *mens rea* ("guilty mind") elements of the offence must be proven, as you learned in Chapter 4.

The type of offence committed determines the kind of trial available to the accused. This chapter focuses on trial by judge and jury. If the accused is tried in a provincial court for a summary conviction or minor indictable offence, trial procedures are similar to what is described in this chapter. No jury is chosen, however, and the proceedings are less formal; the judge alone is the decision maker.

adversarial system the system of law in which two or more opposing sides present their case in court

 Did You Know?

The term "reasonable doubt" has been described as a doubt based on reason and common sense that is "logically derived from the evidence."

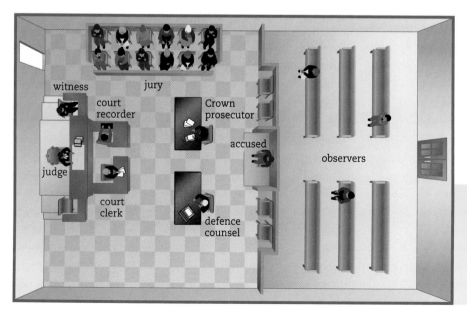

witness · jury · court recorder · Crown prosecutor · accused · observers · judge · court clerk · defence counsel

This diagram shows the participants in the criminal justice system. Do you know what role each individual plays in the trial process?

Courtroom Organization

Canadian trial procedures are adapted from English law and are basically the same in each province and territory. The roles of various people involved in these procedures are outlined on the following pages.

The Judge

Judges are often referred to as "the Bench" or "the Court." The federal government appoints judges of the Superior and Federal Courts and the Supreme Court of Canada. The provincial or territorial judges and justices of the peace are appointed by the lieutenant governor of each province and territory. The judges of the Supreme Court of Canada are formally titled "justices." They are paid by the federal government and are generally chosen from among the highest courts of the provinces and territories or from among lawyers who have had at least 10 years of experience.

Judges must act impartially, that is, without bias. They must not have a preconceived opinion about the case before they hear the evidence.

Judges have full control of the courtroom during preliminary hearings and trials. Judges set the tone for the courtroom and act impartially when presiding over a case. They can exclude the public—and even the accused—if they think this is necessary to administer justice and maintain order. Cameras have only recently been allowed into some Canadian courts. The Ontario Court of Appeal has agreed to allow some appeals to be televised on an experimental basis, making Ontario the first province to televise appeal court proceedings. However, broadcasts of Supreme Court hearings are televised on the Canadian Parliamentary Affairs Channel (CPAC).

This is the interior of the Supreme Court of Canada. It was recently renovated, and more cameras have been installed for recording, giving people full view of the courtroom. In addition, electronic updates include a web-based portal for electronic filing of appeal documents and webcasting of hearings, allowing everyone more access to the court. The Supreme Court of Canada first allowed a camera in its court in 1981 to broadcast its decision in the Patriation Reference case. The Court has an arrangement with the Canadian Public Affairs Channel (CPAC), which allows CPAC to broadcast hearings at a later date. Do you think cameras and other electronic devices should be allowed in all courtrooms? Discuss.

One of the most important roles judges play in criminal court proceedings is deciding what evidence is admissible, since these decisions can greatly influence the outcome of trials. Judges must follow specific rules when allowing evidence into court. Decisions made by judges on the admissibility of evidence (whether to allow it in or restrict its use) can also form the basis for appeals. For example, if a trial judge made an error in allowing into evidence an accused's confession that was not voluntarily made, the accused could appeal the decision.

In a trial without a jury, the judge has numerous other roles. He or she must rule on the credibility (whether the evidence is believable) of witness statements, decide whether the accused is guilty or not, and in cases where mandatory minimum sentences are not involved, they must set the sentence.

Some jurisdictions also appoint justices of the peace, who have less power than judges. Justices of the peace may preside over the court of first appearance, where the charge against the accused (defendant) is first read. Most bail hearings occur before a justice of the peace. They may also issue documents for police, such as search and arrest warrants. In some jurisdictions, justices of the peace may conduct trials for offences against municipal bylaws and provincial laws, such as driving without a licence or speeding under the *Highway Traffic Act*.

Justice of the Peace Jack Chiang is shown here during his swearing-in ceremony in October 2007 in Kingston, Ontario.

 Agents of Change

BERTHA WILSON

Seeing Beverley McLachlin as the Chief Justice of the Supreme Court of Canada might give you the impression that women have always been part of the Court. However, it took 115 years from the time of Confederation in 1867 for a female judge to be appointed to the Supreme Court of Canada—Bertha Wilson, who was the first woman appointed to the Supreme Court of Canada in 1982.

Bertha Wilson was born in Kirkcaldy, Scotland, in 1923 and immigrated to Canada in 1949. She received her law degree from Dalhousie University in Halifax, Nova Scotia. She was called to the Bar of Nova Scotia in 1957 and to the Bar of Ontario two years later. When she had applied to Dalhousie law, the dean suggested she "go home and take up crocheting." Fortunately, she did not listen and persevered (persisted) in her legal studies.

Bertha Wilson had been appointed a judge in the Ontario Court of Appeal in 1975, and then, seven years later, she was named to the Supreme Court of Canada. Her appointment was significant because it championed the role of women in the legal profession. She arrived at the Supreme Court 17 days before the *Charter of Rights and Freedoms* was declared.

Madame Justice Wilson protected the rights of the disadvantaged during her time on the Court, which included many landmark and controversial rulings. Bertha Wilson sat on the Supreme Court of Canada when Dr. Henry Morgentaler challenged Canada's abortion laws. The Court struck down the *Criminal Code*'s abortion laws as being contrary to the Charter, making it legal for any woman in Canada to obtain an abortion. She also sat on the court when the issue of spousal abuse was brought into the public spotlight.

continues…

BERTHA WILSON

This photo of Bertha Wilson as a Supreme Court Judge was taken in 1989.

When Angelique Lyn Lavallee, a victim of spousal abuse, killed her husband and argued self-defence, it was Madame Justice Wilson who allowed the "battered woman defence" and acquitted Lavallee. (For a detailed discussion of the Lavallee case, see Chapter 8.)

When Bertha Wilson passed away in May 2007, the Chief Justice of the Supreme Court wrote:

"In her unassuming and persistent way, Bertha Wilson was a trailblazer who had a profound impact on the administration of justice, the development of law in Canada. To do what Bertha Wilson did took intelligence, vision and courage, all of which this extraordinary woman possessed in exceptional measure."

For Discussion

1. Why is Bertha Wilson considered a pioneer in Canada's legal profession?

2. What issues were decided in two landmark decisions made while she was a Supreme Court of Canada justice?

3. What skills do you think are necessary to be a good judge?

4. In 2008, four out of nine Supreme Court judges were women. These women share in common a dedication to the law and a commitment to supporting the rights and freedoms of Canadians. Do you foresee a day when the majority of Supreme Court judges will be women? Discuss.

The Crown Attorney

Crown attorney the lawyer who prosecutes on behalf of the government and society

Because crime is considered to be an act against society, governments hire lawyers to be **Crown attorneys** (Crown prosecutors). Prosecutors are responsible to see that justice is done. As you have already learned, the burden of proof is on the Crown. This means the Crown attorney must prove beyond a reasonable doubt that the accused committed the offence.

Crown attorneys must disclose all available evidence whether they plan to introduce it or not, even if it may weaken their case. In law, this is called the principle of disclosure, and it ensures that an accused is given the opportunity to answer and prepare a full defence to a charge. Prosecutors also have great influence. For example, they consult with police on cases and decide whether to lay criminal charges. They can also withdraw charges that have been laid.

The Defence Counsel

The **defence counsel** represents the accused to ensure that the accused's legal rights are protected and that a proper legal defence is provided. The accused can represent himself or herself in lower courts, but is encouraged to hire professional counsel. This is reflected in the old saying that persons who represent themselves "have a fool for a client." Because lawyers are trained in procedural and substantive law, they can direct a case through the courts. They will also advise clients on the law involved in the case and how best to proceed. Defence lawyers must represent their clients to the best of their ability, even in cases where the crime is very offensive to the public.

defence counsel the legal representative of an accused

court clerk a person who keeps records and files, and processes documents for a court

court recorder a person who documents court proceedings

The Court Clerk and Court Recorder

The **court clerk** reads out the charge against the accused, swears in witnesses, and handles evidence and much of the paperwork and routine tasks required by the court. The **court recorder** sits near the witness box to record, word for word, all evidence given and all questions and comments made during a trial. Communications are recorded by keying them using shorthand machines or specialized computers, or by verbally inputting them into conelike devices. Because the court relies on an accurate record and may request that evidence be read back, this is a very exacting job. These records are kept and transcripts are made available later, if necessary, for appeals.

The transcript of a trial is extremely important. The court recorder's job is an exacting one that requires attention to detail and precision.

The Sheriff

The **sheriff** and his or her deputies carry out much of the court administration and trial preparation. It is his or her job to make sure the accused appears in court, to find prospective jurors, and to assist the judge. The sheriff also serves summonses (orders to appear in court) and carries out court orders, such as seizing and selling property to settle claims for damages.

sheriff a Crown-appointed official who acts as part of the justice administration system

Other Court Officials

Probation officers may be present in provincial or territorial courts, and judges may ask them to conduct interviews with convicted offenders. Such information may help judges in setting sentences.

Non-profit organizations, such as the John Howard Society, Elizabeth Fry Society, and Salvation Army, may have representatives in court to help defendants. Services to help victims, such as the victim services provided by the Ontario Attorney General and others, are also more easily available than they were in the past.

The John Howard Society of Ontario, which has affiliates across Ontario, provides services to those people who have come into contact with the law, their families, as well as those who are at risk of becoming involved in criminal activity. The society's mission is "effective, just, and humane responses to crime and its causes."

Beginning Motions

At the beginning of a trial, the Crown attorney and the defence may present motions to the judge. One such motion, a stay of proceedings, can stop the trial until further action is taken. In most circumstances, a stay of proceedings stops the trial from proceeding at all. Most often, a stay of proceedings is sought by the defence because the trial has not commenced within a reasonable amount of time. (Remember that the right to a prompt trial is guaranteed under the *Charter of Rights and Freedoms* in s. 11(b).) For example, the defence has been ready to proceed with the case, but the Crown has repeatedly asked for the dates to be changed. The rights of the accused to a trial within a reasonable time have been denied, so a stay of proceedings may be granted. The case of *R. v. Askov*, 1990, was very controversial in this regard, and it led to thousands of cases being stayed. It is discussed in the following Case feature. Other kinds of motions might challenge the legitimacy or admissibility of particular evidence. These motions are generally argued in the absence of the jury.

 ## Case

R. v. Askov, 1990 CanLII 45 (S.C.C.)

For more information, **Go to Nelson Social Studies**

Elijah Askov and three others were charged with conspiracy to commit extortion. The four were arrested and spent almost six months in custody before being released on bail. The preliminary hearing date was set for December 1983 and rescheduled to February 1984 at the request of the accused. It was rescheduled again to July 4, 1984, as agreed to by both sides. Then, because of courtroom scheduling conflicts, the preliminary hearing could not be completed until September—10 months after the arrests. The accused were ordered to stand trial. The earliest trial date available was October 1985, almost two years after the initial arrests. In October 1985, the case was again delayed because other cases had priority. The trial was rescheduled for September 1986, nearly three years after the arrests. The defence moved to stay the proceedings on the grounds that the trial had been unreasonably delayed. This had violated the defendants' rights as guaranteed under section 11(b) of the Charter. The judge agreed and stayed the charges.

The Ontario Court of Appeal ordered the trial to proceed. It found there was no misconduct on the part of the Crown, no indication of any objection by the accused to adjournments, and no evidence of prejudice to the accused. This was appealed to the Supreme Court of Canada, which set aside the appeal court judgment and stayed the proceedings.

The Supreme Court ruled that four factors must be considered in determining whether the delay in bringing the accused to trial had been unreasonable: length of the delay; explanation for the delay; waiver of time period, and prejudice to the accused

The court suggested a guideline of institutional delay of eight to ten months for proceedings in provincial court, and six to eight months from the preliminary hearing until trial.

For Discussion

1. What right is guaranteed by section 11(b) of the Charter?
2. What was the main cause of the delay in this situation?
3. Identify four factors used to determine whether a delay is unreasonable.
4. Why is it so important to have a trial within a reasonable time?
5. Do you think a stay of proceedings should be granted if the trial involves a serious offence such as a criminal assault? Explain.

Review Your Understanding

1. Explain the adversarial system.
2. Compare the role of a Crown attorney to the role of a defence lawyer.
3. Why is it important for judges to be impartial?
4. Why is the role of a court recorder so important to the appeal process?
5. Explain the significance of a stay of proceedings.

6.3 Juries and Jury Selection

Although the jury system is not perfect, it usually satisfies the public more than a trial by judge. A jury lets the public see conflicts resolved by peers, rather than by a judge alone. A jury also reflects the conscience of the community. Juries are expensive, however, and they are used only for the more serious indictable offences. For certain less severe indictable offences, the accused can choose between trial by judge or trial by judge and jury. A judge alone will try the accused for summary conviction offences. Lawyers will advise their clients on whether to opt for a jury or judge alone. Some trials involve highly technical legal defences that might be better understood by a judge. Other cases involve a fact situation that a jury would find sympathetic.

Juries serve an important role in Canada's criminal justice system. Do you know anyone who has ever been asked to serve on a jury?

 Did You Know?

Civil trials in Canada require only six jurors. You will learn more about civil trials in Chapter 11.

Jury Selection

The process of selecting the 12 jurors for a criminal trial is known as **empanelling**. This can take many days. First, a list of jurors is created from an electoral (voting) list of all people living in the area where the court is located. A selection committee headed by the sheriff then randomly picks 75 to 100 names from the list. This large group of people who are potential

empanelling the selection of a jury

jury panel a large group of citizens, randomly selected, for possible inclusion on a jury

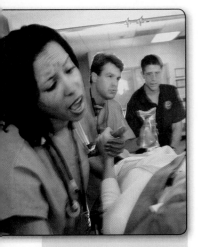

Doctors are exempt from jury duty because they are needed for medical services.

jurors are referred to as a **jury panel**. The people selected are summoned to appear at the court by notice from the sheriff. The more controversial the case, the more people are called. This is to ensure that those who are biased or who have already formed opinions about the case can be eliminated. A prospective juror who does not appear can be issued a warrant and can even be criminally charged. If you are selected from a jury panel to sit on a jury, the complexity of the case and seriousness of the charges facing the accused may determine how long the trial will last.

The legislation in each province or territory outlines who can serve on a jury. Generally, however, prospective jurors must have the following qualifications:

- They must be Canadian citizens.

- They must be at least 18 years of age.

- They must have resided in the province or territory for at least one year.

- They must speak either English or French.

- They must be mentally fit to take on the responsibility.

Jurors are expected to be ordinary citizens with no particular knowledge or skill in the law. That is why certain occupations are exempted from serving on juries. For example, a social worker employed in a federal prison would be exempt from serving on a jury because she or he is too closely connected to corrections work. Judges, lawyers, and police officers would be too knowledgeable about the law, and their experience may influence their thoughts on the case. Medical doctors and veterinarians are also exempted from jury duty because they are considered experts like judges or firefighters. See the chart below for a list of people who are usually exempted from jury duty.

People Usually Exempted from Jury Duty

- MPs, senators, and members of provincial legislatures and municipal governments
- judges, justices of the peace, lawyers, law students
- doctors, coroners, veterinarians
- law enforcement officers, special constables, sheriffs, prison wardens and guards, and spouses of anybody employed in these professions
- people who are visually impaired
- people with a mental or physical disability that seriously impairs their ability to complete jury duty
- anyone who has served on a jury within the preceding two or three years
- anyone convicted of an indictable offence that has not been pardoned

This chart lists the categories of people exempted from jury duty. A prospective juror can also ask to be excused from jury duty in the case of serious hardship, such as a personal illness.

If you want to be excused from jury duty, you can contact the judge where you are expected to appear for the jury selection process. You could be excused from sitting on a jury if you have a personal interest in the case, such as a relationship with a trial participant. You could also be excused if you are unable to speak the language spoken in the trial. If you experience a personal hardship, such as an upcoming scheduled surgery or an illness, you may also be excused. If you had a planned activity, such as a vacation, business trip, or school examinations, you may submit proof of your plans to the judge, and your jury duty may be postponed. If you wish to be excused from jury duty because of your religious beliefs, a justice would consider your request.

Questions Asked of Potential Jurors

- Are you a Canadian citizen?
- Are you 18 years of age or more?
- Do you have good knowledge and command of the English or French language?
- Have you been convicted of an indictable offence for which you have not been granted a pardon?
- Have you been summoned for jury duty in the last three years?
- What is your occupation? Does it fall under any of the exempted categories of occupations listed?
- Do you have a mental or physical disability or medical condition that you feel would not allow you to serve as a juror?

If you receive a form called a Return to Jury Service Notice, you will be required to answer these types of questions to determine your eligibility for jury duty. If you do not complete the form, or you supply false or misleading information, you could receive a fine of not more than $5000 and/or serve six months in jail. In your opinion, should prospective jurors be fined or imprisoned for violating the requirements of the *Juries Act/Jury Act*? Explain.

At the start of a trial, prospective jurors assemble in the courtroom. Cards bearing the name, place of residence, and occupation of each prospective juror are placed in a container, and each person steps forward after his or her name is drawn.

The judge decides what questions prospective jurors can be asked, such as whether they hold any prejudicial ideas about the accused because of his or her race. In selecting a jury, the Crown and defence must consider the value systems of prospective jurors. For example, how might an older male, a feminist, an older female, or a young bachelor view the accused in a case involving obscenity? Ethnicity, religion, age, financial status, occupation, sexual orientation, intelligence, and gender are only a few of the characteristics that are considered.

The Challenges

The Crown attorney and the defence counsel both want a jury that is responsive to their position. To get this, they challenge, eliminate, or accept various prospective jurors. The defence has the first right to challenge a prospective juror. After that, the prosecutor and the defence alternate the right of challenge. Three types of challenges can be used to eliminate prospective jurors:

1. challenge of jury list
2. challenge for cause
3. peremptory challenge

 Activity

To learn more about the jury selection process and the responsibilities of a juror,

 Go to Nelson Social Studies

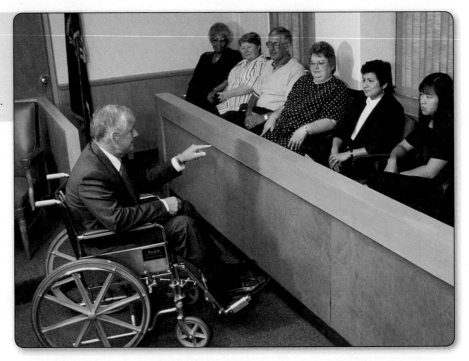

Challenge of Jury List

Either side can challenge the validity of the jury list. However, this is rarely done. It will succeed only if there is evidence that the sheriff or selection committee was fraudulent or biased, or showed wilful misconduct in selecting prospective jurors. For example, the selection committee may have excluded any citizens from a particular ethnic group. However, there is no requirement that there must be a person on the jury who has the same ethnic origin as the accused.

Challenge for Cause

challenge for cause a formal objection to a prospective juror for specific reasons

A **challenge for cause** is made on the basis that prospective jurors do not meet the provincial or territorial requirements governing juries. For instance, perhaps they are not on the jury list or are in a disqualified category (see the list of people usually exempted from jury duty on page 188).

They may also have formed an opinion on the case, or they may not speak and understand English or French. A challenge for cause can be made because the juror may be biased or have an opinion that favours one side or the other in the case. A challenge for cause can be made at any stage of the jury selection process prior to jurors being sworn onto a jury.

Any number of challenges for cause can be made, as long as the judge rules the causes are valid. If one side does challenge for cause, the other side can try to prove the cause is untrue. The judge will appoint two jurors to decide if the challenge should be accepted. In Canada, lawyers can make a motion to be allowed to ask potential jurors about their racial views. If the motion is granted, a question will be carefully worded to help determine if the person would be biased to the Crown or defence position. The issue of racial bias is discussed in the following case, *R. v. Spence*.

Did You Know?

The most common challenge for cause is that the potential juror is biased, either because they are prejudiced in some way or they have prior knowledge about the case.

R. v. Spence, 2005 SCC 71 (CanLII)

For more information, **Go to Nelson Social Studies**

In June 2000, a South Asian (East Indian) pizza deliverer was robbed. A black man named Sean Spence was arrested and arraigned in court on the robbery charge in March 2002.

During the jury selection process, the trial judge warned potential jurors that they would be eliminated if any of them displayed racial prejudice against black people. He allowed the defence counsel to challenge for cause on the basis of potential bias against a black accused. The trial judge refused to allow a challenge for cause to include the East Indian race of the complainant because he regarded the "interracial" element in the facts of this case to be irrelevant. In other words, the judge did not think East Indian jurors would be biased in favour of the victim. The jury was selected, and the accused was convicted at trial.

On appeal to the Ontario Court of Appeal in 2004, defence counsel argued that potential members of a jury who are East Indian might empathize with a victim of the same race. Therefore, this might prejudice the accused in his right to a fair trial by an impartial jury. Counsel wanted the "interracial question" of the victim's East Indian race as well as the race of the accused to be put to the potential jurors: "Would your ability to judge the evidence in this case without bias, prejudice, or partiality be affected by the fact that the accused person is a black man charged with robbing an East Indian person?" The court agreed and set aside the conviction. It concluded that an accused was entitled to have the question relating to the interracial nature of the crime posed to potential jurors.

In June 2005, the Crown appealed to the Supreme Court of Canada. The court allowed the appeal and restored the conviction in a 7–0 judgment. The Supreme Court agreed that it is within the trial judge's discretion to limit a challenge for cause to the race of the accused based on the facts of the case. It is also up to the trial judge to determine whether there is an air of reality to the challenge for cause on the particular circumstances of the case. In the circumstances of this case, the trial judge did not think that leaving out the interracial element was unfair. The only issue of importance to the defence was the identification

Mr. Justice Ian Binnie of the Supreme Court of Canada wrote the unanimous decision in this case.

of the accused. Neither the race of the complainant nor his testimony about the events in question would have shed any light on identification. The interracial element therefore did not need to be included in the question to be asked to potential jurors.

For Discussion

1. What type of challenge for cause was allowed at trial?

2. What question did defence counsel want potential jury members to consider? Why?

3. Why did the trial judge restrict the wording of the question to the race of the accused?

4. Do you think that there should be more opportunities to question jurors as part of the jury selection process? Explain.

Peremptory Challenge

A **peremptory challenge** allows both the defence and the Crown to eliminate a prospective juror without giving a reason. The Crown or defence may simply have a gut feeling about the prospective juror and not want his or her participation in the case. Each side is allowed a set number of peremptory challenges based on the charge:

- very serious charges, such as first-degree murder—20 challenges
- a charge where the penalty is five years or more—12 challenges
- a charge where the penalty is under five years—4 challenges

The judge can also direct a juror to stand aside for any reasonable cause. If a full jury cannot be selected from the remaining prospective jurors, those asked to stand aside will be called again. The defence and the Crown prosecutor can then accept or reject them as jurors. If the full jury of 12 cannot be selected because of challenges, more prospective jurors can be called from the jury list. In extreme circumstances, the judge may order the sheriff to take prospective jurors off the street.

Offences Allowing Trial by Jury

• murder	• seditious (or subversive) offences
• treason	• piracy or piratical acts
• alarming Her Majesty	• inciting to mutiny
• intimidating Parliament or a legislature	• attempting or conspiring to commit any of the above offences
• bribery by the holder of a judicial office	• accessory to murder or treason

Do some of these offences seem outdated to you? Why do you suppose these offences are all still in the *Criminal Code*?

You Be the Judge

R. v. Teerhuis-Moar, 2007 MBCA 120 (CanLII)

For more information, Go to Nelson Social Studies

Sydney Teerhuis-Moar, an Aboriginal man from Winnipeg, had been charged with second-degree murder. Prior to the trial, he challenged Manitoba's *Jury Act*. He argued that the jury selection process in Manitoba, and particularly in Winnipeg, did not lead to juries that were representative of the community. He claimed that fewer Aboriginal people would be selected for jury duty in Winnipeg because the Aboriginal population in the city was only 7 percent, compared to 11.7 percent in the province as a whole. He also argued that fewer Aboriginal people would be selected because of having criminal records, making them not eligible.

The Manitoba Court of Queen's Bench dismissed the claim. It stated that the statistical difference in the percentage of population did not lead to the conclusion that Aboriginal people would be under-represented on a jury. More studies would be needed to verify the information. The accused also did not show any evidence to support his claim relating to people with criminal records. His application to the Court of Appeal was dismissed.

- Do you think that race should be a factor in the jury selection process? Explain.

Jury Duty

After being selected, each juror is sworn in and then sits in the jury box. Prospective jurors who were not selected can leave, but they may have to return for later trials held during that session of the court. Selected jurors may also be required to return for later trials. The judge may waive this requirement, though, particularly if a trial is lengthy.

At the start of a trial, the judge informs jurors of their duties. They may or may not take notes, depending on the judge and jurisdiction. In all trials, however, jurors must not do any of the following:

- discuss the case with anyone other than other jurors

- follow media reports about the case

- disclose any information from jury discussions that is not revealed in open court even after the conclusion of the trial

Every juror must swear an **oath** before the court. The rather archaic language used in the oath has been passed down through Canadian legal history. The oath states that a juror swears to listen fairly and impartially to both the Crown's and defence's case and reach a verdict based solely on the evidence.

JUROR'S OATH

"I swear to well and truly try and true deliverance make between our sovereign lady the Queen and the accused at the bar, whom I have in charge, and a true verdict give, according to the evidence, so help me God."

oath a solemn promise or statement that something is true

After the jury is selected, the judge advises jurors of their duties.

During most trials, jurors go home at the end of each day. The judge may, in rare cases, **sequester** the jury for the entire trial. This means that the jury is separated from external influences until they reach their formal decision—the **verdict**. Sequestered jurors are isolated from their family, friends, and work. They can communicate only with each other and the court officer appointed to look after their needs. They are not allowed to see, hear, or read any media reports in case the trial is being discussed. Sequestering is

sequester to keep the jury together and isolated until it reaches a verdict

verdict the final, formal decision of a trial (for example, not guilty)

used to prevent jurors from being influenced by outside information or by anyone with an interest in the case. Thus, the verdict should be based solely on evidence presented in court, and not on outside opinions or rumours. In all trials, jurors are sent to a deliberation room to reach a verdict.

A juror can be discharged during a trial if he or she is unable to continue for a valid reason. If the jury falls below 10 members, however, a new trial must be ordered.

Sitting on a jury is part of one's civic duty, and, as such, a juror may not be paid. However, jurors may be entitled to a token payment for their services, which increases if the trial is lengthy. Jury pay varies from province to province, with several provinces paying jurors from their first day of jury duty. As of 2008 in Ontario, jurors began receiving a fee of $40 per day on the eleventh day of jury duty. The fee increases to $100 per day if a juror is required to serve for 50 or more days. A travel expense allowance is paid to jurors who live more than 40 kilometres from the court.

Review Your Understanding

1. Describe the steps followed in jury selection.
2. Identify eight categories of people who are excluded from jury duty, and give one reason why you think each category is ineligible.
3. Explain the difference between a peremptory challenge and a challenge for cause.
4. Describe three grounds on which a prospective juror may be challenged for cause.
5. Explain sequestering, and identify the circumstances under which juries are sequestered.

arraignment at the opening of a criminal trial, the charge read to the accused and the plea entered

6.4 Presentation of Evidence

Arraignment

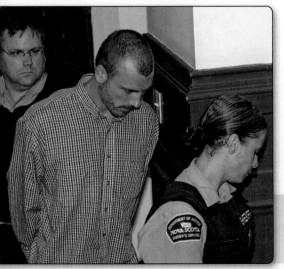

The first step in a trial is the **arraignment**. This is when the charge is read by the court clerk to the accused. The arraignment must include the charge contained in the indictment (the formal written document charging an accused with a crime). Otherwise, an acquittal may result. The accused then enters a plea of guilty or not guilty. If the accused refuses to plead, a not-guilty plea is automatically entered on his or her behalf. The accused is usually arraigned in his or her first court appearance, and re-arraigned for trials in higher courts.

Escorted by sheriff's officers, Michael Mitchelmore is led into the Halifax provincial court for his arraignment in August 2005. Mitchelmore was charged on two counts of first-degree murder.

Crown Evidence

Section 11(d) of the *Charter of Rights and Freedoms* guarantees that any accused person is "presumed innocent until proven guilty." After the arraignment, the onus (responsibility) is on the Crown to rebut (to counter or disprove) this presumption of innocence.

The Crown first presents an opening statement, which summarizes its case against the accused. It then calls evidence such as witness testimony and exhibits. Exhibits may be physical evidence, such as a weapon found at the scene of the crime. Exhibits may also be paper evidence, such as a map of the crime scene drawn by the investigating police officer. All evidence that is relevant, reliable, and fair is admissible, according to the *Canada Evidence Act*. The Supreme Court of Canada has ruled that it is not necessary for the Crown to call obvious witnesses, even the victim, if the relevant evidence that person might provide can be presented in other ways.

Direct evidence is usually obtained from the testimony of witnesses who actually saw the offence being committed. In many instances, however, there may be no such witnesses. Direct evidence is a common kind of evidence, but it is not the most reliable. Eyewitness accounts may be contradictory, and witnesses may not recall what they saw with complete accuracy. For instance, if the witness needs eyeglasses, was he or she wearing them at the time of observing the events in question? Furthermore, memories can change over time. Therefore, how long ago the witness observed the events might affect his or her ability to supply relevant and reliable information.

Circumstantial evidence is indirect evidence. It can show that the accused is most likely the only one who could have committed the criminal offence. Evidence must be proven as it is presented. For example, it must be proven that a glove found at the crime scene is the same one entered as an exhibit. If counsel is claiming that a certain person owned the glove, it must also prove that fact. Some evidence is easily proven. Fingerprints may connect a gun to its owner, or DNA tests may link the accused to the scene of a crime. Once evidence has been presented and proven, the judge or the jury must decide which evidence or testimony they find most convincing.

direct evidence information given by an eyewitness about the event in question

circumstantial evidence indirect evidence not based on personal knowledge

All About Law DVD

"Eyewitness: Unreliable Evidence" from *All About Law DVD*

e Activity

To learn more about the Steven Truscott case,

Go to Nelson Social Studies

In 1959, 14-year-old Steven Truscott was convicted of rape and murder on purely circumstantial evidence. Originally, he was sentenced to hang. Steven Truscott was released after spending 10 years in prison. On August 28, 2007, 48 years later, the Ontario Court of Appeal acquitted Truscott. In July 2008, the Ontario government announced it would pay Truscott $6.5 million in compensation for his ordeal.

Witnesses are questioned by both the Crown and the defence. If the witness is called by the Crown, the defence's questioning is called cross-examination.

examination-in-chief the questions a lawyer asks her or his own witness in court

cross-examination the questions a lawyer asks a witness called by the opposing side

leading question a question that contains the desired answer

directed verdict when a judge withdraws the case from the jury and finds the accused not guilty because the Crown has not proven its case

The **examination-in-chief** (direct examination) is the first questioning of your witness when called to the witness stand. Both Crown and defence can call witnesses. The rules of examination and **cross-examination** apply to both. Because a lawyer interviews witnesses during preparation, he or she knows what answers to expect. Therefore, the lawyer can ask no **leading questions** during direct examination. Leading questions indicate the answer—generally a "yes" or "no" response. Examples of leading questions include: "Did you see the accused driving a yellow car through the red light at 1:45 a.m.?" or "Did you see Alexander at midnight?" Proper, non-leading questions would be: "What happened at the intersection at the time in question?" or "At what time did you see Alexander?"

After the examination-in-chief is finished (also referred to as direct examination), the opposing lawyer cross-examines the witness and is free to use leading questions. The judge and jury then weigh the evidence to decide what evidence is more convincing. Here, the witness's credibility (reliability) is a key factor. The Crown may re-examine the witness about the points brought up by the defence. If the judge permits, the defence may then re-cross-examine. Either side will often ask questions that have little to do with the case, but which may reveal the character of the witness.

The purpose of a trial is to find the truth, and the process of a trial is to test the truth of evidence. In our adversarial system, two sides collide, and when the dust settles, the truth will emerge. This allows each side to get more information from the other side's witnesses. It also allows both sides to uncover any conflicts or contradictions in their testimony. Because the jury must decide the question of guilt solely on the basis of evidence, both sides will try to cast doubt on each other's evidence. Once the Crown has called all its witnesses, it rests its case. It can reopen its case only if the judge decides that it would serve justice to do so.

Defence Evidence

Before it calls any evidence, the defence can make a motion for a **directed verdict**. It will do so if it believes the Crown has not proven its case. If the judge agrees that the essential elements of an offence (*actus reus* and *mens rea*) have not been proven, he or she will instruct the jury to give a directed verdict of "not guilty." In other words, jurors are told what verdict to give.

If the judge rejects the defence motion for a directed verdict, the case continues. The defence then presents its case. Again, the defence only needs to raise a reasonable doubt about whether the accused committed the offence in order to acquit. It does not have to prove that the accused is innocent. It is up to the Crown to prove the guilt of the accused beyond a reasonable doubt.

The defence usually summarizes what it hopes to show and then presents evidence in the form of witnesses. Now the roles are reversed. The defence cannot ask leading questions on their direct examination of their witnesses, but the Crown can do so on its cross-examination. The Crown may also give evidence in reply if the defence raises a new matter that the Crown had no opportunity to deal with during its direct examination. The defence then has the right to present surrebuttal (evidence to counter the Crown's rebuttal evidence).

Steps in Presenting Evidence

1. Crown starts with examination-in-chief of witness.

2. Defence may cross-examine witness.

3. Crown may re-examine witness.

4. Defence may re-cross-examine with judge's permission.

5. Defence presents evidence.

6. Crown may cross-examine witness.

7. Defence may re-examine witness.

8. Crown may make a rebuttal.

9. Defence may make a surrebuttal.

This chart shows the nine steps in presenting evidence. What is the goal of the Crown and the defence in presenting evidence to the jury? Should the Crown have to call the victim as a witness so that the defence has an opportunity to cross-examine him or her? Explain.

Witnesses

Before the trial, the Crown gives the defence a list of Crown witnesses. Either the Crown or the defence may pay witnesses, but only if they are expert witnesses whose special knowledge can help the court. Although witnesses usually appear voluntarily, they may be served a **subpoena** (a court document that orders them to appear). A subpoenaed witness who refuses to appear can be served with an arrest warrant and detained for 30 days. If a judge finds it is justified, the witness can be detained for up to 90 days. Any witness who fails to attend a trial to give evidence may be found guilty of contempt of court and fined or imprisoned for 90 days.

subpoena a court document ordering a person to appear in court

Once the trial begins, if the judge has not already ordered excluding all witnesses, the defence can ask to have witnesses who have not yet testified removed from the courtroom. This is done to keep witnesses from changing their testimony. As each witness takes the stand, he or she must take an oath (swear to tell the truth) on a holy book or make an affirmation (a solemn and formal declaration) to tell the truth.

A witness who knowingly gives false evidence with the intent to mislead the court commits the criminal offence of **perjury**. It is also an offence for a witness to give contradictory evidence. The maximum penalty for both offences is 14 years of imprisonment.

perjury the act of knowingly giving false evidence in a judicial proceeding

"You say you're in for perjury, eh?
— Why should I believe that?"

Perjury is intentionally giving false evidence in court. Do you think a maximum penalty of 14 years of imprisonment is justified? Explain.

Anyone who can understand the nature of the oath and the questions asked by the various parties can be called as a witness. If a witness is found not to be mentally competent, his or her evidence can be declared inadmissible. A child who does not understand the nature of an oath or an affirmation can give unsworn evidence, providing the child understands the importance of telling the truth. In the charge to the jury, the judge should indicate the admissibility of such evidence. Because children may be frightened, the judge may allow them to give evidence from behind a screen and, for certain sexual offences, on videotape.

When children are asked to testify, they must understand the need to tell the truth.

Did You Know?

Section 11(c) of the Charter guarantees the right of an accused not to be compelled to take the witness stand.

credibility the fact or quality of being believable or reliable

The accused does not have to take the witness stand. If the accused has an inappropriate attitude or appearance, it may be in his or her best interests not to do so. This may also be true if the Crown's cross-examination asks the accused questions that could lead to conviction. An accused will discuss with his or her lawyer the benefits and drawbacks of taking the stand. The fact that the accused does not take the stand should not be a factor in determining whether the Crown has proved its case.

The most important aspect of witness testimony is its **credibility**. Witnesses are often asked repeatedly to recall things that they heard or saw. This is done to see if their answers are the same as in earlier accounts. Each side hopes to discredit the other's witnesses. Evidence will often be contradictory, but that does not mean that witnesses are lying. People see things differently, and memory fades. Besides credibility, the weight that should be given to evidence is also significant. It is up to the jury or the judge to decide on the credibility of a witness and the weight his or her evidence deserves.

Questions a Judge or Juror Should Ask of Evidence

☑ Does the witness have an interest in the outcome of the case?

☑ Has the witness been influenced about the case since the offence occurred?

☑ Do other witnesses support this witness's evidence?

☑ Does the witness's testimony conflict with evidence he or she has given earlier?

These are some questions judges and jurors should ask about evidence. What do you think the judge or juror is trying to find out about evidence by asking these questions?

Rules of Evidence

Rules of evidence have developed over the years and are very complex. Most are contained in common law, but there are also provisions in statute law, such as the *Canada Evidence Act*. If the admissibility of evidence is questioned during a trial, the judge will order a ***voir dire***. This is a trial within a trial to decide if evidence can be shown to the jury.

voir dire a type of mini-trial held within an actual trial to decide if certain evidence is admissible

Sometimes it is difficult to determine whether the evidence should be admissible. For example, assume a footprint was found in the mud outside a building where a robbery occurred. The tread markings are similar to those of sneakers owned by the accused. Should the footprint evidence be admitted?

Both the Crown and the defence need an opportunity to argue their positions without a jury being prejudiced by their arguments in case the evidence is not allowed. During a *voir dire*, the jury leaves the courtroom, and the Crown and defence present their positions to the judge. The judge considers the presentations and the rules of evidence and then decides what part (if any) of the evidence is admissible. The jury then returns, and the trial continues.

 **Did You Know?**

A *voir dire* may take days depending on the complexity of the case.

Self-Incrimination

In U.S. movies and TV shows, we often hear characters talking about "taking the Fifth." This is a reference to the Fifth Amendment of the U.S. Constitution against **self-incrimination** (behaviour or evidence that indicates one's guilt). We do not have a Fifth Amendment in Canada. However, section 13 of the *Charter of Rights and Freedoms* does protect witnesses from self-incrimination. It states that evidence witnesses give in court must not be used against them later. This encourages witnesses to answer all questions honestly.

self-incrimination the act of implicating oneself in a crime

The *Canada Evidence Act* states that a witness can object to questions on the grounds of self-incrimination. This act states that evidence from a witness in one court cannot be used against him or her in another criminal court case. The only exception is in a case of perjury to show that the witness lied while previously testifying as a witness. Police can also use evidence a witness has given in court to gain more evidence to lay a charge against that witness. For example, Kyla testifies that she shot the prison guard, and that Gunnar, who is charged with the murder, did not do so. The Crown cannot use Kyla's testimony as a basis for charging her with the murder of the guard. Her admission may lead police to investigate. If they find enough new evidence to indicate that Kyla did indeed commit the offence, they can lay a charge of murder against her based on that evidence alone.

R. v. White, 1999 CanLII 689 (S.C.C.)

For more information, Go to Nelson Social Studies

While changing a tire near Fernie, British Columbia, Lawrence O'Brien was struck by a vehicle and killed. The next morning, Joann White phoned the RCMP. She advised them that while driving the night before, she had swerved to miss a deer and had hit a man. She panicked and left the scene. White gave the same information to an officer who visited her home and who then read her rights. The officer told White that under the *Motor Vehicle Act*, she had to provide a statement if requested to do so by police. The officer told White that this statement could not be used against her in court.

White was charged under section 252(1)(a) of the *Criminal Code* with failing to stop at the scene of an accident. The defence argued that White's various statements to police were involuntary, and that they were obtained in violation of section 10(b) of the Charter. Furthermore, admitting them into evidence would violate the principles of fundamental justice under section 7 of the Charter, because one must not be compelled to incriminate oneself.

- How do you think the courts ruled in this case? Should White's statements be disregarded because of self-incrimination? Explain your opinion. If you were White, what would you have done when the police arrived at your home the day after the accident? Explain.

Review Your Understanding

1. Summarize the order in which evidence is presented in a criminal trial, and state the purpose of each stage of the examination.
2. What is a leading question? Why is a leading question not asked in direct examination of a witness?
3. When would the defence ask the judge for a directed verdict?
4. Compare direct evidence and circumstantial evidence.
5. Who determines the credibility of witnesses?

Types of Evidence

The trial system is complex, as judges rule on whether certain evidence should be allowed or not. Some types of evidence and rules relating to their use are shown below.

Types of Evidence

These are types of evidence that may be admissible in a courtroom. Illegally obtained evidence is not admissible.

- privileged communications
- similar fact evidence
- hearsay evidence
- opinion evidence
- character evidence
- photographs
- electronic devices and video evidence
- polygraph evidence
- confessions

Privileged Communications

Privileged communications are any communications that cannot be presented in court as evidence. Communication between spouses, for example, is privileged. This means that the Crown cannot force the spouse of an accused person to give evidence against the accused based on any communication between them. Of course, the accused's spouse may choose to give evidence for the defence. Some exceptions apply, such as in crimes of violence against the spouse, certain crimes related to sex, and some offences committed against minors.

Other privileged communications include conversations between lawyers and clients, parishioners and clergy, patients and doctors, and so on. The person who receives the communication is the dominant party in a position of power. If that person decides to give evidence based on privileged communication, that evidence is nullified (has no force in court). However, there can be exceptions to rules regarding privileged communications. For example, if a client admits something to his or her lawyer, that information can be brought forward as evidence if the client agrees.

privileged communication
confidential communication that cannot be disclosed

Similar Fact Evidence

Similar fact evidence is evidence that shows the accused has committed similar offences in the past. The Crown generally uses this kind of evidence to imply that the accused has committed the offence again. It is also used to refute defence claims that the offence was a mistake or an accident. Because similar fact evidence discredits the accused's past, it is only admitted in rare situations where it is relevant to the case. In other words, it must be similar to the circumstances in question in the current case. Such evidence can be extremely damaging to the accused's case if the jury gives it too much weight. Generally, the judge will hold a *voir dire*, and the jury will leave the courtroom while the lawyers argue over whether to admit similar fact evidence. The judge will make a ruling on the evidence, and the jury will be allowed to return to the courtroom.

Conversations between a lawyer and his or her client are privileged communications.

R. v. Perrier, 2004 SCC 56 (CanLII)

For more information, Go to Nelson Social Studies

In December 1997 and January 1998, a gang of men invaded family homes in Vancouver, British Columbia, on three occasions. All three home invasions occurred during the day. The attacks were against middle-aged Asian women who had opened the door. In each case, one gang member would pose as a letter carrier and ring the doorbell of the targeted home. When the occupant of the house answered the door, two other gang members would overpower her, and other gang members would join them in the robbery. In all three incidents, the occupants were bound with duct tape while the gang members robbed the homes.

In August 1999, Justin Perrier was convicted for his involvement in the third robbery. In April 2000, he was also convicted on charges of breaking and entering, robbery, unlawful confinement, and possession of stolen property arising from the other two home invasions. During the trial for the first two incidents, the identity of the accused was at issue. While the Crown agreed that membership in the gang rotated, it argued that Perrier was involved in all three incidents and entered similar fact evidence of Perrier's involvement with the gang. The trial judge instructed the jury that evidence could be admitted for all three incidents in proving the guilt of the accused in one or all of the incidents. Perrier was convicted on all charges. His appeal to the British Columbia Court of Appeal was dismissed in October 2003. One court of appeal judge dissented, ruling that the trial judge made an error in instructing the jury by allowing the evidence of gang activity as similar fact evidence.

- What do you think the Supreme Court of Canada ruled in this case? Explain why you think so.

Hearsay Evidence

hearsay evidence information not coming from the direct, personal experience or knowledge of the witness

Hearsay evidence is something that someone other than the witness has said or written who is not in court. For example, Georgina says she heard Silas say he had seen Anton (the accused in a murder trial) stab and kill Gavin. Georgina's statement would be challenged as hearsay evidence because she did not see the murder. Furthermore, Silas (the person who actually made the statement) is not in court to testify about what he actually saw Anton doing to Gavin. Hearsay evidence usually involves a third party who did not see the incident nor even hear what was said at the time in question.

In some circumstances, however, hearsay is admissible, such as when the person who made the statement has died. An out-of-court statement may be admitted as evidence. However, it must show proof that the statement was actually made, not for its content. For example, an out-of-court statement could indicate that a witness was in a location where he or she talked to the accused, but the actual content of this discussion would not be admissible. Hearsay evidence is also admissible if the witness is quoting a person who was dying, as long as the evidence would have been admitted if the person had lived. To be admitted, hearsay evidence must be reliable and necessary to help the judge and jury decide the case.

Opinion Evidence

opinion evidence information based on the thoughts of the witness, usually an expert

Opinion evidence is what an expert witness thinks about certain facts in a case. For example, a pathologist might give opinion evidence as an expert witness on the cause of death after an autopsy. Unless the expert is qualified (declared an expert in his or her field), his or her opinion is generally inadmissible. To be admitted, opinion evidence must be relevant and necessary to help the judge or jury reach a decision. Expert evidence can have a major impact because a judge or jury may see the expert as being infallible (incapable of making a mistake). For that reason, a judge will allow the evidence only if it is on a topic that is outside the "experience and knowledge of a judge or jury."

Character Evidence

The Crown often wants to introduce evidence of any negative character traits and previous convictions of the accused. This kind of **character evidence** is prejudicial (intended to influence the jury to convict). Therefore, the Crown is restricted in its use. For example, the Crown cannot use a series of questions to indicate that the accused has a criminal character or nature. The jury must decide the question of guilt from the facts of the case, not from prior history.

character evidence information indicating the likelihood of an accused committing or not committing the crime

The defence, however, is allowed to introduce character evidence to support the accused's credibility. If convincing enough, this kind of evidence may lead to acquittal. There is a cost, however. If the defence introduces evidence of good character, such as a good school or employment record, the Crown is free to introduce evidence of bad character, including previous convictions. The *Canada Evidence Act* states that witnesses may be questioned about any previous criminal convictions as a way to verify their credibility. This also applies to an accused person who chooses to testify. However, questioning must not attack the credibility of the accused, unless such cross-examination is relevant to the fact that the accused is lying when presenting his or her evidence.

Photographs

Photographs may be entered as evidence if it can be established that they are an accurate portrait of the crime scene. Photographic evidence can be manipulated very easily in today's tech-savvy world. In fact, the software Photoshop has become part of popular vocabulary. It is important to consider who took the photograph, as well as when, where, and how the picture was taken and processed. Often, the photographer and film processor must take the stand to answer questions relating to the accuracy of the photograph. In addition, a judge has the right to not admit photographs that are meant merely to inflame the jury, such as shocking visuals of a murder crime scene.

This sophisticated chip is not only a microphone; it is also a high-powered transmitter.

Electronic Devices and Video Evidence

Evidence obtained through electronic devices or video surveillance will be admitted in court only if *Criminal Code* procedures have been strictly followed. The Code states that electromagnetic, mechanical, or other devices must not be used to intercept private conversations unless this is authorized by a court order or one of the parties involved in the conversation has consented. Court rulings have generally agreed that electronic surveillance must be "treated as a last resort." In other words, physical evidence and witness statements will often be considered first to connect the accused to a crime scene.

The *Criminal Code* also permits police to intercept private conversations without authorization in certain circumstances, if they believe the following:

- that the situation is an emergency

- that interception is needed immediately to prevent an unlawful act that would cause serious harm to any person or to property

- that one of the parties under surveillance is either performing that act or is its intended victim

As well, a person who fears bodily harm can authorize police to intercept his or her private conversations without obtaining judicial permission. This right can be critically important in cases of spousal abuse and stalking.

Video surveillance evidence can be admitted in court. Search warrants are not needed for video surveillance in public places. However, they are required on private property. The judge must set terms and conditions in the warrant that will ensure privacy is respected in those areas in which a person has a reasonable expectation of privacy. For example, the conditions might list what specifically can be filmed around a person's home.

People can take photographs and video footage with their cellphones. Should cellphone images of an alleged criminal incident be admissible in court? Explain.

Polygraph Evidence

In a polygraph (lie detector) test, a person is asked questions while hooked up to a machine that measures changes in blood pressure, respiration, and pulse rate to indicate whether the person is telling the truth. The Supreme Court of Canada (see *Phillion v. R.*, 1977) has ruled that polygraph tests are hearsay and therefore inadmissible as evidence. Polygraph tests are not infallible. There is a concern that a jury might convict an accused based on his or her failure of the test, rather than on the credibility of the evidence presented.

R. v. Oickle, 2000 SCC 38 (CanLII)

For more information, Go to Nelson Social Studies

Several fires involving four buildings and two motor vehicles had occurred in and around Waterville, Nova Scotia. The fires appeared to have been deliberately set. Richard Oickle, a member of the volunteer fire brigade, responded to each fire. He was one of eight people asked to take a polygraph test. Before taking the test, Oickle was informed of his right to remain silent, right to obtain counsel, and right to leave at any time. He was also told that, although polygraph results were not admissible in court, anything he said during the test was. Oickle was told he had failed the polygraph test, which was an "infallible determiner of truth." He was again reminded of his rights and then questioned for an hour. After 40 minutes of further questioning, Oickle confessed to setting fire to his fiancée's car and gave a statement. He was arrested and again informed of his rights.

Oickle's police interview had been videotaped. It showed that at 8:30 p.m., he told police he was tired. They informed him he could call a lawyer. A third officer then interrogated Oickle for more than an hour, and he confessed to setting seven of the eight fires. Oickle was placed in a cell to sleep at 2:45 a.m. At 6:00 a.m., an officer noticed that Oickle was awake and crying, and he asked if he would agree to re-enact the setting of the fires. This, too, was videotaped and showed Oickle being told that he could stop the re-enactment at any time. Oickle was driven to the various crime scenes, where he described how he had set each fire. He was charged with seven counts of arson.

The trial judge ruled that Oickle's statements were voluntary and admissible, and convicted him on all counts. A further appeal to the Nova Scotia Court of Appeal excluded his confession and entered an acquittal. A final appeal to the Supreme Court of Canada resulted in a 6–1 judgment.

- Review the procedures used by the police in obtaining the confession and the different lower court judgments. What do you think the majority of the Supreme Court decided? Why?

Confessions

A **confession** is an accused person's acknowledgment that the charge, or some essential part of it, is true. The *Charter of Rights and Freedoms* states that anyone who is detained or arrested must be promptly informed that he or she has a right to legal counsel before making any statement. Any statement that is taken from an accused person who has not been told of his or her Charter right can later be excluded as evidence. A statement can be either **inculpatory**, which is an admission, or **exculpatory**, a denial. An example of an inculpatory statement would be if the accused said, "I had blood on my hands," because this statement suggests an admission of guilt. An example of an exculpatory statement would be, "I was in another country when the crime happened." This statement places the accused far away from the scene of the crime at the time in question.

How a confession is obtained also affects whether it is admissible in court. If there is reason to believe the confession was not voluntary—that police promised leniency, for example, or subjected the accused to lengthy questioning—the judge may reject it as evidence. Even if such a confession is admitted as evidence, the jury may reject it or give it little weight in reaching its decision, particularly if the jury questions the reliability of the accused's testimony.

confession a statement in which the accused admits that some or all of the charges laid are true

inculpatory demonstrating guilt

exculpatory clearing the defendant of guilt

R. v. Spencer, 2007 SCC 11 (CanLII)

For more information, **Go to Nelson Social Studies**

On September 1, 2001, while driving a vehicle that had been used during three robberies, Brandon Spencer was arrested and charged with 18 robberies that had occurred between November 1997 and August 2001. The vehicle was registered to his girlfriend, Tanya Harrison. The police searched their apartment and found a handgun and watches and jewellery from the August robbery.

Spencer was in custody and was concerned about his girlfriend. Spencer argued in court that he offered to confess to the crimes in exchange for her being given lenient treatment. He also wanted to be able to see his girlfriend. Spencer made several inculpatory statements confessing to some of the robberies and was then allowed to see his girlfriend. He later argued that he was induced to confess in hopes of leniency for his girlfriend and on the promise that he would get to see her. The officer who interviewed Spencer denied making a deal with him.

At trial, the Crown introduced his inculpatory statements. After a lengthy *voir dire*, the statements were admitted into evidence. Spencer was convicted of the 18 robberies. He appealed the decision to the British Columbia Court of Appeal, arguing that his statements were not voluntary and were therefore inadmissible as evidence. Spencer argued that the confession was induced based on the promise that his girlfriend would be treated with leniency.

In a 2–1 judgment in February 2006, the court agreed and ordered a new trial.

The Crown appealed to the Supreme Court of Canada. In March 2007, in a 5–2 decision, the court allowed the appeal and reinstated the convictions. The court held that in considering circumstances where promises are made, the court must determine whether the promise created such a strong inducement that it raised a reasonable doubt as to whether the accused was acting voluntarily. The Supreme Court decided that Spencer's statements were voluntary and that he did not receive an offer of leniency for his girlfriend. While the defence argued that withholding a visit with his girlfriend was a strong enough inducement to make his confession inadmissible, the court disagreed.

For Discussion

1. What deal did the accused allege was made while he was in custody?

2. What is an inculpatory statement?

3. How is a court to treat promises made when there has been a confession?

4. Do you think a trial judge should consider the character of an accused when determining whether a confession was voluntary? Explain.

What is implied by the phrase "a smoking gun"? Why would it be considered damning evidence?

"Oh-oh, we're in trouble!"

Illegally Obtained Evidence

Section 24 of the *Charter of Rights and Freedoms* allows the court to consider its options regarding illegally obtained evidence. In each trial, it must be decided if admitting the evidence in question would bring the "administration of justice into disrepute" (that is, hurt the reputation of the justice system). This determination relies on whether "the reasonable person," fully informed of the facts, would be surprised if a judge allowed the evidence to be admitted. The severity of the offence, how it was committed, and how the evidence was obtained must all be considered.

Types of Evidence

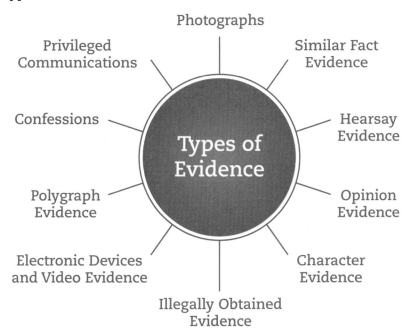

This diagram shows some of the main types of evidence. What types of evidence are not admissible in court? Explain.

Review Your Understanding

1. Explain the concept of privileged communications.
2. Briefly describe each of the following kinds of evidence: character, hearsay, opinion, and similar fact. Provide an example for each.
3. Under what circumstances is a confession inadmissible in court?
4. Describe the present status of each of the following types of evidence in Canadian courts (that is, what rules surround their use as evidence): photographs, videotape recordings, and interception devices.
5. What law gives judges discretion to exclude illegally obtained evidence?

6.5 Reaching a Verdict

The verdict—the decision as to whether or not the accused is guilty—is the culmination of the trial process. It requires that jury members weigh the facts presented and apply these facts to the law.

The Summation

After all witnesses have been called, each side presents its **summation** (a summary of all its key arguments and evidence) to the court. If the defence presented evidence on behalf of the accused, it makes its summation first. The summation is also known as the **closing statement**, or argument. Otherwise, the Crown closes first. No new evidence can be introduced at this time.

summation the formal conclusion that sums up key arguments and evidence, given by each side in a trial

closing statement another term for summation

charge to the jury the judge's instructions to the jury at the end of the trial

The Charge to the Jury

Once summations have been presented, the judge makes the **charge to the jury.** This review of the facts defines and explains the law applying to the case for the jury. For example, the judge might point out that intent must be proven for a guilty verdict. She or he may advise that if the evidence does not establish beyond a reasonable doubt that an offence was committed, the jury might bring a conviction for an attempt. The judge may also indicate how the evidence should be weighed.

Once the judge has finished the charge, either side can challenge it for legal errors. The jury, however, is excluded from the courtroom while the two sides outline any reasons for such a challenge. When the jurors return, the judge may present a recharge. Many appeals result from the judge's charge to the jury.

Adam®   by Brian Basset

What is the judge doing in this cartoon?

Jury Deliberation

To consider its decision, the jury leaves the courtroom in the care of the sheriff. This is known as jury deliberation, because to deliberate is to think about something. One of the jurors is selected to be the foreperson. Unless note-taking was allowed, jurors must rely only on their memory to decide what facts they believe or disbelieve. Because a verdict must be unanimous, the jury may return to the courtroom and ask for certain evidence or laws to be reviewed.

The jury's role is to determine the facts of the case; the judge's role is to determine the law. Jurors should follow a two-step process in applying the facts to the law. First, they should discard any evidence that they do not believe. Second, they should determine the weight that they are going to give to the remaining evidence. The jury can also pose questions to the judge for clarification. The judge hears from both the Crown and defence before answering the question.

The set of facts that the jury believes will determine which law applies to the case, and thus what decision the jury makes. In a murder case, the jury may believe the facts presented by the Crown that indicate that Harry intentionally killed the deceased. Harry would then be convicted of murder. Alternatively, the jurors may believe the facts presented by the defence, which show that the accused did not intend to kill the deceased. The jury might then find Harry guilty of manslaughter. If the jury thinks the incident was an unfortunate accident, the charges may be dismissed.

Finally, the jury must apply the concept of reasonable doubt. If the jury believes the defence's evidence or cannot decide whom to believe, it must acquit. If the jurors have a reasonable doubt, they must acquit the accused, even if they do not believe him or her. In other words, the jury must give the accused the benefit of a doubt.

Did You Know?

Jurors are often referred to as the "triers of fact." That is, they listen to the evidence presented in the courtroom (facts) and make a decision about the guilt of the accused.

You and the Law

To be selected to participate as one of a jury of 12 is a responsibility that should not be taken lightly. In fact, to sit on a jury is considered a civic duty. What personality traits do you think would make an effective juror? Explain.

 You Be the Judge

R. v. Krieger, 2006 SCC 47 (CanLII)

For more information, **Go to Nelson Social Studies**

On September 29, 1999, the accused, Grant Krieger, was indicted by the Court of Queen's Bench of Alberta for unlawfully producing cannabis. Krieger suffers from a debilitating illness and used marijuana medicinally. He legally grew marijuana for his own purposes, but he also provided it to other people for their use. It was for this latter purpose that he was charged with the unlawful production of cannabis. Krieger pleaded not guilty, and he elected a trial by jury.

At trial, on December 3, 2003, Krieger was convicted. His appeal was dismissed by the Alberta Court of Appeal in June 2005. The accused then appealed to the Supreme Court of Canada, arguing that the trial judge directed the jury "to retire to the jury room to consider what I have said, appoint one of yourselves to be your foreperson, and then to return to the court with a verdict of guilty." In other words, the judge told the jury to find Krieger guilty. After this direction was made, the jurors returned to the court and asked for a copy of their oath. Two jurors later asked to be excused from the jury for reasons of religion and of conscience, but the judge denied their requests and reaffirmed his direction for the jury to convict.

• How do you think the Supreme Court of Canada decided the case? Explain.

All About Law DVD

"Grow Ops" from
All About Law DVD

hung jury a jury that cannot
come to a unanimous decision in
a criminal case

If the jury cannot reach a unanimous verdict, it reports this fact to the judge. The judge may review the evidence and ask the jurors to deliberate further. If the jury still cannot reach a decision, and the judge is satisfied that further deliberation will not help them do so, the jury may be dismissed. This is called a **hung jury**, because they are caught or suspended (as in hung up) between guilty and not guilty. The accused may then be tried again in front of a new jury. The decision of the judge to declare a hung jury cannot be appealed.

When the jury does reach a verdict, the foreperson presents it to the court. Both the defence and prosecution can ask that jurors be polled individually. This is to ensure that each agrees with the verdict and has not been pressured to simply agree with the majority. Each juror must then stand and state "guilty" or "not guilty." Then, after being instructed never to disclose anything that occurred in the jury room, the jurors are discharged from their duties.

Case

R. v. Burke, 2002 SCC 55 (CanLII)

For more information, Go to Nelson Social Studies

At the close of Howard Burke's trial for attempted murder on September 18, 1997, the foreman of the jury announced the verdict. The trial court judge, court registrar, and both the defence and Crown counsel heard the verdict as "not guilty as charged." The judge acquitted the accused, and he was discharged from the court. A court officer who had not been in the courtroom was called to escort the jury out of the court. Curious as to the verdict, the court officer asked the foreman what the jury's verdict had been. The foreman answered, "You're kidding, guilty."

The trial judge was quickly informed of the error and an effort was made to locate the jurors. The foreman of the jury and another juror were found in the parking lot, but the remaining jurors had to be contacted at their homes. Two of the jurors were unable to be reached at the time. Court resumed about 25 minutes after it had originally been adjourned. In front of both counsel and one juror, the foreman of the jury confirmed that the verdict had been guilty. Court was rescheduled for an inquiry the next day with the entire jury present. The accused did not attend. During the inquiry into the alleged error, each juror confirmed that their verdict had been "guilty."

Three days later, the accused and the full jury were present at a full inquiry into the proceedings. Upon answering the judge's questions, the foreman testified that he had cleared his throat when announcing the verdict and that he had actually said "guilty as charged." Most of the jurors testified that they had heard the foreman say something like "guilty."

Despite the fact that a publication ban was in place during the trial, two newspaper articles describing the incident were published. The trial judge questioned the jurors on bias. Nine of the jurors indicated they had not been influenced by media reports about the case. Two other jurors indicated they had read or heard reports about the case, but testified that they had not been influenced by these reports. Another juror started to speak about something he had heard in the media about the case, but was cut off by the judge before he could continue with his answer. The trial judge concluded that the jurors had not been influenced or become biased between the time they originally announced the verdict and the time when court was reconvened the next morning. The trial judge contended that he had the jurisdiction to correct his mishearing of the verdict. He changed the verdict from "not guilty" to "guilty." The accused appealed to the Ontario Court of Appeal. In its decision in March 2001, the court dismissed the appeal, concluding that the error involved an accidental slip.

continues...

210 Unit 2 **Criminal Law**

NEL

R. v. Burke, 2002 SCC 55 (CanLII)

In March 2002, the accused appealed to the Supreme Court of Canada where the majority of the court ruled that the appeal should be allowed and a new trial ordered. The court agreed that the error lay in the faulty communication and recording of the verdict and that the judge did have jurisdiction to conduct an inquiry into the error. It concluded, however, that the trial judge conducted an actual bias test. In fact, he should have considered whether the jurors could have been influenced in their decision by reading media reports. This is known in legal terms as a reasonable apprehension of bias. In a 5–4 decision, the majority of the court concluded that the facts raised a reasonable apprehension of bias.

There was a substantial length of time between the original verdict and court reconvening, the accused had been discharged from custody, and the jurors had been exposed to the reaction of the public and to possibly prejudicial media reports. The judge should have ordered a new trial. Four judges dissented, indicating that on the facts of this case, a reasonable person examining all the circumstances would not conclude that there was a reasonable apprehension of bias. In fact, they would see that there was an error in carrying out the court's recording of the true jury verdict.

For Discussion

1. What steps did the trial judge take after he realized the error had occurred?
2. What is a reasonable apprehension of bias?
3. What factors led the Supreme Court to conclude that a reasonable apprehension of bias existed?
4. Do you agree with the majority decision in this case? Why or why not?

A defendant who is acquitted by the jury is permitted to leave. A defendant who has been found guilty will be sentenced. The jury usually has no influence in deciding the penalty, except when an accused is found guilty of second-degree murder. Although not required to do so, the jury may make a recommendation to the judge regarding the number of years that the offender should serve before being eligible for parole. Appeals and sentencing are discussed in Chapter 9.

Did You Know?

In Canada, it is a summary conviction offence for a juror to disclose any information about the jury deliberations. However, in the United States, jurors are often interviewed on television talk shows and news broadcasts about their deliberations.

Review Your Understanding

1. In a criminal trial, who presents its closing statement first?
2. What is the role of the judge in a trial by jury?
3. What is the purpose of the charge to the jury?
4. What happens in a trial in which there is a hung jury?
5. Who presents the jury's verdict to the court?

Should We Have Trials by Jury?

When the Magna Carta was written in 1215, the concept of a jury of one's peers was included. Even to this day, centuries later, the jury system is an instrumental part of the criminal justice process in many democratic countries including Canada, the United States, and Britain. The concept of a trial by jury is so highly valued that it is entrenched in section 11 of the *Charter of Rights and Freedoms* for serious offences. In fact, as a Canadian citizen, one of your civic responsibilities is to agree to sit on a jury if requested. While the jury has been a main part of our judicial system, however, it has not been spared criticism.

On One Side

The jury system has long been praised as an opportunity for citizens to ensure that justice is properly served in the criminal trial process. There are many advantages in a trial by jury system:

- It involves the public in the administration of justice, which also helps to educate the public and reinforce civic responsibility.

- Juries are composed of people from many different backgrounds, which brings fresh perspectives to the courtroom and allows citizens to reject oppressive laws.

Sitting on a jury is your civic duty.

- A jury may base its decision on current social values, rather than strict legal precedent.
- A trial by jury may have advantages for the accused because the defence needs to convince only one juror to favour the accused or have reasonable doubt. A jury's decision must be unanimous. A jury may feel empathy for the accused, especially if the charge is one they identify with.

On the Other Side

Critics of trial by jury have commented that judges are trained to make decisions based on the facts and the law. Therefore, they can render a better decision. Judges must also be independent and impartial and are therefore less likely to be biased or prejudiced. Other disadvantages of trial by jury include the following:

- Some jurors may allow their disgust at the offence—such as child abuse or impaired driving—to cloud their judgment.
- Legal technicalities may confuse jurors. A jury may be swayed by the eloquence of a good prosecutor or defence counsel rather than by actual evidence.

- A jury does not have to present reasons for the decision, whereas a judge must. Reasons often help either side to determine grounds for an appeal.
- Jury trials are more expensive.

The Bottom Line

While the jury system has been criticized, there are safeguards to ensure that justice is served as jurors carry out their responsibilities. The jury selection process is designed to challenge and disqualify those who may be biased. Sometimes potential jurors are even questioned on the possibility of bias. At the end of a trial, if a jury is properly instructed by a trial judge on how to apply the law to the facts of the case, a jury can effectively ensure that a proper verdict is reached on the basis of the evidence presented. A jury is entrusted to perform a serious role in society by ensuring that justice is served in the criminal trial process. A jury not only considers the rights of the accused, but also the interests of the victim and society.

What Do You Think?

1. What are the advantages of a trial by jury?
2. What are the advantages of a trial by judge alone?
3. When do you think a jury trial would be most effective? Explain.
4. When do you think a jury trial would be least effective? Explain.

Chapter Review

Chapter Highlights

- The adversarial system is used in trials.
- Judges must make many significant decisions during a trial.
- The Crown attorney represents society and has the burden of proving the guilt of the accused.
- The rules governing the jury selection process are very specific.
- During jury selection, both the Crown and defence can reject prospective jurors.
- The jury must base its verdict on evidence presented in court.
- Both the Crown and the defence have the opportunity to present evidence and question the other's witnesses.
- A witness's credibility may determine the weight that should be given to his or her evidence.
- A *voir dire* is held to determine the admissibility of evidence.
- The judge determines the admissibility of evidence.
- In his or her charge to the jury, the judge reviews the facts and explains the law as it applies to the case.
- The jury should apply the facts of the case to the law in making its decision.

Check Your Knowledge

1. Identify the participants in the criminal trial process and describe their roles.
2. Outline the process of jury selection.
3. Briefly summarize each step in the criminal trial process.
4. What types of evidence may be considered in Canadian courts?

Apply Your Learning

5. From a newspaper or the Internet, collect five articles concerning criminal law cases. For each case, describe the following:
   a) the offence committed
   b) the statute or legal source of the offence
   c) the evidence that the Crown and the defence could present
6. Prepare an organizer to compare the advantages and disadvantages of trial by jury.
7. With a partner, create a list of interview questions to ask a Crown prosecutor and a defence counsel. Your questions should refer to specifics about their jobs and their roles in the criminal justice system, and relate to what they see as strengths and weaknesses in the adversarial system. Share your questions with the class to generate a class list of questions. Invite a Crown prosecutor and defence counsel to come to your class. During the presentation, make notes on their answers to your questions. Distinguish among opinion, fact, and bias in their presentations.

Communicate Your Understanding

8. Many criminal trials demand that highly technical evidence and legal interpretations must be understood. Should criminal trials make less use of juries and rely more on the expertise of judges? Explain your opinion.
9. Research any of the following organizations that help people involved in the criminal justice system. Your summary should include the name of the organization, its goals, a brief account of the services it provides, and how those services can be accessed.

a) John Howard Society of Ontario

b) Elizabeth Fry Society

c) Salvation Army

d) Aboriginal Justice Learning Network

e) Association in Defence of the Wrongly Convicted

10. Clayton Ruby, one of Canada's most famous defence counsels, describes his view on the relationship between the Crown and the defence: "It is not a war. There is no enemy. It's just all of us trying to deal with a social problem. The trial is an exercise in producing a just result, not a victory, but a just result." Write a response indicating whether you agree or disagree with these statements.

11. Not all people agree that a jury's decision should have to be unanimous. Some legal minds have suggested that a majority decision, or a majority decision of 10 jurors, or a majority decision after the jury has deliberated for a specified length of time, should be valid. Write an argument for or against the proposition that a jury's decision needs to be unanimous.

Develop Your Thinking

12. As a defence counsel, outline what you would do in the following situations. Your client does the following:

a) brings you evidence that would obviously incriminate her

b) admits to committing the offence— an offence you abhor

c) tells you that he is going to have the main witness killed before the trial begins

d) tells you that she did not commit the crime, but knows who did

e) has no respect for the legal process and becomes disruptive during the trial

f) has secretly instructed his friend to burn evidence before police find it

13. For the trial of Socrates more than 2400 years ago, there were 500 jurors. The guilty decision was by a vote of 280 to 220. Are 12 jurors enough to provide a cross-section of society? Explain your opinion.

14. The adversarial system is not the only system of trial procedures. In the inquisitorial system, the judge also finds evidence and examines witnesses, not just the defence and the prosecution. Research the inquisitorial system, and prepare an organizer to show how it differs from the adversarial system.

15. Mr. Justice Ian Binnie commented on jury duty in the case of *R. v. Spence*, 2005: "Our collective experience is that when men and women are given a role in determining the outcome of a criminal prosecution, they take the responsibility seriously; they are impressed by the jurors' oath and the solemnity of the proceedings; they feel a responsibility to each other and to the court to do the best job they can; and they listen to the judge's instructions because they want to decide the case properly on the facts and the law. Over the years, people accused of serious crimes have generally chosen trial by jury in the expectation of a fair result." Do you agree or disagree with Justice Binnie's commentary on jury duty? Explain.

7 Criminal Code Offences

What You Should Know

- How are violent crimes dealt with under the *Criminal Code*?
- What criminal acts are considered property crimes?
- What are some recent changes to the *Criminal Code* that reflect society's changing views?
- What drug offences are found in the *Controlled Drugs and Substances Act*?
- What changes in the criminal law have been made to reduce the occurrence of drinking and driving?

Selected Key Terms

assisted suicide

assault

break and enter

controlled substance

fraud

homicide

manslaughter

murder

robbery

sexual assault

soliciting

street racing

theft

Chapter at a Glance

7.1 Introduction

7.2 Violent Crimes

7.3 Property Crimes

7.4 Other Crimes

7.5 The *Controlled Drugs and Substances Act*

7.6 Driving Offences

Some people say that the way to fight crime is to make tougher sentences and send more criminal offenders to jail. Others say it is better to rehabilitate offenders in the community and deal with the root causes of crime instead. Which side do you agree with?

7.1 Introduction

The *Criminal Code* is a federal statute that is meant to reflect the current social values of Canadians. The actual laws found within the *Criminal Code* may not always mirror what Canadians believe in. However, their interpretation by the courts certainly does do so. This balance between statute law and judicial precedent is what constitutes criminal law in Canada today.

Under the *Constitution Act, 1982*, criminal law is a federal responsibility. That is why all offences are treated the same across Canada. This is very different from the system that exists in the United States, where criminal laws and punishments vary from state to state. For example, a person convicted of first-degree murder anywhere in Canada would be sentenced to life in prison without eligibility of parole for 25 years. In the United States, the same person would face the death penalty if convicted in Texas and life in prison if convicted in Michigan.

In order to best represent the values of society, the government must continue to examine criminal laws. It must amend, remove, and add new laws when necessary. The *Criminal Code* was first enacted in 1892. Since then, it has undergone many amendments and reforms, and amendments continue to occur regularly. For example, changes in values in our society have led to tougher punishments for impaired driving. Technological advances have resulted in new laws to address computer crimes.

The *Criminal Code* outlines clear and concise definitions of what a criminal offence is. It also establishes a range of punishments the judge can impose when a person is convicted of an offence. However, there is another aspect to criminal law in Canada: the courts must interpret (or apply meaning to) the laws based on the facts of each case. There is an ongoing debate in our society about whether judges should be allowed to apply the law and set punishments as they see fit. On the other side, should there be firm guidelines on what constitutes a crime and what is the appropriate punishment?

_e_ Activity

To learn more about Criminal Code offences,

Go to Nelson Social Studies

The Parts of the *Criminal Code*

Part I: General

Part II: Offences against Public Order

Part III: Firearms and Other Weapons

Part IV: Offences against the Administration of Law and Justice

Part V: Sexual Offences, Public Morals, and Disorderly Conduct

Part VI: Invasion of Privacy

Part VII: Disorderly Houses, Gaming, and Betting

Part VIII: Offences against the Person and Reputation

Part IX: Offences against Rights of Property

Part X: Fraudulent Transactions Relating to Contracts and Trade

Part XI: Willful and Forbidden Acts in Respect of Certain Property

Part XII: Offences Relating to Currency

The *Criminal Code* is subdivided into parts that specifically outline criminal offences by category.

7.2 Violent Crimes

Violent crimes include offences against the person and reputation. These are found in Part VIII of the *Criminal Code*. These offences include crimes that are violent in nature and cause harm to the human body. Also included are crimes such as willfully promoting hate toward an individual (offence against a person's reputation). We will focus on six key areas of violent offences in this section: homicide, assault, sexual assault, other sexual offences, abduction, and robbery.

Did You Know?

In 2005 and 2006, the crime rate in Canada for most serious violent offences increased. However, in 2007, the overall violent crime rate in Canada declined by 2.5 percent. In particular, the homicide rate dropped by 3 percent. Other decreases included attempted murder (–5.1 percent), robbery (–4.7 percent), and abduction (–8.3 percent).

Although the national crime rate dropped 7 percent in 2007, Saskatchewan reported the highest crime rate among Canadian provinces for the tenth year in a row. This reflects an increase in crime rates in small urban centres. What other provinces and territories have a high crime rate? Do any of these statistics surprise you?

Canadian Homicide Statistics by Province and Territory, 2006

Province/Territory	Number of Victims	Rate per 100 000 People
Canada Total	**605**	**1.9**
Newfoundland and Labrador	7	1.4
Prince Edward Island	1	0.7
Nova Scotia	16	1.7
New Brunswick	7	0.9
Québec	93	1.2
Ontario	196	1.5
Manitoba	39	3.3
Saskatchewan	40	4.1
Alberta	96	2.8
British Columbia	108	2.5
Yukon	0	0
Northwest Territories	0	0
Nunavut	2	6.5

In 2006, police reported a total of 605 homicides. Of these, 78 were spousal homicides. This was four more than in 2005 and the first increase in the past five years. This rise was due to an increase in the number of men killed by their wives, up from 12 in 2005 to 21 in 2006. What are your thoughts on these statistics? What do you think could explain this increase?

Homicides by Accused–Victim Relationship

Victim Killed by	Number of Victims
Current spouse (includes common law)	62
Ex-spouse (includes separated and divorced)	16
Parent	31
Child	15
Other family	41
Boyfriend/girlfriend (current or former)	15
Close friend or neighbour	42
Casual acquaintance	91
Business relationship	7
Criminal relationship	54
Stranger	75
Unknown	3

Solved and Unsolved Homicides, 2006

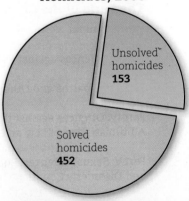

Approximately 75 percent of all homicides in Canada in 2006 were solved (452 out of 605).

Homicide

Killing another human being, directly or indirectly, is defined as **homicide** in the *Criminal Code*. Homicide can either be culpable or non-culpable. A **culpable homicide** happens when a person causes the death of someone else, on purpose or because of recklessness. So, that person is to blame. A **non-culpable homicide** is not an offence. The death was the result of a complete accident, and, therefore, it lacks intent or blame.

homicide the killing of another person, directly or indirectly

culpable homicide blamable or criminal homicide

non-culpable homicide homicide for which a person will not be held criminally responsible

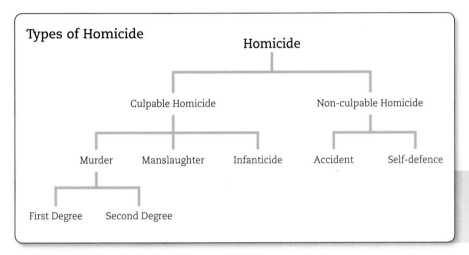

Types of Homicide

What do you already know about these types of homicide?

Murder

Murder is usually defined as the deliberate killing of another person. It is generally understood that there is clear intention to kill. However, it can also occur when there is no intent. For example, a person may set a house on fire. That person is guilty of murder if there was someone in the house and he or she died, and if the person who set the fire knew that someone was in the house. Direct intent is not necessary for murder to exist.

In Canada, murder is divided into two subcategories: **first-degree murder** and **second-degree murder**. First-degree murder occurs if any one of the following situations exists:

murder intentional homicide

first-degree murder the most serious form of homicide, as defined in the *Criminal Code*

second-degree murder murder that does not meet the conditions of first-degree murder

- The murder is planned and deliberate (for example, murder for hire). "Planned" and "deliberate" are not the same thing. Planned refers to a scheme that has been thought out carefully. In addition, the person must have carefully weighed and considered the consequences of his or her actions. Deliberate means the act is not impulsive.

- The victim is a law enforcement agent, such as a police officer or a prison official.

- The death occurs while another crime is being committed. For example, a bank robber may kill a guard even if he or she did not mean to. These crimes include hijacking an aircraft, various sexual assaults, threats or causing bodily harm to a third party, kidnapping and forcible confinement, and hostage taking.

In October 2007, Emrah Bulatci (left) was arrested and charged with first-degree murder after he shot and killed RCMP constable Christopher Worden. Any time a person murders a police officer, the charge is automatically first-degree murder. His case went to trial in 2008.

All other types of murder are classified as second-degree murder. The minimum sentence for both first- and second-degree murder is life imprisonment. The difference between the two has to do with the possibility of parole. Someone convicted of first-degree murder is eligible for parole only after 25 years, and for second-degree murder, after a minimum of 10 years.

In legal terms, the cause of death is known as causation. It is usually an issue in a homicide trial. For the Crown to show causation, it must prove that the accused did in fact cause the death of the victim. The common method of proving this is to use the "but-for" test. But for the accused's act, would the harm have occurred? For example, person X shoots and kills person Y. Applying the but-for test, we ask "But for X's act, would Y have died?" If the answer is no, we must conclude that X caused the death of Y. The legal issue of causation is addressed in the case of *R. v. Nette*, 2001, below.

 Case

R. v. Nette, 2001 SCC 78 (CanLII)

For more information, Go to Nelson Social Studies

On August 21, 1995, Clara Loski, a 95-year-old widow who lived alone in her house in Kelowna, British Columbia, was found dead in her bedroom. Her hands and feet were bound with electrical wire, and a garment was around her head and neck. Also, her home had been robbed.

The RCMP investigation led to the arrest of Daniel Nette. He had made statements to police officers about his involvement in the robbery and the death of Loski. Under section 231(5) of the *Criminal Code*, Nette was charged with first-degree murder. The charge was based on the fact that he had caused her death while committing the offence of unlawful confinement. At the trial, the Crown medical expert testified that Loski died of asphyxiation. He stated, however, that a number of other factors contributed to her death: her age and corresponding lack of muscle tone, her heart problems, and asthma. Nette was found guilty of the lesser charge of second-degree murder. The British Columbia Court of Appeal and the Supreme Court of Canada both dismissed the appeal and upheld the original trial verdict.

The Supreme Court held that the actions of the accused are the test for causation for second-degree murder. How the accused acted must be found to have been a "significant cause of death." In the case of first-degree murder causation, the actions of the accused must be regarded as having been "a substantial and integral cause" of the death. Similarly, for manslaughter, the actions of the accused must be "a contributing cause of death."

For Discussion

1. What was the original charge against Daniel Nette? Why was it appropriate, given the facts of the case?

2. Why was the charge changed based on the definition of "causation"? How was it applied in this case?

3. Madame Justice Louise Arbour of the Supreme Court commented that no reasonable jury could have had any doubt about whether the accused's actions constituted a significant cause of the victim's death. What did she base these comments on?

4. Do you agree with the outcome of this case? Explain.

Manslaughter

Manslaughter is causing the death of a person, directly or indirectly, by means of an unlawful act. Manslaughter is not murder and requires only general intent. For example, if Marina loses control of her car while speeding and kills a pedestrian, she could be charged with manslaughter, not murder. The *mens rea* for manslaughter is that a reasonable person would recognize that the unlawful act—speeding—could physically harm or kill the victim. If Marina had intentionally sped up to hit a specific pedestrian, she would be charged with murder. That is because her actions were based on specific rather than general intent.

Sometimes people charged with murder are convicted of manslaughter. This can happen if the accused successfully uses one of two defences: provocation or intoxication. For a provocation defence, it must be shown that the accused caused another's death "in the heat of passion caused by sudden provocation." Furthermore, the provocation must be a wrongful act or insult and must be something that would cause an ordinary person to lose self-control (excepting drugs or alcohol). Finally, the killing must take place during the loss of self-control. If, after being provoked, the accused has time to plan the killing of the other person, the charge would be murder, not manslaughter. If a person sees a loved one being seriously harmed and kills the aggressor to protect the loved one, this is an example of provocation.

The issue of intoxication is often significant in murder cases. That is because being drunk or high on drugs can affect a person's ability to predict the consequences of his or her actions. The Crown must prove both the killing and the specific intent if the accused uses the intoxication defence. If there is doubt as to whether the accused specifically intended to kill the victim because the accused was drunk or high, the accused must be found guilty of manslaughter, not murder.

Do you think this cartoon depicts manslaughter? Why or why not?

manslaughter culpable homicide that is not murder or infanticide

Review Your Understanding

1. What constitutes a violent crime?
2. What is the difference between culpable and non-culpable homicide?
3. Distinguish between first- and second-degree murder, and describe the penalties for each.
4. Under what circumstances could a charge of murder be reduced to manslaughter?
5. Define causation as it relates to a homicide trial.

 Did You Know?

In October 2006, the government of Alberta passed the *Criminal Notoriety Act*. Its purpose is to prevent people who have been convicted of serious crimes from profiting by retelling the crime (for example, by selling their story to a book publisher). Nova Scotia, Ontario, and Manitoba have similar laws in place.

Assisted Suicide

It is against the law to counsel anyone to commit suicide or to help them accomplish it. Until 1972, it was an offence even to attempt suicide, and those who tried to take their own lives were often prosecuted. **Assisted suicide** continues to remain a controversial issue in Canada. Some chronically ill Canadians have argued that they have the right to assistance when they wish to commit suicide. On the other hand, disability rights groups often oppose legalizing assisted suicide. They believe that people who have disabilities may be pressured to end their lives. So, while suicide and attempted suicide were decriminalized, assisted suicide remains prohibited under section 241 of the *Criminal Code*. The constitutionality of section 241(b) was challenged unsuccessfully by Sue Rodriguez in 1992.

assisted suicide the act of counselling, aiding, or abetting someone to commit suicide

euthanasia mercy killing, usually to relieve suffering

Euthanasia

A related issue to suicide is **euthanasia**, sometimes called mercy killing. This means that one person acts to end another person's life, but usually for compassionate reasons such as ending suffering. There are different levels of consent to euthanasia. For example, Judith, a patient with terminal cancer, has expressed a wish to die by choosing not to undergo aggressive chemotherapy. Under these circumstances, ending her life would be called voluntary/passive euthanasia. On the other hand, Dieter, another patient with terminal cancer, has not expressed a wish to die. Perhaps he cannot express such a wish (for example, because he is in a coma), or perhaps he does not wish to die. Ending his life under these circumstances would be called involuntary/active euthanasia. The main difference is that under voluntary euthanasia, consent is given by the person wishing to die. Under involuntary euthanasia, someone (such as a spouse) gives consent on behalf of the person who cannot speak for himself or herself.

It is often difficult to tell the difference between assisted suicide and euthanasia. A simple way to look at it is as follows. Assisted suicide occurs when a person intentionally kills himself or herself with the assistance of another person. Usually, the person wishing to die is suffering from an incurable or terminal illness. Therefore, he or she is unable to carry out the deed alone. An example of this made headlines in the United States. Dr. Jack Kevorkian, a retired Michigan pathologist, invented the "suicide machine." His machine allowed a person to push a switch to administer a fatal injection through an intravenous needle that Dr. Kevorkian had inserted. He was jailed for second-degree murder after televising an act of assisted suicide. The 79-year-old doctor was released in June 2007 after having served eight years in prison. He claimed that he had participated in at least 130 assisted suicides during his life.

Sue Rodriguez had a terminal disease. She hoped that, when she was no longer able to enjoy life, someone would be able to help her end her own life. However, the *Criminal Code* prohibits giving assistance to commit suicide. Rodriguez challenged this as a violation of her Charter rights. However, both the Supreme Court of British Columbia and the Supreme Court of Canada decided against her. On February 12, 1994, Rodriguez committed suicide with the help of an anonymous doctor.

R. v. Latimer, 2001 SCC 1 (CanLII)

For more information, Go to Nelson Social Studies

On October 24, 1993, Robert Latimer killed his 12-year-old daughter, Tracy. He placed her in the cab of his pickup truck, ran a hose from the exhaust to the cab, and killed her by carbon monoxide poisoning. Tracy was a 40-pound quadriplegic who functioned at the level of a three-month-old. Latimer never denied what he did and explained his actions as a form of "compassionate homicide." In November 1994, a jury convicted him of second-degree murder. He successfully appealed to the Supreme Court of Canada. The court ordered a new trial based on its conclusion that the RCMP had interfered with the jury.

In November 1997, a second jury found Latimer guilty of second-degree murder. The trial judge sentenced him to two years of imprisonment. However, the Saskatchewan Court of Appeal overturned the sentence. It set the minimum sentence for a second-degree murder conviction. This included life imprisonment, with eligibility of parole in 10 years. On January 18, 2001, the Supreme Court of Canada unanimously upheld the decision. Latimer began serving his sentence, and on February 27, 2008, Latimer received early parole. He had served seven years in jail.

Robert Latimer and his wife leave court in 1997 after he was convicted of second-degree murder.

For Discussion

1. Why was Latimer charged with second-degree murder in this case?
2. How does the issue of euthanasia relate to the Latimer case?
3. What is your opinion of the Latimer case and the legal issue of euthanasia as it presently exists in Canada today? Explain.
4. Research the parole board's decision to release Latimer, and examine what they considered before making their decision.

Assault

In Canada, there are three levels of assault, based on the level of severity and corresponding penalties:

Level One: assault
Level Two: assault causing bodily harm
Level Three: aggravated assault

These levels are identified in section 265 of the *Criminal Code*. All assaults have two common elements:

1. The accused must have intent to carry out the attack and cause harm.
2. There must be no consent by the victim (for example, as in a boxing match).

Levels of Assault

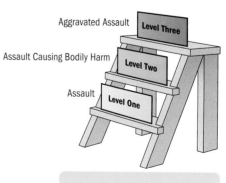

Aggravated Assault — **Level Three**
Assault Causing Bodily Harm — **Level Two**
Assault — **Level One**

The three levels of assault

Canadian Foundation for Children, Youth, and the Law v. Canada (Attorney General), 2004 SCC 4 (CanLII)

For more information, Go to Nelson Social Studies

In February 2004, in a 6–3 decision, the Supreme Court upheld section 43 of the *Criminal Code*. Section 43 is commonly called the "spanking" law. It allows parents, teachers, and caregivers (babysitters and foster parents) to use corporal punishment as "reasonable force" to discipline children. This section of the Code was enacted in 1892, and it has changed little since then. (See also Chapter 13, pages 465–466.)

• Should a parent be charged with assault if he or she spanks a child? Why or why not? Explain your opinion.

Level One Assault

The first level of **assault** consists of one of any of the following actions:

assault the application or threat of force without the other person's consent

- applying intentional force to another person without that person's consent (for example, punching or grabbing someone)

- attempting or threatening, by an act or a gesture, to apply force against someone (for example, waving a fist at someone you intend to hit)

- approaching or blocking the way of another person (for example, aggressive panhandling in major cities like Toronto)

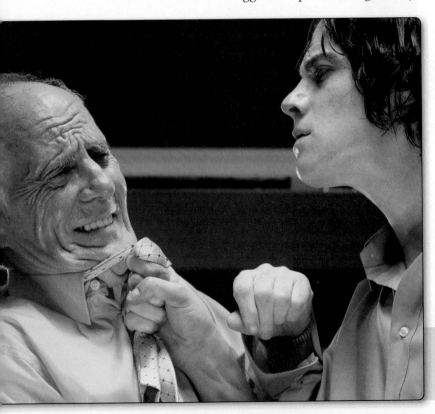

Grabbing or punching someone without that person's consent is an example of Level One Assault.

Harmful words are not assault. The words must be accompanied by gestures. For example, if Rodney tells Adnan, "I am going to belt you," it is not an assault unless Rodney also waves a fist. It is important to note that consent is not necessarily given just because the victim participates in an activity that poses some risk. For example, in Olympic boxing, both fighters consent to being struck with gloved fists. However, they do not consent to being bitten, kicked, or struck below the belt. Assault carries with it a maximum penalty of five years in prison.

Level Two Assault

The second level of assault is **assault causing bodily harm**. It generally involves a physical attack with a weapon, such as a knife or baseball bat. This attack usually causes bodily harm (injury) to the victim, which requires medical attention. Bodily harm is anything that interferes with the victim's health or comfort in more than a fleeting, trifling way. In *R. v. Bertuzzi*, 2004, Todd Bertuzzi of the Vancouver Canucks was charged with assault causing bodily harm. During a hockey game, he punched and severely injured Colorado Avalanche player Steve Moore. (For more on this case, see the Issue feature in Chapter 11 on pages 384–385.) Assault causing bodily harm carries a maximum penalty of 10 years of imprisonment.

Level Three Assault

The third and most severe level of assault is **aggravated assault**. This is an attack so severe that the physical injuries may threaten the life of the victim. It is committed if a person wounds, maims, disfigures, or endangers the life of the victim. However, the *mens rea* required is only to commit bodily harm. Aggravated assault carries a maximum penalty of 14 years in prison.

Sexual Assault

Sexual assault is a specific form of assault that involves any form of unwanted sexual activity. A sexual assault occurs when consent is not given. In 1983, Canada passed Bill C-127. It made changes to the laws of rape, which was the old term used to describe "sexual assault" in the *Criminal Code*. The new legislation grouped sexual assault into three levels. These include acts ranging from unwanted sexual touching to violent physical attacks. The levels of sexual assault parallel the three levels of assault described on pages 223–225.

Level One Sexual Assault

The first level of sexual assault is defined in section 271(1) of the *Criminal Code* as almost the same as criminal assault. The only difference is that it occurs in relation to sexual conduct or when the victim's sexual integrity is violated. It could involve minor physical injury to the victim or no injuries at all. It carries a maximum imprisonment of 10 years. An example is a molestation offence, which is a non-consensual, forced physical sexual behaviour.

Level Two Sexual Assault

The second level of sexual assault is defined in section 272(1) of the *Criminal Code*. It involves sexual assault with a weapon or an imitation of a weapon, threats, or causing bodily harm to the victim. It carries a maximum imprisonment of 14 years.

Level Three Sexual Assault

The third level of sexual assault, the most severe form, is aggravated sexual assault. It is defined in section 273 of the *Criminal Code* as a sexual attack so serious that the victim's physical injuries may even be life threatening. It carries a maximum penalty of life in prison.

An attack with a weapon, such as a knife, is considered Level Two or Level Three Assault, depending on the severity of the injury to the victim.

assault causing bodily harm the second of three levels of assault in criminal law

aggravated assault the most serious of three levels of assault in Canadian law

sexual assault the broad term for the three levels of sexual assault

All About Law DVD
"Abuse of Authority" from *All About Law DVD*

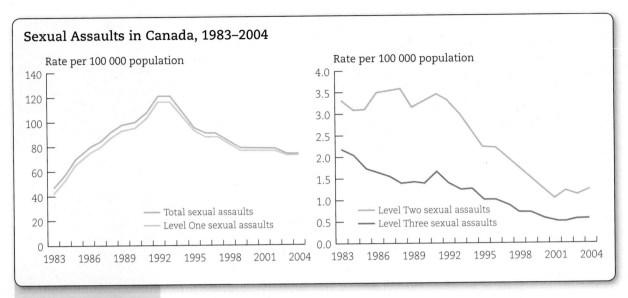

Sexual Assaults in Canada, 1983–2004

Rate per 100 000 population

— Total sexual assaults
— Level One sexual assaults

Rate per 100 000 population

— Level Two sexual assaults
— Level Three sexual assaults

These graphs show the number of sexual assaults reported to the police.

consent agreement given freely and voluntarily

Consent

Consent is a central aspect in any sexual assault. It is defined in section 273.1(2) of the *Criminal Code*. Consent is the voluntary agreement of the accuser to engage in the sexual activity in question. The *actus reus* (act) of sexual assault is the sexual touching to which the victim does not consent. The *mens rea* (intent) of sexual assault can rest on knowledge that the victim gave no consent, recklessness, or willful blindness (the perpetrator avoids asking the victim for consent). Consent is frequently an issue in sexual assault trials, especially since there are usually few witnesses to such assaults.

In *R. v. Ewanchuk*, 1999, the Supreme Court did not allow the defence of "implied consent" to be introduced into Canadian law. Implied consent means that if a victim was being overly flirtatious, for example, it may "imply" that he or she consented to sexual activity. When it comes to consent and sexual activity, the court reaffirmed that "no means no" and only "yes means yes."

Intoxication is also not a defence if the accused "departed markedly from the standard of reasonable care." In other words, if the accused drank so much that loss of self-control was bound to occur, intoxication cannot be used as a defence to sexual assault. The law was clarified following the sensational case of *R. v. Daviault*, 1994 (see the case in Chapter 8, page 271). In this case, the court held that drunkenness can be a defence in a sexual assault case if there is reasonable doubt that the accused could make a clear decision to act with intent. The accused had been drunk during an attack on a 65-year-old partially paralyzed woman. Many Canadians were outraged by this judgment. The *Criminal Code* was later amended with the passage of Bill C-72. This bill clarified the issue of criminal fault by reason of intoxication.

Rape Shield

The rape shield law limits a defendant's ability to cross-examine sexual assault complainants about their past sexual behaviour and sexual history. In *R. v. Seaboyer and Gayme*, 1991, the Supreme Court struck down the rape shield law. The court argued that it violated the rights of the accused. Following this decision, Bill C-49, a new rape shield law, was introduced in 1992. As a result, the *Criminal Code* now prohibits evidence of sexual reputation from being raised in court to challenge the credibility of the complainant. However, the judge can permit this evidence if it will add value to the fairness of the trial. Section 276 of the Code outlines what the judge must consider in determining whether to admit the evidence and in what situations the information should be made public. In the case of *R. v. Darrach*, 2000, in a unanimous 9–0 decision, the Supreme Court confirmed that present rape shield legislation is constitutional.

Age of Consent

Age of consent is the legal age that a person can consent to sexual activity. In the past, the age of consent was 12, which was changed to 14 in 1892. It took nearly a century before Canada raised the age to 16, in February 2008. Where there is a relationship of trust, authority, or dependency (such as a teacher, coach, or doctor), the age of consent in Canada is 18 years. The *Criminal Code* provides what is often referred to as a "close in age" or "peer group" exception. For example, a 14- or 15-year-old can consent to engage in sexual activity with another person who is less than two years older.

In July 2005, Parliament passed a law that increased protection against exploitative sexual activity such as child pornography and prostitution. Included in the law was the creation of a new *Criminal Code* offence of sexual exploitation. This law attempts to better protect young persons between 14 and 18 years of age against predators. Under the new law, it will be up to the courts to decide if a relationship is exploitative of a young person. It recognizes that the age of a person can indicate vulnerability. Other factors, such as the following, are also used to determine if a young person is being exploited sexually:

- Age difference—Is the other person much older than the young person?

- Evolution of the relationship—How did the relationship develop? For example, did it develop quickly and secretly over the Internet?

- Control or influence over the young person—What degree of control or influence did the other person have over the young person? For example, was there an employer/employee or student/teacher relationship?

Abduction

In general terms, **abduction** involves capturing and carrying off a person by force, against his or her will. It is similar to kidnapping. However, in legal terms, it has a different and more precise meaning. Section 282 of the *Criminal Code* defines abduction as "the forcible removal of an unmarried person under the age of 16 from the care of a parent, guardian, or any other person who has lawful care of the child." Foster parents and child welfare agencies are considered guardians. Because the number of separated and divorced families in Canada is rising, so is the number of abductions. In January 1983, abduction by a parent was added to the *Criminal Code* and became a criminal offence. Anyone found guilty of child abduction can be imprisoned for a term up to 10 years.

 Activity

To learn more about rape shield provisions,

 Go to Nelson Social Studies

 Did You Know?

Surveys show that less than 10 percent of women who are sexually assaulted report the assault to the police. In 2005, 6 out of 10 victims who reported being sexually assaulted were under the age of 17.

age of consent the age at which a young person can legally consent to sexual activity

abduction the illegal, forced removal of a child from the custodial parent

Child Abduction in Canada, 2006

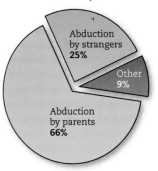

Abduction by parents is rising steadily.

R. v. Dyck, 2008 ONCA 309 (CanLII)

For more information, Go to Nelson Social Studies

In 1988, 11-year-old Christopher Stephenson was grabbed at a Brampton, Ontario, shopping mall. He was sexually assaulted and killed by Joseph Fredericks, a convicted child sex offender. Fredericks had been released and was still on parole. However, he was able to serve the remaining part of his sentence in the community. In 1993, the coroner's inquest into Stephenson's death recommended creating a national registry for convicted sex offenders. This registry would require them to register with local police when they move into a community. A province-wide registry took effect in Ontario on April 23, 2001, the first of its kind in Canada. It was called "Christopher's Law," named after Christopher Stephenson.

On April 25, 2008, the Ontario Court of Appeal dismissed Abram Dyck's challenge of the constitutionality of the sex offender registry. The court ruled that the public's right to safety outweighs the offender's freedoms.

- Should all provinces pass such a law? Why or why not?

Christopher Stephenson was murdered by Joseph Fredericks, shown here (centre) struggling with police after a hearing in 1988.

Canadian 1994 biathlon Olympic gold medalist Myriam Bédard was arrested for abducting her 12-year-old daughter. Bédard had breached a custody order and took her daughter to the United States. On September 20, 2007, Bédard was found guilty and received a conditional sentence with no jail time.

Robbery

In general terms, **robbery** is illegally taking someone's property without permission. For example, if Bobby takes your cellphone without asking, you could call that theft or robbery. In legal terms, robbery has a more specific meaning. It is theft involving violence or the threat of violence using a weapon such as a gun, a knife, or even a stick. When the Crown is basing its case on the threat of violence, it must prove that the victim felt threatened and that there were reasonable and probable grounds for the fear. For example, phrases such as "Empty your till!" or "This is a holdup!" are accepted threats of implied violence.

Similarly, using a finger or fist as a weapon has been accepted in court as a threat of violence. Also, holding an imitation weapon such as a toy gun is classified as using an offensive weapon. The severe punishment for robbery is life imprisonment. This reflects society's revulsion for criminals who steal using violence.

Using a weapon such as a gun or knife is theft involving the threat of violence, and in which the victim feels threatened.

robbery theft involving violence or threats of violence

Robberies in Canada, 2006		
Country/Province/Territory	Number of Robberies	Rate per 100 000 People
Canada Total	**30 707**	**94**
Newfoundland and Labrador	119	23
Prince Edward Island	24	17
Nova Scotia	790	85
New Brunswick	221	29
Québec	6 989	91
Ontario	10 987	87
Manitoba	2 148	182
Saskatchewan	1 474	150
Alberta	3 154	93
British Columbia	4 756	110
Yukon	18	58
Northwest Territories	15	36
Nunavut	12	39

The number of robberies in Canada in 2006 increased by 6 percent from the 2005 rate. Robberies were up in most provinces. The most notable increase (18 percent) was in Saskatchewan, second only to Manitoba. Also, about one in every eight robberies in 2006 involved a firearm. Why do you think the robbery rates across Canada rose? What strategies can a local police force use to help protect its citizens?

Chapter 7 *Criminal Code Offences*

Tackling Violent Crime Act

In February 2008, Parliament passed a new law, the *Tackling Violent Crime Act*. Its aim was to protect Canadians from criminals who commit serious violent crimes. The idea behind the act was to prevent dangerous, high-risk offenders from offending again. It took effect on May 1, 2008. Some of the main points of this act are as follows:

- severe, mandatory jail time for serious gun crimes
- reverse-onus bail provisions for accused in serious gun crimes; offenders must show why they should not be kept in jail while awaiting trial
- three-strikes law aimed at dangerous and high-risk offenders, creating a presumption of dangerousness
- higher penalties for drug-and-alcohol-impaired drivers, including new ways to detect drug-impaired driving
- raise of the age of sexual consent from 14 to 16 years to protect youth from adult sexual predators

To fight impaired driving, the act allows police officers to conduct roadside sobriety exams to test for drugs as well as alcohol. Refusing a test for alcohol or drugs results in a minimum fine of $1000. A maximum sentence for refusing drug and alcohol tests could be as high as five years of imprisonment. Penalties for impaired driving were increased. For a first offence, fines were increased from $600 to $1000. For a second offence, the sentence was increased from 14 to 30 days in jail. A third offence nets 120 days in jail, up from the previous 90 days.

Sexual and violent criminals receive more severe sentences. An offender convicted three or more times of specific violent or sexual crimes must convince the court why he or she should not be declared a dangerous offender. This is known as reverse onus. Peace bonds will be extended and more conditions imposed on those released from jail.

Firearm crimes receive higher mandatory prison sentences. A first offence results in a five-year sentence. A second firearm offence receives a seven-year term in prison. These sentences are for eight specific weapons-related offences. Other serious firearm-related offences such as trafficking or smuggling result in a three-year sentence for a first offence. A second offence nets a five-year sentence.

The *Tackling Violent Crime Act* created two new offences. Breaking and entering to steal a firearm became an indictable offence. So did robbery to steal a firearm. To keep violent criminals off the streets, the act included a reverse onus. Offenders had to show why they should not be held in jail awaiting trial.

To protect youth from sexual predators, the act raised the age of consent from 14 to 16. It included a close-in-age exception. By that, 14- and 15-year-olds were able to engage in sexual activity with partners who were less than five years older.

Justice Minister Rob Nicholson introduced the new legislation as part of his *Tackling Violent Crime Act*. It aims at making sure dangerous offenders do not offend again.

For Discussion

1. What does the act propose to fight impaired driving?
2. How did the act deal with dangerous offenders?
3. What changes in the law deal with weapons charges?
4. How did the act change bail provisions?

1. Explain the difference between assisted suicide and euthanasia.
2. What is the difference among the three levels of assault?
3. What is the difference among the three levels of sexual assault?
4. In what situations is consent not a defence to sexual assault?
5. Describe the elements of robbery.

 Did You Know?

Property that is lost continues to be the property of the owner. So, the old phrase "possession is nine tenths of the law" is not true.

7.3 Property Crimes

At one time, protection of property was one of the most important functions of criminal law. That is why death was a common penalty for theft until just a couple of hundred years ago. Property such as livestock (cattle and horses) was so important to owners that society demanded this extreme punishment. Today, the *Criminal Code* still has major penalties for offences against property. These types of offences make up about two-thirds of all offences listed in the *Criminal Code*. There are five major property crimes (see the diagram below).

 Did You Know?

In 2007, Abbotsford, British Columbia reported 5869 property crimes per 100 000 people. This was the highest rate in Canada.

Types of Property Crimes

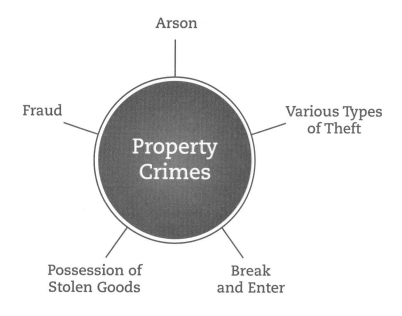

 Did You Know?

The fictional portrayal of crime on television and film, together with media coverage of real crime, has propelled criminal law into the public spotlight. However, one must remember that there is real law and TV law. Often, the fictionalized version tends to distort and sensationalize real law. Journalists further contribute to this hype as they give extensive coverage to crime in newspapers, on the radio, and on television. Therefore, Canadians often think that the crime rate is higher than it really is. Actually, the crime rate in Canada is going down. So, overall, Canadians are very safe.

This diagram shows the five main types of property crime. Each of these is reviewed on the following pages.

Arson

Section 433 of the *Criminal Code* defines **arson** as the act of intentionally causing damage to property by fire or explosion. For example, if a group of teenagers starts a fire that gets out of hand and spreads to nearby buildings, they could be charged with arson. They should have been able to foresee (anticipate) the possible consequences of setting the fire in the first place. Where there is no danger to life, the maximum penalty for arson is 14 years in prison. However, if the arsonist recklessly causes bodily harm to another person, the maximum penalty is life imprisonment.

arson intentionally causing damage to property by fire

In 2006, there were 13 504 incidents of arson reported to police in Canada.

Theft

Theft is one of the most common property offences in Canada. In 2006, it accounted for over half of all property crimes. Theft is defined simply as taking someone's property without their consent or damaging it so severely that it is unusable.

Theft has a number of elements. Each of these must be proven for a successful conviction:

- The act must be fraudulent. This means that the person who is stealing must have intended to do something wrong. In other words, you cannot "accidentally" steal something. The person knows that the property she or he is stealing does not belong to her or him.

- The person taking the item must not have any legal right to it. Having a legal right to an item is known, in legal terms, as **colour of right**. The legal owner needs to be established and whether consent has been given by the owner to someone else.

- The accused must have intent to deprive the owner of the item or convert it to his or her own use. For example, stealing someone's bike and stripping it of parts for one's own use would be considered theft.

theft taking someone's property without her or his consent

colour of right the legal right to a property

? Did You Know?

Theft under $5000 has a maximum penalty of two years, while theft over $5000 can have a penalty of up to 10 years.

Did You Know?

Since February 1, 2008, British Columbians have to prepay for their gas at pumps. Known as "Grant's Law," it protects gas station workers. This was the result of Grant DePatie being dragged to his death while trying to stop a "gas-and-dash" in 2005. While prepayment is common in many U.S. states, British Columbia was the first Canadian province to pass such a law.

In 2006, there were about 160 000 auto thefts reported to police in Canada. There has generally been a downward trend in the number of auto thefts in Canada since 1996. The number has dropped by about 20 percent over the decade.

 ## Case

R. v. Foidart, 2005 MBCA 104 (CanLII)

For more information, Go to Nelson Social Studies

Edwin Foidart was hired by a Winnipeg church to repair their existing pipe organ as part of a major restoration project. In order to do this, Foidart located and purchased a used organ for the church. He planned to use the parts to restore the church's pipe organ. The used organ parts were temporarily stored in a garage on Foidart's property. However, difficulties arose, and the church had to cancel the restoration project. As a result, Foidart was asked to return all the organ parts in his possession. Over time, church members discovered that not all the organ parts had been returned. Some of the parts were found in pipe organs belonging to other churches. The accused was eventually charged with theft over $5000. In his defence, Foidart argued that he had a colour of right to the pieces from the collection. However, he chose not to testify at his trial to this effect.

The trial judge found Foidart guilty of theft. Since the judge had not heard from Foidart as to reasonable belief of colour of right, he could not consider this defence in his decision. Foidart appealed to the Manitoba Court of Appeal. The issue before the court was whether the lack of evidence from the accused himself as to his belief in the ownership of the organ parts was fatal to his case. In a 3–0 decision, the court agreed with the initial trial judge and dismissed Foidart's appeal.

For Discussion

1. How does the definition of theft apply to this case?

2. Explain how the definition of colour of right was applied in this case.

3. Why did the courts conclude that it was necessary for persons to take the stand in their own defence when arguing that they have a colour of right?

4. Do you agree with the Manitoba Court of Appeal's decision? Why or why not?

Identity Theft

Identity theft is the act of stealing someone else's identity, usually for criminal purposes. It has been called the crime of the twenty-first century. In 2005, there were 11 231 reported identity theft complaints in Canada. This crime accounted for over $8.5 million in losses. Identity theft is the fastest-growing form of consumer fraud in North America. Some examples of identity theft include the following:

How can you minimize your risk of identity theft?

Identity theft lineup.

- Mail theft—Thieves steal the mail of victims to get access to their critical information like credit card numbers. Using those numbers, thieves then extend the victim's credit line, apply for new credit cards, and open fraudulent accounts.

- Theft from personal spaces—Thieves target places such as residences, offices, or cars in which the owners have left wallets or purses. Some thieves rely on "dumpster diving." This is the act of rummaging through garbage in dumpsters or trash bins to remove documents containing valuable personal information.

- Misuse of personal data in business transactions—Criminals use special small devices known as "skimmers." They can read the data on a credit card's magnetic stripe when someone swipes the card during a purchase. Identity thieves sometimes install skimmers on the outside of legitimate financial institutions' ATM machines.

- Phishing, spoofing, and pretexting—Criminals can obtain personal data from people online using a technique known as phishing. In such cases, consumers receive "spoofed" e-mails that appear to come from legitimate businesses, such as banks. These e-mails ask consumers to visit spoofed websites that appear to be from the same businesses. Then, consumers are asked to enter personal information. Consumers also receive "pretext" phone calls from persons pretending to be with legitimate businesses, asking for personal information.

- Theft from company or government databases—Identity thieves try to access large databases of personal information. These databases are usually maintained by private companies and government agencies. Criminals steal computer hard drives and hack into databases to obtain this information.

An Edmonton police officer displays a skimmer, a mini video camera used to read PINs at ATMs.

Identity theft is a serious problem for victims. Stolen personal information can be used to open bank accounts or obtain loans or credit cards. It can also be used to gain employment or transfer property from the victim's name. Victims of identity theft may suffer major financial loss as well as damaged reputation or credit ratings. Government and businesses can also be victims of identity theft. If identity theft is used to support terrorist activities, there may be national security implications.

Currently, the *Criminal Code* does not contain a specific identity theft offence. Section 342 contains some new offences dealing with computers and credit/debit cards. However, most of the Code offences relating to property predate the computer and the Internet. In November 2007, Parliament introduced new legislation. If passed, it will create several new *Criminal Code* offences. The new law will make it an offence to obtain, possess, transfer, or sell the identity documents of another person.

Cornered   by Mike Baldwin

3-22 © 2004 Mike Baldwin / Dist. by Universal Press Syndicate

"Do you have another card? This one's been reported stolen."

Identity theft is the fastest-growing form of consumer fraud in North America.

Break and Enter

The law considers **break and enter**, commonly called burglary, a serious offence. The word "break" generally refers to opening something (usually by force), such as a locked door, that was meant to be closed. "Enter" means to go into a place, such as a building, where one has no right to be. In legal terms, they are defined in sections 321 and 350 of the *Criminal Code*. A simple example is someone who enters a home by breaking through a window or glass door.

break and enter entering someone's premises without permission with intent to commit an indictable offence

> **? Did You Know?**
>
> Since peaking in 1991, the rate of break and enters in 2006 has fallen to the lowest level in 30 years. Innovative police programs are some of the reasons for this decline. These programs include targeting high-risk neighbourhoods, the increase in the use of home security devices, and new locks or security bars in homes.

Break and enter, or burglary, is a serious offence.

Possession of Stolen Goods

fraud intentional deceit in order to cause a loss of property

false pretences presenting untruths or false information to induce the victim to act upon it

Section 354 of the *Criminal Code* deals with possession of stolen goods. It is an offence for anyone to possess stolen property and know that it is stolen. For example, if Sonia buys a stolen bicycle from Yolanda, and if Sonia knows that the bicycle is stolen, she is guilty of possessing stolen goods. Anyone found guilty of possessing stolen goods worth $5000 or more can be sentenced to up to 10 years in prison if the offence is treated as an indictable offence. If the value is less than $5000, the sentence is a maximum of two years. If the offence is treated as a summary conviction offence, the sentence is up to six months of imprisonment or a fine of $2000.

Fraud

Section 380 of the *Criminal Code* deals with **fraud**. Fraud is when someone deceives another person on purpose for criminal gain. In order to prove fraud, it must be shown that the accused knew that his or her actions could cause a loss to others. Given the ever-changing complexity of our society, fraud can take many different forms.

Making false statements to obtain credit or a loan is a crime. For example, it is a crime for Connie to apply for a loan and lie about her salary and assets. She could be charged with obtaining credit by **false pretences** under section 361(1) of the *Criminal Code*. A false pretence implies that someone is making a statement that she or he knows is false and that is intended to defraud, as in the case with Connie.

Credit card fraud can take many forms. Credit is a form of money, and the amount of money that can be spent using stolen credit cards can sometimes exceed the amount that one thief can carry away from a bank. Section 342 of the *Criminal Code* describes the offence of credit card fraud.

The *Criminal Code* also states that it is a crime to write a cheque if there is not enough money in the bank account to cover it. It is a defence if the person can prove that she or he believed there were sufficient funds when the cheque was written.

When the value of the fraud exceeds $5000, the offence is considered indictable. This offence carries a maximum 14-year prison term. Fraud for less than $5000 may be either indictable or summary. An indictable offence is punishable with a maximum two-year prison term. The penalty for a summary fraud is a term of up to six months of imprisonment or a fine of up to $2000.

Cost of Credit Card Fraud, 2005 ($ millions)

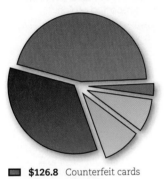

- **$126.8** Counterfeit cards
- **$97.3** Fraudulent applications or use
- **$26.1** Stolen cards
- **$22.5** Lost cards
- **$7.3** Other

In 2005, the RCMP reported $280 million in losses due to credit card fraud.

Review Your Understanding

1. What elements are necessary to convict someone of theft?
2. What is the legal meaning of the terms "break" and "enter"?
3. Explain the concept of "reverse onus" as it applies to the possession of stolen goods.
4. What are some of the problems caused by identity theft?
5. Discuss three types of fraud.

7.4 Other Crimes

This section discusses other *Criminal Code* offences not covered in the previous sections. The six subsections review a variety of crimes ranging from firearms offences to street racing and terrorism. These have nothing in common except that they are all prohibited by the *Criminal Code*. They are grouped together here for convenience only. The following offences are significant because they occur frequently and are of general interest:

- firearms
- street racing
- prostitution
- obscenity
- terrorism
- criminal harassment

Firearms

Firearms in Canada are regulated primarily by the *Firearms Act* and by Part III of the *Criminal Code*. The *Firearms Act* sets out the rules for possessing a firearm. The *Criminal Code* identifies the various weapons regulated by the *Firearms Act*. Penalties for illegal possession or misuse of a firearm are included in both the Code and the act. Provinces, territories, and municipalities may have additional laws and regulations that apply. For example, provinces are responsible for regulating hunting, so they may put restrictions on where people can hunt and on the size of firearms that may be used.

In 1995, Parliament passed the *Firearms Act*. This act required all gun owners to be licensed and registered. Licensing and registration under the *Firearms Act* can be compared to a driver's licence and the registration of a vehicle. A firearms licence shows that the licence holder has met certain safety criteria. He or she has taken a course such as the Canadian Firearms Safety Course and is allowed to possess and use firearms. A registration certificate identifies a firearm and links it to its owner to provide a means of tracking the firearm.

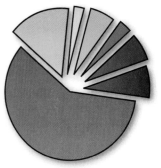

Violent Crime by Type of Weapon in Canada, 2006

- **59.2%** Physical force
- **15.5%** Threat (no weapon)
- **2.4%** Firearm
- **6.2%** Knife
- **3.0%** Club/Blunt instrument
- **6.3%** Other weapon
- **7.4%** Unknown

In 2006, the vast majority of reported violent crimes did not involve a firearm. A firearm was used against only 2.4 percent of victims. Physical force and threatening behaviour were much more common, accounting for three-quarters of all such assaults.

Hunting with a rifle is legal as long as the owner and user have a licence. Also, the firearm must be registered under the *Firearms Act*.

Chapter 7 *Criminal Code Offences* **237**

non-restricted firearm any rifle or shotgun that is neither restricted nor prohibited

restricted firearm a firearm that needs to be registered

prohibited firearm a firearm that a person is not allowed to possess

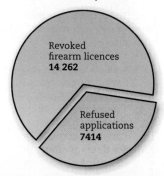

This sawed-off shotgun would be classified as a prohibited firearm.

Firearm Licence Refusal and Revocation, 2008

Revoked firearm licences **14 262**

Refused applications **7414**

As of January 2008, a total of 21 676 firearms applications have been refused and licences revoked in Canada. The following are the main reasons for doing so:
• a history of violence
• mental illness
• potential risk to self or others
• unsafe firearm use and storage
• drug offences
• providing false information

Classes of Firearms

There are three classes of firearms: non-restricted, restricted, and prohibited. **Non-restricted firearms** are ordinary rifles and shotguns other than those referred to below. As of November 2007, non-restricted firearms no longer need to be registered. The reason for this is that they are rarely used in homicides. **Restricted firearms** include the following:

• handguns that are not prohibited

• semi-automatic rifles and shotguns with a barrel shorter than 470 mm

• rifles and shotguns with an overall length of less than 660 mm

Prohibited firearms include the following:

• handguns with a barrel length of 105 mm or less and those using .25 or .32 calibre ammunition

• rifles and shotguns that have been shortened so that their barrel length is less than 457 mm or their overall length is less than 660 mm

• semi-automatic firearms converted to fully automatic

• fully automatic firearms, such as machine guns and assault rifles

Firearm Licences

• To be able to register a firearm, you need a valid firearms licence. This is your authorization to possess and register a firearm and to obtain ammunition. Your licence must be kept current for as long as you possess firearms in Canada. Licence and registration information is contained in the Canadian Firearms Information System. This system is operated by the RCMP and is available to police officers across the country. The types of licences are as follows:

– For Canadian residents 18 and older—The Possession and Acquisition Licence is the only licence currently available to new applicants. It is renewable every five years for a fee of $60. Applicants must have passed the Canadian Firearms Safety Course (CFSC).

– For individuals aged 12 to 17—A Minor's Possession Licence will allow young people to borrow a non-restricted rifle or shotgun for approved purposes such as hunting or target shooting. Generally, the minimum age is 12 years. However, exceptions can be made for younger people who need to hunt to sustain themselves and their families. Applicants must pass the CFSC. Once you turn 18, you will need to apply for a Possession and Acquisition Licence.

Street Racing

Street racing refers to illegal auto races that take place on public roads. They range from spontaneous contests between two cars at street corners to well-organized, complex events. A whole subculture has developed around street racing. It has been glamorized in movies such as *The Fast and the Furious* series, as well as in video games such as *Need for Speed* and *Juiced*. Over the years, street racing has led to serious injuries and loss of life among participants, spectators, and sometimes innocent bystanders and police officers. There were an estimated 10 deaths from street racing in Canada in the first half of 2006 alone. In the Toronto region, 35 people have died since 1999 as a result of street racing.

street racing the criminal offence of driving a vehicle at high speeds in a reckless and dangerous manner

Street racing is a dangerous activity that has led to numerous fatalities and injuries. It was added to the *Criminal Code* in 2006.

In December 2006, Parliament passed a law to address street racing. Section 249(4) of the *Criminal Code* defines street racing as operating a motor vehicle in a race with at least one other motor vehicle. The *Criminal Code* does not make street racing itself a crime. However, it does define dangerous or criminally negligent operation of a vehicle. Under the Code, the penalty for street racing offences is harsher than that for dangerous operation of a motor vehicle and criminal negligence. The penalties for street racing offences are as follows:

- dangerous operation or criminal negligence causing bodily harm — 14 years (instead of 10)

- dangerous driving causing death — life imprisonment (instead of 14 years)

- mandatory suspension of driving licences

Prostitution

prostitution sexual activity in exchange for money

soliciting communicating for the purposes of prostitution

Simply put, **prostitution** is selling sex for money. It is often described as the world's "oldest profession" because it has existed throughout recorded history. The act of prostitution is legal in Canada. However, some activities related to it are illegal. These include soliciting and keeping a common bawdyhouse (a brothel or place of prostitution). **Soliciting** is communicating for the purpose of prostitution. According to the Supreme Court of Canada, such communication must be "pressing or persistent" to be an offence. In December 1985, changes to section 213 of the *Criminal Code* were made to deal with this issue. Under this section, it is not permitted to stop a motor vehicle or to communicate with anyone for the purpose of prostitution. The main goal of section 213 is to reduce the visibility of street prostitution.

Procuring (obtaining or getting) is another illegal activity related to prostitution. It involves directing customers to a prostitute. It also involves living off the earnings of a prostitute. The penalty for procuring is much harsher than the penalties for soliciting or keeping a common bawdyhouse. That is because without the procurer (the pimp), prostitution might not happen at all.

Some Canadians feel that soliciting is a "crime without a victim." Others argue that prostitutes are victims of procuring. Nonetheless, some people believe that this is a moral issue (not a legal one). As such, the government should not interfere. However, legislators are concerned about the issues that surround prostitution, such as its frequency in high-crime areas, its connection with the drug trade, the exploitation of prostitutes by pimps, and the impact of prostitution on neighbourhoods.

Some provinces have moved to protect underage prostitutes. Alberta's *Protection of Children Involved in Prostitution Act* (passed in 2000) allows authorities to pick up suspected prostitutes under 18 years of age. They are taken to a safe house and can be held for up to 72 hours without being charged. The safe house provides an opportunity for the youths to be free from their pimps and to receive counselling.

Some provinces have established additional means of controlling prostitution. For example, the highway and traffic acts in several provinces have been amended to allow police to seize, impound, and sell vehicles used in picking up prostitutes on the street. Also, the person's driving licence can be suspended. In 2002, Ontario passed a civil law that goes even further. Civil courts are allowed to freeze and seize any property bought with the proceeds of prostitution without laying criminal charges.

Urban centres such as Toronto attract prostitution and related crimes.

Review Your Understanding

1. What is the difference between prohibited and restricted firearms?
2. What must a citizen in Canada do to legally possess or use a gun?
3. Summarize some of the newest legislation dealing with firearms.
4. Explain the main aspects of the street racing legislation in the *Criminal Code*.
5. What is the difference between procuring and soliciting in terms of prostitution? What elements must exist for a conviction on soliciting?

Obscenity

Obscenity refers to words, images, or actions that go against moral values. This could range from simple profanity to offensive pictures or videos. The legal definition is described in section 163 of the *Criminal Code*. However, this issue continues to be controversial. The Supreme Court generally follows the "community standards test." It must determine what the community would tolerate. Sex acts that are "degrading or dehumanizing" are considered obscene. The courts frequently must determine whether something is obscene or a work of art. Under the *Criminal Code*, a publication is considered obscene if it exploits sex or contains material on extreme crime, horror, cruelty, or violence.

A variety of offences relate to obscenity. These include making, printing, circulating, mailing, or distributing obscene material. Police can obtain a warrant to seize any obscene materials and then lay charges. Customs officers also have the right to seize materials that they think are obscene. For example, Vancouver's Little Sisters Book and Art Emporium imported books that included gay and lesbian erotica. Under section 163(8) of the *Criminal Code*, they were deemed obscene. Therefore, customs officials seized these and did not allow the material to enter Canada. On December 15, 2000, in *Little Sisters Book and Art Emporium v. Canada*, the Supreme Court supported the rights of customs officers to ban the obscene material from entering the country. However, in this specific case, it objected to the arbitrary targeted practices of the customs agents and confirmed that the onus of proving that material is obscene lies with the customs agency.

obscenity words, images, or actions that are offensive to public morality

Child Pornography

Children are vulnerable and need to be protected from harmful criminal activity. This has led to changes in the *Criminal Code*. Anyone who possesses, produces, distributes, or sells child pornography is guilty of an offence. The penalty for possessing such material is 14 days to five years in prison. The maximum prison term for producing or distributing such material is 10 years. These offences are outlined in section 163 of the *Criminal Code*. In June 2002, Parliament passed a law to protect children from being exploited over the Internet. The new law made it illegal for people to access child pornography online. Also, the law made it illegal to communicate with children online for sexual purposes (section 172.1(1). However, pornography on the Internet is a growing concern since it is difficult to regulate it.

It is important for society to protect children from harmful criminal activity such as child pornography.

R. v. Smith, 2005 CanLII 23805 (ON C.A.)

For more information, **Go to Nelson Social Studies**

Donald Smith ran a website that contained material showing "fantasy violence" against women. The site warned that it contained "nudity and fantasy violence." It included written stories submitted by members and audiovisual material that Smith produced. The audiovisual clips showed topless women with apparent knife and arrow wounds. Actors were used for the clips, and the wounds were created by digital software. There were no explicit acts of sex in the video clips.

Smith was charged under section 163(1) of the *Criminal Code* with making and distributing obscene material. In November 2002, Smith was convicted, and the judge imposed a term of probation and a $100 000 fine. Smith was also prohibited from accessing the Internet. The judge also ordered Smith to turn over his websites to the Crown. Smith appealed this decision on July 7, 2005.

• Do you think Smith's appeal was upheld or dismissed by the Court of Appeal? What would you have done if you were the judge in this case? Should the *Criminal Code* regulate Internet obscenity?

Terrorism

terrorism the unlawful use of force or violence to further certain political or social objectives

Terrorism is any violent action taken for political, religious, or ideological reasons. This includes killing people or harming property to create fear and further the terrorists' goals. Terrorism does not have to take place in Canada. It can be against a Canadian citizen or government located outside of the country.

Motorists from New Brunswick wait to go through U.S. Customs. The Canadian and U.S. governments co-operate to ensure that terrorists do not cross our borders.

The terrorist attacks of September 11, 2001, resulted in several changes to the Canadian *Criminal Code*. The Code now allows the government to publish the names of terrorist groups. Canada has taken action to cut off funds to terrorists. It is now an offence to collect or provide funds for terrorist activities. The government also has the right to freeze any property that is being used in any way to assist a terrorist group. Also, financial institutions must report to the government any assets they have that belong to an identified terrorist group. These changes seriously violate the legal rights of suspects and accused persons. They also raise the issue of freedoms versus security and trying to strike a proper balance between the two. To fight terrorism, Canada passed several new laws. The *Anti-Terrorism Act* became law in 2001. The *Public Safety Act*, passed in 2004, made changes to numerous federal statutes. See the chart on the next page for the highlights of these two laws.

Highlights of the *Anti-Terrorism Act* and the *Public Safety Act*

Anti-Terrorism Act	Public Safety Act
• a legal definition of terrorism • terrorist offences defined • new investigative tools for law enforcement agencies, including more power to use electronic surveillance • new powers for police to arrest suspected terrorists without charge • those with information about terrorist activities must appear before a judge to provide that information • protected classified information in courtroom proceedings	• "interim orders" to deal with immediate threats and emergencies • tighter security over threats to aviation, pipelines, and transmission lines • controls over the export technologies sensitive to national security • prevention of money laundering and the spreading of biological and other weapons by terrorists • powers to arrest and detain within Canada foreign nationals without proper identification • declaring bomb threats and other hoaxes to be criminal offences

This chart outlines the highlights of the *Anti-Terrorism Act* and the *Public Safety Act*. The purpose of these two laws is to identify, prosecute, and convict terrorists operating in Canada.

You Be the Judge

Canada (Attorney General) v. Khawaja (F.C.), 2007 FC 490 (CanLII)

For more information, **Go to Nelson Social Studies**

In 2004, the RCMP raided Momin Khawaja's workplace and home in the Ottawa area. The raid was part of a Canada–Britain investigation. In total, nine men of Pakistani heritage were arrested. On March 29, 2004, Khawaja was the only person arrested in Canada. He was officially charged with several terrorist-related offences. Khawaja was the first man charged under the federal *Anti-Terrorism Act*.

On October 24, 2006, the judge who presided over the case struck down the "motive clause" of the *Anti-Terrorism Act*. This clause defines a terrorist act as one committed for political, religious, or ideological purposes. The judge stated that this clause violated the *Charter of Rights and Freedoms*. The judge wrote that this definition infringed on fundamental freedoms, including those of religion, thought, belief, opinion, expression, and association. However, the judge allowed the trial to go on. Khawaja appealed to the Supreme Court, asking that the charges against him be dropped. His appeal was dismissed in April 2008.

On October 29, 2008, the Ontario Superior Court found Momin Khawaja guilty of five terrorism-related charges. The 29-day trial was considered the first major test of Canada's *Anti-Terrorism Act*, passed in the aftermath of the September 11, 2001, attacks in the United States.

• Do you agree with the court's decision? Why or why not?

This is a courtroom sketch of Momin Khawaja. In 2004, Khawaja became the first person charged under Canada's new *Anti-Terrorism Act* (2001).

Chapter 7 *Criminal Code Offences*

Criminal Harassment

criminal harassment the pursuit or repeated communication with an unwilling victim

Criminal harassment (stalking) is pursuing or communicating with an unwilling victim and with his or her friends and family. Such harassment can range from spying on the individual's home or workplace to actual threats. This offence was added to the *Criminal Code* (section 264) in 1993. It prohibits anyone from repeatedly communicating with or following another person against her or his wishes. The activity causes the person to reasonably fear for his or her safety. It is an indictable offence and is punishable with a prison sentence of up to 10 years.

Criminal Harassment in Canada

- About 88 percent of victims of criminal harassment are harassed by someone they know (ex-partners, spouses, acquaintances, co-workers, or close friends).

- About 12 percent of victims of criminal harassment are harassed by a stranger.

- Although anyone can be a victim of criminal harassment, about 8 out of 10 victims are women, and 9 out of 10 stalkers are men.

Criminal harassment is an indictable offence.

In May 2008, Jack Jordan was convicted of stalking actress Uma Thurman (pictured here) for more than two years. During that time, he would show up on her doorstep or at her movie sets. He also sent the actress a series of creepy love letters.

Review Your Understanding

1. How does the *Criminal Code* define obscenity?
2. What is the purpose of the National Sex Offender Registry?
3. What were some of the changes made to the *Criminal Code* as a result of the September 11, 2001, attacks?
4. Summarize some of the main changes to Canada's terrorism laws as a result of the *Public Safety Act, 2004.*
5. How does the *Criminal Code* define criminal harassment?

7.5 The Controlled Drugs and Substances Act

drug a chemical substance that alters the structure or function of a living organism

A **drug** is defined as "any substance that by its chemical nature alters structure or function in a living organism." This definition is so broad that it includes everything from Tylenol to crack. Of course, not all chemicals with these effects are classified as illegal drugs. Otherwise, tea, beer, cola, and Aspirin would be classed with heroin and cocaine. Certain drugs have been classified as criminal and are restricted by law. Thus, courts have declared that marijuana is not an irrelevant narcotic. It is still on the list of substances defined by Parliament as a controlled drug. The relevant statute that relates to the use of drugs is called the *Controlled Drugs and Substances Act*. It was passed in 1997 and is a combination of the old *Narcotic Control Act* and sections of the *Food and Drugs Act*.

The *Controlled Drugs and Substances Act* makes the possession and selling of a variety of drugs a criminal act. **Controlled substances** are itemized on four basic lists, known as schedules:

- Schedule I—the most dangerous drugs, including narcotics such as heroin and cocaine

- Schedule II—cannabis (marijuana) and its derivatives

- Schedule III—many of the more dangerous drugs previously found in the *Food and Drugs Act*, such as lysergic acid diethylamide (LSD) and Ecstasy

- Schedule IV—drugs that must be controlled but that have therapeutic use, such as barbiturates

There are other schedules in the *Controlled Drugs and Substances Act* besides just these four. Schedules V and VI deal with other medicinal drugs. Schedules VII and VIII deal with cannabis resin (such as hashish) depending on the amount. The act defines a controlled substance as being any substance included in Schedules I to IV.

controlled substance any material listed in the *Controlled Drugs and Substances Act*

Illegal drugs such as Ecstasy (shown here) are listed on Schedule III of the *Controlled Drugs and Substances Act*.

Possession

It is an offence to possess any drug listed in Schedules I to III of the act. However, Canadians are allowed to possess drugs found in Schedule IV for therapeutic use. The chart below summarizes the penalties for possessing drugs found in Schedules I, II, III, and VIII.

Penalties for Possession

Schedule and Substance	Offence	Penalty (maximums)
Schedule I Dangerous drugs	• if a first offence and tried summarily • if a subsequent offence and tried summarily • if tried as an indictable offence	• $1000 fine and/or 6 months • $2000 fine and/or 1 year • 7 years
Schedule II Cannabis (marijuana) and its derivatives	• if a first offence and tried summarily • if a subsequent offence and tried summarily • if tried as an indictable offence	• $1000 and/or 6 months • $2000 and/or 1 year • 5 years less a day
Schedule III Dangerous drugs formerly listed in the *Food and Drugs Act*	• if a first offence and tried summarily • if a subsequent offence and tried summarily • if tried as an indictable offence	• $1000 and/or 6 months • $2000 and/or 1 year • 3 years
Schedule VIII Cannabis resin up to 1 g and cannabis up to 30 g	• if charged under Schedule VIII, always tried summarily	• $1000 and/or 6 months

A person found with one marijuana cigarette is treated less harshly than someone who has a large amount of cannabis. Also, first-time offenders are not treated as severely as those with numerous possession convictions.

Even a small quantity of a drug can get you charged with possession. As long as the drug can be identified, a charge can be laid. In addition, the *Controlled Drugs and Substances Act* adopts the definition of possession given in section 4(3) of the *Criminal Code*. A person is defined as "having possession" even when he or she does not technically own the drug. Having control over a drug can therefore lead to a charge. For example, if five people are sharing a marijuana joint, they could all be convicted of possession. The owner of the house in which the five are smoking the drug is particularly vulnerable, even if he or she does not use the marijuana, because allowing its use in his or her home implies consent.

In prosecuting a drug case, the Crown must first prove possession of a controlled substance. In addition, the Crown must show that there was intent to possess. That is, the accused must know that the substance is a drug. The Supreme Court ruled in *R. v. Beaver*, 1957, that *mens rea* is a necessary element of the offence. Louis Beaver had a package of white powder that he thought was milk sugar in his possession. In fact, it contained a narcotic. The court agreed that Beaver did not know the substance was a narcotic. He was acquitted of possession.

In 2001, the *Controlled Drugs and Substances Act* was changed to allow certain patients to grow or buy their own marijuana. The Marijuana Medical Access Regulations (MMAR) came into effect on July 30, 2001. Canada became the first country in the world to adopt a system regulating the medicinal use of marijuana. This change was a result of the ruling in the *R. v. Parker* case discussed below. Legal users of marijuana must carry an **Authorization to Possess (ATP)** card. This allows them to have marijuana for medical purposes. As of December 2007, 2329 Canadians held ATPs.

Authorization to Possess (ATP) legal authority to possess and produce marijuana for medical purposes

 Case

R. v. Parker, 2000 CanLII 5762 (ON C.A.)

For more information, Go to Nelson Social Studies

Terrance Parker had suffered from epileptic seizures for almost 40 years. Surgery failed to control them. Conventional medicine was only moderately successful. Smoking marijuana, however, reduced the number of seizures substantially. He had no legal source of marijuana, so he grew his own. Police raided and searched his home twice in 1996 and 1997. He was charged with cultivating and possessing marijuana. His defence was that the legislation infringed on his guaranteed Charter rights. Section 7 of the *Charter of Rights and Freedoms* guarantees life, liberty, and security. The trial judge wanted to protect Parker and others like him who need medical marijuana. The judge suggested an exemption for persons possessing or cultivating marijuana for their "personal medically

approved use." The Crown appealed the decision.

The Ontario Court of Appeal agreed with the trial judge. Parker should have the right to grow marijuana for medicinal use. However, the appeal court objected to the trial judge's attempt to amend the law himself. That would change the meaning of the law. On July 31, 2000, the Ontario Court of Appeal unanimously (3–0) declared Canada's marijuana laws unconstitutional. This was because it did not allow for the medical use of marijuana. The judges gave the federal government one year to change the law. After that, marijuana possession laws would be removed from the *Criminal Code* entirely. In July 2001, the law was changed to allow access to marijuana for medical purposes.

continues...

R. v. Parker, 2000 CanLII 5762 (ON C.A.)

Medical marijuana users Terrance Parker (right) and Mary-Lynne Chamney smoke marijuana. They both suffer from epilepsy. On September 19, 2002, a group of seriously ill people crowded the Ontario courthouse in Toronto. They were there to fight for the right to use medical marijuana. In their opinion, failure to do so violated their Charter rights. Do you agree? Explain.

For Discussion

1. What does section 7 of the Charter guarantee?
2. The court declared the prohibition on the possession of marijuana for medical purposes to be "unconstitutional." What does that mean?
3. The Ontario Court of Appeal ruled that Parker needed marijuana to control his epilepsy. Forcing him "to choose between his health and imprisonment violates his right to liberty and security of the person." Do you agree? Explain.
4. Should marijuana continue to be criminalized? Do you think it should be decriminalized or even legalized? Discuss.

Review Your Understanding

1. What is the name of the statute relating to the use of drugs in Canada?
2. What is the definition of a drug? What is the criminal classification of drugs based on?
3. Describe two situations in which someone may be charged with possession while not physically possessing the drug.
4. Is intent necessary for possession? Explain.
5. What changes were made to the *Controlled Drugs and Substances Act* in 2001 in response to the ruling in R. v. Parker?

Drug Trafficking

According to the *Controlled Drugs and Substances Act*, to **traffic** is to "sell, administer, give, transfer, transport, send, or deliver the substance." Section 5 of the act states that no person shall traffic in, or possess for the purpose of trafficking, any substance included in Schedules I, II, III, or IV, or any substance believed to be that substance. The various penalties for trafficking are listed in the chart on the next page.

traffic to sell, administer, give, transfer, transport, send, or deliver a controlled substance

Penalties for Trafficking

Schedule and Substance	Offence	Penalty (maximums)
Schedule I Dangerous drugs	• if tried as an indictable offence	• life
Schedule II Cannabis (marijuana) and its derivatives	• if tried as an indictable offence • if amount trafficked not more than amount specified in Schedule VII (3 kg)	• life • 5 years less a day
Schedule III Dangerous drugs formerly listed in the *Food and Drugs Act*	• if tried as a summary conviction offence • if tried as an indictable offence	• 18 months • 10 years
Schedule VIII Controlled drugs with therapeutic use	• if tried as a summary conviction offence • if tried as an indictable offence	• 1 year • 3 years

The maximum penalties for trafficking vary with the type of controlled substance.

Trafficking has a very broad definition. As a result, prosecutors are free to charge individuals with trafficking even when a simple possession charge might be more appropriate. How much assistance must someone give a drug buyer before the law views it as trafficking? The issue is addressed in the *R. v. Greyeyes* case below.

 Case

R. v. Greyeyes, 1997 CanLII 313 (S.C.C.)

For more information, Go to Nelson Social Studies

In August 1994, Ernest Greyeyes sold five joints of marijuana to an undercover RCMP officer, Constable Morgan. The next day, Morgan asked Greyeyes if he knew where he could get some cocaine. Greyeyes took Morgan to an apartment building. Greyeyes talked to the occupants through the closed door and negotiated a deal. The purchase price was $40 for the cocaine, and the items were exchanged under the door. Morgan drove Greyeyes home and gave him $10 for helping to obtain the cocaine. Shortly after this incident, Greyeyes was charged with trafficking.

At trial, Greyeyes was acquitted. However, the Saskatchewan Court of Appeal overturned the acquittal. Greyeyes appealed to the Supreme Court of Canada. The issue was whether someone can be found guilty of trafficking by aiding or abetting in the sale of narcotics. The Supreme Court dismissed Greyeyes's appeal. It stated that anyone who acts on behalf of a purchaser of narcotics should be treated as a purchaser and not as a trafficker. But, in this case, Greyeyes did far more than act as a purchaser. He clearly aided the traffic of narcotics.

For Discussion

1. Examine the wording of what constitutes the offence of trafficking. Is possession an included element of the offence?

2. What are the elements that are necessary in order to be found guilty of aiding and abetting an offence (see also Chapter 4)?

3. In your opinion, should Greyeyes have been found guilty of possession, possession for the purpose of trafficking, aiding or abetting for the purpose of possession, trafficking, or aiding or abetting in trafficking? Support your opinion.

4. Having police officers pose as drug dealers to catch drug users has been criticized as being unethical. Do you agree or disagree? Why?

Whether someone will be charged with trafficking depends on how much controlled drug is seized. Before 1986, the onus was on the accused to prove his or her innocence. The accused had to prove that he or she did *not* have the controlled drug for the purpose of trafficking. In *R. v. Oakes*, 1986 (see Chapter 2, page 39), the Supreme Court of Canada ruled that this "reverse onus" violated the presumption of innocence contained in section 11(d) of the *Charter of Rights and Freedoms*. Since then, the onus has been on the Crown to prove that the person possessed the controlled drug for the purpose of trafficking. Drug paraphernalia (equipment such as scales or pipes) or large amounts of cash may be used by the Crown as evidence of trafficking.

In 2004, York Region Police seized hundreds of bags of Ecstasy powder, estimated to be worth at least $100 million.

Police often act as undercover agents in stopping the drug trade. The procedures they use to obtain evidence may open the door to an offender's appeal. Police officers posing as drug dealers in order to entrap drug offenders is an example. These practices seem to undermine the integrity of the justice system by giving the police too many powers. Several court rulings have sent a message to police that they may not entrap people. Nor may they use physical violence to obtain evidence. Police also may not undertake "random virtue testing." This is when a police officer encourages someone to commit an offence, even if there is no reasonable suspicion that the person is already engaged in the particular criminal activity. For example, asking someone to traffic drugs when they have never engaged in such an act could be considered random virtue testing.

Police Rights of Search and Seizure under the Act

The *Controlled Drugs and Substances Act* grants police the right to search for controlled substances and drugs. Other rights that are incidental to the search, such as arrest, are granted by the *Criminal Code*. Search and arrest are discussed in more detail in Chapter 5.

Section 11 of the *Controlled Drugs and Substances Act* states that a search warrant can be issued by a justice if police believe that evidence of a drug offence can be located. An officer may act without a warrant if the situation is urgent and it is impractical to obtain one. For example, an officer would be compelled to force a search if the suspect is obviously flushing evidence down the toilet. The act provides that the officer can use as much force as is necessary in these circumstances to enter the premises.

Police officers used a drug search warrant to seize these marijuana plants in Peterborough, Ontario.

Upon entry, the officer can search anyone if there are reasonable grounds to believe that the person possesses a controlled substance. For example, the smell of marijuana smoke or a tip that drugs are being concealed are reasonable grounds for the search. The officer may seize any controlled substances and any items believed to contain them. Objects that may have been used in committing the offence may also be seized. These may include equipment used in the manufacturing of drugs, such as scales.

The *Controlled Drugs and Substances Act* does not give police the power to stop and search a person for drugs in a public place. The *Criminal Code* does authorize this type of search, but there must be reasonable grounds for believing that the person is in possession of a drug. The police are required to establish reasonable grounds before they proceed with the search. Reasonable grounds can include police surveillance, visual or physical signs of drug consumption, or a reliable informant.

Review Your Understanding

1. How does the *Controlled Drugs and Substances Act* define trafficking?
2. What two points must the Crown prove to obtain a conviction for trafficking?
3. Who can be charged with the offence of importing and exporting narcotics?
4. Who has the onus in a trial to prove that an accused person possessed a controlled drug for the purpose of trafficking? What evidence can prove this?
5. Describe a situation in which a warrantless search for drugs would be legal. Explain why.

Impaired Driving Charges, 2002–2006

Year	Number of Charges	Rate per 100 000 People
2002	80 045	255
2003	77 645	245
2004	80 339	251
2005	78 370	243
2006	74 331	228

The impaired driving rate has been dropping since 2004. Can you think of reasons why this might be the case?

7.6 Driving Offences

Motor vehicle accidents are far too common in Canada. Many can be prevented. To try and make the roads safer, the *Criminal Code* deals with a number of offences related to driving. Impaired driving is a concern for most Canadians. Those who drink and drive are penalized by law and criticized by society. The federal government has increased *Criminal Code* penalties for impaired driving. Despite the increase, 74 331 impaired driving charges were laid in 2006 in Canada. That was down 6 percent from 2005 and down 30 percent from 1996. The provinces and territories regulate highways, the licensing of drivers, and alcohol sales. They have introduced measures to deter impaired driving. These include keeping offenders away from motor vehicles by suspending licences and other restrictions.

In February 2008, new legislation was passed called the *Tackling Violent Crime Act*. It took effect and became law on May 1, 2008. The act provides the police with better tools to detect and investigate impaired driving in the following ways:

- It authorizes police officers to conduct roadside sobriety tests to see whether a person is impaired by alcohol, drugs, or a combination of both. They may do this by taking samples of bodily fluids to confirm the presence of the impairing substances.

- It makes it an offence to refuse to co-operate with police demands for physical sobriety tests or bodily fluid samples.

- It allows only scientifically valid defences against impaired driving. This reduces the number of individuals who can avoid conviction on technicalities.

The act also increases the penalties for impaired driving. For example, a minimum sentence of 120 days in jail is now in place for a third impaired driving offence.

You and the Law

In November 2008, Ontario introduced new controversial legislation to crack down on dangerous driving among young drivers. The new law included a ban on more than one teenage passenger in a vehicle driven by a young person. Over 150 000 teens organized themselves through Facebook to cause the government to back down. As a result, the government revoked this part of the new law. Do you believe that the criticism had merit? What other laws affecting young people would you consider protesting through a Facebook website?

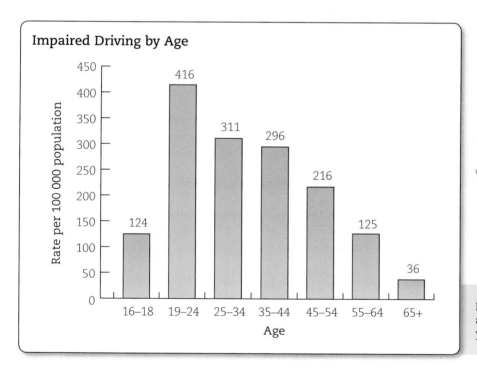

Impaired Driving by Age

Rate per 100 000 population

- 16–18: 124
- 19–24: 416
- 25–34: 311
- 35–44: 296
- 45–54: 216
- 55–64: 125
- 65+: 36

Age

Impaired driving rates are highest among young drivers.

Definition of a Motor Vehicle

The *Criminal Code* defines a **motor vehicle** as any vehicle that is moved "by any means other than by muscular power." In other words, bicycles and skateboards do not qualify. Obviously, automobiles, trucks, motorcycles and scooters are motor vehicles. Others include boats and aircraft. In addition, snowmobiles and all-terrain vehicles (ATVs) are classified as motor vehicles.

motor vehicle a vehicle that moves other than by muscular power, not including railway equipment

Dangerous Operation of a Motor Vehicle

It is an offence to operate a motor vehicle in a way that is dangerous to the public in any public place. A "public place" includes parking lots at shopping plazas and schools. This includes private roads regularly used by the public, such as a private road in a townhouse complex that is shared only by the individuals living there. However, most private property is exempt.

To convict someone of dangerous operation of a motor vehicle, the Crown must establish fault. The standard used is the care that a responsible driver would have exercised. All factors are considered. These include the nature, condition, and use of the public place where the offence occurred. In addition, the amount of traffic at the time and place is important. There does not have to be any "public" present at the time of the offence—only the possibility that someone could have been present. For example, driving at excessive speeds on a road in the middle of the night when there are no other vehicles out can still be considered "dangerous operation of a motor vehicle."

 You Be the Judge

R. v. MacGillivray, 1995 CanLII 139 (S.C.C.)

For more information, **Go to Nelson Social Studies**

On a warm, clear summer day, the beach at Cribbons Point in Nova Scotia was crowded with swimmers and boaters. One of the boaters was Daniel MacGillivray. His boat sped across the water toward a group of boys, who waved their arms and shouted to alert MacGillivray to the dangerous situation. The boat was up at such an angle that MacGillivray did not see the boys. The boat's propeller struck and killed one of them. MacGillivray was charged under section 249(4) of the *Criminal Code* with operating a vessel in a manner that was dangerous to the public and causing the death of the victim. Some witnesses testified that the boat was speeding, and the trial judge found that no one was leaning over the side to look out for dangers.

- If you were the judge in this case, what would you have decided? Was MacGillivray using the proper standard of care in this case? Should he be criminally responsible for the boy's death?

Failure to Stop at the Scene of an Accident

If you are involved in an accident, you must stop at the scene. The law requires you to give your name and address to the other party. If the other party has been injured or appears to require assistance, you must offer to help. This area of law is dealt with under section 252 of the *Criminal Code*.

Call 911 if anyone is injured or there is more than $1000 damage to the vehicles. Also, you must report if you suspect that any of the other drivers involved is guilty of a *Criminal Code* offence (such as driving under the influence of drugs or alcohol). Follow the instructions given to you by the 911 emergency operator. Police will arrive as soon as possible.

If no one is injured and total damage to all the vehicles involved appears to be less than $1000, call your local police for instructions. Police units may be dispatched to the scene. More likely, you may be instructed to report to a collision reporting centre within 24 hours.

The penalty for failure to stop was increased in 1999 because legislators were concerned that impaired drivers were leaving accident scenes to avoid being charged. Occasionally, there are good reasons for leaving the scene of an accident, such as getting help. However, there is no justification if the accused knows an accident has occurred, panics, and leaves. The punishment for failure to stop at the scene of an accident is up to five years in prison. If someone is injured, the maximum sentence is 10 years. If death results, the maximum sentence can be life imprisonment.

Failing to stop at the scene of an accident is an offence in the *Criminal Code*. If someone has been injured, you are required to offer assistance.

Impaired Driving

Impaired driving has become the main criminal cause of death in Canada. Yet offenders have often received sentences that seem trivial compared with the consequences of their actions. Canadians have urged legislators to increase penalties for this offence as a deterrent. Section 253 of the *Criminal Code* describes the offence of impaired driving. Section 255 of the Code outlines punishments for impaired driving charges.

It is not necessary for the vehicle to be in motion, or even running, for a person to be charged with impaired driving. *Mens rea* exists when there is intent to assume the care or control of the vehicle while impaired. In addition, *mens rea* exists when the blood-alcohol level is over 80. *Actus reus* is the action of assuming care or control. Sitting in the driver's seat implies care or control, unless the driver can establish that he or she did not intend to set the car in motion (for example, if the person did not have the car keys or the car did not function). In other cases, such as when the driver is lying down in the car, the Crown must prove beyond a reasonable doubt that the accused was in care or control of the vehicle.

In 1969, Parliament introduced Canada's first-ever Breathalyzer law. It was modelled on British legislation. This law made it illegal for someone to operate a motor vehicle with a **blood–alcohol concentration (BAC)** of more than 80 milligrams of alcohol in 100 millilitres of blood. This is known as a 0.08 reading. The new law also gave police officers the right to demand roadside breath samples and made it an offence to refuse one. In December 1985, the *Criminal Code* was amended to provide for stiffer penalties for impaired drivers. It allowed a blood sample to be taken where a breath sample could not be obtained.

The term "impaired" is not defined in the *Criminal Code*. The court need not factor in a blood-alcohol concentration that would establish the person as impaired. Rather, it is up to the court to determine, on the evidence presented, whether the ability to drive was impaired. It also does not matter how the accused was driving. What is important is establishing that the driver's ability

blood–alcohol concentration (BAC)
a measure of concentration of alcohol in a person's blood

 Did You Know?

In 2005, about 380 668 people were injured in motor vehicle crashes. According to MADD Canada, about 71 413 of these were involved in impaired driving crashes. That is an average of about 196 per day.

Touching fingers to nose or walking in a straight line are two ways that police test drivers for sobriety.

to operate a vehicle is impaired. In other words, you do not have to fail a Breathalyzer test to be charged with impaired driving. A police officer can decide to charge you based on a number of tests (for example, smell, slurred speech, sobriety test, and so on). Taking a Breathalyzer test may certainly support the other evidence, but it is not essential.

An officer may also require a driver to perform a sobriety test, such as walking in a straight line. In such cases, the driver is being detained. Courts have ruled that the demand to perform such tests is valid, as long as the evidence of failing the test is used only to decide whether the person should be asked to submit a breath sample.

The issue of whether a vehicle was in the "care or control" of the accused has been central to many cases. A person standing beside his vehicle after having called a tow truck has been ruled to be in care or control, as has a person who sat in her car for 15 minutes after stopping. The following case also focused on the issue of care and control.

 Case

R. v. Decker, 2002 NFCA 9 (CanLII)

For more information, Go to Nelson Social Studies

On Friday nights, Barry Decker would drive to St. John's, Newfoundland. There, he parked his truck near his friend's home and went partying downtown. He used taxis during the evening. Decker usually stayed at his friend's house overnight and drove home on Saturday morning. A little after 3:30 a.m. on November 20, 1999, Decker returned by taxi to the friend's house but could not get in.

After unsuccessfully trying to locate his friends by cellphone, he decided to sleep in the truck. He lay down and went to sleep, knowing that the engine would shut off in a few minutes as pre-programmed by the remote starter. A few moments later, a police officer found Decker. He had his attention drawn to the vehicle by the fact that the lights were on. Later at the police station, breath samples were taken, and Decker

Being behind the wheel of a vehicle while intoxicated may be enough to establish care or control of the vehicle, even if you are not actually driving and have no intention of driving.

had two readings of 160 milligrams of alcohol per 100 millilitres of blood, double the legal limit. Decker was charged with having care or control of a motor vehicle and operating a vehicle while impaired.

Decker was acquitted. The court found that he did not occupy the driver's seat for the purpose of setting the vehicle in motion. The Crown appealed, but the Supreme Court of Newfoundland (in a 2–1 decision) dismissed the appeal. The courts were satisfied that Decker had no intention of driving based on the long-standing pattern of his behaviour as well as his efforts on the evening in question to find a place to stay.

For Discussion

1. Define "care or control" of a vehicle according to the law. Do you agree with how it was applied in this case?

2. Why did the courts conclude that Decker did not have care or control in this case?

3. Make the argument on behalf of the Crown, arguing that Decker did, in fact, have care or control.

4. Should being in the driver's seat while impaired be enough for a conviction? Explain.

Spot Checks

Some people question the right of the police to stop drivers when they have no reasonable grounds to suspect that an offence has been committed. However, the courts have recognized that the government wants to reduce the problem of drinking and driving. Therefore, the courts have ruled that spot checks are a reasonable limit prescribed by the law.

When stopped in a roadside spot check, a driver may be asked by the police to undergo a **roadside screening test**. The officer will demand that the driver breathe into an approved testing device. The demand may be made only if the officer has reasonable grounds to suspect that the driver has been drinking. It is an offence to refuse the demand. Approved roadside screening devices are described in section 254(1) of the *Criminal Code*. Failing the screening test does not mean one is automatically charged with an offence. The results can be used only to show that the officer had grounds to demand a breath sample. The screening test only provides the police officer with the reasonable grounds to take someone to the police station for a formal Breathalyzer test.

If the roadside test indicates that a breath sample is required, the officer will take the driver to the police station for more breath tests. Because the driver is required to accompany the officer, that person is being detained, and arrest or release should soon follow.

roadside screening test a test given by police to check for impaired driving

 Did You Know?

Sometimes a person cannot give a breath sample (because he or she is unconscious or injured). In these cases, the officer may demand a blood sample. It is taken by a qualified medical practitioner such as a doctor or registered nurse. Two blood samples are taken, and one is available to the accused for independent testing. A warrant must be obtained if the accused refuses to give a blood sample.

Peterborough County OPP takes part in the Reduce Impaired Driving Everywhere (RIDE) program. RIDE is a roadside spot check program that pulls drivers over at random to test for sobriety. It began in 1977 as Reduce Impaired Driving in Etobicoke (a suburb of Toronto) and quickly spread across the province of Ontario. There are similar programs across Canada.

Chapter 7 *Criminal Code Offences*

Increase to Impaired Driving Penalties since February 2008

	Prior to February 2008	Since February 2008
Fine for first-time offence	$600	$1000
Minimum imprisonment term for a second offence	14 days	30 days
Minimum imprisonment term for a third or more offence	90 days	120 days
Maximum imprisonment term if tried as a summary conviction offence	6 months	18 months

In February 2008, section 255 of the *Criminal Code* was amended. The penalties for impaired driving were increased. The punishments also apply to cases where the accused fails an alcohol or drug test or refuses to take such tests when ordered to by the police.

Everyone knows that drinking and driving are illegal and dangerous.

Impaired Driving: Provincial and Territorial

The provinces and territories have the right to regulate motor vehicles. That is why they are trying to keep drunk drivers off the road. Certain laws allow vehicles to be stopped at random. When a police officer stops someone this way, the officer may see or smell alcohol or drugs. He or she may also discover evidence during a safety check. This may lead to further investigation. However, the officer must have grounds for searching the automobile. He or she cannot undertake a search simply on a hunch that the driver is hiding illegal drugs.

The provinces and territories may also suspend the licences of persons convicted under the *Criminal Code*. Therefore, a person may be subject to a fine or imprisonment. His or her driver's licence may also be suspended. The provinces and territories are permitted to suspend a driver's licence for a short period of time (12 to 24 hours) if the driver has consumed even small amounts of alcohol. In Ontario, a driver's licence can be taken away for 12 hours if an approved screening device shows a blood-alcohol level of over 50. Removal of a driver's licence in British Columbia can occur if the reading is over 30. Anyone who drives during this period can, of course, be charged with the additional offence of driving without a licence.

Impaired Driving Licence Suspensions, Ontario

Offence	Penalty
First conviction	One-year suspension of driver's licence
Second conviction	Three-year suspension
Third offence	Lifetime suspension

Provinces and territories have the right to suspend a person's driver's licence if convicted of impaired driving.

Under provincial or territorial law, the offender may have to install an "anti-lock" device on the vehicle. The driver must blow into a mouthpiece located on the dashboard. If the reading is over a set limit, the car will not start. Some provinces require impaired drivers to complete an alcohol education and treatment program before their licence can be reinstated. All provinces have similar restrictions requiring that all new drivers must maintain a zero blood-alcohol concentration (BAC) while driving.

In 2008, the Ontario government passed a new law that allows the civil courts to impound and confiscate a vehicle for the following reasons:

- The vehicle was involved in a drinking and driving offence.

- The vehicle is owned or driven by a person whose licence has been suspended for impaired driving two or more times in the preceding 10 years.

You and the Law

Young drivers are considered high risk by car insurance companies because of their age and the fact that they are new and inexperienced drivers. As a result, they pay higher insurance rates. Do you feel that this is fair? Should all drivers pay the same insurance rates? Explain.

The Cost of Impaired Driving in Ontario

Item	Cost
Legal costs (estimated range)	$2000–$10 000
Criminal Code fine	$1000
Back On Track program	$475
Administrative fee for licence reinstatement	$150
Increased insurance ($4500 extra per year for three years)	$13 500 (estimate)
Ignition locking device	$1300
Total minimum cost* (plus applicable taxes on some items)	$18 425

The cost of being convicted of impaired driving can be very high.

* Other potential costs include property damage, loss of employment income, and uninsured medical costs. Actual costs may be higher.

Review Your Understanding

1. What must a driver do at the scene of an accident in which he or she is involved?
2. What does "care or control" mean regarding a motor vehicle?
3. What procedures must the police follow when administering a roadside test?
4. When can blood samples be taken as evidence of impaired driving?
5. Summarize the provincial and territorial laws that are aimed at reducing drinking and driving.

Do Mandatory Minimum Sentences Work?

Following a violent sexual assault in Banff, Alberta, in August 2008, MP Myron Thompson said he was "disgusted" that a violent attack occurred in his riding. He wants to see longer sentences for violent offenders to prevent such attacks from happening again. "The justice system has to start thinking about the victims. We have to stop putting so much emphasis on the rights of the criminal," Thompson said. Do you agree with his opinion? Explain.

The main purpose of sentencing (as outlined in section 718 of the *Criminal Code*) is to encourage respect for the law and to maintain a just, peaceful, and safe society. Mandatory minimum sentences (MMS) come into play during sentencing. MMS limits the judge's power to reduce sentences. Someone convicted of a crime with an MMS must be punished with a minimum sentence.

In Canada, minimum sentences were first established for firearms offences. That was back in 1977. In 1995, further changes were made to the *Criminal Code*. Today, there are about 40 offences in the *Criminal Code* that carry mandatory minimum sentences. Examples include murder, impaired driving, and various sexual offences involving children.

Some examples of recent changes to mandatory minimum sentences include the following:

- In November 2007, law reforms were introduced to include mandatory jail time for people who produce or sell illegal drugs. Before, there were no minimum sentences for these offences.

- In February 2008, Parliament passed into law tougher mandatory prison sentences for serious gun crimes. The minimum sentence was increased from four years to five years for a first offence. The penalty for second or subsequent offences was increased to seven years.

On One Side

Recent studies on mandatory minimum sentences demonstrate that they do not seem to prevent crime for the following reasons:

- They prevent judges from using their own judgment on how to sentence individuals. As a result, prosecutors and police often choose not to charge people with offences that would automatically land them in jail.

- They sometimes lower conviction rates. This is because juries do not want to convict accused people who face automatic and perhaps unfair prison terms.

- By and large, many offenders sentenced under MMS are not violent. These people were not the intended targets of this sentencing policy.

- Most of the serious and violent offenders were the intended targets of MMS. These offenders usually receive long prison terms anyway. So, mandatory minimum sentences in these cases are not necessary.

Opponents of MMS feel that it is unfair. This system sets sentences without considering the circumstances of particular offenders.

On the Other Side

Supporters of mandatory minimum sentences think that this system will help to meet the goals of imprisonment. Those goals include punishing offenders and keeping them from committing more crimes (at least for a period of time). Another goal is to prevent others from committing similar crimes. Also, unfairness in sentencing would be removed because people who had committed the same crime would receive at least the same minimum sentence.

Mandatory minimum sentences may also be a way of dealing with drug-related crimes. Those arrested on such charges would be more likely to co-operate to avoid extremely long prison sentences. This would help the government put gangs and major drug traffickers out of business.

The Bottom Line

Mandatory minimum sentences in Canada are here to stay. In *R. v. Ferguson*, 2008, the Supreme Court delivered a unanimous landmark ruling. It defended Parliament's right to create mandatory minimum sentences and for judges to carry out these sentences.

What Do You Think?

1. Why has the government of Canada introduced mandatory minimum sentences for certain crimes?

2. Should judges have the power over sentencing for all offences? Explain.

3. Do MMS comply with section 718 of the *Criminal Code*? Explain.

4. Do other countries use MMS? Conduct research to find out what other countries do.

5. What is your opinion on MMS? What offences should they be used for? For what offences should the judge be free to decide the appropriate sentence? Should they be used in Canada's criminal justice system? Explain.

Chapter Review

Chapter Highlights

- Homicide can be either culpable (the person is to blame) or non-culpable (the death was a complete accident and no blame is laid).
- There are three categories for assault and sexual assault charges, depending on the severity of the attack.
- Consent is frequently an issue in a sexual assault trial.
- Arson is the intentional causing of damage by fire.
- Identity theft crimes are on the rise and harm thousands of victims each year.
- Making false statements to obtain credit is considered fraud.
- Weapons are classified as non-restricted, restricted, and prohibited.
- Prostitution is legal, but soliciting for the purpose of prostitution is illegal.
- The courts use the community standards test when determining obscenity.
- The laws concerning use of drugs are found in the *Controlled Drugs and Substances Act*.
- In particular circumstances, individuals can legally use marijuana for medicinal purposes.
- Impaired driving is the main criminal cause of death in Canada.

Check Your Knowledge

1. What are some examples of crimes of violence?
2. Identify the actions that are considered property crimes. Provide examples.
3. Provide examples of laws in the *Criminal Code* that are specifically designed to protect children.
4. Distinguish among the various drug-related offences and provide examples for each.
5. Summarize the main *Criminal Code* offences associated with a motor vehicle.

Apply Your Learning

6. For each of the following incidents, indicate the offence that will be charged, the elements that must be proven for a successful conviction, and the maximum penalty.

   a) The accused killed her child shortly after childbirth.

   b) The accused threatened someone using an imitation weapon.

   c) The accused robbed a bank using a gun.

   d) The accused entered a home and stole a television.

   e) The accused set fire to his friend's car.

   f) The accused pushed his friend down the stairs. The friend died.

   g) The accused was speeding down the street with another car, and a pedestrian was killed when the cars lost control.

   h) The accused was observed by undercover police communicating in a public place for the purpose of buying sexual services.

   i) The accused is stalking someone.

   j) The accused is selling marijuana to students in a park near a school.

   k) The accused is pulled over by police and is asked to undergo a roadside screening test. He refuses.

7. Review the current Canadian *Criminal Code*, and research an area not discussed in this chapter. Provide a report that includes the following:

   - section of the *Criminal Code*
   - area of law that the section deals with
   - what the Crown must prove in order to prosecute the offence
   - the maximum penalty for the offence

Communicate Your Understanding

8. Assume that the next session of Parliament is going to be debating the *Criminal Code* in relation to the following topics:

   - censorship
   - euthanasia
   - legalized gambling
   - decriminalization of marijuana
   - cruelty to animals

   Select one topic to research. Write a letter to your local Member of Parliament outlining your opinion on the topic and showing how to properly balance the interests of individuals and society. Provide examples from the news and how other countries address these issues.

9. Investigate current issues in criminal law by selecting three news articles from print or online sources that deal with criminal law matters. For each article, complete the following:

   a) Briefly summarize the article.

   b) Outline at least two main criminal issues discussed.

   c) Where possible, identify the opinion of the author.

   d) Express your opinion on this criminal matter. Justify your view by providing examples to support it.

10. Research a lobby group in Canada whose main focus is to influence areas of criminal law. Identify the lobby group, summarize its mission statement and what the group is lobbying for, and identify any progress it has made in influencing legislation.

Develop Your Thinking

11. How have changes in the attitudes and values of society brought about changes in criminal law? Support your answer by providing examples of recent changes to criminal law in Canada.

12. The *Criminal Code* specifies a number of offences that are often referred to as "crimes without victims." They include communicating for the purpose of prostitution, obscenity, and keeping a bawdyhouse (brothel). Should the police control such activities, or should people be allowed to decide for themselves whether or not to engage in them? Explain. Explain how there can be victims to these offences.

13. "What people fear most is not the fine but the loss of their vehicle." Express your opinion on this statement about drinking and driving. Support your view by researching current laws that may result in the loss of a vehicle for drinking and driving convictions.

14. A proposal by the Vancouver Police Department would require convicted drunk drivers to display the letter "D" on their car window. In Ohio, judges are permitted to issue a special licence plate to convicted drunk drivers who need their cars for work. Police then know that the car is only to be used for that purpose. In your opinion, should sentencing of impaired drivers include identifying them to the general public? Why or why not?

15. Examine your own community, and identify some of the most pressing criminal issues that exist. Comment on the initiatives that have been taken to address them. Provide some of your own ideas as to why these crimes are common in your community and what can be done to deal with them.

8 Criminal Defences

What You Should Know

- What types of defences are available to an accused person charged with a crime?
- Can some defences lead to a full acquittal?
- How are individuals who commit a crime while suffering from a mental disorder treated in the criminal justice system?
- Is ignorance of the law or intoxication a defence to a criminal act?
- Under what circumstances can provocation be used as an accepted legal defence?

Selected Key Terms

alibi

automatism

battered woman syndrome

defence

double jeopardy

duress

entrapment

not criminally responsible (NCR)

provocation

self-defence

Chapter at a Glance

8.1 Introduction

8.2 The Alibi Defence

8.3 Automatism

8.4 Intoxication

8.5 Defences That Provide a Reason for the Offence

8.6 Other Defences

There are numerous defences available to accused persons in Canada. Some defences are based on the accused stating he or she is innocent, while others provide a reason as to why the accused had no other choice but to commit the offence. A valid defence that is accepted by the court will often lead to an acquittal.

8.1 Introduction

As you learned in Chapter 4, a person accused of committing a crime is presumed innocent. The accused is found guilty *only* if the Crown can prove that the crime was actually committed *(actus reus)* and that the accused had the guilty mind *(mens rea)*. The accused can respond and present a **defence** to the charges. Accused persons can put forth three possible arguments:

- They can deny that they committed the act, disputing the *actus reus*.
- They can argue that they lacked the necessary criminal intent or guilty mind, disputing the *mens rea*.
- They can argue that they have a valid excuse for what happened while committing the act.

Some of these defences are defined within the *Criminal Code* (for example, the defence of mental disorder, which used to be called insanity). Other defences, like self-defence, are considered to be common law defences based on the British common law system.

Various defences are used in criminal law to prove that the accused is not guilty of the offence charged, or perhaps guilty of a lesser one. Several of these defences and the case law that supports them will be discussed in this chapter.

Did You Know?

Judges in Canada are absolutely immune from any civil or criminal action for anything said or done in performing their duties. In other words, they cannot be sued or criminally charged for anything they do or say while performing their duties.

defence the accused's response to criminal charges

alibi a defence that the accused was not at the scene of the crime when it took place

8.2 The Alibi Defence

The best possible defence is an acceptable **alibi** that places the accused somewhere else at the time the offence occurred. For example, Roberto presents an alibi that he was with his friend Yanni at the time the crime took place. The Crown must try to disprove his defence (for example, that Yanni lied for his friend) in order to prove Roberto guilty of the crime. This is the only thing that the defence must disclose to the Crown prior to trial.

An alibi is often presented by the accused upon arrest in a statement made to the police. A full alibi defence includes three parts:

1. a statement indicating that the accused was not present at the location of the crime when it was committed
2. an explanation of the accused's whereabouts at that time
3. the names of any witnesses to the alibi

These parts are necessary if the accused wishes to raise this defence. For example, Ryan is arrested by police for breaking and entering into a neighbourhood home. He tells police that he was at hockey practice on the night in question, and his coach and teammates will confirm this. In this case, Ryan has met all three parts required by the alibi defence. However, if he were home alone that evening, his alibi would be incomplete, satisfying only the first two of the three parts.

The alibi should be supplied early to allow the police and Crown to investigate it properly. Otherwise, it may seem suspicious in court. While the accused is not required to testify in his or her own defence, courts (judges and jury) generally expect an accused to testify and be cross-examined about the alibi. Of course, the Crown still maintains the burden of proving its case beyond a reasonable doubt.

Cornered by Mike Baldwin

6-3 © 2005 Mike Baldwin / Dist. by Universal Press Syndicate

"Look, no matter what happens, if anybody asks, I was here with you the whole night."

The accused must give the name and address of any witness who can support an alibi. Police then investigate the alibi evidence to make sure that the alibi defence is believable. This involves interviewing the alibi witnesses provided by the accused.

R. v. Maracle, 2006 CanLII 4152 (ON C.A.)

For more information, Go to Nelson Social Studies

This is a courtroom sketch of David Maracle. Maracle tried to use the alibi defence to escape a dangerous offender conviction for sexually assaulting a 14-year-old girl.

In May 1997, the complainant, a 14-year-old girl, was grabbed from behind by a man with a gun as she walked on a trail through a wooded park at 7:30 a.m. on her way to school. A cloth was placed over her eyes, which was then replaced by duct tape. She was brutally assaulted three times by her assailant. After the attack, the man duct-taped her wrists and drove off. The victim ripped the tape off her arms and eyes and sought help. She was taken to a hospital where she received medical attention.

In November 1999, David Maracle was convicted of sexual assault causing bodily harm, kidnapping, and carrying a gun for the purpose of committing the indictable offence of forcible confinement. In November 2000, the trial judge found Maracle to be a dangerous offender. The judge ordered him detained for an indeterminate period. Maracle appealed his conviction and sentence to the Ontario Court of Appeal.

The Crown's case had three parts. First, the victim offered some limited identification evidence, even though she never saw her assailant's face. Second, the Crown introduced evidence of a piece of duct tape with the appellant's fingerprint on it. Third, the Crown had DNA evidence in the form of a semen stain on the girl's T-shirt that matched Maracle's DNA profile.

The appellant's main defence was an alibi. In his testimony, he denied that he had ever met or seen the complainant prior to the trial. He also denied attacking her. His alibi was that he was at home on the morning of May 26, 1997. His sister, mother, and brother all supported his alibi.

Maracle further argued that the judge at trial had failed to instruct the jury properly about the "alibi defence" he had presented. He argued that the judge suggested the jury give less weight to the alibi since it was not disclosed to police and the Crown until April 1999, some time after the charges were laid.

In February 2006, the Ontario Court of Appeal ruled unanimously that there were substantial errors in the trial that affected the appellant's alibi defence. This made the trial unfair. They set aside the conviction and ordered a new trial.

For Discussion

1. Identify the three parts of the alibi defence presented at trial.

2. Why did the Ontario Court of Appeal order a new trial?

3. The trial judge asked the jury to consider whether "the alibi was disclosed in sufficient time for meaningful or effective investigation." What did he mean?

4. Do you agree with the decision in this case? Explain.

1. What is a defence?
2. What are three arguments for a valid defence to a crime?
3. Explain the alibi defence and how it works.
4. What three conditions are required for the alibi defence to be accepted?
5. Why must the alibi defence be disclosed to the Crown at the earliest opportunity?

automatism involuntary action by someone who is in a state of impaired consciousness, without control over his or her actions; insane automatism is caused by a disease of the mind

8.3 Automatism

The **automatism** defence is not mentioned in the *Criminal Code*. It has developed over time through common law case precedent. Automatism is defined as automatic functioning without conscious effort or control. In other words, an individual has no control over his or her actions, but is still capable of committing an act (for example, breathing and blinking). At law, there are two types of automatism: non-insane (non-mental-disorder) automatism, and insane (mental disorder) automatism. Both rely upon expert psychiatric evidence. Insane automatism is caused by a "disease of the mind." Non-insane automatism is linked to external factors like sleepwalking. With an automatism defence, the judge must first decide whether a condition exists that will likely present a recurring danger to the public. People with a mental health disability who hear voices telling them to do things against their will would be considered dangerous to others and to themselves. If the judge determines that there is no recurring danger, the case will proceed as a non-insane offence.

Non-Insane Automatism Defence

Non-insane automatism is sometimes called "temporary insanity." Canadian courts have recognized that this state may be the result of the following: a physical blow, physical ailments such as a stroke, hypoglycemia (low blood sugar), sleepwalking (see the *R. v. Parks* case in Chapter 4, pages 124–125), intoxication, or severe psychological trauma. Based on expert testimony, if a judge accepts this defence, the result would be a complete acquittal.

This defence has been used in numerous cases throughout Canadian legal history. For example, in *R. v. Bleta*, 1965, the Supreme Court acquitted Karafil Bleta, who used non-insane automatism as a defence to a murder charge. In this case, Bleta had suffered a serious blow to his head, and while still dazed and confused, stabbed a man with a knife, killing him. Bleta's defence was supported by expert psychiatric evidence presented in court.

In *R. v. Stone*, 1999, the Supreme Court felt it needed to clarify when this defence could be used. The court was concerned that automatism could easily be faked. In *R. v. Stone*, the accused admitted stabbing his wife 47 times. However, he claimed to have done it while in an "automatistic" state brought on by his wife's insulting words. The Supreme Court rejected this defence. It indicated that the burden of proof rests entirely on the accused. The evidence presented to support the defence must be significant.

In April 2002, R.E.M. guitarist Peter Buck was cleared on charges of attacking British Airways staff in an alleged air-rage incident. Buck's lawyers successfully argued that a combination of taking a sleeping pill and drinking "small amounts" of wine had caused Buck to enter a state of non-insane automatism. Buck had not intended to commit an offence.

R. v. Luedecke, 2008 ONCA 716 (CanLII)

For more information, Go to Nelson Social Studies

Jan Luedecke claimed he was suffering from "sexsomnia" when he sexually assaulted a woman at a Toronto party such as this one.

In July 2003, the victim was attending a party in Toronto with a few of her friends. She arrived at about 7:00 p.m., and there were approximately 50 to 60 people present. Over the course of the evening, she had several drinks. At about 2:00 a.m. the following morning, feeling tired, she sat down on a couch and fell asleep, but was abruptly awakened to find a man on top of her having sexual relations with her. Her underwear had been removed and her skirt had been lifted up. She pushed the man onto the floor and proceeded to Women's College Hospital, where she was treated.

Luedecke had spent the evening before the party drinking alcohol and consuming magic mushrooms at a friend's cottage. The next day he drove back to Toronto, arriving at the party around 7:30 p.m. During the evening he drank 8 to 12 beers and several other alcoholic drinks. After having been awake for over 22 hours, he fell asleep at the opposite end of the same couch as the complainant. His next recollection was being pushed by a woman off the couch onto the floor. He testified that he was completely dazed and in shock.

At trial, Luedecke argued the non-insane automatism defence, asserting that his conduct was not the exercise of his conscious will. An expert on sleep disorders testified that Luedecke was acting without logic or reason when he committed the offence. He gave evidence that Luedecke was sleepwalking (somnambulism). The expert concluded that Luedecke was suffering from "sexsomnia" at the time of the offence. This is a term used to describe the occurrence of sexual behaviour during sleepwalking. There had also been other similar incidents in the past with girlfriends.

The defence attorney argued that Luedecke should be found not criminally responsible (NCR) as a result of a mental disorder (see page 267 for an explanation of NCR). However, in November 2005, the trial judge stated that while this was a rare case, he was satisfied that at the time of the incident, the defendant was in a state of non-insane automatism and that his conduct was not voluntary. He concluded that the evidence did not fit the definition of a disease of the mind. Luedecke was therefore acquitted. The Crown appealed, and the Ontario Court of Appeal heard the appeal in February 2008. In a 3–0 judgment in October 2008, the appellate court overturned Luedecke's acquittal and ordered a new trial. However, the new trial should focus only on whether he is not guilty or "not criminally responsible" on account of having a mental disorder that requires treatment in the mental health system.

For Discussion

1. Why did Luedecke present the defence of non-insane automatism in this case?

2. Summarize the sleep expert's evidence in this case.

3. Why do you think the Crown attorney argued that Luedecke should be found not criminally responsible as a result of a mental disorder? Explain.

4. How could this defence be dangerous for women? Do you agree with the final decision in the case? Explain.

Insane Automatism Defence

More and more people with a mental health disability are ending up in the criminal court system. This has forced the various players to reconsider how best to deal with individuals with mental disorders who commit crimes.

In 1992, Parliament made changes to the *Criminal Code* to deal with accused persons with mental disorders. It passed Bill C-30, which created a special section within the *Criminal Code*. Since then, several important cases have come before the courts. These judgments helped establish some clear guidelines on how mental disorder defences should be handled.

A mental disorder, or a disease of the mind, is defined in section 16 of the *Criminal Code*. It states that an individual is **not criminally responsible (NCR)** for a criminal offence providing the following:

- At the time that the act was committed, he or she was suffering from a mental disorder.

- The mental disorder made the individual incapable of appreciating the nature of the act or knowing that the act was wrong.

For example, a person with paranoid schizophrenia may assault someone she or he incorrectly thinks is a threat. In this case, the person with this condition is incapable of understanding that what she or he did was wrong. Under the law, such a person would be considered NCR (not criminally responsible). The NCR defence can be raised by either the accused or the Crown, and whichever party raises the defence incurs the burden of proof. In other words, whoever claims an accused is NCR must be able to prove it in a court.

Prior to an NCR case moving forward, the courts must first determine if the accused is fit to stand trial. A fitness hearing can assess the answers to the following three questions:

1. Does the accused understand the nature of the proceedings? (Does the accused understand that he or she is in court and being tried for having committed an offence?)
2. Does the accused understand the possible consequences of the proceedings? (Is the accused aware that she or he can be sent to jail or to a psychiatric facility?)
3. Can the accused communicate with his or her lawyer?

not criminally responsible (NCR) not criminally responsible because of a disease of the mind

The government has realized that offenders who suffer from mental disorders need to be treated fairly by the criminal system. The Canadian Mental Health Association (CMHA) Mental Health Court Support and Diversion Program provides services to people diverted to the Mental Health Court. These services include helping court clients find the mental health and support services they need and offering information and support to them and their families and loved ones. Staff members of the Court Diversion Program are shown here.

 Did You Know?

The laws in Canada governing insane automatism date back to the 1843 decision of the British House of Lords in the *M'Naghten's Case*. In that case, the accused Daniel M'Naghten, was found not guilty by reason of insanity (mental disorder) after having murdered the prime minister's secretary.

Did You Know?

In the case of *R. v. Newby*, 1991, the accused unsuccessfully used the defence of chronic fatigue syndrome against charges of fraud worth $870 000. The court rejected his defence, found him guilty, and gave him a suspended sentence.

A trial cannot proceed until an accused is deemed to be fit. An accused found to be "unfit" will be sent back to jail or, more often, to a psychiatric hospital until she or he is found to be fit and can then be brought back to court.

Once a person proceeds to trial and is determined to have been suffering from a "disease of the mind" at the time the offence was committed, they are seen as NCR under the law. A trial judge or a provincial review board will then decide the sentence. This board will have to determine whether or not the accused continues to pose a significant threat to public safety. If the accused does not pose such a threat, he or she would be discharged back into society. If the accused does pose a continued threat, she or he will be sent to a psychiatric facility to undergo medical and clinical treatment. The case will be reviewed annually to determine whether the accused continues to pose a "significant risk" (dangerous to society).

 You Be the Judge

Winko v. British Columbia (Forensic Psychiatric Institute), 1999 CanLII 694 (S.C.C.)

For more information, **Go to Nelson Social Studies**

In July 1983, Joseph Winko was arrested for attacking two pedestrians on the street with a knife and stabbing one of them behind the ear. Prior to this incident, he had been hearing voices urging him to harm passing pedestrians. Winko was charged and taken to a psychiatric hospital for treatment. He was eventually charged with aggravated assault, assault with a weapon, and possession of a weapon for purposes dangerous to the public peace. In 1984, he was tried and found not criminally responsible (NCR).

From the time of his NCR verdict until his release, Winko was held at a forensic hospital where he was considered institutionalized. In August 1990, he was released into the Vancouver community with a number of conditions. One of these conditions included reporting to a doctor on a regular basis and taking his medications. In September 1994, he missed a medication injection for the second time. This led to a recurrence of the voices he was hearing at the time of the original offence. Despite occasional breaks from medication, he had never been physically aggressive to anyone since the original offences in 1983.

A three-member panel of the review board of British Columbia considered Winko's status in May 1995, granting him a conditional discharge. He was

released from the hospital under certain conditions. He remained under a court order because the board thought that he was generally harmless. However, the board believed that Winko could become a significant risk to public safety in "certain circumstances." The board suggested that a conditional discharge would best ensure the safety of the public. In July 1996, a majority of the British Columbia Court of Appeal upheld the review board's decision to grant Winko a conditional discharge. Winko further appealed to the Supreme Court. In June 1999, in a unanimous 9–0 decision, the court dismissed the appeal. In its decision, the court made it clear that the review board is required to determine whether the NCR accused is a "significant threat to the safety of the public." In other words, is that person a real risk to do harm to members of the public? If the accused does not pose such a threat, he or she would be *absolutely* discharged. In this case, the board had decided that Winko continued to be a significant threat.

● Do you agree with the ruling in this case? Should the courts be able to decide how long an NCR accused remains institutionalized, or should there be a maximum amount of time put in place, much like regular sentencing? Explain.

The Toronto Mental Health Court— Decriminalizing People with a Mental Health Disability

During the mid-1990s, officials noticed a significant increase in the number of accused persons suffering from mental disorders who were appearing in court. Most were charged with relatively minor offences. It became clear that the regular criminal courts were not equipped to handle these cases. There were delays and inefficiencies in dealing with preliminary issues such as fitness hearings. For the most part, other options for people with a mental health disability were not being fully explored. The accused would often spend several weeks (if not months) in jail waiting for a trial date to be set or for the matter to be resolved.

As well, mentally disordered accused persons were returning to court at an alarming rate because of repeated trouble with the law. In August 1997, this growing problem was brought to the attention of the justice officials. It was proposed that a court be set up to specifically accommodate mentally disordered accused persons. The Mental Health Court was opened in May 1998. It was the first in Canada and one of the first in the world. It was the only one (to date) to address the complex issues involved in dealing with mentally disordered accused persons.

The two primary objectives of the Mental Health Court are to do the following:

1. Deal with pre-trial issues of fitness hearings quickly and efficiently.
2. Try to slow down the "revolving door" of patients with a mental health disability returning to court for minor offences.

The court has also taken on the broader mandate of accommodating mentally disordered accused persons during NCR hearings and disposition hearings.

The Mental Health Court is staffed by two permanent Assistant Crown attorneys for the prosecution and two legal aid lawyers for the defence. There are nine social workers attached to the court. Every day, a psychiatrist attends to perform assessments on any individuals appearing before the court.

Justice Edward Ormston (shown here) was instrumental in making changes to the court system in the area of mental health. The Toronto Mental Health Court has a courtroom devoted to hearing mental health cases, as well as a designated judge. On May 11, 2008, the Mental Health Court in Toronto celebrated a decade of working on behalf of the mentally disordered accused.

The Mental Health Court assists with discharges of accused persons into the community. Staff try to ensure that when an accused leaves the court, he or she has a basic "survival kit." This kit includes identification, a place to live, community psychiatric follow-up, social assistance, and clothing.

For Discussion

1. Identify the reasons why the Toronto Mental Health Court was established.
2. What are the objectives of the court?
3. Do you think that more communities should establish similar courts? Explain.
4. Do you think mental health courts are a good idea? Why or why not?

Review Your Understanding

1. What is the definition of automatism?
2. How are insane automatism and non-insane automatism different?
3. In 1992, Parliament amended the *Criminal Code* (passed Bill C-30). What was the significance of this change?
4. What are the conditions necessary for an NCR ruling?
5. What is the purpose of a "fitness to stand trial" hearing?

8.4 Intoxication

In Chapter 4, you learned the importance of intention. If Christina killed Silvana in front of witnesses, then the act is an established fact. The next step is to ask why Christina did it. Did she intend to kill Silvana, or was it an accident or something in between? Did Christina understand the consequences of her act? If not, she cannot be held criminally responsible. In another example, Janik strikes Fred out of anger. Janik has committed assault, a general intent offence. However, if Janik strikes Fred with the intention to kill him, but only injures him instead, that is aggravated assault. The difference lies in the fact that it is a specific intent offence because the assailant had another criminal purpose in mind (murder) when assaulting the person.

To use intoxication as a defence, the accused must show that he or she did not have the required intent *(mens rea)* at the time that the offence was committed. Any intoxicated person who was unable to form specific intent before striking someone cannot be found guilty of aggravated assault, a specific intent offence. He or she can, however, be found guilty of assault, a general intent offence. All that needs to be proved is that the intoxicated person did strike someone (the *actus reus*). Similarly, a person charged with murder can use the defence of intoxication. If successful, this will lower the conviction from murder (a specific intent offence) to manslaughter (a general intent offence). A judge or jury must decide whether or not the accused understood the consequences of

The defence of intoxication argues that the accused did not have the necessary *mens rea* to be guilty of the crime.

his or her action. In other words, did the accused lack the intent or *mens rea*? If the judge and jury decide that the accused could not foresee the consequences of his or her action, then the accused cannot be found guilty of a specific intent offence.

The role of intoxication in assault and sexual assault cases was discussed in Chapter 7. The law addressing whether intoxication can be a defence was clarified in *R. v. Daviault*, 1994, below. The Supreme Court held that drunkenness could be a defence in a sexual assault case if there is reasonable doubt that the accused could understand the consequences of his actions. In other words, Daviault was not responsible for his actions because he was drunk. This controversial ruling outraged many Canadians. As a result, the *Criminal Code* was changed in 1995 to clarify the issue. Under the new section of the *Criminal Code* (section 33.1), drunkenness is no longer a defence for general intent offences. A drunken person is considered to be criminally at fault if he or she, say, attacks another person, as in the case of an assault or sexual assault.

Did You Know?

RIDE (Reduce Impaired Driving Everywhere) involves police spot checks. Vehicles are stopped and drivers are checked for impairment. In 2007, police in Ontario checked 505 000 cars, boats, and snowmobiles, compared with 616 000 checks in 2001. Although the total number of spot checks in Ontario dropped, provincial funding for RIDE checks is on the rise. It has doubled since 2001 to $2.4 million.

 Case

R. v. Daviault, 1994 CanLII 61 (S.C.C.)

For more information, **Go to Nelson Social Studies**

Henri Daviault was a chronic alcoholic. Ruth Dumais, the victim, was a 65-year-old woman who was partially paralyzed and confined to a wheelchair. In May 1989, Dumais asked Daviault to deliver some alcohol to her. He arrived at Dumais's residence with a 1.1 litre (40-ounce) bottle of brandy. Dumais consumed half a glass of the brandy before falling asleep in her wheelchair. While she slept, Daviault consumed the rest of the bottle. During the night, Daviault wheeled Dumais into the bedroom, threw her on the bed, and sexually assaulted her. Daviault was later charged with sexual assault.

At trial, Daviault testified that prior to being at the complainant's residence, he had consumed seven or eight bottles of beer at a bar. At trial, the defence called a pharmacologist as an expert witness. He suggested that by consuming seven or eight beers and more than a litre (35 ounces) of brandy, Daviault may have experienced "l'amnesie-automatisme," otherwise known as a blackout. In such a state, Daviault's brain would not have functioned normally since he essentially had lost contact with reality. The trial judge found that the accused had committed the offence as described by the complainant. However, he then stated that Daviault should be acquitted

because there was a reasonable doubt as to whether the accused, because of his extreme intoxication, had possessed the minimal intent necessary to commit the offence of sexual assault. When Daviault was found not guilty, the Crown appealed. The court of appeal did not allow the intoxication defence, and Daviault was found guilty. He appealed to the Supreme Court of Canada. In September 1994 in a 6–3 decision, the court allowed the appeal and ordered a new trial. The new trial never took place.

For Discussion

1. Why was Daviault found not guilty at trial?

2. Summarize in your own words the evidence given at trial by the pharmacologist.

3. Justice Sopinka of the Supreme Court said the following in his minority decision: "Society is entitled to punish those who of their own free will render themselves so intoxicated as to pose a threat to other members of the community." What did he mean by this statement?

4. Do you agree with the decision in the case? Why or why not?

The Carter Defence

As you learned in Chapter 7, it is a criminal offence to drink and drive. Being impaired is defined as having a blood–alcohol level (BAC) above the legal limit. The limit is 80 milligrams of alcohol in 100 millimetres of blood. It is measured by having the driver take a Breathalyzer test, which is given by a licensed technician (most often a police officer). The courts have accepted a defence to drinking and driving based on the accused presenting **evidence to the contrary**. This is dubbed the "Carter defence," or the "two-beer defence." It recognizes that machines, and the police officers who operate them, sometimes make mistakes.

evidence to the contrary
evidence that disputes the evidence put forth by the Crown

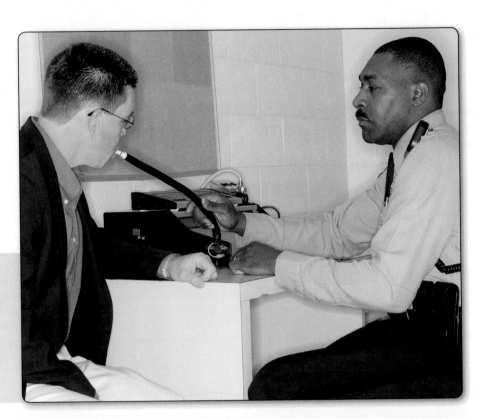

The Carter defence, also known as the "two-beer defence," was used by persons who failed a Breathalyzer test but argued that the test was invalid. It is no longer an acceptable defence in Canada.

In 1985, the Ontario Court of Appeal heard the case of *R. v. Carter*. Breathalyzer tests showed Carter's blood–alcohol level to be at 200 milligrams in 100 millilitres of blood. That was well above the legal limit of 80. Carter provided evidence that he had consumed only two beers before being pulled over by police. Based on this information, an expert calculated that Carter's blood–alcohol concentration should have been below the legal limit. This information represented evidence to the contrary. It disputed the results of the Breathalyzer. Carter was acquitted of his drinking and driving charge.

On July 2, 2008, the *Criminal Code* was changed so that Breathalyzer results could not be questioned. The only exceptions are if there is evidence that the machine did not work properly. Another possibility is if the defence can raise doubt as to whether the machine was operated properly.

R. v. Gibson, 2008 SCC 16 (CanLII)

For more information, **Go to Nelson Social Studies**

In April 2008, in a 7–2 judgment, the Supreme Court upheld the conviction of Robin Gibson and Martin MacDonald. They had failed to convince the court that their charges should be dropped because they did not drink enough to be under the influence, despite failing a Breathalyzer test. The Supreme Court concluded that allowing experts to estimate blood–alcohol concentration is too unreliable. It further concluded that the effects of alcohol vary from person to person and from time to time. The testimony is based on how many drinks an accused person claims to have consumed. As such, the court concluded that the only reliable evidence in such cases is the Breathalyzer test.

- What does this decision say about the future of the Carter defence? Do you agree with this decision? Why or why not?

Today, breath analysis is the most common method of testing for blood–alcohol level. A personal pocket-sized breathalyzer is a reliable device that you blow into to measure the level of alcohol in your blood to test for impairment.

 Did You Know?

In roadside spot checks, police stop random cars. They question drivers in order to determine their sobriety. If the police feel that a driver has been drinking, the officer may request a roadside Breathalyzer test. The roadside spot checks are usually set up on major roadways and off-ramps of highways. They normally occur more often during holidays.

Review Your Understanding

1. What is the difference between general and specific intent offences?
2. How does the defence of intoxication work? What must be proved?
3. Explain the changes to the law as a result of the *Daviault* case.
4. How does the Carter defence work?
5. Recent case law and new legislation have made the Carter defence invalid. Why do you think these changes were made? Do you agree with the new rules? Explain.

Activity

To learn more about
battered woman syndrome,

**Go to Nelson
Social Studies**

8.5 Defences That Provide a Reason for the Offence

There are several ways accused persons can defend themselves. One is by providing a reason why the offence was committed. In these cases, the accused are not denying that an offence took place. Instead they are providing an explanation about why they felt they had no other option but to act as they did (commit the offence).

Battered Woman Syndrome

battered woman syndrome a psychological condition caused by severe domestic violence

The Supreme Court first recognized prolonged abuse as a defence in *R. v. Lavallee*, 1990, when it upheld a jury's acquittal of Angelique Lavallee. Lavallee shot her partner in the back of the head as he left a room one evening. He had told her that he was going to come back and kill her later that night, and she believed him. He had physically abused her for many years. The court found that it was "reasonable" for Lavallee to believe she had no other choice than to use lethal force to defend herself. This groundbreaking decision set a legal precedent, and **battered woman syndrome** became a legal defence. Before this, the danger had to be imminent to use the defence of self-defence (for example, a knife was coming at you).

During the 1990s, the legal system recognized spousal and child abuse as a serious and widespread problem. Police now have clear guidelines on how to deal with and charge abusive spouses. In some communities, police officers themselves will charge the abuser if the abused spouse will not do so.

ABUSE

Violence Against Women + Children

The Truth Hurts

Approximately
3-5 children
in every
Canadian classroom
have witnessed their
mother being assaulted

70% of men
in court-ordered
treatment for
domestic violence
witnessed it
as a child

Ernestine's Women's Shelter
24 HOUR CRISIS LINE

If you or someone you know is being abused, there is help. Call today.

416 746-3701

This poster from Ernestine's Women's Shelter in Toronto is one of many efforts by the shelter to raise public awareness about the realities of violence against women and children. Ernestine's Sharlene Tygesen said, "It's important that we address this issue in the public realm. If we can't address it in public, how can we end it in private?"

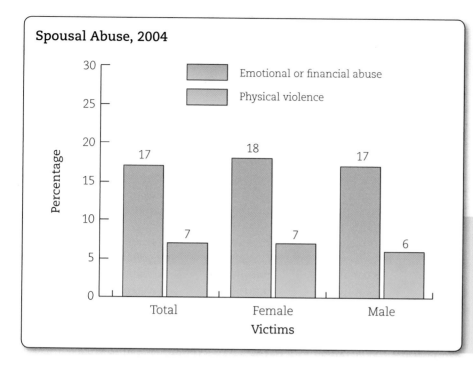

Spousal Abuse, 2004

Emotional or financial abuse

Physical violence

Emotional and financial abuse is 2.5 times more common in spousal relationships than physical violence. Research shows that emotional abuse and/or controlling behaviour often lead to physical violence.

 Case

R. v. Graveline, 2006 SCC 16 (CanLII)

For more information, **Go to Nelson Social Studies**

In August 1999, at approximately 10:50 p.m., Rita Graveline fatally shot her sleeping husband, Michael, with a rifle. At the time of the shooting, the couple were both 51 years old. They had been married for 32 years and had two children. From the beginning of their marriage, Michael Graveline abused his wife. This abuse included humiliating insults and degrading behaviour. At times, the abuse became physical, with threats and attacks.

Rita Graveline was charged with second-degree murder. Her defence at trial was that she had acted in a state of non-insane automatism, as she used the new Lavallee battered woman syndrome defence. The jury acquitted her, but the Crown appealed. The Québec Court of Appeal set aside the acquittal and ordered a new trial. However, Graveline appealed to the Supreme Court. On April 27, 2006, in a 6–1 decision, the court allowed her appeal and restored the acquittal verdict.

For Discussion

1. Why did Graveline argue that she had acted in a state of non-insane automatism?

2. Summarize the evidence given at trial to support her defence of battered woman syndrome.

3. The defence experts concluded that Graveline had acted in a state of automatism brought on shortly before the shooting by her traumatic relationship with her husband and the surrounding circumstances. The Crown agreed that the appellant's amnesia was genuine but argued that it followed rather than preceded the shooting. Why would the Crown make such an argument?

4. How has this case furthered the rights of abused women? Do you agree with the decision in this case? Explain.

Self-Defence

self-defence the legal use of reasonable force in order to defend oneself

At law, you are allowed to defend yourself and your property, but you can only use "necessary" and "reasonable" force. The *Criminal Code* tries to define every circumstance where **self-defence** might occur and the intent of those involved.

The Alberta Court of Appeal gave a clear definition of self-defence in the case of *R. v. Kong*, 2005. Simply stated, a person sometimes has no choice but to use force (even deadly force) to defend himself or herself. When this happens, the person acting in self-defence is considered not criminally responsible. In other words, self-defence is justified for what would otherwise be an unlawful act of assault. The theory surrounding this defence is essentially that the accused is in the right, and the victim got what he or she deserved in being reasonably repelled.

To be able to plead self-defence, an accused must feel that the threat was real. Also, the actions taken in self-defence were reasonable based on how an ordinary person in the same circumstances would have reacted. This test is the most important part of trying to use self-defence successfully at trial.

Section 34(1) of the *Criminal Code* outlines when the use of force is justified. An accused is justified in using force if it is no more than necessary to defend himself or herself. Also, the force used must not be intended to cause death or serious bodily harm. For example, Daniel is walking home from school when he is unexpectedly thrown to the ground by Harmeet. In this case, Daniel is allowed to use reasonable force to defend himself from Harmeet's attack.

Section 34(2) of the *Criminal Code* also states that killing an assailant is justified if a person reasonably believes that his or her life is endangered. For example, Daniel notices the assailant has a knife. In the act of defending himself, Daniel stabs his assailant, and the assailant dies. In this case, Daniel would be able to use self-defence to justify his actions.

Did You Know?

Under section 40 of the *Criminal Code*, you are justified in using as much force as is necessary to prevent someone from unlawfully entering your home.

You and the Law

In a 6–3 decision in February 2007, the Supreme Court of Canada ruled that the 30-year-old practice of using evidence obtained from hypnotized witnesses is unrealiable and should not be used in criminal trials. Do you agree? Explain.

A person acting in self-defence, such as using pepper spray against an attacker, is not criminally responsible for his or her actions, as long as the force used is reasonable and necessary.

R. v. Smith, 2007 ONCJ 47 (CanLII)

For more information, **Go to Nelson Social Studies**

Robert Smith, aged 52, and Walburga Schaller, aged 74, were walking toward each other on a Toronto sidewalk on June 4, 2005. Both were using canes for medical reasons. Neither would yield the right of way to the other, and there was a face off. Eventually, they began to swear at each other and to hit one another with their canes. Smith forced his way past

Schaller, knocking her into a wall, and swatting her with his cane as he passed. He claimed she threatened to break his glasses and had rammed her cane into his stomach. Smith was charged with assault with a weapon. He claimed self-defence for his actions.

• What do you think the trial judge decided? What would you have decided in this case? Explain.

R. v. Paice, 2005 SCC 22 (CanLII)

For more information, **Go to Nelson Social Studies**

In May 2001, Christiano Paice and some friends went to a bar in Moose Jaw, Saskatchewan, to celebrate a birthday. One of Paice's friends and another person began to argue over a game of pool. Paice left his seat at the bar and intervened, separating the combatants.

According to Paice, as he returned to his seat, he was approached by Clinton Bauck, whose friend was involved in the scuffle that Paice had intervened in. Bauck asked Paice, "Do you want to go outside to fight?" Paice agreed. Once outside, Paice and Bauck squared off, exchanging threats, and Bauck pushed Paice several times. Paice eventually swung hard and struck Bauck on the left side of his jaw. Bauck fell backwards, hitting his head on the pavement. While Bauck was down and unconscious, Paice struck him two more times. Some time later, Bauck died as a result of his injuries, and Paice was charged with manslaughter.

The trial judge acquitted Paice. The judge said that, following the deceased's pushing (an unlawful assault), the accused had acted in self-defence within

A person who agrees to fight cannot use the self-defence argument if the other fighter gets seriously injured or killed.

the scope of section 34(1) of the *Criminal Code*. The Saskatchewan Court of Appeal set aside the acquittal and ordered a new trial. Paice appealed to the Supreme Court of Canada. On April 22, 2005, in a unanimous 7–0 decision, the court dismissed the appeal and confirmed the order for a new trial.

For Discussion

1. Why was Paice charged with manslaughter and not murder?

2. Explain the defence of self-defence as it was applied in this case.

3. In her decision, Justice Charron stated that "self-defence under section 34(1) is not available to either combatant in a consensual fistfight because neither could be heard to say that he has been the innocent victim of an unprovoked assault when he has consented to the fight." Do you agree? Explain.

4. What do you think the result will be if a new trial is held? Explain your answer.

Did You Know?

In the 1884 British case *R. v. Dudley and Stephens*, the defence of necessity was used. Tom Dudley and Edwin Stephens were charged with murder after they killed and ate Richard Parker when they were lost at sea without food. The men were found guilty, and their defence failed. The judge had to find them guilty to maintain the precedent that this act was murder. However, the judge gave them only six months or so in prison, which was the "political" way to deal with this problem. They were pardoned by the monarch.

Necessity

The defence of necessity can be used as an excuse for a criminal act committed due to immediate and urgent circumstances. In such cases, accused persons claim that they did not truly act voluntarily. They were forced to act because of certain danger. In other words, they had no other choice. For example, Leslie arrives home to find her mother on the ground having difficulty breathing. She has suffered a heart attack. Leslie picks her up, carries her to the car and speeds off to the hospital for medical attention. If Leslie were to be stopped by a police officer and charged with dangerous driving, she could plead the defence of necessity as a legal excuse to the charges.

Almost half of all fatal collisions involve speeding. Statistics show that drivers who go 30 kilometres per hour over the speed limit on city streets are almost six times more likely to kill or injure someone. Those who go more than 50 kilometres per hour above the limit on highways are nearly 10 times more likely to kill or injure someone.

Canadian courts have reluctantly recognized the defence of necessity. There are several case law examples that clarify the defence. The leading precedent case is that of *Perka v. The Queen*, 1984. There, the Supreme Court stated that the defence applies only in circumstances of imminent risk. The action must have been taken to avoid a direct and immediate danger.

Regardless, necessity can generally be used as a defence to all offences in the *Criminal Code*. In *R. v. Latimer*, 2001 (see the Case feature in Chapter 7 on page 223), Robert Latimer tried to use the defence of necessity to argue against his second-degree murder charge. He was charged in the death of his 12-year-old severely handicapped daughter. The Supreme Court stated that the defence of necessity is narrow and of limited application in criminal law. The court rejected Latimer's argument.

The defence of necessity is rare in Canada. However, the case of *R. v. Ungar*, 2002, on the next page, provides an unusual example of an accused being acquitted on a defence of necessity.

R. v. Ungar, 2002, O.J. No. 2915 (Ont. C.J.)

For more information, **Go to Nelson Social Studies**

Bernard Ungar was a member of Hatzoloh Toronto, a non-profit volunteer organization run by the Orthodox Jewish community of Toronto. The organization was launched in early 1998 to respond 24/7 to emergencies within the Toronto Jewish community. Hatzoloh volunteers are trained emergency medical technicians (EMTs). They provide basic services in a medical emergency until an ambulance arrives to transport the person to a hospital. Hatzoloh volunteers co-operate with the ambulance personnel and assist in any way possible.

Shortly after 12:45 p.m. on March 28, 1999, Ungar received a call that a woman had been hit by a motor vehicle; it was a general call from the dispatcher. Initially, Ungar did not answer the call because it was outside of his calling area. The dispatcher got back on the radio and asked who was closest to the area to assist the woman, at which time Unger responded.

The defence of necessity is extremely difficult to prove. Bernard Ungar was able to use it successfully to ward off reckless driving charges.

Under normal driving conditions, it would take Unger about five minutes to get to the location of the accident, but traffic was stopped. He informed the dispatcher, who told him to "use his imagination" since the woman's life was in danger. Unger put his flashing coloured lights on his roof and drove at high speeds, weaved in and out of oncoming traffic to get to the scene of the accident. He was followed by police the entire time. Ungar arrived at the scene and immediately began providing medical assistance. The ambulance arrived about six minutes later. Police charged Ungar with dangerous driving.

At trial, Ungar argued the defence of necessity since he was faced with a situation that was not only urgent but life threatening. The Crown argued that there was a reasonable legal alternative to Ungar's driving. That was to not do anything and allow the ambulance to arrive when it did. Therefore, he was not entitled to use the necessity defence. The trial judge dismissed the charges and accepted the defence of necessity. He stated that, given the circumstances that Ungar found himself in, every second could mean the difference between life and death. In this case, there was no reasonable legal alternative.

For Discussion

1. Why was Ungar charged with dangerous driving?

2. Explain the defence of necessity as it was applied in this case.

3. In his decision, Justice Lampkin stated that this case should never have come to trial. Do you agree? Explain.

4. Do you agree with the decision in this case? Why or why not?

Duress

duress threat or coercion to force someone to do something against his or her will

The defence of **duress** is similar to that of necessity in that an accused commits a crime in response to some sort of external pressure. In this case, the defence of duress is brought on by a threat of harm by some other person, forcing the accused to act against his or her will. An example would be if Leanne participates in a crime when threatened at gunpoint. Recognizing that the threat is real, Leanne acts against her will to avoid being seriously harmed herself.

The defence of duress is found in section 17 of the *Criminal Code*. It requires threats of death or bodily harm from a person present when the offence is being committed. The defence excludes a long list of offences, including murder. Like the defence of necessity, duress can only be considered when the accused had no realistic choice when deciding whether or not to commit the crime.

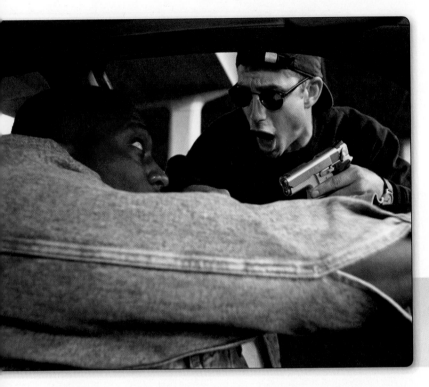

The defence of duress can be used if someone is forced to commit a crime upon fear of immediate death or bodily harm. However, it is often difficult to establish.

You Be the Judge

R. v. Keller, 1998 ABCA 357 (CanLII)

For more information, **Go to Nelson Social Studies**

The appellant, Shane Keller, was convicted of trafficking in lysergic acid diethylamide (LSD). In a written statement, he admitted to picking up at least 10 similar packages during the preceding four months. He claimed, however, that he was compelled to do so under a threat of death or serious bodily harm made by a man he knew as "Shawn." He described Shawn as a big man, over 6 feet 7 inches tall, and a known drug dealer. Shawn threatened that if the appellant did not co-operate, there would be "nasty consequences" and that it would be "over" for him. The appellant interpreted this as a threat of death or serious bodily harm if he did not do what he was told. The trial judge denied his request that the jury be instructed on the common law defence of duress. The Alberta Court of Appeal confirmed that the defence of duress did not apply in this case.

• Why did the defence of duress fail in this case? Explain.

1. Explain the battered woman syndrome defence. Why do you think this has been allowed as a valid defence in criminal cases where the accused has been a long-term victim of spousal abuse?

2. What is meant by "reasonable" when the courts are considering self-defence?

3. What is the difference between sections 34(1) and 34(2) of the *Criminal Code*?

4. Explain the defence of necessity. Why is it difficult to establish in court?

5. How is the defence of duress similar to the defence of necessity?

8.6 Other Defences

There are a number of other defences outlined either in the *Criminal Code* or established through case law precedent.

Ignorance of the Law and Mistake of Fact

Pleading "ignorance of the law" is not an accepted defence. Persons who commit an offence cannot argue that they should not be found guilty because they did not know their actions were against the law. Often, individuals rely on their own knowledge of the law and even seek legal advice that may be incorrect. Regardless of a person's honest (but mistaken) intention, mistaken belief is not a defence.

For example, assume that Jonathan goes hunting with an expired gun licence. He is aware that his licence has lapsed and has every intention of renewing it, but he thinks there is a six-month amnesty period. The grace policy is, in fact, only for three months, and Jonathan's licence has already been expired for five months. Jonathan would be found guilty under the *Firearms Act* in this case, regardless of his honest but mistaken belief that he was not breaking the law.

Sometimes, ignorance of the facts, however, can be accepted as a defence in Canadian law. **Mistake of fact** is a valid defence if it prevents the accused from having the necessary *mens rea* required by law for the crime that was committed. There is a requirement in such a defence that the mistake was genuine and not the result of the accused neglecting to find out the facts. For example, suppose you receive counterfeit money while shopping. When you try to use this money later (for example, to pay a bill with it), you are arrested. You can use the defence of mistake of fact for not knowing that the money was counterfeit, as people do not usually check every bill they receive. As another example, suppose you buy a used bicycle that was advertised in a bulletin board notice.

Ignorance of the law is no excuse. If you go hunting with an expired gun licence, you are breaking the law, even if you think you are within an acceptable grace period before having to renew the licence.

mistake of fact a defence that shows a lack of *mens rea* due to an honest mistake

Later, you are arrested for possessing stolen goods. If you can prove that you did not know the goods were stolen, then your mistake of fact defence will succeed. Unless the brand-new $500 bicycle is offered to you for $40, your mistake of fact would be reasonable.

Entrapment

entrapment police action that induces a person to commit an offence

double jeopardy being tried twice for the same offence

provocation the act of inciting to commit a crime in the heat of passion

Entrapment occurs when police coerce, or forcefully encourage, an individual to commit a crime. The fault lies in the fact that they have no reason to believe that person is already engaged in the particular criminal activity. Of course, the accused has to establish the entrapment. For example, suppose police officers set up an undercover drug operation in a certain neighbourhood, which has been identified as a problem area. Jimmy happens to live in that neighbourhood, but he has never used or sold drugs. Over a period of three weeks, however, he is harassed by an undercover officer to get him drugs. Jimmy eventually helps the officer purchase drugs and is arrested as a result. This is an example of entrapment, since there is no reasonable suspicion that Jimmy was engaged in the criminal activity of drug trafficking.

In *R. v. Mack*, 1988, the Supreme Court recognized entrapment as a defence as well as an abuse of powers by the police. A judge who finds that entrapment has occurred should stay (stop) the proceedings rather than order an acquittal.

e Activity

To learn more about double jeopardy,

Go to Nelson
Social Studies

Double Jeopardy

Double jeopardy means to be tried twice for the same offence. Section 11 of the *Charter of Rights and Freedoms* states that anyone charged and acquitted of an offence cannot be tried for it again. Similarly, someone convicted of an offence cannot be tried again on the same evidence.

In a case of double jeopardy, a pre-trial motion can be made using one of two pleas:

1. In a plea of *autrefois acquit*, the accused states that he or she has already been acquitted of the charge.
2. In a plea of *autrefois convict*, the accused states that he or she has already been convicted on the charge.

The judge then investigates the matter and rules on whether the current charge is based on the same facts as the previous charge that was tried. If so, the judge will dismiss the case.

Provocation

Provocation is defined in section 232 of the *Criminal Code*. It is an accepted legal defence that can reduce a charge of murder to manslaughter. Provocation is a wrongful act or insult that is so significant in nature that it can deprive an ordinary person of the power of self-control. For example, a parent comes home to find that his or her child is being assaulted and attacks and kills the assailant. This person could plead provocation. The offensive act (killing of a person) must be done in the "heat of passion," and the act must occur immediately after the provocation so that there is no cooling-off period.

The principle of double jeopardy is fundamental to Canadian criminal law.

R. v. Humaid, 2006 CanLII 12287 (ON C.A.)

For more information, Go to Nelson Social Studies

Abi Abdel Humaid and the deceased, Aysar Abbas, were married in 1979. Both were engineers, but Aysar was much more successful than her husband, the appellant. She earned over $500 000 a year. In 1996, Humaid had an affair with the family maid. When Aysar found out, she transferred funds from a joint bank account to one in her name only. Aysar and the accused separated for a short time in February 1997. Then, Aysar decided to give the marriage a second chance. Humaid moved back into the family home in April 1997. By the fall of 1999, the marriage had soured.

On October 14, 1999, while out for a walk, Aysar made some comments to Humaid, leading him to believe that she had been unfaithful to him. On hearing this, Humaid testified that he blacked out. He claimed to have no recollection of chasing Aysar along the road and stabbing her 19 times. Humaid was charged with first-degree murder. At trial, he raised the defence of provocation. Humaid was a devout Muslim. He argued that his wife's statements had greater significance because of his Muslim faith. He claimed that it raised the level of insult beyond what an ordinary person in the same situation could tolerate. Humaid argued that he lost self-control and killed his wife in the "heat of passion."

- Were the required elements of the provocation defence met in this case? How would you have decided if you were the judge presiding over this case? Give reasons for your decision.

Abi Abdel Humaid, a devout Muslim, argued that he killed his wife for religious beliefs. Ramandeep K. Grewal (pictured here) is active in women's issues in the Asian community. She argues that some Asian cultures are very male dominated and chauvinistic in many ways. According to Grewal, "It's not a religious conflict; it's a cultural conflict."

Review Your Understanding

1. Explain the difference between ignorance of the law and mistake of fact. In your own words, create an example for each.
2. Police have often been accused of entrapment. Explain how this is possible.
3. What is double jeopardy?
4. Explain the difference between *autrefois acquit* and *autrefois convict*.
5. What does section 232 of the *Criminal Code* say about the defence of provocation?

Should Buy-and-Bust Police Operations Be Unconstitutional?

When engaging in buy-and-bust operations, police have to be careful that they do not cross the line and give the accused the opportunity to use the defence of entrapment.

Police forces in Canada sometimes use informers (some paid) or undercover police agents to obtain information about crimes. With drug cases, infiltrating a group and posing as one of them is often the only way for the police to obtain evidence. In most cases, informers or undercover agents observe the suspect. If necessary, they may need to present the suspect with an opportunity to commit an offence. The police must ensure that the actions of the informer or the undercover agent do not go too far. In such cases, the accused may attempt to use the defence of entrapment to escape charges.

A common tactic used by police is known as a "buy-and-bust" operation. In these situations, undercover police officers try to buy drugs from known dealers. However, there are limits on what police officers can do during these sting operations. Generally, police are expected to uncover criminal activity that is already occurring. They are not supposed to try to provoke innocent citizens into breaking the law.

On One Side

As modern criminals become more sophisticated, police have to be able to employ new tools to keep pace. But these incidents should never see police officers breaching the law while carrying out their duties. When the police are enforcing the *Controlled Drugs and Substances Act*, they often employ "buy-and-bust" operations. An examination of buy-and-bust operations reveals that, overall, they greatly increase the number of arrests. The result is positive public relations for local police forces. This enhances their image and presence in the community. Regardless whether or not the arrests lead to convictions, the fact that there is police presence in the community can help to deter the illegal sale of drugs in troubled areas.

On the Other Side

The strongest argument against buy-and-bust programs is that they often lead to an abuse of the legal process. There is a real risk of goading (pressuring) innocent individuals into committing a crime. Police officers have other ways of investigating, such as surveillance, wire taps, and search warrants. These should be relied upon and might even be more effective. Police sting operations may lead to a decrease in drug operations in the short term. However, the illegal activity sometimes returns after a short lull. Another issue that these programs raise is the possibility of infringements of individuals' Charter rights. The courts must decide whether evidence obtained during a buy-and-bust can be admitted at trial. Critics of these programs argue that they can take a long time to set up. That is why the cost to run such programs can be very high.

The Bottom Line

In *R. v. Barnes*, 1991, Supreme Court of Canada Chief Justice Lamer clarified the legality of buy-and-bust programs. He stated that police should target only those people they suspect are already engaged in criminal activity. He pointed out an exception to this rule when police blanketed an entire neighbourhood known for such crimes.

In the end, when examining these cases, the courts must look for ways to keep a proper balance between stopping criminal activities and not subjecting individuals to unfair investigations by police. Entrapment is unfair. The courts must uphold individuals' legal rights under the *Charter of Rights and Freedoms*. Courts must review police conduct and tactics to ensure that they are acceptable. Canadian courts have placed limits on what police are allowed and not allowed to do and will continue to do so.

What Do You Think?

1. Explain the concept of entrapment.
2. Why do you think truly innocent individuals are sometimes pressured into committing crimes? Explain.
3. Why do police forces regularly set up buy-and-bust programs?
4. What are the arguments against buy-and-bust programs?
5. Are these programs an effective way to stop the sale of illegal drugs in Canada, or are they ultimately pointless? Explain your opinion.

Chapter Review

Chapter Highlights

- A defence is the accused's response to the criminal charges.
- When presenting a defence, an accused is disputing the facts of the case, or he or she is arguing that he or she has a lawful excuse or explanation for what occurred.
- The best possible defence is an acceptable alibi, a defence that places the accused somewhere else at the time the offence occurred.
- Automatism is a state of impaired consciousness during which an individual has no control over his or her actions, but is still capable of committing an act.
- Automatism is classified as either insane or non-insane automatism.
- The defence of intoxication argues that the accused could not form the required *mens rea* at the time the offence was committed.
- Breathalyzer results are considered infallible unless evidence can be produced to show that there was something wrong with the machine.
- Canadian law recognizes prolonged abuse as a form of self-defence.
- Self-defence allows individuals to use force to protect themselves, someone in their care, or their property; the force must be "necessary" and "reasonable" according to the circumstances.
- Canadian courts have been reluctant to recognize the defence of necessity, which is arguing that the accused had to commit the act because of imminent peril or danger.
- The defence of duress requires threats of immediate death or bodily harm from a person present when the offence is being committed.
- Canadian law has not accepted the defence of "ignorance of the law," but the defence of "ignorance of the facts" has been accepted.

- Entrapment can occur if police present a person with the opportunity to commit an offence without reasonable suspicion that the person is already engaged in the particular criminal activity.
- Double jeopardy, being tried for the same crime twice, is prohibited under section 11 of the *Charter of Rights and Freedoms*.
- The defence of provocation can reduce a charge of murder to manslaughter.

Check Your Knowledge

1. Describe a situation in which an alibi can successfully be used as a defence.
2. Identify three examples that would be considered to be non-insane automatism.
3. How has the defence of battered woman syndrome been used in criminal court cases?
4. Explain why the courts have been reluctant to readily accept the defence of necessity.

Apply Your Learning

5. How much force can you legally use to defend yourself or your property? Write a case example to support your response.
6. Find at least five recent criminal cases where a defence discussed in this chapter was used. Use your local newspaper, the Internet, or your library to find the cases. Summarize the cases by answering the following questions:
   a) What are the facts of the case?
   b) What are the criminal charges?
   c) What defence was raised, and what arguments were presented to support the defence?
   d) If there was a decision in the case, identify whether or not the defence was successful.
   e) If there is no decision yet, provide an opinion on whether you think the defence will be accepted by the courts.
   f) Provide a personal opinion on the case.

Communicate Your Understanding

7. You have been asked to prepare a list of questions to ask a forensic psychiatrist to determine if she or he is in fact an expert witness. The psychiatrist has been called to testify in a criminal case where the defence of battered woman syndrome has been raised. Prepare a list of at least 10 questions that you would want answered.

8. Scott Starson was found NCR on criminal charges of uttering death threats. He was detained at a psychiatric facility in Ontario in 1998. While in hospital, he refused the treatment needed to enable him to be discharged. His psychiatrists determined that he was incapable of making treatment decisions for himself. Starson appealed this decision. His case eventually reached the Supreme Court of Canada. In June 2003, the court ruled that Starson was capable of refusing treatment.

Go to Nelson Social Studies

Review the *Starson v. Swazye*, 2003, case in detail. Summarize the facts of the case, the arguments put forth by Starson, the arguments put forth by his doctors, and the reason given by the Supreme Court for their decision. Do you agree with this decision? Why or why not? Present your response to the class. With the rest of the class, debate this issue: Should patients with a mental health disability be allowed to make treatment decisions for themselves?

Develop Your Thinking

9. On August 1, 1995, Ottawa sportscaster Brian Smith was shot and fatally wounded as he walked out of the broadcast centre where he worked. He died the next day. Just a few hours before that, a man turned himself in at the courthouse. Jeffrey Arenburg was charged with first-degree murder and was booked for 60 days of psychiatric assessment. Arenburg was found not criminally responsible for Smith's death. The defence was insane automatism. Arenburg had paranoid schizophrenia. He spent almost 10 years institutionalized in a psychiatric hospital. As a result of this case, the government announced a review of the *Mental Health Act*. On June 23, 2000, *Brian's Law*, a law designed to more adequately deal with mentally disordered individuals who pose a risk to society, came into effect.

Conduct research into *Brian's Law* and summarize the details about this law. Why do you think this law is important?

10. In October 2007, Curtis Fee was arrested for drunk driving after a police officer spotted him weaving across a major highway. At trial, Fee came up with a new defence—the "BlackBerry defence." He indicated that he was not impaired by alcohol when he was arrested, but instead was using his BlackBerry while driving. The trial judge rejected his defence. Do you agree with the judge's decision? Explain.

11. In 1995, Paul Bernardo was found guilty of first-degree murder in the slaying of two Ontario schoolgirls. Before his trial, he had told his lawyer, Ken Murray, where he could locate videotapes of the murders. The police had not discovered these during the search of his home. Later, Karla Homolka, Bernardo's wife, negotiated a lighter sentence in exchange for testifying against her husband. A judicial review confirmed that prosecutors could have avoided making a deal with Homolka if they had had the tapes. In February 1997, Murray was charged under section 139(2) of the *Criminal Code* for obstructing justice. On June 13, 2000, Ken Murray was acquitted of the charges.

Research the lawyer–client relationship in more detail. Should it be allowed as a defence if a lawyer withholds physical evidence that, if disclosed, may incriminate the accused?

From Sentencing to Release

What You Should Know

- What are the objectives of sentencing in the *Criminal Code*?
- What sentencing options are available to a judge?
- What rights does a victim have in the criminal law process?
- What appeal processes are available to the offender and the Crown?
- What is the objective of release?
- What are the various types of release that apply to inmates?

Chapter at a Glance

9.1 Introduction

9.2 The Process and Objectives of Sentencing

9.3 Sentencing an Offender

9.4 Restorative Justice and Victims of Crime

9.5 Appeals

9.6 Canada's Prison System

9.7 Conditional Release

Selected Key Terms

absolute discharge

appellant

community service order

conditional discharge

conditional sentence

dangerous offender

general deterrence

incarceration

long-term offender (LTO)

parole

probation

respondent

specific deterrence

statutory release

suspended sentence

victim impact statement

The Saskatchewan Penitentiary is a maximum-security federal correctional institution. Opened in 1911, it is located in Prince Albert, Saskatchewan. David Milgaard was an inmate here.

9.1 Introduction

Imposing a sentence is one of the most difficult tasks facing a judge. It involves a delicate balance of weighing many factors such as the severity of the crime, the offender's background, and society's views on punishment. It can be called a sentence, a penalty, a disposition, or a sanction. The terms all refer to imposing a punishment and holding an offender accountable for his or her actions.

Once a sentence has been set, either the accused or the Crown may appeal that sentence to a higher court for review. Eventually, the offender may enter a correctional facility. In Canada, this may involve time in a federal penitentiary or provincial jail, depending on the nature and severity of the crime.

In this chapter, you will examine the sentencing and release of offenders. These areas of the law are controversial. Some people seek to punish offenders and want to keep them in prison as long as possible. Others believe that employment, education, and social programs can help offenders to reform and return to the community rehabilitated. In all cases, these theories must be balanced with the concern for public safety.

Most offenders eventually return to society. The system of **conditional release** allows offenders to serve part of their sentence in the community while under supervision. Although the law provides for conditional release, not all inmates qualify for it. Those who do are usually successful in completing their sentences in the community.

Correctional Facilities in Canada, 2005

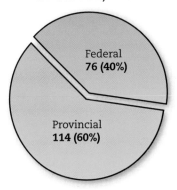

In 2005, there were 190 correctional facilities in Canada.

conditional release a discharge from custody into the community under terms and conditions

Factors a Judge Must Consider

Judges must consider many factors when determining an appropriate sentence.

pre-sentence report a document about the accused's background, used for sentencing

9.2 The Process and Objectives of Sentencing

Sentencing reflects social values. Some people believe that Canadian prisons are too "soft" on inmates and provide too many privileges. Others believe that prisons have many problems. For example, prisons are expensive to run and fail to reform certain criminals. Some people think that non-violent offenders should pay their debt to society in ways other than spending time in jail.

Sentencing may take place right after the accused has been found guilty or many weeks later. A judge may order a probation officer to prepare a **pre-sentence report** about the offender's situation. The report will include interviews with the offender and others who are familiar with the person's history and potential future conduct, and individuals acting as character references. These may include teachers and employers. The judge will consider the report when passing sentence.

The defence and the Crown have the right to call witnesses to testify about the offender's background. The Crown may raise the offender's previous criminal record. The convicted person may also make a statement. If the Crown and the offender disagree on the information presented at the time of sentencing, the judge can listen to sworn evidence.

When passing sentence, the judge must refer to the *Criminal Code*. It specifies the objectives on sentencing and the penalties available. Of course, the judge must also consider that Canadians have the right not to be subjected to "cruel and unusual punishment" according to section 12 of the *Charter of Rights and Freedoms*.

 You Be the Judge

Maljkovich v. Canada, 2005 FC 1398 (CanLII)

For more information, Go to Nelson Social Studies

Vlado Maljkovich was serving a sentence for second-degree murder in the Fenbrook Correctional Institution in Gravenhurst, Ontario. He suffered from an allergy to cigarette smoke. Exposure caused him to get headaches, nausea, and throat irritation. He presented medical evidence to Corrections Canada about his allergies. He also made several complaints, but no action was taken. Maljkovich claimed that Corrections Canada failed to protect him from second-hand smoke. Prisoners had to smoke in designated areas, but the ventilation system did not prevent second-hand smoke from reaching other inmates. Maljkovich argued that this amounted to cruel and unusual punishment under section 12 of the Charter. Maljkovich sued Corrections Canada for damages.

The Federal Court of Canada ruled that Corrections Canada failed to provide Maljkovich with a healthy and safe environment. It awarded him $5000 for the stress and discomfort he suffered. However, the court ruled that the exposure to second-hand smoke was not intended to be a deliberate form of cruel and unusual treatment. Therefore, his exposure was not a Charter violation.

• Do you think an award of damages was appropriate in this case? Why or why not?

Imposing a Sentence

Judges in Canada have a good deal of freedom in imposing sentences. For some offences, there are mandatory minimum sentences, as you will see below. For most, judges have more leeway. For example, someone found guilty of aggravated assault that carries a maximum penalty of 14 years can receive any term up to the maximum. In deciding on a suitable penalty, judges often refer to previous similar cases (precedents). However, judges are not required to follow sentences imposed in similar cases. These are simply guidelines to consider.

When sentencing, a judge may also consider the time spent in custody awaiting trial or sentencing, the circumstances of the convicted person, and the potential for rehabilitation. The victim may also be considered. The judge may ask for a **victim impact statement**. This is a declaration by the victim and others affected by the offence. It describes the impact of the offence on their lives. Victim impact statements are especially significant in cases that may result in lasting harm to the victim or the victim's family.

Victims are able to read their victim impact statement in court.

In recent years, Parliament has toughened its position on certain offences. These include crimes such as harassment or sexual assault. Organized crime is another such area. In these instances, penalties have been increased or mandatory minimum sentences have been set out in the *Criminal Code*.

Parliament has amended the *Criminal Code* to allow for sentences to be served in the community under supervision. Parliament also introduced the label **long-term offender (LTO)**. These are criminals who repeatedly behave in ways that could injure or harm others. People who are likely to reoffend are often labelled LTOs. In its concern for violent crimes, Parliament has also created **mandatory minimum sentences** that must be imposed in certain circumstances. For example, if a weapon is used during a criminal offence, the mandatory minimum prison sentence is four years.

In February 2008, the federal government of Canada passed the *Tackling Violent Crime Act*. This act increased the number of offences that carry mandatory minimum sentences and took aim at serious drug offences. See Agents of Change, Chapter 7, page 230.

victim impact statement a statement made by the victim that describes the effect of the offence on his or her life

long-term offender (LTO) a criminal who repeatedly behaves in a way that could cause serious harm to others and who would likely reoffend

mandatory minimum sentence a minimum punishment imposed by law

R. v. Ferguson, 2008 SCC 6 (CanLII)

For more information, Go to Nelson Social Studies

Michael Ferguson leaves the courthouse on September 30, 2004, after being found guilty of manslaughter.

Michael Ferguson, an RCMP constable, was involved in an altercation with a detainee, Darren Varley. On October 3, 1999, in a cell at an RCMP detachment in Pincher Creek, Alberta, Ferguson shot and killed Varley. The first gunshot hit Varley in the stomach, and the second hit him in the head. Ferguson claimed that he had acted in self-defence and that the gunshots were accidental. He maintained that Varley had attacked him when he entered the cell. The prisoner pulled Ferguson's bulletproof vest over his head and face and grabbed his firearm from the holster. However, earlier at trial, Ferguson said that he had fired the gunshots *after* he regained control of the gun. Expert evidence verified this fact. Further evidence also indicated that there was a three-second delay between the first and second shots.

Ferguson was charged. In the fall of 2004 at the Alberta Court of Queen's Bench, a jury convicted Ferguson of manslaughter. Section 236(a) of the *Criminal Code* sets out a mandatory minimum sentence of four years for the offence of manslaughter with a firearm. The trial judge held that the firing of the second shot was instantaneous and instinctive. He felt that there was no intent to murder Varley. The judge concluded that applying the four-year mandatory minimum sentence amounted to cruel and unusual punishment and a violation of section 12 of the *Charter of Rights and Freedoms*. This is known as a "constitutional exemption." The trial judge imposed a conditional sentence of two years less a day. (A conditional sentence is a penalty for a crime of a term of less than two years that can be served in the community if the offender meets certain expectations.) In May 2006, the Alberta Court of Appeal overturned the original sentence and imposed the mandatory minimum four-year sentence.

Ferguson appealed his case to the Supreme Court of Canada. In a 9–0 decision in February 2008, the court dismissed the appeal and upheld the four-year minimum jail sentence. The court concluded that the mandatory minimum was not out of balance with the harm done in this case. The court did not allow a constitutional exemption from the required minimum sentence. This was consistent with the *Latimer* case discussed in Chapter 7.

For Discussion

1. What was the original sentencing decision?

2. How did the Alberta Court of Appeal decide the case?

3. Summarize the decision of the Supreme Court of Canada.

4. Do you think the *Criminal Code* should set out mandatory minimum sentences? Why or why not?

Purposes of Sentencing

In 1995, Parliament amended the *Criminal Code* to give judges some direction in sentencing. The changes were based on the idea that appropriate sentencing promotes respect for the law. It also helps to maintain a just, peaceful, and safe society. Judges must consider various sentencing objectives and balance these with the circumstances of the criminal case before them. Sentences must have one of the objectives on the next page.

Objectives of Sentencing under the *Criminal Code*

- denounce unlawful conduct
- deter the offender and others from committing offences
- separate offenders from society, where necessary
- assist in rehabilitating offenders
- provide reparations for harm done to victims or to the community
- promote a sense of responsibility in offenders

Judges must consider many of these objectives before imposing a sentence on a convicted offender.

Denouncing Unlawful Conduct

Part of denouncing unlawful conduct is condemning the crime from society's viewpoint. A judge should consider the offender's character and his or her past criminal behaviour. As we saw in Chapter 4, retribution is the idea of giving someone a just reward for her or his actions. It is not a sentencing objective according to Canada's *Criminal Code*. Revenge is also not an appropriate objective in sentencing.

 You Be the Judge

R. v. Kobelka, 2007 ABPC 112 (CanLII)

For more information, **Go to Nelson Social Studies**

In January 2006, Chad Kobelka pleaded guilty to theft, dangerous operation of a motor vehicle causing bodily harm, and flight from police officers. Kobelka was 19 years old at the time he stole an SUV from his uncle. He led police on a lengthy high-speed police chase and finally crashed his vehicle into another, seriously injuring a young couple. The female in the vehicle was 20 weeks pregnant. She delivered her baby prematurely at 36 weeks. It had permanent mental and physical impairments.

In April 2007, a Provincial Court of Alberta judge sentenced Kobelka to 10 years in prison. That was the longest sentence ever given in Canada for these offences. The judge noted that Kobelka had at least 14 opportunities to stop during the police chase but chose not to.

- What sentencing principles do you think the judge considered in determining the sentence in this case? Why? Do you think the judge's sentence was appropriate? Why or why not?

Deterrence

Under the *Criminal Code*, the fundamental purposes of sentencing are: 1) to promote respect for the law; and 2) to maintain a just, peaceful, and safe society. This is accomplished by imposing fair penalties. The Code states that sentencing should deter (prevent) an offender from committing crimes in the future (**specific deterrence**). In addition, all other members of society should be discouraged from committing similar crimes (**general deterrence**). Thus, general deterrence is a sentencing objective for adult offenders under the *Criminal Code*. However, in 2006, the Supreme Court ruled in *R. v. B.W.P.; R. v. B.V.N.* (see the case on page 294) that general deterrence had no role with regard to youth criminals. It should not be used to justify harsher punishments for criminals under the age of 18. See Chapter 10 for more about sentencing principles for youth criminals.

specific deterrence that which discourages the specific criminal from reoffending

general deterrence that which discourages people in society from committing a particular crime

Chapter 9 **From Sentencing to Release**

Case

R. v. B.W.P.; R. v. B.V.N., 2006 SCC 27 (CanLII)

For more information, **Go to Nelson Social Studies**

The Supreme Court of Canada heard the following two appeal cases together in 2006. In 2003, B.W.P. pleaded guilty to manslaughter after another man died from serious head injuries sustained during a fight. When it came to sentencing, the trial judge reviewed the youth's background. He examined B.W.P.'s Aboriginal identity and his minimal criminal record. The judge also noted the positive comments from his family, school, and coaches. Also, tests showed that B.W.P. had a low risk of reoffending.

B.W.P. had served more than three months in pretrial custody. He was sentenced to another 15 months. The Crown wanted B.W.P. to serve two-thirds of the sentence (10 months) in open custody (a group home). The remaining one-third would be served under supervision in the community. Instead, the judge sentenced him to serve just one day of open custody. The remainder would be served in the community. The judge stated that general deterrence (discouraging others from committing the same crime) was not a factor in sentencing youth offenders under the *Youth Criminal Justice Act (YCJA)*. In 2004, the Manitoba Court of Appeal dismissed the appeal. It agreed with the original trial judge. The Crown appealed the decision to the Supreme Court of Canada.

In 2004, B.V.N. pleaded guilty to a charge of aggravated assault related to his involvement with drug trafficking. The judge reviewed B.V.N.'s background. He noted that the accused had an unfortunate family history. He had no convictions for violent crimes. However, he had been suspended from school and then expelled for assault and drug trafficking. Psychological tests revealed that B.V.N. had a high risk of reoffending.

B.V.N. had spent two and a half months in pretrial custody. In addition, he was given a nine-month sentence. The trial judge concluded that general deterrence is only a small factor to be considered in sentencing. The Crown appealed, and the British Columbia Court of Appeal dismissed it, agreeing with the original sentencing judge. Then, B.V.N. appealed his case to the Supreme Court of Canada. He argued that his sentence should be reduced because general deterrence should not be a factor in sentencing.

In June 2006, the Supreme Court of Canada concluded that general deterrence should not be considered when sentencing youths under the *YCJA*. The principles of the *YCJA* allow judges to look at the circumstances surrounding the youths' behaviour. This includes opportunities for rehabilitation and to enable youths to reintegrate into society. As well, youths should be held accountable for their actions. This is done through appropriate penalties that address the harm done. The concept of deterrence is neither mentioned in the *YCJA*, nor did Parliament intend for it to be considered.

The Supreme Court dismissed the appeal in the B.W.P. case. It agreed with the Manitoba Court of Appeal and the trial judge that general deterrence should not be a factor in youth sentencing. In the B.V.N. case, the court concluded that general deterrence did not play a significant role in the sentencing decision by the British Columbia Court of Appeal. Therefore, it did not change the original sentence. Further, B.V.N. had already served his nine-month sentence by the time the Supreme Court had issued its decision.

For Discussion

1. Explain the concepts of general and specific deterrence.

2. Outline the factors considered in determining an appropriate sentence in the B.W.P. and B.V.N. cases.

3. What should judges take into consideration when sentencing youths under the *Youth Criminal Justice Act*?

4. According to the decision in this case, deterrence cannot be used to justify imposing a harsher sentence on a youth offender. Do you agree or disagree with this decision? Why or why not?

Separation of the Offender from Society

According to the *Criminal Code*, one purpose of sentencing is to separate offenders from society. Canada's **incarceration** (imprisonment) rate is not as high as that of Russia or the United States. However, for some critics, the rate is still too high. In recent years, the Canadian government has moved to reduce the number of offenders who are imprisoned. While the 2008 incarceration rate in Canada showed a slight decline, some of these figures are due to the number of adults incarcerated while awaiting their trial or sentencing hearing.

incarceration imprisonment or confinement

International Incarceration Rates, 2008

Country	Number of Prisoners per 100 000 People
Nepal	24
Japan	63
Sweden	79
Canada	108
MEDIAN	125
England and Wales	151
Russia	627
United States	751

Canada has a below-average incarceration rate compared to other countries.

rehabilitate to help an offender successfully reintegrate back into society

recidivism the act of recommitting crimes

Rehabilitation

The *Criminal Code* also states that sentencing should help to **rehabilitate** offenders. This involves restoring a person to good mental and moral health, through treatment and training and addressing the root causes of the criminal activities. Over the years, society has come to view it as an important goal of sentencing. Today, for example, inmates are provided with job counselling and training so that they will be able to reintegrate back into society when they are released. Supervised parole helps offenders prepare for this return to society. This should reduce **recidivism** (repeat offenders committing an offence after release from prison and returning to prison after being convicted of a new offence).

An inmate at the Joliette Institution in Joliette, Québec, learns work skills by sewing underwear in a workshop.

Other Objectives of Sentencing

reparations repayment for harm done to victims and the community

Section 718 of the *Criminal Code* outlines other sentencing objectives. It directs judges to consider **reparations** (repayment) for harm done to victims and the community. It provides alternatives to imprisonment. The *Criminal Code* also states that sentences should reflect the harm done to victims and to the community. Judges should also consider whether offenders have shown any remorse (deep regret) for their conduct.

Considerations in Sentencing

The Criminal Code states that a sentence must be proportional. That means that the severity of the punishment must reflect the harm committed. For this reason, the most severe sentences are handed down for offences that are most harmful to society, such as kidnapping or murder.

mitigating circumstances factors that demonstrate the punishment should be less severe

aggravating circumstances factors that demonstrate the punishment should be more severe

The *Criminal Code* also directs judges to increase or reduce a sentence under certain conditions. For instance, there may be **mitigating circumstances**. These are facts or details that lessen the responsibility of the offender. For example, mitigating circumstances could include whether the crime involved a first-time offender. In other cases, the offender may have a good character or a good employment record. In such cases, the penalty may be reduced. The opposite is true of **aggravating circumstances**. These are details about the crime that increase the responsibility of the offender. In such cases, the penalty may be increased. For example, aggravating circumstances could include evidence showing that an offender abused a position of trust or authority in relation to the victim, or committed the crime in association with a criminal organization.

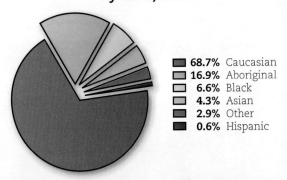

Federal Offender Population by Race, 2007

- **68.7%** Caucasian
- **16.9%** Aboriginal
- **6.6%** Black
- **4.3%** Asian
- **2.9%** Other
- **0.6%** Hispanic

In 2007, the vast majority of offenders in federal prisons were Caucasian. Between 1993 and 2006, the rate of incarceration in federal institutions decreased 5 percent for Aboriginal offenders and 3 percent for Black offenders.

Lastly, in section 718(2), the *Criminal Code* directs judges to do the following:

- give similar sentences for similar offenders committing similar offences in similar circumstances

- not impose consecutive sentences that are unduly long or harsh

- not deprive offenders of their liberty if less restrictive options are available such as serving a sentence in the community

- consider all options other than imprisonment that are reasonable, especially for Aboriginal offenders, who are overrepresented in prisons

R. v. Gladue, 1999, is a landmark judgment for the way in which Aboriginal offenders are sentenced by the courts (see the case on the next page).

R. v. Gladue, 1999 CanLII 679 (S.C.C.)

For more information, **Go to Nelson Social Studies**

On June 3, 1996, Jamie Gladue, an Aboriginal, was charged with second-degree murder and pleaded guilty to manslaughter after jury selection. At age 19, she suspected that her fiancé was having an affair with her sister. She stabbed her fiancé with a knife after being provoked. At that time, she had a blood-alcohol content of between 155 and 165. (Double the legal limit is 160.) Gladue was also pregnant with her second child at the time of the murder. She had been raised by her father from age 11, after her mother left the home.

At the sentencing hearing, the judge considered a number of factors about Gladue. She was a young mother, and her only prior offence was an impaired driving conviction. At the time of the offence, she had a hyperthyroid condition, which caused her to overreact to emotional situations. She had shown signs of remorse and had entered a guilty plea. Her family had supported her, and she had attended alcohol abuse counselling and upgraded her education while on bail. She was pregnant with her third child at the time of sentencing.

The sentencing judge also considered a number of factors concerning the incident. She had stabbed her fiancé twice, the second time while he was fleeing. The remarks that she made before and immediately after the stabbing left no doubt that she intended harm. She was the aggressor. During the time she was on bail, Gladue pleaded guilty to having breached her bail on one occasion by consuming alcohol.

Gladue was sentenced to three years' imprisonment and a 10-year weapons prohibition because the judge considered it to be a very serious offence. Her appeals to both the British Columbia Court of Appeal and the Supreme Court of Canada were dismissed.

Photo by Chris Bolin/*National Post*

Following the 1999 Gladue decision, a new court was established in Toronto. Named after Jamie Gladue, the Gladue court is more sympathetic to the mitigating circumstances of Aboriginal offenders. Assistant Crown Attorney Fred Bartley (left) and Duty Counsel Eugene O'Kanne (right) are shown on the steps of the Toronto courthouse where the Gladue court operates.

The trial decision was in February 1997, and Gladue was sentenced in October, 17 months after the stabbing. The 7–0 Supreme Court of Canada judgment was released in April 1999.

For Discussion

1. What are the mitigating circumstances in this case?

2. What are the aggravating circumstances in this case?

3. If you were sentencing Gladue, what sentencing objectives would you consider? Explain your choices.

4. What sentence would you have imposed on Gladue? Explain.

Review Your Understanding

1. What is the purpose of a pre-sentence report? What might such a report contain?

2. What is a victim impact statement, and what is its purpose?

3. Briefly explain four main objectives of sentencing.

4. What is a proportional sentence?

5. Distinguish between aggravating and mitigating circumstances.

9.3 Sentencing an Offender

For most people, the word "sentencing" means imprisonment. However, society's views about appropriate sentencing have been changing. The prison system is extremely expensive to maintain. That is why **diversion programs** have become more popular. These are the types of sentences that keep offenders out of the prison system. Diversion programs are less costly than prison and avoid the problem of the accused socializing with other convicts. These programs also allow the accused to repay society in a more meaningful way.

diversion program a sentence that keeps offenders out of prison

You Be the Judge

R. v. Millar, 1994 CanLII 7558 (ON S.C.)

For more information, Go to Nelson Social Studies

Scott Millar was charged with first-degree murder in the killing of his father. In a frenzied state and blind with rage, Millar struck the fatal blow. For over 25 years, Millar had been dominated and humiliated by his father. The court found that Millar had been physically, sexually, and psychologically abused in ways that can only be described as cruel, insensitive, inhumane, and unthinkable. The judge noted that this case stood out as one of the most tragic in more than 20 years of criminal law practice. Shortly before the killing, Millar's father cruelly criticized him for his inadequacies and threatened him with a knife. The father's rage was due to Millar's failure to respond to his father's suggestion that it would "be nice to have a glass of milk." If found guilty of first-degree murder, Millar's maximum sentence would be life imprisonment.

• If you were on the jury in this case, would you convict Millar of first-degree murder? Why or why not? What sentence would you impose if you were the judge?

Absolute or Conditional Discharge

For a crime that carries a sentence of less than 14 years, the offender may receive a discharge. These can be either absolute or conditional. An **absolute discharge** is effective immediately, with no conditions attached.

absolute discharge a release without conditions, with no criminal record

A **conditional discharge** means that the accused can avoid a record of conviction provided he or she follows certain conditions laid out by the judge in a probation order at the time of sentencing. (Probation is discussed below.) In either case, no conviction is recorded against the offender. Generally, a discharge is granted when it is the offender's first offence, or when the publicity attached to the case is so negative that it becomes a kind of penalty or deterrent.

conditional discharge a release with terms, which, if successfully completed, results in no criminal record

suspended sentence a punishment that is not carried out as long as the offender complies with conditions

Suspended Sentence and Probation

A judge may give a **suspended sentence** after considering certain factors. These include the character of the accused and the circumstances surrounding the offence. When a sentence is suspended, it is postponed. If the offender meets certain conditions, the sentence will never be served. However, the offender still has a record of conviction and could be placed on **probation** for up to three years. Probation orders can be used in addition to fines and in addition to sentences of less than two years. A suspended sentence cannot be given when there is a mandatory minimum sentence required by the *Criminal Code*. For example, if the offender committed a break and enter with a gun, a mandatory minimum four-year sentence must be given for the weapons offence. Thus, no suspended sentence is possible.

probation a punishment that allows the offender to live in the community under conditions and supervision

A probation order requires that the accused behave. In other words, she or he must keep the peace. The accused must also appear before the court when required. In essence, the offender must do anything else the judge orders. For example, the offender usually reports to a probation officer and agrees to abstain from alcohol or drugs. If the offender breaches probation, the court might reinstate the sentence, and the offender may have to return to jail.

 Did You Know?

In July 2006, Nova Scotia became the first area in Canada to allow the use of electronic ankle bracelets. These are used to track the movements of paroled offenders.

Conditional Sentence

If a sentence is less than two years and the crime carries no minimum sentence, the judge may impose a conditional sentence. In this case, the judge passes sentence but allows the offender to serve the time in the community. The judge must be satisfied that the offender will not endanger the safety of the community. A conditional order is issued, requiring the offender to keep the peace, be of good behaviour, and appear before the court when asked to do so. There may be additional orders to abstain from drugs or alcohol and not carry a weapon, depending on the circumstances of the case.

Allowing offenders to serve their sentence in the community has been hotly debated in Canada. Most prison sentences are less than two years, which is the maximum to be eligible for a conditional sentence. That means that most offenders are eligible. The result is that people who have committed some serious crimes, such as theft without a weapon or even sexual assault, can serve their sentences in the community.

Conditional sentences are intended to be heavier than suspended sentences. In reality, however, there is not much difference in their application by the courts.

Electronic monitoring devices such as this are used for non-dangerous offenders.

R. v. Proulx, 2000 SCC 5 (CanLII)

For more information, **Go to Nelson Social Studies**

In November 1995, Jeromie Proulx had been at a party with friends where he consumed some alcohol. He decided to drive his friends home early in the morning. Proulx had been a licensed driver for only seven weeks when he drove his vehicle erratically, weaving in and out of traffic on the slippery roads. Eventually, he ended up in the oncoming lane of traffic and crashed his vehicle into another car. A passenger was killed in his own vehicle and another seriously injured in the oncoming vehicle. Proulx himself almost died from the injuries he suffered during the crash.

Proulx was charged with dangerous driving causing death and bodily harm. In June 1997, the Manitoba Court of Queen's Bench judge sentenced him to 18 months in jail. The defence argued for a conditional sentence. The judge disagreed, saying that a sentence served in the community would not deter others from committing similar crimes. Only a jail term would denounce the actions of the offender (condemn the crime on behalf of society).

Proulx appealed to the Manitoba Court of Appeal. In October 1997, the court decided that a conditional sentence was warranted as the offender was not a danger to the community. The Crown appealed this decision to the Supreme Court of Canada.

In its landmark decision, the Supreme Court set down a test for conditional sentences. First, the court concluded that a conditional sentence should be used only for terms of less than two years' imprisonment. Second, the offender should not be a danger if released into the community. Third, the court must consider the purposes and principles of sentencing such as denunciation and deterrence. Finally, conditional sentences cannot be used if a mandatory minimum sentence is required by the *Criminal Code*.

In January 2000, the Supreme Court allowed the appeal. It restored the original 18-month term, saying that the sentence was to condemn Proulx's actions and to deter others from committing the same offence.

Both the Manitoba Court of Appeal and the Court of Queen's Bench of Manitoba sit in courtrooms in the Law Court Building (shown here).

For Discussion

1. Why did the trial judge impose a period of incarceration?

2. What conditions must be met before a conditional sentence can be imposed?

3. Why did the Supreme Court of Canada allow the appeal?

4. Do you think conditional sentencing should be used in drinking and driving cases? Why or why not?

How Courts Apply Conditional and Suspended Sentences

Conditional Sentence	Suspended Sentence
Sentence of imprisonment is imposed, but offender is released on a conditional order.	Sentence is not imposed, but offender is released on a probation order.
Offender must remain within the territorial jurisdiction of the court.	Offender may be ordered to stay within the territorial jurisdiction of the court.
Offender may be ordered to attend a treatment program.	Offender may be ordered to attend a treatment program, but only if offender agrees.
Offender may immediately be imprisoned to serve original sentence if conditional order is breached.	Offender may be sent back to trial judge to be sentenced for original offence if probation is breached. Offender can also be tried for breach of probation.

Courts may consider **conditional sentences** and suspended sentences when sentencing offenders.

conditional sentence a prison term of less than two years that is served in the community under conditions

 ## You Be the Judge

R. v. Law, 2007 ABCA 203 (CanLII)

For more information, Go to Nelson Social Studies

Barry Law was convicted of sexual assault. He received a conditional sentence of two years less a day to be served in the community. The conditions included house arrest for the first six months of the sentence. After that, there was a curfew whenever he was not at work for the following 12-month period. He also had to participate in sexual offender counselling. In passing sentence, the trial judge noted that the offender expressed remorse. He was suitable for community supervision because he was a low risk to reoffend. The Crown appealed this sentence.

It argued that the seriousness of the offence justified a minimum three-year prison term, not a conditional sentence to be served in the community. In fact, Alberta case law precedents had established a three-year minimum sentence for serious sexual assaults. The Alberta Court of Appeal overruled the trial judge and sentenced Law to three years in prison. Since this was more than the two-year maximum, there was no question of a conditional sentence.

- Do you think conditional sentencing should be allowed in sexual assault cases? Why or why not?

Review Your Understanding

1. What is a diversion program? What are the benefits of diverting people away from prison?

2. **a)** What is probation, and what might a probation order involve?
   b) Discuss breach of probation.

3. **a)** What is the difference between an absolute discharge and a conditional discharge?
   b) What is the difference between a conditional discharge and a suspended sentence?

4. What is the objective of a conditional sentence?

5. What factors must be present for a judge to consider a conditional sentence?

Suspension of a Privilege

suspension a sentence that removes a privilege, such as driving

Many offences call for the **suspension** of a social privilege. This includes such things as a driver's licence or a restaurant liquor licence. A person whose driver's licence has been suspended will usually have to surrender the actual licence to the court clerk before leaving the courtroom. In many areas, authorities can refuse to issue or renew a licence if a fine has not been paid.

Peace Bond

peace bond a court order requiring a person to keep the peace

A **peace bond** is a court order requiring a person to keep the peace and be of good behaviour for up to 12 months. A peace bond is often used in minor harassment or assault cases. Under the *Criminal Code*, someone who reasonably believes that another person will injure him or her, harm family members, or damage property can apply to have that person enter a peace bond. Once the accused has entered a peace bond, charges may be withdrawn, but other conditions are imposed. Usually the accused has to avoid the person who asked that the bond be imposed and agree not to own any weapons.

Parliament has amended the *Criminal Code* with regard to peace bonds. Now, certain parties may be required to enter into a peace bond on the complaint of a citizen. For example, suppose a citizen swears that someone may commit a sexual offence against someone under the age of 14. The judge may order that person to refrain from having contact with persons of that age. The individual may also be banned from any public area such as a swimming pool or park where persons under that age are present.

compensation something given to make amends for a loss

Someone who is found guilty of vandalism may be required to make restitution. This could involve either washing off the graffiti or repainting to cover it up.

Restitution or Compensation

Restitution or **compensation** requires the offender to repay the victim. The purpose of this penalty is to reduce the impact of the offence on the victim and to compensate him or her.

A victim may ask for restitution at the time of sentencing. The courts consider such compensation in all cases involving harm to property or expenses arising from bodily harm. In granting restitution, the judge may consider a victim impact statement along with the offender's ability to pay. If cash compensation is ordered, payments can be made over time. Restitution can also take the form of work. For example, a group of youths who destroy a homeowner's fence on a night of public mischief might be asked to repair or replace the fence. In addition, the victim can still sue the offender in civil court to obtain anything to which he or she feels entitled. (See Chapter 12 for a discussion on civil law remedies.) The penalty for ignoring a court order granting restitution is imprisonment.

Some communities have programs that bring together offenders and victims and let them work out the compensation themselves. For example, they can determine the type of work offenders can do for the victims. Supporters of this idea believe that it has a more positive effect on offenders than prison sentences would. These meetings also allow victims to tell offenders exactly how the crime has affected them.

Community Service Orders

A judge may sentence an offender to work a certain number of hours for a local organization or on a government project. This is known as a **community service order**. For example, a youth involved in public mischief could be ordered to do community service. This could involve working at a local library placing books on the shelves. Alternatively, it could mean cleaning floors at a town hall.

Community service may enhance the offender's self-worth. In addition, community service allows the offender to associate with upstanding people in the community rather than with criminals in jails. Finally, community service occupies much of the offenders' free time. That way, they do not have idle time to commit other crimes.

High-profile individuals are often sentenced to community service work. For example, a famous person convicted of impaired driving may have to do a presentation at a high school on the dangers of drinking and driving.

community service order a sentence that requires the offender to do specific work in the community under supervision

 You and the Law

In the criminal court system, community service is a common sentence used by judges. What types of community services are performed in your community?

Pardon My Planet

Judges often include community service orders in sentencing. What do you think of community service orders?

Deportation

Non-citizens who commit a serious offence within Canada can be deported. They are usually returned to their country of origin but can also be sent to another country. Usually, the federal government applies to the courts for such a direction. This is known as a deportation order. Under the *Extradition Act*, Canadian residents who commit serious offences in other countries can be extradited (returned) to those countries. There, they will stand trial and receive punishment.

Fines

For individuals who commit summary conviction offences, such as causing a disturbance, the maximum fine under the *Criminal Code* is $2000 and/or six months in jail. No maximum fine is provided for indictable offences. If the penalty for an indictable offence is five years or less, the offender may be ordered to pay a fine instead of going to prison. Where the maximum penalty is more than five years, a fine may be imposed, but only in addition to imprisonment. The judge establishes the amount of the fine.

An offender may ask to have at least 14 days to pay the fine. A **fine option program** is also available for both provincial and federal offences. Instead of paying a fine, an offender can earn credits for doing work similar to community service. In several provinces such as Manitoba, an offender who cannot afford to pay the fine can register with the local community resource centre and "work off" the debt.

fine option program credit for doing community work instead of paying a fine

Imprisonment

In Canada, convicted offenders can go to jail for up to six months for most summary conviction offences. Imprisonment means losing your liberty. Some of these offences—such as uttering threats, sexual assault, and failure to comply with a probation order—carry a penalty of up to 18 months if the Crown proceeds by way of a summary conviction offence. Indictable offences carry sentences ranging from two years to life imprisonment, depending on the seriousness of the crime. For a fuller list of offences and their penalties, see Chapter 7.

A judge decides if the amount of time an offender has been kept in custody before trial will count toward the sentence. The standard rule is that pretrial custody is equal to twice the time when considering a penalty. Thus, a person who has been in custody three months awaiting trial will be considered to have served six months of the sentence. There are two reasons for doubling the pretrial time. First, the offender is not eligible for parole on that time served awaiting trial. Second, there are usually no rehabilitation or recreational facilities available in the pretrial detention facilities.

 Did You Know?

Of all the inmates in federal prisons, 70 percent are high school dropouts, 70 percent have unstable job histories, and 80 percent have substance-abuse problems. Of all the youth in the system, 66 percent have two or more mental health problems.

The forms of custodial sentences available are often subject to public criticism.

For a jail sentence of 30 days or less, the offender is usually kept at the local detention centre. If the sentence is more than 30 days but less than two years, the offender is placed in a provincial prison or reformatory. Sentences of two years or more are served in a federal penitentiary.

People convicted of two or more offences may serve the sentence either concurrently or consecutively, at the judge's discretion. Offenders receive a **concurrent sentence** when they are convicted of two or more crimes and serve both penalties at the same time. Offenders receive a **consecutive sentence** when they are convicted of two or more crimes and the penalties are served one after the other. A sentence of three years for one offence followed by four years for another would result in a total of seven years in prison.

concurrent sentence a penalty for two or more offences, served at the same time

consecutive sentence a penalty for two or more offences, served one after the other

WIZARD OF ID   BY BRANT PARKER & JOHNNY HART

People convicted of two or more offences may be ordered to serve the sentence consecutively or concurrently.

Parliament wants to curb the activities of criminal organizations. That is why it has amended the *Criminal Code* to let judges impose a sentence of up to 14 years on offenders taking part in organized crime. This sentence is always served consecutively. That means that the time is added to any other sentence imposed, up to a total of 14 years. A sentence for an offence related to a terrorist activity must also be served consecutively to any other sentence given.

At the discretion of the judge, offenders may receive an **intermittent sentence**, serving it on evenings or weekends so they can still maintain a job and a family life. An intermittent sentence can be imposed only if the original sentence is less than 90 days. The court would also issue a probation order, outlining the conditions for the offender when not in prison. Conditions often include no alcohol or drugs, evening curfews, and so on.

intermittent sentence a jail term of 90 days or less that is served on weekends or at night

principle of totality the rule of looking at all the circumstances to ensure that a fair sentence is given

The **principle of totality** guides sentencing. This means that someone who is convicted of several violations of the same offence usually does not receive an overly long prison term. For instance, for someone found guilty of 24 charges of passing forged cheques, a year's sentence for each violation (for a total of 24 years) would be severe. A more reasonable total penalty would be two years. However, the penalties should not be so lenient that people are encouraged to commit multiple crimes.

Why do you think
the prison population
differs substantially in
the various countries?

Prison Population Totals, 2006

Rank	Country	Population
1	United States	2 258 983
2	China	1 565 771
3	Russian Federation	892 330
4	Brazil	419 551
5	India	358 368
6	Mexico	217 436
7	South Africa	165 987
8	Thailand	165 316
9	Iran	158 351
10	Ukraine	149 690
...		
44	Canada	35 110

Sentencing Dangerous and Long-Term Offenders

dangerous offender an offender deemed to be a serious risk to public safety due to repetitive behaviours, and is therefore given an indeterminate sentence

Some criminals commit serious violent crimes. Someone who does this repeatedly may be declared a **dangerous offender**. These crimes include manslaughter, attempted murder, or aggravated assault. A dangerous offender must demonstrate one or more of the following conditions:

- a pattern of aggressive behaviour that is unlikely to change
- indifference to the effects of his or her behaviour
- brutality that is abnormal
- sexual impulses that will likely cause injury or pain to others

Marlene Moore was the first woman to be declared a dangerous offender in Canada. Some experts believe that she should never have been labelled a dangerous offender. She never killed anyone. In fact, she was prone to slashing herself and eventually committed suicide at the Kingston Penitentiary for Women.

A hearing is called to decide whether someone is a dangerous offender. Before this, the individual is given a psychiatric assessment. However, prospects for treatment or a cure are irrelevant. The offender is not sentenced on the original offence. He or she receives an **indeterminate sentence**. This means that the offender stays in an institution until authorities are satisfied that he or she is able to return to society and display normal behaviour. The National Parole Board reviews the situation of dangerous offenders regularly. Traditionally, Crown attorneys have used the "dangerous offender" provision for violent crimes (murder, sexual assault, and pedophilia). Recently, they have tried to use this designation for persons charged with reoccurring impaired driving offences.

A long-term offender is someone who behaves in ways that could harm others and is likely to offend again. The category of long-term offender was added to the *Criminal Code* in 1997. It was designed to protect society from sexual offenders. Sometimes the Crown applies for the long-term offender designation if it cannot prove the offender is dangerous. A long-term offender is sentenced for the original offence. That individual then receives an additional sentence of up to 10 years of community supervision.

indeterminate sentence a prison sentence without a fixed end date

Long-Term Offenders in Canada, 2005

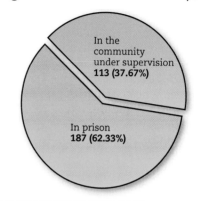

In the community under supervision 113 (37.67%)

In prison 187 (62.33%)

In 2005, there were 300 active long-term offenders in Canada. The majority of these were sexual offenders. Others had been convicted of assault, arson, and even impaired driving causing bodily harm.

People in Red Deer, Alberta, protest the release of convicted sex offender Lorne Donald Mackenzie. Mackenzie was paroled in 2002. His current whereabouts are unknown.

Deacon v. Canada (Attorney General), 2006 FCA 265 (CanLII)

For more information, Go to Nelson Social Studies

Shaun Deacon had a long history of offences against children. He was diagnosed as a homosexual pedophile and named a long-term offender in 1998. In 2001, he was released under a long-term supervision order. When he breached the conditions of the order, he was sentenced to two more years in prison.

In 2004, Deacon was to be released, with conditions. One such condition was that he take medication to control his sexual impulses. Deacon challenged the National Parole Board decision to implement this restriction. He argued that he had a right to refuse to take the medication under section 7 of the Charter, which protects his right to life, liberty, and security of person.

The Federal Court of Appeal ruled that Deacon did have the right not to take the medication. However, the consequences would be that he would be breaking his long-term supervision order and therefore was likely to go back to prison. The court concluded that the medical treatment in this case followed principles of fundamental justice and therefore did not violate section 7 of the Charter.

• Do you agree with this decision? Why or why not?

Capital Punishment in Canada

The law was amended to distinguish between capital and non-capital murder. Capital murders required the death penalty. These were murders that were: 1) planned and deliberate; 2) committed during a violent crime; 3) committed under contract; 4) of a police officer or prison guard while on duty.

After 1962, all death sentences were commuted. In 1967, capital punishment was suspended for five years, except for convicted murderers of police officers and prison guards.

1962

1967

Capital Punishment

There has been much debate in Canada over **capital punishment** (the death penalty). Before 1962, murderers and other criminals in Canada were sentenced to death by hanging. The sentence could be commuted (changed to a lesser penalty) by the federal Cabinet. As the timeline below illustrates, the topic has come up often in Parliament since the 1960s. In 2001, the Supreme Court of Canada confirmed Canada's rejection of the death penalty. The case was *United States v. Burns*, 2001. It also condemned the use of capital punishment worldwide.

capital punishment
the death penalty

 Did You Know?

Between 1867 and 1962, 710 people were put to death in Canada. December 11, 1962, was the date of the last execution, which took place in Toronto.

Review Your Understanding

1. When must a judge consider ordering restitution to a victim?
2. Why are community service orders used?
3. In what situations can a fine be imposed instead of imprisonment?
4. Distinguish among the following types of sentences: consecutive, concurrent, intermittent, and indeterminate.
5. What is the difference between a dangerous offender and a long-term offender?

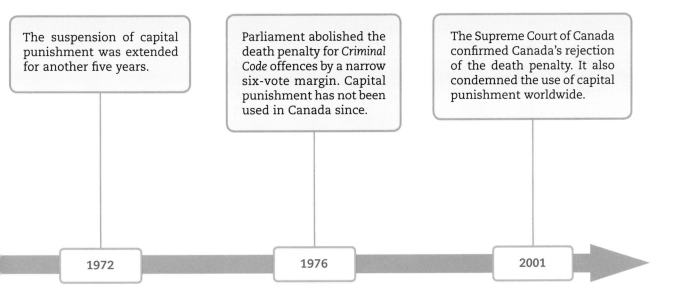

The suspension of capital punishment was extended for another five years. — **1972**

Parliament abolished the death penalty for *Criminal Code* offences by a narrow six-vote margin. Capital punishment has not been used in Canada since. — **1976**

The Supreme Court of Canada confirmed Canada's rejection of the death penalty. It also condemned the use of capital punishment worldwide. — **2001**

The last execution in Canada was in 1962. Canada abolished the death penalty in 1976. In the case of *United States v. Burns*, 2001, the Supreme Court of Canada condemned the death penalty.

Did You Know?

The goal of restorative justice programs is to let victims and offenders meet. The situation must be non-threatening. The federal government changed the *Criminal Code* in 1996 to support restorative justice programs.

9.4 Restorative Justice and Victims of Crime

Restorative justice focuses on healing relationships. Rather than focusing on punishing the offender, it tries to deal with those who have suffered because of the crime, including the offender, the victim, and the community. Until quite recently, criminal law did not consider the suffering of victims of crime. The victim usually did not meet the offender after the criminal incident other than perhaps testifying at the trial. However, under restorative justice, the offender and the victim play major roles in resolving the conflict. Through mediation and discussion, program participants seek ways to fix the damage caused by a crime. For more information on restorative justice, see the Issue features on pages 106–107 and 322–323.

Sentencing, Healing, and Releasing Circles

In Chapter 3, you learned that many Aboriginal communities have unique ways to resolve disputes. Some **sentencing circles** bring together the offender, the victim, and others. Together, they recommend a punishment for the offender. The victim and the community are able to express their views concerning the offence. They may even take part in developing the offender's sentence.

Healing circles are held to resolve the conflict between the offender and the victim. They allow both parties to voice their feelings and to indicate that they have undergone a personal healing.

Releasing circles are held in Aboriginal communities at the end of a sentence. Members of the National Parole Board, the community, and the offender meet. The purpose is to prepare a plan for the successful return of the offender to the community.

restorative justice an approach to crime that emphasizes forgiveness and community involvement

sentencing circle a way of bringing together affected people to help decide an offender's punishment

healing circle a process to resolve conflicts between an offender and the victim

releasing circle a meeting to plan for the successful return of the offender to the community

In this healing circle, Aboriginal people pay tribute to missing First Nations women. This tribute took place outside the Supreme Court in New Westminster, British Columbia, during Robert Pickton's mass murder trial in 2007.

Victims of Crime

The Crown prosecutes a criminal on behalf of society, not on behalf of the victim. The Crown decides on the charge to be laid, introduces the evidence, and asks for a penalty. Although victims assist by giving evidence, their role is usually limited, and they often feel left out of the process. New research has shown that when victims participate in the criminal process, they may recover from the event more quickly. As a result, changes have been introduced to give the victim a larger role.

The federal and provincial governments were concerned about victims of crime. That is why they endorsed the *Canadian Statement of Basic Principles of Justice for Victims of Crime* in 2003. The basic principles provide the following:

- Victims of crime should be treated with compassion and respect.

- The safety and security of victims should be considered at all stages.

- The privacy of victims should be respected.

- Victims are educated about what happens in the criminal justice process.

- Victims are provided with information about support programs available for victims of crime.

In March 2007, the federal government created the Federal Ombudsman for Victims of Crime. An **ombudsman** is an official appointed to hear citizen complaints. This official is impartial and independent of government. The Federal Ombudsman for Victims of Crime provides funding for victim support services. Those services are available across the country. That individual also focuses on specific problems. These include the sexual exploitation of children on the Internet.

Most provinces provide some victim support services. Some services are offence specific, such as sexual assault crisis centres. Others provide assistance to all victims of crime, such as 24-hour crisis and support lines. In some jurisdictions, victim/witness assistance programs provide information about the prosecution process and emotional support during the trial and sentencing. Crown attorneys keep the victims informed of the charges, plea, and sentencing.

Support staff may also assist with the preparation of a victim impact statement. This is a statement about the harm done to the victim and his or her family members. It is usually presented to the judge before sentencing. The statement cannot include any other commentary, such as a suggested sentence. The victim may be allowed to read the statement in court, and may also be called as a witness at a sentencing hearing.

ombudsman a government official appointed to hear and investigate complaints made against the government

Established in 1990, the Victims Services Program of Toronto provides immediate crisis response and support services to victims. Staff include (left to right) Bonnie Levine, Bobbie McMurrich, and Carolyn Moyer.

The *Criminal Code* lets the Crown request restitution for the victim. As we saw earlier, restitution is the act of restoring or repaying the victim in some way. The judge can also consider restitution without the formal application from the Crown. Restitution can be given for the following:

- damage
- loss or destruction of property
- bodily harm
- loss of income
- cost of support and psychological services

Restitution can even be ordered for "indirect" victims. If a stolen car is bought by someone in good faith, and the car is later seized as part of a criminal proceeding, restitution can be ordered to cover the purchaser's losses. Parliament takes restitution seriously. It has given judges the power to insist that the restitution order be paid before any fine that is imposed.

The *Corrections and Conditional Release Act* gives the victim the right to know the offence for which the offender was convicted. Victims are also informed about the length of the sentence and the penitentiary where the sentence is being served. The act also permits victims to attend parole sessions. There, they can provide a statement to help officials assess whether the release of offenders might pose a risk to society. Victims are told the date of the offenders' release, their destination, and any conditions attached to the release.

Other people may be able to show the parole board that they were harmed "as a result of an act of the offender." These include members of a victim's family. Such people may also receive information about the prisoner's release. In some provinces, a victim can register to be told about the movement of the offender within the prison system and if the inmate leaves or escapes. The former is an absence with permission, and the latter is without permission. Victims may also contact the probation officer dealing with community supervision.

? Did You Know?

Between July 2001 and February 2007, 700 victims made statements. This represented 474 parole hearings. Three-quarters of the victims addressed the hearing in person, and the rest were recordings.

At a parole board hearing, the victim sits at the back of the room, away from the actual parole hearing.

MADD Canada

MADD Canada (Mothers Against Drunk Driving) is one of Canada's first victims' rights groups. It helps the victims of drunk drivers and their families. In 1980, Candice Lightner founded MADD in California. Founded in 1990, MADD Canada is the Canadian arm. In 2007, MADD Canada had 85 chapters with approximately 7500 volunteers across the country. MADD Canada works to reform laws against impaired driving and underage drinking. It also promotes safe, sober transportation. MADD Canada makes presentations at schools. In fact, 500 000 high school students and 150 000 elementary students see MADD Canada's presentations each year.

Drunk driving is a serious problem in Canada. Each day, impaired drivers kill nearly four Canadians and injure 187. Approximately 70 000 Canadians are impacted by impaired drivers each year.

In 1999, the federal government passed tougher drinking and driving laws. MADD Canada's lobbying efforts played a large role in these reforms. The government increased the minimum fine for impaired driving from $300 to $600. It also increased the penalty for someone convicted of impaired driving on a suspended licence from two to five years in prison. In 2000, the federal government passed legislation increasing the penalty to life imprisonment for people convicted of impaired driving causing death. Judges can now require convicted drunk drivers to enter treatment programs as part of their sentence. Victims of drunk drivers can read their impact statements in court.

MADD Canada continues to pressure the government for tougher impaired driving laws. MADD Canada supported the federal government's *Violent Crime Reduction Bill* in 2008. The organization believes that police should be able to lay charges at fatal crash scenes. Further, that same year, MADD Canada supported the Ontario government's decision to pass a new civil law. The law allows courts to confiscate (take away) vehicles from repeated drunk drivers. If the owner of a vehicle has had his or her licence suspended for impaired driving more than twice in the preceding 10 years, the vehicle can be taken and sold.

MADD Canada wants the government to lower the legal blood-alcohol concentration from 80 to 50. Some other countries have done this already. It is estimated that there are over 90 000 impaired driving convictions in Canada per year. However, MADD Canada recognizes that there is still a long way to go to put an end to impaired driving in Canada.

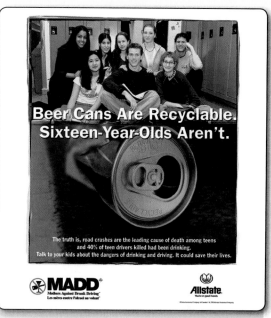

Beer Cans Are Recyclable. Sixteen-Year-Olds Aren't.

The truth is, road crashes are the leading cause of death among teens and 40% of teen drivers killed had been drinking. Talk to your kids about the dangers of drinking and driving. It could save their lives.

MADD Mothers Against Drunk Driving Les mères contre l'alcool au volant

Allstate.

How does an organization like MADD Canada influence the law in Canada?

For Discussion

1. How has MADD Canada addressed the issue of impaired driving in Canada? How has the federal government responded?

2. What rights should a victim have in court?

3. What do you think can be done to reduce impaired driving in Canada?

e Activity

To learn more about MADD Canada,

Go to Nelson Social Studies

Criminal Injuries Compensation Fund

All provinces have some form of victim compensation scheme. This is public money to compensate anyone who is injured in some way when a crime is committed. Victims sometimes turn to the fund because the criminal has no money or has not yet been caught.

The award is intended to cover specific situations, such as the following:

- lost pay
- pain and suffering from injuries
- medical bills and prescriptions
- loss of income by dependants if the victim dies (for example, funeral expenses)
- child support for the offspring of sexual assault

In fact, the fund can cover anything that the board feels is reasonable. Each situation must be verified. However, the victim must return the money if he or she successfully sues the offender for compensation.

Allowing victims to meet offenders in a non-threatening setting is the goal of restorative justice programs. The Centre for Restorative Justice is located in the School of Criminology at Simon Fraser University. It provides a number of programs and services to support and promote restorative justice. The Centre is funded by the Correctional Service of Canada.

Review Your Understanding

1. What are the purposes of sentencing circles, healing circles, and releasing circles? Why do you think these circles are successful in Aboriginal communities?
2. What programs are available to victims at the time of the offence?
3. What programs are available to victims during the trial and sentencing?
4. What programs are available to victims after the offender has been convicted?
5. Outline the right of a victim to receive restitution.

9.5 Appeals

The right to request an appeal of a court decision is an important part of criminal procedure in Canada. Both the accused and the Crown have rights of appeal, as outlined below. The party that makes the appeal request is called the **appellant**, and the other party is called the **respondent**. If the appeal is requested for a reason that is not set out in law, the request will be dismissed. For example, neither side can appeal simply because they did not like the decision. A legal mistake must have been made. Appeal courts were discussed in detail in Chapter 4.

Generally, a period of 30 days is allowed to apply for an appeal. During the appeal time, the accused may apply to be released. If the court agrees to a release, conditions may be imposed.

For appeals of summary conviction offences, the court examines the trial transcript. It may consider a statement of facts in which both

appellant the party who requests an appeal (review) in a higher court

respondent in an appeal, the party who opposes the action sought by the appellant

parties write down the facts as they see them and then agree about what actually occurred. It saves time arguing about things that were already agreed upon by the defence and the Crown. For appeals of indictable offences held in the higher courts, the appellant and the respondent present their arguments. New or "fresh" evidence is admitted only if it would have affected the results of the trial, such as evidence showing that another person did the crime.

Both the Crown and the defence can appeal a conviction, a verdict, a sentence, or rulings on fitness to stand trial for a summary conviction offence if any mistakes were made. The appeal can be based on a mistake about the law or the facts (a question of law or fact). An appeal on the basis of law may question a judge's interpretation of the law; an appeal on the basis of fact is usually based on whether evidence was relevant or credible.

Grounds for Appeal for Indictable Offences	
By the Defence (appeal of a conviction)	By the Crown (appeal of a decision of not guilty)
• a question of law • a question of fact (if the court gives permission) • any other reason that the appeal court believes is worthy	• a question of law • the sentence (if the court gives permission) • a trial judge orders an indictment invalid, or stays the proceedings

An appeal court will consider reasons put forth by the Crown and the defence when deciding whether to grant an appeal.

When a case goes to appeal, the necessary information is collected. This includes a transcript of the evidence taken at trial, charges to the jury, reasons for the trial judge's decision, and possibly a report from the trial judge. The appeal court, which usually has three judges, votes on the final decision. The reason for the majority decision is disclosed, and any dissenting judges may state why they disagree. The court can also rule on which party will pay for the costs of the appeal.

The defence may be successful if the evidence does not support the guilty verdict, if there was an error of law, or if there has been a miscarriage of justice (for example, evidence indicating another person did the crime). The accused is then released. The appeal court may also change the verdict of the original court, change the sentence, or order a new trial. Based on the rule of precedent, the lower courts must follow the decisions of a higher court. For example, if a higher court decided that there was an error in law by the lower court and a new trial was necessary, there would be a new trial.

All About Law DVD
"Isabel Lebourdais" from *All About Law DVD*

Review Your Understanding

1. When can the accused appeal a summary conviction offence decision?
2. What is the difference between a question of law and a question of fact?
3. On what basis can the Crown appeal an indictable offence decision?
4. On what information does the appeal court base its decision?
5. Identify the options the appeal court has in making its decision.

9.6 Canada's Prison System

Canadians differ widely in their opinion of how prisons should operate. They also disagree on how offenders should be treated. Some people believe that offenders should remain in prison for as long as possible—the maximum time allowed by law. Others believe that since offenders are partially shaped by society, the prison system should work to rehabilitate them.

Entering the Prison System

An offender who goes to prison comes under the jurisdiction of provincial or federal **correctional services**. Offenders sentenced to terms of less than two years serve time in provincial jails. Those with longer sentences serve them in federal penitentiaries, which are operated by the Correctional Service of Canada. Each province has its own correctional services regulations. It is responsible for offenders in provincial prisons.

Correctional services are responsible for the following:

- incarcerating all offenders
- processing parole applications
- running probation services

Inmates in provincial institutions serve time in one of three types of facility. The first is a **closed custody** facility. These are reserved for offenders who are dangerous, likely to escape, or are hard to manage. The second is an **open custody** facility. These institutions provide an opportunity for inmates to work. The third type are community correctional centres. These centres offer less security than minimum-security prisons. Inmates in these facilities are allowed to work or go to school every day and return to the correctional facility at night. Many of the residents are inmates on day parole.

There are three levels of security at federal prisons:

1. maximum security (for the most dangerous offenders)
2. medium security
3. minimum security

correctional services government agencies responsible for offenders

closed custody the most secure form of detention in a prison, which is under constant guard

open custody detention that is supervised and allows some supervised access to the community

There are usually no fences or walls surrounding minimum-security facilities, such as this one in Sainte-Anne-des-Plaines, Québec (left). Inmates are generally non-violent and pose limited risk to society. Maximum-security facilities, such as the Kingston Penitentiary in Kingston, Ontario (right), are surrounded by high (6 metre) walls and fences with guard towers. The movement of inmates in maximum-security facilities is rigidly controlled because inmates pose a serious risk to staff, other inmates, and society.

How are offenders assigned to institutions? After sentencing, they are assessed to determine their level of risk and their need for rehabilitation. Next, an institution is selected. This is based on the type of crime the offender committed. Then, officials have to assess the risk of escape. Beyond that, the availability of rehabilitation programs in particular institutions is evaluated. Finally, the location of the offender's family is considered. Authorities also try to place offenders where they will have contact with their own culture and language. Those convicted of first-degree and second-degree murder have to serve at least two years in a maximum-security prison. After that, they can apply to move to a lower-security facility.

In prison, an inmate is assigned to a case management team. This group helps the inmate with rehabilitation. It also encourages him or her to broaden social contacts to include good influences and positive role models. Institutions offer a broad range of programs, including life skills and literacy programs, and treatment programs for substance abuse, sex offences, and family violence. Inmates are also encouraged to enroll in educational programs. They are paid a daily allowance, which can be used at the prison store.

The *Corrections and Conditional Release Act* outlines the discipline procedures of inmates in prison. The act governs the day-to-day management of inmates, including their placement and transfer. It also involves their general living conditions. The act details the discipline, searches, and health care of inmates.

An inmate reads in her room at the women's prison in Joliette, Québec. This is a medium-security facility.

Review Your Understanding

1. List the responsibilities of correctional services.
2. What is the difference between open and closed custody?
3. What is a community correctional facility, and what level of security is provided?
4. Identify the factors considered when assigning an offender to a correctional institution.
5. What determines the location in which an offender spends a prison term?

parole the release of an inmate into the community before the full sentence is served

 Activity

To learn more about parole,

 Go to Nelson Social Studies

A variety of release programs are available to offenders, but they will not always be granted.

9.7 Conditional Release

Conditional release is often referred to as house arrest. It allows the offender to get out of prison and to serve the remainder of the sentence in the community while under supervision. The *Corrections and Conditional Release Act* outlines the rules governing conditional release. The goal of conditional release is to allow offenders to return to society under supervision. This helps to prepare them for the time when they will be released unsupervised. The National Parole Board is appointed by the federal government and has jurisdiction over **parole** for most of Canada. The exceptions are the provincial prisons in Québec, Ontario, and British Columbia. These provinces have their own parole boards. Public safety is the main consideration for determining whether an inmate should be released.

Release Programs for Federal Prison Inmates		
Type of Release	When Granted	Duration
Escorted absences	Any time	5–15 days
Unescorted absences	After one-sixth of sentence is served, or six years, whichever is greater	2 days if in medium security 3 days if in minimum security
Day parole	Before full parole	Daily; return to halfway house
Full parole	After one-third of sentence is served, or seven years, whichever is less	Until completion of sentence if conditions are followed
Statutory release	After two-thirds of sentence is served	Until completion of sentence if conditions are followed

Temporary Absence

Officials may grant inmates absences. These may be either escorted or unescorted absences, depending on the inmate and the reason for the absence. Authorities may grant absences for a variety of reasons, such as the following:

- to participate in rehabilitation programs
- to obtain medical treatment
- to attend significant family events

All offenders are eligible for absences based on medical or humanitarian grounds. For other types of absences, offenders classified as maximum security are not eligible.

During escorted absences, prison staff accompany offenders. Sometimes citizen volunteers do this. From the time offenders enter prison, they are eligible for escorted absences. Those eligible for an unescorted absence also qualify for work release. As the name implies, that program allows inmates to be temporarily released in order to work outside the prison. The National Parole Board must grant permission for certain unescorted absences. These include anyone whose crime involved violence, children, or drugs. Maximum-security offenders are not eligible for unescorted absences.

 Did You Know?

To parole an offender means to release him or her after a portion of the sentence has been served. **Day parole** means releasing the offender during the day, but he or she must return to the institution each night. Day parole allows offenders to go to work or school to prepare for full parole or **statutory release**. An inmate serving a life sentence is eligible for day parole three years before full parole eligibility.

Full parole happens when an offender has served a minimum amount of his or her sentence. This is usually one-third of the sentence or seven years, whichever is less. The date for a review for full parole is automatically set at the beginning of an offender's incarceration. Any judge imposing a penalty of two or more years has the right to increase the minimum time that must be served before parole eligibility. It can be increased up to one-half of the sentence or 10 years, whichever is less. For example, a judge could increase a 20-year sentence by 10 years or a 10-year sentence by 5 years.

During the parole review, a great deal of information is compiled:

- What efforts at reform has the offender made in prison?
- What are the results of a personality assessment?
- Has the offender received and benefited from treatment?
- Does the offender understand the nature and seriousness of the offence?
- Does the offender have a place to live following release?
- Does the offender have any job prospects?

After this information is compiled, a parole hearing is set. The offender and observers may attend the hearing with the board's permission. The board reviews the information before it, which may include submissions from victims who have been harmed by the offender.

The parole board can grant parole, deny parole, or reserve its decision. If parole is denied, the board generally must review the case every two years. If parole is granted, a date is set, and a parole supervisor is assigned. Parole is a conditional system. The parolee is the person who has been granted parole. If that person violates any conditions set by the board, he or she may be brought back to serve the rest of the sentence. If the conditions are respected, parole ends when the original sentence would have ended.

day parole the temporary release from custody of an offender under specific conditions

statutory release an inmate's release from an institution as required by law

full parole an offender's complete release from custody into the community under specific conditions and supervision

Brenda Martin (left) is a Canadian woman who spent more than two years in a Mexican jail accused of fraud. She was transferred to a Canadian prison and paroled in May 2008.

Parole Statistics, 2003–2006

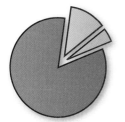

Day Parole

7500 (84%) Completed successfully
1100 (12%) Breach of conditions
400 (4%) New offences

Full Parole

3250 (73%) Completed successfully
800 (18%) Breach of conditions
400 (9%) New offences

While most parolees complete their parole successfully, some parolees do break their parole conditions or commit new crimes.

Parole for Murder

Offenders who have committed murder are subject to different parole rules and conditions. The *Criminal Code* states that first-degree murderers sentenced to life in prison are not eligible for full parole for 25 years. Thus, a life sentence does not mean that the offender will spend life in prison. In fact, most who receive a life sentence are released. However, they do remain on parole and under supervision for the rest of their lives. Those convicted of second-degree murder have their parole eligibility established by the judge at the time of sentencing. This is usually between 10 and 25 years. In a trial by jury, the jury can recommend an appropriate time length for parole eligibility. The judge is not bound by the jury's recommendation. Other considerations when considering an offender's eligibility for parole include the character of the offender, the nature of the offence, and the circumstances in which the offence was committed.

Both groups may be eligible for unescorted temporary absences and day parole three years before their full parole eligibility date. As well, those sentenced to more than 15 years before being eligible for full parole may apply for a judicial review after 15 years. This is referred to as the **faint hope clause**. For example, someone who would not be eligible for parole for 20 years could apply for parole review after 15 years. This clause was introduced to recognize that an inmate may be rehabilitated. Offenders convicted of more than one murder, however, are not eligible for judicial review.

When such an appeal is made, a judge must consider several things:

- the character of the applicant
- the offender's conduct in prison
- the nature of the offence
- victim impact statements and other relevant information

If the judge approves the review, a superior court judge holds a hearing with a jury. The jury must unanimously decide that the parole eligibility period should be reduced. Also, a majority of jury members must decide by how many years.

Accelerated Review

Some offenders are eligible for an **accelerated review**. These include those who are serving their first term in a penitentiary. They qualify if their offence did not involve violence, sex, drugs, or organized crime. These hearings determine the offender's eligibility for early parole. They must be released on full parole unless the parole board can find reasonable grounds to believe the offender is likely to reoffend.

Statutory Release

By law, prisoners are entitled to statutory release. That means that they are able to spend the final one-third of their sentence in the community under supervision. There are some exceptions, however. These include those serving life or indeterminate sentences. Although statutory release is usually automatic, the parole board can add conditions to the release. It can also deny parole to certain offenders.

In February 2008, the National Parole Board granted Robert Latimer day parole. He served seven years in prison. He was convicted in October 1993 of second-degree murder in the death of his 12-year-old daughter, Tracy, who was severely disabled. (For a complete discussion of the *Latimer* case, see Chapter 7.)

faint hope clause reconsideration of parole eligibility for an offender sentenced to at least 15 years in prison

accelerated review a parole board review of an offender's eligibility after one-third of the sentence is served

Royal Prerogative of Mercy

The federal government has the power to grant a **Royal Prerogative of Mercy**. This dates from the days before democracy when the sovereign had the power of life and death over all. Applications are made to the National Parole Board. The board then investigates and makes recommendations to the solicitor general. Under a Royal Prerogative of Mercy, an inmate may have a fine or prison sentence rescinded (revoked). Alternatively, he or she may be issued a **pardon**. One of the most celebrated cases of a pardon in Canada involved Mi'kmaq Donald Marshall Jr. He spent 11 years in prison for a crime he did not commit. A royal commission cleared Marshall of any responsibility.

Royal Prerogative of Mercy the right to revoke a fine or prison sentence or issue a pardon

pardon being excused of a crime

bonding insurance that guarantees the honesty of a person who handles money or other valuables

Criminal Records

For some people, the penalty for having a criminal record may only be embarrassment. For others, it may seriously restrict their job opportunities and ability to travel to foreign countries. For instance, many jobs require **bonding**. Bonding is insurance that guarantees the honesty of a person who handles money or other valuables. A person with a criminal record usually cannot be bonded. Also, some countries, such as the United States, refuse to admit persons with a criminal record. For those with landed immigrant status in Canada, a criminal record could result in deportation.

As of July 24, 1992, the RCMP will remove from its computer system the record of anyone discharged following the court decision. For records prior to that time, the person must apply to the RCMP. Those with convictions can apply to the National Parole Board for a pardon. If successful, the offender's criminal record is kept separate from others. The offender must be free of other convictions during the waiting period. That is generally three to five years after completing the sentence. Provincial human rights legislation prohibits employment discrimination against anyone with a criminal record. The *Canadian Human Rights Act* forbids discrimination based on a pardoned conviction.

Security guards are bonded if they are required to work with cash or other valuables.

Review Your Understanding

1. Who has jurisdiction over conditional release? What factors are considered in a release review?
2. What is the difference between escorted and unescorted absences?
3. What is the purpose of the faint hope clause?
4. Explain the circumstances under which statutory release is allowed.
5. Who is eligible to have a criminal record erased?

Are Restorative Justice Programs Good for Victims?

Restorative justice emphasizes healing for the victim of crime. It also tries to establish accountability for the offender. This system provides a new way to resolve conflict. It emphasizes forgiveness and also involves the community.

Victims' rights have received much more attention in recent years than previously. Canadian governments at various levels have passed laws to protect the rights of victims. They have also tried to involve victims in what happens to those who caused them damage. In 2008, the federal government even created the first Federal Ombudsman for Victims of Crime. This was to give victims a larger role in the criminal justice system.

On One Side

Some Canadians believe that victims should play a major role in restorative justice programs. Corrections Canada has used such programs since the mid-1990s. These bring together victims, offenders, and community members after a crime has been committed. Through mediation and discussion, program participants seek ways to fix the damage caused by a crime.

Restoration programs emphasize healing, forgiveness, and community involvement. They reach out to victims, their families, and offenders. In an effort to prevent future crime, they try to discover why offenders committed the crimes. The process helps victims describe how the crime affected them and their family members. It also permits offenders to explain the reasons for their actions, express their remorse, and compensate the victims. Some victims feel that the process is very positive. It allows them to understand the incident and the offender better. The process also makes it easier for the victim to forgive the offender and feel safe again in the community.

The federal government changed the *Criminal Code* in 1996 to support these programs. It stated that there are other ways of dealing with criminals than simply throwing them in jail. All these alternatives should be considered. Aboriginal offenders should be included in restorative justice programs where possible. Both Aboriginal and non-Aboriginal offenders may participate. These programs seem to be meeting the needs of victims and the community.

On the Other Side

Many victims are afraid to meet their offenders and feel threatened when they do. Some victims say that the crimes committed against them are so terrible that they could never meet the offenders or work with them to find solutions.

Victims' rights groups say that restorative justice programs pay too much attention to offenders. They believe that victims are pressured to get involved with such programs. Instead, they would like to see governments take some of the money spent on restorative justice programs to increase compensation for victims of crime.

However, some of these critics applaud other changes made by the government. For example, amendments made to the *Criminal Code* in 1999 allow victims to read a victim impact statement in court. Judges can also order offenders to pay damages to victims. If an offender does not pay, the victim has the right to go to civil court and seize the assets and wages of the offender.

The goal of restorative justice programs is to let victims meet offenders in a non-threatening setting. Still, many victims decline to participate.

The Bottom Line

Restorative justice programs are useful to victims and offenders. They also benefit governments. These programs are designed to keep offenders out of prison. That reduces the number of cases before the courts, which saves the system money. Although many victims support these programs, they also want laws that punish offenders and prevent crime. Supporters of restorative justice programs think that people who commit less serious offences can benefit from these programs. They say that such offenders will only be hardened in prison. An emphasis on support and treatment programs can help these people rejoin society instead of turning to a life of crime.

What Do You Think?

1. Explain the term "restorative." What are the purposes of restorative justice programs?
2. What role do victims of crime play in these programs? How can they benefit?
3. What criticisms have been made of these programs?
4. How do restorative justice programs seem to be in conflict with victims' groups?
5. Outline your opinions of restorative justice programs and victims' groups. Discuss with a classmate.

Chapter Review

Chapter Highlights

- The defence and the Crown can both make submissions on sentencing.
- A judge uses a variety of information to establish an appropriate sentence.
- The *Criminal Code* outlines the objectives of sentencing.
- The *Criminal Code* directs judges to either increase or reduce a sentence if there are any relevant aggravating or mitigating circumstances.
- Sentences are to be proportional: they are to reflect the degree of harm caused.
- The principle of totality states that an offender should not be sentenced to an overly long prison term.
- Sentences for multiple offences may be served consecutively or concurrently.
- Violent offenders may be classified as dangerous offenders or long-term offenders.
- Restorative justice focuses on healing relationships.
- Sentencing circles are used as a means of healing the offender, the victim, and the community.
- Victims of crime have rights at the time of arrest, trial, sentencing, and parole.
- The rules for appealing judgments and sentences are very specific.
- There are many types of release available to inmates: day parole, escorted absences, unescorted absences, work release, full parole, statutory release, and a Royal Prerogative of Mercy.
- The time for parole eligibility for murderers is specified at the time of sentencing.
- Free pardons and ordinary pardons can be granted by the federal government.
- An offender can apply to have his or her criminal record removed from the police computer system.

Check Your Knowledge

1. Summarize the objectives of sentencing under the *Criminal Code*.
2. Outline the sentencing options available, and provide an example of each.
3. Explain the role of victims at the time of sentencing and during the parole application process.
4. Explain the various forms of conditional release, and provide an example of each.

Apply Your Learning

5. For each of the following situations, indicate whether or not you would impose a conditional sentence, and, if so, what additional requirements you would add on as part of the conditional sentence order. Give the reasons for your decision.

   a) In *R. v. Habib*, 2000, a babysitter was convicted of aggravated assault to an 18-month-old child. The child had a brain injury, a skull fracture, and serious injuries to her eyes, caused by shaken-baby syndrome. The babysitter had acted responsibly when it first appeared that the child required medical assistance. The babysitter was a first-time offender with exemplary reports about her child care. The child recovered well from her injuries.

   b) In *R. v. Dharamdeo*, 2000, a young man was convicted of impaired driving after his car split a lamppost in two and demolished a bus shelter. Later, he was found guilty of impaired driving causing bodily harm for another incident after his car became airborne and struck two other vehicles. One person was injured. In the first incident, he was in violation of his learner's permit, which required that he drive with a licensed driver.

6. For each of the following cases, decide upon a sentence for the offender. Outline the rationale for your decision, including

which sentencing objective is most important. (The maximum sentence allowed for the offence is shown in parentheses at the end of each case.)

a) Welch was 18 years old when he and several others robbed a grocery store of $3200. Weapons and disguises were used. He robbed a small country store 30 days later, and the victim was treated roughly. Welch was apprehended. While out on bail, he and others robbed two Calgary gas stations at gunpoint, departing from the crime scenes in Welch's car. Trial evidence indicated that Welch came from a stable, supportive family, and he had done well in school and in community activities. He had hung around with friends who had a bad influence on him, and he had been somewhat out of control for four years. (life imprisonment)

b) Travis, an M.B.A. student, was charged with the theft of pens, markers, and other items from the University of Western Ontario bookstore. The merchandise was worth just over $17. At the time of the offence, Travis had already purchased $125 worth of goods and had $36 in his wallet. He had been under emotional stress because of problems with his family and with his university studies. Before his trial, Travis apologized to the bookstore management. He also offered to work in the store on a voluntary basis as a penalty for his offence and as a form of compensation. (2 years)

Communicate Your Understanding

7. In recent years, victims have been given more access to the criminal justice system. They are provided with aid at the time of the incident. During the trial, they are kept informed. At sentencing, they are given the opportunity to provide input. They are kept informed of the inmates' imprisonment.

As well, they are allowed to provide input at the time of a parole application. Summarize these rights by drafting your own victims' bill of rights. Outline rights that would provide recognition and support for victims at all stages of the criminal justice process.

8. In your opinion, should the correctional system be allowed to use electronic monitoring to track the location of offenders who are on parole? Explain.

Develop Your Thinking

9. A new federal crime law, the *Tackling Violent Crime Act*, was passed in February 2008 that announced tougher penalties for crimes, including more mandatory minimum sentences. Do you think that mandatory minimum sentences should be included for all *Criminal Code* offences? Why or why not?

10. Some people believe that too many inmates are given some form of conditional release. They also feel that there are too many offences committed by those on release. Is conditional release a valuable use of resources in preparing offenders to return to society? Use the data on release given in this chapter as well as other information to develop and support your opinion on this issue.

11. California has a three-strikes law by which a person convicted of three offences receives life imprisonment. Steven White, a two-time offender, stole a $146 videocassette. Rather than face life imprisonment, he committed suicide. Another person faced life in prison for having stolen four cookies. Do you think that Canada, like California, should institute more severe penalties for repeat offenders? Explain. Support your opinion by researching rates of recidivism in Canada.

10

The Youth Criminal Justice System

What You Should Know

- How do the *Juvenile Delinquents Act*, the *Young Offenders Act*, and the *Youth Criminal Justice Act* differ? How are they similar?
- How are young people treated differently from adults when they break the law?
- What options are available to the police in dealing with young non-violent, first-time offenders?
- What are a youth criminal's legal rights?
- What options are available to judges in sentencing youth criminals?
- When is custody an appropriate sentence for a youth criminal?

Chapter at a Glance

10.1 Introduction
10.2 The *Youth Criminal Justice Act*
10.3 Legal Rights of Youths
10.4 Trial Procedures
10.5 Youth Sentencing Options

Selected Key Terms

alternative measures program

extrajudicial measure

foster home

group home

juvenile delinquent

presumptive offence

young offender

Young Offenders Act (YOA)

youth criminal

Youth Criminal Justice Act (YCJA)

Police report that rate of youths charged with criminal offences declines 26%

Teen gets 10 years for killing family

Fewer youth in court and in custody

STATISTICS CANADA REPORT:

YOUTH HOMICIDES UP 3 PERCENT IN 2006

Grade 11 teen stabbed at school over a cellphone

Violent crimes committed by youth receive increased media attention, as reflected in these headlines.

10.1 Introduction

Youth crime is a hot topic in Canada, and just about everybody has an opinion on it. The headlines on page 326 present conflicting views on youth crime. Most suggest youth crime is on the rise, yet Statistics Canada recently released figures that provide a different picture. Although certain crimes have increased, the overall rate of youth crime in 2006 was 6 percent lower than a decade earlier. It was 25 percent lower than in 1991 (see the graph below).

 Activity

To learn more about youth crime statistics,

 Go to Nelson Social Studies

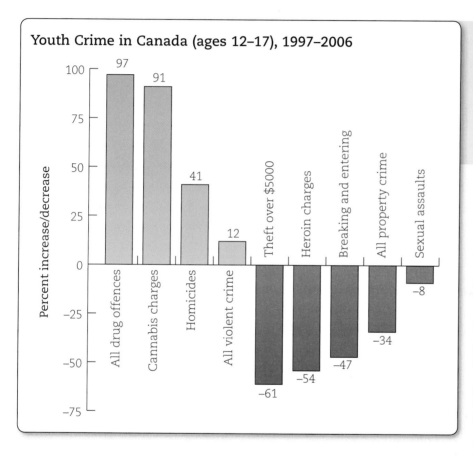

Youth Crime in Canada (ages 12–17), 1997–2006

Percent increase/decrease

- All drug offences — 97
- Cannabis charges — 91
- Homicides — 41
- All violent crime — 12
- Theft over $5000 — −61
- Heroin charges — −54
- Breaking and entering — −47
- All property crime — −34
- Sexual assaults — −8

Which youth crimes have increased since 1997? Which crime has decreased the most? Can you think of any reasons why certain crimes have increased and others have decreased?

young offender a person aged 12 to 17 years old inclusive who breaks the law, as defined under the *Young Offenders Act*

youth criminal a person who is 12 to 17 years old inclusive who is charged with an offence under the *Youth Criminal Justice Act*

juvenile delinquent the historic term for a young offender or youth criminal

Youth Criminal Justice Act (YCJA) current federal legislation that governs youth crime

What to do with **young offenders,** or **youth criminals** (historically known as **juvenile delinquents**), and how they should be dealt with by our criminal justice system is often debated by politicians. When Prime Minister Stephen Harper's Conservative government came into power in January 2006, it lobbied for harsher sentences for youths. This was an effort to cut down on violent crime and repeat offenders. The government argued that these measures would be a deterrent to youth criminals. In November 2007, the government introduced Bill C-25, with amendments to the *Youth Criminal Justice Act (YCJA)*. It provides for tougher sentences for violent crimes and allows courts to consider general deterrence as a youth sentencing objective. (Remember from Chapter 9, page 294, that the Supreme Court had decided in *R. v. B.W.P.; R. v. B.V.N.,* 2006, that general deterrence is *not* a basis for youth sentencing.)

 Did You Know?

According to Statistics Canada, the number of teenagers accused of homicide in 2006 reached the highest point ever. Youth homicide still accounts for just 0.05 percent of youth crime.

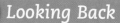
Youth Criminal Legislation: A Brief History

In 1910, teenagers and men had to "break stones for breakfast" in a house of industry. These institutions—also known as poorhouses—were feared by homeless and impoverished youths.

Until the 1890s, there was no clear distinction in Canadian criminal law between youths and adults. Children who broke the law were brought to trial in the same court adults were tried in. If convicted, they were punished as if they were adults. Early prisons were dark, filthy, and overcrowded. Those who committed small crimes, women, and children were placed with hardened criminals. Near the end of the nineteenth century, society realized that children differ from adults in many ways and should be treated differently.

In 1892, Canada changed the *Criminal Code* so that children were tried privately and separately from adults. In 1908, the federal government passed the *Juvenile Delinquents Act*. It was the first legislation to distinguish between child offenders and adult criminals. It also created a separate youth justice system. The age limit for a "juvenile" varied from 7 to 16 or 18 years of age, depending on the province. The act recognized that young people who broke the law were misguided and misdirected "juvenile delinquents," not criminals. They were seen as victims of poverty, abuse, and neglect. Their parents had failed to raise them well, so the state would take over training and controlling the delinquent.

The objective of the *Juvenile Delinquents Act* was to rehabilitate and reform, not to punish. Youths were not charged with specific offences but with "delinquency." The definition of delinquency was so broad that youths could be charged for breaking minor municipal bylaws. Charges could be made for truancy (skipping school), coming home late, or loitering. Youths could also be charged for being "sexually immoral." The meaning of this final charge was open to interpretation by trial judges.

Not surprisingly, the legal rights of juveniles were mostly ignored. Juveniles seldom had lawyers in court.

Youth Criminal Legislation: A Brief History

Because there were no formal guidelines, sentencing was left to the judge's discretion. Sentences ranged in severity from extremely lenient to incredibly harsh. A youth convicted of a minor offence could be sent to a training school for any length of time if the judge thought it was necessary to reform his or her delinquency. Staff decided when the delinquent was rehabilitated and could be released.

As the years passed, it was evident that the act was no longer appropriate. It did not emphasize growing concerns for public safety or the feeling that young people should be held responsible for their behaviour or that youths were not truly being helped or rehabilitated. The need for reform was obvious.

During the 1970s, Parliament made several attempts to write new legislation. *The Young Offenders Act (YOA)* was first introduced in 1970. Over the next 10 years, revisions were made to the *YOA* because of provincial and international criticisms. In July 1982, the governor general gave royal assent to the *YOA*. However, it did not come into effect until April 1, 1984. The delay allowed the provinces to adjust their programs and services.

The *YOA* attempted to make young offenders more accountable for their actions. It tried to protect society to a greater degree from their criminal activity. The minimum age of a young offender was raised from 7 to 12 years old. The maximum age was set at 17 in all provinces and territories. The act did recognize that young offenders should not be held to the same degree of accountability as adults. They should not suffer the same consequences as adults, since they are not fully mature and are still dependent on others. It also recognized the legal rights of youths as guaranteed in the *Charter of Rights and Freedoms*.

However, the *YOA* was criticized for the following:
- not properly addressing serious and violent offences
- an overuse of the court system
- being too soft on the offender
- lacking a clear philosophy on youth justice in Canada

Many Canadians thought the legislation was lacking. After several years of consultation, Parliament

The *Young Offenders Act* tried to balance the legal rights of youth with accountability.

passed the *Youth Criminal Justice Act (YCJA)*. It came into effect on April 1, 2003. It emphasizes the rehabilitation and re-entry of young offenders/youth criminals into society. The *YCJA* is the focus of the rest of this chapter.

For Discussion

1. What were some of the criticisms of the *Juvenile Delinquents Act*?

2. Why was sentencing young offenders to training schools so controversial?

3. What benefits did the *Young Offenders Act* provide over the *Juvenile Delinquents Act*?

4. What is the main emphasis of the *Youth Criminal Justice Act*?

A Century of Federal Legislation for Youth Justice

	Juvenile Delinquents Act	Young Offenders Act	Youth Criminal Justice Act
Dates	1908–1984	1984–2003	2003–
Philosophy	Juveniles are not criminals, but children who need guidance.	Youths are less responsible for crimes than adults.	Tougher sentences prevent crimes, but rehabilitation is important.
Ages covered	7–18, depending on province	12–17, inclusive	12–17, inclusive; youths 14 and older treated more like adults
Youths' rights	no right to a lawyer	must be advised of right to a lawyer	must be advised of right to a lawyer
Court/trial procedures	*Charter of Rights and Freedoms* did not exist until 1982, so it did not apply; hearings closed; transfers to adult court possible	*Charter* applies; hearings open; publication ban on names; transfer to adult court possible for offenders aged 14 and older	*Charter* applies; parents may have to attend; hearings open; no publication ban on names for adult sentences, serious violent offences, or youths considered dangerous
Sentencing	Fine up to $25; placed in foster home or in the care of the government	Many dispositions, including closed and open custody; usual terms 2–3 years, but up to 5 years for murder	Many sentences, including closed and open custody; up to 10 years for first-degree murder

Key similarities and differences in youth justice legislation in the past 100 years

 You Be the Judge

R. v. F.M., 2008 BCCA 111 (CanLII)

For more information, Go to Nelson Social Studies

Shingara Thandi was one of two Indo-Canadian seniors killed by F.M. and T.J.S.

In July 2005, 15-year-old F.M. and 13-year-old T.J.S. robbed and violently assaulted an 83-year-old man. Then they attacked Shingara Thandi with an old wooden baseball bat. They struck Thandi at least three times, resulting in fractures to the side of his head and to the back of his skull. The blows caused severe bleeding, and Thandi died two days later in hospital. The boys were charged with second-degree murder for Thandi's death.

In November 2006, the youths were convicted on the robbery and assault charges. However, they were acquitted on the murder charge. The trial judge convicted them of manslaughter because he was not satisfied beyond a reasonable doubt that the boys knew that the beating was likely to cause death. This is a necessary element of murder. F.M. was sentenced as an adult and received 49 months in prison after receiving a credit of 23 months for pre-sentence custody. T.J.S. was sentenced to 26 months after a credit of nine and a half months. The Crown appealed the acquittal of the second-degree murder charge to the British Columbia Court of Appeal in November 2007. In a unanimous judgment in March 2008, the appellate court dismissed the Crown's appeal.

- Why do you think the Crown's appeal was dismissed? Do you think the boys should have been found guilty of second-degree murder? Why or why not?

10.2 The Youth Criminal Justice Act

Between 1984 and 2003, the broad powers of the *Young Offenders Act (YOA)* led to demands that it be changed. Some critics said it was too "soft" on young offenders. Others said it abused the rights of young people. The *YOA* drastically changed the criminal justice system for young people, and much of it remains in the *Youth Criminal Justice Act*. Both acts reflect how Canadians' views of young people change constantly. The *YCJA* is the third major federal plan in 100 years designed to deal with young people who come into conflict with the law.

The *YCJA* is criminal law and deals with offences under the *Criminal Code*, the *Controlled Drugs and Substances Act*, and other federal laws. These other laws define the offences, while the *Youth Criminal Justice Act* outlines how youths are to be dealt with if charged. It does not apply to provincial laws, such as traffic violations or liquor laws. The *YCJA* states that youths have the same rights as adults under the *Charter of Rights and Freedoms*. It also gives young people additional rights and protections when arrested.

Young Offenders Act (YOA) young offenders law prior to the *Youth Criminal Justice Act*

 Did You Know?

It took seven years, three drafts, and more than 160 amendments for the *Youth Criminal Justice Act* to become law on April 1, 2003.

The Age of Criminal Responsibility

A youth who reaches his or her 18th birthday and commits a crime is considered an adult and faces adult trial procedures and penalties. The minimum age of criminal responsibility has changed over the years. Under the *Juvenile Delinquents Act*, the minimum age for criminally charging a youth was seven years old. The *Young Offenders Act* raised the minimum age to 12 years. It defined any offender between the ages of 12 and 17 as a young offender. This reflects the view that younger children cannot form criminal intent and should not be dealt with in the criminal justice system. Children younger than 12 who get into trouble cannot be charged. They are dealt with under provincial or territorial laws, such as child welfare legislation, or taken home to their parents for discipline. A child can also be placed in a foster or group home or be sent to a mental health facility if he or she has serious behavioural problems. Some critics are still concerned that police cannot charge children younger than 12 even when they commit serious crimes, and they want the age limit set back to seven.

Parliament began a five-year review of the *YCJA* in 2008 to identify areas of concern. Some of the questions being considered are as follows:

- Is it too tough, or not tough enough?

- Is youth crime worse than ever, or are fears exaggerated?

- Should the age of criminal responsibility be reduced from 12 to 7?

- Should deterrence be a factor in sentencing youth criminals for serious crimes?

This chapter will help you answer these and other questions. It will also give you a better understanding about how Canada's youth criminal justice system works and evolves.

Age and Degree of Criminal Responsibility

Age	Classification	Responsibility
0–11 years	child	none
12–17 years	youth	partial
18 years +	adult	full

These classifications apply in Canada today.

 You and the Law

Under the *Youth Criminal Justice Act*, children under 12 cannot be charged with crimes because they cannot form the criminal intent and do not understand the consequences of their actions. However, there seem to be minors committing offences and knowing what they are doing. Should Canada lower the age of criminal responsibility? If so, to what and why?

In 2008, Winnipeg police seized a 10-year-old boy who was thought to have set nearly three dozen fires. Police said the latest string of arsons began March 27 when a Molotov cocktail was thrown at a house. The boy could not be charged under the *Youth Criminal Justice Act* because of his age. He was turned over to a guardian and referred to a provincial education program designed for young children who run up against the law.

- Do you think that child offenders should be dealt with more seriously? Why or why not?

Did You Know?

The Canadian Centre for Justice Statistics stated that Saskatchewan had the highest youth crime rate in Canada in 2006, followed next by Manitoba and Nova Scotia.

Declaration of Principle for the Youth Criminal Justice Act

People believed that the *YOA* lacked a clear philosophy on youth justice in Canada. The *YCJA* provides that philosophy in its Declaration of Principle. It states that the purpose of the youth criminal justice system is to prevent crime by finding out what causes offending behaviour; rehabilitate youths who commit offences; reintegrate them into society; and ensure that they are subject to meaningful consequences for their actions, to promote the long-term protection of the public.

Changes Introduced by the Youth Criminal Justice Act

How has the *Youth Criminal Justice Act* responded to public fears about violent youth crimes?

The *YCJA* introduced some new changes affecting the legal process for youths who commit offences. These are discussed in the next two sections of this chapter and include the following:

- an emphasis on keeping youth who commit minor offences out of court by providing alternative youth sentencing options

- less emphasis on custody as a sentence for non-violent and less serious offences

- guaranteeing youth criminals their basic Charter rights as well as additional rights because of their age

- ending transfers of youth cases to adult court; all cases are now tried in Youth Justice Court

- allowing youth court judges to impose adult sentences for violent youth crimes

- publication of identities of offenders if an adult sentence is imposed, but only after sentencing

- imposing a period of community supervision for youth criminals who have served time in custody

Case

N.A.J. v. R., 2003 PESCTD 60 (CanLII)

For more information, Go to Nelson Social Studies

N.A.J. was sentenced under the *Young Offenders Act* for stealing a boat and taking it for a joyride. He appealed, arguing that he should be sentenced under the YCJA instead.

In September 2002, N.A.J. and his co-accused were drinking and stole a boat. They went for a boat ride with two women they met, and they drank more alcohol. Shortly after they had stolen it, the boat became stuck in buoys, and the coast guard and RCMP were notified.

At the scene, the two young men told the police a false story about a fifth person who owned the boat. According to the story, the owner left when the boat got stuck. Later, the two women told the authorities that this story was not true. N.A.J. and his friend were arrested and charged with joyriding and causing damage to property.

N.A.J. was 16 years old, a first-time offender, and had left school in Grade 7. At the time of his hearing, he had been employed with a government department for nearly eight months. He blamed his behaviour on his surroundings, his associates, and excessive use of alcohol. He was also concerned about compensating the boat's owner for damages to the boat.

At trial, N.A.J. pleaded guilty to the charges. The Crown asked for a term of open custody, followed by a lengthy probation and restitution. The defence asked for a non-custody sentence, restitution, and community service. The trial judge sentenced N.A.J. to three months' open custody, 20 months' probation, 80 hours of community service, and nearly $4000 in restitution.

N.A.J. appealed the open custody imposed in January 2003 under the *Young Offenders Act*. He argued that because his appeal was being heard in June 2003, he should be sentenced under the *Youth Criminal Justice Act*.

For Discussion

1. When did the YCJA become law, and why did N.A.J. want to be sentenced under this legislation?

2. List three factors working in N.A.J.'s favour for having the custody portion of his sentence overturned.

3. What factor is not favourable for N.A.J. to have the custody portion of his sentence overturned?

4. N.A.J.'s appeal was allowed and the custody provision was overturned. Do you agree? Why or why not?

Review Your Understanding

1. Why was the minimum age for charging a youth with a crime raised from 7 to 12?

2. What is the purpose of the *Youth Criminal Justice Act*? When did it become law?

3. What types of offences can a youth be charged with under the YCJA?

4. Outline three of the principles in the YCJA that reflect the act's philosophy on youth justice in Canada.

5. Of the new features in the YCJA, which four are the most important to you? Why?

10.3 Legal Rights of Youths

Police do not have to arrest youths who are suspected of breaking the law. In many cases, police do not automatically charge a youth with an offence. First, they must think about whether there are other ways to hold the youth accountable. There are ways to divert or keep youth out of the justice system that were established under the *YCJA*.

extrajudicial measure measures other than court proceedings for non-violent, first-time youth criminals

alternative measures programs programs under the *Young Offenders Act* for first-time, non-violent offending youth

extrajudicial sanction a more serious punishment for youth criminals that does not create a criminal record

Extrajudicial Measures and Sanctions

Non-violent first-time offenders who are unlikely to re-offend can avoid trial in youth court by taking part in programs of **extrajudicial measures**. These are similar to the adult diversion programs that you read about in Chapter 9. They are designed to keep the matter out of the court system. Under the *Young Offenders Act*, they were called **alternative measures programs**.

The intent of this program is to reduce the number of young people appearing in court. This applies when their first conflict with the law involves a minor or low-risk offence. The most common offences include the following:

- theft under $5000 (for example, shoplifting)
- possession of stolen property
- failure to appear in court
- breach of probation

The most common extrajudicial measures that the police use are as follows:

- taking no further action and returning the youth to his or her parents or guardian
- giving an informal warning, and explaining the consequences of the behaviour
- giving a formal police caution indicating the seriousness of the offence (for example, speaking with the youth and his or her parents about the offence)
- giving a caution from a Crown attorney (similar to police cautions, but are given after the police refer the case to the Crown)
- referring the youth to a community program, such as recreation programs, mental health programs, and child welfare agencies, to which the youth must consent
- referring the youth to an **extrajudicial sanctions** program

Although retail stores may want all shoplifters tried in court, regardless of age, they cannot force police to lay charges if the police feel that extra-judicial measures are more appropriate.

If the police or the Crown do not feel that warnings, cautions, or referrals are appropriate for a youth, they can use extrajudicial sanctions. These are designed to help youths learn from their mistakes before they get criminal records. There is some punishment for the youth's actions, but the case will not go through the court system. In some programs, the young person apologizes to the victim and returns stolen goods. In others, youths work for victims to compensate for damages done. For example, if the youth sprays graffiti on a neighbour's fence, repainting the fence might be appropriate.

Often, apologizing to the victim is part of the sentence. This helps a youth learn from his or her mistakes and avoid a criminal record.

Other programs include counselling, drug and alcohol treatment, special school programs, or a community service order. Community service is the most common program. Youths must work a set number of hours in the community and apologize to the victims. These programs increase the involvement of parents and neighbourhoods in the youth's punishment. They cost less to run than the youth justice court system. The intention of these programs is to rehabilitate youths who have come into conflict with the law.

For example, in Lethbridge, Alberta, three teenagers drove to a construction site where a home was being built and stole some building materials. A neighbour saw the incident, wrote down the vehicle's licence plate number, and called the police. The police located the vehicle and found the youths building a skateboard ramp. The police spoke to the youths and their parents and worked out a plan. First, the youths returned the remaining materials to the construction site. Next, they apologized to the homeowner who owned the material that was stolen. The homeowner estimated the cost of the missing material at about $200. One of the youth's parents paid the money to the homeowner, and the youths agreed to repay the parent. Although this took time out of the officer's, parents', and victim's day, dealing with things in this way provided immediate consequences for the youths' behaviour. This will hopefully make the outcome more meaningful.

To receive extrajudicial sanctions, a youth must admit to having some involvement in the offence, such as admitting being in the area where the offence took place. Although this is an acceptance of some responsibility, it is not a confession of guilt. It cannot be used as evidence in any later court appearance. Youths must be told of their right to consult a lawyer before they take part in a program. Otherwise, to avoid a trial they might confess to something they did not do.

Youths who successfully complete these programs will have all charges against them stayed or dropped. No criminal conviction is recorded. Those who fail to complete the program can be tried on the original charge in a youth court. Youths can refuse to participate in these programs, and if they have a valid defence for the act (see Chapter 8 for more on defences), they should choose to be tried in a youth justice court.

 Did You Know?

We deal with youth under 18 differently from adults for two main reasons. First, they are thought not to have full adult capacity to form intent and understand what they are doing. Second, they may need a second chance as their unlawful behaviour should not ruin the rest of their lives.

R. v. K.(Cr.) and K.(Ct.), 2006 ONCJ 283 (CanLII)

For more information, **Go to Nelson Social Studies**

Two teenage sisters were found guilty of first-degree murder in 2005 in the drowning death of their mother. The sisters supplied their mother with drugs and alcohol. The older sister held their mother's head under water until the mother drowned. The sisters' lawyer argued that the mother was an alcoholic who was in a self-induced state when she accidentally drowned in the tub. But the court also heard that one of the sisters described to a friend how they killed their mother and planned to make it look like an accident. The mother's alcoholism caused her to be abusive. Because of the sisters' ages at the time of the murder, they could not be identified under the *YCJA*.

• Do you think the sisters had a valid defence in this case? Should the mother's alcoholism and possible abusive nature influence the judge's decision? What would you decide if you were the judge in this case?

Which are the three most frequently used extrajudicial measures assigned to youth criminals? Why do you suppose that is?

Extrajudicial Measures and Sanctions Assigned to Youth

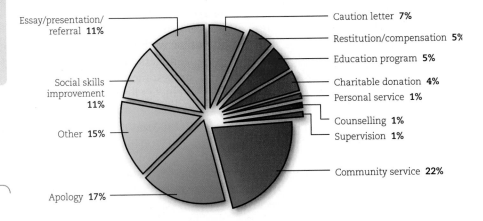

- Essay/presentation/referral **11%**
- Social skills improvement **11%**
- Other **15%**
- Apology **17%**
- Caution letter **7%**
- Restitution/compensation **5%**
- Education program **5%**
- Charitable donation **4%**
- Personal service **1%**
- Counselling **1%**
- Supervision **1%**
- Community service **22%**

 Did You Know?

In September 2008, in a 7–0 judgment in *R. v. L.T.H.*, the Supreme Court of Canada restored a Nova Scotia youth's acquittal in a dangerous driving case. The reason for the acquittal was that the youth likely did not understand what he was doing when he waived his right to legal counsel and to remain silent. The youth had a learning disability, which had a serious effect on his ability to understand.

Arrest and Detention

For serious offences, police must arrest youths, just as they would adults. From the moment the police decide to arrest a youth, certain legal rights and protections come into effect. The legal rights listed in the *Charter of Rights and Freedoms* apply to all youths, just as they apply to all adults. For example, a youth has the right to know the reason for the arrest, the automatic right to consult with a lawyer, the right to apply to be released from custody, and the right to a fair trial. But the *YCJA* provides youth with some additional rights.

Section 25 of the *YCJA* expands upon basic Charter rights by providing additional protections for youths in the youth criminal justice system. During an arrest, the police officer or person in authority—which could include the school principal—must outline the rights in language that the youth understands. They must check that the youth clearly understands these rights. Youths must be told that they do not have to make a statement and that any statement that is made could be used against them in court. Youths must be told of the right to consult a lawyer. They must also be told of the right to have a parent or another adult present during any questioning. Youths who decide to ignore these rights must sign a statement or a waiver proving that they have waived these rights.

 Did You Know?

In 2006, the number of youths not formally charged by the police was 25 percent higher than in 2002.

 ## You Be the Judge

R. v. J.Y., 2007 ABPC 133 (CanLII)

For more information, **Go to Nelson Social Studies**

Two teenage boys were questioned by their school principal about a possible sexual assault of a female student while on her way home from school. The boys admitted their actions, and the principal called the police. The police read the boys their rights and laid criminal charges against them. At trial, the boys' lawyer argued that the principal was a person in authority and that the boys had been denied their Charter protections. As such, their statements should be inadmissible.

- What do you think the judge decided and why? What would you have done if you were the judge in this case?

 ## Case

R. v. R. (B.V.), 2007 ONCJ 31 (CanLII)

For more information, **Go to Nelson Social Studies**

Around 2:00 a.m. in May 2006, a police officer stopped a car driven erratically by B.V.R. The youth had no driver's licence with her, and she only had a class G2 licence. A G2 licence prohibits drivers from having any alcohol in their system while driving. The officer noted the odour of beer in the car and determined that she had alcohol on her breath. A roadside screening device was used, which B.V.R. failed. She was arrested and told about her section 10(b) Charter rights, but she said she did not want a lawyer. She was taken to the police station where she was told her additional *YCJA* rights and cautions. She again said she did not want a lawyer, a parent, or another adult present. She did not sign a waiver to this effect, and there was no audiotaped or videotaped waiver. The breath technician took further breath samples that registered 127 and 118 milligrams of alcohol in 100 millilitres of blood. B.V.R. was charged with impaired driving.

continues...

Police often use roadside screening devices such as this. In B.V.R.'s case, the Breathalyzer results were not admitted as evidence because the police failed to get her to waive her *YCJA* rights in writing.

R. v. R. (B.V.), 2007 ONCJ 31 (CanLII)

At trial, B.V.R.'s lawyer argued that the Crown could not prove that her legal rights under the Charter and the *YCJA* had been respected. There was no waiver of those rights. Without that proof, the lawyer argued that the Breathalyzer readings must be excluded as evidence, under section 24(2) of the Charter. The trial judge agreed. The test results were excluded, and the charges against B.V.R. were dismissed.

For Discussion

1. What additional rights are provided under the *YCJA* for young persons who have been arrested?

2. If a young person declines these rights, why must the youth sign a waiver or have an audiotaped or videotaped waiver taken?

3. What is the purpose or intent of section 24(2) of the Charter, and what impact did it have on this case?

4. Do you agree with the judge's decision? Why or why not?

Police are not allowed to search you without reasonable grounds to believe that you possess evidence of illegal activity.

Searches

In Chapter 5, you learned that police are permitted to search youths and adults without a warrant in certain, limited situations. They must have reasonable grounds to believe the search will uncover evidence that might be lost or disposed of before they can get a search warrant. They can also search a person if he or she lets them. If police ask to search you and you do not say "no," they may assume that you do not object. The police cannot search your car without a warrant unless they have reasonable grounds to believe that an offence is being committed. For example, they might stop you for speeding through a red light, smell alcohol on your breath, and assume you have liquor in your possession. These are reasonable grounds for a search without a warrant.

Given this information, how do police and the courts treat drug searches in schools? The Supreme Court has heard two appeals in recent years. *R. v. M. (M.R.)*, 1998, involved searching a 13-year-old student. It established that a warrant is not needed for a school authority, such as a principal, to search a student. There must be reasonable grounds to believe school regulations were breached and searching the student will reveal evidence proving that claim. Reasonable grounds include information from credible students, a teacher's observations, or both. In *R. v. A.M.*, 2008 (see the case on the next page), the Supreme Court found that using police sniffer dogs without justification or reasonable grounds violates students' privacy rights.

R. v. A.M., 2008 SCC 19 (CanLII)

For more information, **Go to Nelson Social Studies** 🌐

The Supreme Court ruled that reasonable grounds must exist before using sniffer dogs for a drug search in schools.

In 2000, a Sarnia high school principal was concerned about the presence of drugs in his school. The school had a zero-tolerance policy for possession and use of drugs at school. The principal issued an open and standing invitation to the police to bring sniffer dogs into the school. On November 7, 2002, three police officers and a sniffer dog arrived at the school. They asked the principal for permission to conduct a drug search. The principal gave them permission. The police had no knowledge or reasonable grounds to suspect that drugs were present in the school that day. This was simply a random search without search warrants, but conducted with the principal's consent. The police conducted a search, and the students were confined to their classrooms for nearly two hours.

While searching the gymnasium, the sniffer dog showed interest in a backpack. Without getting a warrant, an officer searched the bag. The officer found marijuana, magic mushrooms, and drug-related paraphernalia. The backpack owner, A.M., was arrested and charged with possession for the purpose of trafficking both drugs.

At trial, A.M. argued that the evidence seized should be excluded. He said that his section 8 Charter rights were violated. The trial judge agreed, finding that the sniffer dog and the backpack search were unreasonable. The trial judge commented on how the search violated A.M.'s Charter rights, as well as the rights of all the other students who had been unreasonably detained during the search. The judge acquitted A.M. of the charges in June 2004. A Crown appeal to the Ontario Court of Appeal was dismissed in a unanimous judgment in April 2006. Permission to appeal to the Supreme Court of Canada was granted, and the appeal was heard in May 2007. In a 6–3 judgment on April 25, 2008, the Supreme Court agreed with the two lower courts. It dismissed the Crown's appeal, ruling that the police cannot go into schools or most public places with drug-sniffing dogs and conduct searches without justification. "Completely random" drug searches breach privacy provisions under the *Charter of Rights and Freedoms*.

For Discussion

1. Do you think the sniffer dog search was reasonable? Discuss with a partner who has the opposite view.

2. The Supreme Court majority judgment stated that teenagers may have little expectation of privacy from having their backpacks randomly searched by police, and that this expectation is a reasonable one that society should support. Do you agree? Why or why not?

3. An editorial, "A Balanced Ruling," in the *Toronto Star* on April 28, 2008, stated: "This decision seems like a reasonable compromise between the public interests in keeping schools safe, and the valid, if diminished, privacy rights of students who attend them." Do you agree? Explain.

4. Should Parliament legislate stronger search powers for the use of sniffer dogs in public areas such as bus and train terminals and stadiums? Why or why not?

Detention and Bail

The *Criminal Code* gives youths and adults the same right to bail. The terms of release for youths often impose curfews and forbid contact with victims and certain friends. For many offences, youths are released into the custody of parents or other responsible adults. Generally, youths are not released on their own recognizance. If they are at risk of reoffending or not appearing for trial, they may be sent to a **foster home** or placed under house arrest before trial or sentencing.

foster home a home of an existing family where a young person is placed for care and rehabilitation

As much as possible, youth offenders are kept separate from adult offenders. Youths can only be fingerprinted and photographed when they are charged with indictable offences. To protect youths' rights, police must destroy the photos and fingerprints if the youths are acquitted, the charge is dismissed, or proceedings are discontinued.

Youth detention centres such as this one in Prince George, British Columbia, allow youth offenders to be housed separately from adults.

Victims, school administrators, and police have access to youth court records. Contrary to what many young people believe, the records are not destroyed automatically when a convicted youth reaches the age of 18. The records may be used in adult bail hearings and sentencing. However, after certain periods of time, the documents are no longer available. The time depends on the type of offence and the sentence. The records of youths who receive adult sentences are treated the same as adult records.

You Be the Judge

R. v. L.B., 2007 ONCA 596 (CanLII)

For more information, Go to Nelson Social Studies

In September 2002, two plainclothes police officers in an unmarked car drove by a Toronto high school. They saw a 15-year-old male, F., sitting on a railing near the school entrance. Another 15-year-old male, L.B., was standing far from F. and holding a black bag. The officers believed that, although the two young men were physically separated, they were actually "together." Thinking that the boys looked suspicious, the officers stopped, displayed their badges, and called out "Toronto police."

Without being asked, L.B. walked directly toward the officers, but without the black bag. The officers asked the youths for their names and dates of birth to check their identities. Both officers agreed that they had no cause to detain L.B. or F. They also agreed that both youths could have walked away or stopped answering questions at any time. The officers asked if the bag belonged to one of the youths. The youths claimed they did not know who owned the bag. The officers regarded the bag as abandoned property. They opened it and found a pile of L.B.'s school work and a loaded .22 calibre handgun. Both boys were arrested at gunpoint and charged with possession of a loaded restricted firearm and seven other gun-related counts.

At trial, L.B. claimed that his section 8, 9, and 10(b) Charter rights were infringed. He claimed that the gun should be excluded from evidence under section 24(2) of the Charter. The trial judge agreed that his rights had been violated. The judge excluded the gun evidence and acquitted L.B. The Crown appealed to the Ontario Court of Appeal where the appeal was heard in June 2007.

- Do you think L.B.'s acquittal should be upheld? Why or why not? What is more important in this case: L.B.'s individual rights, or the protection of society against people carrying restricted weapons?

Notice to Parents

Parents or guardians must be notified as soon as possible after their child is detained or arrested. They are encouraged to be present during all steps of the legal process. If their child is found guilty, they must be given opportunities to provide input prior to sentencing. Because their role is important, a judge can order them to attend hearings. Parents or guardians who do not appear may be found in contempt of court. The judge can then issue a warrant for their arrest. Any parent or guardian who promises the court to supervise his or her child and who deliberately fails to carry out these duties can face criminal charges.

 Parents or guardians must be notified as soon as possible after their child has been detained or arrested. They are encouraged to be present during all stages of the legal process.

Review Your Understanding

1. Outline four choices police have when dealing with a youth who has committed a minor first-time offence.

2. What are extrajudicial sanctions, and when are they used? What two conditions must be met before a youth offender can participate in an extrajudicial sanctions program?

3. Under the *YCJA*, what additional rights are available to youths who are arrested?

4. When may a young person be fingerprinted and photographed?

5. What rights and obligations do parents or guardians have when their child is arrested?

10.4 Trial Procedures

Trials under the *Youth Criminal Justice Act* may be held in either a youth or family court, depending on the province or territory. Youth and adult trials are often held in the same facilities but at different times. A judge might hear some adult criminal cases and some youth criminal cases. For example, Ontario's youth court system has two levels. Youths aged 12 to 15 are tried in family court. Youths aged 16 to 17 are tried in provincial court.

Trials for youths and adults follow the same rules of evidence and are equally formal. Defence lawyers usually represent both youths and adults. Both youths and adults can apply for legal aid. The intent of the youth justice system is to deal with youths as quickly as possible and to let them return home quickly.

Did You Know?

Statistics Canada reports that 56 463 youth court cases were completed during 2006–2007. This number is 26 percent lower than in 2002–2003.

A Youth Criminal's Journey through the Justice System

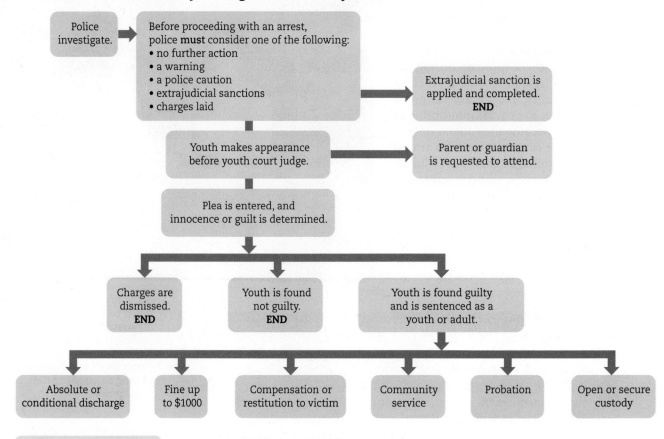

This chart shows a simplified youth court process under the *Youth Criminal Justice Act*.

presumptive offence a serious offence such as murder, attempted murder, manslaughter, aggravated assault, and repeat serious violent crimes

Publication of Identities

Our courts should be open and accessible to everyone interested in them. The *YCJA* lets the public and media attend trials or hearings involving youths. Trials and hearings may be reported, but the identity of the accused can be disclosed only under certain rare conditions. Usually, the identity of a youth involved in the case as a witness or a victim cannot be disclosed. This rule applies to everyone—the media, the defence, the Crown, and even members of the public who might comment on the case on a website.

The names of 14- to 17-year-olds convicted of **presumptive offences** can be reported unless a judge decides that doing so would affect rehabilitation. Presumptive offences are serious crimes such as murder, attempted murder, manslaughter, aggravated sexual assault, and repeat serious violent crimes. For these offences, an adult sentence is appropriate. If youths who are considered dangerous are at large, their names and pictures can be published, although this is rarely done.

A Crown attorney may tell the court at the beginning of a trial that the Crown will not seek an adult sentence in a particular case—even for a serious, violent offence. This means that even if the young person is found guilty, he or she will receive a youth sentence. In this case, the name of the youth cannot be reported or published.

F.N. (Re), 2000 SCC 35 (CanLII)

For more information, **Go to Nelson Social Studies**

F.N., a young offender, was charged with two counts of assault and breach of probation. He appeared in court in St. John's in January 1996, and his name and alleged offences appeared on the court docket (the list of cases being heard). The dockets were kept in the court clerk's possession, but the court had a practice of sending a copy of the court docket to psychologists at both school boards in the St. John's area.

F.N. sought a court order to prevent the court from supplying copies of its weekly dockets to the school boards. His application to the Newfoundland Supreme Court, Trial Division, and his next appeal to the Newfoundland Court of Appeal were both dismissed.

He then appealed to the Supreme Court of Canada. His appeal was heard in November 1999. In a 7–0 judgment in July 2000, the court ruled in his favour and ordered the practice of sending youth court dockets to both school boards to stop.

For Discussion

1. Why do you think F.N. objected to the youth court's distribution of court dockets to the school boards?

2. Why do you think the two Newfoundland courts dismissed F.N.'s appeal?

3. Why do you think the Supreme Court ruled in F.N.'s favour?

4. The Supreme Court judgment stated: "A young person once stigmatized as a lawbreaker may, unless given help and redirection, render the stigma a self-fulfilling prophecy." What does this mean, and do you agree? Explain.

Adult Sentences

Under the *Juvenile Delinquents Act* and the *Young Offenders Act*, youths over the age of 14 who committed very serious offences could have their cases transferred to an adult court. There, they would receive an adult sentence if convicted. Over the years, not many youths were transferred to adult court. The number of transfers varied among the provinces, and the transfer process was complex and took too long.

The *YCJA* has eliminated transfers to adult court. Youths over the age of 14 accused of a violent crime (one that carries a penalty of more than two years in jail) can be treated and sentenced as adults. However, all criminal matters dealing with youths occur in youth court. Lawmakers believe that the lower age limit acts as a deterrent and helps prevent violent youth crimes from happening.

Youth sentences carry different maximum sentences, compared to adult sentences, as shown in the chart below.

 You and the Law

In 2008, the federal Conservative government suggested amending the *Youth Criminal Justice Act* to sentence youth aged 14 and older to life in prison if convicted of first- or second-degree murder. What do you think of this proposal? Explain.

Youth Court Sentences

Crime	Maximum Sentence
First-degree murder	10 years
Second-degree murder	7 years
All other offences where an adult would receive a life sentence	3 years
All other offences	2 years

This chart shows the maximum sentences under the *Youth Criminal Justice Act*. How do they differ from adult sentences? Why do you think there is such a difference between the two types of sentences?

The *YCJA* required youth court judges to sentence youths convicted of certain serious offences as adults unless the youths could convince the court that youth sentences were more appropriate. This *YCJA* sentencing principle was challenged as a violation of the Charter's section 7 right to fundamental justice. The challenge was resolved in a landmark judgment from the Supreme Court of Canada in *R. v. D.B.*, 2008 (see the case below). The judgment still allows judges to give adult sentences to youth criminals aged 14 to 17. It now requires the Crown to prove why a stricter sentence is appropriate. The decision shifted the onus (burden) to the Crown to prove that adult sentences are appropriate. It affirms the principle that youth have a right to be treated differently from adults. Many legal experts believe this ruling is one of the most important judgments on youth justice in Canada in many years.

 Case

R. v. D.B., 2008 SCC 25 (CanLII)

For more information, | Go to Nelson Social Studies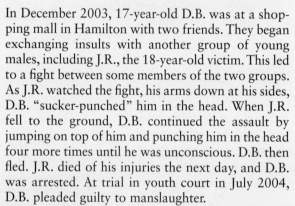

In December 2003, 17-year-old D.B. was at a shopping mall in Hamilton with two friends. They began exchanging insults with another group of young males, including J.R., the 18-year-old victim. This led to a fight between some members of the two groups. As J.R. watched the fight, his arms down at his sides, D.B. "sucker-punched" him in the head. When J.R. fell to the ground, D.B. continued the assault by jumping on top of him and punching him in the head four more times until he was unconscious. D.B. then fled. J.R. died of his injuries the next day, and D.B. was arrested. At trial in youth court in July 2004, D.B. pleaded guilty to manslaughter.

The *YCJA* requires that a youth found guilty of a serious crime receive an adult sentence unless the youth can justify why he or she deserves a youth sentence. D.B. applied to the court, arguing that his section 7 Charter rights were violated. The Crown opposed the application, asking for a stiffer adult sentence for D.B. The trial judge heard arguments from both sides and allowed D.B.'s Charter challenge. The judge imposed the maximum three-year sentence on D.B. under the *YCJA*.

The Crown appealed. In a unanimous judgment in March 2006, the Ontario Court of Appeal dismissed the Crown's appeal and affirmed the trial judge's ruling. The Crown received permission to appeal to the Supreme Court of Canada. That appeal was heard in October 2007. In a 5–4 judgment on

May 16, 2008, a majority of the high court dismissed the Crown's appeal. The judgment stated that it is the Crown's responsibility to prove that youths convicted of violent crimes should be sentenced as adults. D.B.'s three-year sentence was upheld.

For Discussion

1. What does section 7 of the *Charter of Rights and Freedoms* state, and why did D.B. argue that this right had been violated?

2. In his decision, the trial judge stated: "There is no logical reason why it should not be the responsibility of the prosecutor who wants the court to impose an adult sentence to bear the burden of convincing the court." Do you agree? Why or why not?

3. The Supreme Court's majority judgment stated that young people have always been treated differently from adults, but they are still accountable for their acts. "They are decidedly but differently accountable." What does this mean? Do you agree? Why or why not?

4. The Supreme Court minority judgment stated that most people think that sentencing of youth courts is "either too lenient or much too lenient." Do you agree? Why or why not?

1. Why do youth court cases usually take less time to try than adult court cases?
2. What is a presumptive offence? List four examples.
3. Why are the identities of youth criminals protected from media publication? Do you agree that this is a good idea? Why or why not?
4. List three reasons why the YCJA eliminated the transfer of serious crimes to adult court.
5. Why was the case of *R. v. D.B.* such a significant judgment in the history of youth justice in Canada?

10.5 Youth Sentencing Options

Under the *Youth Criminal Justice Act*, the principles of sentencing are as follows:

- to hold offenders accountable for their criminal behaviour

- to consider the victim's needs and concerns

- to impose appropriate sanctions, with emphasis on rehabilitating youths, reintegrating them into society, and protecting society

Balancing different demands makes a judge's task very difficult. Even if the Crown or the defence recommends a specific sentence, the judge still makes the final decision.

Judges must consider the needs of the community. Sentences must help youth take responsibility for breaking the law. We assume that youths are more easily reformed than adults. Judges must choose sentences that will help with rehabilitation and reintegration into society.

Before making a final decision, the judge may hold a sentencing hearing, just as in adult court. The more serious the offence, the more likely this will happen. During the hearing, the judge will usually review a pre-sentence report. The report is prepared by a probation officer or youth justice court worker and is similar to a pre-sentence report in adult court.

e Activity

To learn more about sanctions and programs for youth criminals,

Go to Nelson Social Studies

Common Items Included in a Youth Pre-Sentence Report

- interviews with the youth, the parent(s), and the victim
- any intention by the youth to change his or her conduct
- records of school attendance and performance
- a history of any criminal offences
- the youth's attitude toward the offence
- any background information that provides insight into the youth's character
- a medical and psychiatric profile if there is concern for the youth's state of mind

These are some of the most common items that appear in a youth pre-sentence report.

R. v. C.N., 2006 CanLII 32902 (ON C.A.)

For more information, Go to Nelson Social Studies

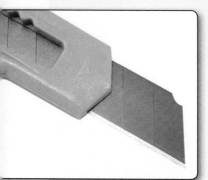

C.N. attacked M.F. with a box cutter or utility knife similar to this one.

In the early morning hours of April 2005, 17-year-old C.N. and three of his friends stalked another young person, M.F., through the streets of Ottawa. C.N. recognized M.F. as the person who had been in a fight with his younger brother about 18 months earlier. When they surrounded M.F., they told him they were going to kill him. M.F. produced a can of pepper spray and sprayed C.N. in the face. When they caught M.F., C.N.'s friends pinned M.F. to the ground while C.N. slashed and stabbed him repeatedly with a box cutter. M.F. suffered serious physical injuries and psychological trauma. C.N. was arrested the same night.

At trial in February 2006, C.N. pleaded guilty to aggravated assault. At sentencing, the judge reviewed the case facts and C.N.'s life. The judge determined that C.N. "is generally described as a polite, courteous, and respectful young man who has strong family support." C.N. had been attending counselling since the incident. The judge also noted that C.N. was drinking alcohol and damaging property. The judge sentenced C.N. to two years' probation, the maximum allowed under the YCJA.

The Crown appealed to the Ontario Court of Appeal, who heard the appeal in September 2006. In a 3–0 judgment, the court allowed the appeal. It changed the sentence to six months of open custody, three months of community supervision, and six months of probation.

• Why do you think the appeal court changed C.N.'s sentence? Which sentence do you think is more appropriate?

Canadians understand that youths who commit a minor first offence where no one is hurt may deserve a second chance. Here, sentencing that emphasizes rehabilitation is appropriate. In the following pages, you will see the different sentences available to judges in a youth court. They range from the most lenient to the most severe.

Absolute Discharges

Youths can receive an absolute discharge for a first-time offence if it is relatively minor. This may be theft under $5000, which is often shoplifting or mischief. Youths receive the discharge when it is in their best interest and does not go against the public good. An absolute discharge means that the youth has been found guilty, but no formal conviction will be entered. The court will take no further action, and the youth is "discharged" from further obligations to the court. If the same youth commits another offence, the judge will see the earlier discharge in the pre-sentence report.

Fines

The absolute maximum fine for youths is $1000. In imposing a fine, the judge must consider the youth criminal's ability to pay and the seriousness of the offence. If the youth has no way of earning money and has no savings, imposing a fine may be senseless. The youth, not the parents or guardians, must pay the penalty for the crime. The youth may ask the court to extend the payment deadline to work off the fine. If the fine is not paid in a reasonable amount of time, the judge may place the youth in custody. Judges may also combine fines with other sentences, such as probation or community service work.

Compensation

A youth criminal may have to pay money to the victim to make up for property damage or lost income. For example, a youth who steals $50 from a friend's purse can be ordered to repay that sum.

Personal and Community Service

Youths who commit crimes often cannot afford to pay fines or compensation to their victims. In the place of money, judges may order youths to work for the victims. For example, if Keith damages his neighbour's prize-winning garden, the judge could order him to do gardening tasks for the victim for a certain period of time. However, the victim must agree. Because victims are often frightened or angered by the offence, they may not want further contact with the offender. As a result, personal service orders are not common. They usually relate to property offences.

When victims reject personal service orders or when youths harm the community, judges may use community service orders. These orders have youths put something back into the community. For instance, 15-year-old Hannah spray-paints graffiti on city property. She may have to paint over or erase the graffiti. She might also be asked to work in a daycare or seniors' centre. The service order cannot take more than 40 hours and must be completed within one year.

Police and Community-Based Programs

Across Canada, community programs help prevent youth crime. The Ottawa Police Youth Centre merged with the Boys and Girls Club of Ottawa. Both groups expanded their programs and reach more youths. This program offers everything from recreational facilities to alternative measures programs for youths charged with drug-related offences. Another project is a poster competition on the issue of sexually exploited teens.

Another example is Manitoba's Youth Fire Stop Program. It is an intervention program run by the Winnipeg fire department. Its aim is to work with youths (mainly under the age of 12) who set fires and cannot be charged with arson under the *YCJA* because of their age. Statistics show that young boys set about 80 percent of fires out of boredom or curiosity. The other 20 percent are youth in crisis. They may be dealing with family breakdowns, violence, or other issues in their homes. By mid-2008, 112 children were referred to this program. Other big cities in Canada have similar programs.

These examples show that it is important to involve police and fire departments in community-based rehabilitation programs. They are often the first to deal with at-risk youths in schools and neighbourhoods. They have the necessary experience and knowledge to deal with them effectively.

If a youth deliberately breaks a neighbour's window, suitable compensation is the cost of the new window.

In 2006, the Ottawa Police Service launched a student-designed poster competition. It was part of the community awareness campaign about sexually exploited adolescents. Jordana Globerman, from Canterbury High School, designed the winning poster (shown here).

Did You Know?

Statistics show that judges give youths probation sentences more than anything else. In 2005–2006, 60 percent of guilty youths received probation.

Probation

A judge can limit a youth's freedom by issuing a probation order. This means the youth criminal is placed under a probation officer's supervision for up to two years. There is no limit to the number of conditions a probation order can contain. One basic condition is that the youth must stay out of trouble while on probation. Other conditions depend on the kind of offences committed and the youth's background.

Youths must receive copies of their probation orders to be fully aware of the conditions. Breaking the terms of probation is a criminal offence. It may lead the youths back to court, where they might receive a longer sentence, including custody.

Standard Conditions of Youth Probation

- ☑ report to a probation officer
- ☑ attend school regularly
- ☑ follow a curfew
- ☑ remain at home with parents
- ☑ not use alcohol or other drugs
- ☑ stay away from malls and stores
- ☑ apologize to the victim
- ☑ perform personal or community services
- ☑ keep the peace and be on good behaviour

Which conditions do you think would be most effective in making a youth criminal take responsibility? Explain.

Custody

Sentencing youth criminals to custody (jail) is a last resort under the *YCJA*. Only violent and serious repeat offenders should be considered for custody. Custody is the most serious sentence in the youth justice system. It is used when youths do the following:

- commit violent crimes and need supervision
- fail to comply with earlier non-custodial sentences

Custody can be either open or secure (closed). Judges decide the kind of custody in which youths will be held.

In *R. v. C.D.*, 2005, the Supreme Court concluded that Parliament designed the *YCJA* to limit using custody when sentencing youth criminals. Rehabilitating youths is foremost in the court's mind.

If a youth turns 18 while in custody, correctional officials may apply to have the offender complete the sentence in an adult facility. Judges must balance the youth's best interests with society's needs. A youth in custody is not eligible for parole or time off for good behaviour. The sentencing already gives a youth special consideration and protection.

Open Custody

Offenders who need more supervision and structure in their lives are given open custody. They can have limited and supervised access to their community. Open custody facilities are designed to rehabilitate youth criminals. They include foster or **group homes**, childcare facilities, and residential wilderness camps. While in open custody, youths attend the school closest to their facility.

group home a home that houses several youth criminals for a set time period for rehabilitation

In foster homes, youths live with other families. These youths are given a few restrictions, such as curfews. Foster parents receive payments from the provincial government for their services. They are usually people who are genuinely interested in children and youths but have no special professional training.

Trained staff operate a group home. Several youths can live there at a time. The setting helps youths learn how to behave responsibly and get along with others. Group homes link with community resources such as schools and rehabilitation programs. Programs may be alcohol- and drug-abuse counselling, anger management, and life-skills training. Youths may also be placed with the Children's Aid Society or a suitable government department such as the Ministry of Community and Social Services.

Secure Custody

Youths who commit serious violent offences or who have a history of offences may be considered a threat to society and sentenced to secure custody. This is also known as closed custody. It is a last resort, and it means that their freedom is totally restricted with little outside contact. Secure facilities usually have barred windows and locked doors. Some are located in separate wings of adult jails or prisons in isolated rural areas. In this case, youth and adult offenders are totally separated.

Important goals in custodial facilities are upgrading education and skills training. Youths may be granted a temporary absence or day release for school. This might also be granted for medical and family reasons. Youths often go to open facilities to finish their sentences, which helps make returning to the community easier.

Custody is followed by community supervision. This supervision is usually about half of the length of custody.

All About Law DVD
"Crime and Punishment, Part 3: The Politics of Punishment" from *All About Law DVD*

Life behind bars is the end of freedom.

R. v. D.J.B., 2007 CanLII 5879 (NL P.C.)

For more information, | Go to Nelson Social Studies |

Police have handcuffed this youth at school before arresting him. Do you think the police should be allowed to handcuff students in schools?

A youth, 14-year-old D.J.B., was convicted of several offences including assault. He was sentenced to a five-month open custody in May 2006. After completing the sentence, he returned home to his parents. Later, he was convicted of more offences, including breach of probation. He was sentenced to a six-month open custody in January 2007. While serving this sentence, D.J.B. left the open custody facility around midnight. He was picked up by the police the next morning and returned to the facility. This happened two more times. In less than one year, D.J.B. escaped three times. He was never at large for long when he escaped, and he did not commit any additional offences while he was at large.

D.J.B.'s family had mental health and addiction issues. He did poorly in school, and his attendance and behaviour were constant problems. At one point, he was suspended after he made a bomb threat. His guidance counsellor described him as "a troubled boy who has become unmanageable." D.J.B. had an extensive youth court record. He was convicted of 21 offences including assaults, thefts, and 15 breaches of various court orders. D.J.B. pleaded guilty to the most recent charges laid against him.

For Discussion

1. Considering D.J.B.'s background, is a non-custodial sentence reasonable for him? Why or why not?

2. How serious were D.J.B.'s offences?

3. Outline three positive factors that the judge could consider when sentencing D.J.B.

4. The Crown and defence recommended that D.J.B. receive a sentence between one and three months in custody. The trial judge sentenced him to eight months in secure custody, followed by 12 months of probation. In your opinion, is this an appropriate sentence? Explain.

Sentences Given to Youths, 2004–2006

	2004–2005		2005–2006		
	Number	% of Total Offenders	Number	% of Total Offenders	% Change
Total number of youth cases	24 916		22 187		–10.7
Custodial supervision					
Secure custody	686	2.8	576	2.6	–16.0
Open custody	592	2.4	547	2.5	–7.6
Total sentenced to custody	1278	5.2	1123	5.1	–12.1
Community supervision					
Probation	21 068	85.8	18 619	84.9	–11.6
Deferred custody and supervision	598	2.4	594	2.7	–0.7
Intensive support and supervision	291	1.2	320	1.5	10.0
Community portion of custody sentence	403	1.6	408	1.9	1.2

This table shows the sentences handed out by youth court judges.

Appeals and Reviews

Under the *Criminal Code*, youths and adults have similar rights of appeal. The *Youth Criminal Justice Act* gives both the convicted offender and the Crown the right to appeal a sentence that seems unfair. The *YCJA* allows for court reviews of all sentences. A review may be requested by youths, their families, or by provincial authorities. Application for a review may be made up to six months after the sentence is imposed. The situation of any youth in custody for more than one year is automatically reviewed at the end of each year. This is intended to allow the courts to change a sentence to reflect any progress the youth may make. The judge conducting the review may keep or reduce the sentence, but never increase it. The review makes it possible for a youth to avoid serving the complete sentence if his or her behaviour shows evidence of reform.

 Did You Know?

If you have a youth court record, on a job application form you can answer "no" to the question, "Do you have a criminal record?" However, you must answer "yes" if you are charged and convicted for something you did after you turned 18.

Review Your Understanding

1. What are the three principles of youth sentencing?
2. What is the purpose of a pre-sentence report? What kind of information does it contain?
3. What is the most lenient sentence a youth can receive? Why is it the best option for most youths?
4. Using examples, distinguish between open and secure custody.
5. What is the difference between an appeal and a review? What are the purposes of each?

Bullying, Drugs, and School Safety: Do Schools Need Heightened Security?

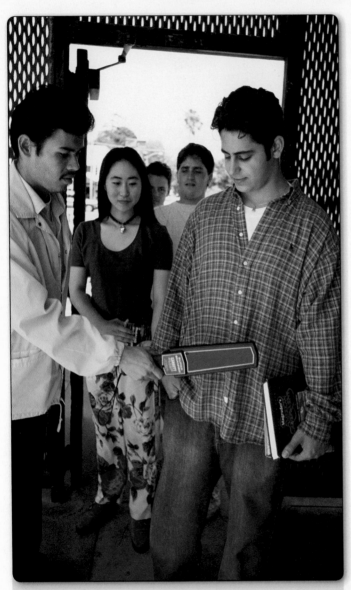

School programs dealing with bullying and violence are much more common and strict than they used to be. Metal detectors are sometimes used at school entrances to check for weapons.

Bullying and cyberbullying hurt others, physically or verbally. They are done over and over, usually to pressure someone with fear or threats. Bullying weakens a student's right to dignity at school. Cyberbullying outside of school comes in many forms. It can be a hateful or threatening e-mail. The bully can impersonate someone online in order to trick another person. A bully might also post pictures online to embarrass someone else. Canadian police say that cyberbullying is increasing, especially among young girls.

Bullying and violence are serious matters in Canadian schools. But has it significantly increased? Some people believe that it has. They believe that it reflects an increase in society in general. Statistics indicate that there is no increase among youths or adults.

However, governments and educators have decided to act on society's behalf. Has this improved anything or just made things worse? Some schools have a no-tolerance policy of drugs and violence. Offenders are kicked out of school and not allowed to return. Is this suitable punishment for students?

On One Side

Educators supporting the tough policies believe that the other side is too soft. Enforcing rules creates a safer environment. Therefore, students will not feel that they need to carry weapons to protect themselves. These educators think that students respect standards only if punishment backs up the standards. The tough policies make students accountable for their actions rather than coddle them. "Good kids" should not suffer for the "bad" few. So, policies like random searches are good things.

Those who support stricter policies favour metal detectors at school entrances. They believe that having police at schools with problem students will help. Punishments should increase. "Bad" students see suspension, expulsion, and jail time as badges of honour. Those supporting strict policies think that will change if corporal punishment returns.

On the Other Side

Critics of tough policies see students as confused and alienated. They do not see teens as thugs. They argue that counselling helps students develop positive self-esteem and self-worth, and this will achieve better results than tough discipline. Positive support programs are more effective than tough policies, such as expulsion. Schools need to teach students proper values and behaviour. Teachers can help students learn, and parents can help students work. Significant change in support is needed to accomplish much over the long term. Building relationships is the way to gain trust and respect for authority figures. It is more subtle than using sniffer dogs and a SWAT team.

In addition, this side feels that tightening security in schools will not resolve anything. Having increased security is based on the notion that all students may be suspects at any time. These measures can teach students that their civil liberties are not protected or valued in society. Instead, administrators should have the time and resources they need to do their jobs.

The Bottom Line

Everyone agrees that schools must be safe. The question remains: How extreme should the measures be to ensure this? Should violent teens be expelled or sentenced to fines and jail time? Or should schools implement more counselling and treatment programs to help troubled teens—including those who are terrified of being bullied?

Governments need to provide enough money for creative, helpful intervention. Taking funds away reduces support for communities on the edge of society. Administrators must report violence that happens in their schools. However, a zero-tolerance policy is harsh and lacks fairness because it is hardest on students who need help the most. Expelling them from school does not help. Students must feel comfortable telling teachers, parents, or the police if they are assaulted or see someone being assaulted. The fear of "snitches get stitches" should go away.

What Do You Think?

1. Conduct an Internet search on violence in Canadian schools. Is it declining, increasing, or staying the same? Prepare a short report on your findings.

2. What does "snitches get stitches" mean? What is good and bad about this attitude?

3. What are educators and governments doing to deal with school violence? Is it enough? Explain.

4. Do you think that zero-tolerance policies work? Why or why not?

5. How does self-esteem relate to violence in schools?

6. What programs do you think would be most effective to reduce school violence? Why?

Chapter Review

Chapter Highlights

- The *Youth Criminal Justice Act* became law on April 1, 2003.
- The *Youth Criminal Justice Act* is criminal law that outlines the rights of youths aged 12 to 17 inclusive, and the procedures for dealing with them.
- A child under the age of 12 is considered too young to be dealt with in the criminal justice system.
- The *Youth Criminal Justice Act* expands the role of rehabilitation services for dealing with youth criminals.
- Youths have the same rights as adults under the *Charter of Rights and Freedoms*. They have some additional rights under the *Youth Criminal Justice Act*.
- Programs of extrajudicial measures and sanctions are designed to deal with youths outside the court system.
- The Supreme Court of Canada ruled that reasonable grounds must exist before using sniffer dogs for drug searches in schools.
- Youths aged 14 years and over can be treated as adult offenders if they commit serious violent crimes, but they are still tried in a Youth Justice Court.
- The names of youths aged 14 to 17 can be published if they have been convicted of a serious indictable offence under the *Youth Criminal Justice Act*.
- Youth criminals are treated differently than adults in court. The Crown must justify why adult sentences are appropriate for youths who have committed violent crimes.
- Sentencing a youth to custody is a last resort under the *Youth Criminal Justice Act*.
- Youths convicted of a criminal offence can be placed in custody when considered a danger to society.
- Youths have the right to appeal a conviction, just like adults do.

Check Your Knowledge

1. Outline the key differences among the *Juvenile Delinquents Act*, the *Young Offenders Act*, and the *Youth Criminal Justice Act*.
2. Explain the legal rights of youths when they are arrested.
3. In your opinion, are extrajudicial measures and sanctions effective? Explain.
4. Outline the sentencing options available to a youth court judge, and give an example of each.

Apply Your Learning

5. Section 42(2) of the *Youth Criminal Justice Act* states sentences for first- and second-degree murder. In paragraph (q), the youth court must order the youth to serve a sentence of no more than 10 years for first-degree murder. The sentence for second-degree murder can be no more than seven years. Are there conditions that justify a youth serving a life sentence for murder? Support your opinion.

6. The media and public are paying more attention to group assaults, or "swarmings." The sense is that there are more assaults and that they are more violent. They also seem to be more senseless and random. Many reported swarmings are unplanned and unorganized or loosely organized. Sometimes racism, prejudice, or hatred is the reason for the assault (for example, attacks on gays and lesbians). Other assaults do not have an obvious cause. Toronto Police Services suggest that about six swarmings happened each day in 2007 in Toronto.

   a) Does swarming occur in your school and, if so, to what extent?

   b) Do you think youths act differently in groups than they do when they are alone?

Communicate Your Understanding

7. Debate the following topics in class. Prepare a brief introduction, and identify the facts and arguments that support your position. Anticipate opposite points of view, and prepare arguments. Conclude with a summary of your position.

   a) The age of criminal accountability should be lowered to seven.

   b) Teens over 14 who commit serious offences should no longer have their identities protected.

   c) Offenders aged 16 and older should automatically be tried in adult court.

   d) Youth criminals aged 14 and older should receive life sentences for first- or second-degree murder.

   e) Zero-tolerance policies are extreme and are not the way to deal with school violence.

8. In 2008, there was a report on safe schools in Toronto. Julian Falconer wrote that female students suffered intense sexual harassment and ridicule. School safety policies treat genders the same way. Most efforts focus on dealing with violence between males. They receive more attention and funding. Bullying, sexual exploitation, and violence against females do not receive the same attention.

   a) Conduct an Internet search, and prepare a summary of the findings of the Falconer Report.

   b) Are there "alarming rates" of harassment and assault on young women in high schools? Conduct an Internet search to determine the answer.

   c) In groups, prepare a brochure or a video presentation of ways to combat bullying and sexual harassment in your school.

Develop Your Thinking

9. Professor Nicholas Bala is a law professor and youth justice expert at Queen's University. He made the following statement about the Supreme Court's decision in *R. v. D.B.* (see page 344): "I think [the Supreme Court judges] have recognized that youth is a distinctive status, not only in terms of physical status, but they have given it constitutional recognition." Write a report or opinion piece of at least one page explaining what the professor means. Do you agree with him? Why or why not?

10. Youth crime is a controversial issue for Canadians. Some people believe in retribution and that we should be tough on youth criminals. Others believe in rehabilitation and that we should work with these youth. We should give them a second chance, and make them productive members of society.

   a) Which is more important when it comes to youth criminals: fairness to the accused, or the safety and protection of society? Why?

   b) Does custody rehabilitate youths? Does it make them positive and productive members of society? Explain.

   c) On the whole, do you think the *Youth Criminal Justice Act* is effective in balancing the interests and protection of society with the rights of youth criminals? Justify your opinion.

   d) You are in a senior high school law class. Are you able to understand the consequences of your actions? Discuss with a partner.

Unit

Civil Law

3

Chapter 11
Resolving Civil Disputes   358

Chapter 12
Negligence and Other Torts   388

"The most advanced justice system in the world is a failure if it does not provide justice to the people it is meant to serve. Access to justice is therefore critical."

—Beverley McLachlin
Chief Justice, Supreme Court of Canada

Resolving Civil Disputes

What You Should Know

- What are the differences between criminal and civil law?
- What is a tort?
- What are the procedures involved in bringing a civil action to trial?
- What are the types of damages and other remedies available for resolving civil disputes?
- What is alternative dispute resolution (ADR), and what are the most common forms?

Selected Key Terms

arbitration
balance of probabilities
class action
default judgment
garnishment
general damages
injunction

litigation
mediation
punitive damages
special damages
statement of claim
statement of defence
tort

Chapter at a Glance

11.1 Introduction
11.2 Crimes and Torts
11.3 Civil Courts and Trial Procedures
11.4 Judgment and Civil Remedies
11.5 Alternative Dispute Resolution (ADR)

Avenue East

Small Claims Courts

ONTARIO DISABILITY SUPPORT PROGRAM (ODSP)

Landlord & Board

Why is small claims court often called "the people's court"?

11.1 Introduction

Civil law is also known as private law. It regulates disputes between individuals. It also regulates disputes between individuals and organizations such as businesses or governments. Society does not have the same interest in regulating civil disputes as it does with criminal matters. Civil disputes only directly concern the parties involved, not all of society. If somebody murders another person, society is concerned. If a neighbour's fence is leaning over onto your property, only you and your neighbour are concerned. If a shopper slips on a wet floor in a store, only the shopper and store are primarily concerned. But, it is likely that the store will change its safety policies after a civil lawsuit. This will make the store safer for the general public.

As you learned in Chapter 4, the main purpose of *criminal law* is to punish the offenders and to protect society from dangerous people. The main purpose of civil law is to compensate for harm. One person may bring an action against the person who committed the civil wrong for **damages** (in the form of a money award) or some other civil remedy (such as a court order stopping something from being done). Review Chapter 1, page 11, for the various categories of civil law.

damages money awarded to a plaintiff for harm or injury suffered

Typical Civil Actions

- Tort law—injuries done by one person to another person's body, property, or reputation and claims arising from serious accidents
- Family law—marriage, divorce, child custody, support claims, division of property, and adoption
- Contract law—failure to pay for work done, something bought but not yet delivered, and non-payment of rent
- Labour law—wrongful dismissal from work, unpaid overtime
- Property law—disputes about ownership of property

These are examples of the most common divisions of civil law and the types of legal actions that would be brought to civil courts.

 You Be the Judge

Rudman v. Hollander, 2005 BCSC 1342 (CanLII)

For more information, Go to Nelson Social Studies

On June 16, 2001, the plaintiff, Barret Rudman broke both elbows when he went over the handlebars of his bicycle. He was braking hard in a "panic" stop to avoid colliding with Charles Hollander's car. Evidence was conflicting about how far apart the car and bike were when Rudman applied his brakes and fell.

Rudman was riding behind Hollander's car as they approached a stop sign. As Hollander's car was reducing speed approaching the intersection, Rudman was increasing speed. The plaintiff had bought the bike six weeks earlier and had never

attempted such a stop before. Rudman claimed that Hollander slowed abruptly and moved to the right, blocking him from passing between Hollander's car and the curb. Hollander testified that he did not apply his brakes until after he heard a noise behind him, stopped to investigate, and saw Rudman and his bike on the ground; there was no collision. There was no evidence such as skid marks indicating a rapid slowing of the defendant's vehicle.

- What do you think the judge decided in this case? Explain.

tort a civil wrong or injury

Civil procedure, trials, judgments, and remedies are examined in this chapter. **Tort** law, a major division of civil law, is the subject of Chapter 12. The word "tort" means a wrong that could be either intentional or unintentional (negligent). Until the nineteenth century, tort law dealt mainly with intentional wrongs such as trespass. What made tort law important was the emergence of negligence, which will be discussed in greater detail in Chapter 12. Important aspects of family law, contract law, and employment law follow in Chapters 13 to 16.

11.2 Crimes and Torts

As you know, Canada's justice system involves both criminal and civil law. Both concern wrongs, and in some cases the same wrong; some actions may involve both a crime and a tort. Publicly, the victim calls the police, who may lay charges, which are then prosecuted by the Crown attorney according to the *Criminal Code*. Privately, however, the person can also sue under civil law for damages.

Some actions involve both a crime and a tort.

Crimes and Torts

If a person ...	It may be a crime of ...	And also the tort of ...
hits another person	assault	battery
breaks into someone's property	break and enter	trespass to land
takes someone's belongings	theft	trespass to goods

Assume that Andrew drives home while under the influence of alcohol after an evening of drinking. He hits Andrea, who is walking home with friends. Society, represented by the Crown, may begin criminal action against Andrew. This could be for careless driving, driving with a blood-alcohol level that is over the legal limit, and impaired driving causing bodily harm. If convicted, Andrew will be punished under the *Criminal Code*.

At the same time, Andrea can begin a civil action. She can sue Andrew for compensation (usually money damages) for her injuries and other losses suffered. It is Andrea's responsibility to bring this civil action. A civil court may award her damages that are "suitable and reasonable" in the court's view for her injuries.

Each action, criminal and civil, proceeds independently of the other. Each case is tried in a different court with a different judge and different lawyers, and there is no set order in which the cases must be tried. But, if Andrew is convicted first in a criminal court, this may help Andrea in her pursuit of damages in a civil action. See the *McIntyre v. Grigg* case on pages 376–377 for a similar case.

People who can prove that they have suffered injury or loss through another person's fault deserve some remedy. Financial payment is the most common and important purpose of tort law from the plaintiff's viewpoint. Some tort actions also contain elements of punishment and deterrence. Interesting tort cases are often followed closely by the media. The publicity may affect the future actions of many people, including the parties involved and the general public. For example, a customer takes action against a fast-food outlet after finding a dead fly in the bottled water. This might have a negative effect on the company's sales and public image (this case is explored in Chapter 12 on page 397, in *Mustapha v. Culligan of Canada Ltd.*). The company would want to avoid another similar lawsuit. Most likely, the negative publicity would cause other bottled-water companies to review and improve their production facilities and quality-control procedures. If a court awarded Andrea substantial compensation in the car accident caused by Andrew, this could have an effect on other careless drivers.

Review Your Understanding

1. Define "tort." Give three examples of torts.
2. List the five main branches of civil law, and provide two examples of each.
3. How can an offence be both a crime and a tort? Give an example.
4. Identify the main purpose of tort law.
5. Explain how a judgment in a tort action might also contain an element of deterrence.

In *Liebeck v. McDonald's Restaurants*, 1994, an American civil jury awarded Stella Liebeck $2.9 million. She suffered third-degree burns when she spilled a cup of hot coffee on her lap. The trial judge reduced the award to $640 000. The parties settled for a confidential amount before an appeal. Many Canadians regard civil suits like Stella Liebeck's as frivolous (silly or wasteful). What do you think?

11.3 Civil Courts and Trial Procedures

Civil actions involving large sums of money or complex issues are tried in your province's supreme court, and they might be appealed to your provincial court of appeal. Some cases might even end up in the Supreme Court of Canada. The role of the courts in civil disputes is to provide a way of resolving conflicts. One court that deals specifically with smaller civil actions is discussed below.

Small Claims Court

Sometimes called "the people's court," **small claims court** provides an informal and inexpensive way for settling disputes. Cases are tried informally by a judge without a jury. The judge allows both parties the chance to explain their side of the story. The parties are not expected to know legal procedures. In most cases, the parties represent themselves in simple disputes, although they may use a lawyer for more complex matters. Many businesses use this court to collect unpaid accounts from customers

small claims court the court to resolve civil claims of $10 000 or less

All provinces and territories have free, easy-to-read booklets with step-by-step procedures for filing a claim. Also, court staff may sometimes have time to answer questions and explain how to fill out the proper forms. Most forms follow a fill-in-the-blank format. The staff cannot provide you with any legal advice or complete the forms for you. It is important to realize that the case cannot proceed until you have completed and filed the necessary paperwork and paid the corresponding court fee.

e Activity

To learn more about filing a claim,

Go to Nelson Social Studies

Typical Small Claims Actions

- breach of contract
- claims for minor accidents
- damage to property
- recovery of property
- unpaid bills
- unpaid loans
- unpaid rent
- unpaid wages

The dollar limit for such claims varies from province to province. It currently ranges from $5000 to $25 000. If the amount of your claim is greater than your province's small claims court limit, you may still sue in that court. It is simpler and less expensive. But, you forfeit (give up) the right to recover the amount over the small claims court limit. A person considering a civil action must carefully choose the court to sue in.

All About Law DVD

"Small Claims Court" from *All About Law DVD*

Small Claims Court Maximums, 2002 and 2008

Province	2002	2008
Alberta	$7 500	$25 000
British Columbia	$10 000	$25 000
Manitoba	$7 500	$10 000
New Brunswick	$6 000	$6 000
Newfoundland and Labrador	$3 000	$5 000
Northwest Territories*	$5 000	$10 000
Nova Scotia	$10 000	$25 000
Ontario†	$10 000	$10 000
Prince Edward Island	$8 000	$8 000
Québec	$3 000	$7 000
Saskatchewan	$5 000	$20 000
Yukon	$5 000	$25 000

*Nunavut does not currently have a small claims division in its court structure. Small claims are heard through the Northwest Territories small claims court.

†Ontario will increase its limit to $25 000 in 2010.

Balance of Probabilities

balance of probabilities the standard of proof in a civil case meaning "more probable than not"

litigation legal action to settle a civil dispute

litigant one of the parties involved in a civil action; the plaintiff or defendant

A civil lawsuit involves two parties: the plaintiff, who is suing, and the defendant, who is being sued. If more than one person or party has suffered the harm, all injured parties should sue together as plaintiffs in one action (a class action). If more than one person is responsible for causing the loss, they all should be sued as defendants. The process of suing is called **litigation**. The parties in the action are the **litigants** (the plaintiff and the defendant). Often, the litigants settle their differences without an actual trial. In the following case, the plaintiff, Ferguson, is suing the defendant, Birchmount Boarding Kennels Ltd., for compensation, claiming that the kennel has caused harm or injury.

Ferguson v. Birchmount Boarding Kennels Ltd., 2006 CanLII 2049 (ON S.C.D.C.)

For more information, Go to Nelson Social Studies

In August 2002, Susan Ferguson and Ross Hagans left their dog, Harley, with Birchmount Boarding Kennels while they went on vacation. The couple adopted Harley in 1994. They had regularly boarded

When people leave their pets with a boarding kennel, they assume that their pet will be safe and protected. Do you think the damages awarded in this case were too high?

him with Birchmount since 1996. This time, Harley escaped from the kennel's enclosed play area and was never found. The kennel co-owner testified that he had examined the fence before and after the incident. He did not see any hole or gap in the fence. The evidence also established that the kennel staff conducted daily inspections of the fence. Of thousands of dogs boarded over the years, only two had previously escaped from the yard.

The plaintiffs sued the defendants for damages for pain and suffering related to the loss of their beloved dog. Ferguson was particularly upset about Harley's escape. She was unable to work and had nightmares. They were successful in small claims court and were awarded $1527.42 in damages plus $1000 in costs. Birchmount appealed, arguing that the damages were too high because Harley was only a dog, not a person. They lost the appeal.

For Discussion

1. Why did Ferguson and Hagans bring an action against Birchmount Boarding Kennels?

2. Summarize the plaintiff's arguments for her civil action.

3. Summarize the arguments made by the defendant.

4. Do you agree with the appeal court's decision? Discuss with a partner.

In several provinces, minors may sue on their own for up to $500. A minor is anyone under the age of 18 or 19, depending on the province. If a minor wants to sue for more than $500, a parent, guardian, or a litigation guardian, must act for the minor.

In a civil action, the burden of proof is on the plaintiff. The plaintiff is not required to prove the case beyond a reasonable doubt, as is required in a criminal trial. Instead, plaintiffs must try to convince a judge that the events most likely took place in the way they claim. This is known in legal terms as proving the case on the balance of probabilities. Of course, the defendant will then try to show that his or her version is what really happened. The judge will decide whose side is more believable and more likely to have happened.

 You and the Law

If you are a minor and want to sue someone for more than $500, a responsible adult must act on your behalf. Why is this required? Do you agree with this legal principle? Why or why not?

Martinig v. Powell River (Corp. of the District of), 2002 BCSC 24 (CanLII)

For more information, 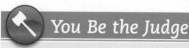 Go to Nelson Social Studies

Powell River is a small community on mainland British Columbia that is known for its recreation facilities.

Colleen Martinig was injured playing softball on a field when she caught her foot in a small hole near first base. The field was owned by the town of Powell River, the defendant. The field was inspected by the parks manager and two coaches before the game as part of the regular maintenance system for the park. Martinig was aware of the uneven field. Martinig sued for her injuries.

• Do you think she was successful in her action? Why or why not?

Before discussing the procedures in a civil action, look at the following chart to compare procedures for both criminal and civil actions.

Criminal and Civil Procedures Compared

Case Factors	Criminal/Public Law	Civil/Private Law
Parties involved	Crown attorney versus accused	Plaintiff versus defendant
Grounds/reason	To determine innocence or guilt of accused	To resolve a dispute
Purpose of action	To punish offender	To compensate for harm
Onus of proof	On Crown attorney	On plaintiff
Burden of proof	Beyond a reasonable doubt	Balance of probabilities
Result of action	Accused is guilty or not guilty	Defendant is liable or not liable for damages
Action taken if defendant is guilty or liable	Accused sentenced	Plaintiff awarded some compensation or remedy

What are the similarities and differences between criminal and civil law procedures?

Civil Trial Procedures

What actually happens during a civil procedure? Assume that Bjorn runs a red light and hits Kate's car, damaging the car and injuring Kate. As in the earlier example involving Andrew and Andrea, the Crown may lay criminal charges against Bjorn for the accident. Kate, too, must decide if she has a valid reason for suing Bjorn. If Kate thinks she has grounds to sue, she must then decide on the proper court (small claims court or her provincial supreme/superior court) in which to proceed. As you have learned, the court in which a civil action is tried depends on the amount of money involved.

You will learn later in this chapter that going to court is not the only option. However, it is often the only way to settle a dispute when the parties have very different versions of the same event.

Filing and Serving a Claim

Assume that Kate's action begins in small claims court. Her first step is to file a **statement of claim**, which must include the following:

- her full name and address
- Bjorn's full name and address
- the amount of money she is claiming
- a brief, clear summary of the reason for the claim

statement of claim the legal document in a civil action outlining the plaintiff's case

If more than one defendant is involved, each one must be named and identified correctly.

After completing the claim, Kate mails or hand-delivers it to the court clerk, along with the required filing fee. The fee is the cost of handling the claim. The amount depends on the amount the plaintiff is claiming. Generally, the larger the claim, the larger the fee. The filing fee is added to the claim by the court. Once the claim has been processed by the court, it must be served on the defendant. It may be delivered personally by Kate, by a friend or business associate, or by a private process-serving agency so that the court knows that the defendant, or a responsible adult, has received the claim.

Criminal charges against a person can be brought as long as the accused is alive. Civil action must be brought within a certain period of time following the event. This is called the **limitation period**, which is outlined in each province's *Limitations Act*. These range from two to five years, depending on the reason for the claim. The claim must be served within six months from its date of issue. If it cannot be served within six months, it can be renewed by a judge.

limitation period a time period imposed by law

When Bjorn receives the claim, he has between 10 and 30 days to respond, depending on the province. He has three main options:

1. Accept total responsibility and settle the claim.
2. File a defence, explaining his version of the event.
3. Do nothing and ignore the claim.

The Crown may lay criminal charges against Bjorn for running a red light and hitting Kate's car. Kate can proceed in a civil suit against Bjorn if she has a cause of action.

Defence or Reply

statement of defence
the defendant's response to the plaintiff's complaint

If Bjorn feels that he does not owe Kate anything, he prepares a **statement of defence**. This is a document that clearly outlines his reasons for disagreeing with her claim. Bjorn may have a number of reasons. He might argue that the light was not red when he went through it and hit Kate's car, or he might say that the brakes on his car failed and he could not stop in time to prevent the accident. If Bjorn enters a defence, a copy of it will be sent to Kate by the court office.

Payment into Court

If Bjorn feels that Kate is entitled to some, but not all, of her claim, he can pay that amount to the small claims court office. Kate will then be notified. She can either accept the amount and drop the balance of her claim, or pursue the case in the hope of obtaining the full amount.

Counterclaim

counterclaim the defendant's suit against the plaintiff for damages or other relief

default judgment judgment for the plaintiff as a result of the defendant's failure to respond to the plaintiff's claim within the time allowed

Bjorn may also make a **counterclaim**, saying that it was actually Kate who was at fault for the accident. He may attempt to claim damages from her for his own loss or injury. A counterclaim must relate to the problem that caused the plaintiff's claim. When a civil action involves damage to vehicles, the defendant will often counterclaim.

In this example, Bjorn defends against Kate's claim and makes one of his own against her. He argues that she began to move before her traffic light had turned green or that she was driving too quickly to stop (or some other reason for his counterclaim). If the case comes to trial, the judge will examine both the plaintiff's claim and the defendant's counterclaim at the same time. The judge will decide who is at fault, what percentage each is at fault, and who will receive what amount from whom (60/40, 80/20, 100/0).

Third-Party Claim

Another option available to the defendant is to involve a third party. This is someone who the defendant feels is partly or completely responsible for the dispute. For example, if Bjorn had his brakes repaired just before the accident, and if their failure was responsible for the accident, Bjorn might involve the repair shop and mechanic as a third party to share some of the blame and the cost. Doing this saves time and money. The case can proceed in the presence of all three parties. Otherwise, Bjorn would have to sue the repair shop separately.

Default Judgment

If Bjorn does not reply to the claim within the required time period, known legally as entering an appearance, a **default judgment** is automatically made against him. This means that Kate wins and is awarded a judgment against Bjorn by default, since he has not responded to the claim. The court considers that the defendant agrees with the claim, and Kate is entitled to recover the amount she claimed plus any related costs.

If the defendant fails to appear in court, a judgment is automatically made against him or her. The gavel is a symbol of justice, but it is an American symbol. Canadian judges do not use gavels.

Out-of-Court Settlement

At any point, either party can make a formal or informal offer to settle the dispute instead of proceeding to trial. The litigants should make every effort to negotiate an **out-of-court settlement**. The plaintiff must balance the proposed offer with the chance of winning the full claim at trial. Kate might prefer to settle for a portion of her claim rather than become involved in a long trial. Settling before a trial saves time and money.

out-of-court settlement when the parties to a lawsuit settle the case before trial

Pre-Trial Conference

A pre-trial conference, or settlement conference, is the last chance for the parties to resolve the dispute before trial. Both litigants will meet with a judge or a court-appointed referee who encourages the parties to settle the claim. The conference allows each party to hear a basic summary of the other's case so there are no surprises at trial. Based on discussions, the judge may give an opinion of the possible judgment if the case moves to trial. Many cases are settled on the basis of this opinion, without going to trial. The parties can discuss matters openly and honestly. The pre-trial conference judge is not the trial judge. If the parties cannot reach an agreement during the pre-trial conference, a trial date will be set.

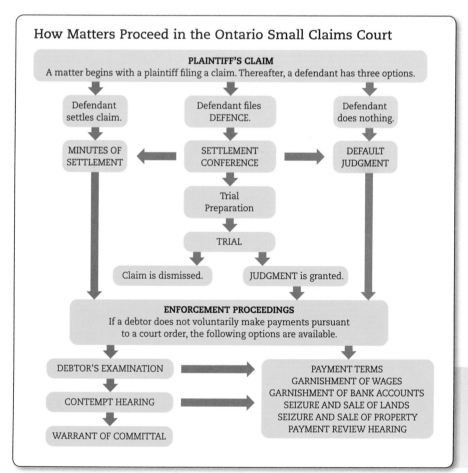

How Matters Proceed in the Ontario Small Claims Court

PLAINTIFF'S CLAIM
A matter begins with a plaintiff filing a claim. Thereafter, a defendant has three options.

Defendant settles claim. → Defendant files DEFENCE. → Defendant does nothing.

MINUTES OF SETTLEMENT ← SETTLEMENT CONFERENCE → DEFAULT JUDGMENT

Trial Preparation

TRIAL

Claim is dismissed.   JUDGMENT is granted.

ENFORCEMENT PROCEEDINGS
If a debtor does not voluntarily make payments pursuant to a court order, the following options are available.

DEBTOR'S EXAMINATION →
CONTEMPT HEARING →
WARRANT OF COMMITTAL

PAYMENT TERMS
GARNISHMENT OF WAGES
GARNISHMENT OF BANK ACCOUNTS
SEIZURE AND SALE OF LANDS
SEIZURE AND SALE OF PROPERTY
PAYMENT REVIEW HEARING

There are three possibilities once a plaintiff files a claim in Ontario Small Claims Court, as shown in this chart.

Civil Procedure in Higher Courts

In higher courts, there are more procedures to help the parties settle their dispute to avoid going to trial. The litigants send legal documents back and forth over several months or even years. This attempts to define and narrow the disputed issues and to assist the judge in understanding the dispute details. Because of this, many cases tried in provincial superior courts take several years before reaching trial. This is called the discovery process.

examination for discovery in civil cases, a pre-trial process to learn the other side's evidence

The **examination for discovery** is a question-and-answer session for the litigants and their lawyers. It can last a few hours or several days. It is typically conducted in a lawyer's office without any court officials present. Its purpose is to limit the possibility of surprises at trial. It provides information about each side's case and allows the parties to reach agreement on certain issues. This reduces court time, saves money, and makes settlement easier.

Both parties must disclose *all* relevant documents, including photos, videotape, and computer files. If material evidence is withheld by one or both of the parties, contempt of court charges could be laid or the case could be thrown out. Either party can question the other under oath. The questions and answers are transcribed by the court reporter and are available at trial. Either party can also ask the court to issue an order permitting inspection of physical objects in the case. In our example, Kate's and Bjorn's cars and photographs from the accident scene might be inspected. If Kate claimed for serious injuries from the accident, Bjorn could request X-rays and medical reports. Often, the parties settle the case after discovery, when both sides realize it would take a lot of time and money to pursue the case any further.

Examination for discovery is a crucial part of most civil actions. In Ontario, discovery hearings will be limited to one day per side, unless the parties involved or the court agree to an extension.

The Trial

If no settlement can be reached, the parties go to court for a trial by judge alone or by a judge and a civil jury of six people (except in small claims court, where only a judge hears cases). In some provinces, civil actions are never tried by a jury. Although juries play a key role in criminal trials, they are not often used for civil actions for damages.

Procedures in a civil trial are similar to those used in criminal trials. Each party has a chance to present his or her case by calling witnesses; parties can also testify themselves if they choose. The plaintiff goes first, followed by the defendant. When all the evidence has been presented, each party sums up his or her case and makes a final argument to the judge. The judge will make a decision to allow none, part, or all of the claim.

 Did You Know?

In 2005–2006, only 23 percent of civil actions in Ontario were jury trials. Most involved actions for motor vehicle accidents.

In a trial by jury, the judge instructs the jury members on the law applicable to the facts of the case. The jury must consider the evidence, as well as questions such as these:

- Who was at fault, and what caused the injuries or loss?
- Is that person totally at fault, or are both parties somewhat to blame?
- How should damages be determined?
- How much should the damages be?

All these factors must be considered in reaching a judgment. (If there is no jury, the judge does all of the above.)

You Be the Judge

Thomas v. Hamilton (City), Board of Education, 1994 CanLII 739 (ON C.A.)

For more information, **Go to Nelson Social Studies**

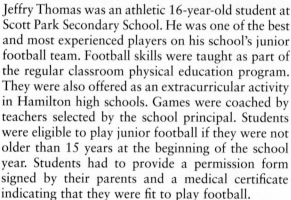

Jeffry Thomas was an athletic 16-year-old student at Scott Park Secondary School. He was one of the best and most experienced players on his school's junior football team. Football skills were taught as part of the regular classroom physical education program. They were also offered as an extracurricular activity in Hamilton high schools. Games were coached by teachers selected by the school principal. Students were eligible to play junior football if they were not older than 15 years at the beginning of the school year. Students had to provide a permission form signed by their parents and a medical certificate indicating that they were fit to play football.

Between 1980 and 1982, Thomas played football and basketball, rode his bike, jogged, and lifted weights four times a week. By the fall of 1982, he was 183 centimetres (6 feet) tall and weighed about 68 kilograms (150 pounds). In October

1982, during a football game, Thomas tackled an opposing player headfirst and went crashing into the punt returner's hip. Thomas was running at jogging speed or faster. The punt returner was running at full speed. All witnesses agreed that the contact between the two players was substantial, and that Thomas's body was extended but his head was not up at the point of contact. He and the other players had been taught to tackle with their shoulders, not their heads, and told that contact should be made with a shoulder. Thomas suffered serious injury to his cervical spine, which left him quadriplegic. Thomas and his family sued the school board and the school football coaches.

- Why do you think Thomas and his family brought a suit against the school board and the coaches? What would you have decided if you were the judge in this case?

Class Action Lawsuits

Class actions are lawsuits that permit groups of people who have suffered similar losses or injuries to come together in one efficient lawsuit. It means that persons who may not have been able to afford to sue on their own can act with others with a common interest against the same defendant. They share the costs of the lawsuit and the outcome. For example, if many consumers are injured because of an allegedly defective product, the key issue is whether the product caused the injuries. In the summer of 2007, a group announced that they planned to launch a class action against OxyContin, made by Purdue

class action a single legal action brought on behalf of all members of a group with a common grievance

A Mississauga, Ontario, banquet hall agreed to pay up to $1 million to guests who launched a class action lawsuit after becoming ill with E. coli poisoning in June 2003. Guests at several functions, including students at a high school graduation party, became ill from the disease. The settlement was distributed among 150 people. Each person received between $500 and $5000, depending on the severity of the symptoms.

Pharma. OxyContin is a painkiller drug that first arrived in pharmacies in the 1990s. It became the number-one pain reliever prescribed by doctors. Since its release, hundreds of fatal overdoses have been reported across Canada. The people in the Atlantic provinces bringing the suit stated that they became concerned when the manufacturer and three of its current and former executives pleaded guilty in a United States court to lying about the drug's risk of addiction. The men must pay U.S. litigants $634.5 million in fines for claiming the drug was less addictive and less subject to abuse than other pain medications.

In early 2008, former users of Merck's painkiller Vioxx and their families had class action suits approved to go ahead in Saskatchewan and Québec. Vioxx was pulled off the market in 2004 after researchers linked it to increased risks of heart problems. The class action suits claim that the painkiller caused the plaintiffs' medical problems, including heart attacks and strokes. Merck plans to appeal these decisions. The company believes each plaintiff's case should be tried separately. In November 2007, Merck agreed to pay $4.85 billion to settle similar claims in the United States.

Canada's federal government is settling a major class action suit involving Aboriginal residential schools. For almost three decades from 1930 to 1970, about 80 000 students were forcefully taken from their families and placed in these residential schools. Their native culture was dismissed. Many suffered sexual and physical abuse (see the timeline below and on page 371). Each of the former residents is to receive compensation of about $10 000, plus $3000 for each year spent in the once-mandatory schools. This will cost the government approximately $2 billion.

Multimillion-dollar class action suits are much more common in the United States. Legal observers suggest that they are coming to Canada. More product liability matters and consumer disputes are being filed. Examples of such suits are for the following:

- manufacturing allegedly defective or hazardous products (for example, asbestos, tobacco, silicone gel breast implants, and certain pesticides like Agent Orange—see Chapter 12, page 418)

This timeline provides an overview of events leading up to the historic settlement for victims of residential school abuse. It is the first time in Canadian legal history that so many courts have been involved in the approval of a class action lawsuit.

Residential Schools

Attendance at residential schools is made compulsory for all Aboriginal children ages 7–15. Children were forcibly removed from families by priests, Indian agents, and police.	There are 80 residential schools in Canada with about 7800 students.	There are 74 residential schools in Canada with about 9300 students.	There are 12 residential schools with 1900 students.	Former students of residential schools begin disclosing sexual and other forms of abuse.
1920	**1931**	**1948**	**1979**	**1980s**

- mass environmental injury, such as chemical spills and contamination
- mass injury, such as results of airplane crashes
- charging cellphone customers for incoming text messages

Threats of class actions have become a concern for manufacturers. They are time-consuming and expensive to defend. Also, companies run the risk of having to pay substantial settlements or court awards. Class action suits can also be brought against employers. Large companies, including Wal-Mart, Starbucks, and Taco Bell, have had to pay unpaid overtime to employees.

Benefits of Joining a Class Action

- They avoid the necessity for hundreds, or thousands, of people to file similar individual lawsuits.
- They seek to ensure that people with similar claims are treated similarly.
- They help eliminate common barriers, such as economic barriers, that prevent people from pursuing legal action.

Which of the benefits of joining a class action lawsuit do you think is the most important? Why?

Review Your Understanding

1. List five examples of cases heard in small claims court.
2. In a civil action, what does the "balance of probabilities" mean? How does it differ from the burden of proof in a criminal trial?
3. What three options are available to a defendant who has just received a plaintiff's statement of claim?
4. What is the purpose of an examination for discovery, and what are its benefits?
5. What is a class action lawsuit, and what are the benefits of joining such an action?

 Did You Know?

In August 2008, separate class action lawsuits were filed in four provinces against Maple Leaf Foods. Up to 20 Canadians died from listeriosis from tainted meat—15 in Ontario. In December 2008, the company agreed to pay up to $27 million to settle these lawsuits.

In 2007, Dara Fresco, an employee of CIBC, filed a $600-million claim with the Ontario Superior Court of Justice. She alleged that the bank failed to compensate workers for overtime. This may be the largest unpaid overtime class action in Canadian legal history.

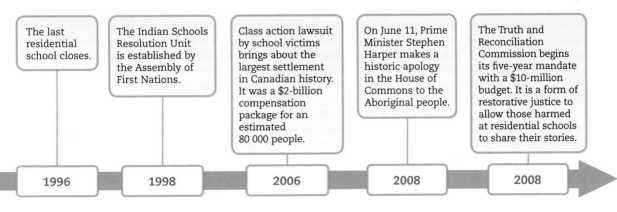

The last residential school closes.	The Indian Schools Resolution Unit is established by the Assembly of First Nations.	Class action lawsuit by school victims brings about the largest settlement in Canadian history. It was a $2-billion compensation package for an estimated 80 000 people.	On June 11, Prime Minister Stephen Harper makes a historic apology in the House of Commons to the Aboriginal people.	The Truth and Reconciliation Commission begins its five-year mandate with a $10-million budget. It is a form of restorative justice to allow those harmed at residential schools to share their stories.
1996	1998	2006	2008	2008

11.4 Judgment and Civil Remedies

At the end of a civil trial, the judge delivers a judgment. In small claims court, the judge often gives an oral judgment while all the parties involved are still present. In higher courts, the judge usually needs some time to review the evidence and the relevant law. A judge is then said to be "reserving judgment." This means that he or she is delaying a decision to review the evidence and write a judgment.

Civil Remedies

Damages for the plaintiff's injury or loss are the most common remedy in tort actions. The intent is to return plaintiffs, as much as possible, to the same position they were in before the loss or injury. In the case of severe injury, such as total paralysis, no amount of money can adequately compensate victims. The major reason for awarding damages in such cases is to help plaintiffs with the cost of future care and to compensate for future loss of income. Judges try to award similar amounts for similar injuries. They review past cases and precedents to determine appropriate awards. Judges are not bound by what other judges have awarded in similar cases. Those awards give them guidance as to the range of damages. There are five types of damages: general, special, punitive, aggravated, and nominal. Plaintiffs may be awarded one or more of these.

General Damages

general damages court ordered compensation for proven losses in a civil action

pecuniary damages a form of general damages for losses that can be reasonably calculated

non-pecuniary damages a form of general damages for losses that do not involve an actual loss of money and thus are difficult to determine

General damages are those that cannot be easily or precisely calculated. They require a judge's or jury's discretion. There are two main categories:

- **Pecuniary damages**—for loss of income and future earnings and the cost of specialized future care

- **Non-pecuniary damages**—for pain and suffering and for loss of enjoyment of life

The word "pecuniary" means related to money. If the plaintiff cannot work because of the defendant's actions, the judge must consider the loss of income. This includes what the plaintiff was earning at the time of the accident and future earnings. The longer the injured plaintiff is expected to live without being able to work, the greater the compensation. If the victim has a job or had definite plans to enter a specific profession or trade, then the average earnings for that occupation may be used. The settlement must be fair to both the plaintiff and the defendant. Other pecuniary costs include costs for future care such as professional help, special equipment, access to facilities, and medication necessary to assist the plaintiff in daily life.

While pecuniary damages may be difficult to determine, calculating non-pecuniary damages is even more difficult. How do you place a price on pain and suffering? What is the loss of enjoyment of life worth to a person permanently injured in an accident? Should an athlete with a promising career and the thrill of winning an Olympic medal be given more for pain and suffering for injuries than a non-athlete? Money cannot always restore what has been injured or lost. It can provide substitutes

Every year many students are injured in physical education classes.

for pleasures that are no longer possible. Compensation can make it possible for an injured plaintiff who can no longer skate or ski to enjoy a winter vacation of a different kind.

 Looking Back

The 1978 Supreme Court of Canada Trilogy

In the United States, there are highly publicized cases in which plaintiffs are awarded millions of dollars. As a result, many Canadians believe cases will be settled the same way. That is not so. Canadian courts take a cautious, or reasonable, and uniquely Canadian approach to cases.

In 1978, three cases (the trilogy) came before the Supreme Court of Canada. They were *Thornton v. Prince George School District No. 57*, *Teno v. Arnold*, and *Andrews v. Grand & Toy Alberta Ltd*. In each, the Supreme Court had to determine appropriate damages for the following, respectively:

- a 17-year-old high school student who fractured his spinal cord in a physical education class resulting in the loss of use of all limbs
- a four-year-old girl who suffered serious brain damage and debilitating physical injuries after crossing the street to buy an ice cream cone
- a 21-year-old man who became a quadriplegic from a traffic accident involving a Grand & Toy driver

The Supreme Court outlined the factors to consider for awards for pain and suffering in very serious cases, those resulting in severe, life-long physical incapacity. The court capped (limited) the maximum award at $100 000 in most cases. These exclude "exceptional circumstances." As well, it is based on how severe the injury is and the victim's disability. The cap is the key difference between the tort liability systems in Canada and the United States. The policy is to control rising claims. It also promotes fairness in personal injury damage awards across Canada.

Since 1978, judges and courts have maintained the cap. The few exceptions were cases where the plaintiff's injuries were more devastating than those of the victims in the trilogy cases. In *Lindal v. Lindal*, 1981, the Supreme Court stated that the cap should increase over time to reflect inflation. In the three decades since the trilogy, the $100 000 limit has risen roughly three times.

Most recently, a judgment from the British Columbia Court of Appeal in *Lee v. Dawson*, 2006,

confirms that the cap is still being followed. Ik Sang Lee was seriously injured in a car accident. A trial jury awarded him $2 million in general damages. The trial judge reduced that award to the cap. At the time of trial, it was $294 600. Both parties appealed. The plaintiff wanted the $2-million judgment restored. The defendant sought a further reduction, but both appeals were dismissed. Leave to appeal to the Supreme Court of Canada was also dismissed, thus keeping the cap in place—for now.

The Supreme Court has not set a cap on general damages for loss of reputation. In *Young v. Bella*, 2006 (see the case on page 374), the court indicated that courts can award general damages above the cap for pain and suffering set by the trilogy. The *Young* decision represents an important development in Canadian law. It should make employers take greater care when giving references that could be harmful.

For Discussion

1. List two reasons why the Supreme Court of Canada established a cap for damages for pain and suffering.

2. What factors should courts consider when awarding damages for pain and suffering?

3. In the case of permanent disability, a key issue to determine is whether the victim's future care should be in a long-term care facility or a modified home or apartment. Although home care is preferable, it is more expensive. In a chart, research the advantages and disadvantages of a long-term care facility versus a modified home environment.

4. In *Lee v. Dawson*, the British Columbia Court of Appeal refused to "overturn the trilogy." Should this trilogy cap be reviewed and removed? With a partner, discuss the advantages and disadvantages of such an action.

Young v. Bella, 2006 SCC 3 (CanLII)

For more information, **Go to Nelson Social Studies**

In 1994, Wanda Young was a student at Memorial University in Newfoundland. She wanted to become a social worker. She gave her final assignment on the treatment of juvenile sex offenders to her professor, Leslie Bella. In it, she illustrated her point that victims of sexual abuse often become abusers. She included a first-person anecdote of a woman who sexually abused a child while babysitting. Young added the source in her bibliography. She did not footnote it in the body of the assignment.

Professor Bella thought the excerpt was from Young's personal experience. Bella believed it was a cry for help, based on Young's own experience. Bella told her director about it. Young was reported to the Child Protection Services branch of the Newfoundland and Labrador government. Young was listed on the provincial child abuse registry. Her name was red flagged in the RCMP and social work communities. These were where she hoped to work after graduation. The report was investigated two years later.

The misunderstanding was cleared up within 24 hours. Young had to explain that the excerpt was a published quote and not about her.

Young took action against the professor and other defendants. She argued that their actions destroyed her chances of becoming a social worker. In 2003, a trial jury found the defendants at fault and awarded her damages of $839 000. In 2004, the Newfoundland Court of Appeal overturned the jury award. It believed that the university had acted in good faith. The university complied with child welfare laws that compel people to report suspected child abuse. It should be protected from any legal actions.

Young appealed this decision to the Supreme Court of Canada. Her appeal was heard in October 2005. In a 7–0 judgment in January 2006, the court allowed her appeal and restored the trial judgment.

For Discussion

1. Why did Wanda Young sue Memorial University as well as Professor Bella?

2. Newfoundland and Labrador's *Child Welfare Act* requires there to be "reasonable cause" to make a report to the Child Abuse Registry. There should be a balance between the protection of children, the protection of persons against unfounded allegations, and the protection of informants. Do you think "reasonable cause" to report existed here? Why or why not?

3. Young was awarded $430 000 for pain and suffering, anxiety, embarrassment, insomnia, and depression, and an additional $409 000 for lost income and future care. Do you think this was a reasonable judgment? Explain.

4. This case suggests that plaintiffs can receive more than the current cap on general damages as long as claims are based on psychological injury and recognized psychiatric illness, and do not arise from catastrophic physical injuries. Do you agree with this principle? Discuss with a partner.

Wanda Young (left) is shown here with her lawyer after she won her appeal in 2006. Young won $839 000 in damages for pain and suffering, embarrassment, depression, and lost income and future care.

Special Damages

special damages compensation for out-of-pocket expenses

punitive damages compensation to punish the defendant for malicious behaviour

Special damages cover out-of-pocket expenses occurring before trial. Receipts are not needed but help to calculate expenses. Such expenses may be ambulance service, hospital costs, therapy, and so on. Lost wages between the accident and the trial are also special damages because they can be calculated precisely.

Punitive Damages

Punitive damages are also known as exemplary damages. They are additional damages to punish offenders for their oppressive, insensitive, or malicious behaviour. Punitive damages are meant to condemn this conduct and to discourage offenders and the general public from behaving in a similar manner. The damages are usually not awarded if the defendant was punished by the criminal court for the same action. They are usually awarded for intentional torts (discussed in Chapter 12).

In January 1994, a fire totally destroyed the Whiten home. The insurance company denied the claim. It alleged that the Whitens were guilty of arson, but the allegations were untrue. In February 2002, in a 6–1 decision in *Whiten v. Pilot Insurance Co.*, the Supreme Court of Canada ordered Pilot to pay Daphne and Keith Whiten $1 million in punitive damages. This was the largest amount ever awarded in Canadian history.

Cornered by Mike Baldwin

"Last year you failed to bring me a new bicycle. This year, I want $250 for the bike and $50,000 in punitive damages."

This is a good example of a frivolous lawsuit for damages.

 ## You Be the Judge

Wolf, Ward, and Luck v. Advance Fur Dressers Ltd. et al., 2005 BCSC 1097 (CanLII)

For more information, **Go to Nelson Social Studies**

In August 2001, the three plaintiffs, Peter Wolf, John Ward, and Carson Luck, travelled to Zimbabwe for a hunting safari. Before leaving, they arranged with the defendant, Advance Fur Dressers Ltd., to process their hunting trophies. The defendant would make arrangements with Canada Customs to pick up the trophies. They would take them to their business in Vernon, British Columbia, to work on them. The defendant would deliver the trophies to the plaintiffs.

The plaintiffs had a successful safari, taking 25 animals, some of which were rare and others which were of exceptional size. The plaintiffs shipped their trophies home and contacted the defendant to state that the crates were on the way. Over the next two years, there was a lot of communication between the parties. Each time the defendant assured the plaintiffs that all was well and the trophies were being processed. In December 2003, the defendant wrote that the trophies were close to completion and would be ready for shipment very shortly. However, this was not true. The company had never claimed the trophies from Canada Customs. They used excuses ranging from a snowstorm, to the death of an employee, to mix-ups in their operations. In fact, the plaintiffs learned that Canada Customs had burned their trophies in 2002 since they had never been claimed.

The hunters sued the defendant for breach of contract, general damages for the destruction of their trophies and mental distress, and punitive damages. They also wanted damages for the full replacement cost each had paid for his trip to Zimbabwe, the hunting safari, and other miscellaneous expenses because each of the trophies had been unique.

- If you were the judge, would you grant this claim? If so, what damages would you award and why? If not, why not?

Aggravated Damages

Aggravated damages are similar to punitive damages. They are awarded when the defendant's behaviour harms the plaintiff. For example, the plaintiff may experience serious emotional shock or suffering because of the defendant. Punitive damages are intended to punish or deter defendants. Aggravated damages compensate the plaintiff for the defendant's intolerable conduct.

For example, a drug company makes a morning-sickness pill. It is later revealed that the pill causes birth defects. An investigation might show that the pill was not properly tested. In this case, the court could assess for punitive damages. On the other hand, an investigation might show that the company knew that the pill caused defects. The knowledge did not stop the company from marketing the pill. In this case, the court could award aggravated damages because of the company's appalling behaviour.

Nominal Damages

Nominal damages are awarded when a judge wants to indicate support for a plaintiff or defendant. The judge awards a small sum, such as $1 to $100. Such an award suggests that, although the plaintiff has suffered little or no loss or harm, he or she has won a moral victory. For example, someone trespasses on another person's property but does not damage anything. Nominal damages may be awarded to tell trespassers that they have affected the owner's right of property use.

aggravated damages compensation awarded for humiliation and mental distress

nominal damages compensation awarded as a moral victory to a plaintiff who has not sustained any actual losses

 Case

McIntyre v. Grigg, 2006 CanLII 37326 (ON C.A.)

For more information, Go to Nelson Social Studies

Hamilton Tiger-Cats wide receiver Andrew Grigg (left) was charged with several serious criminal offences and was sued after hitting a pedestrian, Andrea McIntyre, with his car while driving under the influence in 1996.

On September 13, 1996, Andrea McIntyre was a first-year McMaster University student and an outstanding athlete. She was walking home with friends from the university pub. Andrew Grigg, then a wide receiver with the Hamilton Tiger-Cats, drove through a stop sign. He made a reckless turn, hit a lamppost, and seriously injured McIntyre. She suffered several injuries, including mild brain trauma, a fractured femur, and recurring depression. She would never recover her athletic form.

After Grigg's arrest, a Breathalyzer test showed that his blood-alcohol content was two to three times over the legal limit. Grigg had been drinking at a student pub run by the McMaster Student Union that evening. He was charged with several serious criminal offences. However, Grigg had not been informed of his Charter right to legal counsel before being given a Breathalyzer test. The Crown attorney

continues...

McIntyre v. Grigg, 2006 CanLII 37326 (ON C.A.)

dropped all charges except for careless driving. Grigg pleaded guilty to that charge. He received a $500 fine and a licence suspension.

Six years later, Andrea was still in serious pain and required medication for the rest of her life. She also suffered severe depression and had made two unsuccessful suicide attempts. Her lifetime earning potential was reduced as a result of the accident. She launched a civil action against Grigg and the McMaster Student Union. The Union staff had failed to monitor Grigg's alcohol consumption. In March 2004, the jury awarded McIntyre $250 000 in general damages for pain and suffering. Grigg and his father, who owned the vehicle involved in the accident, were ordered to pay 70 percent of the damages. The McMaster Student Union was found 30 percent liable. The Griggs were also ordered to pay $100 000 in aggravated damages and $100 000 in punitive damages.

The Ontario Court of Appeal heard the defendants' appeal in May 2006. On November 6, in a 2–1 judgment, the appellate court cut the punitive damages award from $100 000 to $20 000. It also struck down the jury's $100 000 aggravated damages award. McMaster's appeal was also dismissed. The *McIntyre v. Grigg* case was the first time in Canada that punitive damages were awarded in an impaired driving case. It broke new ground in Canadian law.

For Discussion

1. What do you think of the trial judgment, the damages awarded, and the division of liability between the Griggs and McMaster Student Union? Discuss with a partner.

2. What are aggravated and punitive damages, and why was each awarded by the trial jury?

3. Why do you think the Ontario Court of Appeal struck down the aggravated damages award, but reduced the punitive damages award?

4. The dissenting justice stated: "All automobile-owning members of society will effectively be 'punished' for the conduct of Mr. Grigg and comparable drivers." What does he mean, and what are the possible implications?

Injunctions

Sometimes a plaintiff is not interested in cash compensation. Suppose that Kasey, Leo, and Ravinder are members of a rock band that rehearses late each evening at their home. Their neighbours, the Lafrattas, feel that they are being unfairly disturbed by the loud music. They ask the band to keep the noise down and they talk to the boys' parents. The Lafrattas then might ask the courts for an **injunction**. This is an order for a person to do or not do something. In this case, a court order to the band members might limit the rehearsals to reasonable hours. Similarly, a factory that is dumping its waste into a lake and polluting it might be subject to an injunction requiring the owners to stop this activity. Another common use of injunctions is to require striking workers to return to work.

Failure to comply with an injunction might result in a contempt of court charge. This could be followed by a fine or jail sentence. Finally, injunctions are increasingly used when a relationship has broken down and one party is harassing the other party. Issuing an injunction might prevent one spouse from selling the matrimonial home, for example. It could order the removal of the problem party from the home.

injunction a court order directing a person to do or not to do something for a specific time period

During the Olympic Games, injunctions are often issued to prevent unlawful use of the Olympic symbols and trademarks, such as this 2010 Olympic mascot.

Contingency Fees

contingency fee an arrangement between a plaintiff and a lawyer where the lawyer will be paid an agreed-upon percentage of the damages at the end of the case

Civil court actions are very expensive. Many people cannot afford to pay lawyer fees and court costs. The concept of **contingency fees** in civil law is common in American television and films. The idea is that a lawyer will take a case and not demand the usual retainer fee in advance. In fact, lawyers sometimes waive those fees altogether and instead agree to deduct a percentage from the judgment. This fee must be determined in advance in a written agreement between the client and the lawyer. If you lose the case, your lawyer receives nothing. Of course, because of the added risk, your lawyer will ask for a corresponding higher fee if he or she wins the case.

Some provinces have guidelines that limit the size of contingency fees. These can be between 20 and 40 percent of the amount of money awarded. The amount is based on the complexity and length of cases. All provincial rules state that a lawyer's fee must not exceed a fair and reasonable limit. The chart below outlines the advantages and disadvantages of contingency fees.

 Did You Know?

Contingency fees are not allowed for criminal and family law cases.

Advantages and Disadvantages of Contingency Fees

Advantages	Disadvantages
• They are practical when the plaintiff has a strong case. • They allow greater access to justice for persons who cannot afford a lawyer and who do not qualify for legal aid. • They are beneficial for class actions and complex personal injury cases.	• They might encourage frivolous lawsuits since clients may have nothing at the start. • Lawyers might take only those cases they are reasonably certain to win. • They could encourage multimillion-dollar lawsuits, as has happened in the United States.

After viewing this chart, do you support the concept of contingency fees? Why or why not?

You and the Law

If you were seriously injured in an accident, do you have any plans about your future—education, employment, and lifestyle—that would help the court determine what types of damages you might receive? Explain.

Review Your Understanding

1. What are the two main categories of general damages?
2. Why is it difficult to determine what damages to award a young child?
3. How do special and nominal damages differ?
4. What is the difference between punitive and aggravated damages?
5. What is a contingency fee? List two advantages and two disadvantages of this system.

Enforcing a Judgment

In a civil case, it is up to the plaintiff to collect any damages awarded. This is known as enforcing the judgment. Getting the defendant to pay damages is not the court's responsibility. For a successful plaintiff to collect damages, the defendant must have one of the following:

- money
- assets that can be seized and sold
- a debt owed to them by someone else or wages that can be seized and paid to the plaintiff

Being awarded a judgment is one thing; collecting on it is quite another. The losing defendant may have little money or may be reluctant to pay. There is an old saying: "You cannot get blood from a stone." This means that you cannot collect money from someone who has none. There are various options available to help plaintiffs receive payment, including examination of the debtor, seizing assets, or garnishment. These are discussed below.

Examination of the Debtor

If the defendant refuses to pay, the plaintiff can request an examination of the debtor. The defendant is ordered to appear in court to satisfy the judge as to whether he or she can settle the claim. The debtor is examined under oath about such things as income and assets. An agreement is usually reached as to how much the debtor can afford to pay. If necessary, instalment payments can be arranged.

Seizing Assets

Another option is to apply to the courts to take legal possession of the defendant's property and sell it to settle the judgment. A court official seizes the assets and notifies the defendant. There is a set period to settle the judgment and redeem (get back) the goods. If this is not done, the goods are sold at public auction. The court deducts all of its costs from the sale and then pays the plaintiff as much of the judgment as possible. Any money left over is returned to the defendant. Certain goods, such as clothing, furniture, utensils, and workers' tools, cannot be seized. The goods must be determined to belong to the defendant before they can be seized.

This is one method of seizing assets. However, it is not what is intended when the court orders taking possession of a person's property to settle a judgment.

Garnishment

A wage **garnishment** is a court order that instructs an employer to deduct a specific percentage of a debtor's wages and pay that to the court. Some people call it having your wages "garnished," but the correct term is "garnisheed." Courts will decide not only whether a portion of your wages should be garnisheed, but also the amount within provincial law guidelines. In turn, the court will give the money to the plaintiff as a payment on the judgment. Provincial labour laws do not allow an employer to fire an employee because of a garnishment order.

garnishment a court order that money owed by a defendant to a plaintiff be paid out of the defendant's bank account or wages

Bank accounts, unpaid rent, and money owing on contracts can also be the subject of a garnishment order. If the defendant cannot afford to have the percentage of wages taken, he or she can apply to the court to have the amount altered. In most provinces, a garnishment order remains in effect for six months, but can be renewed if the entire amount is not paid within that time. There are three ways to stop a wage garnishment (see the chart below).

These are the three ways to stop a wage garnishment.

Three Ways to Stop a Wage Garnishment

- pay the judgment owing to the plaintiff
- file a proposal with the court about your payment plans
- file for personal bankruptcy

Costs

In any civil case, the judge must decide whether to allow court costs or not. Usually, the losing party is required to pay the legal fees and other expenses of the successful party. These costs are based on a fee schedule published by the courts and vary by province. The winning party prepares a bill of costs and gives it to the losing party for payment. However, the amount the judge awards may cover only part of the costs. These can be substantial for long, complex trials in higher courts. The rest of the cost might have to come out of the damage award, and sometimes there is little left over for the plaintiff.

Review Your Understanding

1. List three of the things that a defendant must have before a successful plaintiff can collect damages.
2. How are court costs determined, and who usually pays them?
3. What is the purpose of an examination of the debtor?
4. What procedures are followed when a defendant's assets are seized to pay a judgment award to a plaintiff?
5. Outline the three ways for a defendant to stop a wage garnishment.

11.5 Alternative Dispute Resolution

As you have seen, civil litigation often takes a great deal of time and money. Like criminal courts, civil courts across Canada are backlogged, and it may take several years and thousands of dollars before a case reaches trial. Because of the increasing expense and time-consuming nature of litigation, there is a trend in Canada toward **alternative dispute resolution (ADR)**. As you saw in Chapter 1, on pages 32 to 33, negotiation, mediation, and arbitration are methods used in ADR. This section examines ADR in more detail.

alternative dispute resolution (ADR) a process designed to resolve conflicts without formal trials

Five Advantages of Alternative Dispute Resolution

- It is less expensive than traditional litigation.
- It is much faster than traditional litigation.
- It is less distressing than traditional litigation.
- It may produce a better or fairer result than traditional litigation.
- It often results in a win-win situation that benefits both parties.

Of these five advantages of ADR, which do you think is the most important and why?

Negotiation

Resolving disputes happens all the time. You may have to negotiate with a family member for the use of the family car. Part of the discussion may involve when you will be home with the car. You may try to negotiate a new deadline with your teacher for handing in a major project. Negotiation is an informal and voluntary dispute resolution process between the parties involved. A third party is not involved. The two parties determine the process, communicate with each other, and reach mutually acceptable decisions. Discussions may relate to proof, witnesses, and evidence, and problem solving may be used to consider available options. Any agreement reached can be written into a contract. If negotiation does not work, mediation is often the next step.

ADR Communication Models

Negotiation
Parties communicate with each other and make their own decisions.

The outcome can be written into a contract that is final and binding.

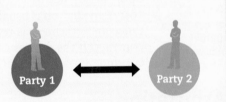

Mediation
A selected neutral third party facilitates parties making their own decision.

The outcome is an agreement to which both parties are committed; the outcome can be written into a contract that is final and binding.

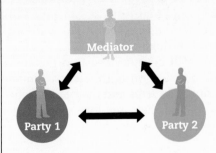

Arbitration
A selected third party receives statements and arguments from both parties and acts as the decision maker.

The arbitrator's decision is final and binding.

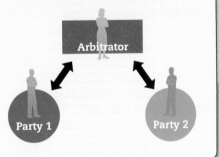

negotiation a process whereby the parties to a civil dispute try to resolve the issues out of court, with or without their lawyers

mediation a process whereby a neutral third person tries to help the parties settle the dispute out of court

arbitration a process whereby a neutral third party hears from the parties and makes a final and binding decision

If you were resolving a dispute with friends, which model would you choose? Why?

Mediation

Mediation is a non-binding process in which the parties appoint a neutral third party—a mediator—to help them reach a mutually acceptable solution to their dispute. It is the most rapidly growing form of ADR. In 1999, Ontario introduced mandatory mediation for certain types of civil actions. The parties involved are required to participate in mediation before a trial is scheduled. Other provinces have adopted this procedure as well. It is becoming a major factor in family relationship disputes, such as child custody, visitation, support payments, and division of property (these issues will be discussed in Unit 4).

The mediator does not impose a solution on the parties. He or she establishes a process to involve the parties in a co-operative decision-making process to settle their dispute. The mediator provides a relaxed, informal, comfortable, and private environment for discussion. The goal is a win-win situation, rather than having a winner and a loser, which is often the case in a trial. Mediators often ask the parties to prepare written statements outlining their versions of the dispute. The mediator reviews these statements and gives the parties a chance to tell their story. At the mediation, the parties can discuss their conflict honestly and openly, and arrive at possible solutions. After learning about the dispute, the mediator tries to get the parties to adjust or settle their dispute based upon his or her assessment of the merits of the claims. The cost of mediation is usually shared equally between the parties. Once an agreement is reached, it can be included in a written contract. If the parties cannot agree, they can walk away and continue with the litigation process.

©Marty Bucella

"Then it's agreed. Bob gets the car, Donna gets the house and all other property goes to the winner of a game of 'Rock, Paper, Scissors.'"

This seems to be a relaxed, informal, but unusual, mediation conference.

Arbitration

Arbitration is a formal process in which the parties involved select a neutral third party or a panel of people with specific technical knowledge. The arbitrator performs a role similar to that of a judge. Arbitration is more formal than negotiation or mediation, but it costs less than litigation. It is the last chance to settle a dispute before thousands of dollars are spent in litigation. Unlike mediation, there may be a winner and a loser.

With arbitration, the parties do not have control over decisions. The arbitrator receives statements about key issues and hears arguments. Both parties can present evidence as well as examine and cross-examine witnesses. Communication flows between the parties through the arbitrator. With his or her specific knowledge, the arbitrator will consider the two positions. She or he usually makes a final, binding decision on both parties. Binding arbitration is often used between professional athletes and their teams when resolving salary disputes. Striking workers and their employers sometimes turn to binding arbitration to resolve contract disputes.

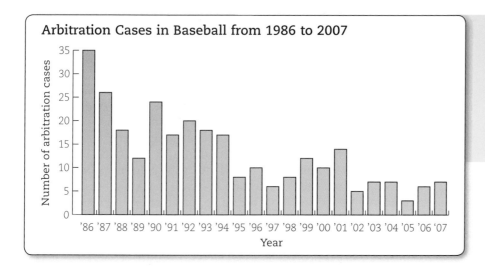

Arbitration Cases in Baseball from 1986 to 2007

Number of arbitration cases (y-axis: 0 to 35)
Year (x-axis: '86 to '07)

The number of baseball salary disputes making it to arbitration has fallen considerably since the peak of 1986. Today, about 90 percent of baseball arbitration cases are settled before the final stage.

Arbitration and Litigation Compared

Factor	Arbitration	Litigation
Speed	Takes days to weeks	Takes months to years
Expertise	Involves an expert	Involves a judge and a jury with limited experience
Procedures	More businesslike but less formal than litigation	Follows formal, complex rules and procedures
Costs	Significantly less expensive than a trial	Can be costly, depending on the length of the trial
Privacy and confidentiality	Conducted in private; not publicly disclosed	Proceedings conducted in public and may be reported by media
Finality	Resolution may permanently satisfy both parties	Resolution may result in divided feelings; there is a winner and a loser

For a serious civil action, would you choose arbitration or litigation?

? Did You Know?

The Canadian Motor Vehicle Arbitration Plan (CAMVAP) helps settle disputes between vehicle owners and manufacturers. It is the largest consumer product arbitration plan in Canada. Although funded by car manufacturers, CAMVAP is an independent body. CAMVAP has about 100 independent arbitrators across the country, most of whom are lawyers.

Review Your Understanding

1. What is ADR? What are the three options available?
2. List two reasons why ADR is being used more often to resolve civil disputes.
3. What is the difference between negotiation and mediation?
4. Distinguish between mediation and arbitration.
5. When is the use of arbitration most effective?

Should the Criminal or Civil Justice System Regulate Violence in Sports?

Canadians have become increasingly vocal about violence in team sports like hockey. On March 8, 2004, many Canadians were shocked when Vancouver Canucks star Todd Bertuzzi sucker-punched Colorado Avalanche rookie Steve Moore. Bertuzzi then jumped him from behind. Moore was hospitalized with three broken vertebrae in his neck and a concussion. He has not played hockey since. Bertuzzi was suspended for 17 months throughout the 310-day NHL lockout. He was banned from competing in the 2004 World Cup of Hockey and in European pro leagues. He also lost just over $500 000 in salary and hundreds of thousands of dollars in product endorsements.

Bertuzzi was criminally charged with assault causing bodily harm. He pleaded guilty and was sentenced to one year's probation and 80 hours of community service. Steve Moore is suing Bertuzzi for almost $38 million. This case went to mediation in December 2008.

Violence in sports is not confined to players. Fans have also been guilty of outbursts of violence. In Europe, incidents of spectator violence have been relatively common at soccer matches. Many fans expect violence, and players and coaches try not to disappoint them. Sometimes outbreaks of violence between teams spark fights between their respective supporters in the audience. Such incidents have caused Canadians to consider how to deal with these outbursts of violence when they happen and how to prevent them.

On One Side

Some fans and players state that some violence is natural and expected in contact sports like hockey, and many players are willing to do anything for victory. They say that risking injury during a hockey game is as much a part of the game as winning and losing. Those who criticize the bodychecking and fights do not really understand the game. Aggression is a basic human condition. It is natural for athletes to let off steam. Players may be upset by questionable calls, heckling fans, pressures of the game, or all three. NHL scouts and general managers constantly search for players who will do battle and come out the winner. Hockey can be mean and ugly. Games are often won in the corner when two big, strong players battle for control of the puck. If violence were eliminated, fan support would decrease and the game would suffer. There are enough rules, penalties, and disciplinary committees to punish those who use too much force. There is no need for criminal or civil action.

On the Other Side

People who oppose violence in sports say that violent behaviour is learned and can be unlearned. At an early age, children who play hockey are taught how to bodycheck to get control of the puck. They see their heroes and role models involved in violent acts and want to copy them. Phrases like "taking him out" and "playing the man" are common. Players are expected to engage in fighting, resist backing down, and support team members who are involved in a fight. There is a fear that this learned violence will become part of the daily lives of children watching and playing the sport.

Fans who oppose violence in sports believe it overshadows the skills of the game. Fighting ruins the game and should be banned. They want criminal and civil action taken against those who use intentional violence. They point out that this type of violence taking place outside the game would be subject to criminal or civil action.

Steve Moore is taken off the ice on a stretcher after Todd Bertuzzi sucker-punched and seriously injured him during an NHL game in 2004. Is this "a natural part" of the game? Explain.

They propose large fines and lengthy—or even permanent—suspensions to deter athletes from engaging in violence.

The Bottom Line

Efforts are being made to understand the nature of violence and deal with it effectively. Violence in sports is no exception. Sports clubs are being pressured to make and enforce tougher rules and penalties for violent behaviour in sports. The media are moving away from sensational coverage of violence in sports. Failure to address the problem at the grassroots level could lead to government action to deal with it.

Some Canadians approve of violence in sports and consider it part of the game. Others feel that violence takes away from the game. In hockey, some violence falls within the rules, and the rest is penalized within the game. Society needs to consider which acts are outside the game rules and require legal action.

What Do You Think?

1. List the differences between the criminal and civil remedies in the *Moore v. Bertuzzi* case.
2. How has the traditional attitude toward violence in sports changed?
3. Assume you are participating in a contact sport. Prepare an argument in favour of using violence in contact sports. Prepare a counterargument that supports criminal or civil action for acts of intentional violence during the game.
4. Should Todd Bertuzzi have been banned from playing hockey until Steve Moore is able to play again? Debate with a partner.
5. In your opinion, is violence in sports a reflection of violence in society? Explain.
6. Conduct an Internet search to find out the results of the mediation in this case or if it ultimately went to trial.

Chapter Review

Chapter Highlights

- Civil (private) law involves disputes between individuals or between individuals and organizations such as businesses or governments.

- Tort law, family law, contract law, labour law, and property law are examples of civil law.

- The main purpose of civil law is to compensate victims for harm or loss suffered.

- Small claims court provides a simple, inexpensive way to settle many civil disputes with a judge and no jury.

- The litigants (parties involved in a lawsuit) in a civil action are the plaintiff (the person suing) and the defendant (the person being sued).

- In civil actions, plaintiffs must prove their case on the balance of probabilities.

- Defendants who receive a claim may file a defence, make a payment into court, or make a counterclaim or a third-party claim.

- A pre-trial or settlement conference is a chance for the litigants to reach a settlement without a formal trial, and many cases are now settled this way.

- Class action lawsuits are brought on behalf of all members of a group with a common interest or grievance. They are becoming more common in Canada.

- There are five types of damages that may be awarded to a successful plaintiff: general, special, nominal, punitive, and aggravated damages.

- An injunction is a court order requiring a defendant to do or not to do something.

- Contingency fees allow greater access to justice for persons who cannot afford a lawyer, but they may be a gamble for the lawyer.

- Alternative dispute resolution (ADR) has become a practical and popular alternative to civil litigation.

- The three ADR models are negotiation, mediation, and arbitration.

Check Your Knowledge

1. Outline the main differences between a civil and a criminal action.

2. Summarize the procedures used in a small claims action.

3. Explain the types of damages available for resolving civil disputes, and provide an example of each.

4. Summarize the remedies available to enforce a judgment against a defendant, and provide an example of each.

5. Outline the three types of ADR and when each might be used.

Apply Your Learning

6. With a partner, discuss the meaning of the following quotation from former American Supreme Court Justice Sandra Day O'Connor:

   "The courts [of this country] should not be the places where resolution of disputes begin. They should be the places where the disputes end after alternative methods of resolving disputes have been considered and tried."

7. Create a detailed original civil action that involves a plaintiff suing a defendant. Your scenario must provide information that supports a claim for some of the types of damages discussed in this chapter. Share your scenario with a classmate. Have him or her identify the evidence that could support each particular damage claim.

8. As you have learned, juries in criminal trials must reach unanimous decisions, while juries in civil actions have to reach majority decisions. Provincial courts of appeal and the Supreme Court of Canada also reach split decisions. Should Canadian law be changed so that criminal trials with juries can reach majority decisions, too? Discuss with a partner, and be prepared to defend your position in class.

Communicate Your Understanding

9. Collect at least five newspaper or Internet articles over a two-week period that discuss or describe civil actions, civil courts, damage awards, and any other issues studied in this chapter. For each article do the following:

   a) Summarize the article in your own words.

   b) Highlight the issue(s) involved.

   c) State and justify your opinion on the issue(s) discussed in the article.

10. Conduct an Internet search for background details on *Liebeck v. McDonald's Restaurants*, 1994 (see page 361 for more information about this case), and discuss both sides of the case. If you had been on the jury, how would you have decided the case? What amount of damages would you have awarded Stella Liebeck, if any? Could McDonald's avoid liability by increasing the size of its warning about the coffee's temperature? Discuss in groups, and be prepared to defend your position.

11. Conduct an Internet search to determine the status or what happened in any of the class action suits mentioned on pages 369–371. Prepare a short summary of the class action, highlighting the key arguments on both sides of the claim. Share your findings with your classmates, and compare the results of these actions. Were they successful and to what extent? If not, why not?

Develop Your Thinking

12. Although the primary function of tort law is to compensate victims, some people feel that it also acts as a deterrent or a penalty. Using original examples from cases you have found in the news, describe two situations in which tort law serves both of these functions.

13. In small groups, conduct an Internet search, and examine the background of Aboriginal residential schools. Why did they exist? Who attended them? What happened to the thousands of students who attended them? (See also the timeline on pages 370–371.) Then examine the background of the class action lawsuit against the schools and the federal government. What was involved? What was the government's final resolution? Share your group's findings with other groups. Discuss how this happened and what can be done to prevent a recurrence of a similar tragedy.

14. Punitive damages function like fines in criminal law. How are they similar? How are they different?

15. Assume that you are involved in an accident that leaves you permanently disabled.

   a) What evidence would you bring forward to justify your claim for loss of future income?

   b) How would such evidence differ for the following people: (i) a six-year-old child; (ii) a 45-year-old chief executive officer of a leading corporation; (iii) a single parent with an eight-year-old child.

12 Negligence and Other Torts

What You Should Know

- What is the difference between an intentional and an unintentional tort?
- What is negligence, and why is it the most important part of tort law?
- In negligence, what are a reasonable person, foreseeability, and causation?
- What are contributory negligence and voluntary assumption of risk?
- What are the main intentional torts?
- What are the main legal remedies and defences for intentional torts?
- How can individuals protect themselves against civil liability?

Selected Key Terms

causation
contributory negligence
duty of care
foreseeability
libel
malpractice

negligence
reasonable person
slander
trespass
vicarious liability
voluntary assumption of risk

Chapter at a Glance

12.1 Introduction
12.2 The Elements of Negligence
12.3 Defences for Negligence
12.4 Special Types of Negligence
12.5 Trespass to Persons and Land
12.6 Defences for Trespass
12.7 Defamation of Character and Its Defences
12.8 The Need for Insurance

Zoe Childs, at the Supreme Court of Canada in 2006. She was rendered paraplegic in a car accident when the vehicle in which she was travelling was hit by an uninsured impaired driver. Childs sued for $6 million in damages. How do you think her case turned out?

12.1 Introduction

In Chapter 11 you learned that a *tort* is "a wrong" that can be either intentional or unintentional. Tort law involves many aspects of your daily life. It involves your personal property, your pets, the sports you play, even your personal freedom and reputation. If you suffer harm or injury to any of these aspects of your life, you may be entitled to sue for damages in a civil court.

Like criminal law, tort law changes with society. For example, people used to drive without seatbelts. They used to ride on motorcycles and bicycles without wearing helmets. However, accident prevention research has shown that using seatbelts and helmets reduces injuries. As a result, provincial governments made such safety devices mandatory. Failure to comply with these laws can reduce or even eliminate the possibility for compensation to an injured person. Tort law may differ slightly from province to province, but the principles are similar. Modern tort law is largely the result of decisions made by judges over many years.

Negligence is the most common and important area of tort law. In common, everyday speech, **negligence** refers to inattention, the possibility of harm, or carelessness in a task. It has a more precise meaning in legal terms. It governs most activities of modern society and has expanded significantly in the last 30 years. Negligence has three key characteristics:

- The action is unintentional.

- The action is unplanned.

- An injury results.

Anyone who carelessly injures a person or damages someone's property should compensate the victim. But carelessness alone does not make someone liable for negligence. Someone must actually be injured or have property damaged by the careless conduct.

For instance, Liam does not clear his icy sidewalk after a winter storm. He is not liable for negligence *unless* somebody falls and is injured. For example, if Aiden slips and falls on the sidewalk, Liam might be liable in any legal action that occurs. Car accidents, injuries to consumers caused by defective products, and medical and legal malpractice (misconduct) are examples of negligence.

Negligence occurs when someone is careless (by not clearing an icy sidewalk, for example), and that carelessness causes someone else to hurt himself or herself.

Did You Know?

Before 1962, most cars were not equipped with seatbelts, and motorists had to buy and install them. Seatbelt use became mandatory in Ontario in 1976. In December 2006, Ontario passed a new seatbelt law stating that every passenger *must* wear a seatbelt. Passengers 16 and older not wearing a seatbelt face a $110 fine.

negligence a careless act that causes harm to another

false imprisonment unlawful physical restraint or detention

nuisance an unreasonable use of land that interferes with the rights of others

There are also intentional torts. When a person deliberately causes harm or loss to another by assault and battery or **false imprisonment**, it is an intentional tort. Trespassing, causing a **nuisance**, and defaming (damaging) a person's reputation are also intentional torts. Intentional torts are the oldest wrongs recognized by the courts and are discussed later in this chapter.

If one person hits another, is it an intentional tort? The answer depends upon a number of factors. The most important element of an intentional tort is intent. As you saw in Chapter 4 on page 126, intent is the true purpose of an act—what a person hopes or desires to result from an action. If Sanjay punches Ravinder squarely in the jaw, harm is clearly intended. But foreseeability (predictability) (see page 393) is also a factor. If your friend Ella throws a snowball at you and it hits you in the face injuring your eye, it is an intentional tort. Ella should have realized that the snowball could hit you and that injury could result. She would be responsible for the damage to your eye. Ella was in control of her actions, and the tort would be considered intentional. The result would be the same if Ella hit a passerby, even if she did not intend to hit that person.

Beware the consequences of throwing an icy snowball.

However, many acts do not result in torts. Some interference with people's rights occurs on a daily basis and is considered acceptable in a busy society. Brushing against bodies on a crowded bus or subway, touching someone lightly to get his or her attention, or taking a shortcut across someone's property are actions that are accepted as a normal part of life. Unless they are done in a hostile manner and cause serious harm or fear of harm, they are not considered intentional torts.

Review Your Understanding

1. Why do you need to know about tort law?
2. What is negligence, and why is it the most common area of tort law?
3. What are the three characteristics of negligence?
4. With examples, distinguish between intentional and unintentional torts.
5. Why is intent the most important element of an intentional tort?

12.2 The Elements of Negligence

The elements of negligence are shown in the table below and are described in more detail on the following pages.

The Potential for a Negligence Action

Elements	Examples in ...			
	a car	a store	a hospital	a law office
Plaintiff is owed a duty of care	Duty to avoid accidents	Duty to ensure store is safe	Duty to provide competent treatment	Duty to provide competent legal advice
Defendant breached duty of care	Drove unsafely; went through a red light	Failed to clean up jam spilled on floor	Amputated the wrong limb	Gave faulty legal advice; client lost right to sue
Plaintiff suffered resulting harm or loss	Plaintiff and/ or plaintiff's car suffered damage	Plaintiff slipped on mess and broke hip	Plaintiff endured unnecessary pain and suffering	Plaintiff lost money arising from potentially successful lawsuit

A negligence action may arise when someone unintentionally harms you. What is needed to prove negligence?

Duty of Care

In a negligence suit, the plaintiff must show that the defendant owed him or her a **duty of care**. You have a duty of care to people when a legal obligation has been placed upon you. For example, it is your responsibility to make sure that your actions do not harm people or their property. This principle is basic to the study of the laws governing negligence. For example, every driver has a duty of care to other motorists, cyclists, and pedestrians to drive in a reasonable manner and to prevent accidents. A driver who drives through a red light and hits your car has breached his or her duty of care to you. If the owner of a shopping centre does not fix a faulty escalator and you are injured on it, a duty of care has also been breached. In our earlier example, Liam owed a duty of care to pedestrians to clear the ice from his sidewalk.

duty of care a specific legal obligation to not harm other people or their property

Did You Know?

In October 2008, in a 3–0 judgment in the case of *Paxton v. Ramji*, the Ontario Court of Appeal justices ruled that doctors cannot owe a duty of care to unborn children because their primary obligation is to the mothers. This decision means that a doctor cannot be sued by a child born with serious deformities caused by a drug that was prescribed to his or her mother.

THE FLYING McCOYS   **BY GARY & GLENN McCOY**

THE FLYING MCCOYS © 2007 Glenn and Gary McCoy. Dist. By UNIVERSAL PRESS SYNDICATE. Reprinted with permission. All rights reserved.

This might be the first motor vehicle negligence lawsuit.

Breach of Duty of Care

Once a duty of care has been established, the court must determine if the defendant breached it. This happens when the defendant fails to meet the expected **standard of care** or degree of care that an ordinary or "reasonable" person would use. This is how courts determine how much care the defendant owed the plaintiff.

standard of care the level of care expected of a person in specific circumstances

reasonable person the standard used to determine if a person's conduct is negligent

The Reasonable Person

Before any negligence claim can be upheld by a court, the court must first be convinced that a duty of care existed. It determines what a **reasonable person** would have expected in a similar situation. The reasonable person is an ordinary adult who has no physical or developmental disabilities. It is someone who people agree is careful, thoughtful, and considerate of others. The reasonable person is not expected to be perfect. Also, the reasonable person is not the same in all circumstances. What is considered reasonable in downtown Vancouver may not be the same as in Milk River, Alberta. This varies from community to community. If the defendant repairs car brakes, the "reasonable person" standard is a reasonably competent mechanic. If the defendant performs surgery, the standard is that of a reasonably competent surgeon. Also, what was "reasonable" 50 years ago is often not the same today.

A person or organization whose conduct falls below the expected standard of care is liable for the results of the negligence. This can be the case even if the party was acting within the law. For example, Anya drives at the posted speed limit during a snowstorm and hits a pedestrian. How would a reasonable person be expected to act? A "reasonable person" might have driven slower. Therefore, Anya may be liable.

The standard of a "reasonable person" is used to determine whether someone is negligent in a tort case. For example, a reasonable person slows down and takes extra care when driving in a snowstorm.

Youths and a Duty of Care

A youth (a child under 12) and a teenager (13 to 18) cannot be judged by the same standards as a reasonable adult. For example, we saw in Chapter 10 that children under the age of 12 cannot be charged with a criminal offence under the *Youth Criminal Justice Act*. However, there is no legislation regarding youth and torts. Since there is no set standard, courts must determine liability based on the facts and the youth's background in each case. The older the youth, the greater his or her responsibility.

Children under the age of six or seven are seldom held responsible. It is generally assumed that they do not understand the consequences of their actions. In any incident involving an older child, the courts consider what a child of similar age, experience, and intelligence might have done. But minors involved in adult activities, such as driving a car or hunting, are expected to meet the adult standard of care. The potential danger from the activity makes it unfair to society to apply a lower standard of care.

You and the Law

Minors involved in adult activities, such as driving a car or hunting, are expected to meet the adult standard of care. What does this mean? Do you agree? Why or why not?

Michaluk v. Rolling River School Division No. 3 et al., 2001 MBCA 45 (CanLII)

For more information, Go to Nelson Social Studies 🌐

Usually, art classes in school do not result in serious harm or injury. However, Dirk Michaluk was not so fortunate when he was seriously injured in his school art class.

The 12-year-old plaintiff, Dirk Michaluk, lost the sight in one eye in an accident during a Grade 8 art class at one of the defendant's schools in Rivers, Manitoba. The class project involved bending coat hangers into mobiles. The teacher gave general instructions, including how to bend the wire. He did not warn students that the wire could spring out of their hands. No specific safety precautions were given. The students were not given safety goggles, which were available in the school. The teacher watched his students and saw that Dirk was working diligently on the project. In the process of bending the wire, it slipped out of Dirk's hands and punctured his eye. He and his litigation guardian brought a civil action against the teacher and the school board for damages and succeeded at trial. The defendants appealed this decision to the Manitoba Court of Appeal.

- Was Dirk Michaluk partly responsible for this accident? What do you think the Court of Appeal decided, and why?

Foreseeability

The concept of **foreseeability** is related to the concept of a reasonable person. Courts typically ask the question: Would a reasonable person in similar circumstances have foreseen (anticipated) the injury to the victim as a result of his or her action? If the answer is yes, the defendant may be at fault and liable. If the answer is no, there is no fault or liability. If the defendant has not met the reasonable person's standard of care, then he or she has breached his or her duty of care. In our earlier example, Liam should have foreseen that somebody might slip and fall and be injured because of the ice on his sidewalk.

foreseeability a reasonable person's ability to anticipate a specific result of an action

Foreseeability is a difficult concept. The courts tend to follow the principle that defendants should not be held responsible for results of actions that could not reasonably be expected. In the earlier example, if Aiden fell on Liam's icy sidewalk, and the gun that he was carrying discharged and injured a neighbour, Liam is not liable for the neighbour's injuries as this was not foreseeable. However, Aiden might be liable if it is found that he was negligent in making sure his gun was secure.

Causation

Once it is established that the defendant has not met the required standard of care, the plaintiff must then prove that the defendant's negligent conduct caused the plaintiff harm. There must be a direct causal connection between the defendant's negligent act and the plaintiff's damages. For example, Liam's failure to shovel his sidewalk caused Aiden's injury. This relationship is called **causation**. Without it, liability for negligence does not exist.

causation when the defendant's action was a direct factor that led to the plaintiff's damages

Once it is established that the defendant's action caused the plaintiff's injury, the court must decide how direct the connection was between the action and the injury. In our example, the connection is very direct. There is no doubt that Liam's lack of action caused Aiden's injury.

The "but-for" test is the technique most commonly used by courts to determine causation. If an accident would not have occurred "but for" the defendant's negligence, this conduct is the cause of the loss. On the other hand, if the accident would have happened anyway, whether or not the defendant acted as he or she did, this conduct is not the cause of the loss. This means that if you can say "but for" the defendant's actions this harm would not have occurred, then causation exists. For example, Chandra is driving slightly over the speed limit through a residential neighbourhood and is startled to see a child falling off her bicycle toward the car. To avoid an accident, Chandra swerves and loses control of her car. She hits a telephone pole, knocks out service to the subdivision, and damages her car. Because the telephone lines are out of order as a result of the accident (and she does not have a cellphone), Lisa is unable to call an ambulance for her husband, who is having a heart attack. Since she cannot drive and is unable to get an ambulance, Lisa's husband dies. Is Chandra responsible for the man's death?

To answer this question, the court would likely find that Chandra's speed was a contributing factor. "But for" her speeding, there would have been no accident, no knocked out telephone service preventing Lisa from calling an ambulance, and her husband would likely not have died. But was his death foreseeable? Was this too far removed for Lisa to sue for damages?

Causation depends on the facts of each case, judged on its own merits. A significant Supreme Court decision in tort law dealing with duty of care, foreseeability, and causation is *Resurfice Corp. v. Hanke*, 2007. It confirmed that the "but-for" test remains the principal rule for determining causation in negligence cases.

 Case

Resurfice Corp. v. Hanke, 2007 SCC 7 (CanLII)

For more information, Go to Nelson Social Studies

A Zamboni machine such as this was the focus of a serious accident that left Ralph Hanke badly burned and disfigured.

In January 1995, Ralph Hanke operated a Zamboni machine at an Edmonton ice rink and was badly burned and disfigured. He had accidentally placed a water hose into the machine's gas tank and overfilled it. It released vapourized gasoline that was then ignited by an overhead heater. This caused an explosion and fire. Hanke sued the manufacturer and distributor of the machine for damages. He claimed that the machine's gas and water tanks were too similar in appearance and placed too close together, making it easy to confuse them.

continues...

Resurfice Corp. v. Hanke, 2007 SCC 7 (CanLII)

In 2003, the judge at the Alberta Court of Queen's Bench dismissed the action. He found that Hanke did not establish the manufacturer's negligence. The tanks were actually different sizes, the gas tank was clearly marked "gasoline only," and Hanke admitted to knowing and recognizing the difference between the tanks.

Hanke's appeal was heard in the Alberta Court of Appeal in May 2004. In a unanimous judgment in May 2005, the court set aside the previous judgment and ordered a new trial. It considered the seriousness of Hanke's injuries and the financial positions of the parties involved. It also considered the possibility that the manufacturer's design may have been a cause of the accident. Before the new trial, Hanke appealed to the Supreme Court of Canada. That appeal was heard on December 12, 2006. In a 9–0 judgment on February 8, 2007, the court allowed his appeal. It restored the trial judgment dismissing Hanke's action.

For Discussion

1. What is the "but-for" test?

2. How did that test apply to this case?

3. Was it reasonably foreseeable that Hanke would mistake the gas and water tanks? Do you think the defendant manufacturer caused or contributed to the plaintiff's injuries? Explain.

4. The Supreme Court's judgment stated: "Foreseeability depends on what a reasonable person would anticipate, not on the seriousness of the plaintiff's injuries or the depth of the defendant's pockets." Explain the meaning of this statement.

Actual Harm or Loss

Finally, in a negligence suit, the plaintiff must prove that real harm or an economic loss occurred because of the defendant's negligence. If nobody was injured as a result of Liam's actions, no loss would have been suffered by anyone, and no legal action would be needed.

The Steps in Proving a Negligence Action

1. Does the defendant owe the plaintiff a *duty of care*?

2. Did the defendant breach the *standard of care*?

3. Did the defendant's careless act *cause* the plaintiff's injury or loss?

4. Was there a direct connection between the defendant's action and the plaintiff's injury or loss? Was what happened *foreseeable*?

5. Did the plaintiff suffer *actual harm or loss*?

This chart summarizes the basic steps in proving a negligence action.

Cornered   by Baldwin

5-31   © 2000 Mike Baldwin / Dist. by Universal Press Syndicate

"Wait, this one's a lawyer. We'd better wash our hands."

Why is this surgeon suggesting his medical team wash their hands before operating on this patient?

Chapter 12 **Negligence and Other Torts**

The First Negligence Case: The Snail in the Bottle

Negligence was not recognized as a tort until the landmark judgment in *Donaghue v. Stevenson*, 1932, from England's highest court. A friend bought May Donaghue a ginger beer in a dark bottle in a pub in Paisley, Scotland. Pouring the drink into a glass, Donaghue found a dead snail in the bottle. The sight of the snail caused Donaghue nervous shock and gastroenteritis that required medical treatment. She sued David Stevenson, the drink manufacturer, claiming he was negligent. He claimed that she could not sue him or his company as there was no contract between them because Donaghue's friend bought her the drink. Donaghue lost at trial but won at appeal.

England's highest court ruled that every person has a duty to take reasonable care for the safety of anyone who might foreseeably be harmed by the person's actions. Since the manufacturer allowed a defective product to be sold, it was only reasonable to hold the company responsible for consumers' safety. The manufacturer should have been able to foresee that its products would be used by people other than the actual purchasers. In its judgment, the court stated: "You must take reasonable care to avoid acts or omissions which you can reasonably foresee would be likely to injure your neighbour."

This ruling on duty of care was the beginning of negligence law. Today, many lawyers claim this decision is the most famous tort case in legal history and a very important precedent. Anyone involved in producing consumer goods may be held liable for negligence if consumers are injured by products when using them routinely. This is the legacy of this landmark case.

The facts in the case on page 397, *Mustapha v. Culligan of Canada Ltd.* (2008), closely resemble the facts in the *Donaghue* case. Many legal experts believe this case is the new, 2008 version.

For Discussion

1. Why would Donaghue claim the manufacturer was negligent?

2. What must a manufacturer be able to prove to avoid liability?

3. Why do many lawyers feel this case is an important precedent?

4. Explain the meaning of the quotation from the judgment.

How would you react if you found a snail in your drink?

Mustapha v. Culligan of Canada Ltd., 2008 SCC 27 (CanLII)

For more information, Go to Nelson Social Studies

Waddah (Martin) Mustapha became violently ill when he found a fly in a water bottle. He sued for damages for the effect this had on his life. His legal action made it to the Supreme Court of Canada, but he lost his appeal.

Waddah Mustapha came to Canada from Lebanon in 1976 at age 16. He and his wife, Lynn, operated a successful hairstyling business in Windsor, Ontario. They kept a spotless home. They considered cleanliness and hygiene of utmost importance. In 1986, they met with a Culligan representative who told them how pure and healthy Culligan water was. They decided to have a dispenser installed in their home. Evidence indicated that the Mustapha family used nothing but Culligan water for their personal use for the next 15 years.

In November 2001, Mrs. Mustapha, who was seven months pregnant, wanted a new bottle of Culligan water installed on their dispenser. As Mr. Mustapha was doing this, they both noticed a dead fly in the sealed bottle of drinking water delivered to their home. Mrs. Mustapha vomited immediately. Mr. Mustapha felt nauseous, had abdominal pain, and later vomited. He was unable to drink water, had nightmares, and underwent a major personality

change. He required treatment and medication. He also feared that his family's health was in danger from the impure water.

The Mustaphas brought an action against Culligan of Canada Ltd. The action was for damages arising from various physical and psychological conditions. They all stemmed from Culligan's negligence in supplying them with impure drinking water. Culligan denied that the flies entered the bottle at their factory. They alleged that Mr. Mustapha greatly exaggerated his injuries. In April 2005, the trial judge ruled in Mustapha's favour and awarded him $341 000.

Culligan appealed this judgment to the Ontario Court of Appeal. In a 3–0 judgment in December 2006, the appellate court overturned the trial judgment. Mustapha sought leave to appeal to the Supreme Court of Canada. His appeal was heard in March 2008. In a 9–0 decision in May 2008, the Supreme Court stated that Mustapha's injuries were not foreseeable by Culligan. His damages award should not be reinstated.

For Discussion

1. In finding in Mustapha's favour, the trial judge concluded that his psychiatric illness was the result of his Middle Eastern cultural sensitivities and the high level of cleanliness maintained by his family in their home. Do you agree with this reasoning? Why or why not?

2. At trial, Culligan presented evidence about the safety standards at its plant. They also argued that no similar complaints had ever been received and that the company's marketing was based on the "absolute purity of its product." Is this an adequate defence? Explain.

3. Was it reasonably foreseeable to Culligan that Mustapha would sustain a psychiatric illness as a result of seeing a fly in the bottle of water? Why or why not?

4. Do you agree with the Supreme Court's decision? Why or why not?

The Burden of Proof

As you learned in Chapter 11, the burden of proof in a civil trial is on the plaintiff. The plaintiff must prove all the required negligence elements. If the plaintiff fails to prove any of these elements, the action fails. Just as in a criminal trial, the defendant does not have to prove anything, but many do present evidence. They show that the plaintiff did not suffer any harm, that the harm was not reasonably foreseeable, or that the defendant's actions did not cause the plaintiff's injuries or loss. Proof exists on a balance of probabilities. The plaintiff's version of the incident must be accepted as "more likely than not" to have happened in order to succeed.

Review Your Understanding

1. Identify the key elements that a plaintiff must prove to succeed in a negligence action.
2. Distinguish between a duty of care and a standard of care in a negligence action.
3. What is the difference between the burden of proof in a civil and criminal trial?
4. What is the connection between foreseeability and a reasonable person?
5. Why is proof of causation so important in a negligence action?

12.3 Defences for Negligence

People sued for negligence can do a number of things. The best defences are claiming that there was no negligence or that the defendant did not owe the plaintiff any duty of care. Another defence is that the defendant lived up to the expected standard of care. Even a plaintiff who is able to prove that there was negligence may not be able to recover as much as expected. If the plaintiff was also negligent in the incident or assumed a risk voluntarily, then damages may be reduced or not awarded at all.

Contributory Negligence

At one time under common law, a plaintiff found to be in any way at fault for an accident was denied the right to claim damages. Society's attitude was that the law should not protect people who do not look after their own safety. But such treatment seemed harsh for plaintiffs who were only slightly at fault for their loss or injury.

Now, if both the plaintiff and defendant are negligent to some degree, damages are divided between them. The division is according to what is known as **contributory negligence**. The court decides which party was more negligent, or whether both parties were equally at fault. The judge considers the elements of negligence discussed earlier in this chapter. The defendant must establish that the plaintiff was partly at fault for what happened and that this negligence contributed to his or her loss. Each province has a *Contributory Negligence Act* or a *Negligence Act*. It allows courts to divide responsibility between the parties.

contributory negligence when the victim's actions caused all or part of the damages suffered

For example, a motor vehicle accident results in a damages award of $80 000. The court finds the defendant 75 percent at fault for driving far too fast and going through a red light. The plaintiff is found 25 percent at fault for driving through the intersection on an amber light and not wearing a seatbelt. As a result of this contributory negligence, the plaintiff receives only $60 000 from the defendant—that is, 75 percent of $80 000. The damages calculated are those that the judge or jury believe are required to fully compensate the injured person for the loss suffered. In other words, contributory negligence costs the victim. It is often used as a defence in accidents when the plaintiff is not wearing a seatbelt.

Major automobile accidents often result in death because passengers did not wear seatbelts. Until 2001, the maximum reduction in Alberta courts for failure to wear a seatbelt was 25 percent. In *Chae v. Min*, 2001, a trial judge reduced Mr. Chae's damage award by 75 percent. This shocking decision was appealed. In *Chae v. Min*, 2005, the Alberta Court of Appeal restored this award back to the more traditional 25 percent. Therefore, Chae received 75 percent of $344 776.

You Be the Judge

Walford v. Jacuzzi Canada Inc., 2007 ONCA 729 (CanLII)

For more information, Go to Nelson Social Studies

Marion Walford's family bought a 1.2-metre-deep above-ground pool in 1994. In July 1996, she bought a used 3-metre slide for the pool. She believed she could install the slide because the pool's manual showed a sketch of a child using a slide. She took the slide to a Pioneer Pools store in Hamilton, Ontario, where she purchased her pool supplies. The manager inspected the slide, told her there would be no problem using it with her pool, and provided her with the parts needed to mount the slide and installation instructions. Walford installed the slide. She established rules for her family to use the slide only feet first.

The next day, Walford's then-15-year-old daughter, Correena, went down the slide crouched on her knees. She entered the water head first, hit her chin on the bottom of the pool, broke her neck, and became quadriplegic. Walford sued Pioneer Pools and their employees, the manufacturer of their pool, and Jacuzzi Canada, the slide's manufacturer. The trial judge ruled that the defendants had not breached any duty to the Walfords and dismissed the action.

In January 2007, Walford appealed the dismissal against Pioneer Pools to the Ontario Court of Appeal. In a 2–1 judgment in October, the court overturned the trial judgment. It placed liability on Pioneer Pools and awarded the plaintiff more than $5 million in damages. But the court also found Correena 20 percent at fault for the accident. Leave to appeal to the Supreme Court was dismissed in April 2008.

This above-ground pool and slide are similar to the ones in which Correnna Walford suffered serious injury, leaving her quadriplegic.

• Why did the court find Correena 20 percent at fault? Do you agree? Why or why not? Now that a further appeal will not be heard by the Supreme Court, what does this mean for the Walford family?

Voluntary Assumption of Risk

The concept of **voluntary assumption of risk** assumes that individuals understand the risks involved in various activities, such as skydiving and bungee jumping, and willingly accept these risks. In negligence cases, defendants must prove that plaintiffs clearly knew the risk involved in their actions and chose to assume that risk. For example, someone who is driving while impaired and causes injury to passengers in his or her car may use this defence. The court assumes that a plaintiff who gets into a car knowing that the driver is drunk voluntarily assumes a risk of injury. The burden of proof is on the defendant. If the defendant can prove that the passengers knew he or she was drunk, the plaintiff will receive reduced damages.

Contact sports such as hockey and football involve physical contact. It is commonly accepted that, to some extent, players accept some risk of injury when playing these types of sports. But what about spectators at sporting events? For example, a fan struck and injured by a baseball at a game will probably not be able to sue the player who hit the ball. The fan should have been aware of such risks. On the other hand, if an angry player threw the bat or ball into the stands and injured a fan, the fan might win a legal action. The injury does not arise from an ordinary or voluntary risk. Generally, risk is stated on the ticket. The ticket holder enters into a contract to attend the event and assumes this risk. If risk is not stated on the ticket, there may be an implication that the person voluntarily assumes the risk merely by observing the activity.

For other activities, like skiing, you must sign a **waiver** before you can participate. The waiver attempts to limit the right to sue for a personal injury if injured, but waivers are not always enforceable. When a waiver is challenged in court, the defendant must show that the plaintiff made a free decision to sign the waiver and was aware of what was being signed.

Crocker v. Sundance Northwest Resort Ltd., 1988, is a landmark judgment involving waivers. An impaired William Crocker signed a waiver to gain entry into a tubing contest at a ski resort. The resort manager discouraged Crocker from participating. Crocker insisted, and the manager made no further efforts to stop him. Crocker was seriously injured. The Supreme Court of Canada determined that the waiver was unenforceable because Crocker was drunk when he signed the form. He had not read its contents nor understood that he was waiving his legal rights. The high court stated that the resort should have taken all reasonable steps to ensure that no one participated in the event while intoxicated. It found the resort 75 percent at fault for Crocker's injuries.

You and the Law

If you were seriously injured while playing a sport at school, what would you have to prove to sue successfully for damages?

Did You Know?

A waiver can significantly limit the right to sue for a personal injury. However, it is not always enforceable.

WHISTLER BLACKCOMB

**RELEASE OF LIABILITY, WAIVER OF CLAIMS,
ASSUMPTION OF RISKS AND INDEMNITY AGREEMENT**
(hereinafter referred to as the "Release Agreement")

**BY SIGNING THIS DOCUMENT YOU WILL WAIVE OR GIVE UP CERTAIN LEGAL RIGHTS,
INCLUDING THE RIGHT TO SUE OR CLAIM COMPENSATION FOLLOWING AN ACCIDENT**

PLEASE READ CAREFULLY!
This Agreement shall apply to all subsequent Season Pass & Card renewals.

1. INITIAL	2. INITIAL	3. INITIAL	4. INITIAL

Barcode#

TO: WHISTLER BLACKCOMB HOLDINGS INC., BLACKCOMB SKIING ENTERPRISES LIMITED PARTNERSHIP, WHISTLER MOUNTAIN RESORT LIMITED PARTNERSHIP, WHISTLER BLACKCOMB EMPLOYMENT CORP. AND HER MAJESTY THE QUEEN IN THE RIGHT OF THE PROVINCE OF BRITISH COLUMBIA (hereinafter collectively referred to as "WHISTLER BLACKCOMB")

ASSUMPTION OF RISKS
I am aware that skiing, snowboarding, participating in snow school lessons, tubing, cycling, mountain biking, hiking and sightseeing (hereinafter collectively referred to as the **"ACTIVITIES"**) involve many risks, dangers and hazards including, but not limited to: boarding, riding and disembarking ski lifts; changing weather conditions; avalanches; loss of balance or control; exposed rock, earth, ice, and other natural objects; trees, tree wells, tree stumps and forest dead fall; the condition of snow or ice on or beneath the surface; variations in the terrain which may create blind spots or areas of reduced visibility; variations in the surface or sub-surface, including changes due to man-made or artificial snow; variable and difficult conditions; streams, creeks, and exposed holes in the snow pack above streams or creeks; cliffs; crevasses; snowcat roads, road-banks or cut-banks; collision with lift towers, fences, snow making equipment, snow grooming equipment, snowcats, snow[...] vehicles, [...] structure[...] [...]ion with oth[...] the failu[...] safely [...]

The waiver of risk is clearly visible on this release form. It should be carefully read before signing it.

Cowles v. Balac, 2006 CanLII 34916 (ONCA)

For more information, **Go to Nelson Social Studies**

In 1996, David Balac and Jennifer-Anne Cowles visited the African Lion Safari (ALS) wildlife park near Hamilton, Ontario. ALS is the only North American facility in which exotic wild animals roam freely in their natural settings while patrons drive their vehicles among the animals. ALS advertised that the visitors were in cages (their vehicles) while the animals were free. When the couple paid their entrance fee, they were given a receipt and pamphlet that contained a map and nothing else. Neither was asked to sign a waiver before entering the park. There were two signs posted outside the park gate warning visitors that they were entering at their own risk. Neither Cowles nor Balac recalled seeing them and nobody drew the signs to their attention.

While driving slowly through the tiger reserve, with all the car windows completely up, they were attacked by a female tiger followed by three other tigers. When the first tiger butted the car, the rocking motion caused Balac's arm or lower body to touch the window switches. This accidentally lowered the windows on both sides of the car, allowing the tigers access to the passengers. The first tiger entered the vehicle through the front passenger window and attacked Balac and Cowles. Two of the other tigers managed to bite Balac's hand through the front driver window.

Balac and Cowles were severely mauled by the tigers before escaping. Both suffered severe physical and psychological injuries. Balac became a virtual recluse as a result of disfigurement and scarring. He will likely never be gainfully employed. Cowles suffered disfiguring hip and scalp injuries that ended her career as an exotic dancer.

They took action against ALS for their injuries. In January 2005, the trial judge ruled that ALS was strictly liable for their injuries. The judge awarded Balac $1.7 million and Cowles $813 000 for pain and suffering, and loss of future income. ALS appealed this decision to the Ontario Court of Appeal in June 2006. In a 2–1 judgment on October 19, the appellate court upheld the trial judgment and the award of damages. An application for leave to appeal this decision to the Supreme Court of Canada was dismissed in March 2007.

This is the open environment of the African Lion Safari. Wild animals roam, while patrons drive their vehicles among them.

For Discussion

1. Did contributory negligence exist in this case? Why or why not?

2. Did Cowles and Balac voluntarily assume a risk, as ALS contended, when they went to the park? Explain.

3. The trial judge wrote: "There is no question … that tigers are dangerous, unpredictable, wild predators. Persons who display such animals in out of control settings should, in my view, be held strictly liable for any damage caused from such display." Explain the meaning of this statement and what the judge meant by "strictly liable."

4. Since Balac was a college student at the time of the attack, his vocation had not yet been established, and his future earning potential still had to be determined. Was his award of $1.7 million appropriate and sufficient? Discuss with a partner.

5. Should the Supreme Court of Canada have heard this appeal? Why or why not?

Inevitable Accident

Sometimes called an "act of God" or *force majeur*, certain accidents are those events that take place through no one's fault. Injury or loss may result from a situation that is unavoidable, no matter what precautions a reasonable person might take under the circumstances. If lightning strikes Yoko's moving car, causing her to lose control and collide with oncoming traffic, Yoko would not likely be held liable. She could not have foreseen such an occurrence and could not have prevented it. This is an inevitable accident.

Review Your Understanding

1. What are the two best defences in a negligence action?
2. What is contributory negligence? Explain using an example that was not discussed in the text.
3. What is voluntary assumption of risk?
4. Identify the two factors that the defendant must prove for the defence of voluntary assumption of risk to succeed.
5. What is an inevitable accident, and how does it affect liability in a negligence action?

12.4 Special Types of Negligence

Among negligence suits, the most common involve motor vehicles, property, and professional services. These are known (respectively) as

- motor vehicle negligence
- occupiers' liability
- professional negligence

Each is discussed in the following section.

Motor Vehicle Negligence

Motor vehicle accidents sometimes lead to both criminal charges and civil actions. For example, the *Criminal Code* contains dangerous and impaired driving offences. Each province has a *Highway Traffic Act* or *Motor Vehicle Act*. It includes a variety of regulations, such as speed limits and seatbelt laws. Violating any section of an act can be considered driver negligence. As you have learned, the burden of proof usually rests on the plaintiff in such an action. However, this burden shifts to the defendant in some cases. Once a plaintiff proves that he or she was struck by another vehicle, the burden of proof shifts to the defendant. Defendants must prove that any loss or injury did not result from their negligence. If there is evidence that both drivers were responsible for an accident to some extent, liability will be split between them. Thus, motor vehicle accidents often involve contributory negligence.

Liability for Passengers

Drivers are responsible, or liable, for their passengers' safety. However, passengers might accept a ride knowing that the driver is intoxicated. On the other hand, they might know that the driver has dangerous habits, such as speeding. In these cases, passengers are presumed to voluntarily assume risk by riding with the driver. Drivers often use the assumption of risk when defending themselves. The defendant must prove that the plaintiff understood and willingly accepted the risk. If the defendant is successful, the plaintiff receives reduced damages.

If the plaintiff is unaware of any danger, there is no voluntary assumption of risk. For example, suppose Macy accepts a ride from Ethan, not knowing that his car has faulty brakes. Ethan has an accident because his brakes failed and Macy is injured. He cannot argue voluntary assumption of risk as a defence, since Macy did not know about the problem.

Seatbelts and Negligence

When worn properly, seatbelts save lives and reduce injuries in auto accidents. Many studies show that wearing seatbelts gives more protection to the public. All provinces and territories now legally require that both drivers and passengers wear them. In fact, highway traffic laws state that drivers have a specific duty of care to ensure that passengers, especially those under 16 years of age, wear seatbelts. The 1994 landmark Supreme Court decision in *Galaske v. O'Donnell* established that all drivers owe a duty of care to child passengers. Drivers are in a relationship of supervision and control over these young passengers.

Failure to wear a seatbelt is one of the most common reasons used by courts and insurance companies to reduce damage awards in vehicle accidents. Drivers or passengers failing to wear seatbelts are not acting as reasonable persons. It can be foreseen that injury can result from this action. More judges are ruling that contributory negligence exists when a person fails to buckle up. Courts consistently reduce damage awards by up to 25 percent for plaintiffs' failure to wear a seatbelt.

Did You Know?

In *Gordon v. Greig*, 2007, the Ontario Superior Court issued a $24-million award to two men severely injured in a car accident. This was the largest award for a spinal cord injury in Canadian history and one of the largest for a brain injury. The plaintiffs' award was reduced by 15 percent for one man and by 25 percent for the other, for failing to wear seatbelts.

Everyone is required by law to wear a seatbelt. Drivers have a specific duty of care to make sure their passengers are buckled up, especially those under the age of 16.

Snushall v. Fulsang, 2005 CanLII 34561 (ON C.A.)

For more information, Go to Nelson Social Studies

Seatbelts on much older cars do not seem as safe and secure as they are in today's vehicles.

In July 1997, the plaintiff, Carol Snushall, was a passenger in a car driven by the defendant, Daniel Fulsang, when his car struck the rear of a van driven by George Vetzal. Fulsang testified that he assumed that Vetzal was going to accelerate. That is why he did not apply his brakes sooner. Once he realized he was wrong, it was too late to avoid the accident.

Fulsang's 1968 car was equipped with lap belts and separate shoulder belts for the driver and the front passenger. Snushall was wearing only her lap belt. She claimed that she did not realize that there was a shoulder belt available. As a result of the accident, she was seriously injured and sustained head and back injuries. The *Highway Traffic Act* states that an occupant is required to wear a seatbelt but not a shoulder belt.

Snushall brought an action against Fulsang. He, in turn, brought a third-party claim against Vetzal (see Chapter 11, page 366, for more on third-party claims). The judge advised the jury that failure to wear a seatbelt would typically result in contributory negligence between 5 and 25 percent. Most cases result in the low end of that range. The jury awarded Snushall just over $900 000 in damages. They found that Fulsang was 80 percent responsible for Snushall's injuries and Vetzal 20 percent responsible. But, the jury also determined that Snushall was 35 percent accountable for her injuries. In other words, the jury only awarded Snushall $585 000, or 65 percent of the total. Fulsang would pay $468 000, and Vetzel would pay $117 000. Snushall and Vetzal both appealed this decision to the Ontario Court of Appeal.

• What do you think the Ontario Court of Appeal decided? Was 35 percent a fair assessment of Snushall's contributory negligence? Should that percentage be higher or lower? Was 20 percent a fair assessment of Vetzel's negligence?

 Did You Know?

According to Transport Canada, about 90.5 percent of all light-duty vehicle occupants in Canada wear seatbelts. More female drivers (93.9 percent) than males (89.8 percent) wear seatbelts. Only 87 percent of drivers under 25 wear seatbelts. This compares to 92.1 percent of drivers 50 and older. Why do you think that the percentage of seatbelt wearers is greater for older drivers?

Vicarious Liability

A vicarious experience is one that is felt second hand or through some substitution. For example, you might get a thrill from hearing a friend talk about a rock concert. In tort law, the principle of **vicarious liability** is when one person is held responsible for another's tort, even though they may have done nothing wrong. For example, Betty loans her car to Lora, who crashes it and injures Amir. Betty may be held responsible because of vicarious liability. In motor vehicle negligence, this liability assumes that vehicle owners have a duty of care to society to lend their vehicles only to those who are competent to drive them safely. It is clearly intended to encourage owners to be careful about who they lend their vehicles to.

Provincial and territorial statutes place liability on both the vehicle driver and owner. Owners are liable for negligence of anyone using their vehicle with their permission (see *McIntyre v. Grigg*, 2006, in Chapter 11, pages 376–377). Even if the owner is not in the car when an accident occurs, both parties are responsible for any negligence. If the owner can prove that the vehicle was stolen and that the driver did not have permission to use it, the owner can avoid liability.

This concept also applies in the workplace. Employers may be (rather than are) liable for torts committed by employees during work hours while carrying out their normal employment duties. There are two main reasons for this principle. First, employers usually have liability insurance to compensate victims for injury or loss, while employees do not. Second, society believes that companies should be responsible for their employees' actions. A finding of vicarious liability requires a strong connection between what the employer asks of the employee and the wrongful conduct.

Finally, parents may be held vicariously liable for their children's torts. Manitoba, Ontario, and British Columbia have all passed a *Parental Responsibility Act*. These acts allow victims to sue parents of children and teenagers under the age of 18 still living at home who intentionally take or damage another's property. Under the *Parental Responsibility Act*, victims need prove only the following:

1. that the child caused the property damage or loss
2. that the defendant(s) are the child's parents
3. the amount of the damage

The parents are liable unless they can prove that the damage was not done on purpose. Or, the parents must prove that they supervised the child and reasonably tried to prevent the damage. So far, very few cases have been tried under this legislation. The following chart outlines the reasons behind the principle of vicarious liability.

> **vicarious liability** in certain relationships, when a person is held responsible for another's tort

 Did You Know?

In the United States, nearly all states have some form of parental responsibility legislation in place.

The Reasons for Vicarious Liability

- It ensures that injured parties can receive damages for harm or injury suffered.
- It protects victims harmed by employees who are unable to pay for the damages they cause while on the job.
- It forces employers to be responsible for their employees' actions.
- It is a way of holding businesses accountable for the risks they create.

The common law principle of vicarious liability has existed for over 200 years.

Occupiers' Liability

occupier someone who supervises and controls a property

Occupiers' liability is about people who enter a property. An **occupier** is someone who controls and supervises a property. This person owes a duty of care to make sure that it is safe for others. The occupier should be able to foresee any harm to others entering the property. For example, occupiers should make sure that handrails and steps at a home's front door are not loose or in need of repair, which could harm a visitor. Store owners should keep floors dry and free of obstructions. Hazards such as clear glass panels and doors should be clearly identified. The chart below lists some common hazardous conditions.

These are common hazardous conditions that occupiers must be aware of and make reasonably safe for visitors on their properties.

Common Hazardous Conditions

- ice and snow that has not been cleared
- unexpected elevation changes
- uneven surfaces (for example, cracks, gaps, potholes)
- slippery surfaces (for example, wet floors, tile flooring)
- missing or loose handrails on stairs
- debris on walking paths or aisles (for example, boxes or fallen produce in aisles)
- inadequate lighting

This sign protects a store from lawsuits arising from negligence. Why are these signs usually so prominent?

To establish the standard of care and the occupier's liability, the common law established three classes of persons who could enter another's property: invitees, licensees, and trespassers.

An invitee is someone on the property for reasons other than social visits. Such a person is owed the highest standard of care. Invitees include students attending school, store customers, service repair personnel, postal carriers, and so on. The standard of care is based on the belief that the occupier and invitee both benefit from their meeting.

A licensee is someone who enters a property with the implied permission of the occupier, for example, a friend who has been asked over to dinner. A licensee is a guest and is usually there for social, not business, reasons. Since no economic benefit is expected to flow to either party, a lesser standard of care is required than for invitees.

Finally, a trespasser is someone who enters a property without permission or a legal right to be there. This includes anyone from a burglar to a wandering or curious person. Guests who overstay their welcome may also be trespassers. Occupiers cannot set traps or cause deliberate harm to trespassers. Once occupiers are aware of a trespasser's presence, they must exercise a reasonable standard of care. Occupiers owe a duty of common humanity even to trespassers. They must act with at least a minimal degree of respect for the safety of all others who come onto the property.

Children and Allurements

Trespassing children have special rights because of their age. A special duty is forced on occupiers when property includes play equipment, such as a swimming pool or a playground. While alluring to children, such equipment may also pose dangers. What is considered an **allurement** varies from case to case. However, an occupier must be able to show that all reasonable

allurement something that is enticing to children and could result in their harm precautions have been taken to prevent any accident that could reasonably have been foreseen as arising from a possible allurement. Taking reasonable precautions may help to reduce, but not eliminate, liability.

Legislators accept that children are attracted to many items. There are laws that owners of such items must follow in order to protect children. Individuals and organizations must build fences of minimum heights around swimming pools and construction sites. Dangerous premises must be marked and blocked.

Occupiers' Liability Acts

Sometimes it is difficult to decide if a person is an invitee or a licensee. For example, Russell invites his business colleague Dean to dinner. Is Dean an invitee or a licensee? If Russell and Dean settle a business transaction during dinner, benefiting both financially, Dean might be an invitee. On the other hand, Russell invited him to dinner on a social occasion, so Dean is also a licensee.

Because of this confusion, several provinces passed *Occupiers' Liability Acts*. They eliminate the difference between invitees and licensees. Occupiers must treat all visitors with a common reasonable standard of care to ensure their safety. Alberta, British Columbia, Manitoba, Ontario, Nova Scotia, and Prince Edward Island have passed this type of act. The remaining provinces still follow the common law categories.

A swimming pool is very alluring to most children. The law requires owners of such allurements to take reasonable precautions to avoid an accident, such as erecting fences.

 Case

St. Prix-Alexander v. Home Depot of Canada Inc., 2008 CanLII 115 (ON S.C.)

For more information, Go to Nelson Social Studies

In November 1999, Deanna St. Prix-Alexander and her family went shopping at an Ottawa Home Depot store. The plaintiff suddenly felt a sharp blow to her neck and shoulder. She felt instant pain, and lost consciousness for a few seconds. She later discovered that a Home Depot employee had accidentally hit her with a heavy box while pulling it off the shelf.

St. Prix-Alexander saw several doctors and specialists about constant headaches, neck pain, and tingling sensations. She started collecting disability benefits in June 2000. An MRI (magnetic resonance imaging) showed that she needed surgery on her spine. She had surgery in 2003. She needed help for almost everything she did for about two months afterwards. She also had to wear a neck brace constantly for five months after her surgery. In 2004, she returned to office work as a public servant until 2006. At that time, she started collecting long-term disability benefits again.

The plaintiff sued Home Depot for $4 million for her injuries. She claimed that she could never work again, although her doctor did not propose that she stop working. In January 2008, the court awarded her nearly $500 000. Most of this award, $400 000, was for her inability to find work of an appropriate nature. She received $75 000 for general damages for pain and suffering.

For Discussion

1. Under the *Occupiers' Liability Act*, what duty of care was Home Depot required to provide to shoppers like St. Prix-Alexander?

2. Why do you think the trial judge found Home Depot and its employee negligent?

3. Do you agree with the plaintiff's claim that she could never work again? Why or why not?

4. Do you agree with the court's decision? Why or why not?

---

1. What trends have developed in judgments regarding passengers who fail to wear seatbelts?
2. What is the principle of vicarious liability? Why are employers vicariously liable for torts committed by their employees during working hours?
3. Outline at least three reasons for the principle of vicarious liability.
4. What is an occupier? What duty of care do occupiers have for persons entering their property?
5. Why have several provinces passed *Occupiers' Liability Acts*?

Host Liability

An emerging area of tort law involves the possible liability of commercial and social hosts. Commercial hosts are places such as bars, restaurants, and service clubs where alcohol is served. Social hosts are private citizens who serve alcohol in their homes. Courts have recognized that people who drink and drive do not consider the duty of care for their own safety, let alone anyone else's. More often now, commercial hosts are being held responsible for letting drunk guests get behind the wheel.

Commercial Hosts

Commercial hosts have a specific duty of care to keep an eye on intoxicated customers and prevent them from driving. Otherwise, they may be held liable for any injuries to third parties. The hosts' duty is to take steps to make sure that patrons who consume alcohol do not injure themselves or anyone they come in contact with.

Activity

To learn more about commercial hosts,

Go to Nelson
Social Studies

Measures for Commercial Hosts to Take to Reduce Liability

- Ensure that all servers have experience and training in recognizing intoxicated patrons.
- Monitor patrons' consumption.
- Do not serve alcohol to people who are intoxicated.
- Ask if the patron has a designated driver or alternate means of transportation.
- Arrange a taxi ride home for the patron.
- Call a family member or friend to come for the patron.
- Take away the patron's vehicle keys.
- Call the police.

These are some of the measures that commercial hosts can take to reduce or eliminate liability if they are sued.

The case *Stewart v. Pettie*, 1995, included a landmark judgment. The Supreme Court ruled that bars, restaurants, and other commercial establishments that serve alcohol have a duty of care. They should be held responsible if a patron drinks too much and then causes an accident that injures or kills someone. The plaintiff, Gillian Stewart, her husband, her sister-in-law, and her brother, Stuart Pettie, were at a Christmas party at an Edmonton dinner theatre. Pettie consumed a large amount of alcohol. Before leaving the theatre, they discussed with Pettie whether he was fit to drive. They all agreed that he was, and they left the theatre. Despite the fact that he was driving below the speed limit, Pettie lost control of the car on an icy patch of road. As a result of the accident, Stewart was rendered quadriplegic. The Supreme Court reviewed the theatre's possible liability. It decided that establishments do not need to prevent an intoxicated person from driving, if the person is accompanied by sober persons who can reasonably be expected to drive.

Recent court decisions suggest a trend toward assigning greater liability to parties whose negligence in supplying alcohol results in injuries to innocent persons. In *Laface v. Boknows Hotels Inc. and McWilliams*, 2006, the 19-year-old defendant, Harry McWilliams, was drinking at a hotel pub and drove away highly intoxicated. Two blocks from the hotel, he drove into a group of people and severely injured five of them. One was the plaintiff, Darin Laface. While at the pub, McWilliams showed obvious signs of intoxication, including slurred speech and staggering. One of McWilliams's friends spoke to the doorman. The friend said that McWilliams was drunk and needed someone to drive his vehicle for him. Nothing was done to prevent McWilliams from driving. The injured parties sued both McWilliams and the hotel. The trial judge divided liability equally between the two parties. An appeal to the British Columbia Court of Appeal was upheld. This was the largest portion of blame ever determined against a pub in an impaired driving civil action in Canada. Allowing McWilliams to drive away from the pub in his condition resulted in foreseeable risk that could have been avoided. By allowing him to drive away, the hotel breached its duty of care. This judgment should be a wake-up call for all bar owners and staff about the duty of care owed to patrons and others with whom they might come in contact.

Bartenders must observe whether a customer is intoxicated and take steps to prevent him or her from driving.

Should hosts be responsible to monitor how much alcohol guests drink?

Social Hosts

Social hosts hold events where alcohol is served but receive no financial benefit. Should they be held responsible for the injuries caused by intoxicated guests to themselves or to others? In early 2006, the Supreme Court heard a landmark case (outlined in the Case feature below) that could affect anyone hosting a party where alcohol is on hand. The Supreme Court had never considered this issue before. Canadian law did not provide a clear answer to the question of host liability. The judgment left the door open to find social hosts liable if they knew (or should have known) that one of their guests was drunk and planning to drive, and they did nothing to prevent it.

 Case

Childs v. Desormeaux, 2006 SCC 18 (CanLII)

For more information, Go to Nelson Social Studies

On New Year's Eve, 1998, Julie Zimmerman and Dwight Courrier hosted a Bring Your Own Bottle (BYOB) house party for relatives and friends. Courrier's friend Desmond Desormeaux was among the invited guests. Desormeaux was a self-described alcoholic with two prior impaired driving convictions. He also had an earlier conviction in 1996 for driving while his licence was suspended. In the past, Desormeaux had frequently slept over at the hosts' home when he had too much to drink, or had taken a taxi home. This time, he did neither.

At about 1:30 a.m. on January 1, 1999, Desormeaux left the party. He drove his car into oncoming traffic, colliding head-on with another car. Seventeen-year-old Zoe Childs and her boyfriend, Derek Dupre, were riding in the back seat of the other car. Dupre was killed, and Childs's spine was severed, rendering her paraplegic. All of the other passengers in both cars were seriously injured. Desormeaux's blood sample taken following the accident was more than twice the legal limit. He pleaded guilty to criminal charges arising from the accident. He received a 10-year prison sentence.

Childs sued Desormeaux and his two hosts for $6 million in damages. The trial judge held Desormeaux liable for the injuries to Childs and the other plaintiffs. He dismissed the action against the hosts. He stated that provincial governments should pass laws to determine social host liability.

Childs appealed this decision to the Ontario Court of Appeal. It also dismissed her claim in a unanimous judgment in May 2004. She then appealed to the Supreme Court of Canada. In a 7–0 decision on May 5, 2006, the high court dismissed her appeal.

For Discussion

1. In its unanimous decision, the Ontario Court of Appeal rejected Childs's appeal for the following reasons:

    - It was a BYOB party, and the hosts did not provide or serve the alcohol.
    - They had no idea how much Desormeaux was drinking.
    - They did not know that Desormeaux was impaired when he drove away from the party.

    Do you agree with the court's reasoning and this decision? Explain.

2. What steps could social hosts take to reduce liability for impaired guests at house parties? List at least four recommendations, and compare your list with others in the class.

3. In the Supreme Court judgment, Chief Justice McLachlin wrote: "As a general rule, a social host does not owe a duty of care to a person injured by a guest who has consumed alcohol ... A person who accepts an invitation to a party does not park his autonomy [freedom] at the door. The guest remains responsible for his or her conduct." Do you agree? Why or why not?

4. Do you agree with the Supreme Court's decision? Why or why not?

Professional Negligence

Recently, tort law has been updated to reflect more closely people's expectations of professionals and the services they provide. "Professionals" include architects, dentists, doctors, engineers, lawyers, pharmacists, and so on. For example, negligence occurs when a pharmacist dispenses the wrong medication. These experts have specialized knowledge and skills, and they must exercise a certain standard of care. This does not mean that they are perfect and never make mistakes. It means that their actions can be compared with the standard of others in the same profession, with the same rank, qualifications, and skills. What would or would not the others do?

The more specialized and qualified the person, the higher the expectations for standard of care. For example, a heart surgeon is held to a higher standard of care than a family doctor is with patients. Although actions have occurred against many types of professionals, the largest body of case law is in the area of medical negligence.

Medical Malpractice

The two main types of medical **malpractice** are negligence and failure to get the patient's **informed consent**. Negligence is the main cause of action in medical malpractice lawsuits. Medical negligence concerns a doctor's duty of care to the patient—that is, whether he or she has provided an adequate standard of care. Surgery always involves some risk. Even surgery that is performed with the greatest duty of care may result in new problems. For example, the patient may not respond as expected and may be worse off, rather than better, after the surgery. A doctor agreeing to provide any medical service has a duty to meet a reasonable standard of care. If the doctor fails to meet this standard, this is medical negligence. If the patient cannot prove negligence, no damages for injuries will be awarded, even if the harm is serious and permanent.

Patients undergoing treatment have the right to know the truth about their medical condition, their treatment options, and the risks involved. They need to decide whether to accept or reject a medical procedure. A doctor's ignorance of a particular risk may not be a successful defence (for example, a possible risky side effect of a drug the doctor prescribed). The law expects such a high standard of care from doctors that a court may rule that the doctor *ought* to have known about that particular risk.

malpractice improper or negligent professional treatment

informed consent agreement to a particular action with full understanding of the risks

 Did You Know?

A group of Canadian doctors founded the Canadian Medical Protective Association (CMPA) in 1901. It was established for their mutual protection against legal actions for alleged malpractice. It had over 71 000 active physicians in 2008. This represents 95 percent of licensed doctors in Canada.

Doctors can be sued for medical negligence if they do not live up to the required standard of care. What standard of care would you expect from your healthcare professional?

Doctors have no right to touch any patient, no matter how sick or close to death, without that person's consent. Medical emergencies are exceptions to this principle, but the situation must be life threatening. In all but these cases, the consent must be informed. If the patient lacks sufficient information to give informed consent, the doctor may be liable for negligence—even assault and medical battery. Negligence may exist if the doctor does not fully inform the patient about the risks involved. Medical battery may exist if the doctor treated the patient without any consent at all, or if aspects of treatment had no consent. Both torts are breaches of a doctor's duty of care to a patient. In determining whether a tort has been committed, the courts must answer this question: Would a reasonable patient, knowing all the risks, have decided against the treatment? If the answer to the question is "yes," then the physician has been negligent. A patient's decision to consent to or refuse treatment must be informed.

Exactly what must physicians tell patients? This issue was settled with the landmark judgment in *Reibl v. Hughes*, 1980. John Reibl accepted Dr. Robert Hughes's advice about the need for surgery. However, the doctor did not tell Reibl that the surgery carried a 4 percent risk of death and a 10 percent risk of stroke during or soon after surgery. Although the doctor performed the operation with proper care and competence, Reibl suffered a massive stroke and was left with partial paralysis. Reibl could no longer continue in his job. Reibl sued for damages and was awarded $225 000, a judgment later upheld by the Supreme Court of Canada.

Since that judgment, doctors must fully disclose any significant or **material risks** involved in the proposed treatment. You cannot consent to treatment unless doctors provide all of the information needed to make informed decisions. Doctors must tell you about known side effects and treatment risks. For surgery, they must tell you about the length of recovery time and the expected quality of life after surgery. A risk might be just a possibility but have serious consequences. Therefore, it is a material risk and you must be told about it. You can give informed consent to doctors only when you are sufficiently informed about all risks.

Is this a possible example of medical negligence? Explain.

material risk a significant possibility of harm from a medical treatment

Review Your Understanding

1. What trend has developed in assessing liability to hosts whose negligence in supplying alcohol results in injuries to others?

2. List at least five measures commercial hosts can take to reduce liability for injuries caused by intoxicated patrons.

3. When might a social host be held liable?

4. Identify five types of professionals, and give an example of negligence for each.

5. What is informed consent, and why is it so important?

12.5 Trespass to Persons and Land

You have learned that there are two main types of torts: unintentional (negligence) and intentional. The main intentional torts are **trespass** to another person (assault and battery, false imprisonment), trespass to land, and nuisance. Each is discussed below.

Assault and Battery

"Assault" in tort law has a different meaning from "assault" in criminal law. In tort law, assault occurs when the victim has reason to believe that bodily harm may occur. Any threat of apparent or immediate danger or violence is an assault. The essential element is the victim's fear. No actual physical contact is necessary. Assault can occur without battery, the follow-through of assault. If someone swings a fist at you and misses, an assault has occurred. You may be awarded damages for the fear you experienced as a result of that action. Pointing an unloaded gun is assault if the victim believes the gun is loaded or feels fear or danger. Uttering threatening words, such as "I'm going to stab you" or "Give me your purse, or it's your life," is assault if the victim has a reasonable belief that the other person intends to carry out the threat. Other examples of assault include unleashing a barking dog, shaking a fist, or a group of people swarming someone in a hostile manner.

    Battery is the most common form of trespass to another person. Battery is the unlawful and intentional touching of a person without that person's consent. It may exist even if no injury results. Kissing, hugging, or touching someone in a sexual manner without the person's consent can be battery, as can spitting at someone, especially if the action is offensive or upsetting to the victim. Pulling a chair out just as someone is sitting down is also battery.

What do you think an impersonal injury lawyer does?

Elements of Assault and Battery

Assault	Battery
• no contact necessary • does not require physical harm done • there must be an intention to cause offensive contact or fear that the intent is there	• harmful or offensive contact • contact must be direct, not indirect • assumes fault on defendant's part unless the defendant can prove he or she did not intend the harm

This chart highlights the key elements of assault and battery in tort law.

Assault and battery are usually tried together. Assault often occurs just before or at the same time as battery. In fact, the difference between these two torts is disappearing. Most cases based on assault include battery. The damages awarded in such actions compensate the victim for harm or loss. If an assault is extremely vicious or committed without reason, the court may also award punitive damages.

Chapter 12 **Negligence and Other Torts**

Arthur v. Wechlin, 2000 BCSC 948 (CanLII)

For more information, Go to Nelson Social Studies

Elton John performs at many concerts around the world and has a large fan base of all ages.

The 38-year-old plaintiff, Shelley Arthur, and a friend attended an Elton John concert at Vancouver's Pacific Coliseum in September 1995. The 43-year-old defendant, Jerry Wechlin, was seated behind them. He yelled out insults and profanity during the concert. Arthur asked Wechlin to stop so she and others could enjoy the concert.

Arthur had a lit cigarette in her hand, and Wechlin told her that smoking was not allowed in the arena. She agreed to put it out if he stopped yelling and disrupting the concert. As she dropped the cigarette, Wechlin thought she was throwing it at him. He grabbed her wrist and held it for a couple of seconds. He lifted her out of her seat, and turned her around, causing her immediate pain. Wechlin believed that Arthur was trying to burn him with her cigarette.

Arthur brought an action for damages. Evidence at trial indicated that Arthur's shoulder and neck were seriously injured by this incident. Her ability to work as a court reporter was severely restricted. The trial judge awarded her nearly $500 000, mainly for lost future income. Arthur was one of the few people in her community skilled in this field. An appeal by Wechlin to the British Columbia Court of Appeal was dismissed in a 3–0 judgment in 2002.

For Discussion

1. On what grounds did the plaintiff base her action?

2. What defence or explanation could Wechlin use to justify his actions?

3. On the balance of probabilities, which version of this incident is more credible? Explain.

4. What is your opinion of the trial judgment? Explain.

False Imprisonment

False imprisonment involves confining or restraining a person without their consent in a specific area. The word "false" means wrongful or unauthorized. "Imprisonment" refers to being confined or not free, but not necessarily in a prison. Wrongful confinement might be a better term for this tort. Confinement may be through physical restraint, barriers, or legal authority. Imprisonment must be a total restriction. A plaintiff must attempt every reasonable means of escape before bringing an action for false imprisonment.

An example is when store detectives hold an innocent person whom they suspect of shoplifting. Physical restraint is not necessary for false imprisonment to happen. If store security stops suspects, who then have a genuine fear of embarrassment if they try to leave, false imprisonment exists. It is enough for a store employee to shout, "Grab that thief!" for false imprisonment to exist.

You saw in Chapter 5 that police might arrest a person without warrant. They might not have reasonable and probable grounds for believing that a crime has been committed. In such cases, the arrested person may sue for false arrest. Like assault and battery, the terms "false arrest" and "false imprisonment" are often used together to mean the same thing.

You Be the Judge

Ward v. British Columbia, 2009 BCCA 23 (CanLII)

For more information, **Go to Nelson Social Studies**

Cameron Ward is arrested as a suspect in planning to throw a pie at Prime Minister Jean Chrétien.

On August 1, 2002, Prime Minister Jean Chrétien attended a ceremony for the opening of the Millennium Gate in Vancouver's Chinatown. On that day, police were on high alert after a man was overheard plotting to throw a pie at the prime minister. While Cameron Ward's clothing was close to the suspect's description, his height, hair colour, and age were all different. Ward was moving away from Chrétien when a police officer confronted him "quite aggressively" and asked if Ward was planning to throw a pie. Ward replied, "No, of course not." Police did not believe him and arrested him for breach of the peace. He was strip-searched and held in jail. His car was impounded and searched, but no pie was found. Ward was detained for several hours after the prime minister had left the area.

Ward was a well-known Vancouver lawyer. He claimed that his Charter rights were violated during this incident. He brought an action for damages against the police officers involved in his arrest, the City of Vancouver, and the provincial government. The trial judge found the arrest was lawful, but that Ward's Charter rights were breached and awarded him damages of $10 100. Ward appealed to the British Columbia Court of Appeal, which granted leave to appeal to the Supreme Court of Canada in June 2009.

• Which of Ward's Charter rights were violated? What decision do you think the appellate court reached and why?

Negligent Investigation: A New Tort

The **negligent investigation** tort allows someone wrongly accused and convicted of a crime to sue police if they cause harm by conducting an investigation negligently or sloppily. This tort was established in the landmark case *Hill v. Hamilton-Wentworth Regional Police Services Board*, 2007. Supreme Court Chief Justice McLachlin stated in the majority judgment: "Police, like doctors or lawyers, must be expected to live up to a reasonable standard of conduct toward those whose lives are in their hands."

In this case, Jason Hill was investigated by Hamilton-Wentworth police in connection with a series of 10 bank robberies. He was arrested and tried for bank robbery in 1996. Evidence against him included a Crime Stoppers tip and a police officer's photo identification of him. It also included eyewitness identifications that suggested the bank robber was an Aboriginal male. Hill is an Aboriginal male. He was convicted and spent more than 20 months in jail. In late 1999, he was acquitted in a new trial after another man was arrested for the robberies originally blamed on Hill.

negligent investigation a tort for improper investigation by police

Louis Sokolov (shown here) was the lawyer who handled Jason Hill's appeal. Hill, an Aboriginal male, was the focus of a landmark court judgment that allowed police to be sued for sloppy investigations.

Hill brought a $3-million civil action for negligence against the police. It was based on their investigation conduct. He attacked the identification evidence of two bank tellers. He did so on the grounds that they were interviewed together with a newspaper photo identifying Hill as the suspect on their desks. He was also critical of the police lineup that consisted of Hill, another Aboriginal male, and 11 Caucasian men. Also, the police failed to adequately reinvestigate the robberies when new evidence emerged that cast doubt on his initial arrest.

Hill's case was dismissed at trial and in the Ontario Court of Appeal. He then appealed to the Supreme Court of Canada. His appeal was heard in November 2006. In a 6–3 decision in October 2007, the Court ruled that police officers and forces can be sued for negligence. However, they sided with the police in this case and ruled that what happened to Hill did not constitute negligence. He was simply a victim of an "unfortunate series of events."

Review Your Understanding

1. What is an intentional tort? Give five examples.
2. Distinguish between assault and battery.
3. When might punitive damages be awarded for assault and battery?
4. What two conditions must exist for a false imprisonment action to succeed?
5. What is the difference between false imprisonment and negligent investigation?

 Did You Know?

In Saskatchewan, farmers must clearly mark farm equipment left in fields in the winter. This is to prevent trespassing snowmobilers from mistaking snow-covered equipment for small hills.

Trespass to Land

Trespass is the act of entering and crossing another person's land without permission or legal authority. As in battery, no specific damage needs to occur for trespass to exist. Simply going on a person's property without permission is a trespass, whether or not trespass was intended. Remaining on that land when asked to leave is also trespass. So is throwing an object onto another person's land, or bringing an object onto another's land and not removing it. For example, cutting down a tree, letting it fall onto a neighbour's property, and not removing it is a trespass. As long as the tree remains on the land, there is a continuing trespass.

Do signs really keep people from trespassing? Explain.

Land ownership gives owners the right to use the land above and below Earth's surface. If Lloyd tunnels through to Sandra's land to access oil there, Sandra can successfully sue for trespass. Similarly, stringing wires or lines over another person's land is trespass. However, statutes permit everyone to use space at certain distances above land. This allows aircraft to fly on regulated flight paths above private property. Occupiers' right to use property is also recognized by provincial landlord and tenant statutes. For example, a landlord who wants to enter a tenant's rented property must notify the tenant in advance.

Nuisance

What is a nuisance, and how does it differ from trespass? A nuisance involves one person's unreasonable use of land that interferes with the enjoyment and use of adjoining land by others. Although trespass is always an intentional tort, a nuisance may be intentional or unintentional. Trespass laws protect the possession and use of property. Nuisance laws protect the quality of that possession and use. For example, if a farmer enters her neighbour's property without permission and reason, she is guilty of trespass. If the same farmer sprays her fruit trees with pesticide and the spray drifts onto a neighbour's property, causing him to fall ill, the neighbour can claim damages for nuisance. Nuisance has been used to try to prevent or obtain damages for excessive odours or noise. Nuisance is also used against factory pollution, and malfunctioning sewage systems. Even a neighbour's barking dog might be considered a nuisance.

Nuisances can be either private or public. A private nuisance recognizes a person's right to the normal use and enjoyment of his or her land, free from harmful or unreasonable interference. Damages will not be awarded for minor annoyances; the harm must be serious and continue for some time. One golf ball hit into a person's backyard from a neighbouring country club is an annoyance. Golf balls hit regularly into that same yard are a nuisance.

A public nuisance is an offence that interferes with the general public's rights, for example, a protest blocking a highway, or blocking public waters. Another example is polluting public waters with insecticides or oil spills. If a majority of people are affected, it is not necessary to prove that everyone has been harmed. Actions for public nuisance are usually brought by government officials on behalf of the public. A successful action often results in a damages award. It may also result in issuing an injunction, for example, a company is ordered to stop dumping waste into a lake.

 You and the Law

As of 2009, nearly 1300 municipalities of various sizes across Canada had passed pesticide restriction bylaws. The largest, with a population of 2.5 million, is Toronto. Has your community passed pesticide legislation?

In June 2008, the United States Supreme Court awarded $507.5 million in punitive damages against Exxon Mobil Corporation. This stemmed from the disastrous 1989 incident when the tanker *Exxon Valdez* ran aground on a reef. As a result, it dumped 11 million gallons (about 42 million litres) of oil into Alaska's Prince William Sound (shown here). This money will be divided among nearly 33 000 fishers, cannery workers, and Alaska residents whose livelihoods were damaged or destroyed by the oil spill. Hundreds of thousands of seabirds and marine animals were also killed.

Nuisance actions are more visible today. Society is more concerned about pollution. This has resulted in more government regulations. Local zoning bylaws try to keep some distance between land used for industry and residents. However, citizens still have the right to take civil action. Occupiers are entitled to make reasonable use of their own property.

Launching a nuisance action against polluters has its pros and cons. How difficult would it be to prove unreasonable interference with the use and enjoyment of your land?

Nuisance Actions Against Polluters

Advantages	Disadvantages
• Individuals may sue polluters without waiting for government to act. • The courts will award compensation to successful plaintiffs for losses suffered. • It may be possible to obtain a permanent injunction to stop a polluter. In some cases, temporary injunctions can be obtained quickly. • An action in tort law may be the only legal remedy for a plaintiff against a polluter.	• Usually, a plaintiff must have a property interest in the land being harmed by pollution in order to sue. • It is difficult to prove that a polluter's activities are directly linked to a specific harm and that such harm could have been foreseen. • The costs of bringing a civil action can be very high. • Many serious environmental problems are global and cannot be addressed through tort law. • The case may not be tried for a long time.

Did You Know?

In September 2007, the Canadian government announced $96 million in compensation for a specific group. The group included people exposed to chemical agents such as Agent Orange. The chemicals were sprayed at the CFB Gagetown military base in New Brunswick. The sprayings happened over seven days in 1966 and 1967. Those who suffered health problems because of the chemicals were paid a one-time, lump sum payment of $20 000 each.

Nuisances are not always linked to environmental concerns. Protests outside courtrooms holding controversial trials are nuisances. They interfere with the free movement of other people in and out of buildings.

The courts decide what is reasonable. They must balance that right against the rights of other occupiers. Courts should only become involved when occupiers in the area can reasonably show they have been inconvenienced. Compensation is not awarded for occasional minor annoyances. The harm must be serious and continue for some time. The normal remedy for a nuisance is an injunction, although damages may also be awarded.

Review Your Understanding

1. How are trespass to land and battery similar?
2. Why is throwing an object onto another's property considered trespass?
3. With examples, explain the difference between a public and private nuisance.
4. In what two ways do trespass and nuisance differ?
5. Besides environmental concerns, what is another common example of a nuisance?

12.6 Defences for Trespass

People who commit intentional torts may not be liable if they can legally defend their actions. Once the plaintiff establishes that the defendant committed a trespass, there are a number of ways a defendant might explain the trespass. The most common defences are as follows:

- consent
- self-defence
- defence of others
- defence of property
- legal authority
- necessity

A defendant may use more than one defence in the same lawsuit. Each defence is discussed below.

Consent

Consent is the most common defence in cases involving trespass, especially battery. Consent must be established by the defendant. A defendant who can show willing consent from the plaintiff is excused from liability in the results. For example, a group of teenagers plays a friendly game of football. During the game, Kevin is tackled and his arm is broken. If Kevin sues for damages, he will not win. He voluntarily agreed to play, and no anger was displayed during the game. Also, he consented while being aware of the risks of the game. This defence is similar to the defence for negligence of voluntary assumption of risk.

Court cases made up of different issues, such as contact sports and medical treatment, have tried resolving how far consent applies. Courts assume that players in certain sports consent to the contact allowed by game rules. For example, football players expect to be tackled, boxers to be punched, and so on. Bodychecking is considered a normal part of hockey. However, if Natalie deliberately slashes Michelle's face, she is using excessive force. She is committing an intentional tort. In this case, Michelle could succeed in a tort action. A criminal charge could also be laid against Natalie, the aggressive player. (See the Issue in Chapter 11, pages 384–385, for more on the issue of violence in contact sports.)

Players in contact sports consent to contact allowed by game rules. Is that what is happening in this hockey game?

Self-Defence

Just as in criminal law, self-defence is a valid defence as long as the force used is not excessive *and* it is reasonable and necessary in the circumstances to prevent personal injury. What is reasonable and necessary depends on the facts of each case. Suppose Julian claims he was defending himself against Scott. Julian must convince the court that he genuinely feared being injured by Scott, and that Scott was struck in self-protection against the threat. The burden of proof rests with Julian. He must prove that his actions were necessary to prevent the attack and that excessive force was not used. Self-defence may even be used as a successful defence if Julian struck the first blow. Julian must convince the court that striking out was the only means of self-protection.

Provocation, which was outlined in Chapter 8 as a possible defence for murder, is not a defence for an intentional tort. If Petra hits Bill for provoking or annoying her to the point where she loses her temper, she has no legal defence. She may be held liable for any injury she causes Bill. But, provocation may reduce the damages that the defendant must pay.

 You Be the Judge

Leonard v. Dunn, 2006 CanLII 33419 (ON S.C.)

For more information, Go to Nelson Social Studies

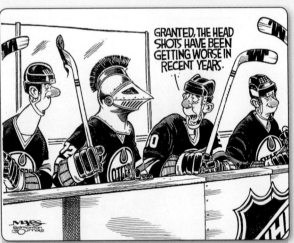

GRANTED, THE HEAD SHOTS HAVE BEEN GETTING WORSE IN RECENT YEARS.

Some fans suggest that hockey games are becoming too violent. Do you think helmets like this will be necessary protection for players in the future?

On February 5, 2004, a recreational, non-contact league hockey game between the Rangers and the Wild Hogs took place in a rink in Aurora, a community north of Toronto. Marc Leonard, 35, played for the Rangers, and Andrew Dunn, 26, for the Wild Hogs. The game was an ordinary one. It was not especially chippy (short-tempered), and few penalties were called. During the third period, the two men collided as they were both jockeying for the puck. The referee blew the whistle and stopped the play immediately to prevent possible escalation of the situation. Dunn then struck Leonard in the face with his gloved hand, breaking off Leonard's two front teeth. This resulted in the need for extensive dental work. The referee called a match penalty on Dunn and issued a five-game suspension.

Leonard brought a civil action against Dunn for damages as a result of his injuries. The case was heard in September 2006. The referee testified this was not a fight and that the collision was not intentional. There was also no evidence to indicate that Leonard had attacked Dunn prior to Dunn striking Leonard. Dunn claimed that Leonard signed a waiver form accepting all risks and must accept that hockey can be a dangerous sport. Dunn also claimed that he punched Leonard in self-defence, and he refused to apologize or admit wrong behaviour.

- If you were the judge, would you have accepted Dunn's argument of self-defence? Why or why not? What do you think the judge decided in this case?

Defence of Others

A third party can come to the aid of someone if it is reasonable to assume that that person is in some degree of immediate danger. This defence occurs most often when a parent comes to the assistance of a child or close relative, or one spouse defends the other. The same principles apply to this defence as to the defence of self-defence.

Defence of Property

Property owners may use reasonable force to eject intruders from their property. The owner must first ask the trespasser to leave. If the request is ignored, then a reasonable amount of force may be used to expel the intruder. However, if the trespasser made a forcible entry onto the property, no request to leave is necessary before force can be used. Again, the amount of force used must be reasonable. The property owner cannot set a deadly or dangerous trap to harm trespassers.

Legal Authority

Sometimes, people such as police officers have legal authority to act in ways that might otherwise result in legal action for assault and battery or false imprisonment. For example, police can hold people in the course of a valid arrest. Many civil actions against police are decided in their favour. They have a legal duty to arrest suspects in a criminal case. Store detectives have the legal authority to arrest suspected shoplifters. They do not have any more rights of arrest than a private citizen. (To review arrest rights, see Chapter 5.)

Police officers that have search warrants can legally defend themselves against trespass claims. Before entering a home, officers should identify themselves and display their search warrant. They should then request entry to the home. Unexpected arrival could lead to serious misunderstanding and possible injury. The safety of both the homeowner and police is at stake.

Some industries can legally release reasonable amounts of smoke, noise, and waste. Similar regulations apply to aircraft and vehicles with sirens. Governments attempt to balance society's right of enjoyment with industry's needs to provide products and services. However, if a business exceeds amounts considered reasonable by law, nuisance actions may be filed.

Necessity

Necessity is also a defence against trespass. If trespassing on the land is necessary, a defendant can be excused from liability. For example, trespassing may be necessary when a storm forces boaters to seek safety on nearby land. The boaters do not have permission to be on the land. However, their defence of necessity would likely succeed. They would be liable for any losses resulting from damages they cause. If you trespass to reclaim your belongings, you could argue that the action was necessary.

Landing on this island in a severe storm might be necessary trespassing.

1. Identify five defences for trespass.
2. When is consent not a valid defence in a contact sport?
3. When is self-defence a valid defence against battery?
4. Who may use the defence of legal authority and in what situations?
5. Explain necessity as a defence against trespass to land.

12.7 Defamation of Character and Its Defences

defamation injury to a person's character or reputation

Defamation is a false statement that damages another person's reputation and may cause financial loss. The attack may be intentional or unintentional. It must lower the person's reputation. It may cause people to avoid him or her. It may expose the person to hatred, contempt, or ridicule. A damaged reputation may result in difficulty in finding or keeping jobs. It may also result in strained friendships.

A person who is defamed can sue for damages. The plaintiff must establish that the defendant's statements seriously injured his or her reputation. Otherwise, only minor damages are possible. Defamation laws, such as provincial *Libel and Slander Acts*, attempt to balance the Charter's freedom of expression and protecting a person's good reputation.

Someone alleging defamation must prove the following:

- The words used by the defendant were false.

- The words referred to the plaintiff.

- The words were read or heard by a third party.

- The words caused economic loss.

The more mean or vicious the remarks, the more serious the tort. Defamation may take the form of slander or libel. Several provinces have removed the distinction between them. They treat all damaging statements as defamation.

Did You Know?

Including a real person's likeness doing something illegal or objectionable in a video game may be defamation.

Slander

slander defamation through verbal communications

Slander is defamation through spoken words, sounds, gestures, or facial expressions. Slander may be unintentional. For example, Niko makes negative comments to Istvan about Istvan himself. If Laura enters the room and overhears the conversation, slander may have occurred. Niko only meant for Istvan to hear the criticism. However, Niko took the risk of having her remarks overheard.

Libel

Libel occurs when someone is defamed in a more permanent visual or audio form. This can happen in radio or television broadcasts, publications, recordings, and so on. Libel does not have to be intentional. If Niko makes negative remarks about Istvan in her private journal, they are not libelous. If someone else reads them, libel may exist.

The Internet is the most important reason behind an increase in libel lawsuits in Canada. For most cases in which damages are awarded, defendants refuse to remove offensive material from the Internet. A writer may be sued for something written in a blog or posted to a discussion board. Removing the material likely avoids a major civil action.

Newspapers often publish the addresses as well as the names of persons arrested for criminal offences. They do so to prevent persons with the same names from being defamed. If a publication is sued for libel, the reporter, the editor, the publisher, and the owner are all liable for defamation. It is often the publisher or owner who pays the damages. The award may be reduced if the defendant makes an apology or prints a correction in another issue of the newspaper.

Defences for Defamation

There are several common defences for defamation of character:

- truth
- absolute and qualified privilege
- fair comment

These defences try to balance protecting a person's reputation with guaranteeing freedom of speech and expression.

Truth

The best defence against defamation is to prove truth. An action will fail if the defendant can show that statements are absolutely true and justified. This is a complete defence, even if the plaintiff's reputation is damaged. Truth is an inadequate defence if someone repeats statements believed to be true that are false. Repeating damaging remarks is as serious as making them in the first place. Editors and publishers are responsible for making sure reporters' stories are completely accurate.

Did You Know?

Casey Hill, an Ontario government lawyer, sued the Church of Scientology for libel. In 1995 in *Hill v. Church of Scientology of Toronto*, the Supreme Court of Canada reaffirmed lower Ontario court decisions. It awarded Hill $1.6 million. This was the largest-ever libel award in Canadian history.

libel defamation in written form

All About Law DVD
"Libel Chill" from *All About Law DVD*

In March 2008, Prime Minister Stephen Harper launched a $3.5 million libel lawsuit against the Liberal Party of Canada for allegations that Harper bribed an independent MP, Chuck Cadman, in return for his support in toppling the Liberal government. In February 2009, Harper abandoned the defamation lawsuit, without costs awarded to either side. Both parties have agreed not to comment further. This was the first time in Canadian history that a sitting prime minister had sued the opposition party for libel.

Absolute Privilege

absolute privilege a defence against defamation for statements made in legislative and judicial proceedings

Many persons in public roles have **absolute privilege**. This includes members of parliament and legislatures, and those taking part in courts, coroners' inquests, and judicial hearings. They can say things openly, honestly, and freely without fear of being sued. Their remarks must be made within the limits of the legislature or court. The principle of absolute privilege is based on the belief that society's interests are best served by open debate—even at the cost of someone's reputation.

Any one of the previously mentioned persons may make a remark outside of the protected location. In this case, the defamed person may take civil action. For example, an MP makes a defamatory remark in the House of Commons. He repeats it to reporters on the front steps of the Parliament buildings. He can be sued for the comment made to reporters on the building steps. The same statement, made in the House of Commons, is protected by absolute privilege.

Qualified Privilege

qualified privilege a defence against defamation for expressing honest opinions as part of a job

malice the intention to harm another

fair comment a defence to defamation for comments made in good faith

People who are required to express their opinions during the course of their work are protected by **qualified privilege**. Its purpose is to encourage free speech on matters of public importance. Qualified privilege will succeed as a defence if the defendant can prove that the statements were made in good faith and without **malice**. If malice is the motive, qualified privilege is not a valid defence.

Under the law, sometimes open and honest communication is more important than protecting a person's reputation. Examples are employers or teachers asked to write letters of reference for employees or students, or credit-reporting agencies asked to provide details on credit rating and ability to meet loan payments. Qualified privilege applies to such people. They act in good faith, and may provide honest yet negative references. They must do so without fear of legal action, even if their remarks turn out to be false and defamatory. This defence is also available to doctors, nurses, and teachers. They have a legal duty to report suspected child abuse.

Elected federal and provincial politicians have absolute privilege within the House of Commons and legislatures. Government officials taking part in local or municipal council meetings have qualified privilege.

Many celebrities, such as Jennifer Aniston, have had to deal with criticism—even malicious slander—from the media.

Fair Comment

Media critics who review various events provide information to the public. **Fair comment**, or the right to criticize, is accepted in our society. Critics should be able to comment honestly on events without fear of legal action. However, if the comments can be proven as malicious, the defendant can be held liable. It is fair for the critic to offer the opinion that an actor's performance in a new film was awful. The critic should not lie about the performance. However, it is not fair for the critic to make malicious comments about the actor's private life. Nor is it fair for a restaurant critic to give a bad review if the critic has a friend at a competing restaurant.

Case

Newman et al. v. Halstead et al., 2006 BCSC 65 (CanLII)

For more information, Go to Nelson Social Studies

Sue Halstead defamed several British Columbia teachers on an Internet website. As a result, the British Columbia Teachers' Federation launched a successful lawsuit against her.

Sue Halstead was a mother of five children in the Comox Valley School District on Vancouver Island. She had a long history criticizing the British Columbia Teachers' Federation (BCTF). She often waged battles with teachers, trustees, and the school board. In 2003, she created a website and Internet chat room called GAFER, Growing Advocacy for Education Reform. They included a page called "B.C.'s Least Wanted Educators." It listed names and photos of teachers who had been criminally charged. It also included teachers, parents, and trustees that she believed were "bullies." She accused several people of misconduct, such as assaults against students, drunkenness at school, smoking pot, and sexual harassment. She alleged the school board

was involved in "unimaginable corruption, crime, and child abuse."

In April 2004, the BCTF filed a defamation action against Halstead. It was on behalf of nine teachers, a retired trustee, and a parent. The teacher Edmund Newman bore the brunt of Halstead's attacks. During the trial, witnesses revealed that Halstead had had normal relations with teachers and trustees until 1997. Then, her behaviour became aggressive and outrageous. No one could suggest why she changed. Halstead did not participate in her trial.

In January 2006, the trial judge awarded the plaintiffs $626 000 in damages. Newman received the greatest individual damages of $150 000. Other plaintiffs received from $1000 to $125 000. The judge ordered $50 000 in punitive damages to be divided among the 11 plaintiffs. Also, the judge issued an injunction against Halstead to shut down her website.

For Discussion

1. What type of defamation is involved in this case?
2. Why did the judge award the plaintiffs punitive damages?
3. Why did the judge issue an injunction against Halstead?
4. The trial judge stated: "Ms. Halstead's shockingly vicious attack upon, and her manifestly fictitious account of, each of the plaintiff's character and conduct is deserving of rebuke...Her actions are malicious and cruel." Do you agree? Why or why not?

Review Your Understanding

1. What is defamation, and what are its two forms?
2. Which of the two forms of defamation is considered the more serious? Why?
3. What is the best defence to the tort of defamation? Why?
4. Distinguish between absolute and qualified privilege.
5. When can fair comment be used as a defence?

12.8 The Need for Insurance

As you have learned, awarding damages to plaintiffs is the most common form of compensation in tort law. In several cases, defendants were required to pay judgments in the hundreds of thousands of dollars. This is often money that few defendants can pay themselves. For this reason, people purchase liability insurance to protect themselves against the possibility of expensive legal actions.

Liability insurance should be purchased to protect against expensive legal actions and unusual lawsuits.

Motor Vehicle Liability Insurance

Today, disputes over motor vehicle accidents often result in civil actions. Lawyers specializing in civil lawsuits may spend more time dealing with these actions than any other type of tort. Several years can pass between the accident and the end of the trial and awarding damages. Someone injured in a vehicle accident can claim special and general damages from the driver. Recently, courts determined that persons indirectly involved, such as relatives, can claim damages. They can use grounds such as mental anguish or loss of companionship of their loved one. Statutes in several provinces allow such claims.

Even minor accidents in which no one was seriously injured can result in damage claims so high that most people are unable to pay them. All car owners in Canada are legally required to purchase motor vehicle liability insurance. The insurance company pays any claims for damages arising from an accident, up to a certain maximum. This type of insurance is called third-party liability insurance. This is because three parties are involved when a claim is made. They are the person who caused the accident, that person's insurance company, and the victim claiming damages.

The law in all provinces and territories requires a minimum of $200 000 of insurance coverage. Damage awards for vehicle accidents are quite high. Many drivers are motivated to buy insurance coverage of $1 million or $2 million. This is far higher than the required minimum.

Some drivers have no insurance. This is illegal in Canada and carries severe fines. People who suffer loss in an accident with an uninsured driver are compensated through special arrangements. In some provinces, a fund run by the insurance industry handles such claims. In the other provinces, the fund is administered by the government. Victims of motor vehicle accidents often have to wait years for damages. Therefore, a limited form of **no-fault insurance** was instituted in some provinces. This type of coverage allows insured drivers to make claims to their insurance companies, regardless of who is at fault. It is designed to put money in the hands of victims immediately, whether or not they are at fault in the accident.

A person who suffers loss beyond what no-fault insurance covers can still bring a tort action for damages. However, if the person wins additional damages from the courts, any no-fault insurance benefits are deducted from the award. Motor vehicle insurance regulations differ across the country. Their details are too complex to be discussed here. You can get details about your provincial or territorial regulations from a local insurance agent.

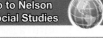

e Activity

To learn more about motor vehicle liability insurance,

Go to Nelson Social Studies

no-fault insurance insurance money paid regardless of who is at fault in an accident

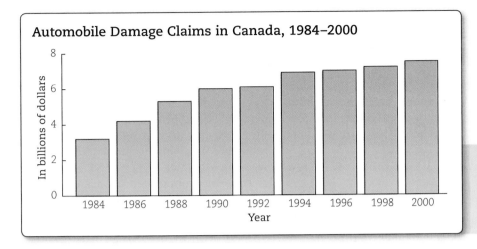

Automobile Damage Claims in Canada, 1984–2000

Automobile damage claims have more than doubled since 1984. What factors might account for this?

Other Liability Insurance

It is now common for people and businesses to reduce losses from possible civil actions by buying insurance. If a court awards damages greater than the limit for coverage, the defendant must pay the difference. This may mean selling possessions or garnisheeing wages. Often, the damages can never be paid fully because the sum is too large to repay in a person's lifetime.

Civil action awards can mean millions of dollars. Large awards are made more often in the United States but are now increasing in Canada. Personal injury accident awards now cost Canadians at least $3.5 billion a year. Such awards cover medical treatment, future care, lost wages, and pain and suffering.

The number of medical malpractice suits and settlement size are increasing in Canada. Most Canadian doctors pay fees to the Canadian Medical Protective Association (CMPA). This organization provides medical insurance that covers legal costs and damage awards for doctors sued successfully for malpractice.

Canadian lawyers are required to purchase malpractice insurance to protect themselves against civil actions from dissatisfied clients. Retail outlets and centres, schools, places of worship (instead of churches), clubs, municipalities, and community organizations purchase insurance. It protects them from lawsuits arising from injuries to persons on their property. Both homeowners and tenants who rent property also buy liability insurance. It covers damages in case of injuries to visitors.

 Did You Know?

The CMPA's 2006 malpractice fees range from $564 a year for charitable, teaching, and research work abroad, to $78 120 for Ontario's obstetricians. These are the highest fees in Canada.

Review Your Understanding

1. What is third-party liability insurance? Who are the three parties?
2. Why might a motorist purchase more insurance than the provincial legal requirement?
3. What is no-fault insurance?
4. What is the purpose of the Canadian Medical Protective Association?
5. Identify three other groups, besides doctors and lawyers, who should purchase liability insurance. Explain why in each case.

Safety or Religion: Which Is More Important When Wearing Helmets?

The Ontario Human Rights Commission (OHRC) has defended an Ontario Sikh man. He is being forced to wear a motorcycle helmet instead of his turban. This violates his human rights and his religious freedom. Baljinder Singh Badesha, a devout Sikh, appeared in a Brampton court in 2008. He argued against a ticket he received for driving his motorcycle without wearing a helmet.

Badesha immigrated to Canada from India in 1989. He learned to ride in India where he was a keen motorcyclist. He got his Ontario motorcycle licence in the summer of 2005. He had been riding for just a few weeks when the police stopped him. He was charged with failing to wear a helmet while driving and received a ticket for $110. He had lived in British Columbia, where there is no mandatory helmet law. He did not know it was against the law to ride without a helmet in Ontario. In Ontario, the test for a motorcycle licence is written, and there is no driving test.

An OHRC attorney, arguing on Badesha's behalf, told the judge that "observant Sikhs are put in the impossible situation of choosing between ordinary, everyday activities and observing their faith. That is religious discrimination."

Baljinder Badesha argues that he should be allowed to ride a motorcycle without a helmet because he is a devout Sikh. Should someone be allowed to disobey a law if their Charter rights are being infringed?

On One Side

In all Canadian provinces, motorcycle drivers had to wear helmets until 1995. In 1995, courts overturned the law in Manitoba and British Columbia after a human rights challenge. Section 104 of Ontario's *Highway Traffic Act* states: "No person shall ride on or operate a motorcycle or motor-assisted bicycle on a highway unless the person is wearing a helmet that complies with the regulations." It is a fact that in motorcycle accidents, helmets save lives. Allowing Sikhs to drive without helmets directly challenges the law's purpose, which is to save lives.

Motorcyclists risk serious head or neck injuries if they do not wear helmets. This increases costs in our public health system. Public health care already costs almost 40 percent of provincial budgets. Crown lawyers in this case argued that helmet laws save the health care system millions of dollars.

On the Other Side

Section 2(a) of the *Charter of Rights and Freedoms* guarantees Canadians freedom of conscience and religion. Baljinder Badesha believes that this freedom includes riding his motorcycle without a helmet. Badesha claims that the law discriminates against Sikhs. Their religion obliges them to cover their hair with only a turban when outside their home. He states: "My religion says we cannot put anything over our turbans. I like to ride a motorcycle, so that is why I fight the case."

Political decisions and case law may support Badesha's claim. In 1990, Baltej Singh Dhillon was accepted into the RCMP. He was told to cut his hair, remove his turban, and shave his beard. Dhillon challenged this in court. Sikhs in the RCMP may now wear turbans, and they do not have to cut their hair or shave their beards.

In *Multani v. Commission scolaire Marguerite-Bourgeoys*, 2006, (see Chapter 2, pages 41–42), Sikhs in Québec won a landmark victory. The Supreme Court overturned a ban on Sikh boys wearing their kirpans (ceremonial daggers) to school. It directed provincial governments and school boards on what they must do to accommodate religious beliefs and freedoms.

The Bottom Line

Wearing a helmet while driving a motorcycle is the law in most provinces. Whether it is a good or bad law is not the question—everyone residing in the province must abide by it, whether they like it or not. Laws are enacted to protect the public, regardless of race, gender, or religion. Laws are not put in place to discriminate; they are there for the best interests of society as a whole. The helmet law does not intentionally discriminate; it applies to all Ontarians equally. Studies show that motorcyclists are three times more likely to be injured than occupants of cars. Helmets prevent up to 73 percent of deaths and up to 86 percent of brain injuries.

But, Sikh men wear turbans to preserve their Sikh identity and acknowledge commitment to their faith. Badesha says that he knows the risks of riding without a helmet and is willing to take them to honour his Sikh beliefs. It seems that the wearing of turbans has become both a human rights and a safety issue.

What Do You Think?

1. Although wearing a turban has never yet been an issue for Canadian firefighters, would wearing a turban be permitted in this profession? Why or why not?

2. In your opinion, should devout Sikhs be allowed an exemption from motorcycle helmet laws? Why or why not?

3. Should anybody who wants to drive a motorcycle without a helmet pay extra insurance and sign a release stating that they will not sue if injured? Discuss with a partner who has an opposing viewpoint.

4. "The helmet law is discriminatory and should not be enforced." Discuss.

5. On March 6, 2008, the trial judge ruled that while the law does violate Badesha's Charter right to freedom of religion, that breach is justified because of reduced health costs and saved lives. A few days later, Badesha indicated that he would appeal this decision. As an appeal court justice, what would your decision be and why? Discuss in small groups.

Chapter Review

Chapter Highlights

- Torts fall into two classes: intentional and unintentional.
- Negligence is the most important and best-known part of tort law.
- Duty of care, foreseeability, and the "reasonable person" are important concepts in negligence.
- The plaintiff must prove his or her tort action on the balance of probabilities.
- Contributory negligence and voluntary assumption of risk are the main defences to negligence.
- An assessment of 25 percent for contributory negligence is the absolute outer limit for seatbelt accidents where the plaintiff was not wearing a seatbelt.
- Vicarious liability—holding a blameless person responsible for the misconduct of others—affects liability for motor vehicle owners and employers.
- Occupiers of property must take reasonable care to make their property safe for visitors.
- Occupiers must take extra precautions to protect children from accidents around allurements such as swimming pools, playgrounds, and construction sites.
- To avoid liability, commercial hosts have a specific duty of care to monitor the behaviour of intoxicated customers and prevent them from driving.
- Doctors must receive informed consent before they touch any patient unless it is an emergency and the patient is unconscious, or to save a life.
- Trespass to a person, such as assault and battery, is a common intentional tort.
- A new tort of negligent investigation exists that allows suspects to sue police for sloppy or inferior investigations.
- Trespass laws protect the possession and use of property, while nuisance laws protect the quality of that possession and use.
- Consent, self-defence, defence of others or property, legal authority, and necessity are the main defences to trespass.
- Defamation of character may be either slander or libel.
- Truth, absolute and qualified privilege, and fair comment are the main defences for defamation.
- The purchase of various types of insurance helps protect against expensive lawsuits.

Check Your Knowledge

1. Outline the elements that are necessary to prove a negligence action, and provide an example for each.
2. Identify the acceptable defences for a negligence action, and provide an example for each.
3. Outline the intentional torts in this chapter, and provide an example for each.
4. Identify the legally acceptable defences for intentional torts, and provide an example for each.

Apply Your Learning

5. Jehovah's Witnesses are members of a Christian faith that does not believe in receiving blood transfusions under any circumstances. Many of them carry cards in their wallets that specifically state they do not want a blood transfusion, in case they are brought to the hospital while unconscious. If a doctor were to disregard this card and perform a blood transfusion anyway, what would happen? Could the doctor be sued for negligence? If you were a nurse or doctor in the emergency room with the doctor in charge, and he or she decided to go ahead and perform the blood transfusion in spite of the card in the patient's wallet, would you support or challenge the doctor? Why or why not?

6. A person attending a sporting event voluntarily assumes certain risks, but not all risks. Using your favourite sport as an example, identify guidelines for which risks are assumed and which are not.

7. List three situations in your life that could result in a possible tort liability. Identify what the torts might be and the risks involved. Outline how risk of loss or injury could be avoided.

Communicate Your Understanding

8. In pairs, choose one of the debate topics below that reflect opinion on the *Parental Responsibility Act*. Conduct an Internet search for background on this legislation, the reasons behind it, and a summary of its highlights. Once you select a debate topic, prepare a brief introduction. Identify facts and arguments that support your position. Anticipate points against your view, and prepare counter-arguments to defend your viewpoint. Conclude with a statement that summarizes your position.

   • I think that parents should definitely be responsible for their children's actions. They bring them up, so they should be punished if they do a bad job.

   • I really do not like the act. Kids should be responsible for what they do. Parents try their best to teach their children the best way to live. Kids know what is right or wrong, and it is their fault.

9. Work with a partner. Collect five articles dealing with negligence or other torts from your daily or weekly newspapers, magazines, or the Internet. Analyze the material and summarize the torts. Identify the parties involved, the injuries or losses suffered by the plaintiffs, and the damages being requested. Summarize the information into case studies to share with your classmates.

10. In small groups, prepare a public awareness campaign that can be used to promote measures for social hosts to take to avoid being sued for actions of intoxicated guests.

Develop Your Thinking

11. Given the tort law standard of the "reasonable person," what standard would developmentally challenged people be expected to meet. Why?

12. Someone who punches another person in the face may be liable for both the tort of battery and the crime of either assault or assault causing bodily harm. (See Chapter 7, pages 223–225, for more information on assault causing bodily harm.) What factors determine whether one or both charges will proceed to trial? Prepare a report to share with your classmates.

13. Divide the class into small groups of equal size. Then, conduct an Internet search to obtain background information on the 1989 *Exxon Valdez* tanker disaster and the pollution of Prince William Sound. Prepare reports on the spill itself, the cleanup process, the results, legal actions, and the current status. Share your findings in class. You might also follow this model to research the Agent Orange health problems at CFB Gagetown, New Brunswick, and prepare further reports for sharing.

Family Law

4

Chapter 13
Marriage, Divorce,
and the Family   434

Chapter 14
Division of Property
and Support   474

"Canada's 2006 census shows that marriage is in decline, and common law unions and single parenthood continue to grow. More children live in single-parent families than ever before. In fact, the single-mother family is now the fastest growing lifestyle in North America. In Canada, women head 83 percent of single-parent families."

—Statistics Canada
from the 2006 census results

NEL

13 Marriage, Divorce, and the Family

What You Should Know

- Is there a "typical" family in the twenty-first century?
- What are the legal (essential and formal) requirements of a marriage?
- How do an annulment, a separation, and a divorce differ?
- What is the key factor in determining custody of and access to children after a divorce?
- Why is mediation commonly used to resolve family disputes?
- What are the most common forms of child abuse?
- What legal options are available to help children in need of protection?

Chapter at a Glance

13.1 Introduction

13.2 The Changing Family Structure

13.3 Legal Requirements of Marriage

13.4 Annulment, Separation, and Divorce

13.5 Children and Divorce

13.6 Children in Need of Protection

Selected Key Terms

adultery

annulment

applicant

best interests of the child

child abuse

common law relationship

custody

divorce

marriage breakdown

monogamy

separation

solemnization of marriage

The formal requirements of the marriage ceremony are the responsibility of the provincial and territorial governments.

13.1 Introduction

Family law deals with the relationships among family members—between husband and wife, same-sex partners, parents and children, and other parties, such as grandparents and step-parents. Governments usually do not interfere in family lives as long as certain functions are fulfilled. Family members are required to do the following:

- register births, marriages, and deaths

- pay taxes

- feed and clothe their children (if they have any)

- educate their children and protect them from harm

- be law-abiding citizens

Federal, provincial, and territorial statutes are the primary sources for Canadian family law. The *Constitution Act, 1867* (formerly the *British North America Act*) divided the power of making marriage laws between the federal and the provincial governments. Section 91(26) gives the federal government jurisdiction over the *essentials* of marriage and divorce. In other words, standard marriage and divorce procedures are nationally recognized.

Section 92(12) gives provincial and territorial governments jurisdiction over the **solemnization of marriage**, the formal requirements of the marriage ceremony. In turn, municipal or local governments are responsible for issuing marriage licences. Section 92(13) gives the provinces power to pass laws about property and civil rights—for example, laws governing property division and support payments on **marriage breakdown**. These issues are discussed in Chapter 14.

solemnization of marriage the procedures required for a legal marriage

marriage breakdown the only ground for divorce in Canada

> Although you must have the legal and mental ability to marry, being in love also helps.

13.2 The Changing Family Structure

The traditional nuclear family consists of a mother, father, and their children. It was the common family model in many developed countries for much of the twentieth century. Traditionally, families formed through marriage, but recently this began to change. Family life changed so much that it is now difficult to talk about a "typical Canadian family." In a 2007 landmark judgment in *A.A. v. B.B.* (see Case on page 436), the Ontario Court of Appeal recognized Canada's first three-parent family. The court ruled that a five-year-old boy can legally have two mothers and a father when it gave legal parental status to the same-sex partner of the boy's biological mother. This case illustrates that the law constantly changes to reflect current social circumstances and values.

A.A. v. B.B, 2007 ONCA 2 (CanLII)

For more information, Go to Nelson Social Studies

A.A. and C.C., a lawyer and a university professor in Ontario, were partners since 1990. They decided to start a family in 1999 with the assistance of their male friend B.B. The two women would be the primary caregivers. They believed it was in the child's best interest that B.B. remain involved in the child's life. A boy, D.D., was born in 2001 and referred to both women as his mothers. The birth mother and sperm donor father were both recognized on D.D's birth certificate. The biological mother's same-sex partner, A.A., was not. D.D. was a bright, healthy, happy boy who was thriving in a loving family that met his every need. He saw his biological father twice a week.

In 2003, A.A. applied to the courts to be recognized as a legal parent. All three parents formed a united front on this court action. A.A. could have become a legal parent by adopting the child. If she had, the father would lose his own legal status, and neither the mother nor her partner wanted that to happen. The trial judge found that all three people had a positive relationship with the child. It was in the boy's best interests to recognize all three persons as legal parents. The judge felt that he did not have the authority to rule in the case under Ontario's *Children's Law Reform Act (CLRA)*. He dismissed the application since the legislation mentioned a child having only one mother and one father.

A.A., supported by B.B. and C.C. and a lawyer representing D.D., appealed this decision to the Ontario Court of Appeal. The appeal was heard in September 2006. In a unanimous landmark judgment in January 2007, the court ruled that a child can legally have three parents.

None of the parents nor the Ontario attorney general intended to appeal this judgment. The Alliance for Marriage and Family, a union of groups supporting traditional Christian marriage and families, asked the Supreme Court of Canada to grant an order adding it as a party to the case. The Alliance wanted to appeal the decision. But, in September 2007, the Supreme Court denied their request. It stated that the Alliance did not meet the test of showing that a public interest would be served by allowing it to appeal this judgment.

For Discussion

1. Why was this such a significant case?

2. The Court of Appeal judgment stated that the law did not foresee the possibility of two women both being parents, "so that over thirty years later the gap in the legislation has been revealed. As a result, the statute does not provide for the best interests of D.D." Do you agree? Why or why not? Discuss with a classmate who has an opposing view.

3. Some critics are calling this decision another unnecessary example of judicial activism (see Chapter 2, page 65) making a mockery of morality and those traditional values on which our nation is founded. Others see this as a landmark in gay rights. With whom do you agree? Explain. Discuss with a classmate who has an opposing view.

4. Do you think this decision will open the door for other "non-traditional families" to consider seeking similar declarations? Explain.

Do you think the number of same-sex parents will increase in the future? Explain.

Statistics Canada now defines a family as follows:

- married couples with or without children
- unmarried couples in a **common law relationship** with or without children
- lone or single parents with children

common law relationship
an intimate relationship between two people who live together but are not married

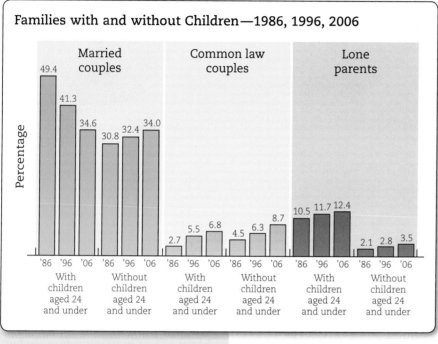

Families with and without Children—1986, 1996, 2006

What trends do these statistics indicate?

 Did You Know?

According to the 2006 census, common law relationships are much more common. In fact, 2.8 million Canadians live together under this arrangement, a 19 percent jump from 2001. They now account for 15.5 percent of all families in Canada.

Couples are marrying later in life. Because of their careers or the costs of raising a family, they sometimes delay having children. Families are smaller, with one or two children. Some couples remain childless, either by choice or for medical reasons. Various relationships redefine today's Canadian families:

- common law and same-sex partners
- blended families with at least one stepchild
- extended families with children, parents, and grandparents sharing home and finances
- two-income families with or without children

Canadian family structures are shown in the pie chart on the next page.

You and the Law

Of the types of Canadian families listed on the left, which is closest to yours? In what types of families do your best friends live?

Family Structures in Canada, 2001 and 2006

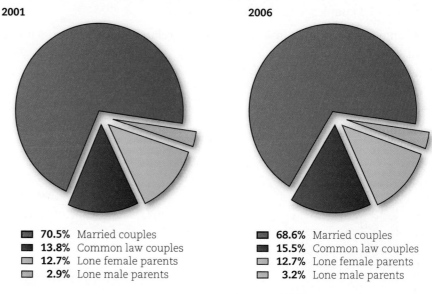

2001

2006

	2001	
■	**70.5%**	Married couples
■	**13.8%**	Common law couples
□	**12.7%**	Lone female parents
□	**2.9%**	Lone male parents

	2006	
■	**68.6%**	Married couples
■	**15.5%**	Common law couples
□	**12.7%**	Lone female parents
□	**3.2%**	Lone male parents

Note: Percentages may not add up to 100 due to rounding.

> What trends do these statistics indicate?

 Did You Know?

According to the 2006 census, married people were in the minority—at 48.5 percent—for the first time in Canadian history. The remaining 51.5 percent of adults were living in common law relationships, or they were divorced, separated, or widowed. During the 1980s, more than 60 percent of Canadians were married.

Family structure reflects social factors. The Canadian population is aging rapidly. Therefore, more generations live in the same home. Until the 1960s, most Canadian immigrants came from Europe. Today, one out of every two immigrants comes from Asia, Africa, the Caribbean, or Central America. In many of these places, caring for aging parents is the cultural norm. New Canadians bring their family customs, traditions, and values with them. Family law is quickly shifting in response to changing family relationships. In fact, during the past 25 years, probably no other area of law has changed as much.

Review Your Understanding

1. Which level of government has jurisdiction over the following:
   a) marriage and divorce
   b) solemnization of marriage
2. What types of issues does family law address?
3. According to Statistics Canada, what are the three types of families in Canada today?
4. What are common law relationships, and how common are they in Canada?
5. What trends did the 2006 census indicate about the changing nature of Canadian families?

13.3 Legal Requirements of Marriage

When two people marry, they enter into a legally binding contract, provided certain requirements are met. If they divorce, they end that contract. Like all contracts, marriage involves both rights and obligations, some of which come into effect only upon divorce. All of this is discussed in this chapter and in Chapter 14.

? Did You Know?

In 2004, the average age of first-time grooms was 30.6 years and 28.5 years for first-time brides. This compares to 33.7 and 31.1 years, respectively, in 2000.

Rights and Obligations of Marriage

- Marriage is a partnership in which each party is expected to make an equal contribution.
- Each spouse has the right to live in the family home. The couple must decide about the possible sale of the home and other assets if they separate or divorce.
- The spouses have a mutual obligation of financial support and an individual obligation of self-support.
- If there are children, partners must determine care, custody, access, and child support in case of divorce.
- Spouses have rights to share in the estate after the death of the other, whether or not the deceased left a will.

These are the most common rights and obligations that couples assume when they marry.

void without legal force; invalid

Essential Requirements of Marriage

Although the federal government controls essential marriage requirements, there is little statute law in this area. Instead, they are determined by common law principles, outlined below. If any essential requirement is lacking at the time of the marriage, the marriage cannot be legally recognized. It is declared **void** (without legal standing). The essential requirements are discussed on page 440.

Because there is little federal legislation, each province and territory has its own *Marriage Act*. Most marriage laws have been passed by the provinces and territories. They are discussed on pages 441–446.

Although marriage is a legally binding contract, it is not necessary to have a lawyer present during the marriage ceremony.

We'll say "I do" after a reduction of the sentence from "till death us do part" to "time served plus 10 years."

BIZARRO
Dist. by King Features

Essential Requirements of Marriage

Mental Capacity

Genuine Consent

Minimum Age

Close Relationships

Unmarried Status

These are the five essential requirements of marriage.

Cornered   by Mike Baldwin

GUNS

"I haven't got time for a whole lot of paperwork. The wedding's tomorrow."

This is a wedding where genuine consent might not be freely given.

consanguinity being closely related by blood to another person

monogamy the state of being married to only one person at a time

bigamy the crime of being married to two persons at the same time

polygamy the crime of being in a relationship or married to two or more persons at the same time

Mental Capacity: To legally marry, you must have the mental capacity or ability to marry. A person who lacks mental capacity because of illness, drugs, or alcohol cannot legally marry. When getting married, both parties must understand the nature of their marriage. They must understand the duties and responsibilities it creates. If mental capacity exists at the time of the marriage, but ceases to exist afterwards, the marriage remains valid.

Genuine Consent: Persons getting married must consent to it freely. If either party is forced under duress or if there is a mistake about the marriage ceremony, the marriage may be declared void. An example of duress is a pregnant girl's parents threatening legal action against the girl's partner if he does not marry her. A mistake is marrying the wrong identical twin. Another is if one of the persons does not speak the language used in the ceremony and believes it to be something else, such as an engagement ceremony.

Minimum Age: Both parties must be old enough to marry. In Canada, the federal government has not established any minimum marriage age. It adopted the English common law minimum ages: 14 years for males, 12 years for females. The basis for these ages is that, generally speaking, females are more mature at 12 than males. Also, males and females reach puberty at these ages. However, all the provinces and territories have legislation requiring a higher minimum age for marriage, and parental consent for a child under a certain age. These ages are discussed on pages 444–445.

Close Relationships: You cannot marry someone closely related to you. Two people who are too closely related by **consanguinity** (blood relationship) or adoption cannot legally marry. For example, brothers and sisters cannot marry, but first cousins are free to marry. Information about who you can and cannot marry is found in the chart on page 441. It is available anywhere marriage licences are issued. In 1991, Parliament abolished further restrictions for marriage partners. For example, a woman may marry her divorced husband's brother or nephew. A man may marry his divorced wife's sister or niece.

Unmarried Status: Both parties must be unmarried at the time of their marriage. In Canada, **monogamy** is the only accepted form of marriage. That is, a person can be married to only one spouse at a time. It is illegal for a person to enter into a second marriage while still married. A person who does so commits **bigamy**, which makes the second marriage illegal and void. Bigamy is still a criminal offence, but very few charges have been laid recently. Before a person can remarry legally, he or she must present a document showing that the earlier marriage has ended. **Polygamy** is also against the law.

Prohibited Close Relationships

A man may not marry his...	A woman may not marry her...
• mother	• father
• daughter	• son
• sister or half-sister	• brother or half-brother
• grandmother	• grandfather
• granddaughter	• grandson

Why would marrying a blood or adopted relative be prohibited?

You Be the Judge

Feng v. Yuen (Estate), 2004 CanLII 35080 (ON C.A.)

For more information, **Go to Nelson Social Studies**

Kam Yuen Sung moved from Hong Kong to Scotland in the early 1960s. There, he and his wife worked hard in the restaurant business and raised their five children. The youngest son moved to Canada around 1987 and was followed by his parents in 1990. The other siblings also came to Canada. While the elder four Sung children grew up, married, and moved away, the youngest son remained at home with his parents. Mrs. Sung died in June 2000, leaving her husband lonely and depressed. In August 2001, Sung married Qi Zi Feng, his housekeeper, but died from cancer in October 2001.

The children challenged the validity of their father's marriage. Medical evidence indicated that at the time of the marriage, Sung required full-time assistance from a caregiver. He suffered from Parkinson's disease, and he needed a respirator to breathe and a wheelchair for transport. He was also taking massive doses of medication for terminal lung cancer. Although Sung was close to all of his children, he did not tell them that he was about to be married, including his youngest son, whom he saw on the day of his marriage.

• On what basis did Sung's children challenge the validity of the marriage? What do you think the court decided about this marriage?

Formal Requirements of Marriage

Provincial and territorial governments have jurisdiction over marriage procedures. They are outlined in the respective *Marriage Acts*.

Formal Requirements (Solemnization) of Marriage

- Issuing marriage licence or banns
- Performing the marriage ceremony
- Establishing age requirements
- Registering the marriage

These requirements for the marriage ceremony are the responsibility of the provinces and territories.

? Did You Know?

According to Statistics Canada, about 60 percent of all weddings in Canada take place during the summer. August is the most popular month, when 21 percent marry. January is the least popular month, when only 2.6 percent marry.

> What do these statistics indicate about marriage in Canada in recent years?

Marriages by Province and Territory

	2003	2005	2007
Canada	**147 391**	**148 439**	**151 695**
Alberta	17 622	18 392	19 837
British Columbia	21 981	20 007	20 697
Manitoba	5 659	5 732	5 796
New Brunswick	3 724	3 686	3 622
Newfoundland and Labrador	2 876	2 806	2 698
Northwest Territories	139	140	139
Nova Scotia	4 742	4 698	4 633
Nunavut	67	69	71
Ontario	63 485	64 677	65 483
Prince Edward Island	823	829	831
Québec	21 138	22 244	22 650
Saskatchewan	4 977	5 000	5 080
Yukon Territory	158	159	158

banns of marriage an announcement of an intended marriage read in the couple's church

This is a copy of an Ontario marriage licence application.

Marriage Licence or Banns

Provincial and territorial statutes require that couples planning to marry either get a marriage licence or have the **banns of marriage** read in their place of worship in some provinces. They can purchase licences at any city hall, civic centre, or township office. In most provinces, couples must wait from three to five days and no more than three months to one year (varying by province) after obtaining a licence to get married. In Ontario, there is no waiting period once the marriage licence is purchased, and it is good for up to 90 days. If couples do not marry within the 90 days, they must reapply for a new licence.

Licence costs vary across Canada. Blood tests and medical certificates are not required to marry anywhere in Canada.

You and the Law

Where can you obtain a marriage licence in your community? How much does it cost?

Re Lin, (1992) 44 R.F.L. (3d) 60

For more information, **Go to Nelson Social Studies**

Shun Liang Lin, a Chinese citizen, met Teresa Tang, a Canadian citizen, when they lived in China. They agreed to marry in Canada. A condition for Lin's entry to Canada was to marry Tang within 90 days. About two weeks after arriving in Canada, the couple had a traditional, non-religious Chinese wedding ceremony. A family elder, who was not a marriage commissioner or clergy member, presided over the ceremony. The couple did not apply for or obtain a marriage licence.

After the ceremony, the couple lived together now and then for two months. It was not clear whether they had sexual intercourse to **consummate** (complete) their marriage. Lin applied to the Alberta Court of Queen's Bench for an order to declare the marriage valid and instruct the Vital Statistics director to issue a marriage licence.

• Do you think Lin succeeded in his application? Explain.

Couples who regularly attend a place of worship may prefer to have their marriage banns announced instead of, or in addition to, buying a licence. In the announcement, the clergy asks the congregation whether anyone is aware of any reason why the couple cannot legally marry. The banns are read at two or three weekly services in a row, depending on the province. Couples must wait at least five days after the last banns are read before getting married. Banns may not be announced if either intended partner was previously married. In this situation, a marriage licence must be purchased.

consummate to validate a marriage by having sexual intercourse

This is an unusual twist to the traditional marriage ceremony.

Marriage Ceremony

Couples can choose either religious or civil ceremonies. Registered clergy members can perform religious ceremonies. A justice of the peace or marriage commissioner may perform civil ceremonies. The marriage must have at least two people who witness the marriage registration. The ceremony may happen how and where the couple marrying wishes. The couple may write all or part of their ceremony, with permission from the person conducting the ceremony.

Nick Skalkos and Sarah LeRiche were married at a Tim Hortons doughnut outlet in Kitchener by a minister of the Universal Life Church. Their rings were honey crullers, which they ate after the ceremony.

Age Requirement

As you have already learned, the federal government adopted minimum ages for marriage from English common law: 14 years for males, 12 years for females. As the chart on page 445 shows, a person must be at least 18 or 19 years old to marry, depending on where he or she lives. Teens who are 16 or older can get married, but they must have written consent from one or both parents. If parental consent is unreasonably withheld, the teen may apply for a court order to dispense with parental consent. The court must review the parents' objections and decide whether or not they are reasonable. However, case law in this area is limited. Below age 16, marriage is permitted by court order only, and only when the young woman is pregnant or has a child. In Ontario, no person under 16 may legally marry, regardless of the circumstances.

Minimum Ages for Marriage in Canada

Province	Age without Parental Consent	Age with Parental Consent
Alberta	18	16
British Columbia	19	16
Manitoba	18	16
New Brunswick	18	16
Newfoundland and Labrador	19	16
Northwest Territories	19	15
Nova Scotia	19	16
Nunavut	19	15
Ontario	18	16
Prince Edward Island	18	16
Québec	18	14 male 12 female
Saskatchewan	18	16
Yukon	19	15

Why is there not a common age to marry without parental consent all across Canada?

You Be the Judge

Re Al-Smadi, (1994) 90 Man. R. (2d) 304

For more information, Go to Nelson Social Studies

Emman Al-Smadi, 14 years old, and her father applied to the court for permission for her to marry Ra'a Ahmed Said, a 27-year-old Jordanian student. Both were of the same religious faith. Evidence showed that, in their faith, once a girl reaches puberty, she may marry if she wishes. She must have her father's consent. Emman cooked, cleaned, and cared for her younger sister once her parents divorced and her father received custody. She confirmed that she freely consented to and chose the proposed marriage. Her father also consented to the marriage. The Child and Family Services director opposed the application, saying that it was not in the best interest of a child under the age of 16 to marry because of parental, cultural, or religious consent. The court dismissed the application. Several months later, a second application was made. It had the additional ground that the now 15-year-old girl was pregnant with Said's child.

- Do you think the second application succeeded? Why or why not?

Registering the Marriage

What is the difference between a marriage licence and a marriage certificate? Municipal or territorial governments issue a licence before you marry, authorizing the marriage. Governments issue certificates after marriages are registered. Every marriage must be registered to establish legal proof of the marriage. The religious representative or person performing the civil ceremony helps complete the marriage registration form. He or she then sends it to the proper Vital Statistics registry. There, the marriage is registered and a legal record is kept.

Spouses can fulfill the essential requirements, marry in good faith, and live together and consummate the marriage. The courts may consider them legally married, even if a formal requirement is lacking. Suppose that a couple marries in good faith by a person they believe to be properly licensed to marry them. They later discover that the person was not authorized to perform marriages. The couple is considered legally married despite the lack of this formal requirement. This problem seldom happens.

Same-Sex Marriages

Same-sex marriages have now been recognized in Canadian law since Parliament passed the *Civil Marriage Act* in 2005. Canada's former definition of marriage was based on the British common law definition, which had been upheld as precedent for hundreds of years. It stated that marriage was "the lawful union of one man and one woman to the exclusion of all others." In other words, only two people of different sexes could legally marry. Although the provinces issue marriage licences and decide who can marry, the federal government controls who can marry whom.

Since 1999, gay men and lesbians sought equal access to social institutions enjoyed by heterosexual Canadians, including the right to marry. Having the same level of love and commitment as heterosexual couples, they felt discriminated against. They believed that their section 15 Charter right to equality was violated. The following timeline highlights key events in legalizing same-sex marriages in Canada.

Did You Know?

In 2004, 75 percent of Canadians under age 30 supported same-sex marriage.

Did You Know?

After the Supreme Court's decision affirming the validity of same-sex marriage, the Alberta government announced that it planned to use the Charter's section 33, the notwithstanding clause, to avoid recognizing same-sex marriage. This became unnecessary when the federal *Civil Marriage Act* was passed.

The timeline below highlights some key events in the process of Canada becoming the fourth country in the world to recognize same-sex marriage.

Same-Sex Marriage Legislation in Canada

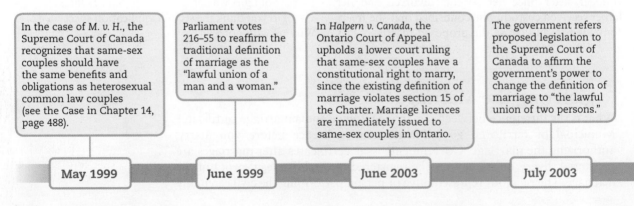

In the case of *M. v. H.*, the Supreme Court of Canada recognizes that same-sex couples should have the same benefits and obligations as heterosexual common law couples (see the Case in Chapter 14, page 488).

May 1999

Parliament votes 216–55 to reaffirm the traditional definition of marriage as the "lawful union of a man and a woman."

June 1999

In *Halpern v. Canada*, the Ontario Court of Appeal upholds a lower court ruling that same-sex couples have a constitutional right to marry, since the existing definition of marriage violates section 15 of the Charter. Marriage licences are immediately issued to same-sex couples in Ontario.

June 2003

The government refers proposed legislation to the Supreme Court of Canada to affirm the government's power to change the definition of marriage to "the lawful union of two persons."

July 2003

Canada was one of the first countries in the world to legalize same-sex marriage. The chart below lists countries and American states that have legalized same-sex marriage and when.

Legalization of Same-Sex Marriage Around the World

The Netherlands	April 1, 2001
Belgium	January 30, 2003
Massachusetts, USA	May 17, 2004
Spain	July 3, 2005
Canada	July 20, 2005
South Africa	November 30, 2006
Connecticut, USA	October 10, 2008
Norway	January 1, 2009

 Activity

To learn more about same-sex marriage,

Go to Nelson Social Studies

The legal concept of same-sex marriage is recent. Most countries still consider a valid marriage to be between a man and a woman only.

Assuming a Spouse's Name after Marriage

After marriage, you can choose to use your own or your spouse's surname. It is not a legal requirement for one spouse to assume the other spouse's surname when they marry. Once you marry, you have three options for your surname:

- assume your spouse's surname (last name)
- assume a combination of your surname and your spouse's surname for a hyphenated surname
- keep your own birth surname

The latter two options are becoming common. Many women feel that keeping their own surname is an important indication of their identity as equal partners in the marriage. As well, many women may have established professional careers and want to keep their name the same for business purposes. Men have similar options when they marry, but more women change their names than men. Procedures for doing this are outlined in each province's or territory's *Change of Name Act*.

A child born to a married couple usually receives the husband's surname or the hyphenated names of both parents. An unmarried woman can give her child her own surname, or she can give the child the father's name if he grants permission or paternity is proven.

 Did You Know?

On June 16, 2008, the California Supreme Court recognized same-sex marriage. As a result, 18 000 couples married over the next five months. However, on November 4, a statewide ballot, Proposition 8, made same-sex marriage illegal by a 52.2 percent majority vote.

 Did You Know?

In Québec, the law states that both spouses must keep their birth names.

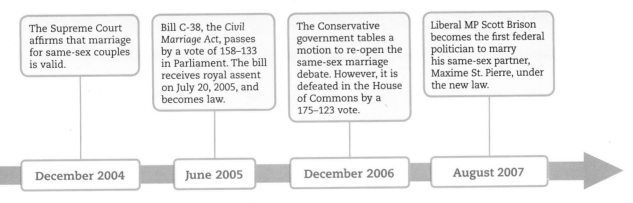

The Supreme Court affirms that marriage for same-sex couples is valid.

Bill C-38, the *Civil Marriage Act*, passes by a vote of 158–133 in Parliament. The bill receives royal assent on July 20, 2005, and becomes law.

The Conservative government tables a motion to re-open the same-sex marriage debate. However, it is defeated in the House of Commons by a 175–123 vote.

Liberal MP Scott Brison becomes the first federal politician to marry his same-sex partner, Maxime St. Pierre, under the new law.

December 2004   June 2005   December 2006   August 2007

This was not what Parliament intended when it passed the *Civil Marriage Act* in 2005.

annulment a court order to set aside a marriage

divorce the legal ending of a marriage

Review Your Understanding

1. What are the five essential requirements of a valid marriage? How does the lack of an essential requirement affect the validity of a marriage?
2. What is the difference between monogamy and bigamy? What effect does bigamy have on a second marriage?
3. Identify the four formal requirements of a valid marriage. How does the lack of a formal requirement affect the validity of a marriage?
4. What is the significance of the *Civil Marriage Act*?
5. Give two reasons why many women keep their birth surname after marriage.

13.4 Annulment, Separation, and Divorce

Marriage is a legally binding contract between two people of legal age. If the spouses want to end their marriage legally, it must be dissolved by the courts through a legal procedure: an **annulment** or a **divorce**. The death of either spouse also terminates a marriage.

Annulment

An annulment is a court order stating that two spouses were never legally married. It allows them to end the marriage without a divorce. Couples usually seek annulments to end marriages that lasted for a very short time.

Grounds for an annulment are specific. They relate to essential marriage requirements, such that the parties could not have married in the first place. A marriage can be annulled for the following reasons:

- a lack of an essential requirement affecting one of the spouses (see the chart on page 440)
- a legal defect in the marriage ceremony
- non-consummation of the marriage

For example, if one of the parties was intoxicated during the ceremony and lacked the mental capacity to marry, the marriage can be annulled. Other examples are if one of the parties was forced into the marriage, one spouse was married to somebody else, or one spouse was under the legal age to marry. Annulments are often based on non-consummation (consummation is the making of the marriage complete by sexual intercourse). The partners must be physically able to have intercourse to consummate the marriage.

Marriages of convenience, such as marriages for immigration purposes, are usually valid. They are not annulled because of non-consummation alone. There must be other important factors present before an annulment is granted.

The Roman Catholic, Jewish, and Islamic faiths also grant religious annulments. These allow a person to marry again within his or her faith. Religious annulments are recognized by the church, but they do not have legal standing. Anyone who obtains an annulment through a religious court must also obtain one through a civil court for it (the annulment) to be legally recognized in Canada.

Case

Torfehnejad v. Salimi, 2006 CanLII 38882 (ON S.C.)

For more information, Go to Nelson Social Studies

Farzad Torfehnejad immigrated to Canada from Iran in 1985 because of Iran's political situation. He became a Canadian citizen in 1989 and obtained an engineering degree. In 2002, at age 38, he thought he should marry. He looked for a suitable person to become his wife. After seeing a wedding video a friend had brought back from Iran, he became interested in one of the guests, Parisa Salimi, and asked about her.

The couple talked on the phone several times a week for months with her parents' permission. He told her he did not own either a home or a car in Toronto and had a student loan of about $25 000. In May 2002, Torfehnejad flew to Iran to see Salimi. Within two weeks, they married and signed an Iranian marriage contract. It included a dowry payment of 500 gold coins by him to his bride. The next day, Torfehnejad returned to Canada. He began sponsorship procedures to bring his wife to Canada. Over the next two years, he gave his wife gifts and cards.

In late 2004, Salimi was granted a visa to come to Canada and arrived the day before her visa expired. She went directly to her cousin's home instead of contacting her husband and applied for welfare. In August 2005, she warned her husband that if he did not give her the promised dowry, she would tell the police that he had threatened her and would have him blacklisted in Iran. In 2006, Torfehnejad asked a judge for an annulment. The annulment was granted.

For Discussion

1. What is a dowry, and why is this dowry agreement unusual? If necessary, conduct an Internet search for the answer.

2. On what grounds would Torfehnejad base his application?

3. How valid was Torfehnejad's application?

4. Why was the applicant's request granted? Do you agree? Why or why not?

Separation

Separation is an intermediate step between marriage and divorce. It occurs when a couple decides not to live together as husband and wife anymore; they "live separate and apart." Sometimes the parties go no further than this. They live out their lives separately, without getting divorced. This most often occurs when one or both spouses belong to a faith that does not recognize divorce.

The phrase "living separate and apart" means that the spouses have separated physically and do not intend to live together again. Usually, one spouse moves out of the family home. A couple can be separated while living under

separation a partial dissolution of a marriage in which the spouses live separate and apart with the intention to end the marriage

the same roof. Canadian law considers a separation valid if either spouse can prove that they sleep separately, share little or no communication, have no common activities, and live separate lives. Unless they get a divorce, the couple is still legally married. Separation does not end a marriage.

During a separation, the couple can live together for up to 90 days in order to get back together, or reconcile. They can do so for one 90-day period, or for many periods that total no more than 90 days. If they do not reconcile, they can proceed to a divorce as if they had not spent this time together.

Couples do not need legal documents when separating. Many negotiate written separation agreements. "Do-it-yourself" separation agreement forms and divorce kits are found in book and office supply stores and on the Internet. These agreements are contracts that are written, signed, and witnessed to make them legally binding. Each spouse should have a lawyer help prepare the agreement, as it outlines his or her position on various issues such as the following:

- child custody

- visitation rights

- spousal and child support

- ownership and division of property and debts

- whether or not the family home is sold

These issues are discussed later in this chapter and in Chapter 14.

The courts are not involved in preparing separation agreements. Once the couple prepares the document, it becomes as enforceable as any other private contract. Spouses should be allowed to determine their own affairs without the legal system involved, as separation agreements are legally binding contracts. However, the courts reserve the right to determine terms on custody and child support, even though the parties may have consented to prior arrangements. The "best interests of the children" is most important. Contract law is discussed in Chapters 15 and 16.

When a married couple separates, it is important for each spouse to have a lawyer to help prepare separation agreements.

Divorce

Divorce is the process that legally ends a marriage. You need it only if you want to remarry. Otherwise, you can live forever legally married to someone from whom you are separated. Divorce procedures are similar to the civil procedures described in Chapter 11. The spouse seeking the divorce is the **applicant**, and the respondent is the spouse being sued for divorce. A divorce may be based on the respondent's **adultery** (voluntary sexual intercourse with someone other than one's spouse). The **co-respondent** is the person with whom the respondent may have committed adultery.

The process begins with an application for divorce. It outlines the grounds for the divorce and other essential information, as shown in the chart below.

applicant the spouse initiating a divorce action

adultery voluntary sexual intercourse by a married person with someone other than the spouse

co-respondent the third party who commits adultery with the respondent in a divorce action

Information for a Divorce Application

- where and when the marriage occurred
- the ground(s) for divorce
- the children's names and ages (if there are any children from the marriage)
- custody of and access to the children
- financial support for the children, and who is responsible for payment
- financial support for the applicant, if it is needed
- division of property and property claims

This is the most important information contained in a divorce application.

Divorce actions are heard in provincial and territorial superior courts. However, about 90 percent of cases are uncontested. They are resolved after months of discussion and negotiation without having a hearing before a judge. Most divorces are uncontested because the spouses want to end their marriage, and there is nothing to argue about. Usually, lawyers represent spouses and offer the evidence to the court without the spouses being present. A judge reads all of this documentation, including the divorce petition. If the judge is satisfied that the agreement is fair to both parties, the divorce is granted.

A divorce is final 31 days after judgment is pronounced. Either party may remarry after obtaining a certificate of divorce from the court. This is the final step in the divorce. The purpose of the waiting period is to give either spouse the right to appeal the divorce or to give them one last opportunity to reconcile. If both parties agree, and if there is a very good reason, the 31-day waiting period may be reduced. This may happen, for instance, if the woman is pregnant and wishes to remarry as soon as possible. However, the judge must be convinced of a special need before reducing the waiting period.

In 2008, Heather Mills received a divorce settlement of £24.3 million (almost $48 million Canadian) from former Beatle Paul McCartney. She asked for more, but McCartney was able to keep most of his fortune, estimated at around £450 million. This divorce makes McCartney the last of The Beatles to get a divorce.

Canadian Divorce Law: A History

The *Constitution Act, 1867*, gave the federal government jurisdiction over divorce. There was no federal divorce law in Canada before 1968 as it still followed the principles of old English common law. Divorce law varied across the country, although most followed England's divorce laws. Until 1968, divorces in Newfoundland and Québec needed a federal act of Parliament (passage of a private statute). Adultery was the basis for most divorces. This was a problem for couples who were simply unhappily married. Society's attitudes toward divorce changed, and more grounds for divorce were needed. The federal government passed the first *Divorce Act* in 1968.

This statute established a divorce law for the first time that applied fully and equally across all of Canada. The act provided two main grounds for divorce:

- marital fault or blame with 15 separate grounds, including mental or physical cruelty, homosexuality, addiction to alcohol or drugs, imprisonment, and desertion
- marriage breakdown—a three-year separation or permanent marriage breakdown

This new ground made divorce more acceptable to those who had been reluctant to petition for divorce on a fault ground.

Over time, legal and other experts continually criticized the grounds for divorce. Pitting spouses against each other and finding fault with one party created considerable pain and suffering during the divorce process. Also, when both spouses agreed that the marriage was broken and could not be fixed, a three-year waiting period was too long. It created unnecessary hardships on the couple. These issues led to the *Divorce Act, 1985*. The act simplified the law, reduced the many grounds for divorce, and responded to social change and pressure for reform.

Under current divorce law, there is only one ground for divorce in Canada: marriage breakdown. This is the origin of the term no-fault divorce. It states that neither party is at fault for the divorce—

What is the cartoonist saying about marriage in this cartoon?

the marriage has simply broken down. This occurs when one of the following conditions exist:

- The spouses have separated for at least one year and were living apart when the divorce petition was filed.
- The respondent committed adultery during the marriage.
- The respondent spouse treats the other spouse with serious physical or mental cruelty and they can no longer live together. Over the years, courts have ruled that mental cruelty includes constant criticism, serious alcoholism, domineering behaviour, and constant refusal to have sexual relations.

For Discussion

1. Research divorce rates from the 1960s to today, and present them to the class in a graph.

2. When was Canada's first *Divorce Act* passed, and what were its two main grounds?

3. Outline the two main reasons for amending Canada's first *Divorce Act*.

4. What is the only valid ground for divorce under the *Divorce Act, 1985*? Identify the three ways this can be proven.

Review Your Understanding

1. Identify two ways of legally ending a marriage.
2. What is an annulment, and what are the grounds for an annulment?
3. What is a separation, and when does it legally occur?
4. What is an uncontested divorce, and why are most divorces uncontested?
5. What is the big difference between the use of marriage breakdown as a ground for divorce between the 1968 and 1985 *Divorce Acts*?

? Did You Know?

In Alberta and British Columbia, the person seeking the divorce is called a plaintiff, and the other spouse is called a defendant.

13.5 Children and Divorce

Today's Canadian children have their own rights and freedoms. They have some *Criminal Code* protection from assault, abuse, or being denied the necessities of life (food, clothing, and shelter). The *Youth Criminal Justice Act* deals with youth crime. Most laws concerning children are provincial or territorial. The chart below lists the legislation that governs **custody** and **access** applications processed under provincial or territorial law. Custody determines which parent the children will live with, and will have care and control of them. Access is about which parent will be given visitation rights and what those rights will be. The *Divorce Act, 1985*, governs such applications under federal law. Parliament adopted the "**best interests of the child**" principle as the only test on which custody and access disputes are resolved.

custody the care and control of a child awarded by the court

access non-custodial parent's right to information and visitation with the child

best interests of the child the principle upon which a judge makes a decision regarding custody and access of children

Provincial and Territorial Laws Affecting Children

Jurisdiction	Name of Legislation
Alberta	*Family Law Act*
British Columbia	*Family Relations Act*
Manitoba	*Family Maintenance Act*
New Brunswick	*Family Services Act*
Newfoundland and Labrador	*Children's Law Act*
Northwest Territories/Nunavut	*Children's Law Act*
Nova Scotia	*Family Maintenance Act*
Ontario	*Children's Law Reform Act*
Prince Edward Island	*Custody Jurisdiction and Enforcement Act*
Québec	*Civil Code of Québec*
Saskatchewan	*Children's Law Act*
Yukon	*Children's Act*

These are the different names for provincial and territorial legislation that governs custody, access, and other matters affecting children.

Judges' responsibilities toward children include the following:

- determining children's fate when their parents separate or divorce
- determining the parents' joint obligations to support their children's basic needs
- removing children from a home if they are abused or neglected
- arranging adoption

But, in all of these cases, courts must consider the "best interests of the child" in making judgments. Although parents are ending their relationship when they divorce, they are not ending their relationship with their children. They still remain parents. Custody and access disputes are the part of family law that affect children most directly and are among the most difficult for courts to resolve.

Recently, the law has moved away from the traditional concepts of custody and access. For example, Alberta, in its 2005 *Family Law Act*, does not mention "custody" and "access." These terms suggest that one parent is the winner and the other the loser. A goal of family law reform is to reduce conflict when relationships fall apart. Therefore, courts may make a parenting order that splits parenting time and duties between the parents and focuses on the child's best interests. These orders may also include grandparents and other people who are important to the child. Although Alberta is moving away from these terms, the next pages refer to "custody" and "access," as these terms are still used in most of Canada.

Custody

How does a judge determine custody and access, and what is in the best interests of the child? The following chart outlines, in no order of priority, some of the key factors judges consider.

You and the Law

If you were the subject of a custody dispute between your parents, which three factors would be the most important for a judge to consider? Why?

Factors Determining Best Interests of the Child
• the child's needs (mental, emotional, and physical health)
• the stability of the home environment
• the belief that keeping siblings together as often as possible is a good thing
• the parent–child relationships and bonding
• the child's culture and religion
• the parenting abilities of each parent and each parent's plan for the child's care
• parental conduct
• the support available from relatives, grandparents, neighbours, and friends
• the child's wishes, depending on age and maturity

The chart above outlines the factors that a judge considers when determining the best interests of the child.

Case

Levine v. McGrath, 2000 CanLII 22447 (ON S.C.)

For more information, Go to Nelson Social Studies

The applicant father, Levine, and the respondent mother, McGrath, lived in London with their two daughters, Amy (aged 13) and Sarah (aged 10). After the couple divorced, McGrath changed jobs and moved to Toronto with the girls. This allowed Amy to get synchronized swimming coaching, involving 25 to 30 hours a week. Although McGrath initiated the idea, both parents agreed that Amy should move to pursue her athletic career. Levine tried to be accommodating and flexible, but he was concerned about Sarah's wishes. He felt that if she wanted to stay in London, she should be able to do so. Sarah felt that she could turn to both parents when she was troubled or wanted advice.

A few weeks after the move, Sarah visited her father. She told him she wanted to stay in London with him in the family home and be with her neighbourhood and school friends. When Levine advised his ex-wife of Sarah's wishes, she refused to consider the idea and ordered him out of her house. Levine applied for an interim court order that Sarah live primarily with him. His application was granted. In addition, an access order gave each parent access on alternate weekends to the daughter not living with them.

Courts try to keep siblings together for the love and support they give each other.

For Discussion

1. In a two-column chart, identify the arguments in favour of and against Sarah's move.

2. Why was separating the sisters not the main concern in this case? Do you agree? Why or why not?

3. Why do you think the father's application succeeded?

4. Do you agree with the court's decision? Why or why not?

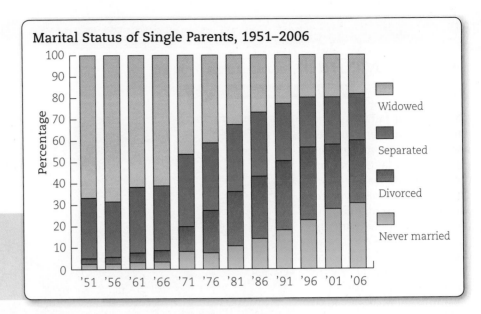

Marital Status of Single Parents, 1951–2006

(chart: stacked bars by year — '51, '56, '61, '66, '71, '76, '81, '86, '91, '96, '01, '06; y-axis Percentage 0–100; legend: Widowed, Separated, Divorced, Never married)

What trends can you observe from these statistics? What is the most surprising information? Explain.

interim custody order a temporary court order for custody of a child

Because male and female roles are changing, judges can no longer rely on the tradition of giving the mother custody, especially for young children. Proof that society's attitude has changed is seen in the increasing number of fathers awarded custody. Men are assuming more parenting and home care responsibilities as mothers become more active in the workforce. The law is beginning to reflect this change.

If parents disagree who should get custody in a divorce, they may go to court for an **interim custody order**. This gives them a temporary decision while they wait for the final one. Usually, interim custody is given to the parent who was responsible for most of the childcare responsibilities. These include the following:

- seeing to the children's educational, cultural, religious, and social development
- taking the children to medical appointments
- planning and preparing the children's meals
- buying, cleaning, and caring for the children's clothing
- interacting with the children after school

Shuffling children between contesting parents is never recommended. Neither is changing a satisfactory custody arrangement. The parent who assumes responsibility for the children at separation is often awarded final custody. The children are settled into that home. Courts are reluctant to disturb children who are settled and doing well. It is not in the children's best interests. The parent with interim or temporary custody has an advantage when the court rules on final custody.

Determining custody is never an easy decision for a judge. Also, a custody decision is never final because children's needs change. A decision that was in the best interest of a three-year-old may not be when he or she is 16. Conditions change, and a custody order can always return to court for review. This may occur several years after the original custody order. Courts are always concerned about the best interests of children until they are adults.

Van de Perre v. Edwards, 2001 SCC 60 (CanLII)

For more information, **Go to Nelson Social Studies**

Kimberly Van de Perre, the 27-year-old applicant, was a Caucasian single woman living in Vancouver. In the spring of 1996, she began an affair with Theodore "Blue" Edwards, the 35-year-old respondent. He was black, and at the time was a professional basketball player for the Vancouver Grizzlies. When Edwards began the affair, he had been married to his wife, Valerie, since 1991 and was the father of six-year-old twin daughters. During the affair, Van de Perre became pregnant. In June, 1997, she gave birth to a son, Elijah. Valerie learned of her husband's affair in 1996, just as she had about two of his earlier affairs.

Kimberly Van de Perre, pictured here with her son, Elijah, smiles after the Supreme Court of Canada awards her sole custody of her son.

When Elijah was three months old, Van de Perre began proceedings for custody and child support. She named Edwards as the boy's father. In turn, Edwards sought sole custody of Elijah. After a lengthy trial, the trial judge awarded Van de Perre sole custody. Edwards was given four one-week access periods a year and shared time at Christmas and on Elijah's birthday.

Edwards appealed this decision to the British Columbia Court of Appeal. He was joined by his wife seeking joint custody of Elijah. They argued that race was an important factor to be considered in deciding custody. In a unanimous judgment in March 2000, the appellate court granted the joint custody application, giving Van de Perre generous access. The court ruled that Elijah would be better off growing up in a black culture in the United States because he would always be perceived as "being black." The court questioned Van de Perre's lack of higher education and her spotty employment record.

Van de Perre appealed this decision to the Supreme Court of Canada. The case was heard in June 2001. The Supreme Court reversed the British Columbia Court of Appeal's decision in a 9–0 judgment in September. It restored the trial judgment, arguing that an appellate court should not intervene in a trial judge's decision made in the best interests of the child.

For Discussion

1. Why do you think the trial judge and the Supreme Court awarded custody to Elijah's mother?

2. In its decision, the British Columbia Court of Appeal stated: "It would obviously be in Elijah's best interests to live with a parent or family who can nurture his identity as a person of colour and who can appreciate and understand the day-to-day realities that Black people face in North American society—including racism and discrimination in various forms." Prepare an argument for and against this position.

3. In its decision, the Supreme Court of Canada stated: "Race is connected to the culture, identity, and well-being of the child… Bi-racial children should be encouraged to positively identify with both racial heritages." Discuss with a partner.

4. Do you agree with the Supreme Court's decision? Why or why not?

Joint Custody/Shared Parenting

joint custody the care and control of a child shared by both parents

shared parenting an arrangement where both parents have equal or similar rights concerning their child's care and custody

Courts are moving away from awarding sole custody of children to just one parent. They do so on the basis that it is in the children's best interests to have as much contact as possible with both parents. This is called **joint custody** or **shared parenting**. Both parents share responsibility for their children. Together, they control their children's upbringing and make the major decisions that affect their children. This is called parallel parenting in British Columbia. It focuses on the children's best interests and not the parents' relationship. This does not mean that the parents must agree on everything. However, they must be able to compromise on and resolve matters such as the following:

- what schools the children will attend, along with extracurricular activities
- their daycare and after-school care arrangements
- health care, such as surgery and braces on teeth
- social contacts and friends
- religious upbringing
- where the children will live, as shared parenting does not mean that the children will reside equally with each parent; in fact, the children will ordinarily reside with only one parent

Joint custody gives the non-custodial parent a significant parenting role. It gives the children a sense of being cared for by both parents. Both parents feel like equal partners in raising their children. Studies also show that divorced fathers who do not live with their children, but have frequent contact with them, are much less likely to avoid their support obligations. This issue is discussed in Chapter 14.

The Ontario Court of Appeal handed down a unanimous judgment in *Kaplanis v. Kaplanis*, 2005. It ruled that battling couples should not be awarded custody unless they show that they can co-operate as parents. In a ruling that might affect joint custody orders, the court said that judges must have solid evidence that parents are able to communicate effectively and work in the best interests of their children before making custody orders.

Joint custody or shared parenting is becoming much more common for the best interests of the child.

If this boy's parents cannot co-operate as parents, joint custody may not be in his best interest.

Access and Mobility Rights

When one parent is granted sole custody of the children, courts usually award access, or visiting rights, to the other parent. Even grandparents may apply for an access order. However, this is a problem if the grandparents are in conflict with one or both of the parents.

Access to a child by the non-custodial parent is usually in the child's best interests. A parent with access usually has the right to do the following:

- Spend time with the children, such as on a weekday evening, weekends, and on special occasions like birthdays and major holidays.

- Receive information about the children's health, well-being, and progress in school.

- Receive advance notice (of at least one month) if the custodial parent intends to move.

But, if a judge feels that a child might be harmed emotionally, physically, or morally by a parent, access might be very strictly controlled or even denied. These situations are rare. An example is a parent whose smoking severely affects a child's asthma.

The courts encourage parents to work out reasonable access terms when the spouses part on good terms. But, if the separation or divorce results in a courtroom battle, the court may outline specific access conditions. The common types of access orders—**reasonable access, defined access,** and **supervised access**—appear in the chart below.

reasonable access non-custodial parent's right to regular visits with the child

defined access a schedule that outlines visitation between a child and the non-custodial parent

supervised access visitation between a child and the non-custodial parent supervised by a third party

Three Types of Access

Reasonable Access

Supervised Access

Defined Access

These are the three common types of access orders.

Reasonable Access: Flexible and regular time spent with the non-custodial parent; the parents have worked out an acceptable agreement preferable to having access strictly outlined, as in defined access

Defined Access: Precise times spent with the non-custodial parent, such as after school, specific weekends, special occasions such as birthdays, and major holidays, including summer holidays

Supervised Access: Also involves a specified time but spent in the presence of a supervisor so that the child is safe; it might be ordered if the parent is addicted to alcohol or drugs or has a history of violent behaviour

Hartwick v. Stoneham, 2000 CanLII 22522 (ON S.C.)

For more information, | Go to Nelson Social Studies

Joseph Hartwick and Allison Stoneham lived together briefly before the birth of their son, Brandon Stoneham, in February 1991. The couple were not married, and they did not cohabit after the child's birth. They signed a separation agreement in June 1994, giving custody of the boy to the mother. It gave increasing access to the father until he was able to enjoy nine hours every other Sunday "unless it was not in the child's best interests."

In September 1999, when Brandon was eight, the mother ended access visits after he asked not to visit his father because the father took little interest in him. Brandon was no longer interested in the activities his dad proposed for their visits. He felt he was "getting too old to go there." He also told a psychologist that his father did not ask about friends, school, or sports activities, nor did he attend his son's hockey or soccer games. Hartwick claimed that when he saw Brandon, he was always rushed, and he could see his son only at times dictated by the mother. Stoneham denied that claim. Hartwick brought an application to restore access.

• How much consideration should the judge give to Brandon's comments and feelings, and why? Do you think the judge restored custody? Why or why not?

Mobility Rights

As more families separate and as society becomes more mobile, mobility rights are an issue before the courts. It is a custodial parent's right to move to another location with his or her children—often away from the non-custodial parent—if the move is reasonable and in the children's best interests. Access orders, like custody orders, are open for review if conditions change. Why might the custodial parent want to move? Common reasons include the following:

- plans to marry someone who lives elsewhere
- desire to return to a former community to be with family and friends
- transfer by an employer
- pursuing better job opportunities
- experiencing serious problems with the non-custodial parent

Canadian courts have ruled that the custodial parent has the right to move the children for reasonable purposes, even if this interferes with the other parent's access rights. What is good for the custodial parent is often presumed to be good for the children. This implies that the right of the custodial parent to create a happy home for the children may be greater than the right of access for the non-custodial parent. This situation was considered by the Supreme Court in a landmark 7–2 judgment, as outlined in the case on the next page.

 You and the Law

If your custodial parent planned to move and take you along, which of the reasons on the right do you think would be the most important? Why? Should you have the right to decide whether you want to go or remain with your other parent? Explain.

Gordon v. Goertz, 1996 CanLII 191 (S.C.C.)

For more information, **Go to Nelson Social Studies**

Robin Goertz tried to prevent his former wife, Janet Gordon, from moving from Saskatoon, Saskatchewan. Gordon planned to move with their seven-year-old daughter to Australia, to study dentistry. She had been granted permanent custody of their daughter, Samantha, when the couple was divorced in a mediated agreement. Both parents enjoyed a warm and loving relationship with Samantha, and Goertz saw Samantha frequently with generous reasonable access. Goertz sought a court order preventing Gordon from moving to Australia. Gordon cross-applied to move to Australia with Samantha.

The trial judge dismissed the father's application, allowing the mother to move. It granted Goertz generous access on one month's notice to visit in Australia. Mother and daughter moved there in 1995. A further appeal to the Saskatchewan Court of Appeal by the father was dismissed, and he appealed to the Supreme Court of Canada. The appeal was heard in December 1995, and in a 7–2 judgment in May 1996, the Supreme Court dismissed the father's appeal, agreeing with the lower court decisions.

For Discussion

1. When these parents separated, what benefits would family mediation provide them?

2. Why do you think all the courts ruled in the mother's favour?

3. Were the courts wrong in allowing the mother to move with Samantha to Australia? Why or why not?

4. What principle was established with this decision?

The decision in *Gordon v. Goertz* established that each case must be decided considering the best interests of the child. Courts are more inclined to examine the impact of the move on the children and not just the needs of the custodial parent. They may also consider other changes that have occurred in everyone's lives between the granting of the original custody order and the proposed move. For example, the father may have remarried with a new family into which the child could easily fit. In addition, it might be in the child's best interests to remain with the father instead of leaving the city, province, or country to go with the mother.

What are some reasons a custodial parent might decide to move with his or her child?

Champion v. Champion, 2008 CanLII 200 (ON S.C.)

For more information, **Go to Nelson Social Studies** ▶

Nancy and Garland Champion were married in July 1998. They separated initially in June 2006 and finally in October 2006. They had two children, Jake (7 years) and Shane (5 years). Mrs. Champion, the applicant, claimed sole custody of their two sons and permission to relocate with her children to Newfoundland. Her husband claimed joint custody, agreed that the children should live with their mother, but he objected to their move to Newfoundland.

The applicant was born in Newfoundland, had family there, and could find full-time work in nursing. Nancy had rental accommodation available to her within walking distance of her parents' home. Her mother could provide childcare while Nancy worked.

In addition, she had a new partner who also had full-time employment waiting in Newfoundland. Nancy had been the children's primary caregiver since birth and made all decisions about the children's needs prior to separation. Since their separation, Garland had no permanent home, was living in a friend's basement, and had nowhere to accommodate the children overnight. Nancy even offered to give up child support if the court granted her permission to move with the children to Newfoundland.

- If Mr. Champion agreed that the children should live with their mother, why did he oppose their move to Newfoundland? What do you think the court decided was in the best interests of the children?

Family Mediation

The *Divorce Act, 1985*, establishes reconciliation as an important objective for couples whose marriage breaks down. It includes a section that encourages family mediation to resolve issues that cause conflict between spouses. In Canada, family mediation is firmly established. It reduces the emotional and economic costs to the partners. It is certainly preferable to battles in a courtroom.

As you saw in the Chapter 1 Issue (pages 32–33) and in Chapter 11 (pages 380–383), alternative dispute resolution (ADR), and mediation in particular, are used more often to resolve family disputes. Family mediation is a voluntary conflict-resolution process. Once they decide to divorce, the spouses meet (usually without their lawyers) several times with a trained mediator to resolve family disputes. Some level of reasonable and positive co-operation between the spouses is necessary for mediation to succeed.

Mediators are usually social workers, psychologists, lawyers or other trained personnel who do the following:

- provide a safe and supportive setting for the spouses and their children
- identify and clarify the issues to be resolved
- ensure that each spouse freely communicates his or her needs to the other to allow for a fair and informed basis for the negotiations
- assist the couple to identify their needs and reach decisions that are satisfactory to all and in the best interests of the entire family, especially the children
- facilitate positive communication and problem solving
- refer clients to appropriate information for effective decision making

- ensure that discussions are respectful and non-threatening
- act in an unbiased, neutral manner to help reach a positive agreement
- do not give legal advice

Family mediation is encouraged by governments and the courts, and its benefits appear in the chart below.

Advantages of Mediation in Family Disputes

- It keeps decision-making powers with those who know the children best—their parents.

- It promotes co-operation and compromise, not competition, thereby reducing hostility and conflict between the parties.

- It provides results that can be mutually satisfying to all parties in the dispute, and they are more likely to honour personal commitments rather than imposed solutions.

- It helps protect family relationships by improving communication and reducing conflict between the parents.

- It may improve parenting because the parents and their children need to reach mutually agreeable decisions.

- It is a confidential process—information learned in mediation cannot be used in other court proceedings, unless the parties agree.

- It is much less costly than litigation, which leaves more money for the children and their parents.

These are the main advantages of mediation in resolving family disputes. Which do you think is the most important?

Mediation is not appropriate for every couple, especially if one of the spouses, usually the wife, has been physically, emotionally, psychologically, or financially abused. Also, mediation may not work when one partner is intimidated by the other partner. In both of these situations, the abused or intimidated person may enter the mediation process lacking equality with his or her partner.

Review Your Understanding

1. What is the only test used in determining custody and access? Why?
2. Identify the factors judges consider in determining custody and access.
3. What is joint custody or shared parenting, and why is it becoming more common?
4. Identify the three common types of access orders, and describe how they differ.
5. What is family mediation? Why is it so firmly established in Canada?

13.6 Children in Need of Protection

Parents have a right to raise their children according to their own personal values and beliefs. All families should have the right to have little government involvement in their lives. But, the pendulum is swinging the other way. Recently, society has recognized that some parents are not raising their children in an acceptable fashion. What is "unacceptable" is not easy to decide. One parent's punishment may be another parent's abuse. Individual values within society vary widely, and methods of child rearing vary with these values. In certain cases, the legal system has the authority to protect the child from his or her family.

Child abuse is one of society's most serious problems. Abused children suffer, often silently, and the damage may last a lifetime. Even worse, children abused today may become future child abusers. Abuse is not confined to any one group of people or any age group. Children from babies to teenagers, from all kinds of homes, and from all types of backgrounds, may be abused. Family members are responsible for most assaults against very young children. This includes immediate and extended family members, as well as people who have been named legal guardians.

Child abuse is any form of behaviour that endangers the development, security, or survival of a child. The chart below outlines the main forms of abuse.

What type of abuse might this child have suffered?

child abuse behaviour that endangers a child's physical, mental, or emotional well-being

Types and Examples of Child Abuse

Types	Definition and Examples
Physical	Deliberate physical force used against a child; for example, shaking, choking, hitting, biting, kicking, burning, or poisoning
Sexual	Sexual activity with a child; for example, incest, touching and fondling genitals, juvenile prostitution, intercourse, sexual exploitation, or involving a child in the production of pornography
Emotional	Attacks on a child's sense of self-worth; for example, constant yelling, insults, rejection, terrorizing, or humiliation. This can be the most difficult type to identify and prove.
Neglect	Failure to look after a child's physical, emotional, and psychological needs; for example, failure to provide adequate food, clothing, shelter, sleep, medical care, and emotional warmth

These are the four main types of child abuse, and examples to recognize each. Which do you think is the most common type of abuse? Why?

Most parents are caring and loving. But, caring for children is often stressful and can sometimes be overwhelming for one or both parents. Young and immature parents may not understand a child's behaviour or may have few support systems such as parents and friends to help them. When parents have financial problems, or a major illness occurs in the family, or personal difficulties arise, parents often "take it out" on their children. In these cases, the law will seek to protect the child while recognizing that the parents may need help with their problems.

Society's concern about neglect and child abuse is reflected in specific legislation. All provinces and territories have legislation, such as *Child Welfare Acts* or *Child and Family Services Acts*, to protect neglected children. British Columbia's legislation is called the *Child, Family and Community Service Act*. Ontario's *Child and Family Services Amendment Act*, passed in 1999, resulted in the most significant change to Ontario's child protection laws in a decade. In most provinces and territories, child protection services are provided by provincial/territorial employees, typically from the Ministry of Community and Social Services, or Child and Family Service Agencies, or by Children's Aid Societies (CAS).

Canadian children are also protected by offences listed in the *Criminal Code*. These include failing to provide the necessities of life, assault, sexual assault, sexual exploitation, sexual touching, and child pornography. As you read in Chapter 7 on page 224, section 43 of the *Criminal Code* states that teachers, parents, and other adults standing in their place are justified in using corporal punishment or corrective force (spanking or hitting) as long as that force is not unreasonable.

Children's best interests are a key concern in today's society. Many people and organizations have called for a total ban on any form of physical punishment of children. They want section 43 declared unconstitutional. It infringes on sections 7 (the security of the person) and 12 (cruel and unusual punishment) of the *Charter of Rights and Freedoms*. Others argue that minor and reasonable physical correction is acceptable as a parenting technique in some cases, including using some force to put an unwilling child in a car seat.

In 2000, an Ontario Superior Court judge ruled that spanking does not violate the constitutional rights of children. The Ontario Superior Court upheld section 43 of the *Criminal Code*. In 2002, the Ontario Court of Appeal upheld this decision. These arguments made their way to the Supreme Court of Canada in the case of *Canadian Foundation for Children, Youth and the Law v. Canada (Attorney General)*.

In a 6–3 judgment on January 30, 2004, the Supreme Court affirmed (agreed with) the lower court decisions. It ruled that section 43 does not violate any Charter rights. If corporal punishment is used properly (not excessively) and only for children aged between 2 and 12, then it is constitutional. For children under two, physical punishment is considered inappropriate. They are too young to learn from the punishment. For children over 12, it is also ineffective. It will likely make them view adults in a negative light as well as possibly hurt them physically. In addition, the court's ruling provided some guidelines as to what the justices considered reasonable and unreasonable force. The chart on page 466 highlights these guidelines.

REPORT CHILD ABUSE.
CALL (415) 431-5133.

Bay Area Child Abuse Councils

Posters like this example help to make society aware of the serious problem of child abuse.

Should spanking or other forms of physical punishment of children be a crime?

 Did You Know?

According to the Department of Justice, abuse of children under age 3 is most often neglect, while abuse of children aged 12 to 15 is most often physical.

Reasonable and Unreasonable Uses of Force

Reasonable Force	Unreasonable Force
• A parent can only use "minor corrective force of a transient and trifling nature." • Corporal punishment must be for "educational" or "corrective" purposes and not be motivated by anger, frustration, or abusiveness. • Inflicting corporal punishment must be limited to the use of the open hand.	• Corporal punishment for children under the age of two is not reasonable. It is harmful to them because it has no corrective value given the limits of their cognitive development. • Corporal punishment of teenagers is not reasonable. It is harmful because it can induce aggressive or antisocial behaviours. • It is not reasonable to use objects such as belts, straps, or rulers due to the physical and emotional harm the use of such objects causes. • It is not reasonable to strike a child on his or her face or head due to the harm these physical acts can cause. • Corporal punishment must not be inhumane, degrading, or harmful, and there must be no lasting bodily harm.

In 2004, in the case of *Canadian Foundation for Children, Youth, and the Law v. Canada (Attorney General)*, the Supreme Court of Canada provided guidelines for parents and others for reasonable and unreasonable actions using corporal punishment with children.

Case

R. v. Swan, 2008 CanLII 10389 (ON S.C.)

For more information, Go to Nelson Social Studies

An Ontario father, Barry Swan, had been married for 37 years and had raised three daughters with his wife. His teenaged daughter, 15-year-old M., lived at home with her parents until June 2006, when she was voluntarily placed in the care of a regional Children's Aid Society (CAS). M. was rebellious, had been sneaking out at night, and was not attending school. Having "run out of answers" about what to do with their daughter, the Swans hoped that the CAS would help them and their daughter. They were most concerned about M.'s boyfriend, who was quite violent and involved with drugs and had a restraining order against his seeing M.

One evening, Mrs. Swan overheard M. making plans to attend a party where her boyfriend was, and told her she could not go. M. left anyway, and Mr. Swan went to look for his daughter and found her at a payphone. He told her that she had to come home and, when she refused to go, he grabbed her shirt and forced her into his truck. He pulled her out of the truck by the arm, and both went into their home. Later that evening, M. sneaked out again, returned

to the payphone, and arranged for someone to pick her up and take her to the party so that she could meet her boyfriend. But, by the time she got to the party, he had left. Her parents then called the police for help in getting their daughter home.

M. told police that her father had assaulted her at the payphone. She did not give a formal statement, and a doctor's report revealed no injuries. Her father was arrested, charged with assault, and was convicted at trial. He appealed his conviction, where his conviction was overturned.

For Discussion

1. Why did the Crown charge Swan with assault?

2. How did the Supreme Court judgment in *Canadian Foundation for Children, Youth and the Law v. Canada* affect this case?

3. Was the father's use of force against his daughter justified? Why or why not?

4. Do you agree with the court's decision? Why or why not?

Reporting Child Abuse

If you know or suspect that a child is abandoned, emotionally mistreated, neglected, or physically abused, you *must* report your information or suspicion, no matter where you live in Canada. People who may have close contact with children, such as doctors, dentists, nurses, teachers and other school staff, counsellors, social workers, daycare workers, clergy, and police officers must immediately report any actual or suspected child abuse to the child services authorities. Failure to do so may result in a fine between $1000 and $10 000, depending on the province or territory.

Procedures for reporting abuse vary throughout Canada. They are summarized in the chart below.

This young boy is just one of many abused children who need protection from their abusers.

Child Abuse Reporting Procedures

Responsible Authority	What to Report
Children's Aid Society	Child's name, address, age, and sex
Provincial child welfare agency	Parent/guardian's name and address
Social worker	Alleged offender's name and address
Police officer	Details of alleged incident
Crown attorney	Your name and address

Depending on your province or territory, you would report child abuse to one of the authorities in the left-hand column. You would report some or all of the information in the right-hand column. What other information could be reported? Why?

Activity

To learn more about reporting child abuse,

Go to Nelson Social Studies

To encourage people to report suspected cases of neglect and abuse, provincial and territorial legislation treats the information received as confidential. The identity of the person making a report is not revealed unless it is necessary for a court hearing. As well, the person supplying the information is protected from legal action, unless the report was made without reasonable grounds or with malicious intent. In that case, the informant may be liable for damages caused to the accused.

Extreme cases of abuse are often easy to identify, but they represent a small percentage of the total picture. Sometimes, cases of severe abuse may not be easy to identify. The injuries may be covered by clothing, or the child may have carefully rehearsed reasons for bruises and cuts. A child's behaviour may indicate a form of abuse. Signs of withdrawal, absence from school, aggression, depression, overtiredness, and a strong need to control others may be evidence that the child is in trouble. Emotional abuse and neglect are the most difficult to identify and prove.

A child's behaviour may be indicative of emotional abuse or neglect.

Child Abuse Registry

The provinces and territories have set up child abuse registries. Each contains reports of abuse, including incident details, the child's identity and that of the alleged abuser, and their relationship. These registries make it harder for parents to cover up acts of abuse. For example, a parent may take the child to different doctors to avoid detection. If medical personnel suspect child abuse, they have quick access to information about suspected abusive parents. A person whose name is entered into the registry must be notified of this fact. Suspects who can prove that no abuse happened can request to have their names removed from the registry. Access to registry information is restricted; it is not available to the general public. For example, in Ontario, the law prohibits police from obtaining information without a search warrant. In some provinces, a person applying for a job involving contact with children may be asked to consent to a name search in the registry.

Sexual Abuse Cases

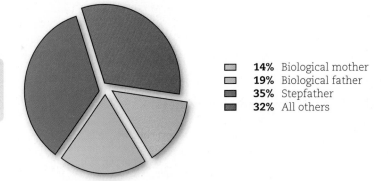

These are the most common sexual abusers from reported statistics.

- **14%** Biological mother
- **19%** Biological father
- **35%** Stepfather
- **32%** All others

Removal of Children

Authorities can obtain a search warrant to enter a home and remove children when there is a strong suspicion that they need protection. If there is a strong reason to have children removed without waiting for a warrant, it can and will be done to protect the children. In October 2000, the Supreme Court of Canada ruled in a 5–2 decision in *Winnipeg Child and Family Services v. K.L.W.* that social workers who reasonably believe children need protection should be able to remove them without warrants. The dissenting judges warned that giving such powers to social workers could lead to abuse in removing children.

Children who are taken from their parents are brought before a family court judge, usually within seven days in most provinces. Parents must be notified of this hearing. The decision to provide protection for a child ultimately rests with the courts. If a court finds that a child is in need of protection, the court may issue one of three types of orders.

Supervision Order

A **supervision order** allows the children to remain in the custody of their parents, under the supervision of the Children's Aid Society or other child protection agency. This might occur when the children require some professional care and attention, yet are still best off at home.

Society (Temporary) Wardship

A **society wardship** allows the legal custody and guardianship of the children to be transferred to a child protection agency on a temporary basis. In most provinces, the period is 12 months. Children are usually placed in a foster or group home during this time. Parents are allowed some visiting rights. At the end of this time, children must either be returned home, made Crown wards and enter long-term care, or be adopted.

Such an order might be needed when the child needs medical care that goes against the parents' religious beliefs. It could also be required when a child is born addicted to drugs because of the mother's addiction during pregnancy. Since there is a risk that these children might not receive adequate care and treatment at home, an order will be issued for support services. A society wardship suggests that a positive child–parent relationship will be restored within time. Parents may usually request a review of supervision or temporary wardship orders, similar to the procedure with custody and access decisions.

Crown (Permanent) Wardship

A **Crown wardship** enables a child to become a permanent ward of a Children's Aid Society. The CAS becomes responsible for the child's care until age 18 (in Ontario, until age 16). The parents lose all rights of control over their child. An example of such a situation would be parents who leave very young children alone, exposing them to possible danger. The children become wards of the state and can be placed with foster parents or given up for adoption. In such circumstances, the consent of the child's parents is not required. Once adoption occurs, the parents have no right to visit their child.

supervision order court order for professional supervision of a child living at home

society wardship a court order granting temporary legal custody of a child to a child protection agency; also called temporary wardship

Crown wardship a court order granting permanent legal custody of a child to the Crown, represented by a child protection agency

 Did You Know?

In July 2008, a family court judge in New Zealand made a nine-year-old girl at the centre of a custody battle a ward of the court so she could change her name from Talula Does the Hula From Hawaii and choose a name she really liked. The judge said, "This court is concerned about the very poor judgment which this child's parents have shown in choosing this name. It makes a fool of the child and sets her up with a social disability and handicap unnecessarily."

Review Your Understanding

1. Describe the four main types of child abuse, and provide examples.
2. Who is responsible for reporting suspected child abuse cases?
3. Why is section 43 of the *Criminal Code* still controversial?
4. What is the purpose of a child abuse registry? If a name has been incorrectly placed in the registry, what can be done about it?
5. What is the difference between a society wardship and a Crown ward? Which is the more permanent?

Should Polygamy Be Legalized?

A polygamous commune has existed in Bountiful, British Columbia, for more than 60 years.

The definition of marriage as a union between a man and a woman changed when same-sex marriages were legalized across Canada in July 2005. The new definition of "the lawful union of two people, to the exclusion of all others" may face another possible change if polygamy is found legal by the courts. Polygamy is an arrangement where one person has relationships with multiple persons of the opposite sex.

Being married to more than one person is a way of life in parts of Africa, India, East Asia, and the Middle East. Polygamous societies have existed for centuries. They are not aberrations (departures from what is accepted as right or normal), despite popular opinion. Polygamous sects also exist in Arizona, Texas, and Utah. They have openly existed for more than 60 years in Bountiful, British Columbia, despite the fact that such a lifestyle is illegal. Canada's polygamy ban is as old as the *Criminal Code* itself. Polygamy was prohibited in

Canada's first *Code* in 1892. Section 293 of our *Criminal Code* makes it illegal with a penalty of up to five years in prison, but it has rarely been enforced.

With sects such as the one in Bountiful, Canadian law is presented with a new challenge. Can the definition of marriage include those who love more than one person? Are Canadians prepared to open their minds and change the definition of marriage again? If two or more women want to marry one man, or vice versa, and they all consent to the union, should the state be concerned?

On One Side

Polygamy is too radical a change for most Canadians. Having more than two people joined in a marital union attacks society's core values and morals, as well as the foundation of marriage. The lifestyle weakens the sacred bond between two persons joined in marriage. It runs counter to Canadian values. Canada has the right to defend the institution of marriage.

Those against polygamy also argue that making it legal means changing other areas of the law, such as property, inheritance, and immigration policies. They argue that such a challenge is something not even same-sex marriages presented. Courts legalized same-sex marriages because they resembled heterosexual marriages—the union of two people only.

Those who are against polygamy are most concerned with the harm it might pose to women and children. They argue that incest, sexual abuse, and child abuse define polygamist societies. This concern should override any cultural or religious freedoms to which polygamists may be entitled. Also, relationships involving one man and two or more women are degrading. They imply that women are not equal to men. This mentality is not legally or morally acceptable in Canadian society. Furthermore, it is not allowed under the *Charter of Rights and Freedoms*.

On the Other Side

The most compelling argument for decriminalizing polygamy is the direct violation of fundamental Charter rights. Polygamy is a lifestyle most frequently associated with religion, in particular the Islamic and Mormon faiths. Some legal experts agree that section 293 of the *Criminal Code* is an obvious infringement of the Charter's section 2 freedom of religion. Therefore, it is unconstitutional.

Other Charter arguments include a direct violation of section 7, the right to "life, liberty, and security of the person." It also violates section 15, the right to "equality before and under the law." Consenting adults should have the freedom to choose how they live and conduct themselves as they want to in their private lives, especially when such choices are religion based. If Canadians can adjust the definition of marriage to include same-sex unions, why not let three or more adults have their love and commitment publicly recognized?

As Canadians' values and morals are constantly changing, polygamy is not such a serious attack. The tolerance level should be raised and people of all lifestyles embraced. Those who support decriminalizing polygamy call for an understanding in a society that already accepts other cultures and religious practices. For example, some of Canada's Muslim community believe in multiple marriages as an interpretation of their Koran (the central religious text of Islam).

Finally, abuse does not necessarily occur within polygamy. Lawmakers should focus on prosecuting abuse and incest, which are separate issues. If women and children are abused, the nature of the relationship is not the concern. Rather, it is the safety of the people involved. If no laws are being broken and the women and children are living in a safe environment, why restrict how certain people or communities live?

The Bottom Line

Both sides of the issue are compelling. One side focuses on preserving core values and traditional marriage. The other side promotes tolerance, understanding, and accepting another definition of a Canadian family. As cases challenging section 293 of the *Criminal Code* find their way into Canadian courts, which one do you think will prevail?

What Do You Think?

1. Immigration to Canada is very high. As immigrants come from parts of the world where polygamy is accepted, should this have an impact on Canadian law? Discuss in small groups.

2. After the legalization of same-sex marriage, is the decriminalization of polygamy inevitable? Why or why not?

3. If the Supreme Court were to rule that section 293 of the *Criminal Code* was a Charter violation and unconstitutional, could it be saved by the Charter's section 1 "reasonable limits" provision (see Chapter 2, pages 38–40)? Provide arguments for both sides of this question.

4. On January 7, 2009, the Brtitish Columbia government charged two leaders in Bountiful, British Columbia, with practising polygamy. The criminal charges are the first ever laid in Canada. Conduct an Internet search to find the latest information on these charges and on the polygamous sect in Bountiful.

Chapter Review

Chapter Highlights

- Families today come in many different forms: married and common law couples with and without children, single-parent families, and same-sex partner relationships.

- The federal government controls marriage and divorce. The provincial and territorial governments control procedures for marriage ceremonies.

- Same-sex marriage has been legal in Canada since July 2005.

- It is not a legal requirement for one spouse to assume the other spouse's surname when they marry.

- An annulment is a court order stating that two persons were never legally married and allowing them to end a partnership without divorce.

- Separation is a middle step between marriage and divorce; the couple lives separate and apart.

- Divorce is the process that legally ends a marriage and is needed only if you want to remarry.

- In Canada today, the only ground for divorce is marriage breakdown, evidenced by a one-year separation, adultery, or mental or physical cruelty.

- Over 90 percent of divorces are uncontested and are granted on the basis of a one-year separation.

- Custody and access disputes are areas of family law that seriously affect children.

- The "best interests of the child" is the only principle on which custody and access disputes are resolved.

- Joint custody, or shared parenting, gives both parents an opportunity to maintain contact with their children.

- Family mediation is a new approach to handling disputes over a marriage breakdown outside of the traditional court setting.

- There are three types of access: reasonable, defined, and supervised.

- The four main types of child abuse are physical, sexual, emotional, and neglect.

- A supervision order and society or Crown wardships are legal procedures for removal from a home of children in need of protection.

Check Your Knowledge

1. Identify the essential and formal requirements of a valid marriage.

2. Distinguish between an annulment and a divorce.

3. Identify the three specific ways to show marriage breakdown has occurred.

4. Outline the purpose and benefits of family mediation.

5. Summarize the various types of child abuse.

Apply Your Learning

6. Louise and Robert had been dating for one year and planned to marry. During their engagement, Robert assumed, from comments made by Louise, that she came from a wealthy family and that her mother was chief executive officer (CEO) of a large national corporation. A week after the marriage, Robert realized that none of this was true. Was their marriage invalid? Why or why not?

7. Review the arguments presented in the *Van de Perre v. Edwards* case (page 457). Should children be placed with adoptive parents who are of the same race, cultural background, and religion as the child? Discuss with a partner, arguing both sides of the issue.

8. From a newspaper or the Internet, collect at least five articles dealing with issues related to children and family law issues discussed in this chapter.

a) Summarize the articles in your own words.

b) Highlight the issue(s) involved.

c) State and justify your opinion on the issue(s) discussed in the articles.

Communicate Your Understanding

9. Using the Internet, research various legal requirements and marriage customs from countries around the world, and prepare a report to share with the class. If possible, obtain visuals to illustrate your report, or prepare a bulletin-board display. In an organizer, compare and contrast these requirements and customs to those of a Canadian marriage.

10. Who should determine the age at which a person can marry—the person, his or her parents, statute law, the courts, or another party? In groups of four, examine this issue and prepare arguments for and against each option. As a group, reach consensus and compare your conclusion with that of other groups.

11. With a partner, discuss the financial, social, and emotional issues of getting married. Make a list of the positive and negative factors involved. Try to reach consensus or agreement on the issues.

12. Debate one of the following topics. Prepare a brief introduction, identify facts and arguments that support your stance, anticipate points against your view and prepare counterarguments to defend your viewpoint, and conclude with a statement that summarizes your position.

- All couples planning to marry must take a life-skills and family planning course.

- Parliament should restore the traditional definition of marriage.

- Women who marry should assume their husband's surname.

- Divorce in Canada is much too easy to obtain.

13. In small groups, create an advertising campaign to use in your school to focus attention on child abuse. This activity could include posters, school announcements, or video and PowerPoint presentations. Highlight what constitutes child abuse and the necessity of reporting child abuse. Also provide information on agencies that deal with child abuse.

Develop Your Thinking

14. Should a marriage in Ontario between two persons aged 15 be valid if the teens somehow managed to obtain a marriage licence and persuade an authorized person to perform the ceremony? Support your opinion.

15. For many children, the problem with access is that the non-custodial parent visits too rarely or not at all. Should the courts do something to force or encourage unwilling non-custodial parents to visit? Would educational programs help? Discuss in small groups, and try to reach a consensus.

16. Assume the role of a family mediator listening to a divorcing couple with two children, aged 7 and 12. What concerns or issues related to the children would you expect the couple to have? Identify these items, and then compare your list with that of a partner. As a mediator, how would you conduct yourself in a family mediation session to facilitate communication between the parties?

Division of Property and Support

What You Should Know

- How is family property divided on a marital breakdown?
- Why is the matrimonial home given special treatment in family law?
- How does the law regard cohabitation?
- When partners separate, how is spousal support determined?
- What is the purpose of the *Federal Child Support Guidelines*?
- What domestic contracts are recognized in law?

Selected Key Terms

cohabitation

domestic contract

equalization

family asset

maintenance

matrimonial home

net family property

self-sufficient

separate property system

spousal support

Chapter at a Glance

14.1 Introduction

14.2 Dividing Family Property

14.3 Common Law Relationships

14.4 Spousal Support

14.5 Child Support

14.6 Domestic Contracts

Following a divorce, it is impossible to cut the couple's home in two, so there are provincial and territorial laws to ensure that both spouses are treated fairly. This was not always the case, however. What do you think happened in the past?

14.1 Introduction

In Chapter 13, you learned that there is one divorce law for all Canadians. *The Constitution Act, 1867*, gives the federal government jurisdiction over marriage and divorce. This includes the following:

- child custody and access (as you saw in Chapter 13)
- support for children
- support for former spouses

Property is always governed by provincial and territorial laws. When a marriage breaks down, these laws control the fair and equal division of the value of a couple's property. This legislation does not exist for common law or unmarried same-sex partners, no matter how long they have lived together. Some legislation provides certain rights for these partners and is discussed in the section Common Law Relationships.

Some couples may want to state their rights, responsibilities, and obligations to each other before they get married in case they divorce. Or, they may want to opt out of legislation that dictates the division of property on marriage breakdown. To help these couples, provincial and territorial legislation now accepts domestic contracts made by both married and unmarried couples. Domestic contracts are sometimes known as prenuptial agreements (prenups), but that term is not recognized in Canadian law. These contracts are discussed in the section Domestic Contracts.

14.2 Dividing Family Property

Under traditional English common law, daughters and married women could not own property. When they married, the husband and wife became a single person, or "one being," in the eyes of the law. This one person was always considered to be the husband, who was also in charge of the family property. This injustice was finally addressed in Britain in 1882 with the passage of the *Married Women's Property Act*. This law granted wives the right to own and control property as though they were single. In Canada, provinces that followed the common law used this statute as the basis for similar legislation. But the **separate property system** often resulted in hardship for women if a marriage ended.

Until the early 1980s, husbands were generally the money earners. Wives usually looked after the home and the children and were homemakers. When marriages broke down, the most common attitude was, "What I paid for is mine, and what you paid for is yours." Since many wives earned little, if any, money, they bought few goods. As a result, husbands owned most of the family property and walked away with it following divorce. The courts did not give the wife an interest in property that was registered in her husband's name. The laws also did not recognize her contribution in the form of household management and home-care duties.

During a marriage, both spouses must financially support each other and any children they have. When the spouses separate, these obligations do not disappear. Provincial legislation deals with support during separation. The federal *Divorce Act* regulates support obligations when couples divorce.

separate property system
a system whereby each spouse owns and controls property as though a single person

Chapter 14 **Division of Property and Support**

If both spouses worked outside the home, the husband usually earned more than his wife. Often, his wages were used for the mortgage payments on their home. Her wages paid the household expenses. When the marriage broke down, the husband was considered the sole owner of the home if it was registered in his name only, which was often the case. Although the wife's wages paid for the family's expenses, which allowed her husband to pay for their home, her financial contribution was not recognized. At best, she might be allowed to keep some items she had paid for (for example, her own car). Clearly, the old property system presented problems. The existing law did not recognize a woman's economic and material contributions to the marriage. This injustice became the focus of public attention in the following landmark case of *Murdoch v. Murdoch*.

 Case

Murdoch v. Murdoch, 1973 CanLII 193 (S.C.C.)

For more information, **Go to Nelson Social Studies**

Irene Murdoch's battle for recognition as an equal partner in her 25-year marriage resulted in legislation that recognized women's rights to an equal share of family property.

Irene Murdoch and her husband, James, worked together for hire on various ranches. In 1947, James and his father-in-law purchased a guest ranch. When they sold it four years later, they divided the profit equally between them. In 1952, James purchased additional property from money partly borrowed from his mother-in-law. The loan was repaid. Over the years, James bought and sold bigger and better ranch properties, always in his name. At all times, the Murdochs lived on and operated one or more of these properties. Irene did not make direct financial contributions to any of these purchases.

During these years, James got a job with a cattle stock association. While her husband was away working for the association, Irene performed or supervised many of the necessary chores on the ranches. This included driving trucks and tractors; haying; mowing; and vaccinating, branding, and dehorning cattle.

In 1968, Irene left her husband after 25 years of marriage. She brought an action for a one-half interest in all lands and assets owned by her husband on the basis that they were equal partners. Irene claimed that payments from her bank account were contributions to the partnership agreement. James claimed that the money he received usually came from his in-laws and was always repaid. As well, all land, livestock, and equipment were held in his name. Income tax returns were filed in his name only. No formal partnership declaration existed between them.

The trial court dismissed Irene's claim for the one-half interest. Her appeal to the Alberta Court of Appeal was also dismissed. In a 4–1 decision, the Supreme Court of Canada ruled that Irene was not entitled to any interest in her husband's land and assets. The court stated that there was no evidence of either a direct financial contribution on her part or a partnership agreement between them. All the work she had done was merely the work "that would be done by any farm wife."

For Discussion

1. Outline three reasons why all three courts dismissed Irene's claim.

2. Was the work done by her typical of that done by any farm or ranch wife? Discuss.

3. How do you think Canadian women felt about this decision?

4. Should marriage be considered a partnership that recognizes contributions in the form of household management and home-care duties? Why or why not?

The lone dissenting decision in the *Murdoch* case was written by Chief Justice Bora Laskin. This was one of Laskin's most significant judgments. It focused national attention on the legal inequities faced by Canadian women. Over the next decade, all provinces and territories passed legislation that recognized women's rights to an equal share of family property on separation or divorce.

Justice Bora Laskin was the 14th Chief Justice of the Supreme Court of Canada from 1973 to his death in 1984. He championed the rights of the disenfranchised.

Provincial and territorial statutes dealing with the division of property following divorce have different names. For example, British Columbia passed the *Family Relations Act*, Alberta and Nova Scotia the *Matrimonial Property Act*, and Ontario the *Family Law Act*. But the basic intent of the statutes is similar. Each recognizes marriage as an economic partnership. The contributions of both spouses—even if one does not earn an income and is a homemaker—are treated with equal importance. This text cannot provide a detailed analysis of each statute. Since the Ontario legislation was the first and the most detailed, it is the focus of this section.

The *Family Law Act*, 1986

In 1978, after the *Murdoch* decision, Ontario passed the first major division of property legislation in Canada: the *Family Law Reform Act*. This act recognized marriage as an equal partnership. It led to the passage of Ontario's *Family Law Act* in 1986. Legally married spouses, which now includes same-sex couples, in all provinces and territories are entitled to share the value of everything acquired during the marriage. There are a few exceptions, which will be discussed later. Common law partners, regardless of the length of their relationship, do not have the same rights. However, they do have some rights to support claims if certain conditions are met. These claims are discussed later in the section Common Law Relationships.

Calculating Family Property and Equalization Payments

The *Family Law Act* provides steps for dealing with property following a marriage breakdown. The legislation does not divide specific property, only the value of the property. This is done through a process called **equalization**. The process is fairly complicated. It usually requires that couples seek advice from a family law lawyer.

First, the law requires that spouses calculate the total net value of all their assets on the date they separated. Almost everything of value to the couple is included, such as furniture, appliances, personal property, financial accounts, and business interests. Determining the value of most of these assets is easy. Complications may arise when determining a pension plan value. In these cases, the couple may want to consult a lawyer or an accountant to assist with the calculations.

Once the value of each spouse's property is established, the couple must subtract the value of any gifts (from someone other than the spouse) or inheritances received. The next step is adding up all the debts on the date of separation. This includes debts such as car loans, mortgages, credit card balances, and so on. If these debts belong to both spouses, then half their value belongs to each spouse. The couple subtracts the total debts from the total assets to determine the total property value on the day of separation.

Next, each spouse creates a list of property owned and debts held on the day of the marriage. The value used for the items is based on the marriage date, not the separation date. Then, each spouse subtracts the value of all debts held on the day of marriage to determine the total marriage-date value of properties.

equalization the process of dividing the value of property equally between spouses when they divorce

> **? Did You Know?**
>
> Frequent flyer points, such as Aeroplan and Air Miles, are a valuable currency and are part of marital property, to be divided when a couple separates.

This is too young an age to be concerned about dividing property when a relationship ends.

After the couple totals their individual property values, the spouse with the greater value of **net family property** gives the other spouse an equalization payment. The payment may be in cash, property, or investment shares, and makes up one-half the difference between the two figures. For example, Françoise has a net family property of $40 000, and Jacques has a net family property of $90 000. The difference between the two totals is $50 000. The *Family Law Act* states that the spouse with the higher total has to pay the spouse with the lower total half of the difference between them. Half of $50 000 is $25 000, so Jacques has to pay Françoise $25 000 as an equalization payment.

net family property the net worth of a spouse on the valuation date

Usually, each spouse keeps the property that he or she is using or that is registered in his or her name. The balancing payment often comes from the proceeds of the sale of their home, a transfer of RRSPs, or a loan. If the equalization payment is a large amount, it may be paid over time instead of in a lump sum.

The following chart summarizes the steps in calculating family property.

Steps in Calculating Family Property and Equalization Payments

Step 1 List and calculate the value of your assets on the date of separation.

Step 2 Subtract the value of gifts and inheritances from the value of assets.

Step 3 Subtract your total debts on the date of separation to provide a total property value on the date of separation.

Step 4 List and calculate the value of your assets, less debts, on the date of marriage.

Step 5 Subtract amount #4 from amount #3 to calculate each spouse's net family property.

Step 6 Deduct the lower net family property from the higher one, and divide the difference by two to determine the amount of the equalization payment.

These are the steps to be followed in calculating net family property and determining the amount of an equalization payment.

The table below shows how this process could be used for an actual couple, Katya and Callum.

An Example of Division of Property

Steps in the Process	Callum		Katya
1. Value of assets at separation	$60 000		$300 000
2. Less: Exemption for inheritance received	35 000		0
3. Less: Debts/liabilities at separation	0		100 000
= Total property value at separation	25 000		200 000
4. Less: Value of assets at marriage	5 000		50 000
5. Net family property	20 000		150 000
6. **End result:** Callum deducts his net family property from Katya's net family property and is entitled to one-half the difference. Half of $130 000 equals $65 000.		$150 000 20 000 $130 000 $65 000	

This example shows the calculation of net family property and how the equalization payment is determined.

Spouses can opt out of an equal division of property by having a marriage contract that exempts certain assets from division. Marriage contracts are discussed in the section Domestic Contracts.

Raymond Sobeski

For more information, Go to Nelson Social Studies

Raymond Sobeski (centre) cuts a celebration cake after winning $30 million from Lotto Super 7.

Raymond Sobeski married Nynna Ionson in 1998. Within a few years, he was unhappy with his marriage. In April 2003, Sobeski discovered that he won $30 million from Lotto Super 7. He decided not to mention this win to anyone, including Ionson. He served his wife with divorce papers after learning of his winnings and before telling her about his big win. He claimed his prize 12 days before the ticket's expiry date in April 2004. He then cancelled his credit cards, bought a series of airline tickets, wrote large cheques for a few friends, and invested most of his winnings. After he claimed his winnings, Ionson filed a legal action against him seeking half of the $30 million. She claimed that the lottery win happened before their divorce was finalized.

- Why would she argue that she was entitled to half of the $30 million? As the judge, what decision would you reach and why?

Unequal Division of Property

Every province and territory intends to distribute marital property equally. However, there are situations in which this might be unfair. Consider the situations presented in the following chart.

These are some examples where dividing property equally may be unfair.

- **Length of the Marriage:** Quon and Meili have been married for only 18 months, and dividing the value of family assets equally may be unfair to Meili. She brought much more property into the marriage than Quon.

- **Length of the Separation:** Jafar and Birrah separated three years ago. Later, they each bought furnishings for their own accommodations. It would be unfair to divide the value of these assets equally. Both Jafar and Birrah bought them for personal use after they separated.

- **Date When an Asset Was Acquired:** Jamie bought an expensive painting for himself just before separating from Laura. He wishes to keep this asset. If Laura did not have time to appreciate or enjoy the painting in their home, Jamie might not have to divide the value of the art with Laura.

- **Gifts and Inheritances:** Rafaela inherited a valuable family antique from a wealthy uncle while she was married to Luciano. This inheritance may be specifically excluded from equal division. It is unfair to make Rafaela share the value of an antique given to her as an inheritance in a will.

Most provincial and territorial statutes have specific laws on equal property division, unless strictly following the law of equal division leads to an unconscionable judgment. The term "unconscionable" means grossly or shockingly unfair and is likely to be applied only in extreme cases. Examples include when the marriage was very short, or when one spouse intentionally and recklessly depleted or squandered his or her assets prior to the separation, such as spending all of the household money betting at the racetrack.

The Matrimonial Home

The **matrimonial home**—the home in which spouses live while married—is generally their most valuable asset. The *Family Law Act* and other similar legislation states that that home applies only to legally married spouses. The statutes say that the home can be a house, a mobile home, a condominium, or any dwelling owned by one or both spouses. For example, Katya and Callum spend part of the year in their Vancouver condominium and the

matrimonial home the home in which the spouses ordinarily reside during their marriage

rest at their chalet in Whistler. Both homes may be considered marital homes if they were "ordinarily occupied" during the marriage. Places that are used only a few times each year for recreational purposes are not marital homes.

It does not matter whose name is on the home ownership papers. Each spouse has an equal right to live in the marital home. Each has the right to not be forced out by the other spouse. And each has the right to share equally in the proceeds if the couple agrees to sell it, unless a marriage contract states otherwise. (See the section Domestic Contracts.)

Katya and Callum lived part of the year in their condo in Vancouver, such as the ones shown here, and part in their Whistler chalet. If the couple also owned a cottage in Ontario or a timeshare in Québec, and these were regularly used by the family, these dwellings would be considered matrimonial homes.

On separation, the courts may grant one spouse exclusive possession of the matrimonial home and its contents for a certain period. This spouse must first convince the court that sharing the home is a practical impossibility. Second, this spouse must show that his or her claim should be preferred over the other's. In other words, remaining in the home is extremely important to him or her. In such a situation, the courts consider each spouse's financial position, the availability of other accommodation, and the best interests of any children. This option is most often used when one spouse has custody of the children and wants to remain in the home until they have grown up and finished school.

After the period of exclusive occupancy ends, the spouses divide the value of the home. This division may involve selling the property and dividing the proceeds. Alternatively, one spouse may buy out the other's interest.

Division of Matrimonial Property

Alan and Patricia were married for three years. Long before the marriage, Alan won money in a provincial lottery and bought $50 000 worth of mutual funds in his own name. During the marriage, the couple bought a $350 000 home, a $30 000 sailboat, and some antiques worth $50 000. All of these assets were registered in Alan's name. Because of some disastrous financial investments, Alan needed cash quickly. He sold the antiques, the sailboat, and their home. Because of this and other marital problems, the couple filed for divorce.

- Would the court divide the value of the matrimonial home equally between them? Why or why not? Would Patricia have a claim to any of Alan's $50 000 worth of mutual funds? Explain.

Significant Legislative Differences

The assets that may be divided upon separation differ among provinces and territories. The *Constitution Act, 1867*, gives each the jurisdiction over property and civil rights. Outside of Ontario, these assets are known as matrimonial property (marital property). Legislation in the western provinces and Québec states that all property acquired by the spouses during marriage is to be divided equally. The Atlantic provinces and Yukon Territory distinguish between family assets and non-family (business) assets associated with one spouse only.

A **family asset** is the matrimonial home and property owned by one or both spouses. It is "ordinarily used or enjoyed by the spouses or one or more of their children for family purposes." Examples include the family cottage, the family car or cars, and money in a joint bank account normally used to run the household (to pay bills). Art displayed in the family home are also family assets. The intent of the law is to allow family assets to be divided equally between the spouses.

Non-family assets (business assets) include stocks and bonds, pension funds, RRSPs, and most business interests. These assets are not divided equally because they are not family property. Instead, they belong to the spouse who purchased them. They are divided with the other spouse only if he or she helped to build up the assets and can prove it. For example, one spouse works to put the other through university or gives up a career to raise children. That spouse has contributed to the future success, earnings, and investments of the other spouse. The chart on the next page summarizes the three legal principles for the division of marital property across Canada.

family asset property owned by one or both spouses and ordinarily used for family purposes

non-family asset property owned by one spouse that is not used for a family purpose; the non-owning spouse does not make any direct contributions to the property

The family cottage can be considered a family asset.

The Principles of Property Division in Canada

1. The property of the marriage is to be divided equally between the spouses unless injustice or inequity would result.

2. The contribution of the spouse who is primarily responsible for childcare and home management must be legally recognized. Such a contribution gives the other spouse an opportunity to acquire property that might not be a family asset.

3. The contribution of each spouse must be legally recognized, whether in the form of money or work, toward the acquisition of property.

matrimonial property property owned by the spouses during their marriage

These are the three principles of law for the division of **matrimonial property** across Canada.

Division of Property on a Spouse's Death

Most married couples prepare wills stating how they want their assets to be divided when they die. Usually, spouses leave their estate to their surviving spouse, and there is no problem.

But, if a spouse leaves nothing to the surviving spouse, the surviving spouse has the legal right to apply to the courts for a division of marital property within six months of death. This gives the survivor the same rights as if the couple had separated just before the spouse's death.

If a spouse dies without a will (intestate), provincial or territorial legislation prevails. It entitles the survivor to a share of the marital property. There is no legal protection for a common law spouse whose partner dies without a will.

"Why do I get the feeling my divorce is final?"

This is not what the courts intend to happen in the division of property.

Review Your Understanding

1. Why did property and family law often result in hardship for women when a marriage ended?

2. Outline four situations in which an equal division of property might be unfair.

3. What is the matrimonial home, and what rights of possession and ownership does each spouse have concerning that home?

4. Summarize the three principles all provinces and territories follow in the division of marital property.

5. Why is a will important for married and common law couples?

14.3 Common Law Relationships

Many people believe that if you live with a partner for a certain length of time, you have a common law marriage and the same rights as married couples. This is *not* true. No amount of time together—3, 5, 10, or 50 years—makes a common law relationship a legal marriage. To be legally married, two persons must have a recognized marriage, as outlined in Chapter 13. Unlike a marriage, a divorce is not necessary to end a common law relationship since the couple was never legally married.

Did You Know?

The term "common law" is no longer used in Alberta laws. The law regarding common law relationships in Alberta recognizes adult interdependent partners. The new law is set out in the *Adult Interdependent Relationships Act*. It has applied in Alberta since June 2003. The term "common law" is still used in the rest of Canada.

Today's support and pension benefits laws recognize that common law couples do *not* have the same rights as married couples.

cohabitation the act of living together in an intimate relationship without being married

Today's laws recognize **cohabitation**, or common law relationships, as being similar to marriages and the partners as "spouses." This is because more couples are choosing to live together and not marry. In all provinces and territories, if a couple lives together without the benefit of a legal marriage, they may have some rights under the law, as you will see later in this section.

According to Statistics Canada, 57 percent of first live-in relationships in Canada are common law.

Property

When married couples separate, they have an automatic right to equal property division and claims between them. This principle does *not* apply to common law couples. No matter how long couples live together, each partner can only ever claim the property owned individually. The partners separate as though they were business partners.

In a common law relationship, property belongs to the person who paid for it. For example, if the partners bought something together, then it belongs to both of them. If one partner pays 30 percent of the price and the other pays 70 percent of the price, then 30 percent of the item's value belongs to one party and 70 percent to the other. If the item was a gift, then it belongs to the person to whom it was given.

The partners may have some property rights based on contributions of work and household maintenance. For instance, a woman's contribution helps her common law partner build a successful and prosperous business. She may be entitled to a share or an interest in the business. However, she has to prove her claim in court to obtain a portion of the asset's value. To prove this claim, the following questions must be considered by the courts:

- How many years have the partners lived together?

- What agreements, if any, did the couple have about each person's contributions and obligations?

- Is there proof that a valid contribution was made?

In 1980, the Supreme Court issued a landmark judgment in the case of *Pettkus v. Becker*. This judgment was the first major recognition of the rights of common law partners by Canadian courts. It is still widely used as a precedent today.

 Did You Know?

According to Statistics Canada, between 2001 and 2006, the average length of time Canadian common law relationships lasted was 4.3 years, compared to an average of 14.3 years for marriages. During that same period, over 2 million Canadians ended a relationship, either through separation or divorce. Just under half were common law relationships.

Pettkus v. Becker, 1980 CanLII 22 (S.C.C.)

For more information, **Go to Nelson Social Studies**

Rosa Becker was awarded half of the couple's interest in land and business despite the fact that the couple was never legally married. In 1986, she committed suicide out of frustration with Canada's legal system and the fact that she received so little from Pettkus of the $150 000 that the Supreme Court had awarded her.

Rosa Becker and Lothar Pettkus met in Montréal in 1955 shortly after they arrived from Europe. She was 29 and he was 24. After a few dates, he moved in with her. She paid for the couple's rent, food, clothing, and other living expenses from her salary, while he saved his entire salary in his own bank account. Becker expressed a desire to be married; Pettkus said he might consider marriage after they knew each other better. By 1960, Pettkus had saved a large sum of money, and they decided to buy a farm. The property was in his name only.

Becker moved to the farm with Pettkus. She participated fully in a very successful beekeeping operation over the next 14 years. The couple never married, but they lived together for 19 years. In 1974, Becker moved out permanently, claiming she was being mistreated. She then filed for a one-half interest in the land and business, which by then was worth about $300 000.

In the original action in 1977, the trial court judge awarded her 40 beehives, minus the bees, and $1500 cash. In his decision, this judge claimed: "Rosa's contribution to the household expenses during the first few years of the relationship was in the nature of risk capital invested in the hope of seducing a young man into marriage."

Becker appealed this decision to the Ontario Court of Appeal. Three judges overturned the trial decision. They stated that Becker's contribution to the beekeeping operation and her relationship with Pettkus had been greatly underrated by the trial judge. Her contribution to the business's success and property acquisition was significant. Becker was awarded half of the interest in all lands owned by Pettkus and in the beekeeping business.

Pettkus was allowed to appeal this decision to the Supreme Court of Canada. In December 1980, the court upheld the Ontario Court of Appeal ruling in a 6–3 judgment. It awarded Becker half of the interest in the assets accumulated by Pettkus during their 19-year relationship.

For Discussion

1. Do couples in a common law relationship have an automatic right to a division of property upon separating? Explain.

2. Why did the Supreme Court rule that Rosa Becker was entitled to a one-half interest in Pettkus's assets?

3. How do you think Canadian women felt about this decision?

4. Should common law couples have an automatic right to a division of property upon separating after three years of cohabitation? Explain.

Nova Scotia (Attorney General) v. Walsh, 2002 SCC 83 (CanLII)

For more information, **Go to Nelson Social Studies**

The exclusion of unmarried spouses from provincial property law in Nova Scotia was challenged by Susan Walsh. Walsh and Wayne Bona lived together for 10 years and had two children. When their relationship ended in 1995, Susan applied for child support and support for herself. She also argued that the definition of "spouse" in Nova Scotia's *Matrimonial Property Act* was unconstitutional. It failed to provide her with the right to an equal division of matrimonial property. This violated her section 15(1) equality rights in the *Charter of Rights and Freedoms*. She lost at trial as the trial judge ruled this was not discrimination within the meaning of section 15, but she won on appeal. A Crown appeal was heard by the Supreme Court in June 2002.

Katherine Briand was one of the lawyers who represented Susan Walsh in her bid to have Nova Scotia's definition of "spouse" declared unconstitutional.

- What do you think the Supreme Court ruled, and why?

Division of Property on a "Spouse's" Death

A surviving common law partner, unlike a married survivor, has no automatic claim to inherit the estate of the deceased. The deceased must leave a will leaving everything to the survivor. If the deceased dies without making a will, the survivor must go to court to claim a share of the estate. However, full title (right of ownership) to any assets owned jointly by common law partners—real estate, furnishings, vehicles, bank accounts—goes automatically to the survivor.

Manitoba's Law

Since June 2004 in Manitoba, the rights of common law and married couples are similar after a certain length of time. Under the *Common Law Partners' Property Act*, once a couple lives together for three years (or one year if they have a child together), the laws affecting the property rights of married couples also apply to unmarried couples or common law relationships. This means that all property acquired while the couple lived together is shared equally—just like married couples. There are some exceptions that are kept separate, such as inheritances.

After living together for similar lengths of time, inheritance rules are the same for both types of couples. This means that if your common law partner dies without a will, or has a will that leaves little or nothing to you, you will still get a fair share of your partner's property.

 Did You Know?

In Québec, 35 percent of couples live together without being legally married. The rate for the rest of Canada is 13.5 percent.

Support

All provinces and territories now recognize that common law partners have the same right to support as married couples, if they live together for a certain period or have a child. For example, common law spouses have the right to request support for themselves if they lived together for three years or more in Alberta and Ontario. They can also make the request if they lived together for less than three years but have a child or adopted a child together. This provision is specifically designed to ensure children's welfare. The principles of support for common law and same-sex partners were further developed in the following Supreme Court of Canada judgment in *M. v. H.*

Case

M. v. H., 1999 CanLII 686 (S.C.C.)

For more information, **Go to Nelson Social Studies**

Two women, M. and H., began a relationship in 1982. They lived in the home that H. had owned since 1974. They shared financial responsibilities equally and launched an advertising business. The business became successful and the couple had enough money for a comfortable lifestyle. This business and other businesses that the couple started provided their primary income. H.'s direct contribution to this business was greater than M.'s but they remained equal owners. M. spent more time managing the home and contributing indirectly through her assistance to H., including a lot of business entertaining. The advertising business was hurt by the economy in the late 1980s, and the couple found themselves in financial difficulty. H. felt M. was taking advantage of her because M. was not actively in the workforce. The business downturn seriously affected the women's personal relationship.

By late 1992, their relationship had fallen apart completely. H. presented M. with a draft agreement to settle their affairs. The challenge of trying to resolve their complicated financial situation caused a great deal of bitterness. M. left the home with some personal belongings. After that, H. changed the locks on the home and excluded M. from the business. M. suffered financial hardship while struggling to become self-sufficient. In October 1992, M. began court proceedings. She claimed that she was entitled to part of the home, a share of the business and cottage, and spousal support. In doing so, she challenged the validity of the definition of "spouse" under Ontario's *Family Law Act*. The definition of common law spouse was restricted to relationships involving people of the opposite sex. In other words, persons in same-sex relationships were not considered "spouses." Therefore, they had no access to the various rights and remedies the act provided to opposite-sex common law spouses.

In early 1996, Justice Gloria Epstein of the Ontario Court of Justice (General Division) gave a landmark judgment. She ruled that the "opposite sex" definition of "spouse" violated section 15 of the *Charter of Rights and Freedoms* and could not be saved under the Charter's section 1 exemption. Justice Epstein declared that the words "a man and a woman" were to be read out (deleted) from the definition of "spouse." They were to be replaced with the words "two persons." H. appealed this judgment to the Ontario Court of Appeal. The trial judgment was upheld in a 2–1 decision in December 1996. Shortly afterward, M. and H. privately concluded a settlement of their financial issues.

In March 1998, the Supreme Court heard the appeal of the Ontario Court of Appeal decision. The Ontario government launched the appeal because it felt it was important to resolve the constitutional issue of whether same-sex couples had a right to seek spousal support. In an 8–1 judgment in May 1999, the court affirmed (agreed with) both earlier judgments. It gave the Ontario government six months to rewrite provincial laws to ensure equal treatment for same-sex spouses.

For Discussion

1. On what basis did M. initiate court proceedings under Ontario's *Family Law* Act?

2. Explain the meaning and significance of Justice Epstein's trial judgment.

3. Why is this case such a landmark judgment?

4. Should a court be able to order a government to rewrite its laws that violate Charter rights? Why or why not?

MADAM JUSTICE GLORIA EPSTEIN

In 1996, Madam Justice Gloria Epstein released her landmark decision in *M. v. H* that the definition of spouse as opposite sex was unconstitutional.

Epstein graduated from Queen's University with a Bachelor of Commerce degree in 1972. After graduation, she lived in Temagami, Ontario. There, she owned and operated the Camp Manito Hotel Resort for two years. In 1974, she began studying law at the University of Toronto. She was called to the Ontario Bar in 1979 and appointed Queen's Counsel in 1992. After practising law with two Toronto firms, Epstein launched her own law firm, Gloria Epstein & Associates. She kept her own practice until she was appointed a justice of the Ontario Superior Court of Justice in late 1993. Epstein presided over all types of cases until her rise to the Ontario Court of Appeal in October 2007.

Justice Epstein is the co-chair of the McMurtry Gardens of Justice project, a sculpture garden celebrating the rule of law and the administration of justice in Ontario. The cover sculpture was the first piece selected for the Gardens.

In February 1996, Justice Epstein released her landmark decision in *M. v. H.* (see page 488). It was reaffirmed by the Ontario Court of Appeal and the Supreme Court of Canada in 1999. She held that it was unfair to exclude same-sex couples from spousal support under Ontario's *Family Law Act*. It violated section 15 of the *Charter of Rights and Freedoms*. As a result, Ontario altered the definition of "spouse" in 67 of its statutes. Ontario also provided same-sex couples with the same treatment under the law as common law couples. The federal government amended all federal statutes to replace the words "of the opposite sex" with the term "survivor" to ensure equal treatment under the law for opposite- and same-sex relationships.

She once owned and operated a fishing camp and is now a justice for the Ontario Court of Appeal. She is a former litigator and an active member of the Canadian Equestrian Federation. In June 1998, Ontario premier Mike Harris assigned to her the delicate task of reviewing the province's treatment of the Dionne quintuplets. All of these accomplishments are just a glimpse into the busy life of the Honourable Madam Justice Gloria J. Epstein.

For Discussion

1. Justice Epstein once said of *M. v. H*: "With my decision, I understand that I was a mere speed bump on the way … to the Court of Appeal and, perhaps, to the Supreme Court of Canada." Explain the meaning of her statement.

2. What impact did this decision have on Ontario and federal law?

The Impact of M. v. H.

In *M. v. H.*, the Supreme Court of Canada found that gay and lesbian couples were similar to heterosexual couples. They form relationships of emotional and economic dependency. The court observed that it was unfair to exclude same-sex couples from **spousal support**. The court's decision was restricted to spousal support under Ontario's *Family Law Act*. However, the court sent a clear message to all provincial and territorial governments. Laws excluding same-sex couples would likely go against section 15 of the *Charter of Rights and Freedoms*. In March 2000, the Ontario government passed a package of amendments to legislation to change the definition of "spouse" to include same-sex partners. Similar legislation was soon passed by all of the provinces and territories, as well as the federal government.

spousal support financial assistance paid by one spouse to another after separation

 Activity

To learn more about common law relationships,

Go to Nelson Social Studies

Review Your Understanding

1. What is the major difference in division of property laws between a married and a common law couple?
2. Outline the questions that a court must consider in dividing property between cohabiting partners.
3. Why was the *Pettkus v. Becker* case such a landmark judgment?
4. Why was the *M. v. H.* case such a landmark judgment?
5. What is the significance of Manitoba's *Common Law Partners' Property Act*?

14.4 Spousal Support

maintenance another term for spousal support

self-sufficient to be able to support oneself financially

Couples who separate often encounter financial problems. This is especially true when one spouse is economically dependent on the other during the marriage. Spousal support or **maintenance** (formerly called alimony) is intended to compensate one spouse for any financial losses suffered because of the marriage breakdown. It assists that spouse until he or she becomes **self-sufficient**. Maintenance is money paid by one spouse to another after a marriage breakdown. Spousal support is not intended to punish or blame the other spouse. It is also not automatic. The spouse in need must apply for support.

Why should one spouse have to support the other after their marriage has ended? For how long should support be paid? It is usually difficult to compare or even predict the amounts a court will award. Each case is different and is decided on its own merits.

Although support rights and obligations differ from province to province, the principles are similar. The two main elements to consider are the needs of the spouse requiring support and the ability of the other spouse to pay.

Both the federal *Divorce Act* and provincial and territorial legislation contain provisions for supporting spouses and children. In the case of divorce, the federal law applies. For separation, provincial and territorial legislation applies.

Factors Affecting Support

As you learned in Chapter 13, the federal government introduced the *Divorce Act* in 1985 that outlined the following objectives for awarding spousal support:

- to recognize any economic advantages or disadvantages arising from the marriage breakdown
- to relieve any economic hardship of the spouses from the marriage breakdown
- to promote the economic self-sufficiency of each spouse

The federal *Divorce Act* and provincial and territorial laws guide judges in determining if support should be awarded and, if so, how much. The following chart outlines the key factors judges consider when determining support.

Provincial Support Legislation

Province/Territory	Name of Act
Alberta	*Family Law Act*
British Columbia	*Family Relations Act*
Manitoba	*Family Maintenance Act*
New Brunswick	*Family Services Act*
Newfoundland and Labrador	*Family Law Act*
Northwest Territories	*Family Law Act*
Nova Scotia	*Maintenance and Custody Act*
Nunavut	*Family Law Act*
Ontario	*Family Law Act*
Prince Edward Island	*Family Law Act*
Québec	*Civil Code of Québec*
Saskatchewan	*Family Maintenance Act*
Yukon Territory	*Family Property and Support Act*

All provinces and territories have different legislation affecting support obligations. Why do you think there is not a single piece of legislation for all the provinces?

Factors to Consider When Determining Spousal Support

- assets and income of each spouse, including present and future earning ability
- ability of each spouse to be self-supporting
- ability of each spouse to provide support to the other spouse, if necessary
- age and physical and mental health of each spouse
- length of time the spouses were married or lived together
- length of time required by the spouse in need to acquire or upgrade job skills
- length of time one spouse spent at home raising the family instead of contributing financially by working outside the home

These are key factors for a judge to consider in determining spousal support.

Notice that the conduct of the spouses is not included in the above factors. The obligation to provide spousal support exists without regard to the other spouse's behaviour. *The Divorce Act* eliminated misconduct or fault from consideration as an issue of support. For example, just because a husband committed adultery does not mean that his wife should receive more support to punish him for his affair.

This was reaffirmed in the 2006 landmark judgment in *Leskun v. Leskun* (see the case on the next page) when the Supreme Court upheld Canada's "no-fault" divorce law.

Chapter 14 **Division of Property and Support**

Leskun v. Leskun, 2006 SCC 25 (CanLII)

For more information, Go to Nelson Social Studies

In 2004, on behalf of the British Columbia Court of Appeal, Justice Mary Southin (shown here) ruled that Gary Leskun must continue support payments because Sherry Leskun was still unable to be self-supporting. In her decision, Justice Southin wrote: "Emotionally, she is bitter to the point of obsession with his misconduct and in consequence has been unable to make a new life."

Sherry and Gary Leskun were married in 1978. During their marriage, Sherry worked and contributed financially to her husband's education. She cashed in RRSP investments and pension benefits so that he could get his postgraduate degree. In 1988, Sherry was laid off from her job at a bank. She also suffered a significant back injury, and several close family members died. Soon after, Gary told her that he wanted a divorce to marry another woman with whom he had been having an affair. The Leskuns divorced in 1999. He was 49 and she was 59. Sherry received one-half of the family assets and was awarded spousal support of $2250 a month. This was to be paid until she returned to full employment. The trial judge also suggested that he was doubtful about Sherry's ability to achieve economic self-sufficiency.

In 2003, Gary asked the court to discontinue support payments. He was now unemployed and in financial difficulty. However, his request was denied. The judge found Sherry was not yet self-sufficient. She still needed spousal support. A further appeal to the British Columbia Court of Appeal in 2004 upheld that decision in a 2–1 judgment.

Gary appealed this decision to the Supreme Court of Canada. His appeal was heard in February 2006. In a 7–0 judgment in June 2006, the court dismissed his appeal. It held that he should continue to pay spousal support. Sherry still suffered physical and emotional health problems, and was unable to return to work to support herself.

For Discussion

1. Why do you think Gary Leskun appealed his case all the way to the Supreme Court of Canada?

2. Canadian courts have held that a person may be entitled to spousal support if she or he is unable to become self-sufficient for health reasons, even years after the marriage ended. Do you agree with this principle? Why or why not?

3. In the Supreme Court's unanimous judgment, Gary Leskun's affair was not considered a factor in the support award. But, the justices recognized that the depression Sherry Leskun suffered was the result of his affair, and the termination of her job made her unemployable and therefore not self-sufficient. Do you agree with the justices? Explain.

4. Do you agree with the Supreme Court's decision in this case? Why or why not?

Self-Sufficiency

After 1985, Canada's legal system focused on the goal of economic self-sufficiency. Once a marriage ends, each spouse may be obligated to seek extra education, employment, or retraining as soon as possible to become self-supporting. Today, both spouses are likely to be employed, particularly if they are younger people. If they earn similar salaries, and if each spouse receives a fair share of all assets upon separation, then support may not be an issue.

Older spouses who have been out of the workforce for many years may find it difficult to support themselves. For example, a woman who was married for 30 years and has few workplace skills may not qualify for a job that allows her to become self-sufficient. In such cases, courts generally do not place a time limit on a support award. Court orders are often left open, to be reviewed after some time.

The goal of Canada's legal system is to see each partner be economically self-sufficient after a marriage breakdown. If one spouse cannot become self-sufficient, the other spouse has a duty to provide support, according to his or her ability to pay. A spouse cannot simply refuse to work and expect to receive support. If the spouse needing support does not try to become self-sufficient, the other spouse may reduce or stop support payments after applying to the courts and receiving a ruling.

If one spouse cannot become self-sufficient, the other spouse must pay spousal support.

 ## You Be the Judge

Moge v. Moge, 1992 CanLII 25 (S.C.C.)

For more information, Go to Nelson Social Studies

Andrzej and Zofia Moge were married in Poland in the mid-1950s. They moved to Manitoba in 1960. During their marriage, he worked full-time outside the home. He did not contribute to the household work or care for their three children. She was a full-time homemaker, caring for the three children. She also worked in the evenings cleaning offices to provide additional income. She had limited formal education and did not speak English well.

They separated in 1973, and Zofia was awarded custody of the children. She received $150 a month for child and spousal support. Andrzej remarried in 1984 and continued to pay support. In 1987, Zofia was laid off and applied and received an increase in support to $400. In 1989, Andrzej applied to end his spousal support obligations. He argued that Zofia had had enough time to become self-sufficient.

Zofia appealed this decision to the Manitoba Court of Appeal. In a 2–1 judgment in 1990, the appellate court ruled that spousal support must continue indefinitely. Zofia was still economically disadvantaged. Andrzej appealed this decision to the Supreme Court of Canada. In a 5–2 judgment in December 1992, the court ruled that Andrzej must continue his support payments indefinitely, even though they had separated nearly 20 years earlier.

- Why did the Supreme Court rule in Zofia's favour? Do you think she should be entitled to ongoing support for an indefinite period? Should spousal support be ended? Explain.

However, a 2008 Alberta Court of Appeal decision in *Shields v. Shields* may reverse the Moge principle of indefinite spousal support for women who spent many years out of the workforce raising children. The Shields decision suggests that once a spouse gains full-time employment, he or she is self-sufficient, even if the spouse was out of the workforce for 15 years caring for children.

 Case

Shields v. Shields, 2008 ABCA 213 (CanLII)

For more information, **Go to Nelson Social Studies**

In 2008, the Alberta Court of Appeal (shown here), in the case of *Shields v. Shields*, ruled against the principle of indefinite spousal support.

Jean and Ken Shields were married in July 1983 and separated in January 1998. They were both 34 years old, and they had two daughters. In September 2000, the Shieldses signed an agreement dividing their property equally, and each took custody of one child. Ken agreed to pay Jean $600 monthly in child support and a lump-sum spousal support of nearly $18 000. Jean retained the right to apply for ongoing spousal support. At that time, Ken earned about $91 000, while Jean earned about $15 000.

Before the marriage, Jean worked as a retail clerk but stopped working when their daughters were born. She remained at home while their children were young. She later returned to full-time work at a meat-processing plant. In early 2002, Ken declared personal bankruptcy after his company failed. He then became a consultant in the oil industry and started a new oil field company. From July 2002 to 2006, his income averaged $132 000 a year. Jean's income averaged $27 000 for the same period.

Jean applied for increased spousal support. In 2006, a judge ordered Ken to pay Jean $1000 a month in spousal support indefinitely, including retroactive payments back to 2002. Ken appealed this decision to the Alberta Court of Appeal. In a 3–0 judgment in June 2008, the court supported his appeal. It limited the spousal payments to only eight years, beginning from the day the marriage broke down. This meant the end of Jean's spousal support.

For Discussion

1. Why did Ken appeal Jean's indefinite spousal support?

2. What arguments would Ken present for his appeal?

3. The Alberta Court of Appeal said that eight years of spousal support was sufficient to compensate Jean for staying at home with the children. They also considered that she was still young enough to upgrade her education to help her reach financial self-sufficiency. Do you agree? Why or why not?

4. In what major way does this decision differ from the Supreme Court judgment in *Moge v. Moge*? With which decision do you agree, and why?

Length of Support

Spousal support is often limited to a short period for short-term relationships with no children, or when a couple is young. Courts usually do not limit the time for spousal support for longer relationships, or for those where there are children. This does not mean that spousal support will go on forever. It just means that courts do not want to guess at what someone's financial situation will be in the future. If one's financial situation greatly changes, one can always go back to court to end spousal support or change the amount.

A spousal support directive that is becoming more common is a "review order." These orders are often made when one spouse has been out of the workforce for a considerable time but is expected to return to the workforce after some retraining. Under a review order, courts state that spousal support amounts can be reviewed after a certain number of years. This gives spouses the chance to return to court to change spousal support orders without having to show that either spouse's financial situation has changed. However, it is not a guarantee that spousal support will be changed. A review order simply allows courts to review the spousal support situation.

Judges may order one spouse to pay the other spouse indefinitely or for a fixed period. A judge may order the support to be paid in weekly, monthly, or yearly payments, or in one lump sum. Either party can apply to the court to have the spousal support order increased, decreased, or stopped if circumstances change. This may arise from a change in salary, remarriage, unemployment, or poor health. A change in circumstances does not mean that the order for maintenance will vary or end.

Judges recognize that one spouse cannot be expected to support two families equally. Indeed, financial problems can strain second marriages more than other problems that go with blended families. When a second marriage results in a blended family, obligations to the first family often take priority. The paying parent may remarry and establish a new second family. Those obligations do not exempt that person from paying child support to the first family. As a result, there may not be enough income to support both families equally. Most judges will at least ensure that the two families are treated equally.

The Supreme Court of Canada issued a landmark judgment in 2003 (*Miglin v. Miglin*, discussed on the next page). It ruled that separation agreements should be final in most cases. But, in certain and limited circumstances where there has been a big change in one spouse's finances, a court may change the agreement to provide continuing support for a needy spouse. This is true even where that spouse has agreed not to ask for spousal support.

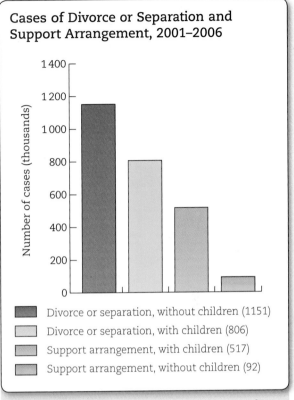

Cases of Divorce or Separation and Support Arrangement, 2001–2006

Number of cases (thousands)

- ■ Divorce or separation, without children (1151)
- □ Divorce or separation, with children (806)
- ▨ Support arrangement, with children (517)
- ▨ Support arrangement, without children (92)

This graph shows the number of cases in Canada of divorces or separation and support arrangement for couples with and without children 23 years and younger, for 2001–2006.

 You and the Law

When a second marriage results in a blended family, obligations to the first family often take priority in determining support orders. What do you think of this legal principle? Explain.

Miglin v. Miglin, 2003 SCC 24 (CanLII)

For more information, Go to Nelson Social Studies

In their separation agreement, Linda and Eric Miglin agreed that she would give up her interest in Killarney Lodge, and he would give up his interest in the family home.

The appellant in this case, Eric Miglin, and the respondent, Linda Miglin, were married in 1979. Five years later as equal shareholders, they purchased Killarney Lodge in Algonquin Park for just over $1 million. They ran it together as a multimillion-dollar family business. He managed the business while she looked after the administrative and housekeeping tasks. Each drew a salary from the business. Between 1985 and 1991, they had four children. The family divided their time between the lodge and their Toronto home. In 1993, the Miglins separated when the children were between two and seven years of age. In 1994, they signed negotiated separation, custody, and child support agreements with expert legal advice.

In the separation agreement, Linda agreed to give up her interest in the lodge in exchange for Eric's interest in the family home, each worth about $250 000. They shared responsibility for raising the children. However, Linda agreed to raise them in their family home in Toronto. A parenting agreement gave Linda $60 000 yearly in child support. Based on this amount, as well as a $15 000 consulting fee for five years that Eric agreed to pay Linda for continuing work at the lodge,

she gave up her right to spousal support "at no time, now or in the future, under any circumstances."

After their divorce in 1997, their relationship became very bitter. Linda found it more difficult than she expected to get back on her feet while raising four children. She applied for sole custody, child support, and spousal support. The trial judge found that her original agreement had been unfair. The judge awarded her spousal support of $4400 a month for five years. Eric appealed this decision to the Ontario Court of Appeal. In a 3–0 judgment in 2001, the appellate court upheld the award of support and extended it for an indefinite period because of a "material change in circumstances."

Eric Miglin appealed this decision to the Supreme Court of Canada. The appeal was heard in October 2002. In a 7–2 judgment in April 2003, a majority of the court reversed the Ontario Court of Appeal's decision to award Linda Miglin support. Seven justices ruled that the original agreement should stand. Each spouse had received independent legal advice over a lengthy period. Also, the distribution of their assets was fair, and the agreement met the federal *Divorce Act* objectives. The two dissenting justices would have awarded Linda support, because the agreement did not consider how difficult it would be for her to become self-sufficient while raising four children.

For Discussion

1. Outline the basis for Linda's case.
2. Outline the basis for Eric's appeal.
3. Why did the Supreme Court of Canada reverse the Ontario Court of Appeal judgment?
4. Some would have liked to see the Supreme Court rule out the possibility of ever opening up separation agreements (which did not happen in this case). Others agreed with the Ontario Court of Appeal that all that is required to review an agreement is a major change in circumstances. Which side of this case do you support, and why? Discuss with a partner with an opposing viewpoint.

Spousal Support Advisory Guidelines

Family law lawyers and judges have expressed concerns that the current Canadian spousal support law differs across the country. This creates a high degree of uncertainty and unpredictability. Aware of these concerns, the federal Department of Justice retained two legal experts to develop spousal support guidelines that could be used to advise the justice system. In January 2005, a draft proposal, the *Spousal Support Advisory Guidelines*, was released for reaction from the legal community. The final version of these guidelines was released in July 2008. It highlights the main differences between the draft and final version.

These guidelines are *not* law, and couples involved in a family law dispute are not bound by them. Their purpose is to provide another tool to help determine how much spousal support should be paid and for how long.

Review Your Understanding

1. What are the two key elements that courts consider in determining spousal support orders?
2. Identify the three objectives for awarding spousal support.
3. Why is conduct or fault not a factor to consider in awarding spousal support?
4. Why are spousal support orders not permanent?
5. What is the purpose of the *Spousal Support Advisory Guidelines*?

14.5 Child Support

Both parents must support their children financially when they live together and after they separate. This responsibility applies to all parents. Even a parent who remarries and starts a new family is still responsible for supporting the children of a previous marriage. The provinces, territories, and federal government share responsibilities regarding child support. The federal *Divorce Act* outlines procedures for determining child support amounts if the parents are already divorced or planning to divorce. Provincial laws apply if the parents have never married, or are separated or planning to separate, but do not intend to divorce.

It is the responsibility of both parents to support their children financially. In 1997, the Canadian Department of Justice released the *Federal Child Support Guidelines*. They were amended on May 1, 2006.

Federal Child Support Guidelines

In the early 1990s, the provincial, territorial, and federal justice ministers began to study child support guidelines. The main goal was to increase support for children who most needed it. Judges needed guidelines that were realistic and reflected the true cost of raising a child. Reform was necessary because support orders varied. Before these reforms, courts all across Canada determined child support on a case-by-case basis. It was based on the children's needs and the parents' abilities to meet these needs. There was no consistency or fairness.

In May 1997, amendments to the *Divorce Act* introduced the *Federal Child Support Guidelines*. This was one of the most significant reforms to Canadian family law in many years. The guidelines were established to do the following:

- Establish a fair system of child support that considers both parents' finances after divorce.

- Reduce conflict and tension by making the calculation of child support simpler and more objective.

- Bring consistency to child support orders while still providing flexibility to families to meet their own circumstances.

- Improve the efficiency of the legal process by giving courts and parties guidance in setting awards and encouraging settlement.

Each province and territory also has guidelines. In all cases, payments are determined based on federal guidelines. They consist of rules and tables for calculating the support that parents should pay toward their children's food, clothing, and shelter. The support amounts are similar in the different guidelines. They do take into account regional economic differences and different provincial income tax rates. For example, effective May 1, 2006, a British Columbia resident who earns $40 000 annually and has one child pays $370 a month. Someone with an annual income of $60 000 and three children pays $1185 a month. A Nova Scotia resident pays $348 and $1113, respectively.

These are typical monthly child support payments under the *Federal Child Support Guidelines* for Ontario residents.

Typical Monthly Support Payments in Ontario

Annual Income ($)	Typical support ($) for			
	1 Child	2 Children	3 Children	4 Children
20 000	172	308	417	506
30 000	270	444	598	724
40 000	367	601	773	915
50 000	462	753	986	1161
60 000	557	902	1177	1403
70 000	647	1043	1359	1618
80 000	719	1159	1511	1799
90 000	798	1281	1668	1985
100 000	877	1404	1825	2170
125 000	1068	1702	2209	2624
150 000	1254	1992	2581	3064

Determining Child Support

The appropriate level of child support depends on the following factors:

- the non-custodial parent's total income

- the number of children to be supported

- the appropriate federal child support table for the province or territory in which the non-custodial parent lives

Usually, it is the non-custodial parent who pays all, or most, of the child support to the custodial parent.

Exceptions to the Tables

Of course, not all children and families are the same. Most families spend more on their children as family income increases, and spending changes with each parent's income. The tables reflect the amount that an average parent with a certain income would spend on his or her children. As well, the custodial parent is expected to contribute a similar share of his or her income to meet the costs of raising the children. In this way, children share in increases and decreases in either parent's income, just as they would if their parents were still married.

Although courts follow these tables closely, exceptions are sometimes made for "special or extraordinary expenses." These may be daycare, medical expenses, some extracurricular activities, private school, and post-secondary education. Both parents share these special expenses in proportion with their incomes. Other exceptions include the following:

- If the table payments would cause undue (excessive) hardship for the paying parent, an exception may be made. For example, a paying parent who has to support other children in a new marriage might be able to claim this. The court would have to examine in detail the financial circumstances of the two households, including any new partners for either parent.

- If the children are 18 or older, the guidelines are a starting point. The court looks at the children's financial needs and their ability to help with their own support. This means that child support payments may be needed when a child is in college or university earning a diploma or degree. Supporting your children is a life-long responsibility. It does not necessarily end when they turn 18, as many believe.

- If there is shared or joint custody, the guidelines may not apply if the paying parent cares for the children at least 40 percent of the time. Here, the court looks at the costs of a shared custody arrangement, including both parents' incomes and the children's needs. Judges have discretion to reduce table amounts when the paying parent has the child for at least 40 percent of the time.

- If the paying parent's annual income is over $150 000, exceptions may be made. The court must first order the table amount for the $150 000. But, the court is then free to order more or less payment, depending on the circumstances.

Child support payments can help the child get a college or university education.

The first test of the *Federal Child Support Guidelines* in the Supreme Court of Canada occurred in the 9–0 judgment in *Francis v. Baker* (discussed below), although it did not affect the majority of divorcing Canadians.

Francis v. Baker, 1999 CanLII 659 (S.C.C.)

For more information, Go to Nelson Social Studies 🌐

In 1997, the Ontario Superior Court awarded Monica Francis child support of $10 000 per month in line with the *Federal Child Support Guidelines*.

Thomas Baker, a Toronto lawyer, and Monica Francis, a high school teacher, were married in 1979. Their first daughter was born in 1983. In July 1985, when their second daughter was five days old, Baker left the family, leaving the children with their mother. After the separation, the mother struggled financially and returned to full-time teaching three months later. Under the separation agreement terms, she received $30 000 a year ($2500 per month) in child support payments and a lump-sum payment of $500 000 to ease her financial problems. The couple divorced in 1987.

In 1988, Francis applied for an increase in child support. After many delays, the case went to trial in 1997. Francis wanted her child support amounts to be made under the new *Federal Child Support Guidelines*. At that time, Francis earned $63 000 a year. Baker had prospered since the separation. He had become the chief executive officer of a large company. He earned $945 538 a year, and was worth an estimated $78 million. When his daughters were in his care, Baker took them on European vacations and to luxury box seats at Blue Jays games and gave them expensive gifts. As well, he paid about $25 000 yearly to send his daughters to private school.

In 1997, the Ontario Superior Court of Justice awarded Francis an increase in child support to $10 000 a month. This was in line with the *Federal Child Support Guidelines* amounts. The amount was upheld on appeal and reaffirmed in a 9–0 judgment by the Supreme Court of Canada in September 1999.

For Discussion

1. The Ontario Court of Appeal's judgment stated: "Children are entitled to live at the standard permitted by all available income, even if that means living better than your basic needs demand." Argue in support of or against this statement. Share your view with a partner.

2. What is the significance of this decision? Do you agree with it? Why or why not?

3. The Supreme Court's judgment stated: "Parliament did not choose to impose a cap or upper limit on child support payments … In my opinion, child support undeniably involves some form of wealth transfer to the children, and will often produce an indirect benefit to the custodial parent." What does this mean?

Children of the Marriage

Under provincial and territorial legislation, parents must support unmarried children living at home until they reach the age of majority. This is either 18 or 19, depending on the province or territory. In addition, some provinces may order continued support as long as the children are enrolled in a full-time educational program. For example, child support may be granted to an adult child for post-secondary education. However, support usually lasts only for the first undergraduate diploma or degree, or until the child turns 23, whichever is first. If a child between 16 and the provincial age of majority leaves home and withdraws from parental control, the obligation to pay child support ends.

You and the Law

For how long do you expect your parents to support you, and why? If you want to study for a post-graduate university degree, should your parents be expected to help pay for that? Why or why not?

Sometimes child support orders include support for adult children who are enrolled in a full-time educational program. The idea is that both parents should continue to be responsible for extra expenses like these, just as they would if they were still married.

You Be the Judge

Haley v. Haley, 2008 CanLII 2607 (ON S.C.)

For more information, Go to Nelson Social Studies

Cheryl and Len Haley were married in 1985. They had a son, Tony, in 1987. The Haleys entered into a separation agreement in 1994. It provided that Len would pay $500 monthly until Tony turned 18 or no longer attended school full-time. Len also agreed to pay half of any post-secondary education costs for his son. By mutual agreement, child support payments were reduced to $300 monthly in 1997. They stopped in December 2005 when Tony finished high school. During the next two years, Tony went through a period of trying to figure out what he wanted to do next and how he could afford it. By early 2007, Tony was accepted into a specialized animation school with good future career opportunities. Total expenses were nearly $12 000 for each of three years. His mother applied to the court to reinstate child support for their son. His father disputed this, arguing that since Tony "chose to strike out on his own," Len's support obligations had ended.

- What do you think the judge decided in this case, and why?

You Be the Judge

Noseworthy v. Noseworthy, 2008 CanLII 32836 (ON S.C.)

For more information, **Go to Nelson Social Studies**

Maureen and Wayne Noseworthy were married in 1971 and divorced in 1982. There was one child, Michael, born in 1980. In 1986, the couple agreed that Wayne would pay $300 a month in child support for as long as Michael resided with his mother and remained a child of the marriage under the *Divorce Act*. Michael went to university in 1999, when his father's support payments increased to $877 a month, and no longer lived with his mother. He obtained his undergraduate degree in 2005 and began law school that fall. Wayne Noseworthy applied to the court to end his support payments to his son.

- What do you think the judge decided, and why?

Cornered by Baldwin

6-23 © 2001 Mike Baldwin / Dist. by Universal Press Syndicate

"Oh yeah? Well my dad's child support payments are bigger than your dad's."

Child support payments are intended to benefit the child, not act as competition among friends.

Tax Treatment

Before 1997, Canadians who paid child support could deduct the payments from their income for tax purposes. The parent receiving child support had to include it as income. Many people questioned the fairness of this law. Since May 1, 1997, child support is no longer deductible for the paying parent and no longer taxable for the receiving parent.

Enforcing Support Payments

Although support enforcement is primarily a provincial or territorial concern, Parliament passed the *Family Orders and Agreements Enforcement Assistance Act* in 1988. It allows the federal government to assist in the enforcement process by doing the following:

- tracking down people who have defaulted on their support orders and agreements

- deducting certain federal money payable to debtors

- refusing to issue important documents, such as passports, to debtors

Finding such individuals is not difficult. Authorities can search data banks listing Canada Pension Plan payments and social insurance benefits. They find the address of a missing spouse or that of his or her employer through the Canada Revenue Agency. The federal statute also permits garnishment of federal payments to the defaulting spouse—such as employment insurance cheques, income tax refunds, and Canada Pension Plan payments—to redirect them to the spouse owed money. (See Chapter 11, pages 379–380 for more information on garnishment.)

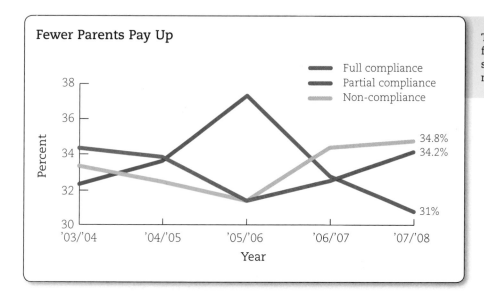

Fewer Parents Pay Up

— Full compliance
— Partial compliance
— Non-compliance

34.8%
34.2%
31%

Percent

30 32 34 36 38

'03/'04   '04/'05   '05/'06   '06/'07   '07/'08
Year

This chart indicates that full compliance with child support orders is still a major problem.

 You Be the Judge

Manis v. Manis, 2001 CanLII 3851 (ON C.A.)

For more information, Go to Nelson Social Studies

Warren and Gail Manis were married in 1985. They had two children, and separated in early 1997. In 1999, Gail was diagnosed with breast cancer, which later spread to her bones. By 2000, she required weekly chemotherapy treatments.

In late 2000, Warren was ordered to pay Gail an equalization payment of just over $415 000, monthly child support of $2300, and monthly spousal support of $4750. As well, Warren was ordered to pay off the mortgage on the matrimonial home and a joint line of credit. He was ordered to provide drug insurance to Gail for her cancer treatment. Finally, he was ordered not to deplete his assets until the equalization payment had been made and the mortgage had been paid off on the matrimonial home.

Warren did not comply with any aspects of the court order. As a result, the home was sold by the bank in August 2001. He depleted his assets and defaulted on the line of credit. He voluntarily declared bankruptcy, even though there was no evidence that any creditors had made demands on him.

Gail brought contempt-of-court proceedings against Warren for his failure to comply with the lower court order. He was sentenced to six months in jail for failing to pay the more than $500 000 owed to Gail. He appealed this decision to the Ontario Court of Appeal. In a 3–0 decision in September 2001, the court dismissed his appeal.

- What is contempt of court, and why was Warren convicted? What message does this send to people who refuse to meet their support obligations?

Provincial Enforcement

Manitoba and Québec were the first provinces to address the serious social problem of parents not supporting their children. They established an enforcement system for defaults on spousal and child support. Support enforcement statutes now exist in all provinces and territories. Examples include Alberta's

Did You Know?

In Alberta, a parent who fails to pay child support can have his or her driver's licence suspended or wages garnisheed (a portion legally deducted). Money is then forwarded to the spouse in need. Newspapers may also print the names and photos of people owing a "significant" amount of support. What are the advantages and disadvantages of this plan?

Activity

To learn more about enforcing child support payments,

Go to Nelson Social Studies

In 2007, Ontario became the second province in Canada (after Alberta) to launch a website that lists photos and personal information about parents failing to make family support payments. Is this a good and necessary idea or an invasion of privacy? Explain.

and Nova Scotia's *Maintenance Enforcement Act*, British Columbia's *Family Maintenance Enforcement Act*, and Ontario's *Support and Custody Orders Enforcement Act*. The provinces and territories also co-operate with one another and with other countries to locate defaulting spouses.

To receive help from an enforcement program, parents must register a child support agreement with the appropriate program in their province or territory. That office then monitors all support payments. It either arranges for payments to be sent to the office or automatically deducts payments from the parent's pay. The office then turns the money over to the parent who is entitled to payment.

In 1992, Ontario's Family Responsibility Office (FRO) became Canada's first automatic wage deduction program. This means that court-ordered support payments are automatically deducted from a parent's paycheque or other income sources. Québec introduced a similar system in late 1995. The other provinces and territories followed the Ontario model.

Support orders are automatically registered with the proper provincial or territorial agency. This ensures that families get the support payments they should be receiving. Once the case is registered, the agency collects support payments from the partner paying support, from his or her employer, or both. These payments are then deposited directly into the recipient's financial institution. If support is not being paid, the agency acts legally to collect money that is owed.

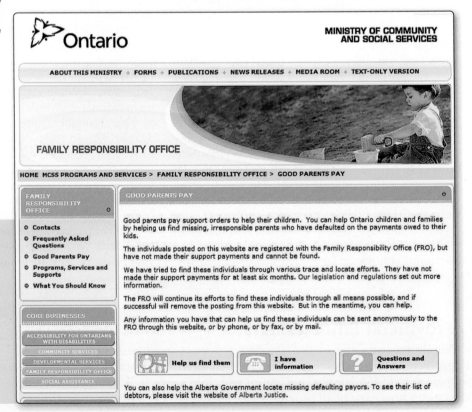

Parental Support

Every province and territory has passed laws that can be used to make adult children responsible for their parents. However, the statutes are not exactly the same everywhere. Making adult children support their needy parents saves taxpayers money. It also maintains the family as a social unit. On the other hand, some people believe that these types of actions should be judged on the quality of care provided by the parent while the children were young. For example, should adult children of abusive parents be forced to support them? Can such private family matters be decided in a courtroom? These cases highlight the role of the family in Canadian society. Given Canada's aging population, it is likely that more cases on this issue will be heard.

Adult children often find they have to support their aging parents in a reversal of roles.

Review Your Understanding

1. Outline the four main reasons for the introduction of the 1997 *Federal Child Support Guidelines*.
2. Identify the three main factors that help determine the appropriate level of child support.
3. Describe four situations in which a court may award more or less than the table amount of support.
4. Does the paying parent stop paying child support when the child reaches the age of majority? Explain.
5. What are governments doing to assist in the enforcement of unpaid support orders?

14.6 Domestic Contracts

One way for partners to ensure that they agree on the division of assets and other legal matters is to prepare a legally binding contract. Thirty years ago, courts seldom recognized such contracts. Legal authorities thought they threatened the stability of marriage and the family unit. Today, these contracts are recognized by the courts, as long as each individual has contributed to the agreement after seeking legal advice. Each partner must retain a separate lawyer. The lawyers must explain how the agreement affects each party before it is signed and dated. They also must see that it is fair to both partners.

Domestic contracts are becoming more popular. They allow couples to air their views on many issues. Issues include how property should be divided if they separate, career plans, raising children, and so on. Contracts help couples anticipate future problems and arrive at solutions in advance. Each contract or agreement must be arranged to meet the individual needs of each family member. Sometimes, the very process of negotiating a domestic contract allows couples to understand that maybe they should not live together or marry after all.

Types of Domestic Contracts

Under provincial and territorial law, "domestic contract" is a general term that refers to any of three types of contracts made between the partners in a relationship. The types of contracts include a **cohabitation agreement**, a marriage contract, or a separation agreement. To be legally binding, the agreement must be dated, written, and signed by the two parties. It also must be witnessed by at least one person who is not related to either partner. Any contract changes must be made in writing, as you will see in Chapter 15. People sometimes refer to these as prenuptial agreements. However, this term is not recognized in Canadian law.

Cohabitation Agreement

A cohabitation agreement is a legally binding contract between common law partners who are cohabiting (living together) or plan to cohabit. They want to make their wishes clearly known to family and friends. It is the common law equivalent of a marriage contract. A cohabitation agreement may be useful to couples who are not legally married and who want a process for dividing their property on separation or death. If the couple marries, their agreement automatically becomes a marriage contract.

Unlike married spouses, common law partners do not have automatic rights to share property when they separate. Whatever assets each person brings into the relationship remain that person's property. However, as you saw in the case of *Pettkus v. Becker* (page 486), the court revisited this position and awarded Rosa Becker an equal share of the property because of the significant contributions she made during her long-term relationship.

You and the Law

If you decide to cohabit or marry, do you intend to prepare a domestic contract? Why or why not?

domestic contract an agreement between partners in an intimate relationship specifying their rights and obligations

cohabitation agreement a domestic contract between two unmarried people who are living together in a common law relationship

There are three types of domestic contracts in Canada: cohabitation agreements, marriage contracts, and separation agreements.

Marriage Contract

A **marriage contract** is a legally binding contract between two people who plan to marry or who are already married. No one enters a marriage with the idea that it will end in divorce. However, marriages do fail. The purpose of the contract is to set out responsibilities during the marriage and the financial impact of separation on each spouse. For example, a couple specifies that one spouse's income should be used for mortgage or rental payments and utility expenses. The other spouse's income is to be spent on household expenses such as food, clothing, entertainment, and miscellaneous items. They might want to decide whether to have separate bank accounts or a joint account. If they buy a car, in whose name will the ownership be registered? By making these decisions, the couple also ensures what happens to these assets upon separation. A marriage contract may be useful for various reasons, as shown in the following chart.

marriage contract a domestic contract between two married people or a couple who plan to marry

Reasons for Marriage Contracts

- One spouse may have more money or financial assets than the other. That spouse may not want to divide assets equally if the marriage breaks down. For example, Ramon's wealthy parents may want to prevent family money from going to Maria if the marriage breaks down. Or perhaps Maria owns art, antiques, or family valuables that have great sentimental value to her. She may feel that Ramon should not share in the rising value of those assets.
- Partners entering a marriage who have children from an earlier marriage may want a contract to protect specific assets for those children. Assets intended for their children would go to them instead of being part of property division. Marriage contracts are becoming common for second and third marriages.
- A marriage contract can be used for dividing property and money earned during the marriage. This allows couples to make decisions that may not agree with provincial and territorial statutes.

These are the main reasons for marriage contracts. Which do you think is the most important, and why?

When a couple draws up a marriage contract, each partner must be honest about his or her financial situation, assets, and liabilities. Courts now recognize all forms of domestic contracts. However, judges tend to set aside unfair contracts that are one-sided and that favour the interests of one party over the other.

Separation Agreements

Separating couples that do not have a marriage contract or cohabitation agreement must settle things with a **separation agreement** or in court. As you saw in Chapter 13, the agreement is a legally binding contract between separating partners. It usually deals with such issues as property division, child and spousal support, custody of and access to the children, and the children's education. It may deal with any other matter of importance to the couple. As a contract, an agreement can be enforced against either party in the same way a court order can be enforced. Contract law is discussed in greater detail in Unit 5.

separation agreement a domestic contract between a separating couple

This cartoon seems to suggest that a marriage contract might make a good marriage vow, but other couples consider marriage contracts "unromantic."

Terminating Domestic Contracts

Married or common law spouses may terminate (end) and destroy their contract by mutual agreement. Alternatively, the contract may include a term ending it automatically. This might be the day when the last child reaches the age of majority. Some contracts allow for review or revision at the end of a certain period. This permits the spouses to adjust their contract to reflect changes in their lives as children are born, careers change, and property is bought and sold.

Review Your Understanding

1. Why should spouses drawing up domestic contracts each have a different lawyer?
2. Identify the three main types of domestic contracts. Why is no standard form available for such contracts?
3. Describe why partners living together might want a cohabitation agreement.
4. Outline three key reasons why a couple planning to marry might want a marriage contract.
5. Describe the most common ways of ending a domestic contract.

In Family Law

Careers in social work, family counselling, and mediation can be both rewarding and exhausting. People entering these fields should be non-judgmental. They should have the ability to empathize and establish rapport with people of all ages. They should enjoy the challenge of negotiating or mediating situations in which emotions run high.

For more information about the course requirements for a Bachelor of Social Work degree at a major university,

Go to Nelson Social Studies

Social worker Elisabeth McGregor began The Compass outreach centre six years ago.

Marriage counsellors often help couples identify their problems and find solutions.

In Focus

Social Worker

Social workers assist people who find it difficult to function well in society. They interview clients to understand their problems and to determine the types of services they need. Social workers interact closely with individuals, families, or groups. Clients include elderly people, people with mental and physical disabilities, and families in crisis.

Social workers help clients build skills to overcome their problems. They work with community agencies to arrange for financial assistance, housing, medical treatment, or legal aid. They also investigate alleged cases of child abuse or neglect and take children into protective custody, if necessary.

Family or Marriage Counsellor

These counsellors help clients overcome problems affecting a relationship with a spouse or family member. They may provide therapy to just one person or to the entire family. Through therapy, clients identify their problems and explore possible solutions. They learn about their family dynamics, and how certain behaviours can cause a family to break apart.

Mediator

Mediators in divorce proceedings are skilled individuals who draw on a background of psychology, counselling, law, and possibly social work. They work with divorcing couples to help them arrive at mutually satisfying solutions. They act as a neutral third party to help couples agree on child custody and access, division of property, and support payments. They foster co-operation and ensure that the legal rights of all parties affected by the divorce are protected.

Career Exploration Activity

As a class, explore career opportunities in social work, family counselling, and mediation that impact family law. Compile the information for a bulletin-board display, or run a law-related career fair.

1. Briefly outline the role and responsibilities of a social worker, a family or marriage counsellor, and a mediator. Use the Internet or your nearest employment information centre.

2. For extended research, interview someone who works in one of these fields. Outline which aspects of the work are most rewarding, and which are more demanding and frustrating. Share your information with the class.

Should Canadians Have Universal Daycare?

All Canadians would agree that it is important for young children to have a safe, healthy environment to stay in while their parents are at work. Whether the government should provide this type of care is widely debated.

Childcare plays a central role in the life of a young child's family. It is often a significant concern in court orders. Daycare costs are high and may be a burden after a marriage breakdown. As a result, Canadians debate whether the government should provide universal daycare—free or affordable daycare for all Canadian children.

In many countries, such as Cuba, Finland, France, and so on, government-funded daycare is already available to all families with young children. Each country has developed its own system for delivering daycare. In every case, the government oversees the program and provides substantial funding.

The province of Québec leads Canada in providing affordable, high-quality daycare for a range of income earners. Before 1997, the Québec government spent $297 million in daycare subsidies. In 1997, it introduced a flat $5 a day rate for each child enrolled in its daycare program. This increased to $7,

with up to $3 more per day for supplies. Before 1997, the average daily cost per child each day was $25. Today, 100 000 children benefit from this program. The government cost has increased to $1.5 billion a year.

In October 2004, the federal Liberal government announced a national childcare system. It promised $5 billion to create 250 000 daycare spaces by 2009, using the Québec plan as a model. When the Liberals were defeated by the Conservatives in the 2006 election, the plan was cancelled. The Conservatives then introduced their own plan. The Universal Child Care Benefit gives parents $1200 a year. This is to "let parents choose the childcare option that best suits each family's needs." This was far from what many parents were demanding.

Despite the high demand for quality daycare, less than a quarter of Canadian children are in a licensed daycare or preschool program. Most families who need childcare must rely on babysitters, nannies, and family members to supervise their children. Sometimes private arrangements, such as unlicensed care offered in a private home, have proven unsafe.

On One Side

Affordable daycare spots are at a premium. Parents manoeuvre to find a place for their children. Supporters of government-funded daycare believe that free or heavily subsidized childcare is similar to free education and health services—the right of all Canadians. Society must provide all young children with a healthy and stimulating environment since they are the nation's future. Studies show that the first six years of a child's life are the basis for all later development. Since children are our future, it seems only right to invest in high-quality daycare. In addition, parents benefit from the peace of mind that reliable daycare provides. All provincial and territorial governments should follow Québec's example. They should commit the money needed for government-funded daycare programs. Single parents in particular often need low-cost daycare to achieve economic self-sufficiency.

On the Other Side

Critics of government-funded daycare believe that those who choose to have children must pay the costs of raising them. Taxpayers are already paying enough. They should not have to assume costs such as daycare expenses that properly belong to parents. They point out that the federal government already allows parents who work outside the home to deduct a portion of their childcare expenses from their income at tax time. They reject the legal argument that single parents should be entitled to low-cost daycare for economic reasons.

A few critics angrily reject the whole notion of daycare. They hold to a traditional view that men should be breadwinners and women should stay at home to raise young children. They say that universal daycare is an inadequate substitute for home-based childcare and may even serve to undermine the family.

The Bottom Line

The pressure on parents to find suitable daycare continues to increase. Some employers provide flexible work hours and other arrangements to help meet the needs of the changing family. However, only 4 percent provide daycare centres for their employees.

Parents continue to pressure the government to pass laws to provide universal daycare. They want daycare facilities that are properly regulated and staffed by qualified childcare workers. The debate continues over who should pay for this service. Should parents be responsible? Or are all Canadians responsible?

What Do You Think?

1. Why has the issue of universal daycare become more important in recent years?
2. How has Québec taken a leadership role in daycare?
3. Do you think that governments and society have "a responsibility to ensure that all young children have a healthy and stimulating environment"? Explain.
4. Conduct Internet searches to find background information on the Conservative, Liberal, NDP, and Green Party proposals for childcare. Compare and contrast the major plans. Which one do you think is best? Discuss. What would be the advantages and disadvantages of employers providing daycare services to their employees?

Chapter Review

Chapter Highlights

- Provincial and territorial governments control property and civil rights.
- Provincial legislation considers marriage as an economic partnership to which the spouses contribute equally.
- Equal division of property legislation does not apply to separating common law partners.
- The matrimonial home is treated differently from the rest of the property brought into or acquired during a marriage.
- Spouses can opt out of an equal division of property by drawing up a domestic contract, but the matrimonial home cannot be included in the contract.
- Although provincial legislation is intended to divide the value of property equally, there are some situations in which this might be unfair.
- When a couple divorces, federal law applies to child and spousal support. When a couple separates, provincial or territorial law applies.
- Self-sufficiency of each spouse is one of the main objectives after marriage breakdown.
- Spousal support is ordered to compensate spouses for the economic sacrifices made during the marriage or for ill spouses who need it and whose former partners can afford it.
- A common law relationship is not a legal marriage, no matter how long the partners have lived together.
- Common law and same-sex partners may be entitled to support if they have lived together for a certain length of time or have a child.
- All provinces have procedures in place to collect child-support payments from defaulting parents.
- There are three types of domestic contracts: marriage contracts, cohabitation agreements, and separation agreements.

Check Your Knowledge

1. Briefly explain the Supreme Court's 1973 ruling in *Murdoch v. Murdoch* (see page 476). What major changes occurred in division of property legislation shortly afterwards?

2. Summarize the factors that are often considered in the determination of spousal support.

3. Identify factors involved in determining the parental obligation for child support.

4. Marriage contracts take some control away from the government and give individuals more control over their personal relationships. What are the advantages and disadvantages of this?

5. In a two-column organizer, compare the rights of married and common law spouses concerning property, support, and inheritance.

Apply Your Learning

6. In *Lampron v. Lampron*, 2006, Jacques Lampron brought an application to terminate monthly child support of $370 for his two children, Isabelle and Paul. Both were over the age of 18 and were still in school. Both children had ended their relationship with their father, calling him a professional thief and stating that they did not want to have anything to do with him. They also advised him in writing that they would refuse permission for their schools to provide him with any information about their education. What do you think the judge decided in this case, and why?

7. In *Contino v. Leonelli-Contino*, 2005, Joanne Leonelli-Contino appealed an Ontario Court of Appeal judgment that reduced the amount of child support her ex-husband, Joseph Contino, had to pay her for their son. Contino agreed to take his son one extra night a week to accommodate his ex-wife's evening course. This increased his access to his son from 39 to 50 percent.

He argued that his payments should be reduced as a result. In an 8–1 judgment in November 2005, the Supreme Court decided that a divorced parent who spends more time with his or her children should not necessarily be able to automatically pay less child support. Do you agree with this judgment? Why or why not?

Communicate Your Understanding

8. From newspapers and the Internet, collect at least five articles dealing with issues relating to children and family law as discussed in this chapter.
   a) Summarize the articles in your own words.
   b) Highlight the issue(s) involved.
   c) State and justify your opinion on the issue(s) discussed in the articles.

9. When a former spouse remarries, for how long should that spouse continue to pay support to his or her first spouse and family? Should a person's first or second family receive economic priority? In your response, detail the factors that should be considered in making this determination and justify your answer.

10. Should provincial and territorial laws be changed to give common law partners the same automatic rights to property division as married spouses? Defend your position.

11. Regarding the *Miglin* decision (see page 496), debate either of the following reactions:
   a) "This case depreciates the value of separation agreements to an all-time low." (an opinion expressed by a family law lawyer)
   b) "It's fantasy to think that you are not going to have a lifetime obligation to someone who has taken herself out of the workforce to wash the socks and raise the kids." (an opinion expressed by another family law lawyer)

Develop Your Thinking

12. Assume that you and the person whom you lived with for five years decide to marry in a civil ceremony. Would you prepare a marriage contract, or would you depend on your province's division of property legislation to settle any disputes if you separate or divorce? Prepare arguments for and against each of these two positions.

13. Explain the meaning of the following statement: "Just because an applicant is a spouse does not create an automatic right to support."

14. After the Wilsons married, Dianne was the main breadwinner. She earned $60 000 a year as a teacher. Her husband, David, had a high school diploma. He worked only occasionally, playing trumpet in a band. For 13 years, David stayed at home looking after their three children and their home. When the couple separated, David applied for monthly spousal support from Dianne to allow him to become self-sufficient.
   a) What factors would David use to argue for spousal support?
   b) Would he succeed in his action? Why or why not?

15. With a partner, assume the role of siblings whose parents have divorced. You live with your mother and her new partner; your father has remarried and has two more children with his new wife.
   a) Prepare an argument for your father continuing to make the same level of support payments as before his remarriage.
   b) Prepare an argument for your father reducing his level of support payments.

Unit

5

Contract Law

Chapter 15
Elements of a Contract 516

Chapter 16
Dispute Resolution 552

"Whether common law or civilian, good law of contract promotes freedom of contract—the freedom of people and groups of people to enter into new transactions and create new wealth."

—Beverley McLachlin
Chief Justice, Supreme Court of Canada

15 Elements of a Contract

What You Should Know

- How does a contract differ from other kinds of agreements?
- What are the requirements for a valid contract?
- How can minors make contracts?
- What groups of people are offered special protection in contract law?
- How are contracts discharged?
- What remedies are available for breach of contract in civil law?
- What protections are available to buyers and sellers regarding transfer of ownership?

Chapter at a Glance

15.1 Introduction

15.2 Agreement or Contract?

15.3 Elements of a Contract

15.4 Discharging a Contract

15.5 Breach of Contract

15.6 Sale-of-Goods Legislation

Selected Key Terms

breach of contract

capacity

caveat emptor

consideration

contract

disclaimer clause

lawful purpose

misrepresentation

offer and acceptance

specific performance

valid contract

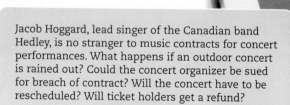

Jacob Hoggard, lead singer of the Canadian band Hedley, is no stranger to music contracts for concert performances. What happens if an outdoor concert is rained out? Could the concert organizer be sued for breach of contract? Will the concert have to be rescheduled? Will ticket holders get a refund?

15.1 Introduction

As a consumer, you have entered into many contracts, often without knowing it. Every time you go to a movie or a concert, ride a bus or subway, buy a CD or DVD, you have made a contract. If you have ever been hired for a job, a contract was formed. Contract law is a fact of everyday life and the basis of business.

Because contracts are so important, the courts have established rules to determine exactly when they are valid. Contract law is mainly private, judge-made common law. It developed over many years as courts heard cases and decisions were recorded in case law.

Once a contract exists, each party has rights and responsibilities to carry out. When these are completed as planned, the contract is successfully discharged. Sometimes circumstances arise that make this impossible. At other times, one party may decide not to live up to the terms of the contract. In this case, a breach of contract occurs.

Because contracts are the basis of all business relationships, they must be binding and enforceable. This chapter will help you understand the elements that make up a contract. You will also discover how contract law deals with such questions as how contracts can be discharged, whether the parties should be held to a contract at all costs, and what legal steps someone can take if a contract is not honoured. This chapter will also explore how the provinces and territories deal with a specific area of contract law—the sale of goods.

Parties often negotiate the terms of a contract.

15.2 Agreement or Contract?

To be a **valid contract**, an agreement imposes rights and responsibilities on the parties involved. But, the courts will not always recognize an agreement as legally binding and enforceable, even if the parties have agreed to the duties imposed. For example, assume that Ryan offers to take Brianna to dinner and a movie and Brianna accepts. Later, Ryan backs out of the invitation. Brianna has no basis to take Ryan to court. Although Ryan made a promise, the agreement cannot be enforced in court. It was simply a social or moral obligation.

All contracts involve agreements, but not all agreements are contracts. A **contract** can be defined as an agreement or promise that the law will enforce. To be a valid contract, the following essential elements (which will be discussed in the next section of this chapter) must be in place:

- offer and acceptance
- consideration
- capacity
- consent
- lawful purpose

valid contract a legally binding agreement

contract an agreement enforceable by law

Elements of a Valid Contract

It is elementary; every piece of the contract must be in place.

offer and acceptance a proposal to a contract that contains all essential terms, followed by an agreement to the proposal by the other party

consideration something of value exchanged between the parties to a contract

capacity the ability to understand the nature and effect of one's actions

lawful purpose a lawful (not illegal) reason or objective

express contract a contract in which the terms are openly declared and known to the parties

implied contract a contract that is inferred by the parties' conduct

For example, at a local store, you find a snowboard that you want to buy. When you take the snowboard to the sales clerk, an **offer and acceptance** takes place. You offer to buy the snowboard at the price advertised, and the sales clerk accepts your offer. After you give your money to the clerk, the clerk gives you the snowboard. Another essential element of a contract has occurred here: **consideration**, the exchange of something of value between the parties.

The other elements of a contract are also involved. You have the legal **capacity** (ability) to enter into the contract. You are of sound mind and are old enough to make the purchase. You also both freely give consent to the contract, in good faith. The clerk does not pressure or trick you into making your purchase, and you do not force the clerk to sell you the snowboard. Finally, the contract has a **lawful purpose**—there is nothing illegal about buying a snowboard, as long as it was not stolen.

A contract that lacks one or more of these essential elements cannot be enforced by either party in the courts.

Types of Contracts

All contracts are either express or implied. An **express contract** can be verbal or written, and it clearly defines all terms and conditions. An **implied contract** is only suggested by a person's actions—nothing is precisely stated or written. Ordering a meal in a restaurant is an example of an implied contract. Your order suggests to the server that you will pay for the meal once you have eaten it. Hailing a taxicab is also an implied contract: the driver assumes you will pay the fare once you arrive at your destination.

All of these actions— ordering a meal, hailing a cab, and signalling a bid at an auction—are examples of implied contracts.

Contracts can also be classified as simple or under seal. Most day-to-day transactions are **simple contracts**. They can be verbal or written, or they can be implied. A verbal contract can be hard to enforce. Without witnesses, it may be impossible to prove that a contract exists at all. Therefore, if possible, contracts should be in writing. Simple contracts need not be very detailed, but they must include the basic terms of the contract, the date, and the signatures of the parties involved.

simple contract a contract that is not under seal

Some transactions require **contracts under seal**. These contracts must be in writing and signed and witnessed "under seal." The seal is usually a red dot or the word "seal." This indicates that the parties have given the contract serious thought, are aware of their rights, and have accepted their responsibilities. In some provinces, deeds to property and mortgages must be signed under seal to be legally binding. The use of seals dates as far back as 3200 BCE, universally adopted by the twelfth century. People pressed family rings or signets into sealing wax, instead of signatures, to finalize a contract.

contracts under seal a formal written contract that is signed, witnessed, and marked with a seal

Changes made to a written contract should be made in writing and initialled by all parties. The courts can ignore any verbal changes or agreements made after a contract is written if the changes contradict or alter the original document. If there is a dispute, the court must be convinced that any verbal agreement was a genuine agreement to change the terms of the original contract.

Signets such as this were used instead of signatures on contracts.

What kind of contract is depicted in this cartoon?

You and the Law

Before you sign a written contract, you should always read the terms of the agreement. Why is this a good idea? Explain.

Review Your Understanding

1. Explain what makes an agreement a legally enforceable contract.
2. Identify the five essential elements of a contract.
3. What forms can a simple contract take?
4. Distinguish between an express contract and an implied contract using examples that are not in the chapter.
5. Explain the significance of a seal on a contract.

15.3 Elements of a Contract

To understand how contract law works, we will examine the five elements of a contract in more detail: offer and acceptance, consideration, capacity, consent, and lawful purpose.

Offer

offeror in a contract, the party who makes an offer

offeree in a contract, the party to whom the offer is made

As you learned in the snowboard example, the essential elements of a legally binding contract include a valid offer and acceptance. One party, the **offeror**, must make a clear, precise offer. The other party, the **offeree**, must accept the offer. In the snowboard example, you were the offeror, and the sales clerk was the offeree. As you prepared to pay for the snowboard, a meeting of the minds took place. Both parties (you and the clerk) clearly understood the rights and responsibilities in the contract that developed.

Serious Intent

As with contracts, offers must contain certain elements to be valid. For one thing, an offer must be definite and seriously intended. For example, Alexander says to Sam, "I'll sell you my Nintendo Wii for $200," and Sam replies, "That's a deal. I'll take it for $200." In this case, both a definite offer and a definite acceptance have taken place. If Sam says, "It looks like a good deal and I'd like to have it," this is not a valid acceptance. Until Sam says "I'll take it," only the offer is valid.

In contract law, a meeting of the minds indicates a mutual understanding and a binding agreement between the offeror and the offeree.

Offers made as a joke or in anger are also not valid. If an automobile stalls in the driveway and the frustrated owner shouts, "I'll sell this piece of junk for a loonie!", any neighbour who takes this as a serious offer will not be able to force the owner to sell the automobile for that price. The owner obviously had no serious intent.

An offeror's words or conduct must indicate both the clear intention and the willingness to carry out the promise if the offer is accepted. For example, "I think I might sell my old iPod for $100" is a vague statement of possible intent. It is not a definite offer.

Definite Terms

The terms of an offer must also be clearly stated. If goods are being sold, then quantity, price, size, colour, terms of sale (when it is to be paid), and the delivery date should be defined. Some terms are implied or assumed to be known. Many goods and services, for example, have a standard price. Consumers are unlikely to ask the price when buying a newspaper or riding the bus.

Invitations to Buy

Are newspaper and magazine advertisements clear and definite offers? What about merchandise featured in a store's retail displays and catalogues? When you go into a supermarket, select goods, and present the goods and your money at the cash register, has a contract been formed?

invitation to treat encouragement, through advertising or display of goods, to prospective buyers to make offers

According to the courts, the answer to all these questions is no. The advertisements, displays, and catalogues are merely invitations by sellers for customers to make an offer to buy the products advertised. This is also known as **invitation to treat**. A retailer does not expect everyone who sees an advertisement to buy the goods.

The basic rule is that customers make definite offers to purchase once they select advertised items or goods from the store's stock. The store's cashier then has the right to accept or reject those offers. In most cases, the cashier accepts the customer's money and hands over the merchandise. Only after all these actions have occurred has a contract been formed and completed.

Generally, an advertisement announcing a big sale on goods is considered an "invitation to treat"—that is, the advertiser invites the public to make an offer.

The Carbolic Smoke Ball Company Case

Normally, advertisements are not considered to be promises that are legally binding on the advertiser. However, the courts may consider advertisements that are worded precisely and with a serious intent to be offers. The case of *Carlill v. Carbolic Smoke Ball Company* [1893] 1 Q.B. 256 England, Court of Appeal, is a classic contract law case. It was the first case to illustrate that advertisers can be held accountable for their statements in advertisements.

The defendant company made and sold a medical preparation called the Carbolic Smoke Ball. The company advertised its product in various English newspapers, stating that a "£100 reward will be paid by the Carbolic Smoke Ball Company to any person who contracts the increasing epidemic influenza, colds, or any disease caused by taking cold, after having used the ball three times daily for two weeks according to the printed directions supplied with each ball. £1000 is deposited with the Alliance Bank, Regent Street, showing our sincerity in the matter."

Mrs. Carlill, the plaintiff, read the advertisement and bought the product at a chemist's store. She used it as directed three times a day from November 20, 1891, to January 17, 1892. Then she caught influenza. When the company refused to pay her the £100, Carlill sued successfully. The defendant company appealed the trial judgment. However, the appeal was dismissed. The court held that the reference in the advertisement to the £1000 deposit indicated the serious intention of the Carbolic Smoke Ball Company to pay.

An offer does not have to be made to one specific person. It is valid and legal to make an offer to an indefinite number of people. This advertisement held an offer to anyone who met the outlined conditions. The defendant company attempted to avoid paying the plaintiff. It argued that the advertisement was merely an invitation to buy. The plaintiff had not

This advertiser had to pay up. Why?

communicated her intention to accept the offer. The court held it was not necessary for Carlill to communicate her acceptance directly to the company. By purchasing the smoke ball and using it as instructed, she accepted a valid and serious offer.

Today, new forms of advertising present consumers with countless offers to buy. Telemarketing promotes goods and services through unsolicited (uninvited) phone calls. This has become very popular with advertisers. Online advertising using the Internet is also popular. Both telemarketing and online advertising keep consumers informed. If advertisers make an offer, they must make sure not to make false claims or misleading statements about their products or services. You will learn more about this in Chapter 16.

The principle of caveat emptor (buyer beware) generally applies to today's shoppers. However, legislatures have passed consumer protection laws to protect buyers. You will learn more about consumer protection laws in Chapter 16. Advertisers must not intentionally deceive consumers by making false claims. Federal and provincial governments have also passed laws that identify unfair, deceptive, and misleading selling practices. These laws also provide consumers who have been victimized by these practices with solutions and compensation.

For Discussion

1. Must an offer be made to one specific person to be considered a valid offer? Explain.
2. How did the defendant argue that there was no contract?
3. Why did the court rule that it was a valid offer?
4. Examine several advertisements in various media (print, radio, and television), and analyze how accurate the claims made are. Present a report to the class.

Communicating an Offer

Obviously, the offeror must communicate the offer to the offeree before acceptance can occur. This can be done in person or by mail, courier, fax, and so on. Because an offer is not valid until it has been received, it is important to know when the offeree becomes aware of it. What happens, for example, if identical offers cross in the mail?

Suppose that Grant writes to Kathleen, offering to sell her a painting for $750. Unaware of this, Kathleen writes to Grant, offering to buy the same painting for the same price. At first glance, it would seem that Kathleen's letter could be considered an acceptance of Grant's offer and that a contract had been formed. But, what if Grant changes his mind after sending the letter? What if one letter never arrives at the intended address? In either case, two separate offers exist. To form a valid contract, an acceptance must be an unconditional reply to a specific offer. The courts would thus assume that no contract was formed between Grant and Kathleen.

An offer can be communicated legally to a specific person or to people in general, as in a reward notice. Suppose you find a lost dog, look at its name and address tag, and then return Sal to his owner. Later, you read a notice that the owner had placed in the newspaper offering a $500 reward for Sal's return. Are you entitled to the reward? No, not legally. When you returned Sal, you did not know of the reward. Therefore, you could not have intended to accept the offer. If you had read the notice first, you would have been entitled to the reward. In this case, by returning Sal, you would have been accepting the offer, thus forming and performing (completing) a contract.

LOST AND FOUND	
Budgie, blue with yellow, lost Yale Town/False Creek area July 26th.	Gold Bracelet, either VGH or McDonald's – FOUND!!! Thanks so much for all the caring calls.
Cat "Lambert" May 31st nr Lgh' d Mall, Orange Wht N/Male Tabby Reward.	MAN'S RING – lost July 29th in Burnaby or at Stanley Park.
Lost "Oscar" Lhasa Apso, honey col. N/M. $500 Reward.	Nokia Cell Phone found Guilford Mall on Sunday July 28th.

For each of these notices, what is the finder's entitlement to a reward?

lapse the ending of an offer because it is not accepted within the allocated time

revocation the cancellation of an offer by the offeror before it is accepted

Terminating an Offer

Unless an offer is accepted, no legal rights or obligations can arise from it. When making an offer, offerors can protect themselves by including a deadline for acceptance. If not accepted by that date, the offer will automatically **lapse** (end). An offer may also be terminated by **revocation**, which means it is withdrawn before being accepted.

If an offer includes no deadline, it remains open for a reasonable length of time before lapsing. How long it will remain open depends on the nature of the transaction. An offer to sell stocks, for example, is open for a much shorter period than an offer to sell a house. Stock prices can change minute by minute.

A verbal offer lapses when the parties leave one another, if it is reasonable to assume that the offeror intended this. For example, Nizar offers to sell Aisha his old laptop computer for $350. If she does not accept the offer before they part company, it lapses. The offeror can also decide to give the offeree time to consider the offer. Nizar could give Aisha seven days to make up her mind. In this case, the offer would be valid until that period had passed or until Aisha accepted or rejected the offer.

An offer also lapses if one party dies or is declared incapable before acceptance takes place. If any of these events occurs after acceptance, the contract is valid as long as the other elements are in place.

Many advertisements contain offers with a deadline for acceptance.

The offeror can also terminate the offer by revoking it. Assume that by the fourth day, Aisha still has not accepted the offer. Nizar changes his mind and clearly communicates to Aisha that the offer is revoked: his laptop is no longer for sale. It does not matter that only four days have passed. Nizar can legally change his mind because Aisha has not accepted the offer.

However, an offer cannot be revoked if the parties have a separate contract that states the offeror cannot withdraw it for a specific period of time. Also, if Aisha gives Nizar a deposit toward purchasing the laptop to show that she is sincere about considering the offer, Nizar cannot withdraw his offer until the seven days have passed. Usually, someone buying a house will make a deposit to keep the house available to him or her alone. This is called **placing an option**. If the purchase is completed, the deposit is applied to the house price. If the offeree does not complete the transaction, the deposit may or may not be returned. This depends on the original terms of the agreement.

placing an option giving a deposit to an offeror

Acceptance

Acceptance can be communicated either in words or by conduct and must follow certain legal rules. For example, you leave your bicycle for repair. The service person agrees to fix it, and you agree to pay the charges. This is acceptance by words or agreement. Many offers are also accepted by performance; for example, you do some type of action to gain a reward. Most offers made over a store counter are accepted without negotiation. To be valid, an acceptance must be unconditional. It must also be made within a specified time and in the manner specified by the offeror.

An offeree may want to accept an offer, but not exactly as presented. In this case, the offeree could make a **counteroffer**, which changes one or more terms of the original offer. For example, Katya offers to sell her car to Dino for $4000. Dino replies, "I would really like to have the car, but I will give you only $3500 for it." Dino has made a counteroffer, which ends the original offer. It is really a new offer to Katya, who can accept or reject it. Of course, Katya can then make her own counteroffer. This process can go back and forth many times. If these negotiations are done through written documents, the exchange is commonly referred to as the battle of the forms.

counteroffer a new offer made in response to the original offer, which ends the original offer

Communicating Acceptance

A contract does not exist until acceptance is communicated to the offeror. It is assumed that offer and acceptance will be communicated in the same way, unless the offer specifies a different way of communicating. For example, a written offer is usually accepted in writing.

Acceptance by Mail

Offers sent and accepted by mail are a part of everyday business; hence, there are legal rules to determine when acceptance is valid. An offer made and accepted by mail becomes a binding contract once a properly addressed and stamped letter of acceptance has been mailed. The postmark is proof of the mailing date. If the acceptance is lost or delayed in the mail, the parties are still bound to the contract as long as the offeree can prove the acceptance was mailed in time.

A postmark, which indicates the mailing date, can be used as proof that an offer was accepted by a certain time.

If the acceptance is lost or does not arrive on time, the offeror may make the offer to someone else. An offeror who fails to specify that acceptance is not complete until the letter is received assumes the risk of loss by Canada Post. The offeree may find it impossible to prove that he or she mailed the acceptance. Because of this, it may be wise for both parties to use registered mail or couriers to send written offers and acceptances to each other.

If an offer does not specify a method of acceptance, a "reasonable method of acceptance" must be used. The courts have interpreted this to mean any method that is at least as fast as the offeror's method of communication. Thus, a mailed offer could be accepted by mail, telephone, or fax. When acceptance of a mailed offer is made in some reasonable manner other than mail, the contract is not formed until the acceptance reaches the offeror. If the mailed offer specifies that acceptance must be by mail, then a faxed or telephoned acceptance is not valid.

An offeror might be tempted to say, "If you do not notify me within five days, I will assume you have accepted my offer." Unfortunately, this would not be legally valid. Acceptance must be expressed actively in words or action.

Negative-option marketing is an exception to this rule. It means that a consumer must take an action in order not to receive an item or service. For example, some book and music clubs automatically send selections unless members return a form before a specified due date. Silence and inaction—in this case, not returning the form—is considered valid because members have a pre-existing agreement with the club.

"Dear Book-of-the-Month Club, I wish to cancel my subscription."

Some book or music clubs automatically send a monthly selection unless the member returns a form by a specific date.

Review Your Understanding

1. Distinguish between an offeror and offeree in a contract.
2. Why must an offer be communicated before it can be accepted?
3. What is a counteroffer, and what effect does it have on the original offer?
4. If an offer does not specify the method of acceptance, what options are available to the offeree?
5. Explain the meaning of this statement: "Remaining silent is not a valid acceptance."

Consideration

The next essential element after offer and acceptance is consideration: the exchange of something of value. In most contracts, consideration for one party is the purchase of a particular item or service; for the other, it is the money paid.

There are two forms of legal consideration: present and future. Present consideration occurs when the contract is formed. Future consideration occurs when one or both of the parties promise to do something in the future. Buying on credit is an example of this. The seller will not receive payment (or consideration) until a later date.

A promise by one person to pay another for services that have already been performed for free is past consideration. Such a contract is not legally binding (see the *Pickett v. Love* case on the next page).

Future consideration occurs in sports all the time. A team may trade a player in the present season for a player to be selected from another team the following year.

Pickett v. Love, (1982) 20 Sask. R. 115 Saskatchewan, Court of Queen's Bench

For more information, **Go to Nelson Social Studies**

Gordon Pickett, the plaintiff, and Brenda Love, the defendant, entered into a romantic relationship in June 1981. They exchanged keys to one another's apartments. Their relationship continued until December 31. Love's feelings started to cool in October, and she told Pickett she wanted to be only friends. However, Pickett persisted in his advances. He gave Love presents, including a watch and the offer of a plane ticket to New Orleans.

Later, Pickett offered to renovate Love's bathroom. She indicated that she would like this but could not afford to pay him for the work. In February 1982, the renovations were completed. Afterwards, Pickett claimed that Love had agreed to pay him what she could each month until the bill was paid, although he was not sure what that amount was. Love indicated to Pickett that their friendship was over and that he was to return the key.

After discovering that Love was seeing a friend of his, Pickett placed a claim on Love's property for $759. The court was not certain as to what had been agreed between the parties, but the judge believed that the plaintiff had done the work in a bid for the defendant's continued affection. Pickett's claim was dismissed.

For Discussion

1. Was there a legally binding contract between the parties? Explain.

2. Did the defendant have an obligation to pay the plaintiff for the renovations? Give reasons.

3. Why did the plaintiff's action fail?

4. What advice would you give to someone entering into a contract?

Suppose a rock collector bought a rock from a vendor at a roadside display for $10. Later, the collector sold the stone—an uncut emerald—for $2 million. Can the roadside vendor legally force the buyer to renegotiate the deal? Explain.

Adequacy of Consideration

The courts are not concerned with the amount of consideration exchanged, as long as one party gives something to the other. The courts will not bargain for you. If someone freely sells something for much less than it is worth, the contract is still binding. Both parties received something of value and benefit. Parties are free to make good or bad bargains, unless evidence suggests that one of the parties was pressured or the consideration is grossly inadequate.

The courts do not regard love, affection, respect, or honour as valuable legal consideration. If your aunt promises to give you a car on your birthday and changes her mind, this is not a contract. It is a gift, and promises of gifts are generally not enforceable.

Capacity

The next essential element is capacity, or the ability to enter into a contract. All sane and sober adults can form contracts. However, there are laws to protect certain groups of people from being exploited in contract situations. As a result, contracts involving minors or persons with a developmental disability or impaired judgment are not legally binding under certain circumstances.

Minors and Contracts

A minor is any person under the age of majority. This is the age at which a person gains full rights and responsibilities in legal matters, including contracts. The age of majority in Canada's provinces and territories is set at either 18 or 19 years. Each province or territory can also restrict the rights and responsibilities that attach to the age of majority. In Ontario and Saskatchewan, the age of majority is 18. However, you must be 19 to legally purchase alcohol and cigarettes. Over the years, the courts have developed laws that determine when and if a minor's contract is valid and enforceable.

The Age of Majority in Canada

- 19 years of age
- 18 years of age

The age of majority varies from province to province in Canada.

Valid Contracts

Minors are obligated to fulfill contracts for **necessaries**. These are goods and services that everyone needs: food, clothing, shelter, education, and medical services. If this were not so, businesses would not enter into any contracts with minors. This might be harmful or damaging to minors in times of need, especially for those nearing the age of majority.

To be considered a necessary, a good or service must reflect a minor's station in life (social position). For example, a mayor's teenaged son may need a tuxedo to attend important functions and formal banquets with his parents. Other students in the same classroom would not have the same need. Even in contracts for necessaries, a minor may not be obligated to pay the contract price if the courts find that terms of the contract were not in the minor's best interests. Only a "reasonable" price must be paid. But what is reasonable? Suppose Emma, a minor, needs a ski jacket and buys one for $400. If she finds an identical coat for $250 at another store, Emma may be obligated to pay only $250, the reasonable price, to the store from which she purchased the coat originally.

Apprenticeship and employment contracts are also considered necessary, if they are beneficial and do not take advantage of minors. However, if the court feels that the minor was overwhelmed by the bargaining power of the other party, the contract will be judged unenforceable. (Chapter 16 deals with employment law.)

necessaries goods and services needed to ensure a person's health and welfare

 Did You Know?

The case *Canadian Taxpayers Federation v. Ontario (Minister of Finance)*, 2004, looked at an election promise (contract) that Premier Dalton McGuinty signed and which he did not follow through on. The courts ruled that these types of contracts or promises are not binding.

Void Contracts

Contracts that are not in a minor's best interests are said to be void (to have never existed). If a person takes unfair advantage of a minor to have the youth enter into a contract, the courts will rule that the contract is prejudicial and has no legal effect.

Voidable Contracts

Contract law has always offered special protection for minors, but it also protects persons and businesses that deal with minors. A contract for necessaries is binding upon a minor, but one for non-necessaries is not. A **voidable contract** is one in which one party (the minor) has the right to make the contract binding or not binding. The general rule is that a minor's contract is voidable at the minor's option—that is, the minor decides whether or not to be bound by the contract. Most minors do complete such contracts, since they entered them in good faith.

It is in the area of non-necessaries that voidable contracts for minors sometimes become an issue. For example, Fiona, who is a minor, purchases a camcorder at the mall, makes a down payment, and takes it home. A week later, she decides she really does not want it. Fiona is not legally bound to complete the payments on her contract, but she must return the camcorder to the retailer and cancel the contract. Fiona may not be able to recover the money she paid before she changed her mind. The reason is that the storekeeper performed his or her obligations under the contract, and Fiona benefited from the use of the camcorder. If there is damage to the camcorder that Fiona did not cause deliberately, the retailer cannot recover the cost from her. The cost of any "wear and tear" is also not recoverable. But, the cost of any deliberate damage can be recovered.

If the retailer learns over the weekend that Fiona is a minor, he or she cannot cancel the contract without Fiona's permission. An adult who enters into a contract with a minor is bound by it if the minor wishes to fulfill its terms.

off the mark   by Mark Parisi

I THINK I CAN FEEL PRETTY SECURE THAT THESE CONTRACTS WON'T BE BINDING...

SUNSWEET PRUNES LAW OFFICES

Does destroying a contract mean you will not be bound by the terms of the contract?

Misrepresentation of Age

If a minor lies about his or her age, this does not change the legal rights of the minor or retailer. It also does not remove the minor's protection under the law. As a result, retailers deal with minors at their own risk. Because of the great protection given to minors, most retailers will sell to minors only for cash. Retailers know that a contract is voidable at the minor's option.

Parental Liability

To protect themselves, many retailers require a parent or other adult to co-sign any contract involving a minor. The parent or other adult is responsible for full payment if the minor does not pay. If a minor uses a parent's credit card and the parent pays the account, it is implied that the parent will do so in the future. Parents who want to cancel this arrangement must notify the retailers involved. Parents are also responsible if they expressly tell a retailer that their child may purchase items for which they will pay. Generally, parents are not responsible for their children's contracts or debts.

Because of the laws protecting minors, many retailers require parents to co-sign contracts involving a minor.

People with Impaired Judgment or a Disability

Contract law treats people with impaired judgment or developmental disabilities in much the same way that it treats minors. It offers them protection. Impaired judgment may be temporary or permanent. It may be caused by illness, disability, hypnosis, or by the effects of alcohol or drugs. If a person's mental impairment requires institutionalization, the person cannot enter into contracts. All others having impaired judgment are still responsible in contracts for necessaries.

As with minors, people with impaired judgment are obligated to pay only a "reasonable" price for necessaries. Any contract for non-necessaries is voidable. The person with impaired judgment must prove that he or she was incapable of understanding what was happening when the contract was formed. The contract must be voided within a reasonable time after recovery, and the goods must be returned. If a person with impaired judgment recovers and continues to benefit from a contract, he or she is bound by the contract.

Review Your Understanding

1. Define consideration.
2. Explain the difference between present and future consideration, and provide an example of each.
3. What groups are protected from being taken advantage of when they enter into contracts?
4. Distinguish between void and voidable contracts made by minors.
5. When are parents liable for contracts that their children may enter into?

caveat emptor a Latin phrase meaning "let the buyer beware"

Consent

Each party in a contract must understand and freely agree to complete it. This is called consent. If you are purchasing a good or service, the principle of **caveat emptor** (buyer beware) applies. This means that the seller is not legally obligated to disclose negative facts that might stop you from making a purchase. You are responsible for checking out claims for the product or service. If either party enters a contract willingly and later discovers that they have made a bad deal, the contract cannot be voided on that fact alone. Parties who enter a contract must accept the consequences of their actions.

Four situations may prevent consent from occurring: misrepresentation, mistake, undue influence, and duress (discussed in the next section).

At a yard sale, the principle of caveat emptor is generally understood to apply.

Misrepresentation

Misrepresentation is a false statement made by one person concerning a material fact. This is a fact that is so important that it causes the other person to enter a contract. Misrepresentation makes genuine consent impossible. It is the most common reason that contracts are voided. There are two kinds of misrepresentation: innocent and fraudulent. The chart below describes the two types of misrepresentation.

misrepresentation a false or misleading statement that is important to the contract

innocent misrepresentation a misrepresentation made in good faith by a person who believed it to be true

fraudulent misrepresentation a misrepresentation made intentionally to deceive the other party

Types of Misrepresentation

Type of Misrepresentation	Examples	Outcome
Innocent misrepresentation exists when a person makes a false statement about a material fact that he or she believes to be true. A seller may repeat facts provided by a usually reliable source, such as a manufacturer.	• Clorinda sells hair colouring to Shamir, repeating the manufacturer's claim that it will last for seven or eight washings. In reality, the colour washes out the second time Shamir shampoos his hair. • A travel agent makes a genuine error while reading a brochure and tells two clients that their total cost for a cruise is $3500. The clients later discover that there is a $750 charge for airfare to get to the cruise ship.	In both cases, the seller is innocent, and the buyer can legally rescind (or cancel) the contract. This is the basic remedy for innocent misrepresentation. It restores the parties to the positions they were in before forming the contract. In other words, Shamir and the clients for the cruise would be entitled to a refund, but not to damages.
Fraudulent misrepresentation occurs if a seller makes a statement about a material fact knowing that it is false. The seller is lying to cheat or defraud the buyer.	• Lisa DeLuca owns a service station on a busy two-lane highway. She learns that a multilane highway will be built nearby, jeopardizing her business. She lists her property for sale. A prospective buyer hears about the proposed highway and asks Lisa about it. She tells the purchaser that the mayor has told her the highway will never be built.	Not only can a buyer rescind a contract formed under such circumstances, he or she can also sue Lisa for damages. The buyer must, however, prove to the court that he or she has suffered some loss from entering into the agreement as a result of the fraudulent misrepresentation.

Both innocent and fraudulent misrepresentation can allow a buyer to rescind a contract.

Mistake

Once a contract has been formed, the law states that it should be carried out whenever possible. It is generally assumed that each party has read and understood the contract and will be bound by his or her signature. Ignorance of the law is no excuse. However, certain types of mistakes, common and unilateral, can make a contract unenforceable. The courts have also recognized two types of unilateral mistakes: clerical and *non est factum*.

Types of Mistakes

Type of Mistake	Example	Outcome	
A **common mistake** occurs if both parties are mistaken about the same fundamental fact of a contract.	• Shani negotiates with Matt to buy his 2000 Pontiac Grand Prix, which Matt keeps in his garage. Unknown to them both, the garage burns down and destroys the car as they are negotiating.	The contract will be void and unenforceable. In fact, there was no car to sell when the contract was made.	**common mistake** an error made by both parties about a fundamental component of the contract
A **unilateral mistake** occurs when one party has made a mistake and the other party knew of the mistake but made no attempt to correct it. There are two types of unilateral mistakes: clerical and *non est factum*.	• You select a utility knife for purchase and tell the store clerk that you want to cut wallboard with it. The clerk, however, knows that the knife will not cut wallboard but says nothing and sells it to you anyway.	The contract will be void and unenforceable.	**unilateral mistake** an error made by one party to the contract
A **clerical mistake** is an error caused by a clerk or store employee, typically involving numbers.	• Séguin and Kirilenko have been discussing the sale of a tractor for some time. Kirilenko offers to sell it to Séguin for $15 000 and agrees to put the offer in writing and to mail it. Kirilenko later writes up the offer and writes the price as $1500, not $15 000. He does not catch the mistake before he mails the offer. When Séguin receives the offer by mail, the error is obvious to him.	Séguin cannot hold Kirilenko to selling the tractor for the price of $1500. The clerical mistake makes the offer void and unenforceable.	**clerical mistake** an error caused by a store clerk or employee
Non est factum, which means "It is not my deed," is a denial by one party that the contract was carried out properly because one of the parties was ignorant of the contract's nature. This type of mistake was more common in Canada when few people were literate. It is rare today because most people know how to read and write.	• A person might be presented with a document to sign and be told it was a will when, in fact, it was a loan guarantee. Later, if the signer went to court over the loan, he or she could plead *non est factum*. The actual document had nothing to do with the signer's intended action.	*Non est factum* may void a contract. However, if a party to the contract is illiterate, it may not serve to void the contract if evidence exists that the party was aware of what he or she was doing in signing the contract.	

Certain types of mistakes may allow a contract to be set aside.

undue influence improper pressure applied on a person to overpower that person's free will

Undue Influence

Undue influence occurs when one person applies improper mental or emotional pressure to persuade another to enter and form a contract involuntarily. It usually happens when one party dominates another. Dominating relationships typically exist between husbands and wives, parents and children, doctors and patients, lawyers and clients, home-care workers and invalids, and so on. Anyone in need can be influenced by the person who meets that need. A contract formed through undue influence lacks genuine consent and is voidable at the victim's option.

Generally, a person who claims that he or she entered a contract because of undue influence must prove that such influence was possible. Action to void the contract must be taken promptly; otherwise, the right to void the agreement may lapse. In the case of *Tribe v. Farrell*, 2006, below, you will see that when an action goes to court for undue influence, the burden of proof shifts to the dominant party (the party accused of taking advantage of another). The dominant party must then prove that he or she did not take advantage of his or her dominant position or use undue influence.

This contract could be set aside because of undue influence.

⚖️ **Case**

Tribe v. Farrell, 2006 BCCA 38 (CanLII)

For more information, **Go to Nelson Social Studies** 🌐

Elderly people are often at risk of being victims of undue influence since they are often forced to rely on others for their personal care.

In August 1996, Georgia Farrell answered an advertisement placed in the newspaper by Jack Tribe offering room and board in return for light housekeeping duties. At the time, Farrell was 48 and Tribe was 83. Farrell did light housekeeping, drove Tribe where he needed to go, did shopping for him, and prepared some meals. She later also provided personal care for Tribe.

When the relationship began, Tribe's will left his entire estate to his son. His son also had a power of attorney, a document that allows the holder to make personal decisions regarding property or medical treatment for another person. In October 1999, Tribe opened a joint bank account with Farrell and transferred $29 000 into the account. They both signed a transfer of ownership of his vehicle to Farrell. While the

document was left undated, she initiated the transfer of ownership after Tribe's death in April 2001. In September 2000, Tribe made a new will leaving his house to Farrell and a new power of attorney document in her name.

Tribe's son, Daniel, took Farrell to court, alleging that the 2000 will and gifts were void because of undue influence. At trial, he alleged that his father had made over $50 000 in gifts to Farrell. He indicated that Farrell did not notify him of his father's serious illness until after his death. Farrell alleged that the son had neglected the care of his father and that she had provided care and companionship for Tribe. He had freely given the gifts of property to her.

After examining the evidence and assessing the witnesses' credibility, the judge ruled that Georgia Farrell had exercised undue influence over Jack Tribe by influencing his decision making. He became physically and emotionally dependent on her. As a result, the judge stated that gifts she had received were void as unconscionable (unfair) transactions. Tribe's 2000 will was also declared invalid.

continues...

Case (continued)

Tribe v. Farrell, 2006 BCCA 38 (CanLII)

The burden of proof shifted to Farrell to disprove undue influence. The judge assessed that Tribe's free will was dominated by Farrell as he was afraid she might leave him if he did not provide her with these benefits. She was unable to rebut the presumption of undue influence. Therefore, the judge held that the joint bank account and the gift of the car were to be set aside and the new will declared invalid.

Farrell appealed to the British Columbia Court of Appeal in 2006, arguing that the trial judge had made errors of fact and law. The court dismissed her appeal.

For Discussion

1. What is undue influence?
2. Why did Jack Tribe's son launch the lawsuit?
3. What did the defendant, Georgia Farrell, argue in support of the gifts?
4. Why did the court rule in favour of Tribe's son?

The spousal relationship presents a special legal situation. For example, a wife tries to void a contract that she either entered into with her husband or entered into for his benefit (such as guaranteeing his debts). She must prove that her husband used undue influence. If she did not receive independent legal advice (from a lawyer other than her husband's), the courts may accept this as evidence that she was subjected to undue influence. For this reason, some lending agencies require a wife who is guaranteeing her husband's loan to sign a statement indicating that she has consulted her own lawyer about her guarantee, and to obtain a certificate of independent legal advice from the lawyer.

Spouses should each receive independent legal advice before guaranteeing each other's loans.

Duress

Duress is similar to undue influence, but more extreme. It occurs when one party uses threats or violence to force another to enter into a contract. The threats may be of physical punishment, detention, or some form of blackmail. The person entering the contract may be the victim. However, the person's spouse, children, or parents may also be targeted. Obviously, a person who has been threatened or beaten into a contract cannot be said to have consented. He or she should be able to avoid any responsibilities under it.

 Did You Know?

The courts developed the concept of undue influence to provide remedies for situations not covered by fraud or duress. As a result, it is more flexible and wider ranging in its application.

Review Your Understanding

1. Identify the four conditions that may prevent genuine consent from occurring in a contract.
2. Using original examples, distinguish between innocent and fraudulent misrepresentation.
3. Distinguish between a common and a unilateral mistake.
4. What is undue influence? Identify four examples of special relationships in which undue influence might arise.
5. What is duress? How does it differ from undue influence?

Lawful Purpose

The last essential element in a legally binding contract is lawful purpose (object). Any contract that is a crime under the *Criminal Code* or that breaks federal or provincial laws is illegal and void. For example, a contract to sell state secrets to a foreign power or terrorist organization is a crime and unenforceable. Other contracts may not break any laws but still may be illegal and void because they go against public policy. This means that the private good of the contracting parties cannot be considered to be more important than the general good of society. Contracts that offend the public good are not enforceable.

Bets and Wagers

Gaming and betting are popular activities in which something of value is exchanged for the chance to win something of greater value. These activities may be addictive and, thus, damaging to society. They are strictly controlled by statute law. Provincial and territorial authorities grant licences allowing charitable groups to raise funds for worthwhile projects through gaming events such as lotteries, bingos, and so on. Most of the proceeds must go back to customers as winnings. Under the *Criminal Code*, it is illegal to operate an unlicensed gambling business.

Betting (making a wager) on the outcome of an event is also allowed under statute law. All territories and provinces have acts that regulate it. Betting on horse races, for example, is allowed and regulated by governments. It is also legal for two co-workers to bet on the outcome of a football game, but the courts will not help the winner to collect. Contracts for bets are not considered important enough to be heard by the courts.

Private businesses can set up slot machines, pinball machines, and video games wherever governments have authorized them. These slot machines can pay out only tokens or merchandise. The pinball and video games can give only free games as winnings, not money. Many municipalities have bylaws to keep game parlours from locating near schools.

Regardless of these restrictions, gambling in Canada is a multibillion dollar industry. It is controlled and dominated by provincial and territorial governments. Government-run lotteries, casinos, and video lottery terminals (VLTs) raised more than $13 billion in 2006. The profits from government-run gambling help fund social, athletic, and cultural groups and projects. However, many critics accuse governments of taking advantage of people who cannot afford to gamble and who may become addicted to gambling, especially through using VLTs. Every year, the Ontario government allocates 2 percent of gross revenues from slot machines at charity casinos and racetracks to the government's problem-gambling program for research treatment and prevention.

The provinces and territories have laws that govern betting at racetracks.

Restraint of Trade

Business contracts may be challenged on grounds of public policy if they are in restraint of trade. Competition is considered necessary for Canada's economic health. Therefore, the courts limit the time that a contract can restrain or restrict trade to a reasonable period. If the period is too long or if the restriction is unreasonable, the contract may be void.

For example, Victor Paslowski owns the only pharmacy in a small community of 3000 people. He enters into a contract to sell his business to Chung Sing Chen. Chung will purchase the business only if Victor promises not to operate another pharmacy within a radius of 100 kilometres of the existing store for 20 years. It is understandable that Chung wants to limit competition, but are these conditions reasonable? The contract might be considered an unreasonable restraint of trade and, therefore, void. The distance involved is probably too great. Customers are unlikely to travel more than 50 kilometres. Also, the 20-year time limit seems unreasonable. It should take Chung only a few years to establish a successful business with the existing customers.

Questions for Contracts Challenged in Court on Restraint of Trade

- Is this contract a restraint of trade?
- Is the restraint against public policy and, therefore, void?
- Is the restraint reasonable for the parties involved?
- Is the restraint reasonable for the public interest?

This chart lists some questions to ask of contracts challenged in court on restraint of trade.

The reasonableness of a restraint depends on various factors. These factors include the size of the community the business serves, how necessary the business is to the community, the type of business, the available competition, and the length of the restriction. Courts only support restraints of trade that give a buyer a reasonable amount of time to establish a reputation. After a reasonable period, the seller should be able to start a similar business.

The courts are reluctant to restrict an employee's ability to earn a living by moving from one business to another similar business. Employees who have access to confidential information or trade secrets may have to accept certain restraints in their contract. Such a contract is called a **restraint of employment contract**. A promise not to work for a competitor for a certain period after leaving the present employer is likely to be binding.

restraint of employment contract restrictions in an employment contract

Review Your Understanding

1. Distinguish between "illegal" and "void" as these terms relate to contract law.
2. Give an example of a contract that might be against public policy.
3. Summarize the four questions that must be considered if a contract is challenged in court as a restraint of trade.
4. Why are courts reluctant to enforce restraint of employment contracts?
5. When might a restraint of employment contract be enforceable?

15.4 Discharging a Contract

Once the parties agree and the essential contract elements are in place, an enforceable contract exists. However, all contracts must end eventually. This usually happens after the parties fulfill their obligations, or through performance. Contracts can also be ended by mutual agreement, impossibility of performance, and breach of contract.

Performance

Performance is the most common way to discharge (end) a contract. For example, a promoter contracts a rock group to give an outdoor concert during Canada Day celebrations. The concert sells out, and the group puts on its show. The promoter then pays the group, as agreed. Because all parties have performed their obligations, the contract has been discharged. If the group has been contracted to give six shows over the summer, the contract will be discharged once they have played all six shows and been paid by the promoter.

What if one party to the contract offers to perform and the other party refuses to accept? According to contract law, the first party is no longer obligated to attempt to perform his or her part of the contract. He or she may take legal action against the other for breach of contract.

These students signed a contract to paint this house. Once they finish and the owner pays them, each party will have performed its part of the contract, and the contract will be discharged.

Mutual Agreement

Parties to a contract may agree to cancel it. For example, if few tickets sell for the Canada Day rock concert, both parties could decide it is not worthwhile to continue the contract. Parties may also cancel one contract by agreeing on a new one. The promoter could negotiate a new agreement with the rock group to perform on another date. Some contracts may include a provision that foresees an event that will end the contract. For example, the contract between the promoter and the rock group would be cancelled if a certain number of tickets are not sold by a certain date.

Impossibility of Performance

Under earlier English common law, parties were responsible for meeting all of the contract obligations even if events later made this impossible. It was felt a contract should anticipate all circumstances that could make performance impossible. It should cover these in specific terms or conditions. For example, a farmer's contract to sell wheat might include a term covering the crop destruction by an early frost, flooding, or drought. People now buy insurance as protection against unforeseen circumstances.

The courts now sometimes excuse parties from performing their contracts when events after the agreement is made make this impossible. For example, the Canada Day rock concert cannot take place because a huge storm erupts. When a contract cannot be performed because of this kind of situation, or because the subject matter has been destroyed (for example, a concert hall is levelled by a fire or a tornado before the concert happens), a **frustration of contract** (the impossibility of performance) occurs.

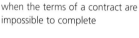
Did You Know?

In the landmark case of *Taylor v. Caldwell* (1863), a music hall rented to hold a concert was destroyed by fire before the concert could be held. The contract was held to be frustrated.

frustration of contract
when the terms of a contract are impossible to complete

When events such as a severe rainstorm make it impossible for a contract to be performed, a frustration of contract occurs.

The existence of a law can also make certain transactions impossible to perform. Suppose that real estate developers draw up a contract to build an apartment complex on a piece of land. Before construction begins, they learn the property lies on Aboriginal burial grounds. By law, nothing can be built there, so the contract is frustrated. A contract must have a lawful purpose if it is to be enforceable.

Review Your Understanding

1. Explain discharge by performance.
2. How does discharge by mutual agreement work?
3. How can a contract be terminated by mutual agreement?
4. To what extent were parties to a contract obligated to fulfill it under English common law?
5. What condition must exist for a contract to be discharged by impossibility of performance?

15.5 Breach of Contract

breach of contract failure to perform an obligation owed to another under a contract

breach of condition failure to perform an essential term of a contract, entitling the injured party to treat the contract as ended

breach of warranty failure to perform a term of a contract, entitling the injured party to damages

Breach of contract is the opposite of performance. It occurs when one party does not fulfill its obligations. If a fundamental part of the contract is breached, it is a **breach of condition**. In this case, the injured party can end or terminate the contract and sue for damages. If the rock group did not show up for the Canada Day concert because it accepted a better offer from another promoter, this would be a breach of condition. The original promoter could sue the group.

If the breach of contract is minor, a **breach of warranty** exists. In this case, the injured party cannot rescind or terminate the contract. For example, Noah orders a specific make and colour of car with a racing stripe painted on each side. The car that is delivered to him conforms in every respect except for the racing stripes. This is a breach of warranty since the omission is minor. Noah has several choices: He can ask the dealer to paint the stripes, he can deduct the cost of the stripes when he pays for the car, or he can sue for damages to obtain the money to have someone else do it.

The amount of damages awarded depends on the financial loss the injured party suffers. This is likely more for a breach of condition than for a breach of warranty. As you have seen in Chapter 11, civil legal actions are often costly and time-consuming. It often makes more sense for parties in contract disputes to use alternative dispute resolution procedures such as mediation or arbitration.

Substantial Performance

The law protects the party inconvenienced by a breach of contract. However, the rule of substantial performance also protects a party who has fulfilled most, but not all, parts of the contract. In the case of Noah's missing car stripes, the dealer is protected. What if Noah simply no longer liked the car? The rule of substantial performance prevents him from using the missing racing stripes as an excuse to break the contract. Because the dealer fulfilled most of the terms of the contract, so must Noah.

Tanaquil was rear-ended in a vehicle collision. She went to her local garage for repairs to her vehicle. The body shop repairs are excellent, but she says the paint colour is wrong. Is this a breach of condition or a breach of warranty? Explain.

This list provides key clauses that should be included in a contract.

Contract Checklist

- ☑ specific obligations
- ☑ when it is to end
- ☑ provisions for breach of contract
- ☑ conditions for delivery of goods
- ☑ conditions for performance of a service
- ☑ compensation if a party does not meet its obligations
- ☑ circumstances that might prevent completion
- ☑ how either party might end the contract

Remedies for Breach of Contract

Once parties have entered into a legally binding contract, they are bound to perform the agreement. Still, breaches of contract do occur. The following remedies are available to the party injured by the breach.

Damages

Damages are awarded to compensate the injured party for any losses, not to punish the party that breached the contract. They are meant to place the injured party in the same position they would have been if the contract were completed. Specific types of damages that might be awarded were discussed in detail in Chapter 11, on pages 372–376.

The jury's not awarding damages. You sued for loss of self-esteem and they're going to help you find it...

Damages are awarded as compensation, not as punishment.

Mitigation of Loss

The courts expect whoever is injured by a breach of contract to take reasonable steps to reduce or prevent any losses that the breach may cause. This is known as **mitigation of loss**. For example, Rimma refuses to accept a truckload of vegetables that she ordered from Omar. Omar must try to find another buyer. Not only that, he must do so quickly to reduce spoilage and prevent greater damages. If Omar has to sell the vegetables for a lower price, he can sue Rimma for the difference. However, he cannot simply leave the produce to rot and then sue Rimma. Similarly, if an employee sues for damages after being wrongfully dismissed, he or she must make an effort to mitigate losses by looking for another job.

mitigation of loss the expectation that a person injured by a breach of contract will take reasonable steps to reduce any losses that the breach caused

Liquidated Damages

To avoid court disputes, many contracts specify **liquidated damages**. This is a sum of money that the parties agree to in advance to settle any breach of contract that might occur. For example, a renovation contract might include a term that sets the sum of money the renovator will pay for each day that work continues beyond the contract completion date. The sum is meant only to compensate the injured party, not to punish the renovator.

liquidated damages a sum of money stipulated in a contract to settle a potential breach

Specific Performance

In most cases of breach of contract, monetary damages are an adequate remedy. But, what happens when money is not enough? For example, you find a piece of heritage jewellery on the Internet, and your bid of $500 wins the auction. Later, the dealer returns your cheque and says she is keeping the piece for herself. In this breach, the court may order **specific performance**. This means that the precise terms of the original contract must be honoured. The dealer would have to sell you the piece of jewellery for $500, as promised.

The courts likely award an injured party specific performance if a breach involves one-of-a-kind items such as homes, art, antiques, and so on. Since no two pieces of land are the same, the courts often award specific performance for a breach of contract involving land. However, if the land is purchased for development or investment, the courts are less likely to do so. This is because the purchaser could buy a different parcel of land for these same purposes.

specific performance a court order that requires a person to fulfill the terms of a contract

? Did You Know?

The most common remedy when a contract is breached is monetary compensation.

Specific performance is not available if the courts have to supervise carrying out the order to determine if it is satisfactory. For this reason, a contract for a personal service, such as painting a family portrait, cannot be specifically enforced. As well, an employee cannot be forced to work for an employer. An employer usually cannot be forced to keep a particular employee. In cases involving these kinds of services, either an injunction or money damages are awarded.

 You Be the Judge

Chan v. Chadha Construction et al., 2000 BCCA 198 (CanLII)

For more information, Go to Nelson Social Studies

If a home builder did not finish a home as promised, what remedy should the court order?

In 1989, the defendant, Chadha Construction, sold a home that it had built for the Chan family. However, it did not make all the changes and repairs that it agreed to do at the time. Later, the Chans sued. They said that Chadha had breached the contract by providing an incomplete house. In 1998, the trial judge ordered specific performance. The judge ordered Chadha to do the repair work under the supervision of an engineer of the Chans' choice. The plaintiffs appealed, saying that specific performance was an inappropriate remedy. In effect, it required the original builder to do the repair work 10 years after the original construction.

- Do you think damages or specific performance should have been ordered in this case? Explain.

Injunctions

When ordered as a remedy for a breach of contract, an injunction is the opposite of specific performance. It requires the defendant not to do something. For example, Ziyi's employment contract contains a non-competition clause. It states that she may not conduct research for any other laboratory during the term of her contract and for a period of time after the contract ends. Ziyi breaks the contract and does research for the competition. Her initial employer may seek an injunction to stop her from doing this. Injunctions are usually granted at the court's discretion when damages are considered inappropriate.

Privity of Contract

privity of contract a contractual relationship between two parties

To succeed in a court action over breach of contract, the plaintiff must be able to prove **privity of contract**—that is, a contractual relationship with the defendant. Normally, a person who is not directly involved in the contract, or a third party, cannot take legal action. There are exceptions, however. The beneficiary of a life insurance policy can sue the insurance company if it refuses to pay the benefit. The original contract would have been between the insured person, who is now the deceased, and the insurance company.

Rescission

When an important condition of a contract is breached, the injured party can try to have the contract rescinded (cancelled). **Rescission** (cancellation or revocation) returns the parties to their original positions before the contract was formed.

rescission the cancellation of a contract

You Be the Judge

Kitchen Craft Connection v. Dennis, (1999) 50 C.L.R. (2d) 239 Ontario Superior Court of Justice

For more information, **Go to Nelson Social Studies**

What would you do if you hired someone to do a job such as build and install a new kitchen, and you were dissatisfied with the work? Could you simply refuse to pay the contractor?

The defendant, Dennis, contracted Kitchen Craft Connection to build and install kitchen cabinets. After they were installed, it was clear that the cabinets and the installation were defective. The plaintiff was given the opportunity to fix the problems on two occasions, but was unable to complete the contract within the agreed-upon time. Dennis declined to make the payments under the contract. The plaintiff, Kitchen Craft, sued for the money owed. The defendant made a counterclaim to have the contract rescinded and to have the money that had been paid returned.

- Should the contract be rescinded and the defendant given a refund? Explain.

Limitation of Actions

If an injured party has the legal right, he or she should take court action as soon as possible after a breach of contract has occurred. As time passes, evidence may get lost or be forgotten; witnesses may move or die.

Certain laws also impose specific time limits. The *Statute of Limitations*, provincial limitations acts, and limitations sections in certain federal and provincial laws set fairly similar time limits that apply to contracts. If action is not taken within the time allowed, the claim is barred—that is, the courts will not help to enforce it. The standard time limit for contracts, other than real estate, is six years from the time of the breach.

All About Law DVD
"Copyright Concerns" from *All About Law DVD*

Review Your Understanding

1. What is the difference between a breach of condition and a breach of warranty? How does each affect a contract?
2. Explain the difference between damages and an order for specific performance.
3. How does an injunction differ from an order for specific performance?
4. What is meant by this statement: "A party must mitigate its losses"?
5. What is the importance of a statute of limitations?

15.6 Sale-of-Goods Legislation

In 1893, the British Parliament passed the *Sale of Goods Act*. This was England's first law to legislate the sale of goods. Since then, each province and territory in Canada has passed similar sale-of-goods acts. In Québec, these laws are part of the *Civil Code*.

The sale of goods is a specific area of contract law. It deals with contracts in which the seller transfers the ownership of goods, in the present or in the future, to the buyer for monetary consideration. In an **absolute sale**, ownership passes to the buyer when the contract is fulfilled. Barter transactions exchange only goods and services, not money. Therefore, they are not covered by sale-of-goods laws. In sale-of-goods acts, "goods" refer only to personal property, such as furniture, clothing, appliances, and other movable possessions. Items such as stocks, bonds, and cheques—and services—are covered by other acts.

absolute sale a sale whereby ownership passes to the buyer when the contract is fulfilled

Title, Delivery, and Payment

Most written contracts specify the time when ownership of goods (title) passes to the buyer. This is important because the owner must accept the burden of loss if the goods are lost, stolen, damaged, or destroyed. If no agreement is made, the provincial or territorial sale-of-goods legislation outlines how to deal with these situations.

Delivery involves transferring ownership from seller to buyer. It usually takes place at the seller's place of business. There may be agreements that state otherwise. However, the seller is usually responsible for delivering the goods to the buyer at the location specified in the contract.

Most contracts state the time and method of payment, but sale-of-goods legislation provides for payment at the time of delivery. If no price is agreed upon, a "reasonable price" is due. Non-payment does not automatically allow the seller to reclaim the goods, unless the buyer has agreed to such action. The seller can, however, charge interest and take legal action against the buyer. If the buyer has breached the contract, the seller must attempt to mitigate any loss.

Why is the concept of title to the goods important in these circumstances?

Express Conditions and Warranties

As you read earlier, it is important in a breach of a sales contract to know whether a condition or a warranty is involved. If it is difficult to determine which of the two is involved, the courts will decide.

An **express condition** is both essential to the contract and clearly outlined in it. For example, Miyoshi draws up a contract with Lingaard, a carpenter, to build her a maple cabinet. If he builds a walnut cabinet, Miyoshi can refuse to accept it. Lingaard has broken the express condition, which makes the contract void.

express condition an essential term of a contract clearly outlined within it

Express warranties are specific promises that manufacturers and retailers make to consumers about the performance, quality, and condition of goods. Also known as guarantees, they are usually given to a buyer in the form of a certificate along with the purchase. Limited warranties last for a certain period, such as six months or one year. For example, a car warranty generally covers the cost of parts and repairs for a certain number of kilometres or years, whichever comes first.

When a written contract contains express warranties, any verbal promises the seller makes are not binding. There is an exception, however. If a buyer makes a purchase relying solely on the seller's advice and information, any verbal promises the seller makes are binding. Such a contract may be rescinded under provincial consumer protection legislation.

Warranties and conditions that are not written into a contract but that are stated clearly in displays and advertisements are also binding on the seller. If the manufacturer, not the seller, makes the warranty promises, then a contract exists between the buyer and the manufacturer.

So-called secret warranties also exist. For example, a certain car model has a defect but the manufacturer alerts only dealers, not the public. The manufacturer promises dealers to cover repair work related to the defect. Even though the defect may not be identified in the buyer's warranty, and even if the buyer's warranty has expired, this secret warranty may still be in effect. It is up to the consumer to find out if such a warranty exists. He or she must then complain to the dealer or manufacturer about the problem.

express warranty a stated promise that goods or services will meet certain standards

Always keep a product warranty in a safe place in case you need it some day.

Warranty Checklist

When buying a product that has an express warranty, or guarantee, check the following:

- ☑ who holds it
- ☑ what it covers
- ☑ how long it lasts
- ☑ if it can be extended

What other terms would you add?

implied condition a term of a contract that is not explicitly stated but is presumed by law

Implied Conditions and Warranties

Implied conditions and implied warranties are promises in law that sellers make to buyers through implication or suggestion. They are described in sale-of-goods legislation and include the following basic promises:

- The seller has title to the goods and the right to sell them.

- The articles or goods are of merchantable quality (suitable for sale) and suitable for the required purpose.

- The goods supplied correspond to the samples or descriptions provided to the buyer.

Because each of these is a part of every sale of goods, they are examined more closely on the following pages.

 You and the Law

Locate the packaging contents from an electronic item that you or a family member has recently purchased. Does the product contain an express warranty? If so, from whom? What does the warranty cover, and how long does it last?

Title

It is implied that the seller has title to the goods and, therefore, the right to sell them. If the goods belong to someone else, the true owner can demand that they be returned—even from a buyer who has paid for them in good faith. To be compensated, the buyer would have to take legal action against the seller for breach of condition. This is one reason you should search title before buying, for example, a used car.

If a seller has clear (good) title to the goods, they legally belong to the buyer after the contract of sale has been fulfilled. The buyer can then use the goods in any way, including reselling them. It is further implied that the seller does not give the right to anyone else to use the goods.

Quality and Suitability

When making purchases, buyers should check goods carefully. In some cases, there is an implied condition that the products will be of good quality and fit for use. Buyers often know very little about specific products. They must be able to depend on sellers to be honest. A buyer may indicate to the seller how the goods are to be used and that he or she is relying on the seller's knowledge and judgment. Then there is an implied condition that the goods will be fit and suitable for the buyer's purpose.

merchantable quality fit for intended use; suitable for sale

A buyer may be able to get a refund if a product is not of **merchantable quality**—that is, fit to be used for its normal purpose. For example, a lawn mower must be able to cut grass, a CD burner to make CDs, and so on. Merchantable quality goods are normally saleable, but not always. For example, electrical goods must be approved by an accredited certification organization—such as CSA International—and display a certification mark. Say you buy a desktop computer in the United States, then pay the duty and taxes to bring it back to Canada. It may not have been certified according to the standards set by certification organizations in Canada. This means that it goes against provincial regulations and is not saleable in Canada, even though it works perfectly.

CSA International Certification Marks	
CSA®	certified for the Canadian market
CSA® US / CSA® NRTL	certified for the U.S. market
CSA® C US / CSA® NTRL/C	certified for both the Canadian and U.S. markets

There are different certification options available to manufacturers. However, in most cases, a sample of the product has been tested against applicable standards and found to meet those requirements for the particular market.

Sale by Description or Sample

If you buy a product based on a description, sample, or both, there is an implied condition that the goods you receive will match the description or sample. The seller must tell the buyer that the goods are samples. They must be of merchantable quality and visibly free of defects. In any sale by description or sample, a buyer must be allowed to compare the delivered goods with the sample.

An example of sale by sample is buying certain grades of lumber after looking at sample pieces displayed in the store. A sale by description is buying a sofa online based on photographs and descriptions on the retailer's website. If you later visit the retailer's store to select your fabric from samples, this is a sale by description and sample.

If delivered goods do not match the description or the samples, the buyer has the right to return them and rescind the contract. The buyer, however, must examine the goods and act as quickly as possible. A buyer who accepts goods without examining them does so at risk. It is probably too late to do anything if the buyer discovers later that the goods are not exactly what was ordered.

If you buy a product without asking the seller's advice—for example, a brand-name product—the seller cannot be held responsible if you, the buyer, are unhappy with the purchase. However, the manufacturer can be held liable for the tort of negligence if the product is faulty and the buyer is injured through its use.

This is a website for ordering candles and other products. Would this be sale by description or sample or both? Explain.

Checklist for Buying a Used Car Privately

Legal points to consider:

- ☑ Caveat emptor, or buyer beware, applies.
- ☑ Generally, the sale is "as is."
- ☑ Implied warranties generally exist regarding fitness for the purpose.
- ☑ If the seller makes any representations, get them in writing.
- ☑ Check the vehicle's registration and accident history.
- ☑ Check title: Are there any liens on the vehicle?

When buying a car privately, take the time to check the title, condition, and history of the vehicle.

disclaimer clause a provision in a contract that denies the buyer certain rights or protections

Disclaimer Clauses

Many sellers try to reduce the risk of being sued for breach of implied warranties and conditions by adding **disclaimer clauses** to contracts. These are often printed on the back of standard sales contracts. Typical wording might be: "There are no conditions, express or implied, statutory or otherwise, other than those contained in this written agreement." A contract might also stipulate that the sale is "as is."

These clauses seek to remove protections from the buyer. Therefore, they are not binding unless the seller brings them to the buyer's attention. For example, if the disclaimer appears on the back of a contract, there must be an indication on the front of the contract that additional terms are on the back. Or, if the disclaimer clause is in the "fine print," it may have to be highlighted in some way. Most provinces and territories carefully regulate these disclaimers in consumer contracts.

"They'll be ready in a month. It's not my fault you couldn't read the fine print."

Always read the fine print or have someone you trust read it for you.

Mayer v. Big White Ski Resort Ltd., 1998 CanLII 5114 (BC C.A.)

For more information, Go to Nelson Social Studies

Why do you think ski resorts have to include disclaimers in contracts with skiers?

Signing the release was a condition on the application form for the pass.

The release clause indicated in large type and heavy black ink:

Waiver of claims, Assumption of Risk and Indemnity Agreement. By signing this document you will waive certain legal rights, including the right to sue. Please read carefully!

The court held that the plaintiff made no effort to read the release despite opportunities to do so. Not only did he sign the release, Mayer had to print his name and address just below the printed summary. The court concluded that Big White had taken reasonable steps to bring the release to Mayer's attention and that it was a condition of the contract. There was consideration for the contract and the passes were issued. The release was held to be binding and enforceable, and Mayer's appeal was dismissed.

In March 1995, Bernard Mayer was injured while skiing at Big White Ski Resort in British Columbia. He collided with a snowmobile operated by resort employee Eric Bobert. Mayer sued Big White for negligence. Big White successfully moved to have the action dismissed, relying on a waiver (release clause) that Mayer had signed.

Mayer appealed, arguing that Big White failed to take reasonable steps to bring the release to his attention. He also argued that there was no present consideration (see page 525 for more on consideration). His wife had completed the season's pass application form and included a cheque earlier. Mayer testified that when he picked up the pass at the busy resort, he signed the agreement without reading the release, just as he had in previous seasons.

For Discussion

1. Why did Mayer bring an action against Big White Ski Resort Ltd.?

2. Outline Mayer's arguments against the ski resort in his appeal.

3. What was the consideration for the contract?

4. What steps did Big White take to bring the release of liability to the attention of Mayer?

Remedies of the Buyer and Seller

If a sales contract is breached, there are remedies for both buyers and sellers. If goods are not delivered, or if goods do not match the samples or descriptions, the buyer need not pay for the goods. As discussed earlier, the buyer can also rescind the contract or sue for damages or specific performance.

For the seller, breach of contract usually means that the buyer has not paid for the goods. Under the various sale of goods acts, the seller has certain remedies that reflect who has title to the goods—seller or buyer.

Remedies for the Seller when a Breach Occurs over a Sale of Goods	
Non-delivery	If the goods have been sold but not delivered, the seller can keep them until the buyer pays. This is often referred to as the **right of lien**.
Stoppage in transit	If the goods are in transit and the seller learns that the buyer cannot pay the amount owing, the seller can order the carrier not to make the delivery. If the goods are intercepted, they can be returned to the seller or sent to another location.
Resale goods	Resale goods stopped in transit are often resold. First, however, the seller must notify the buyer of the intended resale so that he or she has one last opportunity to pay to obtain the goods.
Damages	If the buyer has the goods, the seller can sue for the full price. If the goods are still in the seller's possession, the damages sued for might represent the expenses involved in finding a new buyer and any difference in the resale price of the goods.

This chart shows the most common remedies available to a seller when the buyer cannot pay for the goods.

right of lien if goods have been sold but not delivered, the right of the seller to keep the goods until the buyer pays

 Did You Know?

In 1996, the General Assembly of the United Nations adopted the Model Law on Electronic Commerce. Drafted by the UN Commission on International Trade Law, it set international standards that allow electronic communications to have the same legal weight as paper documents.

Review Your Understanding

1. What types of transactions do the sale of goods acts cover?
2. What is the difference between express and implied conditions and warranties? Use original examples of each.
3. List three implied obligations that sellers have to buyers under sale of goods acts.
4. Define "merchantable quality." What can a purchaser do if the goods are not of merchantable quality?
5. What is a disclaimer clause, and when might it have no legal effect?

E-Commerce: The Changing Nature of Business Transactions

When you enter an online contract, the offeror must make sure that the terms and conditions are brought to your attention. You have an obligation to read the contract before clicking "I agree."

Commerce conducted over the Internet (e-commerce) is transforming business. Around the world, lawmakers are creating new laws to deal with the realities of buying, selling, and forming contracts online. Technology has even made it possible to create a digital signature that is personal, verifiable, and protected by encryption (coding). This is a major breakthrough, because all formal contracts must be signed.

In Ontario, the *Electronic Commerce Act, 2000*, sets out the conditions that electronic communication must meet to satisfy the legal requirements for written communication. It governs how electronic contracts are formed, used, and enforced in Ontario.

When are online contracts enforceable? As a consumer, if you click "I agree" when you are downloading software or when you are purchasing a gift online, are you bound by the terms of the agreement? How do businesses ensure that contracts are enforceable when consumers accept their online offers? What types of electronic contracts are available?

On One Side

There are two main forms of electronic contracts. A click-wrap contract requires the offeree to scroll down through all the terms and conditions presented. The offeree must expressly agree by clicking an "I accept" or "I agree" button. For example, a website may contain this type of contract for software purchases. A browse-wrap contract often contains a statement that indicates that using the website or software indicates that the user accepts the terms. These terms, however, may not have been brought to the attention of the user. Therefore, problems may arise with respect to the enforceability of such contracts.

What should you do when you contract online? You should always read the terms and conditions before you click "I agree." To be safe, you could even print off a hard copy of the agreement and read it to understand what you are getting into before you click "I agree." That way, you will also have a hard copy of the contract should a future dispute arise.

A business that creates an online contract should also make sure that it brings the terms and conditions to the user's attention. Sometimes the online contract contains a statement placed in a separate box or in bold print. For example, "I have read the terms and conditions carefully and agree to the terms and conditions set forth." The user can then accept or decline the offer. If users do not agree to the terms and conditions, they are generally denied access to click through the contract.

On the Other Side

Lack of notice to the terms and conditions in an online contract could result in the contract being unenforceable. For example, a website contains a browse-wrap contract, where users must review terms that are buried in the contract. That contract may be unenforceable. While scrolling through online pages on a website may seem like turning the pages of a hard copy contract, a business should always bring the terms and conditions to the user's attention.

An online contract may contain terms that may be potentially advantageous only to the business seller. These terms should be brought to the attention of the parties to the contract. Otherwise, the contract may be unenforceable. When the terms of an online contract are considered unconscionable (unfair), the same common law principles of contract law apply and the contract may be unenforceable.

Resolving contract disputes with online transactions can also be difficult. Prior to entering the contract, the accepting party may not have read or noticed that the laws of a different country apply to resolving a dispute. For example, someone in Toronto makes an online contract with a New York company. He or she does not realize that the agreement states that California laws govern the contract. When negotiating contracts, it is important for you to be aware of what laws apply to resolve contract disputes.

The Bottom Line

Traditional contract law principles still apply to the formation of electronic contracts. In order to have a binding contract over the Internet, the terms and conditions of the offer must be clearly stated. The offeree (the person accepting the offer) must communicate their acceptance to the offeror (the person extending the offer), and there must be consideration between the parties to the contract. What happens if you do not read the terms and conditions of the offer? The court, except in the case of fraud, will not likely intervene for you. As with all types of contracts, online and written, a savvy buyer should always read the terms of the contract before clicking "I agree."

What Do You Think?

1. What law governs online contracts in Ontario?
2. Explain the difference between a click-wrap and a browse-wrap contract.
3. What should consumers do before they click the "I agree" button on an online contract?
4. When might an online contract be unenforceable?

Chapter Review

Chapter Highlights

- The law of contracts is the basis of business and is founded on judge-made common law.
- The essential elements of a valid contract are offer and acceptance, consideration, capacity, consent, and lawful purpose.
- The legal requirements of a valid offer and acceptance are serious intent, definite terms, and proper communication of the offer and acceptance.
- Telecommunications technology has created new tools that benefit businesses and consumers and also create new areas of contract law.
- Present and future consideration create a legally binding contract, but past consideration does not.
- Minors and people with impaired judgment enjoy special protections under contract law.
- Contracts formed through undue influence or duress are void.
- Contracts can be discharged by performance, mutual agreement, impossibility of performance or frustration, or breach of contract.
- Civil remedies available for breach of contract include damages, specific performance, injunctions, or rescission.
- A breach of condition is the breaking of a fundamental term of the contract. A breach of warranty involves the breach of a minor term.
- In assessing damages, courts will determine whether a party has attempted to mitigate its loss.
- The *Statute of Limitations* or the limitations acts of each province set up the time periods within which a claim under contract law must be acted upon.
- Sale-of-goods legislation is designed to offer protection to the buyer and seller by codifying implied conditions and warranties.
- Sellers often use disclaimers in an attempt to exempt them from liability.
- There are remedies available to a buyer and seller if a breach occurs over a sale of goods.

Check Your Knowledge

1. Identify the elements that must be present for a contract to be valid, and provide an example of each.
2. What groups of people have extra protection in contract law? Provide an example for each.
3. Outline circumstances in which consent to a contract can be declared invalid.
4. In a restraint-of-trade action, what factors are considered in determining the reasonableness of the contract?
5. Briefly describe the various methods used to discharge a contract.
6. What civil remedies are available for breach of contract? Give an example of the appropriate use of each remedy.

Apply Your Learning

7. Cranston offers to sell a sailboard to Parker for $1000. Parker is prepared to pay the price and mails a properly stamped and addressed envelope with his acceptance by return mail. Cranston does not receive Parker's letter of acceptance. What must be established to prove a binding contract between the parties?
8. Hearing cries for help, Andrea jumps into the swimming pool and rescues an elderly man. He is grateful and asks her to return later that afternoon for a $100 reward for saving his life. However, instead of paying her the reward, he simply thanks her once again. Is Andrea entitled to the reward? Why or why not?
9. Katco Manufacturing sold plastic pipe to the Centre '99 arena. The pipe was to be used as part of the ice-making equipment at the hockey and skating rink. The diameter of the pipe supplied was smaller than what was called for in the purchase order. After installation, the pipe cracked and split in several places. The arena owners took legal action for damages.

a) Outline the arguments the arena owners would make in their claim for damages.

b) What arguments would Katco Manufacturing likely make in its defence?

10. Spencer purchased several cases of canned lobster for his specialty food store from the defendant seafood company, a Prince Edward Island processor of frozen and canned fish products. Several of his customers returned the products as inedible. After being examined by federal food inspectors, the entire lot of canned lobster was destroyed. Spencer claimed damages from the processor for his loss.

a) Under what area of law would Spencer sue?

b) What argument would support his claim?

11. While Elini is trying to adjust her snowmobile engine, her neighbour, Dimitri, offers to help. He owns and operates the local snowmobile agency and makes the adjustments. Neither of them discusses money.

a) Can Dimitri later sue Elini for the cost of his services? Explain.

b) If Elini had offered to pay Dimitri at the end of the month, would this be legally enforceable? Explain.

12. Rachelle contracts to build a cabinet for Greg by a certain date for $800. As time passes, Greg begins to doubt that Rachelle will meet the deadline. He promises her another $100 in return for her promise to finish the project by the agreed-upon date. Rachelle finishes the cabinet on time and sends Greg a bill for $900.

a) Is Greg legally bound to honour his promise to pay Rachelle the extra $100? Explain.

b) Give legal arguments for both Rachelle getting the extra $100, and Greg not having to pay the extra $100.

Communicate Your Understanding

13. Consider the following statement: "If they do things right, the parties to a contract create their own legal rights and duties." Create a written contract in which you agree to cut a neighbour's lawn for the summer. Make sure that it includes the following:

a) a definite time period

b) how often the lawn is to be cut

c) whether any other maintenance is involved, such as raking

d) the amount of payment and when it is to be received

e) any circumstances that may cause the contract to end early

f) the scheduled termination date for the contract

Develop Your Thinking

14. The law has changed from the time when caveat emptor was the main defence a seller used in a contractual dispute with a buyer.

a) In what situations does caveat emptor still apply today?

b) Should statutes protect consumers, or should it be a responsibility for consumers to educate themselves before entering into contract relationships? Explain.

15. Explain the meaning of the following statement: "Consumers must be honest and must be prepared to accept their responsibilities in the marketplace."

16. Explain the following statement made by an English judge, Sir George Jessel (1824–1883): "A creditor might accept anything in satisfaction of a debt … He might take a horse, or a canary if he chose."

16 Dispute Resolution

What You Should Know

- What federal and provincial laws protect consumers?
- How can consumers protect themselves from being taken advantage of?
- What are the different classes of tenancy?
- What are the rights and duties of a tenant and landlord?
- What is the nature of the employer–employee relationship?
- What procedures must unions and employers follow to negotiate a collective agreement?

Selected Key Terms

collective agreement
Competition Bureau
cooling-off period
independent contractor
landlord
lease

misleading advertising
sublet
telemarketing schemes
tenant
union
workers' compensation

Chapter at a Glance

16.1 Introduction

16.2 Consumer Protection

16.3 Landlord and Tenant Law

16.4 Employment Law

All of these situations can end up in dispute. What if you buy something and are unhappy with it? What if your landlord will not fix the leak in your bathroom? What if your employer tries to pay you less than minimum wage? In these situations, you may need to turn to the law to resolve your dispute.

16.1 Introduction

By this point in your life, you have probably already been involved in a situation involving some aspect of dispute resolution. For some of you, a part-time job may have created some level of frustration because your employer failed to pay you the legally required minimum wage. For others, you might have bought something that did not meet your expectations, and now you feel ripped off. In the very near future, many of you will be going to college or university or entering the workforce. Living on your own will mean signing a housing rental agreement involving thousands of dollars. As a consumer in today's society, there may be many times when things do not go the way you had expected them to go. In these situations, you need to know when to turn to the law to resolve these disputes.

This chapter will focus on three specific aspects of dispute resolution: consumer protection, landlord and tenant agreements, and employment law. A good understanding of your rights and the laws for these three topics will benefit you as you enter into a consumer contract, sign a lease, or take a job.

16.2 Consumer Protection

The global marketplace in the world today is more complex. This means that consumer protection laws are becoming more important. Telemarketing and Internet fraud have raised consumer concerns about deceptive and unlawful activities in the marketplace. They have also forced police and intelligence agencies to co-operate internationally when necessary. National borders alone cannot stop these activities.

Since the late 1960s, governments in Canada have passed legislation to protect consumers. These laws are meant to do the following:

- Ensure that consumers are given accurate information.

- Protect consumers from hazardous or dangerous products.

- Regulate activities around the sale of goods.

Sometimes federal and provincial laws overlap, which gives consumers some choice in seeking help or compensation. It also means some confusion about which laws apply in which situations. Because these laws differ from province to province, they cannot be covered in detail in this textbook. Federal and provincial governments, however, do provide information on their websites and through free booklets. You may want to refer to these if you need detailed, up-to-date information.

Federal Laws

Federal laws such as the *Competition Act* treat dishonest business conduct and **misleading advertising** as offences against society. The **Competition Bureau** is a department of Industry Canada. It oversees consumer protection under these laws and looks into complaints that fall under various federal acts. These include the *Competition Act, Consumer Packaging and Labelling Act*, the *Textile Labelling Act*, and the *Precious Metals Marketing Act*.

Many young people move out on their own and have to sign rental agreements. These can involve thousands of dollars. So, it is important to know how to deal with disputes if necessary.

 Did You Know?

The banking industry in Canada spends over $100 million a year to prevent, detect, and deter fraud. It also uses this for other crimes against banks. This includes criminal activity resulting from identity theft.

misleading advertising advertising that makes a representation to the public that is false or misleading

Competition Bureau a federal agency that oversees competitive markets and protects consumers

Federal Legislation on Consumer Protection

Act	Responsibilities
Competition Act	• governs most business conduct in Canada • contains both criminal and civil provisions aimed at preventing anti-competitive practices in the marketplace
Consumer Packaging and Labelling Act	• a criminal statute relating to the packaging, labelling, sale, importation, and advertising of pre-packaged and certain other products
Textile Labelling Act	• a criminal statute relating to the labelling, sale, importation, and advertising of consumer textile articles • requires that textile articles bear accurate and meaningful labelling information to help consumers make informed purchasing decisions, such as the name of each fibre present
Precious Metals Marketing Act	• a criminal statute relating to the marking of articles containing precious metals • provides for the uniform description and quality markings of articles made with gold, silver, platinum, or palladium to help consumers make informed purchasing decisions • prohibits the making of false or misleading representations related to precious metal articles

These are some of the federal statutes that protect consumers.

The Competition Bureau is mainly responsible for protecting and promoting competitive markets. It also enables informed consumer choice. It administers and enforces the four acts outlined in the chart above. There are several specific areas that the bureau investigates and prosecutes. These include conspiracy, misleading advertising, and the protection of personal information.

 You Be the Judge

Paul Barnard and Telemarketing

For more information, **Go to Nelson Social Studies**

As of September 30, 2008, Canadians who do not want to be contacted by telemarketers can register their phone number at no charge with the National No-Call Registry. This prevents them from receiving future telemarketing calls. Why do you think the government created such a list?

Paul Barnard was a senior manager of DataCom Marketing. He was charged under the deceptive telemarketing provisions of the *Competition Act*. Barnard had telemarketers contact businesses in Canada and the United States. DataCom relied on the "assumed sale" technique, and implied that the businesses had ordered a directory listing in the past. The telemarketers also suggested that someone in the company had already authorized an order. In fact, they had not. DataCom successfully deceived more than 50 000 businesses. The businesses did receive a business directory, which they had ordered under false pretenses. DataCom charged each business between $200 and $500. The total cost of DataCom's telemarketing scam was estimated at $150 million over a 10-year period.

DataCom's telemarketers failed to disclose several things required by law: the purpose of the call, the company they represented, and the nature and price of the product. These are required by the *Competition Act* telemarketing provisions. In April 2008, Barnard was found guilty for his involvement in a business directories telemarketing scam.

• What punishment should Barnard receive? Justify your answer. Suggest ways individuals and companies could avoid such scams in the future.

Conspiracy

Conspiracy to reduce competition (and thus consumer choice) takes three main forms: price fixing, market sharing, and bid rigging. Price fixing occurs when competitors enter into an agreement to set prices so that consumers have no choice. In market sharing, they split the market geographically, or by customer, to reduce competition. Bid rigging happens when they reach a secret agreement among themselves. For example, paving companies might secretly coordinate their bids on a highway project to guarantee that one of them gets the contract at an inflated price.

The Competition Bureau investigates allegations about competitors engaging in price fixing. Price fixing is also called **cartel** activity. A cartel is an agreement between a combination of multiple businesses not to compete with each other. Those found guilty of participating in a cartel can be liable for up to five years of imprisonment and/or a fine of up to $10 million. Anyone suffering loss or damages as a result of a cartel may start a civil action against cartel participants. They do so in order to recover damages.

cartel a form of price fixing where multiple businesses agree to control the production, sale, and price of goods to restrict competition

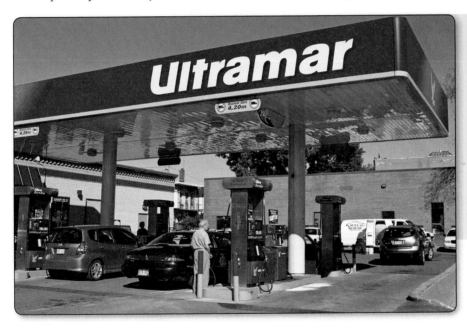

On June 12, 2008, the Competition Bureau laid criminal charges against 13 individuals and 11 companies, including Ultramar. They were accused of fixing gasoline prices at various Québec gas stations. Three of the companies and an individual pleaded guilty. The fines totalled just over $2 million against the companies and $50 000 against the individual.

Misleading Advertising

Advertisers are allowed to be creative in describing products. However, they cannot deceive consumers. This is called "misleading advertising." Sometimes, though, sales clerks, store displays, and advertisements do make false claims. For example, a store advertises a "great sale price" for a new computer system. Buried in the fine print of the warranty is a requirement to send the computer to Japan for any servicing—at the buyer's expense! In this case, the advertisement could be considered misleading. A seller who knowingly or recklessly makes a false or misleading representation can be criminally charged under the *Competition Act*. The offending party may be ordered to cease the activity or pay monetary compensation.

 You and the Law

"Sticker shock" is the surprised response to the unexpectedly high actual ticket price, including all extra charges. In the airline industry, the final price could be as much as 50 percent higher than the advertised price. Have you or your family ever experienced "sticker shock"? Should the government of Canada pass a law requiring all airlines to advertise prices that include all charges? Explain.

Maritime Travel Inc. v. Go Travel Direct Inc., 2008 NSSC 163 (CanLII)

For more information, **Go to Nelson Social Studies**

You have many choices available to you when booking a vacation. All the companies in the travel industry have to act fairly in this very competitive market. In 2000, the Office of Consumer Affairs launched the Canadian Consumer Information Gateway. This is an innovative web-based portal designed to improve and promote public access to consumer information. The gateway provides fast, convenient access to consumer information from more than 400 departments and agencies.

Maritime Travel is a long-established travel agency. Its head office is in Halifax. It supplies travel packages to southern destinations. Go Travel Direct is a direct-sale tour operator, with its head office in Ottawa. In 2000, Go Travel Direct entered the Halifax market and opened an office there. Go Travel Direct began to advertise. It sold itself as a tour operator with whom customers could book directly without going through a travel agency. Starting in January 2003, Go Travel Direct ran ads in Halifax's *The Chronicle-Herald*. It compared its price for a trip to a specific southern property to Maritime Travel's price for the same location.

Maritime Travel then started legal action against Go Travel Direct with regard to the advertisements. Maritime Travel argued that the ads were false and misleading under the federal *Competition Act* (section 52). To maintain its business, Maritime Travel was forced to lower its prices to match those offered by Go Direct Travel. The court reviewed all of the advertisements that were presented as evidence. It concluded that several Go Travel Direct ads had been false and misleading. The prices advertised were never meant to be honoured. They were simply advertising gimmicks. As well, the travel packages that Go Travel Direct offered were not exactly the same as those offered by Maritime Travel. This was the reason for the price difference. The Nova Scotia Supreme Court ruled in favour of Maritime Travel. It awarded the company damages of $216 842 because of Go Travel Direct's misleading advertising.

For Discussion

1. Explain how section 52 of the *Competition Act* applies to this case.

2. Summarize the arguments presented by Maritime Travel.

3. Does this decision suggest that competition for travel should be limited in some way? Explain.

4. Examine your local paper, and compare travel advertisements to see if any of the ads appear to be misleading. Summarize and report back on your findings.

Deceptive Marketing

Deceptive marketing involves unfair business practices and fraud. **Telemarketing schemes** to defraud people are commonly called scams. They are so widespread that they have been referred to as an epidemic. In 2007, it was estimated that over 4000 Canadians were victims of mass-marketing fraud. This resulted in the theft of over $18 million. One project known as "Operation PhoneBusters" is an example of how police and consumers have joined to fight the problem.

PhoneBusters was established in January 1993. It acts as the Canadian anti-fraud call centre. It is run by the Ontario Provincial Police, the Royal Canadian Mounted Police (RCMP), and the Competition Bureau. PhoneBusters tries to educate the public about specific false telemarketing pitches. The organization also collects evidence and other material for law enforcement agencies. PhoneBusters is the central agency in Canada that collects the information on telemarketing schemes and fraud. This is in an effort to prevent future similar crimes from taking place.

telemarketing scheme a deceptive marketing scheme conducted through unsolicited phone calls

Consumer Tips: How Can I Recognize a Scam?

Scam	Examples
It sounds too good to be true.	• You have won a big prize in a contest that you do not recall entering. • You are offered a once-in-a-lifetime investment that offers a huge, guaranteed return. • You are told that you can buy into a lottery ticket pool that cannot lose.
You must pay or you cannot play.	• "You're a winner!" but you must agree to send money to the caller to pay for delivery, processing, taxes, duties, or some other fee to receive your prize. Sometimes the caller will even send a courier to pick up your money.
You must give them your private financial information.	• The caller asks for all your confidential banking and/or credit card information. Honest businesses do not require these details unless you are using that specific method of payment.
Will that be cash … or cash?	• Often criminal telemarketers ask you to send cash or a money order rather than a cheque or credit card. Cash is untraceable and cannot be cancelled. Criminals also have difficulty in establishing themselves as merchants with legitimate credit card companies.
The caller is more excited than you are.	• The criminals want to get you excited about this "opportunity" so that you will not be able to think clearly.
It is the manager calling.	• The person calling claims to be a government official, tax officer, banking official, lawyer, or some other person in authority. The person calls you by your first name and asks you a lot of personal or lifestyle questions.
The stranger calling wants to become your best friend.	• Criminals love finding out if you are lonely and willing to talk. Once they know that, they will try to convince you that they are your friend—after all, we do not normally suspect our friends of being criminals.
It is a limited opportunity, and you are going to miss out.	• If you are pressured to make a big purchase decision immediately, it is probably not a legitimate deal. Real businesses or charities will give you a chance to check them out or think about it.

This table outlines typical techniques used by criminals to pull people into a scam.

Illegal Marketing Practices—Ontario Hydro Energy and Toronto Hydro Energy Services

For more information, 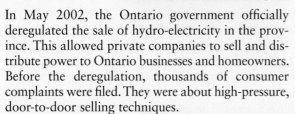 Go to Nelson Social Studies

In May 2002, the Ontario government officially deregulated the sale of hydro-electricity in the province. This allowed private companies to sell and distribute power to Ontario businesses and homeowners. Before the deregulation, thousands of consumer complaints were filed. They were about high-pressure, door-to-door selling techniques.

In April 2002, the Ontario Energy Board fined two electricity retailers for heavy-handed sales tactics. It was found that Ontario Hydro Energy and Toronto Hydro Energy Services' door-to-door agents misled consumers about prices. Agents also misrepresented who they worked for or used undue pressure to get contracts signed. In one case, an agent told a consumer that his electricity rate would drop by 25 percent if he signed at the door, but that was not true. Sales agents did not give consumers copies of their contracts. In another case, an agent entered a residence without being invited. The agent badgered the homeowner and would not leave. Some agents also suggested that homeowners' electricity could be cut off if they did not sign the contract.

Ontario Hydro Energy was fined $46 500 for incidents involving seven customers. Toronto Hydro Energy Services was fined $10 000 for incidents involving two customers.

• Do you think the fines issued in these two cases were adequate? Should the fines for illegal marketing practices associated with electricity sales be greater than for other goods sold door to door? Explain.

 Activity

To learn more about identity theft,

 Go to Nelson Social Studies

Personal Information Checklist

☑ age   ☑ weight
☑ name   ☑ height
☑ medical records
☑ ID numbers
☑ credit and loan records
☑ employee files
☑ student files

Information that can be found in a telephone book is not considered to be personal information. Why?

Protection of Personal Information

As Canadians are doing more business over the Internet, more private and personal information enters cyberspace. To protect consumers, the federal government passed the *Personal Information Protection and Electronic Documents Act* in 2000. It came into full effect on January 1, 2004. The act covers all businesses regulated by the federal and provincial governments, including banks, airlines, and telecommunications companies.

The act regulates when customer and employee personal information can be collected, used, and disclosed. Organizations generally must get consent before using or disclosing personal information. Under the act, businesses must also have effective security measures to protect that information. Consumers and employees must also be able to check this information.

In order to fight the increase of identity theft incidents in Canada, Parliament introduced Bill C-27 in November 2007. However, the bill failed to pass into law because of the October 2008 federal election. The bill would make it illegal to use another person's identity documents, such as passport, credit cards, or driver's licence in order to commit fraud. Criminals found guilty of fraud can serve up to five years in jail. They may also have to reimburse their victims for the costs resulting from fraud. As you learned in Chapter 4, offences involving fraud and impersonation are prosecuted under the *Criminal Code*. However, there is nothing that outlaws someone from possessing another person's information. That is why identity theft legislation is needed.

Ultimately, consumers should be cautious when sharing personal information. They should ask how it will be used, why it is needed, who else will be seeing it, and how it will be protected.

How Do Thieves Steal an Identity?

Method	Examples
Dumpster diving	Thieves rummage through trash looking for bills or other papers with your personal information on it.
Skimming	Thieves steal credit/debit card numbers by using a special electronic storage device when processing your card.
Phishing	Thieves pretend to be representatives from a financial institution or a company and send fake messages to get you to reveal your personal information.
Change of address	Thieves divert your billing statements to another location by completing a change of address form.
Stealing	Thieves steal wallets and purses; mail, including bank and credit card statements; pre-approved credit offers; and new cheques or tax information. They steal personnel records or bribe employees who have access to them.

Identity theft often begins with the misuse of your personal information, such as your name and social insurance number, credit card numbers, or other financial account information.

 Case

R. v. Stucky, 2006 CanLII 41523 (ON S.C.)

For more information, Go to Nelson Social Studies

David Stucky ran two successful direct-marketing companies in Toronto, known as the Stucky Companies. The companies employed as many as 120 people. They created between 20 to 30 promotions and sent out up to 30 000 promotional pieces each month. In July 2002, Stucky was charged under section 52 of the *Competition Act* for false or misleading advertising. The charges were a result of over 20 million pieces of direct mail "lottery promotions" sent to random consumers in the United States, Great Britain, Australia, or New Zealand. The Stucky Companies were located in Toronto, and the mailings came from Canada. However, no materials were mailed to anyone in Canada.

The lottery promotions created the impression that recipients could win a substantial sum of money. The Crown argued that the "lottery promotion" included several parts. The size of the entire jackpot related to what the consumer could realistically expect to win was exaggerated. The promotions did not disclose the probability of winning anything. There was a suggestion that the promotions were associated with a governmental or quasi-governmental organization. This made them seem more legitimate.

The case focused on the question of whether the mailing was meant to be misleading. Stucky argued that the *Competition Act* only applied to mailings sent to people in Canada. No one in Canada received a lottery promotion. Therefore, the Crown had failed to prove an essential element of the offences charged against Stucky. Stucky argued that he must be acquitted on all counts. The court concluded that in this case, an offence did exist. The mailings intentionally made false or misleading claims with the intent to deceive the consumers who received them. However, the charges were dismissed. The judge accepted Stucky's position that the act covered only mailings sent to people in Canada.

For Discussion

1. What is contained in section 52 of the *Competition Act*?

2. What was the Crown's position in this case, and what facts supported this position?

3. Explain Stucky's defence to the charges.

4. Do you agree with the decision in this case? Explain your position.

Provincial Laws

The provinces and territories also have consumer protection acts. The names vary, but the acts allow consumers to seek compensation against offenders. Provinces and territories also have the equivalent of the federal Consumer Protection Bureau. It is normally a branch of the ministry that deals with consumer affairs and commercial relations.

Provincial and territorial legislation also protects consumers in areas such as door-to-door sales, loan scams, credit reporting, and disclosure of credit costs, discussed below.

Door-to-Door Sales

Door-to-door (direct) sales have offered buyers convenience and ease for generations. On the other hand, some door-to-door sellers have been using high-pressure tactics for just as long. This is one reason why sellers have to register with the provincial Consumer Protection Bureau. Many consumers find themselves caught off guard or pressured to buy a product or service they do not want or need by aggressive sales agents who knock on their door unsolicited. Once an aggressive seller gets a foot in the door, he or she might not leave until the resident agrees to buy the products.

Laws recognize this type of pressure tactic and so have established a **cooling-off period**. During this time, a buyer can cancel a contract with a door-to-door seller without giving any reason, whether or not the goods have been received and/or paid for. For example, the consumer protection acts of Ontario, Alberta, Nova Scotia, and British Columbia set their cooling-off period at 10 days. To cancel, the buyer must notify the seller of the desire to cancel within the cooling-off period. The best way to do this is by registered mail or by delivering the letter personally. This entitles the consumer to a full refund.

cooling-off period a set period of time during which a buyer can cancel a contract made with a door-to-door seller without giving any reason

Do you know anyone who has been confronted by an aggressive door-to-door seller?

This table outlines tips on dealing with door-to-door sellers.

Tips on Buying Door to Door

- Be careful when allowing strangers into your home. Let them in only if you have asked the company to send someone to your house for a product or service demonstration. Make sure the seller has identification.

- Ask yourself if you really need the product or service right now. Do not buy on impulse.

- Never give out personal or financial information, such as your credit card or bank account number, unless you know the selling company's reputation.

- Never sign a contract without reading and fully understanding it. Do not sign anything with blank spaces.

- Do not be pressured or rushed into a purchase. Common high-pressure tactics are setting time limits ("buy today and save 50 percent") and forcing customers to make hasty decisions—often with the promise of a "special" offer. You can take the information and ask the seller to come back when you have had time to consider the purchase.

- Do not feel embarrassed about protecting yourself. If you feel threatened in any way, ask the seller to leave. If you are at all suspicious, call the police.

R. v. Purity One Inc. (Jeffrey Clapper), 2005

For more information, Go to Nelson Social Studies

Under Ontario's *Consumer Protection Act*, consumers have 10 days to cancel a contract for any reason if it was signed in their home. In this case, the consumer paid for a vacuum cleaner and air purifier after receiving an in-home demonstration. The following day, the consumer tried to cancel the cheque, but it had already been cashed. The consumer then delivered a registered letter to Jeffrey Clapper of Purity One Inc. to cancel the contract within the 10-day cooling-off period. The consumer cancelled the contract but never received a refund.

• Purity One Inc. and Jeffrey Clapper were charged under Ontario's *Business Practices Act* for engaging in an unfair business practice. They were also charged under the *Consumer Protection Act* for failing to refund money under a direct sales contract as required by law. How do you think the courts ruled in this case? Explain.

Loan Scams

Consumer ministries also try to protect consumers against dishonest lending and borrowing practices. Often, this is done through public education campaigns and by giving consumers free advice. Some companies advertise that they can guarantee a loan even if you have bad credit or no credit rating at all. In Ontario, as in many other provinces, it is illegal for lenders to charge consumers a payment fee (advance fee) before they receive the loan. In these loan scams, brokers charge the consumers fees, swearing that the loans have been secured. Then, the loans are never delivered. Such illegal advance fee loans generate millions of dollars annually in Canada.

 Did You Know?

Retailers are not legally required to offer refunds or exchanges. Consumers should check each store's policy before making a purchase—and get it in writing.

Credit Reporting

Consumers are encouraged to know their credit rights as a form of consumer protection. Equifax Canada and TransUnion Canada are the two businesses that collect credit information on individuals. They report it to credit-granting institutions such as retailers and banks.

Canadian federal and provincial laws identify who can review a consumer's credit report and for what purposes. Consent is needed for anyone to get a copy of someone else's credit report. There must be legitimate business reasons and an acceptable reason to get the report. For example, you want to rent an apartment. The landlord can ask for your consent to request a report on your credit history. This helps determine if you can make the monthly rental payments.

When you apply for a loan or credit card, you will be asked to complete and sign an application form that includes written consent giving permission to the credit grantor to check your credit report. Consumers can see a record of who has requested their credit report and when. These records are kept for three years.

Disclosure of Credit Costs

To make sure consumers know the cost of buying goods on credit, provincial legislation requires **full disclosure** of all credit costs. This means that consumers must receive a detailed statement of the cost of credit in dollars and

full disclosure a requirement that a consumer receive a detailed statement of the cost of credit and a true annual rate of interest expressed as a percentage

cents and as a true annual rate of interest expressed as a percentage. This lets consumers compare credit terms so they can shop around for the best interest rates. Consumers are not bound to contracts that do not provide full disclosure.

The Better Business Bureau—Promoting Trust in the Marketplace

The Better Business Bureau (BBB) is a non-profit public service organization financed by the private business sector. It operates 14 local bureaus across Canada. The BBB promotes trust and ethical business practices. It performs rigorous and ongoing evaluations of businesses. In 2005, the Canadian BBBs provided consumers with over 2.3 million "reliability reports." The organization helped resolve over 14 000 complaints.

The BBB began in the United States in 1912 and in Canada in 1935. Today, there are over 140 offices located throughout Canada and the United States. The international headquarters are in Arlington, Virginia.

The BBB works toward building trust between buyers and sellers. It defines and promotes the standards of excellence that set the best businesses apart from the rest. This is achieved by the following methods:

- collecting complaint histories and other information about businesses
- providing consumers with unbiased reliability reports to help them in their purchasing decisions
- evaluating businesses against objective standards and permitting only those businesses that meet and uphold those standards to join the BBB

The BBB maintains an information website. It provides businesses and consumers with an ongoing source of important consumer and marketplace information. News releases about consumer alerts and consumer advice as well as marketplace scams are provided and regularly updated. A list of all BBB-accredited businesses can be found on the BBB website.

The BBB joins with businesses to address concerns in the marketplace. In 2007, the BBB and Microsoft Canada partnered in a number of awareness activities. They focused on informing and educating businesses and consumers on the impact that pirated software had on themselves and the marketplace.

The Better Business Bureau helps build trust in the marketplace. Its website provides consumer and marketplace information to help people make better buying decisions.

The goal was to teach consumers how to protect themselves from unknowingly purchasing counterfeit software. These types of partnerships greatly benefit and protect consumers.

For Discussion

1. How does the Better Business Bureau build trust between buyers and sellers in the marketplace?
2. What is the significance of the BBB accreditation program?
3. How has the BBB partnered with businesses to address concerns in the marketplace?
4. Select a product or service that you are interested in, and research whether the companies are BBB-accredited.

Review Your Understanding

1. What purpose does the Competition Bureau serve? Identify the four main federal laws it is responsible for.
2. How does PhoneBusters help to protect consumers?
3. How is personal information protected in Canada?
4. Identity thieves have a variety of ways to obtain an individual's personal information. What are some of these methods? Explain.
5. Identify some of the areas of law and specific provincial and territorial legislation that protect consumers.

16.3 Landlord and Tenant Law

Landlord and tenant law applies to people who rent property and those who rent it to them. A **landlord** is a party that owns property and agrees to allow another party to use it in return for payment. A **tenant** is a party that rents a property from the landlord. (A party can be a person or a corporation.) This section examines residential tenants only, not commercial ones.

landlord the property owner who agrees to allow another party to occupy or use the property in return for payment

tenant the party that rents the landlord's property

Most likely, you will rent an apartment or a house at some point in your life.

Law governing the landlord and tenant relationship developed from English common law. Each province or territory has passed legislation that applies to residential tenancies. It tries to reduce the number of disputes the courts must resolve. Each province or territory has also enacted human rights legislation that prevents landlords from discriminating among prospective tenants.

The laws governing residential tenancies differ from one province or territory to the next. Therefore, it is important to understand the laws of the area in which you live. You should know your rights and responsibilities as a landlord or tenant.

 Did You Know?

If a landlord has a "no pets" policy, he or she may refuse to rent to a pet owner who is applying to rent.

Types of Tenancies

lease a contract between a landlord and tenant for the rental of property

lessor the property owner who rents out premises

lessee the tenant who occupies rented premises

The contract between a tenant and a landlord is called a **lease**. (It is also sometimes referred to as a tenancy agreement.) In it, the landlord is called the **lessor**, and the tenant is the **lessee**. The lease identifies the parties to the lease, the property to be rented, the amount of the rent, and the period of the tenancy. The tenant is entitled to use the property exclusively for the length of the lease.

A lease can be verbal or written. Many people prefer a written lease because it details the rights and duties of both parties. However, even without a written lease, a tenancy agreement can still exist. A critical aspect of landlord and tenant law is that the residential tenancy acts of each province and territory outweigh other agreements entered into by a landlord and tenant. In other words, landlords and tenants cannot "opt out" of the provincial or territorial statutes that created their relationship.

Many of the provincial and territorial statutes are so detailed that people sometimes question the need for a lease. However, each province or territory requires the landlord to provide the tenant with a copy of the signed lease.

There are several types or classes of tenancy. It is important to know the kind of tenancy you are entering into. This will determine how much notice you or your landlord must give to terminate the lease.

This table outlines the two classes of tenancy. Knowing which kind of tenancy agreement you are entering into is important, and it should be outlined in the lease. Before you sign a lease agreement, make sure you read the terms of the contract carefully.

Classes of Tenancies

Class of Tenancy	Description
Fixed-term tenancy	This is the rental of property by a tenant for a certain time and expiring on a specific date. No further notice is required by either party. For example, Hakim and Miranda rent a winter cottage for three months beginning January 1. The parties know that the tenancy will end on March 31.
Periodic tenancy	This is the rental of property by a tenant for some regular period of time, such as a week or a month. It is renewed at the end of each period by agreement, such as the payment of rent. For example, if Andrew's rent is paid monthly, the periodic tenancy is month to month.

When more than one person enters into a tenancy agreement, all parties are liable for their own portion of the rent. They are also liable for the total amount if the other renters do not pay. Therefore, if one tenant leaves before the lease ends, the remaining tenants must pay that person's share of the rent. If only one person enters into a tenancy agreement, he or she is liable for the entire amount of the rent under the agreement.

Young renters are often enthusiastic about sharing the rent, but under a tenancy agreement, each person is liable for the whole rent if one person fails to pay. How do you think such a situation could be prevented?

Entering into a Tenancy Agreement

As you read earlier, the parties in a landlord and tenant relationship cannot ignore the residential tenancy laws in their area. Leases must reflect the local laws where the rental property is located. Terms that do not reflect these laws are void.

If a term of a residential tenancy agreement is broken, the landlord or tenant can take the matter before an adjudicator (such as a rental housing tribunal) to resolve the dispute. You may already be familiar with the ways in which agreements are broken. The landlord could raise the rent without reason or refuse to do repairs or provide sufficient heat. The tenant could fail to pay rent on time or disturb others in the building on a regular basis. If a breach occurs, the innocent party may not be freed from his or her obligations, even if he or she takes legal action. For example, if John takes legal action to force Kim, his landlord, to fix his leaking faucet, he may still have to pay rent. The landlord may also take legal action to evict the tenant. The landlord must still fulfill all of his or her responsibilities to the tenant until the tenancy is terminated.

Parts of a Tenancy Agreement
• name and address of the landlord
• name of the lessee
• period of possession of the rented accommodation
• statement that the lessee is granted exclusive possession
• specific address of the property to be rented
• amount of rent to be paid and when it is to be paid
• services or utilities included in the rent (e.g., water, hydro, snow shovelling, etc.)

A tenancy agreement should specify all of these items, at the very least.

It is possible to use a standard lease form, which is available at stationery stores. You simply buy the form and fill in the blanks. Some provinces have approved a standard form lease that must be used. Leases usually contain clauses about rent, a **security deposit**, repairs, liability for injury, rules about quiet and privacy, and payment of utilities and taxes.

security deposit a sum of money tenants pay at the beginning of a tenancy

Rent

The exact amount of the rent, and when it is due, should be specified in the tenancy agreement. These agreements usually specify that payment is due at the beginning of the month. The tenant is responsible for delivering the rent payment to the landlord. Rent is overdue the day after it should have been paid. Some leases state that a penalty will be charged (so much per day) until the rent payment is received. Tenants may decide, for convenience, to provide postdated cheques to their landlords, but they do so at their own risk. The practice of insisting tenants provide postdated cheques has been abolished in some provinces and territories to protect the tenant.

If the tenant does not pay the rent that is due, the landlord might give him or her a brief grace period. If payment is still not received, the landlord can give notice of termination (an eviction notice). However, the tenant can still stay in the premises. The landlord must apply for an order from the appropriate body to have the tenant evicted. This may be a rental housing tribunal or other body. The landlord *cannot* forcibly remove the tenant. Only a legal authority, such as the sheriff, can evict the tenant, and she or he must act on an order issued by an appropriate body.

If the landlord plans to increase the rent at the end of the periodic or fixed-term lease, then notice in writing must be given to the tenant. **Rent control** was first legislated in many areas across Canada as a temporary way to control and regulate the amount of rent increases. However, rent control is now a permanent part of most provincial and territorial legislation. This means that rents can increase only by a certain percentage each year. In Ontario, the 2008 annual increase was limited to 1.4 percent. This was the lowest guideline since the introduction of rent regulation in Ontario in 1975.

rent control a form of government-mandated law setting a maximum price that landlords may charge tenants

Did You Know?

The allowable rent increase in British Columbia in 2008 was 3.7 percent, but there was no rent control in Nova Scotia.

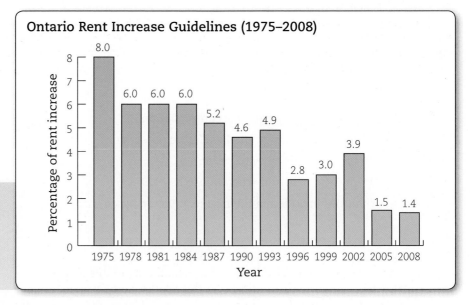

Since rent control was introduced in Ontario in 1975, the rate of allowable rental increases has dropped significantly. Why do you suppose that is?

Security Deposits

Tenants usually must pay a security deposit when they sign a lease. The laws of the province or territory clearly specify how these deposits should be used, such as to cover unpaid rent or damages. The security deposit is held in trust by the landlord until the end of the tenancy. Landlords have the right to ask for a security deposit. However, they cannot ask for any amount they wish. The security deposit is often equal to the value of one month's rent. If the tenant fails to pay all rent owing, the security deposit can be used to cover the amount owing in areas that allow this.

In some provinces and territories, the security deposit can be used to pay for damage done by the tenant. This often leads to disputes because the two sides often disagree on what constitutes damage, or what it will cost to repair it. If the two sides cannot agree, the matter can be referred to a mediator.

Repairs

Generally, landlords must maintain the rental unit and the residential complex in a good state of repair so that it is "fit for habitation." The building and the units must comply with local health, safety, and housing standards. This includes getting rid of mice, cockroaches, and other pests on the premises. Since the dwelling is the landlord's investment, maintenance and most repairs are considered his or her responsibility. It would be unfair to have tenants make repairs that would benefit the landlord and future tenants.

Generally, tenants are responsible for keeping the rental unit clean. They are also responsible for any damage they cause to their own unit or to the complex. In addition, they are responsible for damage caused by other occupants in their apartment or by guests. For this reason, tenants often get insurance not only to cover their own possessions, but also to protect themselves from third-party damages or injuries to guests. For example, if Sam's young nieces and nephews visit him and overfill the bathtub, he is responsible for the resulting damage. If Sam is insured, his insurance company may agree to pay for the damage.

Tenants have the right to a well-maintained property, and residential tenancy laws help them enforce that right. Tenants must first tell the landlord about any needed repairs. If the landlord fails to respond, tenants should complain in writing. This provides them with a dated, written record of their notification to the landlord.

Landlords have an obligation to supply tenants with a unit that is fit for habitation. What could you do if you lived in this flooded apartment and the landlord refused to fix this problem?

If nothing is done to address the tenant's issues after a reasonable amount of time, he or she can pay for repairs and deduct the cost from the next month's rent. However, they can later be found liable if the repairs were not really required or cost too much. For this reason, tenants may decide to apply to an adjudicator with a government landlord and tenant review board to end the tenancy, to lower the rent, or for an order to have the repairs done. Tenants may be entitled to reduced rent if they lose privileges or are inconvenienced by repairs.

Landlords and tenants bring different interests to residential tenancy agreements. Landlords are running a business and trying to make a profit. Tenants are contracting for an essential service for themselves and their families, often in a tight marketplace. Because disputes happen, it is important for the parties to deal with each other in writing. They should keep copies of correspondence and records of conversations. In this way, landlords can help to protect their business investments, and tenants can help to protect their homes.

Quiet Enjoyment and Privacy

You have the right to enjoy your rental property, free from interference by someone else. This is known as quiet enjoyment. This right can be upheld against the landlord and other tenants.

The law says that the landlord cannot enter your rented premises unless there is an emergency, proper notice has been given, or you agree to let the landlord in. Entry is usually allowed only during daylight hours or as otherwise agreed between the landlord and tenant. In Alberta, the landlord cannot enter on a holiday, which includes Sundays. If a tenant has a different day of religious worship, the tenant must give the landlord written notice of that day. A landlord can then enter on a Sunday, but not on the day that is the tenant's day of religious worship.

One reason a landlord may give notice of entry is to show the unit to prospective renters or buyers. The law says that the landlord has the right to show the premises to potential tenants during reasonable hours, as long as the tenant or the landlord has given notice to terminate the tenancy. The landlord has no right to stop political canvassers from entering the building. However, tradespeople can be restricted. Neither the landlord nor tenants can alter the locks without the consent of the other. This is meant to stop a landlord from evicting a tenant or to prevent the tenant from obstructing a landlord's lawful access.

Playing the drums is perfectly legal, but not if it interferes with someone else's right to quiet enjoyment of a rental property. How would you schedule drum practice if you shared a house with other tenants?

Utility Services and Property Taxes

Municipal bylaws require certain services to be provided to a tenant to make the premises habitable. These vital services include water, heat, electricity, garbage collection, and sewage disposal. Other services are supplied at the discretion of the landlord or the tenant. These include telephone, Internet, cable, and snow removal. If vital services are not provided, the tenant should first inform the landlord. If there is no response, municipal inspectors should be notified. After inspecting the premises, they can order the services to be provided or order the landlord to do the necessary repairs. If the landlord refuses to comply, the tenant can apply to the courts or to a government board such as the Landlord and Tenant Board in Ontario. It is a serious offence for a landlord to withhold vital services.

The lease should state who is responsible for paying for optional services. If the lease does not state the payment responsibilities for services, or if there is no lease, the person who hires someone to provide a service—for example, snow removal—is liable for the cost. The landlord is also responsible for paying the local property taxes. The tenant's share of the taxes is included as part of the rent.

Landlord and Tenant Responsibilities

Landlord Responsibilities

- Make sure the rental unit is reasonably safe by having proper doors and locks.
- Give a tenant a receipt when rent is paid in cash.
- Do repairs and keep the unit in good condition.
- Pay the utility bills if utilities are included in the rent.
- Investigate any complaints about a tenant disturbing other tenants.
- Live up to any tenancy agreement and legislation of the province.

Tenant Responsibilities

- Pay the rent on time.
- Keep the unit and the building clean.
- Repair as soon as possible any damage the tenant and his or her guests cause.
- Make sure not to disturb other people.
- Make sure not to endanger the safety of others.
- Live up to any tenancy agreement and provincial laws.

The table above outlines the responsibilities of landlords and tenants.

Tolea v. Ialungo, 2008 BCSC 395 (CanLII)

For more information, Go to Nelson Social Studies

Mihaela Tolea fell down a flight of stairs through a metal gate, similar to the one pictured here. She claimed that the gate was not properly installed, which breached duty of care.

In 1974, Mary Ialungo (the defendant) purchased a home in Coquitlam, British Columbia. She intended to rent it to tenants. She relied upon her son, Vito, to look after the property. This included maintaining, inspecting, and renting the property. Inside the premises, there was a staircase between the ground floor and the upper level. At the top of the stairway was a metal gate. It was installed in 1979 or 1980 by the tenants who were living there at that time. The gate was secured by a spring-loaded bar and latch, which was bolted to the railing.

Mihaela Tolea (the plaintiff) and her family moved into the premises on March 15, 2002. On October 4, 2002, Tolea fell through the gate and down the staircase suffering serious injuries. Tolea sued both Mary and Vito Ialungo for injuries and damages caused as a result of her fall. Tolea claimed that she fell because of the defendants' negligence in permitting a hazard—the gate—to remain on the premises. She claimed that the gate had been installed in a dangerous manner contrary to building code standards. Tolea argued that the defendants owed her a duty of care that required them to ensure she would be reasonably safe in using the premises.

The Ialungos argued that they were not aware of any problem with the gate. None of the previous tenants had a problem with it in the 22 years before the plaintiff's accident. Evidence was presented that Vito had inspected the premises before renting it to the Toleas. Also, Tolea and her husband inspected the property before moving in. Neither noticed any problem with the gate, nor did they raise any concerns about it with the defendants. Between March and October, the plaintiff and her family used the stairs daily, reporting no problems with the gate. The judge in this case ruled that there was insufficient evidence to conclude that the defendants breached any duty of care owed to the plaintiff. The judge concluded that it was an accident for which no one should be held legally liable. The plaintiff's claim was dismissed.

For Discussion

1. What is meant by "duty of care" when it comes to a landlord's responsibilities?
2. What evidence was presented by the plaintiff to support her claim?
3. How did the defendants fulfill their "duty of care" responsibilities toward the plaintiff?
4. Do you agree with the decision in this case? Explain your position.

 Did You Know?

The Centre for Equality Rights in Accommodation (CERA) is an Ontario-based non-profit human rights organization formed in 1987. It promotes human rights and challenges discrimination in housing. CERA supports improved protection under Ontario's *Human Rights Code* for low-income families with children, young people, and other disadvantaged groups.

Changing or Terminating a Tenancy

A tenancy can end in a number of ways. The tenant can move out at the end of the lease, or move out during the lease period. The tenant can **sublet** or assign the tenancy to another person. The landlord can terminate the tenancy for reasons specified in the residential tenancy legislation. Alternatively, the tenancy can be terminated because both the landlord and tenant agree to it. Each of these scenarios is examined below.

sublet to rent out leased premises by a tenant to a third party

PARDON MY PLANET   *BY VIC LEE*

NO, THIS ISN'T A PRE-NUPTIAL AGREEMENT – IT'S A RENTAL AGREEMENT. IT STATES THAT IF YOU PLAN TO LEAVE ME, YOU GIVE THIRTY DAYS' NOTICE AND LEAVE ME IN THE SAME CONDITION YOU FOUND ME IN.

Why do you think that rental (tenancy) agreements are important for landlords? Why are they important for tenants?

Surrender of the Lease

After entering into a lease, a tenant's circumstances may change. He or she might lose a job, drop out of school, or go through some other change. If the tenant decides to surrender the lease and leave the premises, that person is still responsible for the rent for the remainder of the lease. However, the law requires that landlords attempt to minimize the tenant's losses. That is, the landlord has a duty to re-rent the unit as quickly as possible. In a tight rental market, the unit may be rented as soon as the former tenant leaves. In that case, the former tenant may be responsible for only reasonable out-of-pocket expenses to the landlord, such as advertising the availability of the unit.

Assignment and Sublet

The terms "**assignment**" and "sublet" have different meanings. An assignment occurs when a tenant gets a replacement tenant and waives the right to repossess (regain possession of) the rental unit. The new tenant pays rent directly to the landlord. The original tenant is still liable for the terms of the lease (such as having to pay rent) if the new tenant defaults.

assignment the transfer of a right under a rental contract to another person

A sublet occurs when a tenant rents out the premises (either in part or as a whole), but keeps the right to repossess. For example, Hiroshi, a university student, rents an apartment on an annual basis. He sublets to other students in the summer with the agreement that he will move back into the apartment in the fall, when his school year starts. Hiroshi is liable for all the terms of the tenancy agreement, including the obligation to pay rent, until the lease term ends. The summer tenants, called the subtenants, pay the rent to Hiroshi, who then pays the landlord.

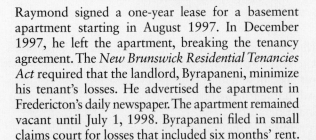

FOR SUBLET

Bonnie Doon house, bsmt. suite, private entrance, share utils. 3 appl. Fenced pet OK, $500/mo. Quiet street.

172 St. and 64 Ave., 2 bdrm apt., with dishwasher, indoor pool & daycare on site. Heat water incl. $600/mo. Walking distance from shopping.

Downtown, newly reno. 2 bdrm apt., stove, fridge, dishwasher, balcony, parking incl., $775/mo. Close to LRT.

Millcreek house, 1 bdrm. main flr. $650/mo. 4 appl., dble gar. Available immediately.

Meadowlark apt. 1 bdrm, $350/mo., all utils. incl. No pets. Close to bus and hospital. Available Nov. 1.

What would be the advantages and disadvantages of subletting?

For an assignment or sublet, the landlord may charge the original tenant a reasonable fee for any expenses incurred. This may include drawing up a new lease for the new subtenant.

Although tenants can assign or sublet, the landlord usually wants to meet the new tenant. The landlord can demand that the original tenant obtain permission to assign or sublet. In the past, landlords often withheld such permission. They preferred to rent an empty apartment to a new tenant rather than have someone take over an existing lease. Today, if the tenant finds someone to sublet the apartment or to whom the contract can be assigned, the landlord cannot unreasonably deny permission. If the landlord does so, the tenant can apply to the courts for permission to sublet to a specific person. The only tenants who do not have the right to sublet or assign are residents of public housing because of the long waiting lists.

You Be the Judge

Raymond v. Byrapaneni, 2001 NBCA 8 (CanLII)

For more information, **Go to Nelson Social Studies** 🌐

Raymond signed a one-year lease for a basement apartment starting in August 1997. In December 1997, he left the apartment, breaking the tenancy agreement. The *New Brunswick Residential Tenancies Act* required that the landlord, Byrapaneni, minimize his tenant's losses. He advertised the apartment in Fredericton's daily newspaper. The apartment remained vacant until July 1, 1998. Byrapaneni filed in small claims court for losses that included six months' rent.

Byrapaneni had three other vacant units available in the same building at the same time that he was trying to rent the Raymond apartment. Raymond had permission to sublet the apartment. There was an understanding that he remained liable if the subtenant did not pay the rent. Raymond met with a family who told him that they were interested in renting a basement apartment. In January, the family rented an apartment on the third floor of the building. This was despite the fact that Raymond had told them that his unit was available. When asked at trial why they did not take the Raymond apartment, they indicated that the landlord had told them it was not available. The landlord disputed the family's statement.

- Should Raymond have to pay the six months' rent that was owing while the apartment was vacant? Why or why not?

Termination by Notice

Neither a landlord nor a tenant can terminate a lease on a whim. It is allowed only on certain grounds (which must be set out in the written notice). For example, each province and territory requires a certain length of notice.

Situations that allow a landlord to terminate a tenancy are usually one of two kinds:

1. The tenant has committed a serious breach. For example, Emma and Olivia cause undue damage, fail to pay rent to Alissa (the landlord), or disturb others.
2. The landlord wants to change the use of the premises (for example, convert the building to condominiums or move in his immediate family members).

Issuing an eviction notice is the last step in the process of removing an undesirable tenant.

If the landlord serves notice to terminate a tenancy because the tenant has committed a breach of the tenancy agreement, the tenant may be given some time to correct the situation. If the tenant does not correct the problem and does not leave, the landlord can apply to an adjudicator or the court to obtain a **writ of possession**. This document allows the landlord to regain possession. If necessary, the landlord can call the sheriff to enforce the writ.

When the landlord wants to change the use of the premises, the tenant may be able to challenge the lease termination. Usually, the landlord must prove that he or she will be changing the use of the rental unit according to what is set out in the notice of termination. In addition, it is illegal for a landlord to harass a tenant with the intent of getting him or her to vacate.

writ of possession a legal document authorizing a landlord to repossess a rental property and evict the tenants

---

 You Be the Judge

Yukon Housing Corp. v. Kirsten Atkins, 2008 YKTC 54 (CanLII)

For more information, Go to Nelson Social Studies

The landlord (Yukon Housing Corporation) provided the tenant (Kirsten Atkins) with a written notice of termination dated August 21, 2007. It terminated the tenancy effective September 7, 2007. The landlord relied on section 93(2) of the *Landlord and Tenant Act*. The corporation alleged that Atkins had committed a substantial breach of the tenancy agreement. This involved the failure by Atkins to provide the landlord with financial information despite numerous requests.

Atkins appealed the eviction notice to the Housing Advisory Board. It upheld the eviction notice but gave Atkins until December 31, 2007, to produce the required income information. On January 3, 2008, the landlord issued a second termination notice. Atkins again appealed the eviction notice to the board. The

second eviction notice was upheld. Following the decision, Atkins wrote to the board. She asked that the time allowed for supplying the information be extended to February 29, 2008. The board agreed to this request. However, Atkins failed to provide the information to the landlord by that date. A third letter of eviction was sent out on March 28, 2008. As of the date of the trial, Atkins still lived on the premises.

On May 23, a judge ordered that the tenancy end as of May 31, 2008. He ordered that the landlord be allowed to regain possession of the premises. As part of the order, he issued a warrant to the sheriff to enter the premises and give possession to the landlord.

- Do you think terminating a tenancy agreement should take this long? Was it justified in this case? Why or why not?

Review Your Understanding

1. What is a tenancy agreement? Who are the parties to it?
2. What types of clauses should be included in a lease?
3. What responsibilities does the tenant have when it comes to rent? What can the landlord do if a tenant fails to pay his or her rent?
4. Summarize the specific responsibilities that both a landlord and tenant have regarding repairs, quiet enjoyment and privacy, and utilities and property taxes.
5. Identify and explain the ways either the tenant or landlord can change or terminate the tenancy.

16.4 Employment Law

Employment contracts are some of the most important contracts you enter into. They determine what you earn and what kind of lifestyle you can afford. Today, employees negotiate contracts with their employers either directly or indirectly. They may do this as individuals or through **unions**. Unions are organizations that represent groups of employees in contract negotiations.

Even with contracts, employers and employees still come into conflict. This can result in changes to employment law. To balance the powers of employers and employees and to bring peace to the workplace, statutes have been passed. Minimum wages, hours of work, occupational health and safety, and human rights are some key areas of employment law now governed by federal, provincial, and territorial legislation.

union an organization that represents and negotiates for the employees of a particular business

The Employment Relationship

All employment relationships are based on contracts. They must have all the essential elements that you studied in Chapter 15. This is true even if the work is casual or part-time, or the employment contract was made informally or verbally. In an employer–employee relationship, a person is hired to work under someone's direction for a certain number of hours per week. It is usually in the employer's workplace and using the employer's equipment. The law governing this relationship is covered under employment statutes. The laws set standards for wages, work hours, overtime, vacation pay, and so on. Employment legislation also sets requirements for occupational safety and working conditions. All employment contracts must meet the minimums set by these statutes.

An employer must provide the employee with supervision, a workplace, and equipment.

Contracts between employers and employees are usually negotiated individually. Contract terms generally include a statement about whether the job is permanent, the rate of pay, work hours, holidays, and benefits. Benefits can include medical, dental and life insurance, pension plans, and so on. The employer may pay all or part of the benefit costs for the employee. Contracts can also be negotiated between employers and unions.

Cornered
by Mike Baldwin

12-24 © 2004 Mike Baldwin / Dist. by Universal Press Syndicate

"I agreed to guide you. My contract says nothing about pulling a sleigh."

Identify some of the essential parts of an employment contract. Why are such contracts important?

 Did You Know?

In 1894, the Government of Canada created Labour Day. It introduced legislation that made the first Monday in September a national holiday. Labour Day is a time to spend with family and friends. It is a celebration of the social and economic contributions workers make to Canadian society.

Terms of Employment

- human rights legislation
- employment standards and safety legislation (statutes)
- trade union legislation (often called "labour law")
- common law of employment contracts

The chart above outlines some of the types of laws that govern the employment relationship. Employment terms must not violate human rights laws.

 Did You Know?

On October 12, 2007, the Ontario government declared the third Monday in February to be an official public holiday known as Family Day. Family Day is also recognized in Alberta and Saskatchewan.

Employer–employee relationships that are not covered by legislation usually rely on common law (except in Québec, which has its own code). Contract law developed over the years as courts heard and decided on employment disputes. In settling these disputes, judges dealt with both verbal and written contracts. They have also interpreted terms that were both implied (understood to exist) and expressed (clearly written out).

Chapter 16 **Dispute Resolution**

Laws Affecting Employers and Employees

For many years, employer–employee law was referred to as the law of master and servant. The employer was the master and the employee the servant. Although those terms are no longer used, the relationship continues to exist: employees work for employers. Employers direct employees in what, how, where, and when work is to be done. Employers also provide the means to do the job. A complex network of common law and federal, provincial, and territorial legislation now applies to the employer–employee relationship. If an employer does not perform his or her fundamental common law duties, the employee may sue. If the employee breaches any of his or her basic duties, the employer has **just cause** (the legal right) to fire the employee.

just cause the legal right to take an action, such as firing an employee

Employer and Employee Responsibilities under Common Law

Employer Responsibilities

- Pay the agreed-upon wage or salary.
- Pay agreed-upon employee expenses.
- Provide a safe workplace, which includes hiring workers with necessary skills.
- Provide the type of work the employee was hired to do.
- Let the employee have a second job, as long as it is non-competitive.
- Assign work that is legal.
- Honour the terms of the employment contract.
- Give reasonable notice of an intention to terminate the contract of employment.

Employee Responsibilities

- Be punctual and take only permitted leaves of absence.
- Obey legal and reasonable orders.
- Be loyal, honest, and competent.

Common law lays out the basic duties of the employer and employee in terms of the employment contract.

Federal Employment Legislation

The courts would be overwhelmed if they had to settle every employment dispute. For this reason, all levels of government passed laws that set standards for employment, wages, working conditions, termination notice, and so on.

As you learned in Chapter 1, the *Constitution Act, 1867*, gave the provinces jurisdiction over property and civil rights. The right to enter into a contract is a civil right. Therefore, most statutes for employment are provincial. As a result, the law varies across Canada. The main federal employment statute is the *Canada Labour Code*. The Code applies only to those industries in which the federal government has jurisdiction. These industries include the following:

- occupations under federal jurisdiction, such as banking, the post office, and national defence
- employees of Crown corporations, such as the Canadian Broadcasting Corporation (CBC), VIA Rail, and the Bank of Canada
- workers in industries that connect one province or territory to another, either through transportation or physical connections, such as bridges, pipelines, and airfields

 Did You Know?

The *Canada Labour Code* applies to only 10 percent of employees in Canada. However, it is a model and leader for employment legislation across the country.

Human Rights in Employment

As you learned in Chapter 3, all levels of government passed human rights legislation to promote equality. The legislation also protects individuals from both intentional and unintentional discrimination. These laws extend to many areas of life, including employment. Human rights legislation is powerful and prevails over employment contracts and legislation in most disputes.

The federal *Canadian Human Rights Act* and most provincial and territorial human rights codes and acts prohibit discrimination on a number of grounds. Each jurisdiction also has a human rights commission to administer and enforce human rights legislation.

Prohibited Grounds of Discrimination

The *Canadian Human Rights Act* and all the provincial and territorial human rights legislation prohibit discrimination on some or all of these grounds.

Cole v. Bell Canada, 2007 CHRT 7 (CanLII)

For more information, Go to Nelson Social Studies

Employment law in Canada requires an employer to make a reasonable accommodation for employees in special situations, such as breastfeeding. When it comes to breast-feeding, discrimination against women continues to be a common practice in society, particularly in employment.

Hayley Cole began working at Bell Canada in 1987. She held various positions within the company. In February 2000, she took maternity leave from work to give birth to her second child. Cole's son was born on February 27, 2000. He had a congenital heart defect that required extensive surgery. Given his condition, her doctor recommended that she breastfeed him for as long as possible to strengthen his immune system. Upon returning from maternity leave, Cole asked the company to provide her with a work schedule that would allow her to go home and breastfeed her child at the same time every day. Her request was denied.

Cole filed a complaint with the Canadian Human Rights Commission. She argued that by turning down her request for a modified work schedule, Bell Canada discriminated against her based on her sex and family status. The Canadian Human Rights Tribunal heard the case. It ruled that by denying Cole's request for unpaid time off work each day to nurse her child, Bell had discriminated against Cole on the basis of her sex within the meaning of the *Canadian Human Rights Act*.

The tribunal further found that Bell had no policy on accommodating employees with respect to breastfeeding. Bell had failed to prove that having to accommodate Cole's request would have caused undue hardship to Bell. The tribunal ordered that Bell take measures to prevent this discrimination from occurring in the future. It awarded Cole compensation for pain and suffering.

• Do you agree with the decision in this case? How could Bell have accommodated Cole's request?

Discrimination is prohibited—not only on the job, but also in employment interviews, hiring practices, and advertisements. Therefore, prospective employees cannot be asked about their religion, marital status, political beliefs, and so on. Sometimes an employer must set a job requirement that excludes people, which is discriminatory. To be acceptable under human rights legislation, the requirement must relate directly to the ability to do the job. As long as the requirement is reasonable and valid—or a bona fide occupational requirement—it is acceptable.

For example, a moving company wants to hire some students for part-time work. It advertises that the job requires students who are strong enough to lift large furniture and appliances. The company could not place an advertisement saying that applicants must be of a certain height, weight, colour, race, or sex. These characteristics have nothing to do with strength. They are not valid job requirements. If challenged, employers have to prove that the job requirement is valid.

If a job requirement has a negative impact on a social group, this is known as adverse effect discrimination. In this situation, the employer must take steps to accommodate people who are negatively affected. This is known as the employer's duty to accommodate.

Harassment is another area that is covered in human rights legislation. It has been described as a course of abusive or distressing comments or conduct that is unwelcome. This could include hostility or intimidation by others in the workplace based on gender, race, or religion. Another example of harassment is when a person in a position of power forces an employee to do something to keep his or her job. Every person has the right to be free from harassment in the workplace and from working in a poisoned work environment.

Anyone who is harassed may take action against those responsible. An employer who ignores complaints of harassment can be held liable. There are two distinct kinds of harassment: personal harassment and sexual harassment. Personal harassment is abusive behaviour directed at a specific person or persons. Harassment involving sexual comments and actions is known as sexual harassment.

 Did You Know?

In a 5–2 decision in *Mckinney v. University of Guelph*, 1990, the Supreme Court of Canada ruled that mandatory retirement at age 65 violated section 15 of the Charter. However, such a violation was justified as being reasonable under section 1 of the Charter. By July 2009, all provinces in Canada eliminated mandatory retirement legislation.

All About Law DVD

"Defrocked Doc" from *All About Law DVD*

Everyone should be able to work in a safe and healthy workplace, without fear of violence. In 2004, more than 356 000 incidents of workplace violence were reported. These included sexual assault, robbery, and physical assault. Of these, nearly 75 000 injuries were documented.

You and the Law

A 2008 study has found that half of Ontario youths aged 12–14 have part-time jobs, compared to 42 percent in British Columbia. Teens must be 15 to work in a factory, but only 14 to work in a store or office. What age do you think is appropriate to begin working part-time? Explain.

Did You Know?

In December 2006, the Ontario government passed the *Education Amendment Act (Learning to Age 18)*. This act required students to stay in school until age 18. Do you agree with this? Why or why not?

Provincial and Territorial Employment Legislation

Each province and territory in Canada has employment legislation that gives employees basic protection. Some acts relate to specific occupations, such as teaching, medicine, accounting, and so on. Other acts and codes are more general. Employment standards acts or codes vary across the country. Each covers key terms of employment and establishes certain minimums.

Minimum Age

In Canada and most industrialized nations, employment law offers youths special protection. School is compulsory in most of Canada until the age of 16. This is generally the minimum age at which a youth can work full-time. For youths under 16, work hours are restricted. That is, employers usually cannot hire youths under the age of 16 to work during school hours or late at night during the week.

Minimum Wage

Each province and territory sets its own minimum hourly wage rate. Governments increase the rate to help employees keep up with living costs or to encourage people to take jobs. Businesses, on the other hand, may pressure governments to keep minimum wages from rising. This helps keep business costs low. Some occupations, such as farm workers, resident caretakers, and restaurant servers, have special minimum wage rates.

Hourly Minimum Wages in Canada, September 2008

Province or Territory	Adult	Student, Youth, or Inexperienced
Alberta	$8.40	None
British Columbia	$8.00	$6.00
Manitoba	$8.50	None
New Brunswick	$7.75	None
Newfoundland and Labrador	$8.00 ($10.00 as of July 2010)	None
Northwest Territories	$8.25	None
Nova Scotia	$8.10	$7.60
Nunavut	$8.50	None
Ontario	$8.75 ($10.25 as of March 2010)	$8.20
Prince Edward Island	$7.75	None
Québec	$8.50	None
Saskatchewan	$8.60 ($9.20 as of May 2009)	None
Yukon Territory	$8.58	None

Why do you think the minimum wage is not the same for all provinces and territories?

Work Hours

The standards for work hours are inconsistent across Canada. In many provinces and territories, full-time employees can work between an 8- and 12-hour day and 40 to 48 hours per week. Overtime pay is paid to workers who work greater than the legislated maximum number of hours. Overtime pay is usually paid at time-and-a-half.

Work Hours in Canada, 1996

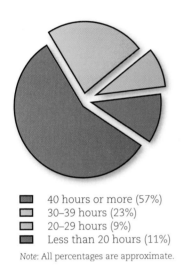

- ■ 40 hours or more (57%)
- ☐ 30–39 hours (23%)
- ☐ 20–29 hours (9%)
- ■ Less than 20 hours (11%)

Note: All percentages are approximate.

Work Hours in Canada, 2006

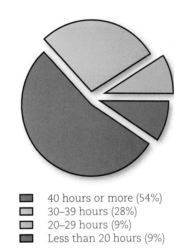

- ■ 40 hours or more (54%)
- ☐ 30–39 hours (28%)
- ☐ 20–29 hours (9%)
- ■ Less than 20 hours (9%)

> In Canada, the number of employed persons working at least 40 hours per week has decreased from 1996 to 2006. What do you think are some of the reasons for this trend? What do you think are some of the labour issues associated with the number of hours workers are expected to work each week?

Statutory Holidays

All full-time employees must be allowed to take off statutory holidays, with pay. These holidays include New Year's Day, Good Friday, Victoria Day, Canada Day, Labour Day, Thanksgiving, Christmas Day, and Boxing Day. As well, they must pay for special provincial or territorial holidays. These include New Brunswick Day, British Columbia Day, and Ontario and Alberta's Family Day. Generally, employees must work for at least three months before being eligible for statutory holiday pay. They must also work regular shifts before and after the holiday. Pay for working a holiday is usually double the regular rate. Even though Sunday shopping is common across Canada, employees have the right to refuse to work on Sundays. Employees who work on a Sunday must be given an alternative day of rest during the week.

Vacation

Employees are usually entitled to two weeks of annual vacation, with pay, after having worked one year for an employer. They often receive more annual vacation time the longer they work for their employers. Employees who do not take an annual vacation are entitled to vacation pay. It is calculated as 4 percent of the employee's yearly earnings, but may increase for long-term employees.

Leave of Absence

A **leave of absence** allows an employee to take a period of time off work without the fear of losing her or his job. Depending on the employer, extended leaves of absence are taken with no pay or partial pay. One of the most common types of leaves of absence is maternity or parental leave. Maternity leave is granted to mothers who have given birth and who have worked the required period of time before taking leave. Parental leave is available to both men and women and adoptive parents and is 35 weeks in length. The federal government pays for maternity and parental leave (through the Employment Insurance program), but employers can pay employees more if they choose to. By combining maternity and parental leaves, a mother can take a total leave of one year. A worker cannot be dismissed or laid off because of pregnancy or adoption, as this would be considered discrimination.

Did You Know?

The *United States Family and Medical Leave Act* provides for only 12 weeks of maternity leave, and it covers only those who work for larger companies. Of 21 high-income countries, the United States has the least generous policies in this respect.

Cornered by Baldwin

4-26 © 1999 Mike Baldwin / Dist. by Universal Press Syndicate

"I need time off to go back to college and party. Fraternity leave."

Would this be a reasonable request by an employee? Under what special conditions should an employer provide a leave from work?

Termination and Dismissal

Employment standards legislation sets minimum periods of termination notice in the employment contract. An employee who resigns or quits must give the employer one or two weeks' notice, depending on the length of employment.

An employer must give notice when dismissing an employee without cause. The period normally ranges from one to eight weeks, again depending on the length of employment. An employer can dismiss the employee immediately, without notice, but must pay him or her termination pay. Notice is not required if an employer dismisses an employee for just cause. Grounds could include any breach of the employee's common law duties, including fraud, theft, and serious misconduct (for example, stealing or lying). The onus is on the employer to prove that cause exists.

Employees dismissed without proper cause or notice can sue the employer for wrongful dismissal. In some provinces, they may also be entitled to severance pay, which recognizes an employee's many years of service. An employee who is dismissed for just cause is not entitled to receive termination or severance pay.

Honda Canada Inc. v. Keays, 2008 SCC 39 (CanLII)

For more information, **Go to Nelson Social Studies** 🌐

Kevin Keays started work in 1986 at Honda's assembly plant in Alliston, Ontario. He was a model employee and was promoted to team leader in the quality engineering department. It was expected that he would show his fellow department members how to operate Honda's new global computer system. Some years after joining the company, Keays started having health problems. These forced him to miss work. He had glowing reports as a dedicated and conscientious employee for most of his work categories. However, he received negative reports about his attendance. His missing work affected the smooth operation of his department. It also affected his ability to satisfy the requirements of Honda's "lean" and efficient operations.

In 1996, he was diagnosed with chronic fatigue syndrome (CFS). He was off work and on and off disability insurance for two years. In 1998, he returned to work full-time following the termination of his insurance benefits. He soon began to miss work again and was falling asleep at his workstation. Keays tried to work out an accommodation with Honda. The frustration of trying to do so and the need to get medical notes for each of his absences (which was not required for other ill employees) aggravated Keays's symptoms and increased his absences. Honda referred him to two doctors. The doctors suggested that there was nothing wrong with him.

Keays hired a lawyer, who sent Honda a letter. It outlined his concerns and an offer to work toward a resolution. Honda decided that they no longer accepted the legitimacy of Keays's absences. Keays was fired in March 2000 after 14 years of employment. He sued Honda for wrongful dismissal. In 2005, the trial judge awarded Keays two years' salary and $500 000 in punitive damages. Honda appealed to the Ontario Court of Appeal. In September 2006, the appellate court unanimously upheld the finding of wrongful termination. The majority of the court ordered that the punitive damages be reduced from $500 000 to $100 000. In a 7–2 decision in June 2008, the Supreme Court of Canada ruled in favour of Honda. They dismissed the punitive damages ordered by the lower courts but upheld the two years' salary award.

Honda was involved in a wrongful dismissal lawsuit over an employee who missed work because of an illness. What accommodations should employers have to make to sick employees?

For Discussion

1. Why was Keays unable to work?

2. What requests did Honda make of Keays, and why was he eventually fired from his job?

3. Do you agree with the Supreme Court's decision in this case? Explain.

4. Justice Bastarache wrote for the majority of the Supreme Court in this case. The justice stated that "courts should only resort to punitive damages in exceptional cases." The conduct meriting punitive damages awards must be "harsh, vindictive, reprehensible, and malicious," as well as "extreme in its nature and such that by any reasonable standard it is deserving of full condemnation and punishment." Given this explanation, why did Honda's actions in this case not merit punitive damages to be awarded to Keays?

Health and Safety Legislation

Every year, thousands of Canadians are injured on the job. Some die from job-related injuries and illnesses. These injuries cause great human suffering and they cost businesses billions of dollars in lost work days and related costs. All provinces and territories have legislation, often called the *Occupational Health and Safety Act*. It sets workplace standards. Under these acts, employers must provide workers with a safe and healthy workplace. They must also provide training in work and safety skills.

Employees must assume some degree of risk related to work. However, any employee may refuse to work in unsafe conditions without fear of being fired. In most areas, any business with 20 or more employees is required to have a joint health and safety committee. This committee is made up of both managers and employees. It must meet regularly to ensure the act is being followed. If working conditions are unsafe, the committee can order work to stop until the situation is corrected.

Employers are also obligated to provide employees with **Workplace Hazardous Materials Information System (WHMIS)** training. WHMIS is the national Canadian system of identifying hazardous materials in the workplace. This system teaches employees how to interpret the symbols for hazardous materials and how to handle and store them. Employees also learn how to neutralize hazardous products in case of accidents.

Workplace Hazardous Materials Information System (WHMIS) a system of classifying and providing information about materials dangerous to workers

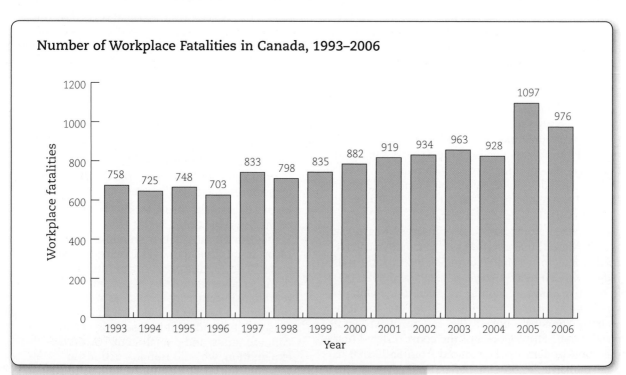

Number of Workplace Fatalities in Canada, 1993–2006

Year	Workplace fatalities
1993	758
1994	725
1995	748
1996	703
1997	833
1998	798
1999	835
2000	882
2001	919
2002	934
2003	963
2004	928
2005	1097
2006	976

All employers have the duty to ensure their workplace is safe for employees.

Canadian statistics show that one in seven young workers is injured on the job. The leading causes of death are machine injuries and electrocutions. All workers, especially young workers, need to be aware of their rights in the workplace. For example, you have the *right to know* about unsafe materials and/or dangerous machinery in the workplace. Workers should receive proper health and safety training. This includes learning how to identify workplace hazards and knowing the proper course of action when there is an accident or spill. You also have the *right to participate* in your workplace's safety practices. Workers should report any unsafe practices or conditions they observe. Many workplaces also have health and safety committees where workers can go for advice and information. Finally, you have the *right to refuse unsafe work*. Workers who believe that the work they must do or the equipment they must use is unsafe, can stop their work immediately. They can contact the supervisor or health and safety representative to correct the unsafe situation before continuing with their job.

Did You Know?

According to WorkSafeBC, 41 workers under the age of 25 are injured on the job each day.

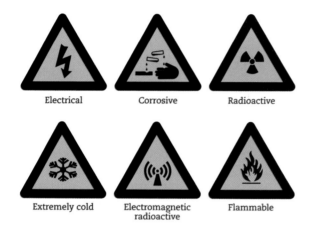

Electrical	Corrosive	Radioactive
Extremely cold	Electromagnetic radioactive	Flammable

Symbols such as these are used to identify the various kinds of hazards that can be present in work environments. All workers should be able to recognize each of these symbols in the workplace and know what they mean.

Workers' Compensation

Workers' compensation is a kind of no-fault accident insurance for employees. It is available throughout Canada. In the past, workers who suffered job-related injuries or illnesses had to sue the employer to get compensation. Most workers could not afford to challenge their employer. Workers' compensation was designed to eliminate this need and to pay compensation quickly. Workers' compensation boards were developed in Canada in the early twentieth century. Workers' compensation was also meant to spare employers from having to face frequent lawsuits and large damage settlements. Benefits are paid to an injured employee, regardless of who caused the accident. Under workers' compensation legislation, employers pay premiums into a workers' compensation fund. The amount they pay depends on the number of employees and the industry's safety record.

Each government has also established a workers' compensation board. If a work-related injury or illness occurs, the employee is supposed to report it to the board as soon as possible. The board then investigates the claim, at no cost to the employee. If the claim is approved, the injured employee is paid for all expenses and a percentage of his or her salary. The board will also pay for retraining, if needed.

workers' compensation a scheme for paying benefits to employees injured on the job or suffering workplace-related health problems

Activity

To learn more about workers' compensation,

Go to Nelson Social Studies

Unions

Workers in Canada fought for many years for the legal right to have unions represent them collectively (as a group) in dealings with employers. It was felt this would give employees more power in the employer–employee relationship. Unions are legal today. The law that applies to them in Canada is often referred to as "labour law."

Unions can benefit both employers and employees. Many businesses are too big to deal with employees individually. Instead, in a unionized workplace, the employer (or management) negotiates with the union representatives. This process is called **collective bargaining**.

Statistics suggest that union members find strength in numbers. The employment contract that a union negotiates with an employer is a **collective agreement**. Its terms and conditions are usually more favourable for employees than statutory employment standards discussed earlier in this chapter. Increased bargaining power can result in improved job security, wages, safety, and benefits.

collective bargaining
negotiation between an employer and a union on behalf of its members

collective agreement
the contract resulting from collective bargaining between a union and an employer

The Winnipeg General Strike of 1919, where more than 30 000 workers of all occupations went on strike to demand the right to collective bargaining, was a key moment in Canadian labour history.

Union Certification

Provincial and territorial labour legislation and the *Canada Labour Code* deal with collective bargaining, workplace health and safety, and employment standards. This legislation also establishes labour relations boards. These boards control, supervise, and regulate the formation and operation of unions. They help to maintain relations between unions and employers. In general, labour tribunal decisions are overruled by the courts only if they are found to be unreasonable.

Unions, or union branches, can be formed either inside or outside a business. If formed inside, workers organizing the union drive try to sign up co-workers. If formed from the outside, an existing union tries to recruit workers as new members. When a new auto plant opens, an existing union may try to sign up employees and gain the right to represent them in negotiations with the employer.

To get the right to represent employees, the union must apply to a labour relations board for certification (official recognition). A union is certified only if the majority of employees (more than 50 percent) support it. The union can verify this for the board by submitting signed membership cards, by a representative vote, or both.

Some employers may be against union representation. They may threaten or intimidate workers to stop them from joining a union. Union organizers may also threaten or coerce workers to join. In either case, this intimidation is forbidden under labour legislation as an unfair labour practice.

Lavigne v. Ontario Public Service Employees Union, 1991 CanLII 68 (S.C.C.)

For more information, Go to Nelson Social Studies

Francis Lavigne taught at a community college similar to the school shown here. He was forced to pay union dues even though he disagreed with some of the ways the union was spending this money. Should employees have the right to opt out of paying union dues?

Francis Lavigne taught at the Haileybury School of Mines, a community college, since 1974. As part of a mandatory clause in the college's collective agreement, union dues were automatically taken off his pay. Lavigne objected to some of the union's spending, such as contributions to the New Democratic Party and disarmament campaigns. He felt he should be able to "opt out" of paying union dues, especially if they were used for expenses he did not support. Lavigne went to court to stop the deductions.

The trial judge ruled that the *Colleges Collective Bargaining Act* and the collective agreement were of no force and effect. They forced Lavigne to pay union dues for purposes not directly related to collective bargaining. The judge ruled that Lavigne's freedom of association, guaranteed by section 2(d) of the *Charter of Rights and Freedoms*, was infringed. Furthermore, this was not justified under section 1 of the Charter.

The Ontario Court of Appeal reversed this judgment. It ruled that the union's use of dues was a private activity by a private organization. Thus, the Charter did not apply. It also ruled that there was no infringement on Lavigne's freedom of association. He was free to associate with others and to oppose the union.

Lavigne appealed to the Supreme Court of Canada. On June 27, 1991, the court delivered a unanimous 7–0 decision. The court agreed with the trial judge that Lavigne's freedom of association was violated. However, it found that the violation of association was justified under section 1 of the Charter. The court also ruled that paying union dues was not a private activity. The appeal was dismissed.

For Discussion

1. According to the trial judge, in what way was Lavigne's freedom of association infringed upon?

2. What was the main reason the Ontario Court of Appeal reversed the trial judge's decision?

3. Do you agree with the Supreme Court of Canada's decision in this case? Explain.

4. Justice Sopinka of the Supreme Court stated in his decision that "an opting-out formula could seriously undermine the unions' financial base and the spirit of solidarity so important to the emotional and symbolic underpinnings of unionism." What did he mean by this statement? Do you agree?

Did You Know?

In 2007, almost 4.5 million workers were union members in Canada. This was an increase of 39 020 over 2006 membership numbers. As a result, union membership as a percentage of all paid employment in Canada was 30.3 percent for 2007.

Union Membership in the Workplace

Labour law allows for different union-membership arrangements in a union-represented workplace. In a closed shop, all employees must belong to the union. In an open shop, not all workers must belong, but the union always campaigns for membership.

Other agreements can be written into the terms of the union contract with the employer. In a union shop, the employer can hire non-union members. However, each employee must join the union within a certain time. In an agency shop, non-union workers are permitted, but they must pay union dues.

Union members do not have to be actively involved in their union. They do have to pay dues and follow union rules. Members elect the union executive, which plans union activities. The executive's main responsibility is to prepare the union's negotiation position in collective bargaining. Many unions also create programs to help members develop professional and personal skills. The general membership is asked to vote only on important issues, such as accepting an employer's contract offer.

If the business is large enough, union members elect a shop steward to represent them. Any union member who wants the union to take action on a work-related complaint must take the complaint to the shop steward. The steward then takes the complaint to the union executive. If it decides to take action, it notifies the employer that it has a **grievance**. This is a formal complaint alleging a violation of the collective bargaining agreement. If the grievance cannot be resolved, the union may take it through a more formal arbitration process.

Once a union has negotiated a contract it is satisfied with, it will present the contract to its members at a meeting and ask them to vote on it. This meeting is referred to as a ratification meeting.

grievance a work-related complaint made by an employee, the union, or management when it is thought that the collective agreement is not being followed

Collective Bargaining

A union's main purpose is to represent members in collective bargaining with the employer. A union has the right to represent employees exclusively. In return, members expect their union to win them favourable contract terms. This includes wages, benefits, working hours and conditions, training, grievance procedures, and so on.

During contract negotiations, the union gives the employer the terms that it wants in the collective agreement. The employer studies the terms, discusses them with union negotiators, and then makes an offer. The union executive must consider the offer and recommend that the membership accept or reject it.

If the executive thinks the offer may be acceptable, it presents the offer to the membership for a vote. The executive may send the offer to members for a vote even if it knows it will be rejected. This may show the employer the extent of worker solidarity—that employees are united in their position.

As negotiations go back and forth, they can become harsh and confrontational. Both sides, however, must bargain in good faith (genuinely work toward an agreement). If either side hides information or refuses to discuss certain matters, the other party can complain to the labour relations board. If the board finds the party guilty of unfair labour practices, it will be penalized.

Mediation and Arbitration

Labour legislation specifies the procedures for collective bargaining. If the parties cannot reach an agreement on their own, they may have to seek alternative dispute resolution (ADR) (see Chapter 11 for more on ADR). In this case, the labour relations board appoints a mediator. He or she attempts to resolve disputes through compromise and voluntary agreement. When negotiations between the union and the employer break down, mediation helps the two parties find acceptable middle ground.

If both sides reject the mediator's recommendations, they can request that an arbitrator be appointed. The parties may have to agree in advance to binding arbitration. It means that a neutral third party determines the contract terms. In such cases, the arbitrator's decision is final. This may leave conflicts between the employer and union members unresolved, only to break out at a later date. That is why binding arbitration is generally avoided.

Strikes

A **strike** is the ultimate weapon a union can use, but it is usually legal only after negotiations have failed. Tensions may be so high, however, that union members will walk out in a wildcat strike before being in a legal striking position. Wildcat strikes are rare because employees who take this extreme job action have breached their employment contract and can be fired. Courts can also issue injunctions to prohibit wildcat strikes.

 Did You Know?

All provinces have legislation that prohibits certain workers from striking. Across Canada, police, firefighters, and hospital employees (among others) do not have the right to strike. They are required to settle their disputes through binding arbitration. These jobs are considered essential services. They are considered necessary to prevent danger to life, health, and safety.

strike a work stoppage or partial withdrawal of service by union members to further their contract demands

 Did You Know?

In *Fraser v. Ontario (Attorney General)*, in a 3-0 judgment on November 17, 2008, the Ontario Court of Appeal ruled that Ontario farm workers have the right to unionize. The court said that the *Agricultural Employees Protection Act* "substantially" impairs their Charter right to freedom of association. This act prevented farm workers from collective bargaining. The decision affects an estimated 32 000 workers each year, including 16 500 migrant farm workers from Mexico and the Caribbean.

Once a union can legally strike, it may set up picket lines outside the workplace to make its position known to the public.

During a strike, employees are still legally employees, even though the business is not paying them. Sometimes a worker breaks the strike and crosses the picket line. The union often disciplines such people, usually through fines or by cancelling their union memberships. Many unions have strike funds or borrow money so that striking members can be paid something.

Picketing must be lawful and peaceful. Picketers can try to persuade people not to enter or do business with the employer. They cannot use force, block roadways, or commit libel on the placards they carry. Section 423 of the *Criminal Code* prohibits strikers from using violence to intimidate or prevent a person from doing anything that he or she has a lawful right to do in the workplace. In *Harrison v. Carswell*, 1975, the Supreme Court of Canada ruled that employees have the right to strike. However, they may not picket on private property if the owner asks them to leave.

An employer who thinks that a strike is illegal, damaging to property, or dangerous to the public can seek an injunction that requires the workers to return to work or to stop illegal picketing. The government can pass legislation to force employees back to work while the contract is still under dispute. Such legislation may include mandatory negotiations, mediation, or arbitration.

Lockout

lockout an employer's refusal to open the workplace to employees as a labour dispute strategy

The employer's ultimate weapon is a **lockout**. This means that the employer refuses to let employees into the workplace while the contract is in dispute. As with a strike, this action may be used legally only after a given period of time once negotiations have failed. Lockouts are unusual, however. It is usually in the employer's best interest to keep the business operating if employees are willing to work.

Employees of CBC Radio walk the picket line outside the broadcaster's headquarters on Front Street in Toronto. The lockout lasted nearly two months, from mid-August to mid-October 2005. It involved 5500 workers.

Collective Agreement

Once the union and the employer have come to a tentative agreement, the union membership votes on the package. Usually, only a simple majority is required for the package to become the collective agreement (formal contract).

Once the agreement is in force, there still may be many occasions in which one party feels that the other is not fulfilling its obligations. In this case, the two sides meet and try to resolve the matter; if unresolved, it is referred to arbitration.

Independent Contractors and Self-Employment

An **independent contractor** is someone who is hired by a business or person to do a specific job. The independent contractor establishes the work hours, uses his or her own equipment, and is self-directed. To earn money during summer vacation, for example, Hanuf builds landscaped retaining walls for his clients. He creates his own designs and uses his own supplies and equipment. Hanuf is an independent contractor.

Businesses and individuals often hire independent contractors to provide work or services. The contractors may be hired to do anything from cutting grass, to installing a new kitchen or walkway, to editing a textbook, to programming a website. As the word "independent" suggests, they are in business for themselves. They are not in an employer–employee relationship with the clients who hire them. This fact has important implications in tax law, tort law, and labour law.

In the new economy that emerged in the late 1970s and early 1980s, many businesses downsized. Whole departments were dismissed. The businesses later rehired many of these people as independent contractors, not as employees. In this way, businesses do not have to pay Canada Pension Plan, employment insurance, or other employee benefits. This can cut a business's wage and benefit costs by up to 20 percent. Anyone who hires an independent contractor is not liable for injuries suffered by the contractor, or by a contractor's employees, while the contract is being carried out.

There are also advantages to being independent contractors. First of all, they can control their own work and be their own bosses. They can take whatever profits they make, but they must also take any losses they incur.

Employers are increasingly moving away from traditional employer–employee relationships and are adopting more business relationships with independent contractors (or self-employed workers). A student who runs a small business cutting grass all summer is an example of an independent contractor.

Chapter 16 **Dispute Resolution**

Many people who perform services for others, such as doing home improvements, are independent contractors. They use their own tools and are paid directly by the client.

Did You Know?

Alberta has nearly 8000 Aboriginal independent contractors, mainly in arts and culture, accommodation and food, and construction.

Independent contractors often supply their own tools. They are usually responsible for paying for the materials and the costs of any employees who are needed to complete contracts. Those who hire employees take on full employer responsibilities. They should be fully aware of employment law.

Independent contractors are also described as self-employed. The number of self-employed people in Canada has grown dramatically as technology and the economy changed. It has also grown as businesses downsize and try to keep the number of full-time employees to a minimum.

Sometimes there are questions about whether a worker is self-employed or actually employed by the client. According to various court decisions, the worker is an employee (and therefore not self-employed) if the following conditions exist:

- The worker does not own the tools or equipment required for the work.

- The worker does not control decisions about how and when to work.

- The worker has been hired for the long term rather than for specific tasks.

- The worker is not responsible for losses or cannot keep profits.

Review Your Understanding

1. What areas of law can an employee consult to find the terms of employment?
2. List the common law duties that employers and employees have to each other.
3. Describe the advantages and disadvantages of workers' compensation to both employers and employees.
4. What is the goal of a union?
5. Why would a person want to be an independent contractor instead of an employee?

In Contract Law

Negotiating agreements or contracts is a demanding career. This field of work requires men and women who are logical, self-confident, persuasive, and tactful. They should be good speakers who can think "on their feet" and remain focused on the goal in a highly charged situation. Most of these jobs also have the safety or well-being of others in hand, which is a big responsibility.

For more information about the course requirements for a contract law career,

 Go to Nelson Social Studies

An employee relations specialist (right)

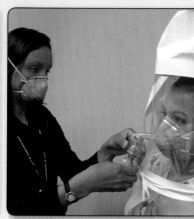

An occupational health and safety specialist

In Focus

Occupational Health and Safety Specialist

Occupational health and safety specialists (inspectors) make sure that working conditions are as safe as possible. They help to promote better health and safety practices to prevent harm to workers and the general public. These specialists work often for the government. They must inspect and enforce safety standards. They impose fines when necessary as outlined by each province's occupational health and safety laws. They may also have to study, redesign, and update working environments. If an accident occurs, they help investigate the causes. They recommend corrective action to make sure that a similar accident does not happen again.

Employee Relations Specialist

Employee relations specialists develop policies and programs on personnel and labour relations. They negotiate collective agreements for employers. They advise employers on interpreting the agreements. They may administer employment equity programs and investigate harassment complaints. They represent employers in hearings called to resolve disputes between employers and employees involving collective agreements. They advise employers and employees on how to properly comply with federal and provincial regulations, policies, and procedures about human-resource related matters.

Paralegal

Paralegals, also known as legal assistants, are qualified through education, training, or work experience to perform certain legal work as authorized by law. Without a paralegal, the work would be performed by an attorney. Paralegals can work for a law firm or their own company. They prepare and proofread legal documents and maintain client files. As they gain experience, they may research court records and judgments handed down in previous cases. In Canada, legislation for paralegals is continually evolving. As such, they must receive training, carry liability insurance, and report to a public body that can investigate complaints.

Career Exploration Activity

As a class, explore career opportunities in contract law. The information you compile can be included with the material you have gathered from the other career profiles to complete your career bulletin-board displays or to use in a law-related career fair.

1. Contact an occupational health and safety specialist, employee relations specialist, or paralegal, and arrange to job-shadow her or him.

2. Interview the person, and outline the role, responsibilities, skills, and education needed for this career. Share your findings with the class.

Should Alcohol and Drug Tests of Employees Be Allowed?

Safety and security are very important matters today. In fact, they are so important that some businesses have imposed mandatory drug and alcohol tests on employees. Airlines, for example, perform drug tests on pilots, on whose skills customers' lives depend. But what about industries where the need is not so obvious?

In Canada, there are no laws forcing employees to undergo mandatory alcohol and drug testing in the workplace. Each employer decides when alcohol and drug testing is necessary to confirm that an employee is physically fit to perform assigned work in a safe manner. As such, the legality of these tests has been considered by the courts on a case-by-case basis.

In the United States, the case law and decisions from the U.S. Supreme Court generally support compulsory drug-and-alcohol-testing programs in both the public and private workplace. This support has even entered the school system. The U.S.

In 1989, the oil Tanker *Exxon Valdez* sank, spilling oil in Prince William Sound in the Gulf of Alaska. The captain was suspected of being intoxicated. See page 417 for more detail.

Supreme Court handed down a 5–4 decision in the *Board of Education of Pottawatomie County v. Lindsay Earls et al.*, 2001. It decided that it was reasonable for students to submit to random drug testing in order to participate in school activities, such as athletics and clubs.

In 1990, the Toronto-Dominion Bank introduced drug testing. New employees had to provide urine samples for analysis. If cocaine, cannabis, heroin, or codeine was detected, employees were sent for counselling or treatment at the bank's expense. Employees who refused to be tested were fired, as were those who tested positive three times.

As more businesses took on these tests, rights became a concern. In 1998, the Federal Court Appeal Division ruled that Toronto-Dominion's drug testing trespassed on employees' human rights. It discriminated against people with drug addictions. As a result, the bank suspended the tests.

In 1995, a board of inquiry appointed under the Ontario *Human Rights Code* reviewed Imperial Oil's drug-testing policies. The policies began after the *Exxon Valdez* disaster. The board decided that the policies breached Martin Entrop's civil liberties. Entrop was demoted in 1991 after disclosing that he had received treatment for alcoholism in 1984. He stated that he had not had a drink in seven years. In its decision, the board ruled that alcoholism is a disease. As a disability, it is a prohibited ground of discrimination. Entrop was awarded $21 000 for mental anguish and was given his job back. However, he had to agree to undergo psychological treatment and provide breath samples whenever the company wanted them.

Canadian case law suggests that it may be reasonable for employers to subject employees to mandatory testing as a condition of employment in safety-sensitive jobs.

The courts have defined such jobs as ones in which incapacity from drug or alcohol impairment may result in injury to the employee, others, or the environment. To use the tests, employers must demonstrate a legitimate safety concern, or they must demonstrate a reasonable and probable belief that an employee is impaired by or dependent on alcohol or drugs. Employees can challenge the testing as being unreasonable, unnecessary, discriminatory, or a violation of human rights legislation.

On One Side

The Toronto-Dominion Bank argued that employees handle huge amounts of money. Those who abuse drugs would be putting customers' money at risk. The bank also held that the *Charter of Rights and Freedoms* and human rights codes were not meant to protect illegal drug users. Mandatory drug testing helps to maintain values of honesty and trust, which are vital to banking.

Imperial Oil developed its drug-testing policy after the 1989 sinking of the oil tanker *Exxon Valdez*. The resulting oil spill was an environmental disaster. The captain, who had struggled with alcoholism, was suspected of being intoxicated. He was later acquitted of any wrongdoing. The company still believed that it was in its best interests to develop a testing policy for its employees to ensure the health and safety of the general public.

On the Other Side

Alan Borovoy of the Canadian Civil Liberties Association has argued that mandatory employee drug testing should be outlawed: "Such tests are a needless invasion of privacy that will tell you a lot about a person's lifestyle but virtually nothing about an employee's ability to do the job."

Borovoy has called drug tests degrading. However, he and other critics accept breath tests for employees. These tests measure only one thing: the level of alcohol impairment, which affects the employee's ability to do the job.

The Bottom Line

These cases reflect how human rights commissions and the courts try to balance society's need for safety and security with an individual's right to privacy. Some people believe businesses must be able to test employees to create a safe and secure environment for everyone. Besides, if people do not agree with the conditions of employment, they can work elsewhere. They have that choice.

Others agree with the Canadian Human Rights Tribunal that employers should not be the enforcers of criminal law. Critics concerned about civil liberties worry that employers will not stop with urine tests. Would blood tests be next? Gene tests? Investigations of medical records and family histories? Electronic monitoring?

What Do You Think?

1. Some high schools use breath tests at school dances. Students who refuse to be tested cannot enter, and parents/guardians are notified if their children are impaired. Are you in favour of this policy, or is it an invasion of individual rights? Explain.

2. Describe the main arguments for and against mandatory drug testing of employees. Which side do you most agree with and why?

3. For the following occupations, decide whether mandatory drug testing should be a condition of employment, and provide a brief explanation for your decision:
   - **a)** teacher
   - **b)** airline pilot
   - **c)** police officer
   - **d)** pharmacist
   - **e)** bank teller
   - **f)** receptionist
   - **g)** school-bus driver

Chapter Review

Chapter Highlights

- Today, business is more global and complex. As a result, consumer protection laws are becoming more important.
- Federal and provincial legislation protects consumers against unfair, harmful, or deceptive business practices.
- As Canadians do more business over the Internet, protecting personal information is a necessity.
- Deceptive marketing involves unfair business practices and fraud. Telemarketing schemes to defraud people are commonly called scams.
- The *Canadian Human Rights Act* and provincial and territorial human rights acts and codes apply to accommodation rentals.
- A lease should outline the rights and duties of the landlord and the tenant as set out in the province's or territory's residential tenancy legislation.
- The landlord and tenant must look to the common law, the statute law, and the lease for conditions that apply to their relationship.
- The landlord or tenant should give a notice of termination if he or she wishes to end the tenancy before the end of the tenancy agreement.
- Common law, statute law, and the employment contract govern the employer–employee relationship.
- Employment legislation sets standards for minimum wages, work hours, overtime and vacation pay, leaves of absence, and rules for termination and dismissal.
- The prohibited grounds for discrimination listed in human rights legislation apply to the workplace.
- In collective bargaining, a union negotiates with an employer to get the best contract for all its members.

Check Your Knowledge

1. Outline actions that would be considered offences under the *Competition Act*, and provide an example that is not in the text to illustrate each type of offence.
2. Identify some of the conditions that a tenant should check into when entering a lease.
3. Summarize the rights and responsibilities of both a landlord and tenant.
4. Identify and briefly explain the various types of laws that affect the employer–employee relationship.
5. When hiring an employee, what issues should an employer be aware of concerning discrimination?

Apply Your Learning

6. A door-to-door seller, Kirk, tried to persuade a couple to buy some aluminum siding for their home. The home had been newly painted and was in good repair. When the couple said that they did not need any siding, Kirk told them he had a great deal for them. The couple listened to the deal and then signed the contract. A day later, they realized that they really did not want the siding.

   a) What can the couple do, if anything, about getting out of the contract they signed?

   b) How should the couple go about communicating their intention to end the contract? How long do they have to change their minds?

7. A newly married couple, Albert and Sophia, rented an apartment in downtown Vancouver. The landlord had advertised the apartment in the newspaper as having air conditioning with an indoor swimming pool and sauna facility. These items were not, however, mentioned in the lease that they signed. When the couple moved in, the landlord failed to supply air conditioning for one month during the summer, and the swimming pool and sauna were not

usable for nearly five months. The couple complained to the landlord but were not satisfied with his response. They took their complaint to the rental housing tribunal to resolve the dispute. Should the tribunal grant the couple any sort of compensation in this matter? If so, what compensation should be given?

Communicate Your Understanding

8. You have been hired by a consumer protection agency to produce a pamphlet that will alert the public to the dangers of telemarketing fraud. Contact your local Better Business Bureau or use the Internet and other media to research the following for your pamphlet:

   a) some examples of deceptive telemarketing scams

   b) some signs that you might be the potential target of this fraud

   c) how consumers can protect themselves

9. Use the Internet to access the laws that apply to landlords and tenants in your province or territory. Prepare a report for one of your classmates, assuming that he or she will be renting an apartment in the future. Indicate the specifics for each of the following:

   a) the time period that the landlord has to deliver a copy of the lease to the tenant

   b) the time period that the landlord must give the tenant before taking action when the rent is not paid

   c) who is responsible for repairs and maintenance

   d) what a security deposit can be used for, and the amount of interest that must be paid on it

   e) the title of the office in the province or territory to whom complaints can be addressed

   f) the length of notice that must be given to terminate each type of tenancy

10. Write a letter to your landlord indicating that you want to end your tenancy on April 30, the end of your one-year lease. Include all the information that you think is essential.

11. In 1946, Supreme Court of Canada Justice Ivan Rand delivered a landmark arbitration decision. It followed a 100-day strike by Ford autoworkers. His decision was called the "Rand Formula." It requires an employer to deduct a portion of the salaries of all employees within a bargaining unit to go to the union as union dues. Research this historic labour case. Present a short summary of the case, the decision, and an explanation as to why this case was so critical for labour unions. Some have argued that the "Rand Formula" was the greatest protection Canadian workers were ever given. Others say it violates a worker's freedom of association under the Charter. What do you think? Explain.

Develop Your Thinking

12. Landlords have a large investment in their properties, but these are also tenants' homes. Some say the laws favour tenants too much. Others say the laws favour landlords too much. Imagine that you are a tenant. What tenancy laws would you want to change if you could to protect yourself? Why would you change them? Now imagine that you are a landlord. What tenancy laws would you want to change if you could to protect your investment? Why would you change them?

13. Monitoring of computers in the workplace is increasing. Software can record what is on an employee's monitor every few seconds and keep track of all e-mails, websites visited, and chat-room conversations.

    a) Should employers be allowed to monitor employees' computers at work? Why or why not?

    b) Imagine you are an employer. Develop guidelines for computer use by your employees. Include penalties that will be imposed for workers who violate the guidelines.

Constitution Act, 1982
Schedule B
Part I

CANADIAN CHARTER OF RIGHTS AND FREEDOMS

Whereas Canada is founded upon principles that recognize the supremacy of God and the rule of law:

Guarantee of Rights and Freedoms

Rights and Freedoms in Canada

1. The *Canadian Charter of Rights and Freedoms* guarantees the rights and freedoms set out in it subject only to such reasonable limits prescribed by law as can be demonstrably justified in a free and democratic society.

Fundamental freedoms

Fundamental Freedoms

2. Everyone has the following fundamental freedoms:

(a) freedom of conscience and religion;

(b) freedom of thought, belief, opinion and expression, including freedom of the press and other media of communication;

(c) freedom of peaceful assembly; and

(d) freedom of association.

Democratic Rights

Democratic Rights of Citizens

3. Every citizen of Canada has the right to vote in an election of members of the House of Commons or of a legislative assembly and to be qualified for membership therein.

Maximum Duration of Legislative Bodies

4. (1) No House of Commons and no legislative assembly shall continue for longer than five years from the date fixed for the return of the writs at a general election of its members.

Continuation in Special Circumstances

(2) In time of real or apprehended war, invasion or insurrection, a House of Commons may be continued by Parliament and a legislative assembly may be continued by the legislature beyond five years if such continuation is not opposed by the votes of more than one-third of the members of the House of Commons or the legislative assembly, as the case may be.

Annual Sitting of Legislative Bodies

5. There shall be a sitting of Parliament and of each legislature at least once every twelve months.

Mobility Rights

Mobility of Citizens

6. (1) Every citizen of Canada has the right to enter, remain in and leave Canada.

Rights to Move and Gain Livelihood

(2) Every citizen of Canada and every person who has the status of a permanent resident of Canada has the right

(a) to move and take up residence in any province; and

(b) to pursue the gaining of a livelihood in any province.

Limitation

(3) The rights specified in subsection (2) are subject to

(a) any laws or practices of general application in force in a province other than those that discriminate among persons primarily on the basis of province of present or previous residence; and

(b) any laws providing for reasonable residency requirements as a qualification for the receipt of publicly provided social services.

Affirmative Action Programs

(4) Subsections (2) and (3) do not preclude any law, program or activity that has as its object the amelioration in a province of conditions of individuals in that province who are socially or economically disadvantaged if the rate of employment in that province is below the rate of employment in Canada.

Legal Rights

Life, Liberty and Security of Person

7. Everyone has the right to life, liberty and security of the person and the right not to be deprived thereof except in accordance with the principles of fundamental justice.

Search or Seizure

8. Everyone has the right to be secure against unreasonable search or seizure.

Detention or Imprisonment

9. Everyone has the right not to be arbitrarily detained or imprisoned.

Arrest or Detention

10. Everyone has the right on arrest or detention

(a) to be informed promptly of the reasons therefor;

(b) to retain and instruct counsel without delay and to be informed of that right; and

(c) to have the validity of the detention determined by way of habeas corpus and to be released if the detention is not lawful.

Proceedings in Criminal and Penal Matters

11. Any person charged with an offence has the right

(a) to be informed without unreasonable delay of the specific offence;

(b) to be tried within a reasonable time;

(c) not to be compelled to be a witness in proceedings against that person in respect of the offence;

(d) to be presumed innocent until proven guilty according to law in a fair and public hearing by an independent and impartial tribunal;

(e) not to be denied reasonable bail without just cause;

(f) except in the case of an offence under military law tried before a military tribunal, to the benefit of trial by jury where the maximum punishment for the offence is imprisonment for five years or a more severe punishment;

(g) not to be found guilty on account of any act or omission unless, at the time of the act or omission, it constituted an offence under Canadian or international law or was criminal according to the general principles of law recognized by the community of nations;

(h) if finally acquitted of the offence, not to be tried for it again and, if finally found guilty and punished for the offence, not to be tried or punished for it again; and

(i) if found guilty of the offence and if the punishment for the offence has been varied between the time of commission and the time of sentencing, to the benefit of the lesser punishment.

Treatment or Punishment

12. Everyone has the right not to be subjected to any cruel and unusual treatment or punishment.

Self-Crimination

13. A witness who testifies in any proceedings has the right not to have any incriminating evidence so given used to incriminate that witness in any other proceedings, except in a prosecution for perjury or for the giving of contradictory evidence.

Interpreter

14. A party or witness in any proceedings who does not understand or speak the language in which the proceedings are conducted or who is deaf has the right to the assistance of an interpreter.

Equality Rights

Equality Before and Under Law and Equal Protection and Benefit of Law

15. (1) Every individual is equal before and under the law and has the right to the equal protection and equal benefit of the law without discrimination and, in particular, without discrimination based on race, national or ethnic origin, colour, religion, sex, age or mental or physical disability.

Affirmative Action Programs

(2) Subsection (1) does not preclude any law, program or activity that has as its object the amelioration of conditions of disadvantaged individuals or groups including those that are disadvantaged because of race, national or ethnic origin, colour, religion, sex, age or mental or physical disability.

Official Languages of Canada

Official Languages of Canada

16. (1) English and French are the official languages of Canada and have equality of status and equal rights and privileges as to their use in all institutions of the Parliament and government of Canada.

Official Languages of New Brunswick

(2) English and French are the official languages of New Brunswick and have equality of status and equal rights and privileges as to their use in all institutions of the legislature and government of New Brunswick.

Advancement of Status and Use

(3) Nothing in this Charter limits the authority of Parliament or a legislature to advance the equality of status or use of English and French.

Proceedings of Parliament

17. (1) Everyone has the right to use English or French in any debates and other proceedings of Parliament.

Canadian Charter of Rights and Freedoms **599**

Proceedings of New Brunswick Legislature

(2) Everyone has the right to use English or French in any debates and other proceedings of the legislature of New Brunswick.

Parliamentary Statutes and Records

18. (1) The statutes, records and journals of Parliament shall be printed and published in English and French and both language versions are equally authoritative.

New Brunswick Statutes and Records

(2) The statutes, records and journals of the legislature of New Brunswick shall be printed and published in English and French and both language versions are equally authoritative.

Proceedings in Courts Established by Parliament

19. (1) Either English or French may be used by any person in, or in any pleading in or process issuing from, any court established by Parliament.

Proceedings in New Brunswick Courts

(2) Either English or French may be used by any person in, or in any pleading in or process issuing from, any court of New Brunswick.

Communications by Public with Federal Institutions

20. (1) Any member of the public in Canada has the right to communicate with, and to receive available services from, any head or central office of an institution of the Parliament or government of Canada in English or French, and has the same right with respect to any other office of any such institution where

(a) there is a significant demand for communications with and services from that office in such language; or

(b) due to the nature of the office, it is reasonable that communications with and services from that office be available in both English and French.

Communications by Public with New Brunswick Institutions

(2) Any member of the public in New Brunswick has the right to communicate with, and to receive available services from, any office of an institution of the legislature or government of New Brunswick in English or French.

Continuation of Existing Consitutional Provisions

21. Nothing in sections 16 to 20 abrogates or derogates from any right, privilege or obligation with respect to the English or French languages, or either of them, that exists or is continued by virtue of any other provision of the Constitution of Canada.

22. Nothing in sections 16 to 20 abrogates or derogates from any legal or customary right or privilege acquired or enjoyed either before or after the coming into force of this Charter with respect to any language that is not English or French.

Rights and Privileges Preserved

Minority Language Educational Rights

23. (1) Citizens of Canada

Language of Instruction

(a) whose first language learned and still understood is that of the English or French linguistic minority population of the province in which they reside, or

(b) who have received their primary school instruction in Canada in English or French and reside in a province where the language in which they received that instruction is the language of the English or French linguistic minority population of the province, have the right to have their children receive primary and secondary school instruction in that language in that province.

(2) Citizens of Canada of whom any child has received or is receiving primary or secondary school instruction in English or French in Canada, have the right to have all their children receive primary and secondary school instruction in the same language.

Continuity of Language Instruction

(3) The right of citizens of Canada under subsections (1) and (2) to have their children receive primary and secondary school instruction in the language of the English or French linguistic minority population of a province

Application Where Numbers Warrant

(a) applies wherever in the province the number of children of citizens who have such a right is sufficient to warrant the provision to them out of public funds of minority language instruction; and

(b) includes, where the number of those children so warrants, the right to have them receive that instruction in minority language educational facilities provided out of public funds.

Enforcement

Enforcement of Guaranteed Rights and Freedoms

24. (1) Anyone whose rights or freedoms, as guaranteed by this Charter, have been infringed or denied may apply to a court of competent jurisdiction to obtain such remedy as the court considers appropriate and just in the circumstances.

Exclusion of Evidence Bringing Administration of Justice into Disrepute

(2) Where, in proceedings under subsection (1), a court concludes that evidence was obtained in a manner that infringed or denied any rights or freedoms guaranteed by this Charter, the evidence shall be excluded if it is established that, having regard to all the circumstances, the admission of it in the proceedings would bring the administration of justice into disrepute.

General

Aboriginal Rights and Freedoms not Affected by Charter

25. The guarantee in this Charter of certain rights and freedoms shall not be construed so as to abrogate or derogate from any aboriginal treaty or other rights or freedoms that pertain to the aboriginal peoples of Canada including

(a) any rights or freedoms that have been recognized by the Royal Proclamation of October 7, 1763; and

(b) any rights or freedoms that now exist by way of land claims agreements or may be so acquired.

Other Rights and Freedoms not Affected by Charter

26. The guarantee in this Charter of certain rights and freedoms shall not be construed as denying the existence of any other rights or freedoms that exist in Canada.

Multicultural Heritage

27. This Charter shall be interpreted in a manner consistent with the preservation and enhancement of the multicultural heritage of Canadians.

Rights Guaranteed Equally to Both Sexes

28. Notwithstanding anything in this Charter, the rights and freedoms referred to in it are guaranteed equally to male and female persons.

Rights Respecting Certain Schools Preserved

29. Nothing in this Charter abrogates or derogates from any rights or privileges guaranteed by or under the Constitution of Canada in respect of denominational, separate or dissentient schools.

Application to Territories and Territorial Authorities

30. A reference in this Charter to a province or to the legislative assembly or legislature of a province shall be deemed to include a reference to the Yukon Territory and the Northwest Territories, or to the appropriate legislative authority thereof, as the case may be.

31. Nothing in this Charter extends the legislative powers of any body or authority.

Legislative Powers not Extended

Application of Charter

32. (1) This Charter applies

(a) to the Parliament and government of Canada in respect of all matters within the authority of Parliament including all matters relating to the Yukon Territory and Northwest Territories; and

(b) to the legislature and government of each province in respect of all matters within the authority of the legislature of each province.

Application of Charter

(2) Notwithstanding subsection (1), section 15 shall not have effect until three years after this section comes into force.

Exception

33. (1) Parliament or the legislature of a province may expressly declare in an Act of Parliament or of the legislature, as the case may be, that the Act or a provision thereof shall operate notwithstanding a provision included in section 2 or sections 7 to 15 of this Charter.

Exception Where Express Declaration

(2) An Act or a provision of an Act in respect of which a declaration made under this section is in effect shall have such operation as it would have but for the provision of this Charter referred to in the declaration.

Operation of Exception

(3) A declaration made under subsection (1) shall cease to have effect five years after it comes into force or on such earlier date as may be specified in the declaration.

Five Year Limitation

(4) Parliament or a legislature of a province may re-enact a declaration made under subsection (1).

Re-enactment

(5) Subsection (3) applies in respect of a re-enactment made under subsection (4).

Five Year Limitation

Citation

34. This Part may be cited as the *Canadian Charter of Rights and Freedoms.*

Citation

Appendix B: Citation References

The source of most of the cases that appear in *All About Law*, 6th edition, is the electronic case reporting website, CanLII, the Canadian Legal Information Institute, which includes complete court judgments. A few of the cases were unavailable on the CanLII site, and selected case law reports were used instead. The information below provides the full names of the sources listed in abbreviated form in **Appendix C: Table of Cases.**

Neutral Cites (Electronic)

ABCA	Alberta Court of Appeal
ABPC	Alberta Provincial Court
ABQB	Alberta Court of Queen's Bench
BCCA	British Columbia Court of Appeal
BCPC	British Columbia Provincial Court
BCSC	British Columbia Supreme Court
CHRT	Canadian Human Rights Tribunal
FC	Federal Court of Canada
FCA	Federal Court of Appeal
MBCA	Manitoba Court of Appeal
NBCA	New Brunswick Court of Appeal
NFCA	Newfoundland and Labrador Court of Appeal
NLPC	Newfoundland and Labrador Provincial Court
NSSC	Nova Scotia Supreme Court
ONCA	Ontario Court of Appeal
ONCJ	Ontario Court of Justice
ONSC	Ontario Superior Court of Justice
ONSCDC	Ontario Superior Court of Justice (Divisional Court)
PESCTD	Prince Edward Island Supreme Court, Trial Division
SCC	Supreme Court of Canada
YKTC	Yukon Territorial Court

Case Law Reports

C.L.R.	*Construction Law Reports*
Man. R.	*Manitoba Reports*
R.F.L.	*Reports of Family Law*
Sask. R.	*Saskatchewan Reports*

Internet Citations

These charts show the elements of a citation for a neutral online citation and for a citation in a case-reporting series of books. In this text, most cases use a neutral citation followed by a reference to the Nelson Social Studies website.

NEUTRAL (Online) CITATION

R.	v.	Ferguson,	2008	SCC	6	CanLII
Regina or *Rex* (Latin for "queen" or "king") represents society	*versus* (Latin for "against")	defendant (accused)	year of decision	Supreme Court of Canada; the court hearing the case	number assigned by the court	Canadian Legal Information Institute, which provides access to full case decisions on the Internet

Cowles	v.	Balac,	2006	CanLII	34916	(ON C.A.)
plaintiff (person suing)	*versus* (Latin for "against")	defendant (person being sued)	year of decision	Canadian Legal Information Institute, which provides access to full case decisions on the Internet	number assigned by the legal information service	Ontario Court of Appeal

CASE-REPORTING SERIES CITATION

R.	v.	Bates	(2000),	35	C.R.	(5th)	327	(Ont. C.A.)
Regina or *Rex* (Latin for "queen" or "king") represents society	*versus* (Latin for "against")	defendant (accused)	year of decision	volume number	name of reporter where case is reported (e.g., *Criminal Reports*)	series	page number	jurisdiction (federal, province, or territory) and court (e.g., Ontario Court of Appeal)

Langille et al.	v.	McGrath	(2000),	233	N.B.R.	(2d)	29	(N.B.Q.B.)
plaintiff and others (Latin *et alia* for "and others")	*versus* (Latin for "against")	defendant	year of decision	volume number	name of reporter where case is reported (e.g., *New Brunswick Reports*)	series	page number	jurisdiction (federal, province, or territory) and court (e.g., New Brunswick Court of Queen's Bench)

Appendix C: Table of Cases

The following is an alphabetical list of all cases appearing in All About Law, 6th Edition.
At the end of each entry, boldfaced numbers refer to page numbers in this book. For example,
A.A. v. B.B. is located on page 436.

A.A. v. B.B., 2007 ONCA 2 (CanLII) **436**

Arsenault-Cameron v. Prince Edward Island, 2000 SCC 1 (CanLII) **62**

Arthur v. Wechlin, 2000 BCSC 948 (CanLII) **414**

British Columbia (Public Service Employee Relation Commission) v. BCGSEU, 1999 CanLII 652 (S.C.C.) **94**

Canada (Attorney General) v. JTI-Macdonald Corp., 2007 SCC 30 (CanLII) **44**

Canada (Attorney General) v. Khawaja (F.C.), 2007 FC 490 (CanLII) **243**

Canadian Foundation for Children, Youth and the Law v. Canada (Attorney General), 2004 SCC 4 (CanLII) **224**

Carlill v. Carbolic Smoke Ball Company [1893] 1 Q.B. 256 England, Court of Appeal **522**

Champion v. Champion, 2008 CanLII 200 (ON S.C.) **462**

Chan v. Chadha Construction et al., 2000 BCCA 198 (CanLII) **540**

Charkaoui v. Canada (Citizenship and Immigration), 2007 SCC 9 (CanLII) **55**

Childs v. Desormeaux, 2006 SCC 18 (CanLII) **410**

Cole v. Bell Canada, 2007 CHRT 7 (CanLII) **578**

Council of Canadians with Disabilities v. VIA Rail Canada Inc., 2007 SCC 15 (CanLII) **98**

Cowles v. Balac, 2006 CanLII 34916 (ON C.A.) **401**

Deacon v. Canada (Attorney General), 2006 FCA 265 (CanLII) **308**

F.N. (Re), 2000 SCC 35 (CanLII) **343**

Feng v. Yuen (Estate), 2004 CanLII 35080 (ON C.A.) **441**

Ferguson v. Birchmount Boarding Kennels Ltd., 2006 CanLII 2049 (ON S.C.D.C.) **363**

Francis v. Baker, 1999 CanLII 659 (S.C.C.) **505**

Gordon v. Goertz, 1996 CanLII 191 (S.C.C.) **461**

Grant v. Dempsey, 2001 NSSC 20 (CanLII) **18**

Guerin v. The Queen, 1984 CanLII 25 (S.C.C.) **82**

Haley v. Haley, 2008 CanLII 2607 (ON S.C.) **501**

Hartwick v. Stoneham, 2000 CanLII 22522 (ON S.C.) **460**

Honda Canada Inc. v. Keays, 2008 SCC 39 (CanLII) **583**

Kitchen Craft Connection v. Dennis, (1999) 50 C.L.R. (2d) 239 Ontario Superior Court of Justice **541**

Lavigne v. Ontario Public Service Employees Union, 1991 CanLII 68 (S.C.C.) **587**

Leonard v. Dunn, 2006 CanLII 33419 (ON S.C.) **420**

Leskun v. Leskun, 2006 SCC 25 (CanLII) **492**

Levine v. McGrath, 2000 CanLII 22447 (ON S.C.) **455**

M. v. H., 1999 CanLII 686 (S.C.C.) **488**

Maljkovich v. Canada, 2005 FC 1398 (CanLII) **290**

Manis v. Manis, 2001 CanLII 3851 (ON C.A.) **504**

Maritime Travel Inc. v. Go Travel Direct Inc., 2008 NSSC 163 (CanLII) **556**

Martinig v. Powell River (Corp. of the District of), 2002 BCSC 24 (CanLII) **364**

Mayer v. Big White Ski Resort Ltd., 1998 CanLII 5114 (BC C.A.) **546**

McIntyre v. Grigg, 2006 CanLII 37326 (ON C.A.) **376**

Michaluk v. Rolling River School Division No. 3 et al, 2001 MBCA 45 (CanLII) **393**

Miglin v. Miglin, 2003 SCC 24 (CanLII) **496**

Moge v. Moge, 1992 CanLII 25 (S.C.C.)

Multani v. Commission scolaire Marguerite-Bourgeoys, 2006 SCC 6 (CanLII) **41**

Murdoch v. Murdoch, 1973 CanLII 193 (S.C.C.) **478**

Mustapha v. Culligan of Canada Ltd., 2008 SCC 27 (CanLII) **397**

N.A.J. v. R., 2003 PESCTD 60 (CanLII) **333**

Newman et al v. Halstead et al, 2006 BCSC 65 (CanLII) **425**

Noseworthy v. Noseworthy, 2008 CanLII 32836 (ON S.C.) **502**

Nova Scotia (Attorney General) v. Walsh, 2002 SCC 83 (CanLII) **487**

Pettkus v. Becker, 1980 CanLII 22 (S.C.C.) **486**

Pickett v. Love, (1982) 20 Sask. R. 115 Saskatchewan, Court of Queen's Bench **526**

R. v. A. M., 2008 SCC 19 (CanLII) **50, 339**

R. v. Asante-Mensah, 2003 SCC 38 (CanLII) **149**

R. v. Askov, 1990 CanLII 45 (S.C.C.) **186**

R. v. B.W.P.; R. v. B.V.N., 2006 SCC 27 (CanLII) **294**

R. v. Burke, 2002 SCC 55 (CanLII) **210**

R. v. C.N., 2006 CanLII 32902 (ON C.A.) **346**

R. v. Clayton, 2007 SCC 32 (CanLII) **156**

R. v. Collins and French, 2006 BCSC 1531 (CanLII) **127**

R. v. D.B., 2008 SCC 25 (CanLII) **344**

R. v. D.J.B., 2007 CanLII 5879 (NL P.C.) **350**

R. v. Daviault, 1994 CanLII 61 (S.C.C.) **271**

R. v. Decker, 2002 NFCA 9 (CanLII) **254**

R. v. Dillon, 2006 CanLII 10745 (ON S.C.) **161**

R. v. Dyck, 2008 ONCA 309 (CanLII) **228**

R. v. F.M., 2008 BCCA 111 (CanLII) **330**

R. v. Feeney, 1997 CanLII 342 (S.C.C.) **171**

R. v. Ferguson, 2008 SCC 6 (CanLII) **292**

R. v. Foidart, 2005 MBCA 104 (CanLII) **233**

R. v. Gibson, 2008 SCC 16 (CanLII) **273**

R. v. Gladue, 1999 CanLII 679 (S.C.C.) **297**

R. v. Goodine, 1993 CanLII 5379 (NB C.A.) **131**

R. v. Graveline, 2006 SCC 16 (CanLII) **275**

R. v. Greyeyes, 1997 CanLII 313 (S.C.C.) **248**

R. v. Hall, 2002 SCC 64 (CanLII) **166**

R. v. Harrison, 2008 ONCA 85 (CanLII) **151**

R. v. Humaid, 2006 CanLII 12287 (ON C.A.) **283**

R. v. J.Y., 2007 ABPC 133 (CanLII) **337**

R. v. K.(Cr.) and K.(Ct.), 2006 ONCJ 283 (CanLII) **336**

R. v. Keller, 1998 ABCA 357 (CanLII) **280**

R. v. Kerr, 2004 SCC 44 (CanLII) **18**

R. v. Kobelka, 2007 ABPC 112 (CanLII) **293**

R. v. Krieger, 2006 SCC 47 (CanLII) **209**

R. v. L.B., 2007 ONCA 596 (CanLII) **340**

R. v. Latimer, 2001 SCC 1 (CanLII) **223**

R. v. Law, 2007 ABCA 203 (CanLII) **301**

R. v. Lindsay, 2005 CanLII 24240 (ON S.C.) **132**

R. v. Luedecke, 2008 ONCA 716 (CanLII) **266**

R. v. MacGillivray, 1995 CanLII 139 (S.C.C.) **252**

R. v. Mann, 2004 SCC 52 (CanLII) **51**

R. v. Maracle, 2006 CanLII 4152 (ON C.A.) **264**

R. v. Millar, 1994 CanLII 7558 (ON S.C.) **298**

R. v. Nette, 2001 SCC 78 (CanLII) **220**

R. v. Oakes, 1986 CanLII 46 (S.C.C.) **39**

R. v. Oickle, 2000 SCC 38 (CanLII) **205**

R. v. Paice, 2005 SCC 22 (CanLII) **277**

R. v. Parker, 2000 CanLII 5762 (ON C.A.) **246**

R. v. Parks, 1992 CanLII 78 (S.C.C.) **124**

R. v. Perrier, 2004 SCC 56 (CanLII) **202**

R. v. Proulx, 2000 SCC 5 (CanLII) **300**

R. v. Purity One Inc. (Jeffrey Clapper), 2005 **561**

R. v. R. (B.V.), 2007 ONCJ 31 (CanLII) **337**

R. v. Singh, 2007 SCC 48 (CanLII) **163**

R. v. Shanker, 2007 ONCA 280 (CanLII) **159**

R. v. Smith, 2005 CanLII 23805 (ON C.A.) **242**

R. v. Smith, 2007 ONCJ 47 (CanLII) **277**

R. v. Spence, 2005 SCC 71 (CanLII) **191**

R. v. Spencer, 2007 SCC 11 (CanLII) **206**

R. v. Stucky, 2006 CanLII 41523 (ON S.C.) **559**

R. v. Swan, 2008 CanLII 10389 (ON S.C.) **466**

R. v. Teerhuis-Moar, 2007 MBCA 120 (CanLII) **192**

R. v. Tessling, 2004 SCC 67 (CanLII) **52**

R. v. Ungar, 2002, O.J. No. 2915 (Ont. C.J.) **279**

R. v. White, 1999 CanLII 689 (S.C.C.) **200**

R. v. Williams, 2003 SCC 41 (CanLII) **128**

Raymond v. Byrapaneni, 2001 NBCA 8 (CanLII) **572**

Re Al-Smadi, (1994) 90 Man. R. (2d) 304 **445**

Re Lin, (1992) 44 R.F.L. (3d) 60 **443**

Resurfice Corp. v. Hanke, 2007 SCC 7 (CanLII) **394**

Rodriguez v. British Columbia (Attorney General), 1993 CanLII 75 (S.C.C.) **49**

Rudman v. Hollander, 2005 BCSC 1342 (CanLII) **359**

Sauvé v. Canada (Chief Electoral Officer), 2002 SCC 68 (CanLII) **47**

Shields v. Shields, 2008 ABCA 213 (CanLII) **494**

Siadat v. Ontario College of Teachers, 2007 CanLII 253 (ON S.C.D.C.) **101**

Snushall v. Fulsang, 2005 CanLII 34561 (ON C.A.) **404**

St. Prix-Alexander v. Home Depot of Canada Inc., 2008 CanLII 115 (ON S.C.) **407**

Thomas v. Hamilton (City), Board of Education, 1994 CanLII 739 (ON C.A.) **369**

Tolea v. Ialungo, 2008 BCSC 395 (CanLII) **570**

Torfehnejad v. Salimi, 2006 CanLII 38882 (ON S.C.) **449**

Tribe v. Farrell, 2006 BCCA 38 (CanLII) **532**

Van de Perre v. Edwards, 2001 SCC 60 (CanLII) **457**

Walford v. Jacuzzi Canada Inc., 2007 ONCA 729 (CanLII) **399**

Ward v. British Columbia, 2009 BCCA 23 (CanLII) **415**

Willoughby v. Gallant, 2000 PESCTD 62 (CanLII) **530**

Winko v. British Columbia (Forensic Psychiatric Institute), 1999 CanLII 694 (S.C.C.) **268**

Wolf, Ward and Luck v. Advance Fur Dressers Ltd. et al., 2005 BCSC 1097 (CanLII) **375**

Young v. Bella, 2006 SCC 3 (CanLII) **374**

Yukon Housing Corp. v. Kirsten Atkins, 2008 YKTC 54 (CanLII) **573**

Glossary

A

abduction the illegal, forced removal of an unmarried person under the age of 16 from the person who has lawful care of the child (e.g., the custodial parent)

abetting encouraging, inciting, or urging another person to commit a crime

Aboriginal rights the guarantee that the rights and freedoms entrenched in the *Charter of Rights and Freedoms* cannot interfere with any Aboriginal, treaty, or other rights of the Aboriginal peoples of Canada

absolute discharge a sentence in which, while the offender is found guilty, no conviction is recorded and the offender is free to go without conditions

absolute privilege a defence against defamation for statements made in legislative and judicial proceedings

absolute sale a sale where ownership passes to the buyer when the contract is fulfilled

accelerated review an early consideration (review) by the parole board of an offender's eligibility (e.g., once one-third of the sentence is served); allowed only under certain conditions

access in family law, the right of the non-custodial parent to visit the child(ren) when the parents separate; in human rights law, a term used to describe the ability to gain entry into a facility or service

accessory after the fact someone who, after a crime is committed and knowing that it was committed, receives, comforts, or helps the criminal so that he or she can escape

accommodation removing a barrier or changing a policy so discrimination does not occur

accused the person charged with an offence; the defendant in a criminal trial

actus reus a Latin phrase meaning "a wrongful deed"; the physical act of a crime, which together with mens rea, makes a person criminally liable

adjournment a postponement of court business

administrative law outlines the relationship between citizens and government boards and agencies

adultery voluntary sexual intercourse by a married person with someone other than his or her spouse

adversarial system the system of law in which two opposing sides each present their case in court

age of consent the age at which criminal law recognizes the legal capacity of a young person to consent to sexual activity

aggravated assault the third, most serious of three levels of assault in criminal law; assault that wounds, maims, disfigures, or endangers the life of the victim

aggravated damages compensation payable in a civil action that awards money to a plaintiff for the defendant's outrageous conduct; somewhat similar to punitive damages

aggravating circumstances factors that increase the responsibility of the offender, and that may increase the penalty

aiding assisting someone to commit a criminal offence. Usually, the person is not present when the crime is committed, but has knowledge of the crime and has helped through advice, actions, or financial support. If enough aid is given, the person's participation in the crime may be upgraded to the charge of conspiracy.

alibi a defence that the accused was in a different place, not at the scene of the crime, when it took place

allurement something that is inviting or enticing to children and could result in their harm; for example, a swimming pool or bells on an ice cream truck

alternative dispute resolution (ADR) a collective term for processes (e.g., negotiation, mediation, arbitration) designed to settle or resolve conflicts without formal trials

alternative measures programs programs under the *Young Offenders Act* for first-time, non-violent offending youth

amend to change or alter existing legislation (laws)

amending formula the procedure to change (amend) Canada's Constitution without the involvement of the British Parliament

annulment a court ruling that a relationship was never a marriage

appeal referring a case to a higher court

appearance notice a legal document detailing the criminal offence the accused is charged with, and the date the accused must attend court

appellant the party that requests an appeal in criminal court—either the defence or the Crown

applicant the spouse initiating a divorce action, as opposed to the respondent

arbitration an alternative dispute resolution process in which the arbitrator hears from both sides and makes a final decision; more formal than negotiation and mediation; may be binding arbitration

arraignment the first stage in a criminal trial, in which the court clerk reads the charge to the accused and a plea is entered

arrest to legally detain a person and charge him or her with a criminal offence

arson intentionally or recklessly causing damage to property by fire or explosion

assault in criminal law, the term for the three levels of assault (assault, assault causing bodily harm, aggravated assault); in tort law, the threat of danger or violence (rather than any actual contact, which is battery in tort law)

assault causing bodily harm the second of three levels of assault in criminal law; assault that interferes with the victim's health or comfort in a significant way (not a minor hurt or injury), or assault involving a real, threatened, or imitation weapon

assignment the transfer of a right under a rental contract to another person (e.g., a tenant finds a replacement to assume the lease and gives up the right to repossess the premises)

assimilation the process of being absorbed into the prevailing culture; made similar in customs and views

assisted suicide aiding and abetting someone to commit suicide

attempt an effort or a try; an act done with the intent to commit an offence

Authorization to Possess (ATP) legal authority to possess and produce marijuana for medical purposes

automatism a state of impaired consciousness during which an individual has no control over his or her actions, yet is capable of committing an act (either insane or non-insane automatism)

B

bail hearing a hearing before a judge or justice of the peace to determine whether an accused can be released from jail before trial and with what conditions; supposed to happen within 24 hours of arrest

balance of probabilities the basis on which a judge decides a civil action; based on which party has presented the case with a greater likelihood of fact and truth; compare to proof beyond a reasonable doubt in criminal cases

banns of marriage an announcement of an intended marriage, read in the couple's church

barrier to equality anything that prevents someone from participating fully and equally in society

battered woman syndrome the psychological condition caused by consistent and/or severe domestic violence (both mental and physical)

battery intentional physical contact that is harmful or offensive to the other person; the completion of an assault in tort law

best interests of the child the principle upon which a judge makes a decision regarding custody of and access to children

bigamy the act of being married to two persons at the same time

bill a proposed law; a draft form of an act or statute

blood–alcohol concentration (BAC) a measure of concentration of alcohol in a person's blood; often expressed as milligrams (mg) of alcohol in 100 mL of blood (e.g., "a blood–alcohol concentration of 80" means 80 mg of alcohol in 100 mL of blood; this is currently the legal alcohol limit)

bona fide occupational requirement a legitimate, reasonable necessity (requirement) of a job; a possible defence against unfair discrimination in hiring and other employment situations

bonding insurance that guarantees the honesty of a person who handles money or other valuables

breach of condition failure to perform a major or very important part of a contract, entitling the injured party to treat the contract as ended

breach of contract failure to perform an obligation owed to another party under a contract

breach of warranty failure to perform a minor term of a contract, entitling the injured party to damages, but not allowing that party to terminate the contract

break and enter to enter another's premises without permission by breaking or opening anything that is closed; also called burglary

burden of proof the onus of bringing forth proof (evidence) in order to prove someone's guilt to the court

C

capacity the ability to understand the nature and effect of one's actions, such as entering into marriage; the legal ability to enter a contract

capital punishment the penalty of death for committing a crime

cartel a form of price fixing where multiple businesses agree not to compete against each other

case law recorded written decisions of judges; also known as common law

causation the relationship existing between the defendant's action and the plaintiff's loss that would not have occurred "but for" the defendant's actions; in murder trials, the cause of death

caveat emptor a Latin phrase meaning "let the buyer beware"; a principle in contract law

challenge for cause a formal objection to a prospective juror for reasons such as the juror's knowledge of the case or lack of impartiality

character evidence evidence used to indicate the likelihood of an accused committing or not committing the crime

charge to the jury after the summations in a trial, a judge's instructions to the jury (e.g., review of the facts or of points of law)

child abuse any behaviour that endangers a child's physical, mental, or moral well-being, including physical, sexual, and emotional abuse and neglect

circumstantial evidence information (evidence) that relates only indirectly to the alleged offence

citation a reference to a legal case listing all the relevant information such as the plaintiff and defendant, the year of the decision, and so on

citizen's arrest detainment or arrest of a person by a person other than a police officer

civil law a term for private law governing the relationships between individuals; also a term for the legal system of Québec

civil rights the rights of citizens (e.g., to political and social freedom and equality), which limit the power a government has over its citizens

class action a single legal action brought on behalf of all members of a group with a common interest or grievance

clerical mistake an error caused by a store clerk or employee, typically involving numbers

closed custody detention in a prison under constant guard; the most secure form of custody

closing statement another term for summation

Code of Hammurabi one of the earliest known sets of written laws, recorded by King Hammurabi of Babylon in 1750 BCE

codification the process of assembling a system of laws into one statute or a body of statutes (e.g., the Code of Hammurabi, Canada's *Criminal Code*)

cohabitation the act of living together without being married

cohabitation agreement a domestic contract that outlines the rights and obligations of two unmarried people who are living together in a common law relationship

collective agreement the contract resulting from collective bargaining between a union and an employer

collective bargaining negotiation done by a union on behalf of all its members concerning wages, hours, and other conditions of employment

collective rights the rights of the group, rather than of the individual

colour of right the legal right to a property; anything that shows a person has true ownership of something

common law a system of law based on past legal decisions; also known as case law

common law relationship a close relationship between two people who live together as a married couple but who are not legally married

common mistake an error made by both parties concerning a fundamental fact of a contract

community service order a sentencing option in which the judge demands that the offender do some specific work in the community under supervision

compensation something given to make amends for a loss (e.g., damages to an injured plaintiff); also called restitution; in criminal law, a sentencing objective

Competition Bureau a department of Industry Canada that oversees consumer protection and looks into complaints made under various federal acts

complainant a person who makes an allegation of discrimination

concurrent sentence a penalty (sentence) for crimes in which penalties for two or more offences are served at the same time

conditional discharge a sentence in which, while the offender is found guilty, no conviction is recorded and the offender is free to go, but must meet certain expectations (e.g., probation orders) in order to avoid a criminal record and a new sentence

conditional release a discharge from custody into the community where the offender has to meet certain expectations (conditions) and is supervised to some extent

conditional sentence a penalty (sentence) for a crime of a term of less than two years that is served in the community if the offender meets certain expectations

confession a statement by the accused in which he or she admits to the crime or acknowledges that some or all of the charge laid is true

consanguinity being closely related by blood to another person

consecutive sentence a penalty (sentence) for crimes in which penalties for two or more offences are served one after the other

consent agreement given freely and voluntarily, in good faith

consideration something of value exchanged between the parties to a contract; categorized as past, present, or future consideration

conspiracy an agreement or arrangement between two or more people to commit an unlawful act

constitutional law outlines the structure and powers of the federal and provincial governments

consummate to validate or complete a marriage by having sexual intercourse with your spouse

contingency fee an arrangement between a plaintiff and a lawyer where the lawyer will be paid an agreed-upon percentage

of the eventual settlement at the end of a trial

contract an agreement enforceable by law, including express and implied contracts, simple contracts, and contracts under seal

contract law outlines the requirements for legally binding agreements

contract under seal a written contract in formal language, signed and witnessed, and with a red seal to signify serious intent

contributory negligence negligence on the victim's part that helps bring about (contributes to) his or her own injury or loss; a partial defence for negligence

controlled substance any material, including both illegal drugs and drugs legally prescribed by doctors, listed in the *Controlled Drugs and Substances Act*

cooling-off period the time during which a buyer can cancel a contract with a door-to-door seller without giving any reason, whether or not the goods have been received and/or paid for

co-respondent the third party who commits adultery with the respondent in a divorce action

correctional services government agencies responsible for probation services, the imprisonment and supervision of inmates, and inmates' parole

counterclaim a defendant's claim in response to the plaintiff's claim, aimed at reducing or removing the defendant's liability

counteroffer a new offer made in response to the original offer that varies from or qualifies the original, and so brings the original offer to an end

court clerk a person who keeps records, files, and processes documents for a court

court recorder a person who documents (records) all spoken evidence, comments, and questions during court proceedings

credibility the fact or quality of being believable or reliable

Criminal Code the body of public law that declares actions to be crimes (criminal offences), and prescribes punishments for those crimes

criminal harassment pursuing or communicating with an unwilling victim and with his or her friends or family; also known as stalking

criminal law the body of public law that declares acts to be crimes and prescribes punishments for those crimes

criminal negligence wanton and reckless disregard for the lives and safety of other people

criminal offence an action that is considered a crime, as defined in the *Criminal Code*

criminalize to impose a criminal penalty on something that Canadians feel is so immoral that it must be a criminal offence in the *Criminal Code*

cross-examination the questions a lawyer asks a witness called by the opposing side

Crown attorney in criminal matters, the lawyer prosecuting on behalf of the Crown and society; an agent of the attorney general

Crown wardship a court order granting permanent legal custody and guardianship of a child to the Crown, represented by a child protection agency such as the Children's Aid Society

culpable homicide blameworthy or criminal homicide (the killing of another person), as in murder, manslaughter, or infanticide

custody in criminal law, actual imprisonment or physical detention; in family law, the care and control of a child awarded by the court

D

damages money awarded by a civil court to a plaintiff for harm or injury suffered; categorized as general, special, punitive, aggravated, and nominal

dangerous offender a person who has committed serious personal injury and who meets certain criteria to be given this

designation, resulting in an indeterminate sentence; similar to long-term offender

day parole an offender's release from custody during the day under specific conditions, with each night spent in an institution or halfway house; usually a step toward full parole

decriminalize to remove an act from the *Criminal Code* that Canadians no longer feel is severely immoral; thus, the act is no longer a criminal offence (although it may still be illegal)

defamation injury to a person's character or reputation; often characterized as slander or libel

default judgment a decision made in the plaintiff's favour when the defendant in a civil action does not dispute the claim within a reasonable time

defence the accused's response to criminal charges; the accused is either disputing the facts of the case, or arguing that he or she has a lawful excuse or explanation for what occurred

defence counsel the legal representative of an accused

defendant in criminal law, the person charged with an offence; in civil law, the party being sued

defined access the right of the non-custodial parent to certain prearranged visits with the child(ren), such as on weekends, birthdays, and certain holidays

democratic rights the right of the people to elect governments

detain to keep in custody or temporarily confine

direct evidence information (evidence) given by a person who witnessed the event in question (e.g., testimony of a bystander who saw an assault take place)

directed verdict a judge's direction to the jury, after the Crown presents its evidence, to find the accused not guilty because the Crown has not proven its case

disclaimer clause a provision in a contract that denies the buyer certain rights or protections; the seller has an obligation to bring this clause to the buyer's attention

disclosure an early stage in criminal proceedings where the Crown attorney and the defence counsel meet so that the Crown can reveal all evidence it has against the accused; charges may be dropped if the Crown's case is not strong enough

discrimination treating individuals or groups unfairly or differently because of such characteristics as race, sex, religion, age, or disability

diversion program sentences that keep offenders out of prison (e.g., suspended sentence, probation)

divorce the legal dissolution or ending of a marriage

domestic contract a cohabitation agreement, marriage contract, or separation agreement; made between two partners in a relationship and concerning property and obligations to each other

double jeopardy to be tried twice for the same offence

drug a chemical structure that alters the structure or function of a living organism

duress forcing someone to do something (such as commit a crime or sign a contract) by threatening harm

duty counsel a criminal defence lawyer on duty at the court and police station to give legal advice to those just arrested or brought before the court

duty of care a specific legal obligation to not harm other people or their property; a key principle of tort law

E

empanelling the selection of a jury

employment equity the principle that treatment of all employees should be based on their abilities, and be fair, just, and impartial; these programs are generally aimed at women, Aboriginal peoples, visible minorities, and people with disabilities

enact to pass a proposed law, which is known as a bill, into legislation

entrapment police action that encourages or aids a person to commit an offence

entrenched fixed firmly or securely in law; specifically, made part of Canada's Constitution so that it can only be changed by an amendment to the Constitution

equality rights protection from discrimination

equalization the process of dividing the value of property equally between spouses when they divorce

euthanasia painlessly putting to death, as an act of mercy, a person suffering from an incurable and disabling disease

evidence anything that is used to determine or demonstrate the truth in a court of law

evidence to the contrary evidence that disputes the evidence put forth by the Crown; a rebuttal of the charges

examination for discovery a pre-trial process in civil cases in which each side discloses all evidence, and certain issues are discussed and agreed upon; similar to disclosure in criminal cases

examination-in-chief the first questioning of a witness during court proceedings; also called direct examination

exculpatory denying something, as in exculpatory evidence clears the defendant of guilt

express condition an essential term of a contract clearly outlined within it

express contract an oral or written contract in which the terms and conditions are clearly defined and understood by the parties; the opposite of an implied contract

express warranty a clear and open promise that goods or services will meet certain standards; also called a guarantee

extrajudicial measure an alternative to the formal youth court trial; a consequence or punishment designed to hold a non-violent, first-time youth criminal responsible without creating a youth criminal record

extrajudicial sanction a more serious punishment intended to hold a youth criminal responsible without creating a criminal record; a midpoint between an extrajudicial measure and a youth court trial

F

faint hope clause the provision that allows an offender sentenced to more than 15 years before becoming eligible for full parole (e.g., a murderer) to have his or her parole eligibility reconsidered

fair comment a defence to defamation; the right to criticize openly and honestly without malice, as in a movie or theatre review

false imprisonment unlawful physical restraint or detention

false pretences illegal lying or misrepresentation; presenting untruths or false information knowingly and with fraudulent intent to induce the victim to act upon it

family asset property owned by one or both spouses and ordinarily used and enjoyed for family purposes by the spouses and/or any children; as opposed to non-family assets

family law outlines the area of law that regulates aspects of family life; deals with relationships between spouses or partners, and parents, grandparents, and children

feminist one who believes in the social, economic, and political equality of the sexes

feudal system a political, social, and economic system prevalent in Europe between the ninth and fifteenth centuries; based on the relationship between lord and vassal (servant)

fine option program an alternative to paying a monetary penalty (fine) in which the offender can earn credit for doing community work

First Nations a term originated by Aboriginal peoples to describe themselves and recognizing that they belong to distinct cultural groups with sovereign rights based on being Canada's first inhabitants

first-degree murder the killing of another person that is planned and deliberate, in which the victim is a law enforcement agent, or that is related to committing or attempting other crimes that are particularly offensive to society (e.g., hostage taking, sexual assault, hijacking an airplane)

forensic science the application of biochemical and other scientific techniques (e.g., human tissue or fibre analysis) to criminal investigations

foreseeability the ability of a reasonable person to expect or anticipate the result of a certain action

foster home a form of open custody for youth criminals, placing the youth in the home of an existing family for care and rehabilitation for a set time period

fraud intentionally deceiving the public or a person in order to cause a loss of property

fraudulent misrepresentation an untrue statement, or one that gives a false impression, about specific goods or services, that is made knowingly and with the intent of deceiving

frustration of contract when the terms of a contract are made impossible to accomplish or perform

full disclosure requires that a consumer receive a detailed statement of the cost of credit in dollars and cents and as a true annual rate of interest expressed as a percentage

full parole an offender's complete release from custody into the community under specific conditions and supervision

fundamental freedoms basic freedoms, including freedom of expression and freedom of religion

G

garnishment a court order requiring that money owed by a defendant to a plaintiff be paid out of the defendant's bank account or wages

general damages compensation payable in a civil action that is not easily calculated and requires the judge's discretion (e.g., for pain and suffering, lost future income, loss of enjoyment of life)

general deterrence that which prevents or discourages people in general from doing something

grievance a formal, work-related complaint made by an employee, the union, or management when it is thought that the collective agreement is not being followed

grounds of discrimination categories or types of discrimination

group home a home that houses several youth criminals for a set time period for rehabilitation; operated by trained staff and non-profit agencies

H

habeas corpus a document that requires a person to be brought to court to determine if he or she is being legally detained; from the Latin term meaning "you must have the body," that is, there must be grounds for detention

healing circle an option within restorative justice that attempts to resolve conflicts between an offender and his or her victim

hearsay evidence information (evidence) not coming from the direct, personal experience or knowledge of the witness

homicide the killing of another person, directly or indirectly

human rights rights that protect one from discrimination by other individuals

hung jury a jury that cannot come to a unanimous decision in a criminal case

hybrid offence criminal offence that may be tried, at the Crown's option, as a summary conviction offence or indictable offence, with the corresponding less or more severe punishment

I

identity theft using someone's personal information, without his or her knowledge or consent, to commit a crime such as fraud or theft

impartiality a principle of justice holding that decisions should be based on objective criteria, rather than on the basis of bias, prejudice, or preferring the benefit

to one person over another for improper reasons

implied condition an essential term in a contract that is not expressed formally but is suggested by the buyer

implied contract a contract that is suggested or understood without being openly and specifically stated; the opposite of an express contract

incarceration imprisonment or confinement

inculpatory admitting to something incriminating, as in inculpatory evidence demonstrates guilt

independent contractor a person who sells services to clients and who maintains a separate business himself or herself, unlike an employee

indeterminate sentence a penalty (sentence) ordering imprisonment for a period that is not fixed, during which the situation is reviewed periodically to see if the offender can safely return to society; often used for dangerous offenders

Indian the term used in the *Constitution Act, 1982*, to describe First Nations peoples who are not Inuit or Métis

indictable offence a severe or particularly serious criminal offence (e.g., murder, treason), which has a correspondingly severe penalty, and which proceeds by way of a formal court document called an indictment

information a written complaint, usually made by a police officer under oath, stating that there is reason to believe that a person has committed a criminal offence

informed consent agreement to a particular action with full understanding of the risks, as with patients and medical procedures

infringed broken or violated, as in an agreement or right that is infringed

injunction a court order directing a person to do or not to do something for a specific time period

innocent misrepresentation an untrue statement, or one that gives a false impression,

about specific goods or services by someone who thinks the statement is true

intent the true purpose of one's actions; the state of a person's mind who knows and desires the consequences of his or her actions; a key characteristic of the tort of negligence

intentional discrimination treatment of others that is unfair (on the basis of prejudice or stereotype) and on purpose

interim custody order the care and custody of a child awarded by the court temporarily to one parent

intermittent sentence a penalty (sentence) for a crime that may be served on weekends or at night, allowing the offender to keep a job; only available for sentences of less than 90 days

invitation to treat encouragement, through advertising or display of goods, to prospective buyers to make offers

J

joint custody the care and control of a child awarded by the court to both parents; also called shared parenting or parallel parenting

judicial activism judges who put their own personal views and values into their court judgments

jurisdiction authority or power to do something, such as make laws

jury panel a large group of citizens, randomly selected, for possible inclusion on a jury

just cause the legal right to take an action, such as firing an employee

juvenile delinquent a child between the ages of 7 to 18 who committed delinquencies under the *Juvenile Delinquents Act*

L

labour and employment law laws that govern the relationship between employers and employees

land claim assertion of the right to certain lands, as in claims to land long-used by Aboriginal peoples

landlord the property owner who agrees to allow another party to occupy or use the property in return for payment

language rights protection of both English and French as Canada's two official languages; stipulate that both languages have equal importance in Parliament and in all of Canada's institutions

lapse the termination, or ending, of an offer because it is not accepted

lawful purpose a lawful (not illegal) reason or objective

leading question a question that prompts the witness to give a desired answer

lease a contract between a landlord and tenant for the rental of property; also called a tenancy agreement

leave of absence time granted away from work for a specified period and purpose, such as maternity, parental, and adoption leaves

legal aid legal services paid for by the government, available to persons unable to afford a lawyer

legal rights safeguards for a person's procedural rights in the criminal justice system

legalize to make an act completely legal; that is, it is not in the *Criminal Code*, nor is it punishable by a fine

lessee the tenant who occupies rented premises

lessor the property owner who rents out premises

libel defamation in a printed or permanent form, such as pictures, printed words, or video

limitation period the period of time after an event occurs during which a civil claim can be filed

lineup a group of people who are lined up by the police so that a witness to a crime may say which person committed the crime

liquidated damages a sum of money that the parties to a contract agree to in advance to settle any breach of contract that might occur

litigant one of the two parties involved in a civil action; the plaintiff or defendant

litigation a lawsuit; the legal action to settle a civil dispute

lobby trying to influence the government to pass laws that would support one's cause and/or benefit the organization the lobbyist represents; many lobbyists are paid by a company or institution

lockout an employer's refusal to open the workplace to employees; a strategy used in labour disputes

long-term offender (LTO) a criminal who repeatedly behaves in a way that could injure, kill, or cause psychological harm and, in the case of a sexual offender, would likely re-offend

M

maintenance another term for spousal support

malice the desire to harm another; active ill will

malpractice improper or negligent professional treatment by someone with expertise, such as a doctor or lawyer

mandatory minimum sentence a required minimum sentence that must be served for the commission of specific *Criminal Code* offences

manslaughter killing another person by committing an unlawful act with only general intent

marriage breakdown the only ground for divorce under the *Divorce Act, 1985*

marriage contract a domestic contract between two married people or a couple who plan to marry; concerns the division of property and obligations to each other

material risk any major or significant possibility of harm or suffering from a medical treatment

matrimonial home the home in which the spouses live during their marriage

matrimonial property property owned by the spouses during their marriage; also called marital property

mediation an alternative dispute resolution process in which a third party tries to get opposing parties to reach a compromise or mutually acceptable agreement; also used in family law

mens rea a Latin phrase meaning "a guilty mind"; the knowledge, intent, or recklessness of one's actions, which together with *actus reus*, makes one criminally liable

merchantable quality fit for intended use; suitable for sale

misleading advertising advertising that makes a representation to the public that is false or misleading in a material respect

misrepresentation an untrue statement, or one that gives a false impression, about specific goods or services; can be innocent or fraudulent

mistake of fact a defence whereby a person did not have the necessary mens rea to commit a crime because the person honestly did not know that he or she was committing a crime

mitigating circumstances factors that moderate or lessen the responsibility of the offender, thereby possibly reducing the penalty

mitigation of loss the expectation that a person injured by a breach of contract will take reasonable steps to reduce or prevent any losses that the breach caused

mobility rights the right to enter, remain in, and leave Canada and to move from province to province within the country

monogamy the state of being married to only one person at a time

motive the reason for committing a certain act

motor vehicle a vehicle that is drawn, propelled, or driven by any means other than muscular power, not including railway equipment

murder intentional homicide (killing of another person); has two classes: first-degree murder and second-degree murder

N

necessaries goods and services needed to ensure a person's health and welfare (e.g., food, clothing, shelter); as opposed to non-necessaries

negligence a careless act that causes harm to another

negligent investigation a new tort allowing the wrongly accused to sue police for negligence in cases of inferior or shoddy investigation

negotiation an alternative dispute resolution process that is informal and voluntary with the intent of reaching a compromise or mutually acceptable agreement

net family property the total value of a couple's assets, less any debts, on the date of separation; a figure needed to calculate any equalization payments

no-fault insurance insurance that is paid promptly to the injured party by the insurer, regardless of who is at fault in an accident

nominal damages compensation payable in a civil action and awarded as a moral victory to a plaintiff who has not suffered substantial harm or injury

non-culpable homicide homicide (the killing of another person) that is not criminal but was caused completely by accident or in self-defence

non-family asset valuable items, such as investments and a business, owned by a spouse, that are not divided between spouses in the event of a separation; as opposed to family assets; also called business assets

non-pecuniary damages a form of general damages for losses that do not involve an actual loss of money (e.g., for loss of enjoyment of life) and are difficult to determine

non-restricted firearm any rifles and shotguns that are neither restricted nor prohibited

not criminally responsible (NCR) having no criminal responsibility for an offence committed because of a disease of the mind

notwithstanding clause the provision (clause) in the *Charter of Rights and Freedoms* allowing provinces and territories to create laws that operate in spite of certain contradictions with the Charter

nuisance an unreasonable use of land that interferes with the rights of others to enjoy their property; could be either public or private

O

oath a solemn promise or statement that something is true

obscenity words, images, or actions that go against moral values

occupier someone who controls and physically possesses a property

offer and acceptance a proposal that expresses the willingness of one party to enter into a contract, followed by an assent by the other party in words or deed; also called a "meeting of the minds"

offeree in a contract, the party to whom the offer is made

offeror in a contract, the party who makes an offer

ombudsman a government official appointed to hear and investigate complaints made by private citizens against government officials or departments or agencies

open custody supervised detention that allows some supervised access to the community (e.g., to work); less guarded than closed custody

opinion evidence evidence based on the thoughts of the witness, usually an expert in his or her field (e.g., a coroner commenting on cause of death)

out-of-court settlement a resolution to a civil dispute made to each party's satisfaction before the matter proceeds to trial

P

pardon being excused of a crime

parole releasing an inmate into the community before the full sentence is served

patriation bringing legislation back under the legal authority of the country to which it applies

pay equity equal payment for work evaluated as equal in worth

peace bond a court order requiring a person to keep the peace and behave well for a specific period of time

pecuniary damages a form of general damages for losses that can be reasonably calculated, such as loss of future earnings and cost of future care

peremptory challenge a formal objection to a potential juror for which no specific reason is given, unlike a challenge for cause

perjury the act of knowingly giving false evidence in a judicial proceeding with the intent to mislead

placing an option giving a deposit to an offeror

plaintiff the person suing in a civil action

plea negotiation a negotiation in which the Crown and the defence attempt to make a deal, usually resulting in a guilty plea to a lesser charge than the original charge, thus resulting in a lesser penalty

points system a method of evaluating applicants for independent immigration, using categories and points

polygamy being in a relationship with or married to two or more persons

polygraph test a process that measures a person's changes in blood pressure, perspiration, and pulse rate to indicate if he or she is telling the truth; these tests are not admissible in Canadian courts

precedent a legal decision that serves as an example and authority in subsequent similar cases; basis for the rule of precedent—the legal principle in which similar facts result in similar decisions

prejudice having a preconceived opinion of a person based on the person's belonging to a certain group; the opinion itself

preliminary hearing a hearing with the purpose of seeing if the Crown has enough evidence to justify sending the case to trial; it also gives the accused a chance to hear the details of the case against him or her

pre-sentence report an account (report) prepared for the court prior to the accused's sentencing that sets out his or her background

presumptive offence a serious offence such as murder, attempted murder, manslaughter, aggravated assault, and repeat violent crimes

principle of totality the rule or concept of looking at the whole (e.g., when an offender has committed several crimes, the sentences should not amount to an overlong prison term)

private law outlines the legal relationship between private citizens and between citizens and organizations; main types include family, labour, tort, contract, and property law

privileged communication confidential communication (e.g., conversations, letters) that a person cannot be required to present in court as evidence

privity of contract a contractual relationship between two parties

probation a sentence that allows the offender to live in the community under the supervision of a probation officer, instead of serving a term of imprisonment; requires good behaviour and other conditions imposed by the judge; common for first-time offenders

procedural justice fairness in the processes that resolve disputes

procedural law outlines the steps involved in protecting our rights

prohibited firearm a weapon that a person is not allowed to possess, including some handguns, rifles and shotguns that have been shortened, semi-automatic firearms that have been converted to fully automatic, and fully automatic firearms

property law outlines the relationship between individuals and property

prosecute to initiate and carry out a legal action; in criminal law, a Crown attorney prosecutes an accused

prostitution sexual activity in exchange for money

provocation committing a crime during the heat of passion

public law controls the relationships between individuals and the government; main types include criminal, constitutional, and administrative law

punitive damages compensation payable in a civil action in addition to general and special damages to punish the defendant for a "high-handed and malicious" attitude; also called exemplary damages

Q

qualified privilege a defence against defamation for those whose work requires that they express honest opinions, such as teachers and doctors, unless malice is evident

R

read down to rule in court that a law is generally acceptable, but unacceptable in that specific case; as opposed to strike down

read in to add a term to a law that changes the law, but still allows it to be upheld as constitutional; the law does not need to be struck down

reasonable access the right of the non-custodial parent to flexible and regular visits with his or her child(ren)

reasonable and probable grounds a set of facts or circumstances that would cause a person of ordinary and prudent judgment to believe beyond a mere suspicion

reasonable limits clause the provision (clause) in the *Charter of Rights and Freedoms* stating that the Charter rights and freedoms are not absolute, and therefore can be limited if there is justification

reasonable person the standard used in determining if a person's conduct in a particular situation is negligent

recidivism relapse into crime; the return to prison of repeat offenders

recklessness a state or instance of acting carelessly or without regard for the consequences of one's actions

recognizance a legal document that the accused must sign, in which she or he acknowledges the charge laid and promises to appear at a specified court date; sometimes accompanied by a payment to the court

rehabilitate the process of helping an individual who has committed a crime to see that his or her actions were wrong, and reintegrating him or her into the community; a sentencing objective

releasing circle an option in restorative justice and Aboriginal communities in which the offender, National Parole Board members, and community members meet to plan for the offender's rejoining the community

remedy a method for a person to enforce her or his rights in court

rent control a form of government-mandated law setting a maximum price that landlords may charge tenants

reparations repayment for harm done to victims and the community

rescission the cancellation or revocation of a contract

resolution discussion a discussion held before a trial between the defence lawyer and Crown attorney to see if the case can be resolved without going to trial

respondent in a court case, the party (e.g., the Crown) who opposes the appeal requested by the other party, the appellant; in a discrimination case, the person who is alleged to have committed an act of discrimination

restitution the act of making good, restoring (e.g., returning something stolen to its rightful owner or compensating in another way); a sentencing objective

restorative justice an approach to the law and crime that emphasizes healing, forgiveness, and community involvement; includes sentencing, healing, and releasing circles

restraint of employment contract an employment contract that puts certain restraints on the employee (e.g., an employee privy to trade secrets might not be able to work for the competition)

restricted firearm a firearm that needs to be registered; includes handguns that are not prohibited, certain semi-automatic rifles and shotguns, and rifles and shotguns that are shorter than 660 millimetres

retribution a deserved penalty or punishment for a wrong or crime; vengeance

reverse onus when the burden of proof is placed on the defence rather than on the Crown (e.g., in a bail hearing involving a serious criminal charge, the accused is responsible for proving why he or she should be released from custody)

revocation in contract law, the cancellation, or taking back, of an offer by the offeree before it is accepted

right of lien if goods have been sold but not delivered, the seller is entitled to keep the goods until the buyer pays

rights and freedoms the things that Canadians are allowed to do, and the things that Canadians can expect of the government, as guaranteed in the *Charter of Rights and Freedoms*

roadside screening test a test given by a police officer to anyone who is driving or who has care and control of a motor vehicle to indicate whether the driver's ability to drive is impaired by drugs or alcohol

robbery theft involving violence, threat of violence, assault, or the use of offensive weapons

Royal Prerogative of Mercy under a Royal Prerogative of Mercy, an inmate may have a fine or prison sentence rescinded (revoked) or may be issued a free pardon or an ordinary pardon

rule of law the fundamental principle that the law applies equally to all persons and that neither an individual nor the government is above the law

S

search the police procedure in which officers look for evidence that may be used in court

search warrant a legal document issued by a judge authorizing the police to search a specific location at a specific time for a specific reason

second-degree murder intentional homicide that does not meet the conditions of first-degree murder

security deposit a sum of money that tenants pay at the beginning of a tenancy (usually to the landlord)

self-defence the legal use of force, possibly even deadly force, in order to defend oneself

self-incrimination the act of implicating oneself in a crime; behaviour indicating one's guilt

self-sufficient to be able to support oneself financially; a consideration of the *Divorce Act* that each spouse has an obligation to support herself or himself within a reasonable period of time after a divorce

sentencing circle an option in restorative justice that brings together affected people (victim, offender, police, etc.) to help sentence (decide the penalty for) the offender

separate property system an approach to the division of family property that allows each spouse to own and control property as though a single person

separation a partial dissolution of a marriage in which the spouses live separate and apart

separation agreement a domestic contract between a separating couple, dealing with such issues as support and division of assets and property

sequester to keep the jury together and away from non-jurors until the jury reaches a verdict

sexual assault the broad term for the three levels of sexual assault (the most serious of which is aggravated sexual assault), which parallel those for assault

sexual harassment unwelcome actions or conduct toward another person of a sexual nature

shared parenting an arrangement by which both parents have equal or similar rights concerning their child(ren)'s care and custody; also known as joint custody

sheriff a Crown-appointed official who acts as part of the justice administration system (e.g., serving court documents)

simple contract a contract that is either express or implied, oral or written, and not under seal

slander defamation through spoken words, sounds, or actions

small claims court the lowest level civil court where disputes involving money or property are resolved simply, inexpensively, and informally by a judge without a jury

society wardship a court order granting temporary legal custody and guardianship of a child to a child protection agency, such as the Children's Aid Society

solemnization of marriage the various steps and procedures, including the ceremony, leading to marriage

soliciting communicating for the purposes of prostitution

special damages compensation payable in a civil case for specific out-of-pocket expenses (e.g., prescription drugs, vehicle repairs, lost income)

specific deterrence that which discourages or prevents criminals from re-offending

specific performance a court order that requires a person do something previously promised in a contract

spousal support financial assistance paid by one spouse to another after a relationship or marriage breakdown; also called maintenance

standard of care the level of care, or degree of caution, expected when a reasonable person is carrying out an action

statement of claim the legal document in a civil action outlining the plaintiff's case against the defendant, and the desired remedy

statement of defence the defendant's response to the plaintiff's complaint, outlining the defendant's version of the event

Status Indians First Nations people who are registered legally under the *Indian Act*

statute a law or act passed by a government body, such as Parliament or a provincial legislature

statute of limitations a time limit within which a charge must be laid (not applicable to indictable offences)

statutory release an inmate's release from an institution as required by law; except for certain offences, once two-thirds of the sentence is served

stay of proceedings a court order to stop the trial proceedings until a certain condition is met

stereotyping judging, or forming an opinion of, one person of a group and applying that judgment to all members of the group

street racing driving a vehicle at high speeds in a reckless and dangerous manner; considered a criminal offence

strike a work stoppage or partial withdrawal of service by union members to further their contract demands; types include general, sympathy, and wildcat strikes

strike down to rule in court that a law is invalid and no longer in effect

sublet a tenant's renting out of his or her rented premises to a third party while keeping the right to repossess

subpoena a court document ordering a person to appear in court for a specific purpose (e.g., as a witness)

substantive law consists of rules that outline a person's rights and obligations in society

suffrage the right to vote in political elections; franchise

summary conviction offence a minor criminal offence (in contrast to an indictable offence), which is tried immediately (summarily) without a preliminary hearing or jury

summation the formal conclusion, which recapitulates (sums up) key arguments and evidence, given by each side in a trial (i.e., the defence and the Crown); also called a closing statement

summons an order to appear in criminal court

supervised access the right of the non-custodial parent to visit with the child(ren) under the supervision of a third party, such as a grandparent or social worker

supervision order a court order requiring that a professional supervise a child needing protection, but the child stays at home

suspended sentence a delayed or held-off sentence; if the offender meets certain conditions, the judge never does decide on a penalty; like a conditional discharge, but the offender has a record

suspension a sentence that removes a privilege, such as driving

T

telemarketing scheme a deceptive marketing scheme aimed at defrauding people; also known as "scams"

telewarrant a legal document issued by a judge over the phone, by fax, or by e-mail for the arrest of an accused, and naming or describing the accused as well as listing the alleged offences

tenant the party that rents (pays money for the use of) the landlord's property

terrorism the unlawful use of force or violence against persons or property in order to intimidate or coerce a government and the civilian population in an attempt to further certain political or social objectives

theft taking someone's property without their consent

tort a wrong or injury, other than breach of contract, that may be intentional or unintentional; the basis of tort law

tort law outlines the area of law that holds a person or organization responsible for the damage caused by their actions against another person

traffic selling, administering, giving, transferring, transporting, sending, or delivering a controlled substance

Treaty Indians individuals not registered under the *Indian Act* but who can show legal descent from a band that signed a treaty with the federal government in Canada

trespass to enter or cross another's property without consent or legal right

U

undertaking a court document that the accused signs to swear that he or she will attend a specified court date and meet any conditions of release laid down by the judge

undue hardship a financial or health and safety risk that makes it impossible to accommodate a complainant in a discrimination case

undue influence improper pressure applied by one person on another in order to benefit from the result (e.g., a will)

unilateral mistake an error made by one party and recognized, but not corrected, by the other party; a one-sided mistake

unintentional discrimination actions that appear to be neutral but that effectively discriminate against most members of a group; sometimes called adverse effect discrimination

union an organization whose purpose is to represent and negotiate for the employees of a particular company or industry

V

valid contract a contract (agreement enforceable by law) that includes all the essential elements: offer and acceptance, consideration, capacity, consent, legal purpose

verdict the final, formal decision of a trial (e.g., not guilty)

vicarious liability occurs when a person is held responsible for another's tort, even though the person being held responsible may not have done anything wrong

victim impact statement a statement made in court by the victim and others affected by the offence that describes the impact of the offence on their lives

void without legal force; invalid, as in a marriage or contract

voidable contract a contract that may be valid or void at the option of one or both parties

voir dire a type of mini-trial held within an actual trial to decide if certain evidence is admissible

voluntary assumption of risk the acceptance of a possibility of harm or suffering; a partial defence for negligence

W

waiver a document signed by a plaintiff, releasing the defendant from liability in the event of an accident or injury

warrant a legal document issued by a judge to order the arrest of the accused, and naming or describing the accused as well as listing the alleged offences

willful blindness pretending not to see something, even though a person knows what is going on

workers' compensation paying benefits to employees injured on the job or suffering workplace-related health problems

Workplace Hazardous Materials Information System (WHMIS) a system of classifying and providing information about dangerous materials so that workers can be trained to deal with them effectively and safely

writ of possession a legal document authorizing a landlord to repossess a rental property and evict the tenants

Y

young offender a person aged 12 to 17 years old inclusive, who breaks the law as defined under the *Young Offenders Act*

Young Offenders Act (YOA) federal legislation that replaced the Juvenile Delinquents Act in 1984; was replaced by the Youth Criminal Justice Act in 2003

youth criminal a young person who is 12 or older but less than 18 charged with an offence under the *Youth Criminal Justice Act*

Youth Criminal Justice Act (YCJA) federal legislation that replaced the *Young Offenders Act* in 2003

Index

A

Abduction, 227–228
Aboriginal people
  Aboriginal title, 81–82
  Assembly of First Nations (AFN), 80
  assimilation, 79–80
  collective rights, 79–80
  criminal sentencings, 296–297
  equality, 83
  government powers, 28
  Indian Act, 79–80, 82, 107
  influence on law, 13
  justice systems, 106–107
  land claims, 80–81
  Nunavut, 81
  releasing circles, 310
  residential schools, 80, 370–371
  rights, 63, 79, 83
  Royal Proclamation of 1763, 79
  Status Indians, 107
  treaties, 79, 83
  Treaty Indians, 107
  White Paper, 80–81
Absolute discharges, 298, 346
Absolute privilege, 424
Accelerated review, 320
Acceptance, 517–518, 524–525
Access, 91, 453–454, 459, 475
Accessories, 131
Accommodation, 95–96, 578–579
Accused persons, 145, 146
  alibis, 263–264
  bail hearings, 164–166
  confessions, 205–206
  defence evidence, 196–198
  defined, 146
  interpreter rights, 54, 60
  legal rights, 48–49, 54
  presumption of innocence, 39, 57, 195, 263
  previous records, 123
  procedural justice, 116–117
  searches, 153
  testimony, 57, 198–200
Act of God, 402
Acts, 29
Actus reus, 124, 129, 181
Administrative law, 10
Adultery, 451–452
Adversarial system, 181
Age of consent, 227, 230
Aggravated assault, 225
Aggravated damages, 376
Agricultural Employees Protection Act, 589
Aiding and abetting, 131, 248
Alcohol and drug testing, 594–595
Alibis, 263–264
Alimony, 490–497

Allurements, 406–407
Alternative dispute resolution (ADR), 32–33, 380–383, 589
  See also Arbitration; Mediation
Alternative measures programs, 334
Amending formula, 26–27
Amendments, 30, 115, 118
American Revolution, 22–23
Annulment, 448–449
Anti-terrorism legislation, 55–56, 130, 153, 242–243
Appeals, 15, 314–315, 351
Appearance notices, 146
Appellants, 314
Arbitrary decisions or detention, 20, 54, 160
Arbitration, 32, 381–383, 589
Arraignment, 134, 164, 194
Arrest, 54, 145–149, 161–162
Arson, 232
Assault, 128, 223–225, 413
Assembly of First Nations (AFN), 80
Assignments, 571–572
Assimilation, 79–80
Assisted suicide, 49, 222
Association in Defence of the Wrongly Convicted (AIDWYC), 137
Attempt to commit a crime, 129
Authorization to Possess (ATP), 246
Automatism, 265–268, 275

B

Bail hearings, 146, 164–166
Balance of probabilities, 362–363
Banns of marriage, 441–443
Barrier to equality, 78
Battered woman syndrome, 274–275
Battery, 413, 419
Becker, Rosa, 486
Bédard, Myriam, 228
Best interests of the child, 453–454, 456, 460–461
Better Business Bureau (BBB), 562
Bid rigging, 555
Bigamy, 440
Bill of Rights (U.S.), 22
Bills, 29–30
Binnie, Ian, 191
Biometrics, 166–167
Blood–alcohol concentration (BAC), 253, 272–273
Bona fide occupational requirement, 93–94
Bonding, 321
Borovoy, Alan, 172, 595
Branches of government, 29
Breach of contract, 517, 538–541, 547

Breach of warranty, 538
Break and enter, 235
Breathalyzer tests, 253–255, 272–273
Briand, Katherine, 487
British North America Act (BNA Act), 27, 74, 119, 134
Buck, Peter, 265
Bulatci, Emrah, 220
Burden of proof
  civil cases, 363–364
  criminal cases, 38, 184, 364
  defined, 38
  negligence, 398, 402
  non-insane automatism defence, 265
  undue influence, 532
  voluntary assumption of the risk, 400
Burglary, 235
Business assets, 482
But-for test, 220, 394
Buy-and-bust operations, 284–285

C

Cadman, Chuck, 423
Cameras in courtrooms, 182
Canada Labour Code, 576
Canadian Bill of Rights, 25–26, 76, 77
Canadian Charter of Rights and Freedoms
  case analysis, 38–39
  criminal proceedings, 145–146
  democratic rights, 46–47
  development, 26–27
  division of powers, 28
  enforcement, 65–67
  equality rights, 60–61
  fundamental freedoms, 37, 41–45
  human rights cases, 96
  landmark decisions, 58–59
  language rights, 61–64
  legal rights, 48–60, 120
  mobility rights, 47
  notwithstanding clause, 38–40
  presumption of innocence, 57
  reasonable limits clause, 37–39
  remedies, 64–65
  rights and freedoms, 38
  youth crimes, 331
Canadian Confederation, 79
Canadian Constitution, 27, 37, 83, 119
Canadian Consumer Information Gateway, 556
Canadian Human Rights Act, 94–98, 577

Canadian Medical Protective Association (CMPA), 411, 427
Canadian Motor Vehicle Arbitration Plan, 383
Canadian Statement of Basic Principles of Justice for Victims of Crime, 311
Capacity to enter into a contract, 517–518, 526–529
Capital punishment, 308–309
Cartel, 555
Carter defence, 272–273
Case law, 15–17, 20
Causation, 220, 393–395
Caveat emptor (buyer beware), 522, 529
Centre for Equality Rights in Accommodation (CERA), 570
Chamney, Mary-Lynne, 247
Character evidence, 203
Chiang, Jack, 183
Child abuse, 464, 467–468
Child abuse registry, 468
Child custody, 453–458, 468
Child pornography, 241
Children in need of protection
  child abuse, 464, 467–468
  child abuse registry, 468
  corporal punishment, 465–466
  Crown wardship, 469
  legislation, 465
  orders, 469
  removal of children, 468
  sexual abuse, 468
  society wardship, 469
  supervision order, 469
Child support, 497–504
Childs, Zoe, 388
Chinese Exclusion Act, 85
Christopher's Law, 228
Circumstantial evidence, 128, 195
Citations, 16–17
Citizen's arrest, 148–149
Civil law
  actions, 359
  burden of proof, 363–364
  class actions, 362, 369–371
  contingency fees, 378
  vs. criminal law, 364
  defendants, 362
  defined, 9–11
  judgments, 378–380
  lawsuits, 362
  minors, 363
  plaintiffs, 362
  procedures, 364–369
  remedies, 372–377
Civil rights, 21, 25–26, 89, 92, 172
Clark, Glen, 63
Class actions, 362, 369–371
Closed custody, 316, 349

Code of Hammurabi, 12–14, 34
Codes, 13, 22
Cohabitation, 483-484, 506
Collective agreements, 591
Collective bargaining, 586, 588–589
Collective rights, 79–80
Colour of right, 232–233
Common law, 120
    codification, 20–21, 25
    contracts, 517
    defences, 263, 265
    defined, 15–16
    detention, 51
    divorce, 452
    employment law, 576
    marriage age, 444
    police conduct, 150
    pre-1982 courts, 120
    property rights, 475
    rules of evidence, 199
Common law relationships, 437
    cohabitation agreements, 506
    interdependent partners, 484
    vs. marriage, 484
    property rights, 485–487
    same-sex, 488–490
    statistics, 437, 485
    support, 487–488
Community service order, 303
Commuting, 309
Compensation. See Restitution
Competition Act, 553–556, 559
Competition Bureau, 553–555
Complainants, 93
Concurrent sentences, 305
Conditional discharge, 299
Conditional release, 289, 318–321
Conditional sentences, 288, 299–301
Conditions, 542–544
Confessions, 183, 200, 205–206, 207
Consanguinity, 440
Consecutive sentences, 305
Consent, 226, 419, 517, 520, 529
Consideration, 517–518, 525–526
Conspiracy, 130, 133
Constitution (U.S.), 22
Constitution Act, 1867, 27–28, 435, 452
Constitution Act, 1982, 26–27, 40, 119, 217
Constitutional exemption, 292
Constitutional law, 10, 26

Constitution of the Iroquois Nations (Great Binding Law), 13
Consumer protection
    Better Business Bureau (BBB), 562
    bid rigging, 555
    Canadian Consumer Information Gateway, 556
    cartel activity, 555
    Competition Act, 553–556, 559
    Competition Bureau, 553–555
    conspiracy, 555
    cooling-off periods, 560
    credit reporting, 561
    disclosure of credit costs, 561–562
    door-to-door sales, 560
    Federal laws, 553–559
    full disclosure, 561–562
    identity theft, 558–559
    loan scams, 561
    market sharing, 555
    misleading advertising, 553, 555
    personal information, 558
    Personal Information Protection and Electronic Documents Act, 558
    PhoneBusters, 557
    price fixing, 555
    provincial laws, 560–562
    purpose of laws, 553
    refunds, 561
    scams, 557
    sticker shock, 557
    telemarketing, 554, 557
Contingency fees, 378
Contract law, 11
Contracts
    acceptance, 517–518, 524–525
    breach, 517, 539–541, 547
    capacity, 526–529
    careers related to, 593
    caveat emptor, 522, 529
    checklist, 538
    conditions, 542–544
    consent, 520, 529
    consideration, 517–518, 525–526
    damages, 539
    defined, 517
    delivery, 542
    disclaimers, 545
    duress, 533
    electronic, 548–549
    employment, 574–575
    express, 518

    frustration, 537
    illegal, 534
    impaired judgment, 529
    implied, 518
    impossibility, 537
    injunctions, 540
    intent, 520–521
    invitations, 521
    law, 359
    lawful purpose, 534
    limitation of actions, 541
    liquidated damages, 539
    merchantable quality, 544
    minors, 527–528
    misrepresentation, 530
    mistake, 531
    mitigation of loss, 539
    mutual agreement, 536
    necessaries, 527
    non est factum, 531
    offers, 517–518, 520–524
    payment, 542
    performance, 536–537
    privity, 540
    remedies, 539–541, 547
    rescission, 541
    restraint of employment, 534
    restraint of trade, 534
    revocation, 523–524
    right of lien, 547
    sale of goods acts, 542
    simple, 519
    specific performance, 539–540
    substantial performance, 538
    terms, 521
    title, 542, 544
    under seal, 519
    undue influence, 532–533
    valid, 517
    void, 527, 532, 534
    voidable, 528–529, 531–532
    warranties, 538, 543, 545
Contributory negligence, 398–399
Controlled Drugs and Substances Act
    Authorization to Possess (ATP) card, 246
    buy-and-bust operations, 284–285
    drugs, 244–245
    medical marijuana, 246–247
    penalties, 245, 248, 258
    possession, 245–246
    search and seizure, 249–250
    trafficking, 247–249
Cooling-off period, 560

Corporal punishment, 224, 465–466
Correctional facilities. See Incarceration
Corrections and Conditional Release Act, 312, 317–318
Counsel
    defence, 168, 181, 184, 185
    duty, 161, 173
    guarantee, 25, 162, 205
    inform at arrest, 147, 162
    legal aid, 54–55, 163
    right, 54
    trial, 168
Counterclaims, 366
Court clerks, 185
Court recorders, 185
Courtrooms, 181
Courts, 65–67
Credibility, 180, 183, 196, 198, 203, 204
Credit card fraud, 236
Criminal Code
    changes, 119
    corporal punishment, 224, 465–466
    criminal offences, 114
    defined, 114
    enactment, 118
    limits and duties, 120
    parts, 217
    penalties, 57
    sentencing, 296
    substantive laws, 9–10
    See also under specific offences
Criminal harassment, 244
Criminalizing of behaviour, 115
Criminal law
    appeals courts, 134–135
    burden of proof, 39, 181
    careers, 139
    court system, 134–136
    criminal procedure. See Criminal procedure; Evidence
    cruel and unusual punishment, 57
    defined, 10
    elements of offence, 124
    federal responsibility, 217
    interpreters, 60
    justice system, 116
    offences, 114
    presumption of innocence, 57
    self-incrimination rights, 60
    stay of proceedings, 57
    Tackling Violent Crime Act, 230, 251, 291

and torts, 360, 384–385
trial, 57
See also Appeals;
Criminal Code;
Criminal procedure;
Defences; Evidence;
Sentencing; Trials;
and specific offences
Criminal negligence, 127
Criminal Notoriety Act, 221
Criminal offences, 112, 114,
115, 118, 120
Criminal organizations,
132–133
Criminal procedure
case diagram, 174
vs. civil, 364
court appearances, 173
evidence, 146, 152–153,
169–170
rights under *Canadian
Charter of Rights and
Freedoms,* 145–146
See also Criminal Code;
Criminal law;
Defences; Evidence;
Trials; *and specific
offences*
Criminal records, 321
Cromwell, Thomas, 182
Cronk, Eleanore, 152
Cross-examination, 196, 198,
203
Crown attorneys, 181, 184
Crown wardship, 469
Cruel and unusual
punishment, 57, 290
Culpable homicide, 219
Custody, 147, 164, 453, 475
Cyberbullying, 6

D

Damages, 359, 372–377, 378,
393
Danforth, Pat, 99
Dangerous offenders, 306–307
Daycare, 510–511
Day parole, 318–319
Death penalty, 308–309
*Declaration of the Rights of
Man and of the Citizen,* 23
Decriminalizing of behaviour,
115, 269
Defamation, 422–425
Default judgments, 366
Defence counsel, 185
Defence lawyers. *See* Counsel
Defences, 263
battery, 419–421
defamation, 423
negligence, 398–402
trespass, 419–421
See also specific defences
Defendants (civil), 11, 362

Defendants (criminal).
See Accused persons
Defined access, 459
Delivery of goods, 542
Democratic right to vote,
46–47
Demonstrations, 7, 44–45
Denunciation, 293, 300
Deportation, 303
Detention, 54, 154, 160
Deterrence, 293–294, 300
Diefenbaker, John, 25, 76
Directed verdict, 196
Direct evidence, 195
Direct examination, 196
Disabled persons, 91–92,
98–99
Disclaimers, 545
Disclosure, 168
Discovery process, 368
Discrimination
disabled persons, 91–92,
98–99
employment, 577–579
defined, 71
grounds, 97, 100, 577
immigrants, 85–87
workplace, 95
Dispute resolution. *See*
Alternative dispute
resolution (ADR)
Diversion programs, 298
Division of powers, 28
Divorce
access, 453–454, 459
adultery, 451–452
application, 451
best interests of the
child, 450, 453–454,
456, 460–461
child support, 450,
497–504
co-respondent, 451
custody, 450, 453–458,
468
defined, 296
defined access, 459
Divorce Act, 1985,
452–453, 462
family mediation,
462–463
family property, 479
*Federal Child Support
Guidelines,* 497–498,
500
history, 452
joint custody, 468
jurisdiction, 452, 475
kits, 450
legislation, 453
matrimonial home, 481
matrimonial property,
482
mobility rights, 460–461
no-fault, 452

parties, 451
property division,
478–481, 483
reasonable access, 459
reconciliation, 462
respondent, 451
self-sufficiency, 493–494
separation agreements,
506–507
spousal support,
490–497
supervised access, 459
uncontested, 451
waiting period, 451
See also Marriage
DNA, 170
Doctors, 411–412
Domestic contracts, 506–508
Dominion Elections Act, 72
Door-to-door sales, 560
Double jeopardy, 282
Dowry, 449
Driving offences
dangerous operation,
251–252, 279
failure to stop, 252–253
speeding, 278
street racing, 114–115,
239
*Tackling Violent Crime
Act,* 230
See also Impaired
driving
Drugs. *See Controlled Drugs
and Substances Act*
Drug testing, 594–595
Drunk driving. *See* Impaired
driving
Duress, 280, 533
Duty counsel, 161, 162, 173
Duty of care, 391–392, 570

E

Edwards, Henrietta Muir,
74–75
Egale Canada (Equality for
Gays and Lesbians
Everywhere), 90
Electronic contracts, 548–549
Electronic monitoring, 299
Empanelling, 187
Employee relations specialists,
593
Employment law
accommodation,
577–579
alcohol and drug testing,
594–595
Canada Labour Code,
576
civil actions, 359
collective agreements, 591
collective bargaining,
586, 588

common law duties,
576
contracts, 574–575
defined, 11
discrimination, 577–579
dismissal, 582
equity, 78
Family Day, 575
Federal legislation, 576
harassment, 579
health and safety,
584–585
holidays, 581
human rights, 577
independent contractors,
591–592
International Day of
Mourning, 584
Labour Day, 575
leaves of absence, 582
lockouts, 590
minimum age, 580
minimum wage, 580
pay equity, 77
provincial laws, 576,
580–591
retirement, 579
strikes, 589–590
termination, 582
unions, 574, 586–589
vacation, 581
workers' compensation,
585
work hours, 581
Workplace Hazardous
Materials Information
System (WHMIS),
584
Enacting criminal law, 118
Entrapment, 282–285
Entrenched rights, 46, 58
Epstein, Gloria, 489
Equality rights, 60–61, 71
Equalization, 478–480
Escorted absences, 318
Euthanasia, 222–223
Evictions, 566
Evidence
admissibility, 199
character, 203
circumstantial, 128, 195
collection, 169
confessions, 205–206
defined, 169
direct, 195
DNA, 170
electronic devices,
203–204
eyewitness, 197
forensic science tests,
169–170
hearsay, 202
illegally obtained, 207
opinion, 202–203
photographs, 203

polygraph tests, 204–205
presentation, 197
privileged communications, 201
rules, 198
similar fact, 201–202
to the contrary, 272
types, 200, 207
video, 203–204
voir dire, 199
weight, 198
Examination for discovery, 368
Examination-in-chief, 196
Examination of debtor, 379
Exculpatory, 205
Executive branch, 29–30
Exemplary damages, 375
Express contract, 518
Express warranty, 543
Extrajudicial measures, 334–336
Exxon Valdez, 417, 594

F

Faint hope clause, 320
Fair comment, 424
Fairness, 116
False imprisonment, 390, 414
False pretenses, 236
Families, 437–438, 462–463, 510–511
Family assets, 482
Family counsellors, 509
Family Day, 575
Family law, 11, 359, 435, 477–478
See also Children in need of protection; Divorce; Marriage
Family Law Act, 477–478
Famous Five, 74–75
Federal Child Support Guidelines, 497–498, 500
Federal Courts, 135–136
Federal government, 29
Federal Ombudsman for Victims of Crime, 311
Feeney Warrant, 171
Feminists, 72
Ferguson, Michael, 292
Feudal system, 14
Fines, 299, 304, 346–347
Fingerprints, 164, 166
Firearms, 230, 237–238, 258
First-degree murder, 219
First Nations, 79, 83
Fontaine, Phil, 80
Force majeur, 402
Forensic science tests, 169–170
Foreseeability, 393
Foster homes, 340, 348–349

Fraud, 236, 530
Fresco, Dara, 371
Full disclosure, 561
Full parole, 318–319
Fundamental freedoms, 41–45

G

Gambling, 533
Gangs. *See also* Criminal organizations
Garnishments, 379–380
Gavels, 366
Gay rights, 88–90
General damages, 372–373
General deterrence, 293
Gosnell, Joe, 63
Governor General, 29–31
Grant's Law, 233
Great Binding Law, 13
Grewal, Ramandeep K., 283
Grievance, 588
Grigg, Andrew, 376
Group homes, 348

H

Habeas corpus, 19, 164, 166
Halstead, Sue, 425
Harassment, 579
Harper, Elijah, 83
Harper, Stephen, 423
Hazardous conditions, 406
Head tax, 85–86
Healing circles, 310
Hearsay evidence, 202
Hells Angels, 132
Helmets, 428–429
Hill, Jason, 415, 416
Hofsess, John, 49
Homicide, 218–223
Homolka, Karla, 175
Host liability, 408–410
House arrest, 289, 318–321
House of Commons, 29–30
Human rights
Canadian Bill of Rights, 25
careers, 105
defined, 21, 71, 92
development, 22
employment law, 577
laws, 71, 94–105
legal case analysis, 96
remedies, 96, 103
Human Rights Code (Ontario), 100–102
Humphrey, John, 24
Hung jury, 210
Hybrid offences, 121, 123

I

Identity theft, 234–235, 558–559

Ignorance of the law, 281
Immigrants, 84–88
Immoral behaviour, 115
Impaired driving
blood–alcohol concentration (BAC), 253, 272–273
blood samples, 255
care and control, 254
Carter defence, 272–273
civil damages, 376–377
defined, 253–254
drugs, 250
elements, 253
host liability, 408–410
MADD Canada (Mothers Against Drunk Driving), 313
motor vehicle, 251
penalties, 256
rate, 250
Reduce Impaired Driving Everywhere (RIDE) program, 255, 271
sobriety checkpoints, 54
spot checks, 255
Tackling Violent Crime Act, 230, 251
Impartiality, 117
Implied contract, 518
Incarceration
assignment to institution, 317
Canadian, 299
closed custody facilities, 316
community correctional centres, 316
conditional release, 289, 318
correctional services, 316
costs, 290
defined, 295
inmates, 304
international, 295, 306
release programs, 318
Saskatchewan Penitentiary, 288
sentences, 304
smoking, 290
youth offenders, 348–350
Inculpatory, 205
Independent contractors, 591–592
Indeterminate sentence, 306, 307, 309, 320
Indian, 79
Indian Act, 79–80, 82, 107
Indictable offences, 121, 122, 123
Indictments, 121–122, 138, 194, 315
Indirect victims, 312

Inevitable accidents, 402
Information documents, 146, 158
Informed consent, 411–412
Infringed rights, 58, 65
Injunctions, 377, 540
Insane automatism, 267–268
Insurance, 426–427
Intent, 331
attempts, 129
children, 331
crimes, 125–127, 129
defined, 126
incapacity to form, 129
Intentional discrimination, 93
Intentional torts, 390
Interim custody order, 456
Intermittent sentences, 305
International Day of Mourning, 584
Internment camps, 86–87
Interpreter rights, 54, 60
Intoxication, 226, 270–271
Invitees, 406

J

Jean, Michaëlle, 31
John Howard Society of Ontario, 185
Johnson, Audrey, 77
Joint custody, 458
Judges, 182–183, 263
Judicial activism, 65
Judiciary, 29, 65–67
Jurisdiction, 28
Jury trials
challenges for cause, 190
charge to jury, 208
deliberation, 209–210
empanelling, 187
hung jury, 210
importance, 212–213
jury duty, 193–194
jury selection, 187–192
offences allowing, 192
panel, 188
peremptory challenges, 189, 192
sentencing, 211
sequestration, 193–194
Just cause, 576
Justinian Code, 12
Juvenile delinquents, 327, 328
Juvenile Delinquents Act, 328, 330–331

K

Kevorkian, Jack, 222
Khawaja, Momin, 243
Kidnapping, 227
King, Mackenzie, 87
Knowledge, 128

L

Labour and employment law.
  See Employment law
Labour Day, 575
Lady Justice, 3, 117
Land claim, 80
Landlord and tenant law
  applicable law, 563, 565
  assignments, 571–572
  Centre for Equality
    Rights in
    Accommodation
    (CERA), 570
  changing tenancies,
    571–572
  discrimination, 573
  duty of care, 570
  eviction, 566
  fixed-term tenancies,
    564
  joint tenancies, 564
  landlords, 563, 569–570
  leases, lessees, and
    lessors, 564
  periodic tenancies, 564
  quiet enjoyment, 568
  rents, 565–566
  repairs, 567–568
  responsibilities, 569
  security deposits,
    565–566
  subletting, 571–572
  surrender of lease, 571
  taxes, 569
  tenancies, 564
  tenancy agreements, 565
  tenants, 563, 569
  termination of tenancies,
    571–573
  utilities, 569
Language rights, 61–62
Lapse, 523
Laskin, Bora, 477
Latimer, Robert, 223, 320
Lawful purpose, 517–518,
  534
Laying charges, 148
Leading question, 196
Leases, 564
Leaves of absence, 582
Lee, Ralph Lung Kee, 85
Legal aid, 161, 162, 163–164
Legal authority, 421
Legal Education and Action
  Fund (LEAF), 77
Legalizing of behaviour, 115
Legal rights, 36, 37, 38, 40,
  48–60
  accused persons, 48–49
  arrest, 54
  counsel, 54
  cruel and unusual
    punishment, 57
  defined, 48
  detention, 54–56

interpreters, 54, 60
legal aid, 54–55
life, liberty, and security
  of the person, 48–49
privacy, 51–53
search and seizure,
  50–51
self-incrimination, 60
stay of proceedings, 57
at trial, 57
  See also Accused persons
Legislative branch, 29–30
Lepofsky, David, 92
Lesbian rights, 88–90
Lessees and lessors, 564
Libel, 423
Licensees, 406
Life, liberty, and security of
  the person, 48–49
Limitation of actions, 541
Limitation period, 365
Lineup, 155
Liquidated damages, 539
Litigation, 362, 383
Litigation guardians, 363
Lobbying, 7, 80
Lockouts, 590
Long-term offenders (LTO),
  291, 307

M

Macphail, Agnes, 73
MADD Canada (Mothers
  Against Drunk Driving),
  313
Magna Carta, 13, 19–20, 22,
  212
Maintenance, 490–497
Malice, 424
Malpractice, 411
Mandatory minimum
  sentences, 258–259,
  291–292, 299–300
Manslaughter, 221
Marijuana, 53, 140–141,
  246–247
Market sharing, 555
Marriage
  age, 440, 444–445
  annulment, 448–449
  banns, 441–443
  bigamy, 440
  breakdown, 435
  ceremonies, 444
  Civil Marriage Act, 446
  close relationships,
    440–441
  consent, 440
  Constitution Act, 1867,
    435
  death of spouse, 483
  domestic contracts,
    506–508
  dowry, 449

Family Law Act,
  477–478
  jurisdiction, 435, 439,
    441, 475
  licences, 435, 441–443
*Married Women's
  Property Act,* 475
  mental capacity, 440
  monogamy, 440
  names, 447
  polygamy, 470–471
  property rights,
    475–477, 483
  registering, 445–446
  requirements, 440–441
  rights and obligations,
    439
  same-sex, 89, 446–447
  separation, 449–450
  solemnization, 435
  statistics, 442
  terminations, 448–452
  See also Common law
    relationships; Divorce
Marriage contracts, 506–507
Marriage counsellors, 509
*Married Women's Property
  Act,* 475
Martin, Brenda, 319
Material risks, 412
Matrimonial home and
  property, 477, 481, 482,
  483, 487
McClung, Nellie, 72, 74–75
McGregor, Elisabeth, 509
McIntyre, Al, 114
McKinney, Louise, 74–75
McLachlin, Beverley, 3,
  58–59, 69, 357, 515
Mediation
  defined, 381, 382
  discussion of, 32–33
  family, 462–463
  human rights cases, 103
  mediators, 509
  model, 381
  unions, 589
Medical malpractice, 411–412
Meech Lake Accord, 83
Mens rea, 124, 181
Mental disability, 267–269
Merchantable quality, 544
Mercy killing, 222
Milgaard, David, 137, 288
Mill, John Stuart, 120
Minimum wage, 580
Minors, 363, 527–528
Misleading advertising, 553
Misrepresentation, 530
Mistakes, 531
Mistakes of fact, 281–282
Mitigating circumstances, 296
Mitigation of loss, 539
Mobility rights, 47, 460–461
Monogamy, 440

Moore, Marlene, 306
Morgentaler, Henry, 48
Mosaic Law, 12
Motions, 186
Motive, 128
Motor vehicles
  accidents, 252–253
  dangerous operation,
    252
  defined, 251
  driving offences, 230,
    250–257, 278–279
  helmets, 428–429
  insurance, 426–427
  negligence, 402–404
  seatbelts, 389, 399,
    403–404
  spot checks, 255
  See also Driving
    offences; Impaired
    driving
Multicultural rights, 63
Municipalities, 28, 31
Murder, 219–220, 320
Murdoch, Irene, 476
Murphy, Emily, 73–75
Mustapha, Waddah (Martin),
  397

N

Napoleonic Code, 13
National Parole Board,
  307, 310, 318, 320–321
National Sex Offender
  Registry, 226
Necessity, 278–279, 421
Negligence
  burden of proof, 398
  but-for test, 394
  causation, 393–395
  contributory negligence,
    398–399
  defined, 389
  duty of care, 391–392
  elements, 391, 395
  foreseeability, 393–395
  harm, 395
  host liability, 408–410
  informed consent,
    411–412
  intent, 389
  malpractice, 411–412
  manufacturer liability,
    545
  material risks, 412
  motor vehicles,
    402–404
  occupiers' liability,
    406–407
  professional negligence,
    411–412
  reasonable person, 392
  standard of care, 392
  vicarious liability, 405

voluntary assumption of
    risk, 400–401
waivers, 400
youth, 392–393
Negligent investigation,
    415–416
Negotiation, 32, 381
Net family property, 478
Nisga'a people, 63
No-fault divorce, 452
No-fault insurance, 426
Nominal damages, 376
Non-culpable homicide, 219
Non est factum, 531
Non-family assets, 482
Non-insane automatism,
    265–266, 275
Non-pecuniary damages,
    372–373
Non-restricted firearms, 238
Not criminally responsible
    (NCR), 266, 267–268, 276
Notwithstanding clause, 38,
    40
Nuisance, 390, 417–418
Nunavut, 81

O

Oaths, 193, 197–198
Obscenity laws, 43, 241–242
Occupational health and
    safety specialists, 593
Occupier, 241
Occupiers' liability, 406–407
Occupiers' Liability Acts, 407
Oda, Beverley, 119
Offences, 121–123
Offers, 517–518, 520–524, 531
Ombudsman, 311
Onley, David, 91
Ontario Human Rights
    Commission, 102–104
Open custody, 316, 348–349
Opinion evidence, 202–203
Opt-out clause, 38–40
Organized crime, 132–133,
    305
Ormston, Edward, 269
Out-of-court settlements,
    367
Override clause, 38–40

P

Paralegals, 593
Pardons, 321
Parents
    abductions, 227
    liability for child's
        contract, 528
    *Parental Responsibility
        Act,* 405
    same-sex, 436
    single, 456

support of, 505
vicarious tort liability,
    405
Parker, Terrance, 247
Parlby, Irene, 74–75
Parliament (British), 20, 27
Parliament (Canadian), 29
Parole
    accelerated review, 320
    correctional services,
        316
    day, 316, 318–319
    defined, 318, 319
    early, 320
    electronic monitoring,
        299
    full, 318–320
    National Parole Board,
        307, 310, 318, 320,
        321
    provinces, 318
    return to society, 295
    Royal Prerogative of
        Mercy, 321
    as sentencing factor,
        289
    statutory release, 318,
        320
    victim input, 312
Parties, 131
Patriation, 27
Pay equity, 77
Payment, 542
Payments into court, 366
Peace bond, 302
Pecuniary damages, 372
Penitentiaries. *See*
    Incarceration
Peremptory challenge, 192
Perjury, 197
Permanent wardships, 469
Personal information, 558
*Personal Information
    Protection and Electronic
    Documents Act,* 558
Persons Case, 74–75
Pesticide legislation, 417
Philosophes, 22
PhoneBusters, 557
Photographs, 166, 203
Placing an option, 524
Plaintiffs, 11, 362
Plea negotiations, 175
Pleas, 173
Points system, 88
Poisoned environment, 95
Police
    arrests, 146–149
    buy-and-bust operations,
        284–285
    control of conduct,
        150–151
    drug searches, 249–250
    duties, 149–153
    entrapment, 282

limits on behaviour,
    145–146
police services, 151
undercover, 249
Police caution, 54
Polluters, 418
Polygamy, 440, 470–471
Polygraph tests, 153, 154,
    204–205
Possession of stolen goods,
    236
Precedent, 15–16
Prejudice, 92–93
Preliminary hearings, 134, 173
Pre-sentence report, 290
Presumption of innocence, 39,
    57, 195, 263
Presumptive offences, 342
Pre-trial conferences, 367
Price fixing, 555
Principle of totality, 305
Private law. *See* Civil law
Privileged communications,
    201
Privity of contract, 540
Probation
    breach, 299
    correctional services,
        316
    defined, 299
    end, 319
    hearing, 319
    murder, 320
    officers, 185, 299
    orders, 299, 304–305
    parolee, 319
    review, 319
    statistics, 319
    suspended sentence, 301
    youth offenders, 348
Probation officers, 185, 299
Procedural justice, 116–117
Procedural law, 9
Procuring, 240
Professional negligence,
    411–412
Prohibited, 114, 116
Prohibited firearms, 238
Property crimes, 231–236
Property law, 11, 359
Prosecution, 113, 119
Prosecutors, 117, 123, 143,
    181, 184
Prostitution, 240
Provincial Court of Appeal,
    135–136
Provincial Courts, 134, 136,
    173
Provincial government, 29
Provincial laws, 31, 100
Provincial Supreme Court,
    134, 136, 173
Provocation, 282
Public law, 9–10, 119
Public place, 252

Public Safety Act, 242–243
Punitive damages, 375, 376,
    377

Q

Qualified privilege, 424

R

Rape and shield laws,
    225–227
Read down (a law), 64
Read in (a law), 64
Reading the caution to the
    accused, 147
Reasonable access. 459
Reasonable and probable
    grounds, 145–146, 160
Reasonable doubt, 181
Reasonable limits clause,
    38–39
Reasonable persons, 392
Rebick, Judy, 43
Recidivism, 295
Recklessness, 127
Recognizance, 165
Reduce Impaired Driving
    Everywhere (RIDE)
    program, 255, 271
Rehabilitate, 295
Releasing circles, 310
Remedies
    breach of contract,
        539–541, 547
    defined, 48
    failure to pay child
        support, 503
    human rights cases, 96,
        103–104
    rights and freedoms
        infringement, 64–65
Rents, 565–566
Reparations, 293, 296
Rescission, 541
Residential schools, 370–371
Resolution discussions, 175
Respondents, 93, 314
Restitution, 14, 302, 312,
    347
Restorative justice, 106,
    310–311, 314, 322–323
    See also Victims' rights
Restraint of employment
    contract, 535
Restraint of trade, 534
Restricted firearms, 238
Retirement, 579
Retribution, 14
Reverse onus, 165, 250
Revocation, 523
Right of lien, 547
Rights and freedoms, 37–38,
    64–65, 79
Roadside screening test, 255
Robbery, 229

Rodriguez, Sue, 49, 222
Rosenberg, Marc, 69
Royal assent, 30
Royal Prerogative of Mercy, 321
Royal Proclamation of 1763, 79
Rule of law, 19–20

S

Sale of Goods Act, 542
Same-sex couples
    marriage, 446–447
    support, 488–490
Same-sex parents, 436
Scams, 557
Seals, 519
Searches
    controlled substances, 249–250
    defined, 155
    exceptions, 158
    grounds, 155–156
    laws, 50–51
    rights, 157–158
    warrants, 145, 155, 157, 249–250
Seatbelts, 389, 399, 403–404
Second-degree murder, 219, 220
Secure custody, 349
Security certificates, 56
Security deposits, 565–566
Security of the person, 48–49
Seizing assets, 379
Self-defence, 276–277, 292, 420
Self-incrimination, 60, 199–200
Self-sufficient, 474, 488, 490, 492, 493, 494, 496
Senate, 29–30
Sentencing
    Aboriginal people, 296–297
    absolute discharge, 298
    aggravating circumstances, 296
    capital punishment, 308–309
    community service orders, 303
    commuting, 309
    concurrent, 305
    conditional discharge, 298–299
    conditional sentences, 292, 299–301
    consecutive, 305
    constitutional exemptions, 292
    dangerous offenders, 306
    denunciation, 293, 300

deportation, 303
deterrence, 293–294, 300
diversion programs, 298
electronic monitoring, 299
factors, 289
fines, 304
incarceration, 304–306
intermittent, 305
long-term offenders (LTO), 291, 307
mandatory minimum sentences, 291–292, 299–300
mitigating circumstances, 296
objectives, 293
peace bonds, 302
pre-sentence reports, 290
principle of totality, 305
probation, 299, 301, 305, 316
proportional, 296
rehabilitation, 291, 295, 317
reparations, 293, 296
restitution, 302, 312
separation of offender from society, 295
suspended sentences, 299, 301
suspensions of social privilege, 302
victim impact statements, 291
victims, 311–312
youths, 293–294
See also Incarceration; Parole; Probation; Victims' rights
Sentencing circles, 106, 310
Separate property system, 475
Separation (marriage), 449–450, 475, 477, 478, 479, 480, 481, 506
Sequester, 193
Settlement conferences, 367
Seven Years' War, 79
Sex offender registries, 226, 228
Sexual assault, 225–227
Sexual exploitation, 227
Sexual harassment, 77, 95, 579
Shankar, Corey, 159
Shared parenting, 458
Sheriff, 185
Shoplifting, 129, 148
Significant risk, 268
Similar fact evidence, 201–202
Simple contract, 519
Slander, 422
Small claims court, 361–362, 367

Sobeski, Raymond, 480
Sobriety checkpoints, 54
Social workers, 509
Society wardships, 469
Sokolov, Louis, 416
Solemnization of marriage, 435
Soliciting, 240
Southin, Mary, 492
Spanking, 224, 465–466
Special damages, 375
Specific deterrence, 293
Specific performance, 539–540
Sports violence, 384–385
Spot checks, 271, 273
Spousal abuse, 274–275
Spousal support, 490–497
Stalking, 244
Standard of care, 392
Stare decisis, 16
Statement of claim, 365
Statement of defence, 366
Statements, 162–163
State of mind, 126
Statistics Canada, 433
Status Indian, 107
Statute law, 20–21, 29
Statute of limitations, criminal, 122
See also Limitation of actions
Statute of Westminster, 27
Statutory releases, 318–320
Stay of proceedings, 57, 186
Stereotyping, 92–93
Sticker shock, 555
Stowe, Emily, 72
Street racing, 114–115, 239
Stewart, Jane, 63
Strikes, 589–590
Striking down (a law), 64
Sublet, 571–572
Subpoenas, 197
Substantive law, 9
Suffrage, 72–73
Suicide, 49, 222
Summary conviction offences, 112, 121–122
Summation, 208
Summons, 148
Supervised access, 459
Supervision orders, 469
Supreme Court of Canada, 15, 135–136, 182
Suspended sentences, 299, 301
Suspensions of social privilege, 302
Suzuki, David, 86

T

Tackling Violent Crime Act, 230, 251, 291
Tasers, 176–177
Telemarketing, 554, 557
Telewarrants, 158

Temporary absences, 318
Temporary insanity, 265–266, 275
Temporary wardships, 469
Tenancies and agreements, 564, 565
Tenants, 563, 569
Terrorism, 242
    See also Anti-terrorism legislation
Theft, 232–233
Third-party claims, 366
Third-party liability insurance, 426
Title, 542, 544
Toronto Mental Health Court, 269
Toronto Women's Literary Club, 72
Tort law, 11
Torts
    absolute privilege, 424
    assault and battery, 413
    consent, 419
    and criminal law, 384–385
    defamation, 422–425
    defence of others, 421
    defence of property, 421
    defined, 359–360
    fair comment, 424
    false imprisonment, 414
    intentional, 390
    legal authority, 421
    libel, 423
    necessity, 421
    negligent investigation, 415–416
    nuisance, 417–418
    qualified privilege, 424
    self-defence, 420
    slander, 422
    trespass, 416, 419–421
    See also Negligence
Traffic, 247
Training schools, 329
Treaties, 79
Treaty Indian, 107
Trespass, 388, 390, 406, 413–422
Trial courts, 134
Trials, 195–196
Trudeau, Pierre Elliott, 26–27
Truscott, Steven, 195

U

Unconscionable judgments, 481
Undertakings, 165
Undue hardship, 95
Undue influence, 532–533
Unescorted absences, 318

Unintentional discrimination, 93
Unions, 574, 586
United Nations Commission on Human Rights, 24
United Nations Human Development Index (2007–2008), 21
United Nations Model Law on Electronic Commerce, 547
United Nations Universal Declaration of Human Rights, 24
Unwritten law, 15

V

Valid contract, 517
Van de Perre, Kimberly, 457
Verdicts, 193, 208, 210
Vicarious liability, 405
Victim impact statements
    appeals, 320
    defined, 291
    factor in sentencing, 289
    read in court, 291, 322
    restitution orders, 302
    victim support services, 311
Victims' rights
    Canadian Statement of Basic Principles of Justice for Victims of Crime, 311
    compensation fund, 314
    Corrections and Conditional Release Act, 312, 317–318
    Federal Ombudsman for Victims of Crime, 311
    indirect victims, 312

MADD Canada (Mothers Against Drunk Driving), 313
    restitution, 302, 312
    restorative justice, 310–311, 314, 322–323
    role in criminal process, 311–312
    support services, 311
    youth crimes, 347
    See also Victim impact statements
Video evidence, 203–204
Violent crimes, 218–230.
    See specific offences
Visiting rights, 453–454, 459
Void, 439
Voidable contract, 529
Voir dire, 199
Voluntary assumption of risk, 400
Voting rights
Aboriginals, 73, 79
Asian Canadians, 87
generally, 46–47
women, 72–73

W

Waivers, 400
Ward, Cameron, 415
War Measures Act, 86
Warranties, 538, 543, 545
Warrants, 145–148, 157–158, 171
Weapons charges, 230
See also Firearms
White Paper, 80–81
Willful blindness, 126
Wilson, Bertha, 183–184
Wilson, Cairine, 74

Winnipeg Political Equality League, 72
Witnesses, 197–198, 276
Women
    employment equity, 78
    feminists, 72
    Legal Education and Action Fund (LEAF), 77
    lesbians, 88–90
    in military, 75–76, 78
    pay equity, 77
    Persons Case, 74–75
    political equality, 73
    rights, 73–76
    suffrage, 72–73
    in workforce, 73
Workers' compensation, 585
Workplace Hazardous Materials Information System (WHMIS), 584
Work release, 318
Writ of possession, 573

Y

Young Offenders Act (YOA), 329–330, 331 334
Young, Wanda, 374
Youth crime
    age of responsibility, 331
    court process, 342
    delinquents, 328
    history, 328–330
    Juvenile Delinquents Act, 328, 330–331
    school violence, 352–353
    statistics, 327, 332, 341, 348
    young offenders, 327

Young Offenders Act (YOA), 329–330, 331, 334
Youth Criminal Justice Act (YCJA)
    absolute discharges, 346
    adult treatment, 343–344
    age of responsibility, 331
    appeals, 351
    application, 331
    arrests, 336–337
    bail, 340
    changes, 332
    community programs, 347
    community service, 347
    compensation, 347
    custody, 348–350
    defined, 327
    detention, 340
    disclosure of identities, 342
    diversion programs, 334–336
    enactment, 327, 329, 331
    fines, 346–347
    notices to parents, 341
    pre-sentence reports, 345
    vs. previous legislation, 330, 332
    probation, 348
    purpose, 332, 335
    records, 340, 351
    review, 331, 343
    searches, 338–339
    sentences, 343, 345, 351
    trials, 341

(t.)=top. (b.)=bottom, (c.)=centre, (l.)=left, (r.)=right

4: J. DeVisser/Ivy Images; 5: Amanda Edwards/Getty Images; 6: © John Birdsall/ The Image Works; 9: Reprinted by permission of Carswell, a division of Thomson Canada Limited; 14: Nancy Carter/North Wind Picture Archives; 15: The Granger Collection, New York; 19: © Bettmann/Corbis; 20: Karen Bleier/AFP/Getty Images; 21: (table) Human Development Report 2007/08, © 2007 by the United Nations Development Programme. Published 2007 by Palgrave Macmillan. Reproduced with permission of Palgrave Macmillan; 22: John Hancock (1737–93) signs the American Declaration of Independence, 4th July 1776 (colour litho), American School, (18th C.) (after)/Private Collection, Peter Newark American Pictures/The Bridgeman Art Library; 23: © Visual Arts Library (London)/Alamy; 25, 26: Duncan Cameron/Library & Archives Canada/ (PA-112659, PA-111213); 27, 2–3: (t.) Ron Bull/*Toronto Star*; 30: (c.) © 2008 Jupiterimages Corp, (b.) Library of Parliament/Roy Grogan; 31: The Canadian Press (Tom Hanson); 32: © Ed Hore, 36, 2: (b.) The Canadian Press (Kevin Frayer); 37: © Ted Soqui/Corbis; 40: (t.) © Les. Ladbury/Alamy, (b.) © Stock Connection Blue/Alamy; 41: (t. r.) © mevans/iStock, (c. l.) © Jaspreet Ghuman; 42: The Canadian Press (Fred Chartrand); 43: The Canadian Press (Paul Chiasson); 44: Revised from photograph provided by the Non-Smokers' Rights Association, Toronto ON Canada; 45: The Canadian Press (Tom Hanson); 47: The Canadian Press (Ryan Remiorz); 48: Photoresearchers/First Light; 49: The Canadian Press (Chuck Stoody); 50: Jeff T. Green/Getty Images; 51: CBS Photo Archive via Getty Images; 52: The Canadian Press (Walter Tychnowicz); 53: *Moncton Times and Transcript*/The Canadian Press (Viktor Pivovarov); 54: Vince Talotta/*Toronto Star*; 56: The Canadian Press (Ryan Remiorz); 59: The Canadian Press (Tom Hanson); 61: Ivy Images; 62: © Passport Canada/Government of Canada. Reprinted with permission; 63: The Canadian Press (Nick Procaylo); 70: © Simon Wilson; 71: John Giustina/Iconica/Getty Images; 73: © Canada Post Corporation {1985}. Reproduced with Permission; 74: © John Fowler; 76: Lieut. Michael M. Dean/Canada. Dept. of National Defence/Library and Archives Canada/ PA-141885; 77: Courtesy and with permission of LEAF; 78: The Canadian Press (Allauddin Khan); 79: Library & Archives Canada/By the King, a proclamation: George R./AMICUS 746814; 80, 3: (b.) The Canadian Press (Ryan Taplin); 81: The Canadian Press (Fred Chartrand); 82: Courtesy and with permission of Martin Zlotnik; 83: The Canadian Press (Wayne Glowacki); 84: (table) Statistics Canada, "Immigrant population by place of birth and period of immigration (2001 Census)," <http://www40.statcan.gc.ca/l01/cst01/demo24a-eng.htm> Extracted on Feb. 20, 2009; 85: (t.) The Canadian Press (Aaron Harris), (b.) Peter Power/*Toronto Star*; 86: Courtesy and with permission of Diana Domai; 87: Library and Archives Canada/C-027645; 89: Rick Madonik/*Toronto Star*; 90: Aaron Vincent Elkaim/*Toronto Star*; 91: Richard Lautens/*Toronto Star*; 92: Vince Talotta/*Toronto Star*; 93: Sense of Belonging logo is the © copyright of the United Nations Association in Canada <www.unac.org>. Reprinted with permission; 94, 99: The Canadian Press (Fred Chartrand); 97, 98, 104: Source: Canadian Human Rights Commission 2006 Annual Report/http://www.chrc-ccdp.ca/publications/ar_2006_ra/page2-en.asp AND http://www.ohrc.on.ca/ en/resources/annualreports/ar0607/pdf /Authored by the Canadian Human Rights Commission. Reproduced with permission of the Ministry of Public Works and Government services, 2008; 100: prism_68/Shutterstock; 101: Courtesy and with permission of Fatima Siadat; 105: Debbie Hill/UPI/Landov; 106: *Winnipeg Free Press*/The Canadian Press (Joe Bryksa); 112, 113, 121, 122, 127, 134: (c.) © 2008 Jupiterimages Corp; 114: The Canadian Press (Richard Lam); 117: © David R. Frazier Photolibrary, Inc./Alamy; 119: The Canadian Press (Sean Kilpatrick); 123: Michael Kelly/Stone/Getty Images; 124: *The Globe and Mail*/The Canadian Press (Erik Christensen); 125: Jeremy Woodhouse/Blend Images/Getty Images; 126: AP Photo/Zollfahndungsamt Stuttgart; 129: © John O'Brien from cartoonbank.com. All rights reserved; 130: Hummer/Taxi/Getty Images; 131: InnerShadows/iStock; 132: *Kitchener Waterloo Record*/The Canadian Press (Brent Foster); 134: (b.) D. Tanaka/Ivy Images; 135: (t.) Al Harvey/The Slide Farm, (c.) © Eduard Hueber/archphoto.com, (b.) © Garry Black/Masterfile; 137: Scott Gries/Getty Images; 139: (l.) Bruce Campion-Smith/*Toronto Star*, (r.) Ron Bull/*Toronto Star*; 140: The Canadian Press (Gregory Smith); 143: (Question #8 stats) Statistics Canada, *General Social Survey, Cycle 18 Overview: Personal Safety and Perceptions of the Criminal Justice System*. Table 1D– "Population aged 15 and over by general satisfaction with personal safety, by CMA, catalogue no. 85-566-XIE (2004). Table 1B– "Population aged 15 and over by feelings of safety waiting for or using public transportation alone after dark, by CMA, 2004; 144: The Canadian Press (Andrew Vaughn); 145: Rene Johnston/*Toronto*

Star; 146: Copyright King Features Syndicate. Reprinted with permission—Torstar Syndication Services; 147: Daniel Allan/Photographer's Choice/Getty Images; 147, 153: OPP Flashes (insignia) are registered trademarks (® ™) of the OPP and are reprinted with permission of the OPP; 148: SW Productions/Photodisc/ Getty Images; 150: Michael Stuparyk/*Toronto Star*; 151: David Cooper/*Toronto Star*; 152: Courtesy of Justice Eleanore Cronk; 154: © Anna Clopet/Corbis; 155: David Cooper/*Toronto Star*; 156: The Canadian Press (Paul Chiasson); 157: Ron Bull/*Toronto Star*; 158: © Jeffrey L. Rotman/Corbis; 159: Steve Russell/ *Toronto Star*; 160: *Toronto Star*/The Canadian Press (John Mahler); 161: Darrin Klimek/Digital Vision/Getty Images; 162: By permission of Dave Coverly and Creators Syndicate, Inc; 163: (graph) Reprinted with permission/Torstar Syndication Services (Source: Statistics Canada); 164: © 2008 Jupiterimages Corp; 165: AP Photo/*Knoxville News Sentinel*/Michael Patrick; 167: © Guy Zimmerman; 168: © Michael Newman/PhotoEdit; 169: Rene Johnston/*Toronto Star*; 170: The Canadian Press (Jonathan Hayward); 171: Al Harvey/The Slide Farm; 172: Jim Rankin/*Toronto Star*; 174: Reprinted with permission of Torstar Syndication Services; 175: The Canadian Press (Frank Gunn); 176: Source: TASER International/T. Hoy, S. Vokey/The Canadian Press; 177: *The Gazette*/ The Canadian Press (Jim Slosiarek); 179: (Question #7) Excerpted from "The morality of copping a plea," by Steve Maich, *Maclean's*, July 9, 2007; 180: The Canadian Press (Adrian Wyld); 182, 191: © Supreme Court of Canada (Philippe Landreville); 183: Michael Lea/*Kingston Whig-Standard*; 184: The Canadian Press (FLS); 185: (c. r.) © Amelia Kunhardt/The Image Works, (b.) Logo is copyrighted to and reprinted with permission of the John Howard Society of Ontario; 187: Michael Kelley /Stone/Getty Images; 188: © 2008 Jupiterimages Corp; 190: © Dennis MacDonald/Alamy; 193: The Canadian Press (Jane Wolsak); 194: *Halifax Chronicle Herald*/The Canadian Press (Tim Krochak); 195: The Canadian Press (Adrian Wyld); 196: © Guy Cali/Corbis; 197: © Rex May/www.cartoonstock.com; 198: © Jim Pickerell/The Image Works; 201: Stockbyte/Getty Images; 203: © Jeffrey L. Rotman/Corbis; 204: © Tokyo Space Club/Corbis; 206: © The New Yorker Collection 1990 Gahan Wilson from cartoonbank.com. All rights reserved; 208: Adam @ Home © (1991) by Universal Press Syndicate. Reprinted with permission. All rights reserved; 212: The Canadian Press (Mona Shafer Edwards); 216, 110 (b. l.): © 2008 Jupiterimages Corp; 220: The Canadian Press (Jeff McIntosh); 218: (table homicides by relationship) Adapted from Statistics Canada, *Homicide in Canada, 2007*. By Geoffrey Li. Component of Statistics Canada catalogue no. 85-002-X (Juristat), vol. 28, no. 9, October 2008. Table 7– "Solved homicides by accused-victim relationship Canada"; 218: (table homicides by province/territory) Statistics Canada, *Crime Statistics in Canada, 2006*. By Warren Silver. Component of Statistics Canada catalogue no. 85-002-XIE (Juristat), vol. 27, no. 5. Table 3– "Selected criminal code incidents, Canada and the provinces/territories, 2006"; 221: © Dan Reynolds/www.cartoonstock. com; 222: The Canadian Press (Chuck Stoody); 223: The Canadian Press (Kevin Frayer); 224: Oppenheim Bernhard/Stone/Getty Images; 225: © Justin Leighton/ Alamy; 226: (graphs) Statistics Canada, Chart– "Total sexual assaults and level I sexual assaults reported to police, Canada, 1983 to 2004," Canadian Centre for Justice Statistics, Uniform Crime Reporting Survey <http://www.statcan.gc.ca/ pub/85-570-x/2006001/figures/4054027-eng.htm> Extracted Feb. 20, 2009. AND Chart– "Level II and level III sexual assaults reported to the police, Canada, 1983 to 2004," Canadian Centre for Justice Statistics, Uniform Crime Reporting Survey <http://www.statcan.ca/english/research/85-570-XIE/2006001/figures/ figure13.htm> Extracted Feb. 20, 2009; 228: (t.) Michael Stuparyk/*Toronto Star*, (b.) The Canadian Press (Jacques Boissinot); 229, 110–111: (t.) Erik Dreyer/ Stone/Getty Images; 229: (table) Adapted from Statistics Canada, *Crime Statistics in Canada, 2006*. By Warren Silver. Component of Statistics Canada catalogue no. 85-002-XIE (Juristat), vol. 27, no. 5. Table 3– "Selected criminal code incidents, Canada and the provinces/territories, 2006"; 230: (bulleted list) Reprinted with permission/Torstar Syndication Services, (photo): The Canadian Press (Fred Chartrand); 232, 237, 238, 241: © 2008 Jupiterimages Corp; 233: izusek/iStock; 234: (t.) © 2008 by Mike Baldwin 'Cornered', (b.) *Edmonton Sun*/The Canadian Press (Brendon Dlouhy); 235: (t. r.) © 2008 by Mike Baldwin 'Cornered', (b.) Altrendo Images/Getty Images; 239: AP Photo/Frank Wiese; 240: Tara Walton/ *Toronto Star*; 242: The Canadian Press (Robert F. Bukaty); 243: The Canadian Press (Tammy Hoy); 244: Mark Von Holden/WireImages/Getty Images; 245: ImageState/Jupiterimages; 247: The Canadian Press (Kevin Frayer); 249: (t.) Tony Bock/*Toronto Star*; 249 (b.), 110–111: (c. b.) *Peterborough Examiner*/The Canadian Press (Clifford Skarstedt); 250: (table) Adapted from Statistics Canada, *Crime Statistics in Canada, 2006*. By Warren Silver. Component of Statistics Canada catalogue no. 85-002-XIE (Juristat), vol. 27, no. 5. Table 1– "Federal statute incidents reported to police, by most serious offence, Canada, 2002 to 2006"; 251: (graph) Statistics Canada, *The Daily*, Nov. 7, 2003. Chart "Rates of impaired driving highest among young drivers" <http://www.statcan. gc.ca/daily-quotidien/031107/dq031107b-eng.htm> Extracted Feb. 20, 2009; 253: Ron Bull/*Toronto Star*; 254: (t.) Doug Menuez/Photodisc/Getty Images, (b.) Bill Ivy/Ivy Images; **255:** Carolos Osorio/*Toronto Star*; **258:** G. Campbell/Shutterstock; **262, 266, 272, 276:** © 2008 Jupiterimages Corp; **263:** © 2008 by Mike Baldwin 'Cornered; **264:** © Marcela Prikryl. Reprinted with permission. Image provided courtesy of the *Hamilton Spectator*; **265:** The Canadian Press (Max Nash); **267:** Bill Ivy/Ivy Images; **269:** Peter Power/*Toronto Star*; **270:** Howard Pyle/Photolibrary; **273:** Gabriela Hasbun/Aurora/Getty Images; **274:** © Ernestine's Women's Shelter. Reprinted with permission; **275:** (graph) Statistics Canada, *Family Violence in Canada: A Statistical Profile, 2007*. Statistics Canada cat. no. 85-224-XIE (Canadian Centre for Justice Statistics). Fig. 1.6–"Emotional and financial abuse is 2.5 times more prevalent in spousal relationships than physical violence"; **277:** Andy Batt/Workbook Stock/Jupiterimages; **278:** Stefano Maccari/Shutterstock; **279:** Josiah Davidson/Photographer's Choice/Getty Images; **280:** Jack Star/PhotoLink/Getty Images; **281:** Yvette Cardozo/Photolibrary; **282:** © Graham Harrop; **283:** Tory Zimmerman/*Toronto Star*; **284:** Taxi/Getty Images; **288:** The Canadian Press (Thomas Porter); **291:** Bob Breidenbach-Pool/Getty Images; **292:** *Lethbridge Herald*/The Canadian Press (David Rossiter); **295:** The Canadian Press (Ryan Remiorz); **296:** (chart) Reprinted with permission/Torstar Syndication Services (Source: Correctional Service Canada, 2006 Census); **297:** Photo by Chris Bolin/*National Post*; **299:** © Dwayne Newton/PhotoEdit; **300:** Danita Delimont/Alamy; **302:** © cjpdesigns/Shutterstock; **303:** Pardon My Planet (I Need Help) © Vic Lee. King Features Syndicate; **304:** © Graham Harrop; By permission of Johnny Hart and Creators Syndicate, Inc.; **306:** (table) © International Centre for Prison Studies, Kings College, London UK <http://www.kcl.ac.uk/schools/law/research/icps> Reproduced with permission; **306:** (photo) Sun Media Corp.; **307:** *Red Deer Advocate*/The Canadian Press (Randy Fiedler); **310:** The Canadian Press (Chuck Stoody); **311:** Vince Talotta/*Toronto Star*; **312:** © National Parole Board (Gov. of Canada). Reprinted with permission; **313:** © MADD Canada; **314:** Reproduced with permission of the Centre for Restorative Justice, School of Criminology, Simon Fraser University, Burnaby, BC; **316:** (l.) The Canadian Press (Ryan Remiorz), (r.) M. J. Turnbull/Ivy Images; **317:** The Canadian Press (Ryan Remiorz); **319:** The Canadian Press (Fred Chartrand); **320:** The Canadian Press (Tom Hanson); **321:** © Jeff Greeberg/PhotoEdit; **323:** © Michael Newman/PhotoEdit; **328:** Archives of Ontario (ACC 6520 S13459); **329, 349:** © 2008 Jupiterimages Corp; **330:** Sam Leung/*The Province*; **332:** © Adrian Raeside; **333:** Ruddy Gold/A.G.E. Foto Stock/First Light; **334:** David Young-Wolff/Stone/Getty Images; **335:** © Tom Carter/PhotoEdit; **337:** © Dennis MacDonald/PhotoEdit; **338:** © Spencer Grant/PhotoEdit; **339:** AP/David Duprey; **340:** © Ron Manning/Prince George Youth Custody Center; **341:** © Michael Newman/PhotoEdit; **346:** Polina Lobanova/Shutterstock; **347:** (t.) Mark Atkins/Shutterstock, (b.) Copyright © 2008 Canterbury High School, Ottawa-Carleton District School Board. Design courtesy of the Visual & Media Arts Department, Jordana Globerman. Funding for this project is provided by the Government of Ontario through the Ministry of the Attorney General, Ontario Victim Services Secretariat Community Grants Program; **350:** Nick Vedros/Photolibrary; **351:** (table) Statistics Canada, The Daily, Nov. 21, 2007, "Adult and youth correctional services: Key indicators," Table –"Composition of average count of the youth correctional population"; **352:** © Michael Newman/PhotoEdit; **358:** Bill Ivy/Ivy Images; **361:** AP Photo/Joe Marquette; **363, 357:** Tina Rencelj/Shutterstock; **364:** Al Harvey/The Slide Farm; **365:** GeostockPhotodisc/Getty Images; **366, 388, 370:** © 2008 Jupiterimages Corp; **367:** (chart) © Charles Foster/Justice Matters. This chart shows most but not all of the procedures that may be involved in a small claims court action. Not shown, for example, are counterclaims, motions, or enforcement procedures involving the sheriff's office; **371:** The Canadian Press (Aaron Harris); **372:** Tatyana Makeyeva/AFP/Getty Images; **374:** *The St. John's Telegram*/The Canadian Press (Keith Gosse); **375:** © 2008 by Mike Baldwin 'Cornered'; **376:** *The Hamilton Spectator*; **377:** The Canadian Press (Sharon Doucette); **382:** © Marty Bucella; **383:** Reprinted with permission/Torstar Syndication Services (Source: www.hardballtimes.com); **385:** The Canadian Press (Chuck Stoody); **388, 356:** *Ottawa Sun*/The Canadian Press (Jeff Bassett); **389:** © WoodyStock/Alamy; **390:** Ivy Images; **391:** The Flying McCoys © 2007 Glenn And Gary McCoy. Dist. By Universal Press; **392, 416:** (b.) © 2008 Jupiterimages Corp; **393:** Photo courtesy of Marianne Mangan; **394:** © Christinne Muschi/Reuters/Corbis; **395:** © 2008 by Mike Baldwin 'Cornered'; **396:** GK Hart/Vikki Hart/Photodisc/Getty Images; **397:** photo by Rob Gurdebeke, *The Windsor Star*; **399:** (t.) © Luis Santana/iStock, (b.) © Peter Arnold, Inc. (Martha Cooper)/Alamy; **400:** © Whistler Blackcomb, an Intrawest Resort. Reprinted with permission; Mike Slaughter/*Toronto Star*; **403:** © Frank Huster/wink/Jupiterimages; Courtesy of Seven82 Motors, Queensland Australia; **406:** © Chris Fertnig/iStock; **407:** © Jerry Schiller/Shutterstock; **409:** Effinity Stock Photography/iStock; **410:** Barry Gnyp/UpperCut Images/Getty Images; **411:** By permission of Johnny Hart and Creators Syndicate, Inc; **412:** © Mike Flanagan/www.cartoonstock.com; **413:** © Graham Harrop; **414:** Peter Endig/dpa/Landov; **415:** The Canadian Press (Chuck Stoody); **416:** (t.) Ivy Images; **417:** Natalie B. Fobes/*National Geographic*/Getty Images; **419:** © Diademimages/Dreamstime; **420:** © Malcolm Mayes/Artizans; **421:** Peter McBride/Iconica/Getty Images; **423:** The Canadian Press (Chris Wattie); **424:** C.J. LaFrance/Getty Images; **425:** Karen McKinnon/*Vancouver Sun*; Cartoon by Pascal Elie; **428, 356:** (inset) *The Globe and Mail*/The Canadian Press (J.P. Moczulski); **434, 458** (b.), **467:** (b.) © 2008 Jupiterimages Corp; **435:** Courtesy of Patricia Sands-Anis; **436:** Rachel Epstein/PhotoEdit; **437–438:** (graph, pie charts) Reprinted with permission from *The Globe and Mail*; **439:** Bizarro (new) © Dan Piraro. King Features Syndicate; **440:** © 2008 by Mike Baldwin 'Cornered'; **442:** (t. table) Adapted from Statistics Canada, Summary Table– "Marriages by province and territory," <http://www40.statcan.ca/l01/cst01/famil04.htm> Extracted Feb. 20, 2009, (b. l.) © Queen's Printer for Ontario, 2008. Reproduced with permission; **443:** Pardon My Planet (I Need Help) © Vic Lee. King Features Syndicate; **444:** *Kitchener Waterloo Record*/The Canadian Press (Peter Lee); **448:** © Graham Harrop; **450:** © Christoph Vorlet/Laughing Stock/Jupiterimages; **451:** Photo by ITV/Rex Features/The Canadian Press; **452:** HERMAN ® is reprinted with permission from LaughingStock Licensing Inc., Ottawa, Canada. All rights reserved; **455, 433:** (b.) Courtesy of Karen Spencer; **456:** (bar graph) Reprinted with permission from *The Globe and Mail*; **457:** The Canadian Press(Richard Lam); **458:** (t. l.) Kain Zernitsky/Stock Illustration Source/Getty Images; **461:** © Randy Faris/Corbis; **464:** © Jessica Jones Photography/iStock; **465:** (t.) Rachel Epstein/PhotoEdit, (b.) Dan Atkin/Alamy; **467** (t.), **432:** Lucille Khornak/Taxi/Getty Images; **470:** The Canadian Press (Jonathan Hayward); **474:** Paul Vismara /Stock Ilustration Source/Getty Images; **475:** © Sonya Etchison/Shutterstock; **476:** © Mathieson & Hewitt Photographers; **477:** The Canadian Press (Fred Chartrand); **478:** Pardon My Planet (I Need Help) © Vic Lee. King Features Syndicate; **480:** RPJ/*Toronto Star*; **481:** © Steve Rosset/Shutterstock; **482:** Dick Loek/*Toronto Star*; **483:** © Jerry King/www.cartoonstock.com; **484, 433:** (t.) Todd Davidson/Stock Illustration RF/Getty Images; **485:** Pardon My Planet (I Need Help) © Vic Lee. King Features Syndicate; **486:** The Canadian Press (Denis Paquin); **487:** Courtesy of Katherine Briand; **489:** Courtesy of Justice Gloria Epstein; **492:** Steve Bosch/*Vancouver Sun*; **493:** Caro/Alamy; **494:** © Duane S. Radford/Lone Pine Photo; **495:** (graph) Adapted from Statistics Canada, *Child and Spousal Support: Maintenance Enforcement Survey Statistics, 2006/2007*. By C. Martin and P. Robinson, (Canadian Centre for Justice Statistics). Statistics Canada cat. no. 85-228-XIE, March 2008. Chart 1– "Cases of divorce or separation between 2001 and 2006, in ten provinces"; **496:** © Jack D. Kozlowski; **497:** images.com/Corbis; **499, 509** (r.), **510:** © 2008 Jupiterimages Corp; **500:** *Toronto Star*/The Canadian Press (Vince Talotta); **501:** © Andresr/Shutterstock; **502:** © 2008 by Mike Baldwin 'Cornered'; **503:** Reprinted With Permission/Torstar Syndication Services; **504:** © Queen's Printer for Ontario, 2009. Reproduced with permission; **505:** D. Anschutz/Digital Vision/Getty Images; **506:** Michael Newman\PhotoEdit; **508:** HERMAN® is reprinted with permission from LaughingStock Licensing Inc., Ottawa, Canada. All rights Reserved; **509:** (l.) Carlos Osorio/*Toronto Star*; **516:** The Canadian Press (Paul Lapid); **517, 528** (t.), **532:** (t.) Mark Parisi/Atlantic Feature Syndicate; **518** (all), **519** (t.), **541, 548:** © 2008 Jupiterimages Corp; **519:** (b.) Peanuts: © United Feature Syndicate, Inc.; **520:** © Jonathan Nourok/PhotoEdit; **521:** Graham Barclay/Bloomberg News/Landov; **523:** (b.) Graca Victoria/Victoria Visuals/iStock; **524:** Ivy Images; **525:** (t.) © Jorodo/www.cartoonstock.com, (b.) The Canadian Press (Frank Gunn); **526:** Mauricio Duenas/AFP/Getty Images; **528:** (b.) Blend Images/Getty Images; **529, 532:** (b.) Burke/Triolo Productions/Jupiterimages; **533:** © Michael Newman/PhotoEdit; **534:** The Canadian Press (Michael Burns Jr.); **536:** © Dick Hemingway; **537:** Kevin Dietsch/UPI/Landov; **538:** Michael Rosenfeld/Stone/Getty Images; **539:** © Graham Harrop; **540:** Dick Loek/*Toronto Star*; **542:** Gene Blevins/Reuters/Landov; **543:** © Country Lane Gazebos. Reprinted with permission. All rights reserved; **544:** Courtesy of CSA International; **545:** (t.) Courtesy of Crafty Candles, (c.) Ivy Images, (b.) © 2008 by Mike Baldwin 'Cornered'; **546:** Ivy Images; **552:** (b.) © Jim West/The Image Works; **552** (t. l.), **552** (t. r.), **553, 554, 556** (t. l.), **563, 570, 578, 579:** © 2008 Jupiterimages Corp; **555:** The Canadian Press (Paul Chiasson); **557:** (table) Excerpted and adapted from Phone Busters™, The Canadian Anti-fraud Call Centre, http://www.phonebusters.com/english/recognizeit_consumertip.html; **560:** © Images-com/Corbis; **562:** Reprinted with permission of the Council of Better Business Bureaus, Inc. Copyright 2009. Council of Better Business Bureaus, Inc., 4200 Wilson Blvd., Arlington, VA 22203. World Wide Web: http://www.us.bbb.org; **564:** PM Images/Stone/Getty Images; **567:** Andrew Stawicki/*Toronto Star*; **568:** C Squared Studios/Photodisc/Getty Images; **571:** Pardon My Planet (I Need Help) © Vic Lee. King Features Syndicate; **573:** The Canadian Press (Lenny Ignelzi); **574:** The Canadian Press (Lenny Ignelzi); **575, 585:** © 2008 by Mike Baldwin 'Cornered'; **583:** The Canadian Press (Paul Vernon); **585:** © Stephen Finn/Shutterstock; **586:** Source: Public archives of Manitoba, PAM N-12296; **587:** Paul Irish/*Toronto Star*; **588:** Rick Eglinton/*Toronto Star*; **589:** Peter Power/*Toronto Star*; **590:** *Toronto Star*/Stuart Nimmo; **591:** © Ken Hurst/Shutterstock Images; **592:** © Anne Kitzman/Shutterstock; **593:** (r.) *Waterloo Regional Record*/The Canadian Press (David Bebee), (l.) *Halifax Chronicle-Herald*/The Canadian Press (Peter Parsons); **594:** The Canadian Press (John Gaps III)